OVERLAND WEST

The Story of the
Oregon and California Trails

VOLUME II

1849–1852

THE OVERLAND ROUTE
From Alonzo Delano's *Life on the Plains*, 1849. Author's collection.

With GOLDEN VISIONS BRIGHT *Before* THEM

Trails to the Mining West
1849–1852

WILL BAGLEY

UNIVERSITY OF OKLAHOMA PRESS ❀ NORMAN

ALSO BY WILL BAGLEY

A Road from El Dorado: The 1848 Trail Journal of Ephraim Green

Frontiersman: Abner Blackburn's Narrative

West from Fort Bridger: The Pioneering of Immigrant Trails across Utah, 1846–1850 (with Harold Schindler)

This Is the Place: A Crossroads of Utah's Past (with Pat Bagley)

The Pioneer Camp of the Saints: The 1846 and 1847 Mormon Trail Journals of Thomas Bullock

Scoundrel's Tale: The Samuel Brannan Papers

Army of Israel: Mormon Battalion Narratives (with David L. Bigler)

Blood of the Prophets: Brigham Young and the Massacre at Mountain Meadows

Always a Cowboy: Judge Wilson McCarthy and the Rescue of the Denver & Rio Grande Western Railroad

Innocent Blood: Essential Narratives of the Mountain Meadows Massacre (with David L. Bigler)

So Rugged and Mountainous: Blazing the Trails to Oregon and California, 1812–1848

The Mormon Rebellion: America's First Civil War (with David L. Bigler)

Playing with Shadows: Voices of Dissent in the Mormon West (with Polly Aird and Jeffrey Nichols)

Library of Congress Cataloging-in-Publication Data

Bagley, Will, 1950–

   With golden visions bright before them : trails to the mining West, 1849–1852 / Will Bagley.

      p. cm. — (Overland West : the story of the Oregon & California Trails and the creation of the mining West ; v. 2)

   Includes bibliographical references and index.

   ISBN 978-0-8061-4284-5 (hardcover : alk. paper) — ISBN 978-0-87062-418-6 (special edition : alk. paper) 1. Overland journeys to the Pacific. 2. Frontier and pioneer life—West (U.S.) 3. California—Gold discoveries. 4. California National Historic Trail—History. 5. Oregon National Historic Trail—History. 6. West (U.S.)—History—1848–1860. I. Title.

   F593.B138 2012

   304.80978—dc23

2012008720

The paper in this book meets the guidelines for permanence and durability of the Committee on Production Guidelines for Book Longevity of the Council on Library Resources, Inc. ∞

1 2 3 4 5 6 7 8 9 10

*For
Laura,
for so much*

The principal part of our company are bound for California with golden visions bright before them, and their distance undoubtedly makes them more enchanting. We have all sorts of men from every part of the Union, lawyers, doctors, farmers, mechanics, storekeepers, brags, boys, & nothings. Some very decent, some very clever & many about half drunk all the time.

Pardon Dexter Tiffany to "My Dear Wife"
6 May 1849, Missouri Historical Society

Dust was plentier than pleasure; pleasure more enticing than virtue. Fortune was the horse, youth in the saddle, dissipation the track, and desire the spur. Let none wonder that the time was the best ever made.

The Annals of San Francisco
1854

Anything connected with the Gold Rush is best begun when you're young; you may see the end of it when your beard has turned snow white.

Dale Morgan to Robert Greenwood
16 December 1965, California State Library

CONTENTS

x

ILLUSTRATIONS

Maps

PREFACE

The discovery of gold on the American River in January 1848, the acquisition of Mexico's northern provinces nine days later, and the subsequent rush to California are pivotal events in American history. After the first overland emigrant party set its course for California in 1841, trails to the West evolved slowly, but the first decade of wagon travel to the Pacific saw the region politically rearranged. The West in 1840 belonged to the Indian nations, Mexico, and the Hudson's Bay Company (the HBC). The United States governed nothing beyond the Missouri River. The HBC had been "Here Before Christ," or at least since 1821, but the British Empire abandoned its claim to the Oregon Country below the 49th parallel in 1846, freeing President James K. Polk to conquer virtually all of Mexico's vast frontier from the 42nd parallel to the Rio Grande and the Sea of Cortés. With the Treaty of Guadalupe Hidalgo, the United States paid fifteen million dollars to acquire a half million square miles of territory. The treaty incorporated today's Southwest, expanded the nation by 25 percent, and achieved Polk's dream of creating a continental nation.

A year later, the rush to plunder a great bonanza defined how the West, with the singular exception of Mormon country, would be populated and developed. By John Unruh's careful calculation, the overland wagon road up the Platte River and over South Pass brought 18,847 Americans to the West Coast and the Great Basin before 1849. California's gold disrupted this slow, steady pattern of exploration and trail blazing and ignited an international frenzy that transformed all the country beyond the Continental Divide. The region's mineral wealth inspired the overland trail to grow a host of new tentacles and underwrote the rapid settlement of today's Colorado, Nevada, Idaho, Montana, and Wyoming. Trails and the mines they made possible set the stage for the Transcontinental Railroad, and the new roads demanded long and bloody campaigns to confine the Indian nations to reservations devoid of the resources needed to support their traditional ways of life. In many respects the rush for riches over the Oregon and California trails created the American West we know today.

By 1849 a network of rough faint tracks and traces, which could generously be called wagon roads, crisscrossed the Great Plains, the Rockies, the Great Basin, and the Columbia River country. Pioneers had worked out passable and relatively safe routes over the Western Cordillera guarding the Pacific. Trading posts and supply stations had multiplied, while ferries served a few particularly dangerous river crossings. Adventurers, veterans of the Mexican-American War, and old mountaineers opened cutoffs that sometimes shortened the trek and connected an increasingly complex web of trails and outposts. The expanding settlements in the valley of the Great Salt Lake provided much-needed vegetables and grain, fresh animals, and a winter refuge for stragglers. The trails, it seemed, had evolved in anticipation of some great and unheralded event.

News of the California gold discovery came at a critical moment in the young republic's history. Before 1849, eccentrics, compulsive gamblers, and down-on-their-luck farmers, whose families often started moving west from Jamestown and Plymouth Plantation, formed the large majority of those who went overland to the Pacific. Except for a few adventurers who went west to have a good time, people came to Oregon and California seeking health, cheap land, and a milder climate—a fresh start in a new home, a chance to win a better life. Gold fever changed what had been a slow trickle of pioneering families into a flood of male fortune hunters and freebooters. Some had been the young lifeblood of their communities, but many came from society's margins and had nothing to lose.

Between 1849 and 1852, the trails to Oregon and California grew like wandering vines. This study pays particular attention to the relentless transformation of a few faint traces into the "road across the plains," revealing how quickly emigrants and entrepreneurs responded to the demands of increased traffic, failing resources, and a rough-and-ready frontier economy to blaze new trails or shorten existing ones. Never rigidly constrained to a narrow track, these roads changed from year to year, wandering across a floodplain, abandoning a worn-out track, or seeking the always-elusive shortcut. This process sometimes had catastrophic results—as those who took the illusive shortcuts of Stephen Meek, Lansford Hastings, and Peter Lassen learned. But over time, this evolution created a quicker and safer road to the West.

The 1849 gold rush conjured up the California Dream and an enduring American legend, but it had even more portentous consequences. As if by magic, the metallic capital flowing from the Sierra Nevada spawned instant cities up and down the Pacific Coast. The legend of a golden king's lost city had animated European imaginations ever since Cortés swindled Moctezuma: now the golden stream of a new El Dorado fueled an international boom, thawing the economic ice age that had gripped the United States since the Panic of 1837. The patterns and practices of resource exploitation, economic expansion and exhaustion, cultural and political allegiances, and ethnic conflicts created during this crucial epoch still define the Golden West. This Gilded Age produced an opulent literary legacy, notably thousands of overland journals and recollections ranging from simple chronicles describing the availability of grass and water to masterpieces such as Alonzo Delano's *Life on the Plains* and Sarah Royce's *A Frontier Lady*. Perhaps the era's most abiding bequest is the American belief that it is possible to get rich quick, a strange faith that was virtually unknown before the rush for California's gold.

This is character-driven history filled with a crowd of inspired, crazed, determined, resolute, lovable, desperate, and determined gamblers—and that accounts only for the women who set out to strike it rich. Good men did seek their fortunes on the frontier, but their vivid accounts depict many gold seekers as ruthless, cowardly, violent, merciless, reckless, despicable, deranged, and dirty scoundrels. Few fortune hunters had any intention of staying in the West longer than it took to amass a "pile"—a comfortable fortune. Even fewer saw their golden dreams come true. Before this brief, glittering era ended, its flood of gold liberated a national economy shackled by a lack of capital, a voluntary mass migration stripped New England and the Midwest of many of its best and brightest sons, and water cannons churned much of the Mother Lode into mud and silt that choked California's rivers and destroyed its great fisheries. A dozen and then a hundred and finally a thousand boomtowns sprang up across the West. And of the 310,000 Indians estimated to have inhabited California before contact with Europeans, the 1860 federal census would find only 17,798.[1]

Traditional histories of overland roads paint this mass migration as a heroic epic of progress that opened new lands and a continental treasure house to the blessings of civilization, Christianity, and the Constitution. Tales of the trails became an integral part of our national myth, but the transformation of the American West between 1840 and 1870 is a more complex and contentious story than the legend pretends. The men and women who converted a vast "wilderness" into an American agricultural and industrial dynamo could scarcely believe how quickly this economic and demographic revolution took place: they could not have been any more surprised at the speed of their conquest if they had turned lead into gold. Telling even part of this story—how Americans used old wagon roads and forged new ones between 1849 and 1852 to redefine a nation—is as daunting as trying to eat an elephant. Anyone naïve enough to attempt to write a multivolume history of such an epic must do it one bite at a time, but only a fool would not let the creature's shape define how to carve it up. The heart of the elephant is the gold rush—especially its defining year, 1849. As it happens, this volume's many

---

[1] Hurtado, *Indian Survival*, 194.

chapters about 1849 provide the most detailed physical description of the overland trail found in the series.

Since it has been done so often and so well, telling a story of such sweep is no easy matter. This retelling of the tale relies on the voices of the people themselves to describe the adventures of each year's emigration from 1849 to 1852, when the Oregon and California trails saw their most intense use. The designation of 1852—the date picked by California historian H. H. Bancroft—as the end of the gold rush is completely arbitrary.[2] To capture a sense of the journey and its terrain, this book follows the western trek of the Forty-niners and Oregon-bound soldiers and settlers in detail. As the 1849 rush to California commenced, crested, and collapsed, those who led the way had radically different experiences from the companies following in their wake. Travelers took different routes depending on when they reached various points along the trail as the mad march became "a long race for the best grass and the first chance in the gold field."[3] The start of the rush became a heated contest to see who could first cross two thousand tough miles, so the first chapters use the classic narrative model of a race; later ones describe the experiences of those who were caught up in the middle of a mass migration and how the stragglers and wanderers of 1849 narrowly avoided disaster—or did not.

The work's next section describes travel over the next three years. Each focuses on what was unique about that particular passage without forcing readers to march over the trail once more. The perspective of a century and a half offers new ways to analyze the experience, but these chapters focus on the people who crossed the plains and their stories—how they recorded making the trek or recalled it through the veil of memory, and the impact the experience had on their lives. Integrated into this chronological account are aspects of life on the trail, such as the roles of women and children; violence, law, and order; bison and bird hunting; epidemics and stampedes; reactions to the new land and its alien landforms; and most important, the ever-changing relations between overlanders and Indians.

The book ends with a critical examination of the impact overland wagon roads had on the rush for gold and the subsequent history of the American West. The initial race to exploit California's mineral wealth defined the nature of the subsequent social upheavals, spurred settlement from Nebraska to the West Coast, and provided the template for mining development, the economic foundation of the region's economy and culture. Hundreds of new sources have emerged over the last two decades, and wherever possible I have relied on them to tell the story. It is a privilege to share the potent prose of such talented writers as Mary E. Brush,

---

[2]Bancroft, *History of California,* 7:696n1.
[3]Hittell, "Reminiscences of the Plains and Mines," 195.

Lewis Tremble, P. Dexter Tiffany, and Chloe Ann Terry. Their words offer visceral insights into the experience of going "the plains across," and how their encounter with the place and its vast spaces transformed both them and the western land. Native voices are at the heart of this story, but few sources provide any reliable record of their perspectives. Indians appear as others saw them, often as apparitions or caricatures whose voices speak only in someone else's language. Yet these narratives offer surprising insights into how the tribes reacted to the strange and apparently crazy intruders on their ancient homelands.

Crossing the Oregon and California trails could be as harrowing as fighting in the Civil War. Like any tumultuous transition, this one came only with untold suffering, sacrifice, and sorrow. For gold-seeking Forty-niners, Oregon-bound farmers, and Mormon pilgrims the cost was high, but for America's Indian peoples it was ruinous. The fraction of the West's Native inhabitants in 1840 who survived until 1870 saw their cultures devastated and the resources they depended upon shot down, dug up and plowed under, or turned to mud or dust. After the adventures of their golden youths, many of the apparent winners of the struggle to master half a continent—male Anglo-Saxon Protestants—faced hardscrabble poverty in old age. For the women who went west with them, the cost in lives, pain, and shattered dreams was even higher. Male and female, they entered their decrepitude having "seen the elephant": in the argot of the age, they had seen the best and worst the world had to offer, and more. Whatever trials they had to endure, they were proud people who carried an undying memory of the trails they had crossed to their graves. Their story is fraught with meaning. I have tried to tell it, as Forty-niner Charles Dexter Cleveland wrote, to "pleasantly engage the mind, satisfy natural curiosity, and in the indefinite years to come, be some resource to posterity, in a classic way."[4]

---

[4]Cleveland, Autobiography, 67.

Editorial Procedures

This volume follows the editorial procedures outlined in *So Rugged and Mountainous,* the first volume of *Overland West.* Briefly, quotations reproduce the source's spelling and use "*sic*" sparingly. Editorial alterations appear in square brackets. I have corrected obvious transcription errors, standardized capitalization and punctuation, and edited and occasionally resequenced sources for readability rather than academic formality. For example, I adjusted capitalization rather than follow the [a]ggravating [c]ustom of bracketing such changes. Underlined text is italicized and crossed-out text omitted. Footnotes are as short as possible, listing only author, title, date, and page number to provide telegraphic citations to the bibliography, which is divided into two sections with complete information on primary sources (by author rather than editor for published journals and memoirs) and secondary sources (including books, articles, government documents, theses, and dissertations). I have italicized book titles and put article, website, thesis, and dissertation titles in quotation marks. Manuscript citations appear in plain text without quotation marks. Where available, newspaper citations are to page/column: for example, 2/3. I have avoided listing online addresses, which are always in flux, but the text of many of these documents can be found on the internet.

With
GOLDEN VISIONS
BRIGHT
Before
THEM

PROLOGUE

When the California gold rush began, Americans had a vague notion of "The California and Oregon Trail," which was, after all, the title of Francis Parkman's popular book. Newspapers had long featured letters from the trail, but as gold fever swept the restless young nation, it created an unquenchable thirst for accurate descriptions of the road to the Pacific. The art of photography was not yet a decade old, and the only authentic paintings depicting life on the plains were hidden in private collections. Books by bold men who had made the long and perilous journey, such as John C. Frémont, Edwin Bryant, and Lansford W. Hastings, were in high demand, but reliable information about how to take a wagon across the prairies, deserts, and mountains of the nation's new empire was scarce indeed.

That changed quickly. By the fall of 1850, anyone in Peoria or Saint Louis with an imagination and fifty cents to buy a ticket could "fancy himself in an air balloon, overtaking and passing the emigrants on the road, witnessing their distress, and seeing the country and the nature of the obstacles they have to contend with." At Peoria on 18 September, James Wilkins, an enterprising English-born artist who had crossed the plains the previous summer, began exhibiting his "Immense Moving Mirror of the Land Route to California, by the South Pass of the Rocky Mountains, Embracing all the Scenery from the Missouri River to San Francisco." This panoramic painting, a primitive precursor of a motion picture, consisted of three painted scrolls about ten feet tall that covered some 3,600 square yards of canvas—as much as three thousand running feet of art, but realistically probably half that. During its initial run, crowds had to be turned away every night without a chance to see this "splendid artistical work." Wilkins had a hit on his hands, for his images revealed "the stupendous difficulties the emigrant wagons have to encounter in the longest wagon travel in the world"—the awfully steep ascents, the river crossings, the terrific descents, indeed, every obstacle they had to contend with—"all with the safety and comfort of sitting at your own fireside."[1]

---

[1] See "Immense Moving Mirror of the Land Route to California," an advertisement in the *Missouri Republican*, 6 October 1850, in Wilkins's journal, *An Artist on the Overland Trail*, 3–17.

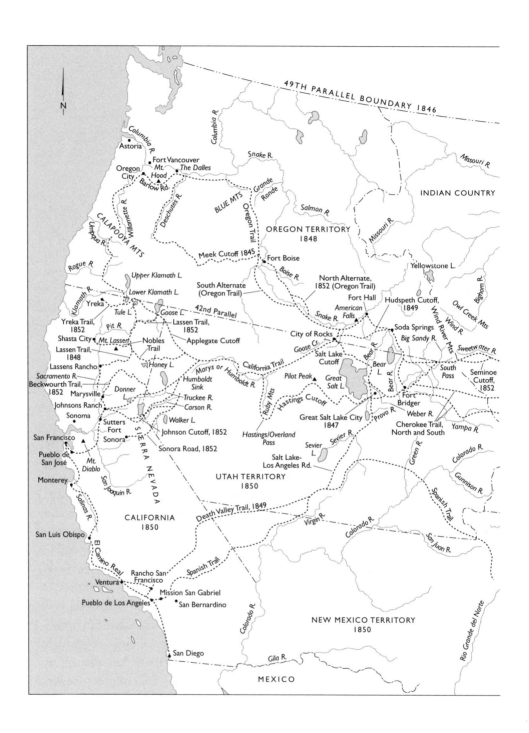

49TH PARALLEL BOUNDARY 1846

Columbia R.

Astoria

Fort Vancouver

Oregon City

Mt. Hood

The Dalles

Barlow Rd.

Columbia R.

Snake R.

Grande Ronde

BLUE MTS

Oregon Trail

Salmon R.

Missouri R.

INDIAN COUNTRY

OREGON TERRITORY 1848

Deschutes R.

Willamette R.

CALAPOOYA MTS

Umpqua R.

Rogue R.

Meek Cutoff 1845

Fort Boise

Boise R.

Missouri R.

Yellowstone L.

Bighorn R.

Upper Klamath L.

Lower Klamath L.

South Alternate (Oregon Trail)

North Alternate, 1852 (Oregon Trail)

Fort Hall

Hudspeth Cutoff, 1849

Owl Creek Mts

Yreka

Tule L.

Goose L.

42nd Parallel

Snake R.

American Falls

Soda Springs

Big Sandy R.

Wind River Mts

Wind R.

Yreka Trail, 1852

Lassen Trail, 1852

City of Rocks

Sweetwater R.

Klamath R.

Pit R.

Shasta City

Mt. Lassen

Nobles Trail

Applegate Cutoff

Goose Cr.

Salt Lake Cutoff

Bear R.

Bear L.

South Pass

Lassen Trail, 1848

California Trail

Pilot Peak

Great Salt L.

Fort Bridger

Seminoe Cutoff, 1852

Lassens Rancho

Marys or Humboldt R.

Ruby Mts

Hastings Cutoff

Weber R.

Yampa R.

Sacramento R.

Beckwourth Trail, 1852

Marysville

Donner L.

Humboldt Sink

Humboldt R.

Great Salt Lake City 1847

Provo R.

Cherokee Trail, North and South

Johnsons Ranch

Sonoma

Sutters Fort

Sonora

Truckee R.

Carson R.

Walker L.

Johnson Cutoff, 1852

Hastings/Overland Pass

Sevier L.

Sevier R.

Green R.

Colorado R.

Gunnison R.

San Francisco

Pueblo de San José

Mt. Diablo

Sonora Road, 1852

Salt Lake-Los Angeles Rd.

Monterey

San Joaquin R.

SIERRA NEVADA

UTAH TERRITORY 1850

Spanish Trail

Salinas R.

CALIFORNIA 1850

Death Valley Trail, 1849

Virgin R.

Colorado R.

San Juan R.

San Luis Obispo

El Camino Real

Spanish Trail

Colorado R.

Rancho San Francisco

Ventura

Mission San Gabriel

Pueblo de Los Angeles

San Bernardino

NEW MEXICO TERRITORY 1850

Rio Grande del Norte

San Diego

Gila R.

MEXICO

N

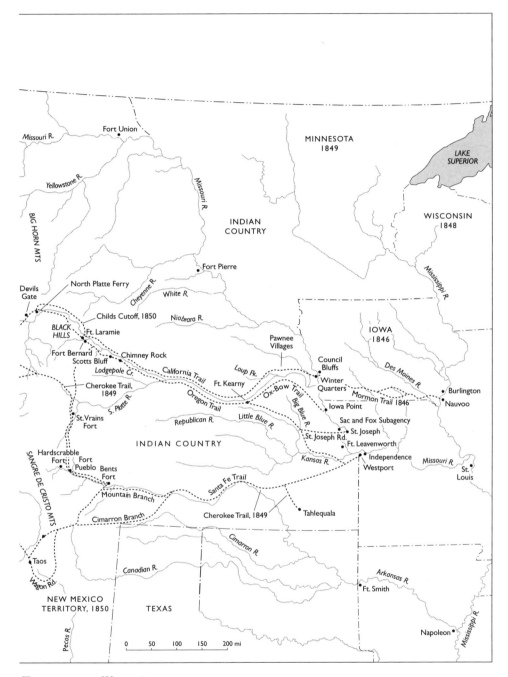

The following labels appear on the map:

Missouri R.

Fort Union

MINNESOTA 1849

LAKE SUPERIOR

Yellowstone R.

Missouri R.

BIG HORN MTS

INDIAN COUNTRY

WISCONSIN 1848

Fort Pierre

Mississippi R.

Devils Gate

North Platte Ferry

Cheyenne R.

White R.

Childs Cutoff, 1850

Niobrara R.

IOWA 1846

BLACK HILLS

Ft. Laramie

Fort Bernard
Scotts Bluff

Chimney Rock

Lodgepole Cr.

California Trail

Pawnee Villages

Loup Fk.

Council Bluffs

Des Moines R.

Cherokee Trail, 1849

Ft. Kearny

Winter Quarters

Mormon Trail 1846

Burlington

Nauvoo

S. Platte R.

Oregon Trail

Ox-Bow Trail

Big Blue R.

Iowa Point

St.Vrains Fort

Republican R.

Little Blue R.

Sac and Fox Subagency

St. Joseph Rd.

St. Joseph

INDIAN COUNTRY

Ft. Leavenworth

SANGRE DE CRISTO MTS

Hardscrabble Fort

Fort Pueblo

Bents Fort

Kansas R.

Independence

Westport

Missouri R.

St. Louis

Mountain Branch

Santa Fe Trail

Cimarron Branch

Cherokee Trail, 1849

Tahlequala

Taos

Canadian R.

Cimarron R.

Arkansas R.

Ft. Smith

Wagon Rd.

NEW MEXICO TERRITORY, 1850

TEXAS

Pecos R.

Napoleon

Mississippi R.

0   50   100   150   200 mi

THE OVERLAND WEST, 1852

Between 1849 and 1852, the Oregon-California Trail added a host of alternates, shortcuts, and toll roads, notably the Cherokee, Beckwourth, Nobles, and Yreka trails; the Hudspeth, Childs, Georgetown, Seminoe, Kinney, Slate Creek, and Johnson cutoffs; and the Golden Pass Road. Meanwhile mining camps sponsored roads to Marysville, Auburn, Shasta City, Downieville, Columbia, Volcano, Grizzly Flat, and Sonora. Cartography by Bill Nelson.

5

After an extra week in Peoria, the show opened in Saint Louis to even greater acclaim. "There are but few who do not know the route, so far as mere descriptions can convey an idea of it," observed the *Missouri Republican.* The best informed, who had read and heard much about the trail west, had almost no idea what it actually looked like. Wilkins's panorama gave people a unique pictorial image of the road to El Dorado. At a time when print ruled and newspapers carried only primitive graphics, most Americans knew as much about the appearance of the surface of the moon as they did about the landscape of the Far West. Streaming pictures like Wilkins's changed all that.[2] His artwork captured the trail's "beauties and its terrors—its advantages and privations—the beautiful vallies and plains—the fearful mountain ascents, and deserts—the crossings of dangerous rivers, and desert plains—the scarcity of grass and water, and the many straits to which the traveler is sometimes forced."

The panorama, along with its supporting broadsides and lectures, faithfully recorded what Wilkins had seen on his trip, "giving the public a pretty accurate knowledge of the difficulties our emigrant wagons have to encounter." Unlike most of his fellow Forty-niners, Wilkins ascended the east bank of the Missouri River before crossing near old Fort Kearny at today's Nebraska City and heading for Fort Childs, now the new Fort Kearny. By 1849 a complicated network of trails started from Missouri to Iowa, but they all converged near the new army post. From the fort, Wilkins's panorama proceeded "up the valley of the Platte to the fording of the south fork, where the stream is nearly a mile in width, crossing Ash Hollow, to those well-known land marks CASTLE BLUFFS, COURT HOUSE ROCK AND CHIMNEY ROCK" and "to those picturesque and grotesque shaped rocks of enormous size known as SCOTT's BLUFF." The first scroll, like the first stage of the journey, ended at Fort Laramie.

After crossing the deep and difficult Laramie River, the trail left the Great Plains and entered the Black Hills of Wyoming. "Here mountain scenery commences, which continues changing into every possible variation of character, for upwards of a thousand miles." Wilkins's scrolling pictures jumped from the North Platte Ferry to Independence Rock, "a noted landmark," ignoring Emigrant Gap, the Poison Spring, Avenue of Rocks, Willow Springs, Prospect Hill, Horse Creek, and the Saleratus Lake. The panorama picked up again at "*Devil's Gate,* so called from the mountains being cleft in twain their whole breadth, in order to let pass the Sweet Water river, forming a terrific chasm, the walls of which are perpendicular and over 400 feet high." Emigrants ascended the Sweetwater past Split Rock, forded

---

[2]While Wilkins toured with his panorama, 350,000 Britons paid a shilling each to see a badly drawn "Diorama of Fremont's Overland-Route" at London's Athenaeum and Egyptian Hall. Spence and Jackson, *Expeditions of John Charles Frémont,* 3:152.

(*left*) The mouth of Ash Hollow
(*right*) Court House Rock

the Three Crossings or slogged over one of two deep sand routes, crossing the river four more times before climbing up Rocky Ridge: "Here get a distant view of the Snowy Mountains, the white peaks glittering in the sun, till we imperceptibly pass the Dividing Ridge!"

Wilkins's surviving sketches reflect the problem South Pass posed for artists, since the long ascent of its wide valley to the spot "where the waters flow into the Pacific" was hardly dramatic. West of South Pass at the "parting of the ways," Wilkins chose the Old Oregon Trail, which avoided the long, parched crossing of the Green River barrens via the Sublette Cutoff. He visited Fort Bridger, "a secluded post for trading with the Indians"—and now emigrants. From the fort, the trail ascended the Muddy to cross into the Bear River Valley, "the most fertile and home-like on the whole route," where the Sublette route rejoined the old road. The artist did not portray the "well-known camping places" or natural wonders at Soda Springs and Steamboat Springs. Wilkins was now at the back of the massive emigration, and "came the cutoff" John J. Myers and Benoni Hudspeth had opened in July, which avoided the old detour north to Fort Hall. At another parting of the ways, where the Oregon Trail headed down the Snake River, Wilkins turned south with the California Trail to climb Raft River. The panorama's second scroll ended "with a view of the City of the Rocks, so named from its resemblance to a city." Wilkins was the second man known to apply the name to what is now Idaho's City of Rocks National Reserve.

(*left*) Devils Gate
(*right*) Castle Rock (the City of Rocks)

The third scroll began at the foot of Granite Pass on Goose Creek. The trail passed the inscriptions and gargoyles that decorated Record Bluff and Raven Cliff, found much-needed grass and water at Rock and Chicken springs, and finally reached the Hot and Cold Springs in Thousand Springs Valley, where a century later film star Jimmy Stewart built the Wine Cup Ranch. "We next come to Humboldt or Mary's river, well remembered by every Emigrant, from its length, (down which he pursues it for 300 miles, till it sinks in the ground,) and from the poisonous waters near its sink." At one of the last oases on the filthy stream, Wilkins was one of the few stragglers not seduced by the Applegate-Lassen Trail—the terrible "Cherokee" shortcut or Death Route—which added hundreds of miles to the journey. When he arrived in September, there was hardly a blade of grass left on the last hundred miles to the Truckee and Carson rivers. For natives of the American heartlands, the stark playa called the Sink of the Humboldt was the most alien spot on the entire road to California; for Forty-niners, it was by far the hardest. The panorama portrayed horrific scenes at Sulphur Springs, and the Sandy Desert was "strewn with the skeletons of stock and property of every description" until it reached a "repose at Carson River." Wilkins portrayed Carson Valley as the "Valley of a thousand springs, similar to Salt Lake Valley" with its many hot springs and the terrific scenery—terrific in the sense of *terrifying*—of the canyon that began the ascent of the Sierra Nevada.

"Here is said to be THE BACK BONE OF THE ELEPHANT," the panorama's promoters proclaimed, referring to the mascot of every Forty-niner's hardships and

EMIGRANT TRAIN PASSING THE WIND RIVER MOUNTAINS
English immigrant James M. Hutchings published thirteen "Views Drawn from Nature by George Baker in 1853" as a pictorial letter sheet titled "Hutchings Panoramic Scenes—Crossing the Plains." For the cost of a forty-cent stamp, lonely miners could mail a letter sheet and share the experience of "seeing the elephant" with the folks back home. Baker's drawings provide insight into what James Wilkins's lost panorama probably looked like. Author's collection.

fears. "Scenery awfully grand; descent of the Mountains," and, at last, "arrival at the Gold Mines. Dry Diggings; Weatherville [Weberville]; Gold Digging; Sutter's Fort; Sacramento City; San Francisco." Here the panorama, like the wagon road, brought spectators and "the great Caravan of 1849" to the end of the trail: the new El Dorado.

Very few could be "indifferent to the trials or fate of the Pilgrims to the land of gold," and few knew the anxieties, dangers, and grief associated with the overland route to California better than Wilkins, who reached home at Saint Louis on 30 January 1850 after a trip to Panama on the steamer *Unicorn*. "On his return he set himself to work to elaborate his sketches," the *Missouri Republican* reported. He completed them after "eighteen months of patient observation and toil on the part of himself and his assistants. We can hardly conceive of any thing so interesting to our people as a faithful sketch of such a spectacle." Wilkins's massive scrolling image of the road west struck a chord with his countrymen. The panorama appeared in Cincinnati, Louisville, and Frankfort before a return engagement at Saint Louis in March 1851. The life and action of the artist's images gave Midwesterners a new understanding of the beautiful and sublime scenery of the West. "All have relations, or friends who have passed over this route within the last two years," the *Republican* noted the day after the panorama's premier. The painting conveyed, the paper believed, "more distinctly than words could do, a correct and vivid idea of the fatigues, the danger, and anxiety to which the emigrants were and are liable."

Despite its success, the painter's immense moving mirror did not spare the artist a life of genteel poverty. Although he lived for almost another forty years, neither fate nor the gold rush would be kind to the *"gold stricken"* James F. Wilkins. On returning home, he learned "the strange facts that have come to light" about the deaths of his wife and daughters from cholera. The vultures holding his dead family's debts swept away what little property Wilkins had accumulated by the fruit of his pencil. Cholera and gold fever had, he wrote, "carried off all I hold most dear."

For many Americans like Wilkins, the gold rush cost a great deal. Perhaps five thousand people died from diseases or accidents on the trail west between 1849 and 1852. Many families would never hear again from a father, son, or brother. Some simply vanished, but others disappeared into the rootless population left stranded in El Dorado or joined the ranks of prospectors who spent the rest of their lives wandering the West, always seeking the next big strike. For others it was much worse. Bands of California Indians that had never seen white people before 1849 would be decimated by 1852 and extinct by the end of the century. The frenzied quest for gold uprooted the Sierra foothills and generated a flood of mud, poisoning California's great rivers and destroying a natural resource as productive as Alaska's salmon fishery. The great rush to seize the region's wealth came at incalculable cost to the nation, but it purchased an immense treasure: today's American West.

CHAPTER 1

MEN OF ENTERPRISE
AND ADVENTURE

The Rush Begins

California's gold was no secret to the *Californios,* who—along with their Native allies and enemies—formed a large majority of the population when the United States acquired the province in February 1848. This knowledge was already a generation old when they flocked to San Feliciano Canyon in 1842. A year later the agent of Yankee trader and Mexican citizen Don Abel Stearns deposited 18.34 ounces of placer gold from these mines in the U.S. Mint in Philadelphia.[1] The sight of a glittering nugget, such as the one James Marshall noticed in the tailrace of a sawmill he was building in January 1848, was nothing new, but Marshall's discovery started California's second bout with gold fever. Not much happened until May, when Samuel Brannan, a retired Mormon preacher and partner at a trading post in the former bunkhouse at Sutters Fort, bought up every pick, shovel, and Indian basket he could find. Brannan was nobody's fool, but until that point his business had to rely on gold from the pockets of travelers "wishing to cross the mountains with pack animals" and barter; "California banknotes"—cattle hides worth about a dollar—served as his primary medium of exchange. Rumors about gold were already rampant, but the gold dust coming over his counter and a quick visit to the mines confirmed its existence. No one in San Francisco had paid much attention to the stories, but when Brannan charged up Montgomery Street on 10 May 1848 waving a bottle of gold dust in one hand, swinging his hat with the other, and shouting, "Gold! Gold! Gold from the American River!" everything changed. By the middle of June "the abandonment of San Francisco was complete," Brannan's newspaper announced.[2]

California's military governor, Colonel Richard Mason, set out for the goldfields in July 1848 to investigate the wild stories coming from the American River and see

[1] Cutter, "The Discovery of Gold," 13.
[2] Brannan, *Scoundrel's Tale,* 255, 262–68.

where most of his soldiers had gone. The stories were all true; he reported on his return to Monterey, "the most remarkable part of it is that it is not exaggerated." Four thousand men were scattered along the river's South Fork digging from one to three ounces of gold per day from the streams and gulches. One small ravine disgorged gold worth upward of $12,000. "I could not have credited these reports, had I not seen, in the abundance of the precious metal, evidence of their truth," Mason wrote.[3] Even his officers could hardly credit "the gold-digger's stories" the colonel brought back.

Lieutenant Edward Ord asked permission to go and see for himself, along with Captain A. J. Smith of the First Dragoons. On their way, they found farms and villages almost deserted. The officer in charge of the port of San Francisco had already collected $40,000 in duties, all paid in raw gold. The officers dined with "twenty well-dressed happy-looking civilians" who all downed one or more bottles of champagne, each worth three days of Ord's pay. Smith and Ord sailed for Sacramento with Sam Brannan, now well on his way to becoming California's first millionaire. They ascended the Sacramento River with "some half-dozen runaway sailors and a grogshop keeper or two" to a landing, where "half a dozen motley set of vagabonds, (whites, Indians, negroes, kenakas, Chinese and Chilenos)" greeted their launch. John Sutter helped the officers find horses. By sunset they were riding toward the Mormon diggings along the American River. The next morning they went to see "the gold washers at work."

At Mormon Island, named after the Mormon Battalion veterans who made the first big strike, the officers found three hundred men digging, panning, and rocking primitive cradles that produced two ounces per man for a morning's work. "We looked on in wonder and astonishment for an hour, to see by what a simple process men were all around us getting rich," Ord wrote. Mormon families camped at every spring or patch of grass, "perfectly contented with their luck." The officers spent the evening chatting about their prospects "in the newly established city on the shores of the Salt Lake." The Saints, as they called themselves, were preparing to leave El Dorado to join Brigham Young in their new Zion in the Great Basin, saying they "had *gold enough*." Within a month they had blazed a wagon road over Carson Pass.

On Sunday Ord visited the dry diggings. Working with a borrowed washer, in fifteen minutes the officers extracted more than an ounce of pure gold from less than a peck of dirt. Ord estimated almost every man along the American River's South Fork was, without exception, "making from two ounces to two hundred dollars per day, when they chose to work." Three fourths of them "were either runaway sailors or soldiers, or men who had left home suddenly, and might be called a drinking, fighting but not a working population." Under "the enterprising gold-loving

<hr>

[3]Taylor, "California and New Mexico," 529–31.

Yankees," Ord predicted California would export from six to ten million dollars' worth of gold annually within ten years. Men from Oregon, southern California, and then Mexico and Chile soon joined the frenzy, and the craze for the shiny metal left the army without enough men to guard its ordnance. Ord saw "towns without men—country without government, laws or legislators—and, what's more, no one disposed to stop to make them." Even the grizzly bears and great herds of wild elk and antelope near the well-traveled road to the goldfields had "not had time to get out of the way of the tide of gold hunters rolling over the plains."[4]

These Immense Additions to Our Territorial Possessions

As his presidency came to its end, James K. Polk struggled mightily to persuade Congress to provide a government for the Mexican-American War's greatest prize—Alta California, the vast territory south of the 42nd parallel stretching from the Continental Divide to the Pacific. California's mineral wealth "and other advantages" would attract a large population, but Polk feared that "among the emigrants would be men of enterprise and adventure" who would "probably organize an independent Government, calling it California or the Pacific Republic, and might induce Oregon to join them." Sectional politics complicated the issue, since the fate of slavery was inextricably bound up in the future of this newly conquered province, but Congress took no action to prevent losing California to a band of reckless and ambitious opportunists.

The president rode to his successor's inauguration at the U.S. Capitol with the president-elect, Zachary Taylor, who "was free in conversation." The subject of California came up, "which drew from Gen'l Taylor the expression of views & opinions which greatly surprised me," Polk confided to his diary. California and Oregon were "too distant to become members of the Union," Taylor said: it would be better for them to form an independent government. Although aghast at the implications of Taylor's rambling, Polk said nothing. If Congress failed to extend the protection of law to California, "there was danger that that fine territory would be lost to the Union by establishment of an Independent Government," he wrote. "Gen'l Taylor's opinions as expressed, I hope, have not been well considered." Polk, of course, was horrified that all his work to build a continental nation was about to be squandered and undone. He concluded Taylor was a well-meaning old man, but the general was "uneducated, exceedingly ignorant of public affairs, and, I should judge of very ordinary capacity."[5]

---

[4]Ord to Pacificus Ord, 26 August 1848, "The Gold Region," *Defiance Democrat,* 9 February 1849. For additional background, see Owens, *Riches for All,* 1–28.

[5]Polk, *The Diary,* 4:231, 233, 375–76. In September 1848, Senator Thomas Benton's letter "To the people of California" suggesting they form an independent government appeared in the *New York Herald.* Benton sent the letter to California with John C. Frémont. Denouncing Benton's arrogance, Polk wrote, "The inference is plain enough that he means they shall make Colonel Fremont the Governor of the Independent Government they shall form." Ibid., 4:136–37.

In his last message to Congress on 5 December 1848, President Polk had already announced news that would forestall his successor's vague plan to abandon the lands the United States had purchased from Mexico with the Treaty of Guadalupe Hidalgo. "The Mississippi, so lately the frontier of our country, is now only its center," Polk observed. The acquisition changed not only the frontier—as Richard White quipped, the place where white people got scarce—but the very definition of the American West, which now encompassed all the lands between the Missouri River and the Pacific Ocean. Its conquests made the United States nearly as large as the whole of Europe. "It would be difficult to calculate the value of these immense additions to our territorial possessions," he added. Polk then confirmed the news the *New York Herald* first reported in August. "It was known that mines of the precious metals existed to a considerable extent in California at the time of its acquisition," Polk noted. "Recent discoveries render it probable that these mines are more extensive and valuable than was anticipated." He went on to say that the extraordinary tales of gold would "scarcely command belief were they not corroborated by the authentic reports of officers in the public service."[6] Colonel Mason confirmed the stories and estimated the gold in the conquered province would pay for the war with Mexico a hundred times over. Two days after Polk's message, the War Department put on display physical proof of the president's claims: a tea caddy containing 230 ounces—more than fourteen pounds—of California gold that Mason had sent to Washington.

Cholera would kill James K. Polk three months after he left the presidency. If he had calculated that his announcement of the gold discovery would promote a surge of emigration to the West Coast, the result could not have pleased him more. The California gold rush created one of the largest voluntary migrations in history. By early June 1849, a Fort Laramie trader told John W. Gunnison, eleven thousand wagons and forty-four thousand emigrants were on their way to Oregon, California, and Utah.[7] Along with the older settlers, a convention in Monterey expressed their desire to become part of the Union when it created a state constitution on 13 October 1849. A month later, voters elected Oregon Trail veteran Peter H. Burnett governor of the provisional state of California.

The gold rush began a new era in overland trail history. The previous decade had seen the creation of well-established wagon roads to the Pacific, but fewer than 20,000 people had used them to venture west before 1848. (By contrast, between 1840 and 1850 the population of Illinois swelled by 375,287 souls.) The trails to Oregon and California continued their dynamic evolution for the next twenty years,

---

[6]Watson, "Herald of the Gold Rush," 299; Polk, Fourth Annual Message, in Papers, Library of Congress, 1848.
[7]Gunnison, Diary, 7 June 1849, 35.

but by 1849 the era of heroic pioneering was over. More than 100,000 people would
set out for the West Coast in 1849 and 1850 to test whether the trail blazed by
Indians, fur traders, explorers, missionaries, soldiers, speculators, and farmers was
a viable "Road across the Plains."[8] Gold mania added new routes to the California
Trail. For the first time, westbound wagons used the Salt Lake Cutoff to return
to the main trail at City of Rocks. In July 1849, the Hudspeth Cutoff supplanted
the northern detour to Fort Hall. Cherokee gold seekers from today's Oklahoma
opened two entirely new ways to get from the South Platte River to Fort Bridger
in 1849. Known as the Cherokee Trail, the new traces followed the Arkansas River
to Pikes Peak and crossed the Continental Divide along the general line of today's
Interstate 80. Like other alternates, these additions relieved the immense pressure
livestock and people put on pastures and springs along the main trail.

The disease that killed the retired president at Nashville crept up the Mississippi River Valley, slaying thousands in the unhealthy river towns. Cholera swept
through the crowded hordes of gold seekers, who carried it to the tribes of the Great
Plains. In a year that marked an explosion of American energy and enterprise, the
devastating epidemic of 1849 proved a grim harbinger to the peoples of the plains.

As Contagious as the Itch: Gold Fever

As cholera worked its insidious way up the Mississippi, another equally potent epidemic was sweeping America. "We want words to convey an idea of the extent of
the gold fever in New York," the *Philadelphia Public Ledger* reported on 22 December
1848. "At church, in the theatre, at the table, in every hotel, the talk is of California."

Before 1848, no wagon had ever passed between Oregon and California, overland veteran Peter Burnett recalled, but the fever struck Oregon early enough for
Burnett to begin organizing a train late that summer. "It occurred to me that we
might be able to make the trip with wagons," he wrote, so he asked former Hudson's
Bay chieftain John McLoughlin if he thought it was practical. "Without hesitation
he replied that he thought we could succeed." On 10 September 1848 Burnett led
a party of forty-six wagons and between 150 and 200 men south from Oregon
City. Forty miles north of the Sacramento Valley, they met the lost, starving, and
disorganized remnant of the train Peter Lassen had led west from the Humboldt.
The Oregonians saw no "evidence of any work having been bestowed upon the
road by the emigrants." Burnett's pioneers easily cleared the trace of fallen timber
and loose rock. By the end of October they had blazed a wagon road from the
Willamette Valley to the Sacramento Valley. Perhaps two thirds of Oregon's male

---

[8]The number is John Unruh's conservative estimate; see *The Plains Across,* 119–20.

population followed before year's end.[9] This was not good news for the women and children left behind. "Every thing was prosperous until the breaking out of the gold fever in California, when the men, most of them left the plow and the ax in search of the glittering dust," Betsey Bayley wrote from Yamhill County.[10]

Back in the States, "The gold excitement spread like wildfire, even out to our log cabin in the prairie, and as we had almost nothing to lose, and we might gain a fortune, we early caught the fever," recalled Luzena Wilson. "It sounded like such a small task to go out to California, and once there fortune, of course, would come to us."[11] Incredible fantasies of instant wealth animated an astonishing number of Forty-niners, and credible sources fed the mania. "I have seen the gold; I have handled it; I have it now in my possession to the amount of thousands of dollars; and what is most cheering, the quantities appear to be inexhaustible," wrote Donner party veteran James F. Reed. "All who have worked in digging gold, from 4 to 6 hours in a day, have from 800 to 2000 dollars, collected within the last 60 days. This is difficult to be realized, but it is true."[12]

The hysteria became a worldwide phenomenon, attracting thousands from Central America and Polynesia, spreading to South America, crossing the Pacific to Australia and China, and finally infecting Europe.[13] "Many die unheeded, many come off rich," wrote California's military governor, "but there are ten arriving from each quarter of the globe to replace every one who goes—Chinese, Sandwich Islanders, Chilians, Peruvians, Prussians, Mexicans, French, English, Irish, outnumber as yet the Americans, but the latter will soon have their share."[14] As Malcolm Rohrbough observed, "When California discovered gold, the world discovered California."[15]

Gold fever, John Berry Hill recalled, "was as contagious as the itch. If you took it, brimstone and grease wouldn't cure you. The only remedy was to go to the mines and try your luck."[16] Why did Americans respond so enthusiastically to the call of California's gold? Some claimed the noblest of motives. "Our object is to endeavor to make something in California so as to support them in their old days as well as to enable us to remove them from unpleasant recollections," wrote Alexander Graham, seeking to justify abandoning his aging family.[17] Francis A.

---

[9]Burnett, *Recollections*, 254–55; "Meeting of Emigrants—The New Road," *California Star & Californian*, 18 November 1848, 2/3.

[10]Bayley to Griffith, 20 September 1849, in Holmes, *Covered Wagon Women*, 1:38.

[11]Wilson, *Luzena Stanley Wilson*, 1.

[12]"From California. A Letter from James F. Reed," 11 August 1848, *Illinois Journal*, 29 June 1849, 2. Although printed too late to influence Forty-niners, such reports contributed to the even larger 1850 emigration.

[13]For the worldwide impact of the gold craze, see Rohrbough, "We Will Make Our Fortunes," 55–70; Browning, *To the Golden Shore*, 74.

[14]Smith, "California—Letter from Gov. Smith," *Bangor Whig and Courier*, 26 June 1849.

[15]Rohrbough, *Days of Gold*, 20.

[16]Hill, *A Gold Hunter*, 16.

[17]Graham to "Dear Barbour," 19 May 1850, Beinecke Library.

Hardy said he was leaving all that was dear to him on earth "to procure the means (if possible by industry, honesty and persevereance) to render my family (a wife and infant son) comfortable and happy."[18]

The dismal state of the capital-starved American economy, still mired in a deep depression brought on by the Panic of 1837 that even the war with Mexico did little to dispel, provided a bottom-line motive for individuals to head to California. "It was a period of National hard times and we being financially involved in our business interests near Clinton, Iowa, longed to go to the new El Dorado and 'pick up' gold enough with which to return and pay off our debts," recalled Catherine Haun, rather delicately obscuring the mountain of unpaid bills she and her new husband left behind.[19] James A. Tate set out for "the much famed Land of Gold in California, to repair a ruined fortune."[20] Dr. Charles E. Boyle felt "determined to make one mighty effort to disenthrall myself from the slavery of the detested sin of being poor, and here I am on my way to California."[21]

"The fever has got a deeper hold on me," Joseph H. Purdy confessed as he contemplated the risks and rewards of a trek to the mines early in 1849: he decided to cut in half his previous estimate of the required time and personal risk. A man could not make a better investment than to grubstake an underfunded Argonaut, he assured his brother. His joint-stock company's charter guaranteed the repayment of any investments and one half of the profits. "By this you will see," Purdy wrote, "that the capitalist risks nothing but the interest on his capital." Purdy's surefire moneymaking machine never left Ohio, but he was spinning a golden dream that would become a model for generations of Americans.[22] The desire to get rich quick was not yet embedded in the country's soul, but El Dorado's dazzling promise of financial liberation without great effort had wide appeal.

In the American West, the California gold rush changed everything. More than any other single event, it permanently transformed the nature of transcontinental wagon travel. Unlike the handful of land-hungry pioneers who had opened the trails, these thousands of gold seekers "came not to settle or build but to plunder." The Oregon Trail became the California Road. In addition to its enormous numbers, the great rush from 1849 to 1852 had characteristics that distinguished those who made the trek during those years from those who traveled the trails to the Pacific before and after.[23] Previous migrations consisted mostly of farming families

---

[18]Hardy, Journal, 25 April 1850, Beinecke Library.

[19]Haun, "A Woman's Trip Across the Plains in 1849," 166.

[20]Tate, Diary, 1849, Western Historical Manuscripts. Tate died shortly after reaching California.

[21]Boyle, Diary, 2 April 1849, serialized in the *Columbus Dispatch*.

[22]John Purdy to James Purdy, 23 February [?], 3 and 28 March 1849, BYU Library.

[23]Unruh, Jr., *The Plains Across*, 7. Three of the best recent studies of the California gold rush are Rohrbough, *Days of Gold;* Eifler, *Gold Rush Capitalists;* and Johnson, *Roaring Camp.*

in which women and children often outnumbered the men, but the Forty-niners proved to be largely young males.[24] Alongside a leavening of gamblers and criminals, they included a surprising number of educated professional men from respectable families—men who were bedazzled by the prospect of instant wealth, especially when contrasted with the limited opportunities available in the cash-strapped economies of the South and Midwest. Commenting on the California emigrants in January 1849, the *New York Herald* found them to be "remarkably orderly, respectable, and intelligent" and mourned the loss of "the finest portion of our youth."[25]

During the gold-inspired migration, older states lost young men in numbers that increased the phenomenon's likeness to a war. The gold craze resembled war fever at its hottest pitch. El Dorado had broad appeal, but it was especially attractive to the population most enchanted by the prospect of military glory. As in war, the cost of California fever would be measured in thousands of deaths and ruined lives. "Destiny of almost every Shade Must Mark the history of Such a vast number Marching to a far distant & in Many respects destitute Country," wrote Daniel Burgert. While pondering the many graves that lined the trail in 1849, he concluded, "our people are rightly Characterized for enterprize & despite distance & danger, the most remote point of our Country has only to [divulge] its hidden resources to Secure a population."[26] Gold seekers shared the faith that it was America's "manifest destiny to overspread the continent allotted by Providence." Jane McManus Storm Cazneau probably coined the redundant slogan in 1845; in January 1849 her magazine said the immense wealth flowing from the conquered province showed "that 'manifest destiny' being fulfilled."[27] No Forty-niner appears to have used the catchy phrase in a journal, but they understood the concept. "This westward march will open a new field to the extention of Liberty and drive savage barbarity and Mexican stupidity before the march of civilization and enterprise," one wrote on the Fourth of July.[28]

More than 100,000 adventurous souls crossed the northern and southern wagon roads to California in 1849 and 1850, and gold fever lured even more people to sail to the goldfields. They came from virtually every trade and profession, including a striking number of physicians and lawyers. "It is surprizing to see how many doctors are going to California," wrote William Rothwell. "Every train has 2 or 3.

---

[24]Experts estimate that women comprised between 5.7 percent (Faragher, *Women and Men on the Overland Trail*, 195) to 10 percent (Read, "Women and Children," 6) of gold rush overland parties.

[25]Browning, *To the Golden Shore*, 103–104.

[26]Burgert and Rudy, Diary, 18 May 1849, Mattes Library, 21. Five weeks after writing this, Burgert drowned at the North Platte ferry.

[27]Anonymous, "Californian Gold," 4. For evidence Cazneau wrote the editorial long credited to her editor, John L. O'Sullivan, see Hudson, *Mistress of Manifest Destiny*, 60–62, 209.

[28]Van Dorn, Diary, 2 July 1849, Beinecke Library.

About every tenth man is a 'professional character.' "[29] Thirty wagons and 127 men formed Hagan Z. Ludington's Star Brilliant Company No. 1, including "2 Physicians and Chemists; Blacksmiths, Carpenters, Wagon-makers, and tradesmen of every kind with tools of every description," plus a number of men who had been across the plains and to San Francisco, all under the command of the wealthy and influential B. C. Brayton, who could speak Spanish, French, and several Indian languages. Ludington trusted they could make the journey in one hundred days (a note appended to his letter claimed his party "made the trip in just 96 days"). Evidence indicated the extravagant reports from El Dorado were true: "I have seen a great deal of the gold brought from there," Ludington wrote, "and our prospects are very flattering for our pockets [to be] full of the gold dust."[30]

Every age group joined the rush west. They came from virtually every state in the Union, and diarists reported meeting Mexican, English, Irish, Norwegian, Continental French, and Italian emigrants, along with entire parties of "Dutchmen"—meaning anyone from Northern Europe. Louis Nusbaumer wound up in Death Valley, but he started his trek with the German California Mining Company.[31] "Met a Mexican family from St. Louis, formerly from San Antonio, with an old poor grey horse packed for California, all alone, very dark skinned, left a train he traveled with," Peter Decker reported while ascending South Pass.[32] Charles Boyle met the same Mexican "going alone to the diggings" with his family. "He had started with the Telegraph train but had left them on account of bad usage."[33] Edmund Booth and a man named Clough headed for the goldfields despite being unable to hear—and Clough could not speak a word. Gordon C. Cone met Booth, a most singular beaing, hiking alone along the Humboldt: "He writes a good hand, is well educated, and communicates altogether by means of writing on a slate that he carri[e]s with him for that purpose."[34] The golden army included such notables as author Edward Bryant and Colonel William Hamilton, a "small, active, smart looking man" who was the son of Alexander Hamilton.[35]

The season followed a hard winter, and the spring "was cold and wet which made the grass late and traveling slow," John Hudgins complained.[36] Bad weather delayed most of the emigration about two weeks, but the moisture provided abundant grass to sustain the thousands of animals being driven west. "The

---

[29]Rothwell, Notes of a Journey, 11 May 1850, Beinecke Library, 47.
[30]Ludington to "My Dear Father," 4 May 1849, California State Library.
[31]Nusbaumer, Erlebnisse einer Reise nach den Goldregionen Californiens, Bancroft Library.
[32]Decker, The Diaries, 15 June 1849, 97.
[33]Boyle, Diary, 15 June 1849.
[34]Booth, Edmund Booth (1810–1905), Forty-niner, 6; Cone, Journal, 19 September 1849, BYU Library, 114–15.
[35]Lord, "At the Extremity of Civilization," 91.
[36]Hudgins, California in 1849, Western Historical Manuscripts.

THE INDEPENDENT GOLD SEEKER

This Forty-niner was fully equipped with all the necessities for an enjoyable 1,900-mile trek to California. Courtesy California History Room, California State Library, Sacramento.

unusual severity of last winter in the mountains and the great fall of snow has just given us a rainy spring, [and] this has been our salvation for we have passed over fair feed for our cattle where old mountaineers and guide books tell us no feed could be found," John M. Muscott wrote. "We have now no fears of a scarcity of grass for our cattle the rest of our journey."[37] Eastbound Mormons told Andrew Lopp Murphy that forage "was 500% better than it has ever been before." By season's end, practically every blade of grass on the trail had vanished into the maws of hungry horses, oxen, mules, or bison.[38]

From the start and with increasing intensity, the rush resembled a horserace. "There is a great many families a-going very ill prepared," wrote Joshua Sullivan. "Those that go ahead will stand the best chance."[39] Companies competed to see who could leave the frontier first, and diarists happily noted overtaking and leaving behind other trains. All too often this led to the brutal overtaxing of teams, and heavy loads and hard duty combined to ruin many animals before they reached Fort Laramie. As Edward Jackson observed, abuse and poor grass "bring ponies almost onto their marrow bones."[40] Men stayed on the road until midnight or later seeking water, grass, or relief from the heat of the day. Charles Boyle observed, "We always found our horses travel faster and farther at night than in day time."[41] Seeing trails crowded with the canvas tops of prairie schooners and growing piles of abandoned food, property, and hardware amplified the desire to reach the gold-fields before all the wealth disappeared. As the season wore on, wagon trains and pack parties traveled farther and harder. Desperate conditions gave rise to waves of theft and random violence. As the great rush intensified, it was every man for himself—and the devil take the hindmost.

The Cheapest, Best and Most Expeditious Route: Passages to the Goldfields

As the nation struggled to absorb a third of Mexico, slavery stopped the political reorganization of America's newly conquered Southwest in its tracks. Congress dallied until September 1850 before granting California statehood and creating New Mexico and Utah territories. But while Washington dithered, Colonel Mason's tea caddy of gold did more than ignite a mass migration. Frontier politicians had spent decades lobbying the federal government to take an active role in protecting

[37]Muscott to Robbins, 10 June 1849, California State Library.
[38]Murphy, Diary, 12 June 1849, Western Historical Manuscripts.
[39]Sullivan to "Dear Wife," 8 May 1849, California Letters, Oregon Historical Society.
[40]Jackson, Journal, 25 August 1849, BYU Library.
[41]Boyle, Diary, 23 July 1849.

the overland wagon road. Except for sponsoring a few topographical expeditions to the West that produced invaluable maps but explored little unknown country, Congress did nothing to promote or protect the trails until after declaring war on Mexico on 11 May 1846. Eight days later Congress created the Regiment of Mounted Riflemen to establish, administer, and garrison military posts on the Oregon Trail at the "earliest practical date." It allocated a mere $3,000 to cover each fort's cost—and the army sent the regiment to Mexico. After distinguished service at Churubusco and Chapultepec, the unit was discharged, scattered, and finally reconstituted in August 1848 under Colonel William Loring. On 10 May 1849, the Riflemen left Jefferson Barracks in Saint Louis to begin a two-thousand-mile march to Oregon and fulfill its original assignment.[42]

Robert Morris of the Riflemen, brevetted captain for gallantry at Chapultepec, received problematic orders to command a twenty-five man escort for "General" John Wilson, whose kinsman Zachary Taylor had appointed him navy agent and "Principal Indian Agent" for Alta California. Wilson hired James Mason Hutchings, a talented British artist who signed on as the train's carpenter; Hutchings thought Wilson looked "like a plain, honest old farmer, one that is shrewd enough to know what is right, and tactful enough to know how get it." Despite this positive first impression, Wilson was a wily, dogmatic, and temperamental country lawyer from Missouri who proved neither diplomatic nor modest. Hutchings considered Morris an officer and a gentleman, but Wilson wrote a long report denouncing the young war hero as inexperienced, incompetent, vain, and unfit for command. The general's entourage included his wife and two daughters in a family carriage; three sons; a doctor; a botanist; plus seven teamsters to drive the seven government wagons carrying Wilson's law books, baggage, 225 pounds of rope, and "substantial household property as we thought would have enabled us to go to housekeeping." Historian Fred Rogers thought the trek might have been "the most expensive overland journey of the time by a government official."[43]

Captain Howard Stansbury of the Topographical Engineers reached Fort Leavenworth too late to accompany the Riflemen. On the last day of May, he set out with eighteen men and five wagons with orders to correct or confirm John C. Frémont's 1843 maps of the "practicable wagon route," particularly all the "notorious positions, such as Fort Kearny, Fort Laramie, the South Pass, and Fort Hall." He was to survey the Great Salt Lake, evaluate Fort Hall and determine the best way to supply the fort if it became an army post, keep a journal, and make a "correct map of your route." Stansbury was to "neglect no subject of interest," including the

[42]Settle, *March of the Mounted Riflemen*, 13–16, 21, 69, 98n109, 129.

[43]Ibid.; Bruff, *Gold Rush*, 259, 620n206; Rogers, "Bear Flag Lieutenant," 157; Culmer, "'General' John Wilson," 323; Morris, Journal, Beinecke Library.

Mormons and how they were faring in their new home. A small emigrant party sought the expedition's protection, including Mrs. Charles C. Sackett, whose cheerfulness and vivacity "beguiled the tedium" of the trek, while her fortitude and patience "set an example worthy of the imitation of many of the ruder sex."[44]

The U.S. Army finally established its first permanent Oregon Trail military post when a volunteer regiment began building Fort Childs in 1848 at the head of Grand Island on the Platte River. Almost immediately the name was changed to Fort Kearny—after the famed frontier officer Stephen Watts Kearny, who was struck down that fall by a mosquito in Mexico. The low-lying spot was in the heart of Indian country at the confluence of several trails but was not the perfect location for a military station. "Fort Kearny is a sort of one-horse affair, stuck down in the mud on the wrong side of the river, and a long distance from wood and every other comfort," wrote one critic. He thought the site "must have been selected by some person who did not know what he was doing."[45]

For those who went to California on their own dime and not at the government's expense, the question of the hour was this: "Which was the cheapest, best and most expeditious route to reach San Francisco?"[46] There were three ways to get to the West Coast in 1849—"the Plains across, the Horn around, or the Isthmus over." The long voyage around Cape Horn was safest and easiest. Several primitive routes across Central America offered the quickest way to reach the goldfields—and both waterborne routes were safer than walking to California. Along the East Coast, companies quickly chartered ships to sail to the Pacific: within days of Polk's announcement, it was impossible to book a passage to the land of gold. About 16,000 Argonauts rounded the Horn in 1849; an estimated 4,624 hardy souls sailed to Panama, crossed to the Pacific, and then competed to buy a ticket to San Francisco.[47] Some 11,229 Argonauts followed them in 1850 and in 1851 opened another route across Nicaragua.[48] As a captain in the U.S. Fourth Infantry learned in 1852, it was not a tropical vacation. "The horrors of the road, in the rainy season, are beyond description," wrote Ulysses S. Grant, recalling the scores of men, women, and children who died crossing Panama.[49]

"In 1852 there were but three routes by which one could reach the Pacific Coast," wrote Theodore Potter, who said a man's choice "depended absolutely upon the amount of money which he had on hand." With $300, he could take a steamer from New Orleans to Nicaragua or Panama, cross to the Pacific, and sail to California in

---

[44]Madsen, *Exploring the Great Salt Lake*, 2–6, 22–23, 25n38.

[45]"S.M.B.," 1 July 1852, *Missouri Republican*, in Watkins, "Notes," 239–40.

[46]Webster, *Gold Seekers of '49*, 18.

[47]Unruh, *The Plains Across*, 401.

[48]Folkman, *The Nicaragua Route*, 163. Folkman estimated that 456,103 passengers used the Isthmian routes by 1869.

[49]Grant, *Papers of Ulysses S. Grant*, 1:251–52.

about thirty days. For $150 he could sail around Cape Horn "and reach the Golden Gate in any time from three to six months according to the season." If he lacked funds, he could work his way across the "so-called American Desert, and after spending anywhere from four to six months on the way would reach the golden valleys of California."[50] Neither Potter's numbers nor his logic was precise, since guidebooks estimated $750 was the minimum cost for a sea voyage. Careful records of expenses indicate they ranged from $600 to more than $1,200. Tradition held that half of those who went by sea reached San Francisco with empty pockets. "I would not think of setting off on such a trip again without $1000, not counting passage money," wrote one.[51]

Location played a key role in which route a traveler chose. People living east of the Alleghenies generally favored the sea routes, whereas those to the west were much more likely to go overland. New Yorkers and New Englanders usually chose the convenience and relative safety of a sea voyage, but a few of them "preferred the novelty, the sport, and the adventure of a trip by land to the tedium of a sea voyage."[52] After New Hampshire native Kimball Webster compared the dangers of "a protracted detention on the Isthmus and the tediousness of a long, monotonous journey via Cape Horn," he decided an overland crossing "would be an interesting and romantic journey and one not entirely free from difficulties and hardships."[53]

By the time the great rush began in 1849, some twenty-five hundred wagons had crossed the Oregon Trail, which was no longer a trail but a wagon road, albeit with some rough spots in the Cascade Range. After 1845 many of those wagons surmounted the Cascades over the Barlow Road or reached the Willamette Valley by the southern route from the Humboldt. In contrast, the California Trail was still—as Peter Lassen called it in July 1848—the "California trace," a shifting set of tracks laid down by about four hundred wagons. It was what guidebook author T. H. Jefferson described as "a simple wagon trail—part good, and part very bad."[54] The precise route varied from year to year along a line still being worked out by trial and error. The two Sierra crossings that became the most important corridors on the California Road—the Lassen Trail and the Carson Pass wagon road—opened only on the very eve of the rush. By the end of the great migration of 1852, the Oregon Trail and the California Trace were transcontinental wagon roads, great national highways.

---

[50]Potter, *Autobiography,* 25.

[51]Lewis, *Sea Routes to the Gold Fields,* 10–11.

[52]H., "Pencillings by the Way," *Alta California,* 21 September 1850, 2/2.

[53]Webster, *Gold Seekers of '49,* 19.

[54]Lassen, "From the Emigrants," 16 July 1848; Jefferson, accompaniment to *Map of the Emigrant Road,* 1. The estimated number of wagons is derived from Unruh's estimate, using a ratio of five emigrants per wagon for Oregon and six emigrants per wagon for California. See *The Plains Across,* 119–20.

Besides the main road up the Platte River, by 1849 there were other ways to cross the plains. Historian John Unruh calculated nine thousand Forty-niners crossed the "so-called southwestern trails," using the Santa Fe, Gila, and Spanish trails; another fifteen thousand tramped across northern Mexico in both 1849 and 1850.[55] Based on a detailed study of additional evidence, Patricia Etter, the leading expert on the southern route, estimated that twenty thousand emigrants used southern routes in 1849 alone.[56] Another web of overland pack trails known as the Zuni Trail crossed what James Collier described as "Alps on Alps and nothing but Alps."[57] For those who wanted to take wagons from Santa Fe to California there was only one practical choice: the rough trace called Cooke's Wagon Road, the passable track Captain Philip St. George Cooke and his Mormon volunteers blazed in 1846 that crossed Guadalupe Pass to Tucson. In October 1849, Forty-niners blazed an alternate trail over Apache Pass, a route Interstate 10 later followed.

The Spanish Trail, opened in 1829 and 1830 as a trading route, was the oldest path between Santa Fe and Los Angeles, but this rugged track had few attractions in 1849. "The way from Santa Fe to the little Salt Lake goes through elevated plains, and as is indicated on the map, is known by the name of SPANISH TRAIL," wrote German guidebook author Bruno Schmölder. "From here on, the way goes southward, through a generally barren valley, over the Vega de Santa Clara, a luxuriant overgrown mountain meadow, by way of the Rio Tinto, down to the coast. This stretch is rather difficult to travel because of the many rocky places."[58] D. Hoyt's notes seem to describe an attempt to go from Santa Fe to Salt Lake in 1849, but his party gave up after their guide deserted and they barely escaped several flash floods.[59] Wagons had traveled this route to southern California and had since 1837, Antoine Leroux claimed in 1853; he was referring to Isaac Slover and William Pope, who "with their wagons and two Mexicans, went from Taos that way."[60] In 1848 a single Mormon wagon had reached Salt Lake after traversing the western half of the "rather difficult" Spanish Trail from Los Angeles, but it was hardly a wagon road. Gamblers who risked leaving the established trail to test an unproven shortcut made a dangerous bet, as the owners of the hundred or so wagons who wound up in Death Valley in 1849 learned.

---

[55]Ibid., 401.

[56]Etter, *To California on the Southern Route*, 13, 15, 19–20. Etter defined "Southern Route" broadly, but did not include most routes across northern Mexico. In a 1995 article, she estimated that 15,000 gold seekers crossed New Mexico and forded the Colorado River at Yuma. See Etter, "To California on the Southern Route," 2.

[57]William Brisbane, in Etter, *To California on the Southern Route*, 57.

[58]Schmölder, *Der Führer für wanderer nach Californian*, Huntington Library translation, 25/96. Today the name "Old Spanish Trail" is popular, but the route was neither old nor Spanish—Mexican and American traders opened it in 1830.

[59]Hoyt to "Mr. Sosey," 20 January 1850, *Missouri Whig*.

[60]Foreman, "Antoine Leroux," 374. Bancroft, *History of California*, 5:722, dated Slover's return with a colony from New Mexico to about 1841 to 1843. No other source reports wagons using the Spanish Trail.

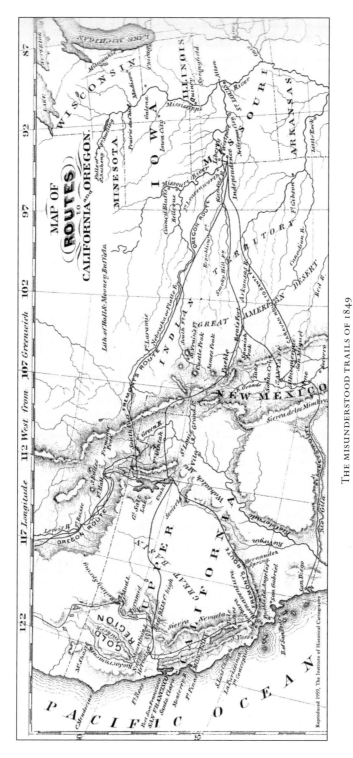

THE MISUNDERSTOOD TRAILS OF 1849

Published in the most popular American guidebook, Oliver Gray Steele's *Map of Routes to California and Oregon* (Buffalo: Hall and Mooney Lithograph, 1849) approximated John C. Frémont's western wanderings but failed to show where the Oregon-California Trail actually went. From Carl I. Wheat, *Mapping the Transmississippi West*.

Ignorance about the way west created a huge demand for reliable information about the trail. Frémont's bestselling reports and his excellent, if not flawless, maps experienced a new surge in sales, and travelers regarded them as holy writ. Commercial guidebooks varied in quality, ranging from Joel Palmer's excellent *Journal of Travels over the Rocky Mountains* to Lansford Hastings's suspect *Emigrants' Guide* to Joseph E. Ware's widely denounced *Emigrants' Guide to California.* New York presses quickly released authentic and fabricated trail guides to meet the insatiable thirst for information about how to get to California. T. H. Jefferson's useful *Map of the Emigrant Road* appeared early in 1849 for three dollars per copy. Four detailed charts listed campsites along with an *Accompaniment* brimming with practical advice from someone who had been there.[61] Jefferson's guide featured the only useful maps, but it was not widely available—Dexter Tiffany may have had made a copy, but Goldsborough Bruff was the only Forty-niner who certainly possessed one. As George Stewart observed, "if more of them had had the map, the summer of '49 would have seen fewer graves along the Humboldt."[62] At the other end of the spectrum was Henry I. Simpson's *Emigrant's Guide to the Gold Mines,* rushed into print in 1848, which Dale Morgan condemned as an outright fraud.[63] Francis Parkman's account of his adventures on the Oregon Trail in 1846 appeared as *The California and Oregon Trail,* a title Parkman disliked, since he went no farther west than Fort Laramie. He considered the publisher's insertion of *"California"* a trick to generate publicity.[64] Translations of Edwin Bryant's *What I Saw in California* appeared in Amsterdam and Brussels, and bibliographic research reveals that in 1849 California guidebooks were issued by presses in Leipzig, Grimma, Weimar, Hamburg, Amsterdam, Moscow, London, Paris, and Christiania, Denmark.

Dozens, if not hundreds, of these guidebooks described the way west, and some of these ephemera have disappeared entirely.[65] Many of the best emigrant diaries, notably Goldsborough Bruff's, began as notes for trail guides. Within a year the 1849 migration had produced several useful waybills by James Abbey, Giles S. Isham, and Riley Root. More fraudulent trail accounts appeared in 1850, notably William Beschke's completely imaginary *Dreadful Sufferings and Thrilling Adventures of an Overland Party of Emigrants.* "Guides got up by persons in the States who have never passed over the plains," authors Philip L. Platt and Nelson Slater complained in 1852, "are of very little practical use to the traveler."[66] Edwin Patterson, who was

---

[61]See Morgan, *Overland in 1846,* 237–44.

[62]Jefferson, *Map of the Emigrant Road,* 8.

[63]For Morgan's quotation and a list of similar guidebooks, see Myres, ed., *Ho For California!*

[64]Parkman, *Letters,* 39. Later editions carried the title popular today, *The Oregon Trail.*

[65]For example, see multiple mentions of Walker's Guide and John Udell's reference to "Heighter's Guide" in his *Incidents of Travel to California.*

[66]Platt and Slater, *Travelers' Guide,* xvi.

working on his own guidebook and camped with Platt at Thousand Springs Valley in 1852, helped explain why his *Travelers' Guide across the Plains* was so highly admired. Platt was "driving an ox team, having wintered with his family at Fort Laramie, and taken an early start. He has a roadometer attached to his wagon, and intends publishing a Guide Book. I looked over his manuscript and find it very correct."[67]

Emigrant opinions about the quality of overland guidebooks varied. Like many others, Asa C. Call recommended William Clayton's *Latter-Day Saints' Emigrants' Guide to Salt Lake,* which was, "as far as it goes, the most reliable work of the kind that I have seen." Other authors, notably journalist Joseph E. Ware, had never seen the trail they described. "Many of these guide books are an outrageous imposition, especially Ware's," Call wrote. "It hits the truth scarcely as often as the almanacs do the weather—for they usually do know enough to put down warm weather for August and snow for January; and his 'guide book' seems to be *all* guess work."[68] Relying on Hastings, Bryant, Clayton, and Frémont, Ware cobbled together "the most informative of all the guidebooks issued at the beginning of the gold rush," but it had many flaws. *Emigrants' Guide to California* praised the Humboldt River as "rich and beautifully clothed with blue grass, herds grass, clover, and other nutritious grasses," and he lined its bank with imaginary timber, claiming the valley furnished "the requisite for the emigrants' comfort, in abundance."[69] This was rank nonsense, and many who had bought his guidebook did not hesitate to say so. Bennett C. Clark called it "perfectly worthless."[70] Ware and other authors had "made a great deal of money, but have ruined thousands," complained S. F. Rodmon.[71] In Ware's defense, at least one overlander recommended it.[72]

At Salt Lake in 1849, Ira J. Willis capitalized on his trail experience to extend William Clayton's guide from Salt Lake to the gold mines. Willis and his Mormon agents sold handwritten copies for a dollar apiece, although Goldsborough Bruff bought his copy, "written in the most illiterate manner," of "Best Guide to the Gold Mines" for fifty cents at City of Rocks.[73] A later traveler came to a balanced perspective on the quality of information available about the trail. "I procured maps which proved more or less inaccurate and guide books which only served to make confusion worse confounded," wrote Randall Henry Hewitt. "As a rule guide books must be considered carefully and then acted upon generally."[74] After

---

[67]Patterson, Diary and Letters, 22 June 1850, Mattes Library.

[68]Call, "From Utah," 20 September 1850, 13.

[69]Caughey, *The California Gold Rush,* 53–54; Ware, *Emigrants' Guide,* 32.

[70]Clark, "A Journey," 20 July 1849, 31.

[71]Rodmon, "From California," 17 August 1849.

[72]Dr. George W. Davis to Waltus Watkins, 6 December 1850, Beinecke Library.

[73]Paden, "The Ira J. Willis Guide," 192–207; Bruff, *Gold Rush,* 1207–1208.

[74]Hewitt, *Across the Plains,* 71.

traveling twenty waterless miles due to poor directions, Edward Jackson expressed a widespread sentiment: "Confound the Guide books!"[75]

A few promoters envisioned revolutionary ways to reach the New El Dorado: some even dreamed of a transcontinental air service. "Said an old Dutchman, where we staid all night, to us seriously," New Yorker John Muscott wrote near Saint Joseph, " 'Why did you not take your passage in the balloon, that the papers say is fitting up in New York to take passengers to California?' " As his guests struggled for an answer, the Dutchman recognized the wisdom of their course: " 'I *just reckon* it cost a *heap* more to travel that way.' "[76] Citizens of Boston were preparing a "light train" of cars, engines, and balloons "to Navigate the air to carry passengers And goods to the gold diggings," Mormon apostle Wilford Woodruff told Brigham Young. He warned they might "burst there boiler & run off the track" over the Salt Lake Valley and rain down hot water, boilers, engines, cars, balloons, sails, dry goods, and men—but there was no cause for alarm since it would be only "a shower of the march of intellect, internal improvement, ingenuity, and yankee Notions."[77] Those who set out for California soon learned it would take more than Yankee notions to reach the land of gold.

ROUGH AND READY: JOINT-STOCK COMPANIES

As gold fever spread, dazzled Americans spontaneously created dozens, if not hundreds, of "joint-stock companies" to finance the journey and subsequent mining operations. Essentially they were extended partnerships in which all members paid a fee to entitle them to a share of the spectacular profits that seemed certain to await anyone willing to venture to the valley of the Sacramento. Massachusetts alone dispatched at least twenty-two such overland organizations, plus another 102 that went by sea.[78] The names of the Wolverine Rangers, Buckeye Rovers, Ohio Volcano Mining Company, Savannah Boys, Illinois California Bound Invincibles, and Piqua Independent California Company honored hometowns or states. Others adopted more colorful monikers: the Spartan Band, the Helltown Greasers, the Telegraph Train, the Rough and Ready Company, the Darby Plains California Company, the Enterprise Company, the Banner Company, and the California Rangers.[79]

---

[75]Jackson, Journal, 27 August 1849, BYU Library, 79.

[76]Muscott to Robbins, 27 April 1849, California State Library, 3.

[77]Woodruff, *Wilford Woodruff's Journal*, 15 February 1849, 3:419.

[78]Potter, *Trail to California*, 13–15.

[79]The most thoroughly documented gold rush joint-stock company is probably Michigan's Wolverine Rangers. See Cumming, *Gold Rush*; Webster, *Gold Seekers of '49*; Goldsmith, *Overland in Forty-Nine*; and Swain, *The World Rushed In*, 51, 451–65, which include company constitutions.

Citizens of the young nation were devoted to democracy, so many gold rush parties drafted complicated constitutions that would have been better suited to running small republics. Former Virginia legislator Joseph S. Watkins's party of seventy Tennesseans had both republican and military governments, "a constitution and by-laws, a president and vice-president, a legislature, three judges, and court of appeals, nine sergeants, as well as other officers." The officials considered the drudgery of camp chores and standing guard beneath their dignity, a stance that "produced murmuring, which ripened into actual rebellion." Watkins petitioned the aristocracy in the legislature to change the constitution, but "no member was found willing to present a petition which compromised his own privilege." Thirteen wagons defected, and the traveling republic and its sublime government "fell to pieces by the weight of its own machinery and exclusive privileges."[80]

These charters sometimes required members to refrain from bad conduct and to observe the Sabbath—"And no member of this Association is to perform any unnecessary labor upon the Sabbath day," the constitution of the Painesville Mining Association directed.[81] They often contained a temperance pledge and a promise to refrain from other bad habits. "No gambling of any kind shall be indulged in by the members of this Association, either among themselves or with others," read article 10 of the Columbus and California Industrial Association's constitution. "Nor shall any member be allowed to use any kind of intoxicating drink, unless administered under medical advice."[82] Grounds for expulsion from the Columbus Mining and Trading Company included neglect of duty, gambling, intemperance, and embezzling company property.[83] Such resolutions were easier to make than to keep. By early June 1849, Charles Boyle's Mess no. 3 "had tapped the brandy keg belonging to the outfit's medicine chest." By the time they reached the upper Sweetwater five days later, the company "divided the brandy as it was decreasing daily, and some of us wished to preserve a little for an occasion of sickness, and it was not likely to last where it was."[84]

As historian David Potter noted, the joint-stock companies created a paradoxical combination of collectivism and individualism. Some of these organizations, such as William Z. Walker's, "voted to break up our camp and each man look out for himself" before they left the frontier. Few such enterprises survived to reach Fort Laramie, let alone the goldfields.[85] The handful that did make it to California almost always quickly disbanded. "The first business of the company after getting

[80]Delano, *Life on the Plains,* 17 June 1849, 84–85.

[81]Mathews, *Mathews Family,* 277.

[82]"Constitution," *Ohio Statesman,* 15 February 1849.

[83]Purdy to James Purdy, 23 February 1849, BYU Library.

[84]Boyle, Diary, 9 and 14 June 1849.

[85]Potter, *Trail to California,* 13–15; Walker, Diary, 26 April 1849, BYU Library.

through was to dissolve," Mead Turney wrote from the Yuba River in 1849. "After getting off the road, where the force of circumstances held them together, they spontaneously separated."[86] Whether a large company arrived by land or by sea, most broke up "for a very natural cause—it was easier for men to get along alone, or a few banded together, than in heavy parties."[87] While traveling down the Humboldt River, Israel Hale summed up the problem thus: "I have seen enough on this trip to satisfy me that a copartnership or stock company will not do. The reason is: men do not think alike."[88]

The theories and idealism that led to large, highly structured, and closely regulated wagon parties, especially those that left the Missouri frontier in 1849, soon had to confront the reality of life on the trail. Such outfits quickly broke up into more manageable units that seldom totaled more than thirty wagons. By 1852 most trains reflected a more natural and better-adapted organization. "There were few single team or single family outfits, all such attached themselves to some group," recalled John K. Stockton. "These groups were made up of relatives, friends or neighbors, or those belonging to the same religious denomination, or drawn together by some common bond." Despite the strong influence of family and community, these overland outfits were hardly exclusive. "The fame of American gold had reached Europe," Stockton wrote, "and our train numbered those from every civilized nation."[89]

The Pleasures of Going to See the Elephant

One small but wealthy band of Forty-niners hired twenty-six-year-old William Stinson, who claimed to be a veteran of five or six years on the plains, to guide them to California. No less an authority than Kit Carson allegedly recommended him as a skilled guide. Stinson knew something about marketing, too, for he promised his clients "a sight of all the elephants on the route, in other words, of all the interesting objects on our journey."[90]

The origin of the phrase "to see the elephant" goes back to 13 April 1796, when sea captain John Crowinshield landed the first pachyderm in America.[91] Hachaliah Bailey made a fortune exhibiting a series of elephants, beginning in 1815 with the exceptionally talented Old Bet, who met a violent end when a New England farmer shot her for defiling the Sabbath. The saying appeared as early as 1834, and an 1872

---

[86]Turney to Uri Seeley, 16 December 1849, in Mathews, *Mathews Family,* 319.
[87]"California Affairs," *Bangor Whig and Courier,* 17 August 1849.
[88]Hale, "Diary of a Trip to California," 14 August 1849, 107.
[89]Stockton, The Trail of the Covered Wagon, 1929.
[90]Muscott to Robbins, 27 April 1849, California State Library, 1, 5.
[91]Goodwin, "The First Living Elephant in America," 256.

compendium of Americanisms said it meant "to have seen all and to know every-thing." Before that, an English writer defined it as being "up to the latest move" or "down to the latest trick." Once elephants began appearing in circus parades in the late 1830s, the phrase spread like wildfire. On his way to Santa Fe in 1841, George Kendall heard a hunter return to a camp and say wearily, "I've seen the elephant." The greenhorn reporter provoked a gale of laughter when he asked the old scout if he had seen a "real, sure-enough" elephant, but as Kendall learned, "When a man is disappointed in any thing he undertakes, when he has seen enough, when he gets sick and tired of any job he may have set himself about, he has seen the elephant." Early on, wrote historian George Hammond, the expression acquired its secondary but more famous meaning "of having seen and been disappointed, of having labored and failed." Mary MacDougall Gordon thought the saying was popularized by the gold rush, where it meant "to face a severe hazard or to gain experience through ordeals."[92] Different people saw the elephant in different ways at different times—during the Civil War, it described a soldier's first experience with the savagery of combat. The expression "roughly meant 'to see it all,'" David L. Bigler noted. For gold seekers, the phrase captured the romance that drew them west.[93]

The vastness of the Great Plains, the challenges of the Rocky Mountains, and the deserts of the Green River Country offered westbound travelers plenty of opportunities to become acquainted with the beast, but some anticipated meet-ing him even before they crossed the Missouri River. While fording the Grand River in Iowa, Elizabeth Bedwell "saw a few hairs of the Elephants tail."[94] Not far away, James Tolles had to wade into a river to clear a ford that high water had washed out: "this looks a little like the Elephant," he wrote.[95] "If we have not had a glimpse of the *Elephant* himself today we have at least seen the showbill of him," William Renfro Rothwell commented while still on the Missouri River. "There is a great deal of talk now about the Elephant," he wrote home a week later. "It is thought we will get to see him soon. He is ranging this side of the mountains."[96] Cholera terrified overlanders. At Saint Joseph Gordon Cone said two doctors with his party "have seen the Elephant, have dissuaded as many as they could, and are makeing their arrangements to go back."[97]

From the start, the trials of the trail were enough to make one emigrant turn back, having "seen the Elephant and eaten its ears."[98] A day's journey from Fort

---

[92]Hammond, "Who Saw the Elephant?" 3–7; Reid, *Overland to California,* 31n20.

[93]Bigler, "The Elephant Meets the Lion," 1.

[94]Bedwell, Journal of Road to Oregon, 15 May 1852, Mattes Library.

[95]Tolles, Journal of My Travels, 28 April 1849, BYU Library, 10.

[96]Rothwell, Notes of a Journey, 16, 28 April, 5 May 1850, Beinecke Library.

[97]Cone, Journal of Travels, 23 May 1849, 12.

[98]Mattes, *Great Platte River Road,* 62.

THE ELEPHANT

During the gold rush, the phrase "going to see the elephant" became synonymous with going to California. Whether they saw the elephant on the trail or in the mines, it essentially meant, "Now I've seen everything." Author's collection.

Laramie, William Riley Murray "met some return waggons (seen the elephant) they told us we could get no more grass for 100 miles ahead after crossing the Platte."[99] The beast intimidated thoughtful travelers like Samuel Stover, who met wagons on the back track from the North Platte Ferry whose parties cautioned, "The elephant is just on ahead"; he hoped not to see him.[100] Some downplayed their encounters with the pachyderm: "And I have seen the *elephant,* surveyed him from head to tail—at all hours and in all moods," Franklin Grist commented at Fort Kearny, "and my opinion is that on the whole he is neither so good nor so bad as he is made out to be."[101] Others were warlike in their defiance: "We are told that the Elephant is in waiting, ready to receive us," wrote James D. Lyon. "If he shows fight or attempts to stop us on our progress to the golden land, we shall attack him with sword and spear."[102] Horace Ladd was more realistic: "Our motto is to go ahead till we see the Elephant, and if we cannot conquer him we will try to go around him."[103]

However imposing the beasts that dwelt east of the Rockies may have seemed, rogue elephants haunted the deserts of the Snake River plain and the Great Basin. The fiercest of the breed lived near the crest of the Sierra Nevada and the Cascades. Many met the creatures on the Black Rock Desert or at the Sink of the Humboldt, on the Forty-mile Desert or on the slopes of the Blue Mountains. "From the sink, I saw tracks of the Elephant—hundreds of emigrants lost their all, between the sink and Truckies River," Charles Lockwood wrote from Sacramento. "I do not recollect being out of sight of dead, or dying Cattle, Horses, or Mules—a distance of 30 miles." But it was "from the summit of Sierra Nevada, to the Gold Mines, you find the elephant in his most formidable shape, with sundry *Horns* and *Tusks,*" Lockwood warned.[104] If travelers were lucky enough to escape the deserts and Indians with animals and outfit intact, like Charles Turner they were certain to see the elephant among the peaks and passes of "the Sierra Nevada, where the Boys say the 'Elephant' stays, and they think they had a fair view of him."[105]

"Oh the pleasures of going to see the Elephant!!!" an exasperated Lucy Rutledge Cooke wrote after a tough crossing of the Bear River.[106] "I have walked two-thirds of this twenty-four hundred mile trip; been out of 'grub' part of the time—the very time, too, I had to work the hardest; and must say that I cannot regret having taken the journey," Edwin Patterson said after reaching the goldfields. "I have never, yet, seen the elephant, nor do I believe any one else, who came over with

[99]Murray, Diary, 5 July 1849, Mattes Library.

[100]Stover, *Diary,* 4 July 1849, 20.

[101]Grist to "Dear Mother," 20 June 1849, University of North Carolina.

[102]Mattes, *Great Platte River Road,* 61.

[103]Ladd, 8 July 1849, in Cumming, *Gold Rush,* 65.

[104]Lockwood to "Respected and highly esteemed friends," 7 December 1849, Missouri Historical Society.

[105]Turner to "Dear Bro. & Sister," 23 August 1849, in Mathews, *Mathews Family,* 307.

[106]Cooke, "Letters on the Way to California," 4:288.

the same outfit, has had any cause to complain," he claimed. Those who did, he concluded, "had no curiosity to gratify—no ambition to sustain him in difficulties, or who is constitutionally too lazy to enjoy good health. We are at length here, in the land of our golden dreams, and shall endeavor to make up for lost time."[107]

To Fit Themselves Out:
Preparing for the Road to El Dorado

For years thriving frontier emporia at Independence, Westport, and Saint Joseph had offered a variety of services for westbound emigrants. When demand exploded in 1849, towns to the north such as Weston and Council Bluffs joined in the competition for the lucrative trade as business boomed all along the Missouri frontier. Merchants offered complete outfits to take a family across the plains, and craftsmen built specially designed wagons in which both families and fortune seekers could make the journey in style and comfort. Travelers gradually shifted their preferred departure point northward, encouraged by popular overland guides such as Hosea B. Horn's, which touted Council Bluffs as "the natural crossing of the Missouri River, on the route destined by nature for the great thoroughfare to the Pacific. This was the road first selected by *nature's civil engineers,* the buffalo and the elk, for their Western travel."[108]

The basic outfit needed to cross the plains consisted of a wagon and its teams or pack mules and packs, plus a six-month supply of food, cooking and camping gear, bedclothes, a water keg and a few buckets, tools, perhaps a tent and a small stock of medicine, and enough clothing and footwear to make the trip and ideally last another year. "We felt that surely we must be armed to the teeth after crossing the border," David Leeper recalled. Most Forty-niners did not feel properly outfitted without a rifle, revolver, shotgun, and Bowie knife.[109] Knowledgeable overlanders stocked items to trade with the locals, and T. H. Jefferson listed Mackinaw blankets, flintlock guns, powder and ball, knives, hatchets, squaw awls, whiskey, tobacco, beads, vermillion, and flints as *"Goods in demand among Indians."* Jefferson advocated forsaking wagons entirely. "Packing is the safest and most expeditious, and in some respects preferable, even for women and children," he wrote.[110] Many carried a supply of alcohol for whatever need might arise. Forty-niners soon learned that hard cash could solve a host of problems or even purchase a life-restoring essential like water on the Forty-mile Desert.

[107]Patterson, Diary and Letters, 16 July 1850, Mattes Library.
[108]Horn, *Horn's Overland Guide,* [vi].
[109]Leeper, *Argonauts of 'Forty-nine,* 12.
[110]Jefferson, *Map of the Emigrant Road,* 1, 17.

On the eve of the rush, Peter Lassen advised people thinking about crossing the Rocky Mountains how to fit themselves out. The veteran trailblazer advocated traveling lightly. He recommended a wagon with tolerably high wheels and no fewer than four yoke of good strong oxen and "bringing no loading but what will be absolutely necessary on the road—meat and bread, or bread stuffs," and as few cooking and other utensils as possible—"and these of the lightest kind, no extra bedding; nor useless chests, trunks, boxes, &c." Such trumpery would inevitably have to be thrown out "as thousands of others have done," he warned, and might kill some of their oxen.[111] Few Forty-niners heeded Lassen's warning, which was not widely reprinted, but such sensible advice was slow to be appreciated. "The theory that prevailed in 1848–49 in regard to the weight and strength of wagons and teams that would enable them to stand the journey had been completely reversed before we went out," John Parkinson recalled. Heavy wagons carrying a year's worth of provisions simply wore out teams. When his family set out in 1852, "the needed supplies were definitely known; and everything in the outfit was made as light as possible consistent with the strength necessary to stand the wear and tear of the journey."[112]

It was hard to fit the basic necessities for a two-thousand-mile journey into a wagon that could haul only a single ton. Novices felt compelled to purchase "mining tools, cooking utensils, sheet iron, stoves, horseshoes, kegs of powder, quantities of lead and all other things," Mark D. Manlove noted, and they littered the trail all the way to Fort Laramie.[113] Frontier merchants quickly learned to retrieve the abandoned items and sell them the next season. "I suppose I have seen more than a wagon load of bacon and beans I can't say how many. Some have throwed away flour Some powder and mining tools, cooking stoves, peaches, and in fact every thing," wrote William Franklin Knox. "If we had known about these things we might have come empty this far and got everything we wanted for nothing."[114]

Overland travelers found that an ordinary light farm wagon was best adapted for the journey, but oversized and customized wagons were not uncommon. Margaret Frink's wagon "was designed expressly for the trip, it being built light, with every-thing planned for convenience." As the wife of a successful Indiana merchant, Frink was able to travel in style. Her wagon "was so arranged that when closed up, it could be used as our bedroom. The bottom was divided off into little compartments or cupboards," and the interior was "lined with green cloth, to make it pleasant and soft for the eye, with three or four large pockets on each side, to hold many little

[111]Lassen, "From the Emigrants," 16 July 1848, 1/2.
[112]Parkinson, "Memories of Early Wisconsin and the Gold Mines," 2.
[113]Manlove, An Overland Trip, California State Library.
[114]Knox to "Dear Father," 25 May 1849, Mattes Library, 2.

A "String Box" straight ox wagon

Most overlanders favored simple "straight" wagons, shown here in a Nick Eggenhofer image depicting an ox harness that became popular after the gold rush. From the artist's *Wagons, Mules and Men: How the Frontier Moved West*. Courtesy Evelyn E. Herman.

conveniences,—looking-glasses, combs, brushes, and so on." After loading the bottom of the wagon box with provisions and baggage, her husband covered it with a floor that supported an India-rubber mattress "that could be filled with either air or water, making a very comfortable bed. During the day we could empty the air out, so that it took up but little room." Frink also had a feather bed and pillows, and the couple stayed at hotels and farmhouses every night until they crossed the Missouri River. Her husband lashed a small sheet-iron cooking stove behind the wagon and purchased two five-gallon India-rubber bottles for desert crossings.[115]

Although they were novices, William Henry Hart and his three companions showed considerable insight when they determined the kind of wagon they wanted in 1852 and "ordered it built in the best style." Their "outfit consisted of four yoke of oxen, young sound healthy animals, a string box wagon without springs and with a cover of heavy Duck doubled." The wagon had a deck or false floor built in sections so they could remove it at will, and they filled it full to the roof with bags of corn. "About a foot or more of the forward part of the wagon was partitioned off to contain our cooking utensils, tools, and small articles of daily use,

---

[115]Frink, "Adventures of a Party of Gold Seekers," 61–62.

which included our iron Camp Kettles, Tin, Coffee, & Tea Pots water Buckets Frying Pan, Stew Pan, Axe, Hatchet, Auger, chisel & such tools," Hart wrote. For provisions they "laid in a stock of Bacon, Dried Beef & Venison, Dried apples & Peaches, Flour, Crackers, Sugar Tea, Coffee, Rice, Beans, Saleratus, Pepper, Salt, &c &c." They had a practical fifteen-gallon water keg and a good supply of halter rope. "Our Tar Bucket was slung under the hind axle tree and extra ox Bows and a yoke were fastened under the wagon body." At the Grand River crossing on the Rock Island road across Iowa, Hart saw "a great variety of styles of wagons of all shapes and sizes. Some had made their wagon bodies like scows so that they use them as ferry boats." Most wagons had two or three yoke of cattle "and once in a while we see a light wagon with one yoke, very few have over 5 yoke. Then there are horse teams with light wagons and 2, 4 or 6 horses. Some have plain white cotten covers like ours, others oiled or painted," Hart reported.[116]

Wagons came in all colors—red and green were particularly popular—and overlanders found other ways to personalize their rolling homes. "It is quite amusing to note the different mottoes on the wagon covers, such as 'From Danville, Ill., and bound for Oregon,' 'Bound for California or bust,'" E. W. Conyers reported.[117] On her way to California in 1860, Lavinia Porter saw similar fanciful legends such as Pikes Peak or Bust, and Root Hog or Die. She "met these teams coming back, and underneath their legends was the scrawled term 'Busted' or 'The Hog's Dead.'"[118]

Overlanders also used carts and carriages to head west. Carts had proven to be the most efficient vehicles during the fur trade, but they were not widely used during the gold rush. A carriage had started for California in 1843 with one of the first westbound wagon trains, but it made it no farther than the Raft River. The Mormon Pioneer Camp took three carriages all the way to the Salt Lake Valley in 1847 and brought at least two of them back to the Missouri River in the fall, so they proved able to survive at least the first part of the Oregon Trail. T. H. Jefferson offered some interesting advice: "A light one-horse Rockaway, or pleasure wagon, with patent axles and hubs, containing from three to five hundred pounds weight, and drawn by two horses, will perform the journey more speedily, and probably as well, as any wagon."[119] Many appreciated carriages, coaches, Dearborns, and drays for their comfort and speed, but these vehicles were not well adapted to the difficult mountain crossings on the road to the Pacific. The Pioneer Line left

---

[116]Hart, Diary, 1 February, 1 March, 21 April, and 12 May 1852, BYU Library, 7–10, 47–48.

[117]Conyers, "Diary," 25 May 1852.

[118]Porter, "By Ox Team to California," 220.

[119]A Long Island carriage builder developed the Rockaway carriage, which was similar to a New England "Pleasure Wagon," in the early 1830s. The design let the driver and passengers sit on the same level under an extended roof and became popular as a "'democratic' wagon for American tastes." The Oregon Historical Society offers plans for a Rockaway Coupe on its website. Eventually, the Rockaway influenced the design of the limousine.

Independence with twenty fine new six-passenger spring wagons, but Captain Thomas Turner, the proprietor, had to abandon five of them at Independence Rock. Turner later attempted to get the line's few surviving carriages over the Sierra, but it does not appear he succeeded.[120] Experience taught many emigrants that they were unlikely to get their carriages over the worst parts of the road. Many such rigs acquired from gold seekers enlivened the streets of Great Salt Lake City.

The obvious disadvantages of vehicles as fragile as carriages did not prevent people from trying to take them overland. While waiting for a companion to die on the Fourth of July, Bennett Clark found an abandoned four-wheeled "Dearbourn" carriage.[121] Not only did Harriet Buckingham have a mule-drawn carriage to ride in when her family headed west in 1851, she had a hired hand to drive it.[122] Jane Kellogg's husband bought a light horse carriage to take her and her mother to Oregon.[123] Overlooking the junction of the Independence and Saint Joseph roads in May 1850, Francis Hardy could see "hundreds of men & some women on horses and mules & hundreds more on foot & riding in wagons, carts, & carriages, all in motion & bound for California, Salt Lake or Oregon (many of these for the latter place were women & children, some of the latter at the breast)."[124] Near the Loup Fork in 1852, E. W. Conyers saw "a splendid four-horse coach in which is seated four richly dressed young ladies and two young girls, aged about 10 and 12 years, and a young man who was handling the lines." They were clearly enjoying themselves, for "one of the young ladies was making music on an accordeon, another was playing on a guitar; all were singing as they trotted past, gay as larks."[125]

The problem with such vulnerable vehicles was getting them all the way over the trail, as Francis Sawyer learned the hard way. Her husband bought a single-horse carriage for her at Saint Joseph and a mule named Jennie that she adored. "My mule and carriage go along so nicely and comfortably," Sawyer wrote. "She never stops for mud-holes. She is the best animal we have." On the Humboldt, her party harnessed her beloved Jennie to a wagon "and put one of the wagon mules into the carriage. I did not admire the change, but submitted, and sure enough, bad luck came of it." The mule mired down while crossing a slough, "and before they could unharness him, he began jumping and kicking and broke one of the shafts to the carriage. I was so sorry I felt like crying, for I thought I would have to leave my carriage behind." But Thomas Sawyer "went to work and mended it, so that now it is almost as stout as it ever was."

[120]Tiffany, Diary and Letters, 12 July 1849, Missouri Historical Society; Reid, *Overland to California,* 129.
[121]Clark, "A Journey," 3 July 1849, 25.
[122]Buckingham, "Crossing the Plains ," 18.
[123]Kellogg, "Memories," 1852.
[124]Hardy, Journal, 17 May 1850, Beinecke Library.
[125]Conyers, "Diary," 25 May 1852.

Crossing the Forty-mile Desert was easier in 1852 than it had ever been before, Francis observed, but the journey still took its toll. Near Gold Canyon her husband concluded their four-horse wagon was too hard on the mules and not worth hauling over the Sierra Nevada, so he sold it for $25. The men built packsaddles and "put some light things into my carriage," she reported, planning to "drive it as far as it will hold out." This was not far: the "rough, rocky, and difficult" trace up West Carson Canyon had stones as large as hogsheads littering the road. "Our carriage broke down, and we had to abandon it. One wheel got fastened between two rocks and broke all to pieces." The Sawyers packed everything on mules and made it to Placerville four days later, but they discovered that their dog "had been left behind somewhere." The beloved carriage, which had actually crossed the California border, was history, but Thomas Sawyer, who must rank among the most devoted of all husbands and dog owners in trail history, went back twelve gritty miles and rescued the wandering pet. "We had a very dusty road to-day," Francis wrote. "I tell you I was glad to be in California at last."[126]

All Starving Together: Provisions

The question of how much food it would take to cross the plains was one of life and death. "We had laid in a bountiful supply of provisions, for such a journey required a vast amount," wrote Margaret Chambers, recalling how her family prepared for their 1851 trek when she was seventeen. "None but those who have cooked for a family of eight, crossing the plains, have any idea of what it takes."[127] Joseph Ware certainly did not. His popular 1849 guidebook calculated it would cost a little less than $21 per person to buy a larder large enough to make the trip.[128] A lack of insight into proper nutrition further hampered gold rushers, especially men. "Many laid in a very bad supply of provisions, and this unwholesome diet proves more than a match for their stomachs," observed Asa Call in 1850.[129] Dale Morgan considered Platt and Slater's *Traveler's Guide* of 1852 to be "one of the more distinguished among the overland guides." It recommended a variety of provisions that would "keep well across the plains—such as flour, corn meal (kiln-dried), hard-bread, crackers of different kinds, side bacon and hams, tea, coffee, sugar, different kinds of dried fruits, beans and rice; to which may be added some pickles, a little vinegar, and some good butter," with "the whole amount to be not less than 300 pounds to each man; it should be more rather than less."[130]

---

[126]Sawyer, "Kentucky to California," 11 May, 26 July, 7, 11, 15 August 1852, 4:85, 87, 108, 112–14.
[127]Chambers, *Reminiscences*, 42.
[128]Ware, *Emigrants' Guide to California*, 7. Ware also failed to add his cost estimates correctly.
[129]Call, "From Utah."
[130]Platt and Slater, *Travelers' Guide*, v, xvii–xviii.

Provisioning was a complicated process. Prices were high on the Missouri frontier, so careful travelers like John Tucker Scott shipped provisions down the Illinois
and Mississippi rivers and up the Missouri to avoid paying the premium. They
arrived at Saint Joseph "all stored & in good order" in early May. Scott soon had
the supplies loaded and was ready to start the following day—assuming he could
get across the river.[131] Supplies had to be carefully stored. "The food was packed
in crates, made very tight, to keep out dust and moisture. These were fitted into
the bottom of the wagons and on top of them, bedding, clothing and other necessities were packed," recalled John Stockton. "We had dried apples, peaches and
pumpkin, sorghum molasses, made from sugar, furnished our sweets. The maple
sugar was molded into cakes, and was looked upon as a luxury."[132] As the women
in her 1852 overland party prepared for the trip, they "busied themselves in laying
in supplies of medicines and the many little delicacies and necessaries that only a
woman would think of, and of which a man would never dream," Mary Alexander
Variel reported.[133] Each wagon should take a twenty-gallon water cask, Joseph E.
Ware advised, which was about twice the size trail veterans suggested.[134]

Many overlanders considered coffee every bit as vital for a successful journey
as food, if not more so. "There is no getting along without coffee on these plains,"
wrote John Hawkins Clark. Gold seekers considered the brew so essential that it
commanded a dollar a pound on the trail. "As for coffee I believe I could make it
better than any other man on the plains before we got through, and it is an article
that we could well afford to take pains with, there being no food obtainable on
that trip so refreshing, invigorating and cheering as real good coffee," boasted
William Hart. "It seemed to put every man in good spirits to strengthen him up
and increase his powers of endurance. We drank it every morning and made tea
generally in the evening."[135] Sugar was a welcome luxury—Alonzo Delano saw
four men demolish one hundred pounds in only ninety days. No matter how well
prepared travelers might be or the amount of food they took along, their diet seldom satisfied the hunger the continual hard work created. "It is astonishing what
appetites we had, and how much the stomach could digest," Delano observed. "It
seems almost insatiable."[136]

Reflecting its surprising influence on American culture, the rush for riches
drove innovative developments in food preservation. James MacDonald thought
a concoction known as the "meat biscuit" was "the greatest article of food ever

---

[131]Scott, "Journal of a Trip to Oregon," introduction, 5:31.

[132]Stockton, The Trail of the Covered Wagon, 1929.

[133]Variel, "A Romance of the Plains," Mattes Library.

[134]Ware, Emigrants' Guide to California, 6.

[135]Clark, "Overland to the Gold Fields," 29 May 1852, 245; Hart, Diaries, 25 April 1852, BYU Library, 30–31.

[136]Delano, Life on the Plains, 30 July 1849, 161.

brought on these plains. It is worth its weight in gold." Texas real-estate promoter Gail Borden developed the product, which was made of dehydrated meat mixed with flour, expressly for the 1849 California trade. "We shave or pound it up, cover it with cold water, let it soak soft, fill it up with hot water, boil it and season it to taste, then break some flour in it," MacDonald wrote in 1850. His party used it once and sometimes twice a day but did not use one-sixth of their supply before crossing South Pass. "It is most excellent," MacDonald reported.[137]

Scurvy was the most pernicious consequence of the lack of vitamin C in most trail provisions. The British navy had issued lime and lemon juice to prevent the disease for almost a hundred years, but despite this knowledge, the lack of fresh vegetables made scurvy the scourge of the trail. "Scurvy has been the poison bane of the last emigration," one Forty-niner warned from Sutters Fort. "Apple and peach fruit and rice are as useful articles of food as can possibly be taken on the road," he wrote. This veteran advised each man to take three-quarters of a bushel of dried fruit, along with "a plenty of pickles, ¼ bushel of onions, and ½ bushel of beans to each man."[138] A former sea captain told Margaret Frink at Saint Joseph how to defend "against the scurvy, from which so many California emigrants suffered in 1849." The next day Frink bought a supply of acid to take the place of vegetables, and she took along pickles, which with vinegar was a common preventive for this devastating disease.[139]

Canned vegetables had been available since Napoléon's time, but cans were usually too heavy to transport effectively, although there were exceptions. "This evening I indulged myself with a can of Lewis' fresh lobster (the last one)," wrote artist James Wilkins on the Lassen Trail in 1849. "And after a hard days ride and four months hard living, you may believe me when I say I enjoyed it with as great a gusto as ever man did a meal in the wilderness." Perhaps he bought it from J. E. Tracy in Saint Louis, who in March 1849 had "on hand a large quantity of different kinds of MEATS, put up in cans hermetically sealed, expressly for the use of persons going to California."[140] Francis Sawyer went fishing in Bear River to celebrate the Fourth of July at Soda Springs and then cooked a good dinner. "We had canned vegetables, fish, rice cakes, and other little dishes."[141]

Emigrants reported finding shellfish in Raft River or Cassia Creek near City of Rocks. "We found a fine lot of Clams in this streem which we caught and had a

---

[137]MacDonald to "Dear Mary," *The Trek,* 3 July 1850, 135. For Borden's career, see Frantz, *Gail Borden.* Despite MacDonald's enthusiasm, Borden lost $100,000 on the meat biscuit and faced a similar disaster with his next invention, condensed milk, until the Civil War made him rich.

[138]M. M. to Chambers and Knapp, 24 January 1850, in Wyman, *California Emigrant Letters,* 89–90.

[139]Frink, "Adventures of a Party of Gold Seekers," 2:57, 64.

[140]Wilkins, *An Artist on the Overland Trail,* 4 September 1849, 68n42.

[141]Sawyer, "Kentucky to California,"4 July 1852, 103.

regular clambake," Elisha B. Lewis wrote. "They were very good and answered very well for a change."[142] Where the road crossed Raft River, Edmund Booth tried roasted and fried mussels. "Some liked them. Some did not."[143] Others were less finicky: "We made a dinner of the Muscles we caught in the creek," Joseph Wood reported. "We could not boil them tender but they made a good *substitute for a change*."[144] "We caught some trout last night and a few mussels," George Bonniwell wrote. "We have lived so long on bacon that anything in the name of a change is very acceptable."[145] In "the wild, strange valley of Goose Creek," Joseph Middleton saw piles of blue shells. Alonzo Delano ate a meal of freshwater clams and crabs collected from the creek. The boiled crabs proved palatable, but "even with a hungry stomach and long confinement on salt bacon," he could not relish the clams.[146]

The universal complaint about trail diets was their monotony. "Food at least is very common with us. We have slap Jacks and bacon for breakfast. Bacon and Slap Jacks for dinner and for supper we have the same that we had for Breakfast—Slap Jacks and Bacon," mourned Richard Keen. "Some of the boys begin to talk of Scurvy."[147] Visions of the healthful fare they had left behind haunted many gold seekers. "We have lived on dry provisions so long that we often think of our tables at home covered, at this season, with every kind of vegetable, cherries, and early apples," B. R. Biddle wrote near Goose Creek. "We all need a change of diet."[148]

There were, however, covered wagon cooks who showed a great ability to innovate and improvise. Some made a concoction called "push" by pouring flour mixed with water into hot bacon fat as a substitute for butter.[149] On the road in Iowa, Chloe Terry baked thirty-six loaves of bread over two days. "We cut it in slices, & then dry it verry dry then it will do to take across the plains & not mold," she wrote.[150] "I made a blackberry pie for supper, very good—all it lacked was cream," Belinda Cooley Pickett proudly noted near the headwaters of the Humboldt after traveling fifteen dusty miles during the day. She rolled her crust on the bottom of her bread pan using a tent peg in place of the rolling pin and bread board she had thrown away, along with her family's tent, to lighten the load. The boys slept under the wagon. "I hang quilts around the wagon. This is really going to California," Pickett noted.[151]

[142]Lewis, Overland to California, 5 August 1849, Beinecke Library, 41.

[143]Booth, *Edmund Booth (1810–1905), Forty-niner,* 24 August 1849, 11.

[144]Wood, Diary, 29 July 1849, Huntington Library.

[145]Bonniwell, Gold Rush Diary, 7 July 1850.

[146]Middleton, Diary, 28 August 1849, Beinecke Library, 97; Delano, *Life on the Plains,* 153.

[147]Keen, Diary, 18 July 1852, State Historical Society of Iowa, 77.

[148]Biddle, "Journey to California," 21 July 1849.

[149]Tiffany, Diary and Letters, 4 June 1849, Mattes Library, 46.

[150]Terry, Diary, 5 May 1852, Washington State Historical Society.

[151]Pickett, Covered Wagon Days, 31 July 1853, Mattes Library.

Nature and the Indians provided a tremendous source of food, especially toward the end of the trail. "We met bushes of wild currant, small and tart," wrote Irish adventurer William Kelly, "and being a good antiscorbutic, I recommended each mess to pull as many as would make a good pie, which we found palatable as well as wholesome."[152] Indians along the Oregon Trail were great traders, Georgia Hughes recalled, who sometimes had "salmon, both dried and fresh, and sometimes huckleberries which they exchanged for whatever we had, usually clothing or bread. Money they did not want. They did not even know what it was."[153] Gold seekers told of marvelous meals in unlikely places. "I had a most excellent dinner," P. Dexter Tiffany wrote after a midday repast at Fort Kearny. "We had boiled codfish dressed with Eggs mashed potatoes, fried ham, boiled rice & apple pies together with the finest of bread & milk."[154] Edward Jackson got a coffeepot full of milk from an emigrant and used hardtack to make a first-rate "ship bread pudding in apple pie order."[155]

Gold rushers ran out of supplies for a host of reasons. Platt and Slater's *Traveler's Guide* recommended stowing food in the bottom of the wagon: "In this way, it may be kept good at least half the way across."[156] Such advice hinted at a hard reality of crossing the plains: it was extremely difficult to keep provisions from getting wet while fording rivers, to prevent the universal dust and sand from seeping into even the most well-sealed containers and contaminating their contents, or to stop or slow the relentless process of spoilage. "Nearly everything we eat or drink has salt in it, and nearly everything is hot," complained B. R. Biddle.[157] The sheer weight of supplies was another reason overlanders usually ended their treks desperately hungry. "Provisions are getting scarce with many trains that threw away a great part of them in the first part of the journey, expecting to be able to get through long before they will," observed Gordon Cone after reaching the Carson River.[158]

The reckless ran out of food before reaching the Black Hills. "Many of the emigrants are in great distress. Some are going badly prepared for the trip," Robert James reported from Fort Laramie. "Some are packing on their own backs and begging their way, some of whom have given out without provisions or friends." Those who ran out of provisions could "not get supplied at the forts, as they have but a scanty supply on hand and are living on half rations."[159] Reports of Forty-niners dumping huge amounts of supplies influenced those who followed in 1850

[152]Kelly, *Excursion to California*, 274.

[153]Hughes, Recollections, Oregon Historical Society, 3.

[154]Tiffany, Diary and Letters, 7 June 1849, Mattes Library, 49.

[155]Jackson, Journal, 26 June 1849, BYU Library.

[156]Platt and Slater, *Travelers' Guide*, xvii.

[157]Biddle, "Journey to California," 15 August 1849.

[158]Cone, Journal of Travels, 27 September 1849, BYU Library, 126.

[159]James, "From the Clay Emigrants," 18 May 1850, *Liberty Tribune*, 21 June 1850, 1:4.

to set out with too little food. William Holcomb believed the suffering on the trail in 1850 was greater than it ever was again because the Forty-niners took too much and those who set out a year later took too little. Holcomb's party reached Humboldt Sink "entirely without grub except for a few rose-buds," and "after three days subsistance on rose-buds we were compelled to live on nothing." He and his companions almost lost hope and pledged their word of honor to bury anyone who died with his head pointing toward California. Almost miraculously, they stumbled upon seventy-five pounds of abandoned food.[160]

Provisions were "very scarce on the road and sell extraordinary high" at the Sink of the Humboldt in 1850, "and it is feared there will be a good deal of suffering in consequence of this before the emmigrants all reach California," Francis Hardy wrote. Here several diarists recorded coming to an accounting, for "many are out of money and nearly out of provisions," Hardy observed.[161] James Abbey was fortunate: his party "cooked the last provisions we had on the route" the day they reached the goldfields, but most emigrants that year ran out of supplies long before the trail ended.[162] "We have got a hard time of it. We are on one biscuit apiece for each meal while we lay still," George Bonniwell wrote at the Sink. "Almost everybody is out of provisions and packing, and the destruction of property on this road is very great. And what it will be to those that are behind, the Lord knows. God have mercy upon his people."[163] At the same place, "We See Human Suffering here almost beyond Description," William H. Kilgore wrote. "Some have lost their provisions by accidents in Crossing Deep waters, others did not Start with a Sufficient quantity to last them through. Some others have by accident got Separated from their Company and consequently have no provision." A few desperate folks had "a little parched Corn (a Scanty Substinance for a traviling man)," Kilgore observed, but "Some have neither money or provision. Some are butchering their miserable Poor oxen and Selling the bones (for it Cannot be Said to be beef) out at twenty five Cts a pound, and when they have Sold out they will go through a foot."[164]

Cattleman Cyrus C. Loveland drove a herd of cattle to California in 1850. "There are a number of emigrants that have been entirely out of provisions for several days and it appears that their only dependence for something to eat is on our drove of cattle from the manner in which they flocked around the train," he recorded. His party killed two beeves, and such a crowd gathered that the butcher did not have room to work. "Provisions are very scarce," Loveland wrote at the Sink. "Our

[160]Stewart, *California Trail,* 209; Holcomb, Sketch of the Life, Bancroft Library, 23, 24.

[161]Hardy, Journal, 4 August 1850, Beinecke Library, 146–47.

[162]Abbey, *California,* 19 August 1850, 60.

[163]Bonniwell, Gold Rush Diary, 27 July 1850.

[164]Kilgore, *The Kilgore Journal,* 23 July 1850.

mess has just ate the last of our breadstuff and fruit. We have one mess more of beans and then beef is our only show."[165] Rushing to meet the enormous demand, traders in California loaded up pack mules with bacon and flour and headed east over the Sierra; they often charged a dollar a pound or more for their wares. An emigrant offered a man named Shoemaker "$2.00 a pound for flour & bacon but we have none for them for love nor money."[166] Along the Carson River Francis Hardy saw a pound of flour traded for a first-rate wagon.[167]

Many parties took cows and had one luxury that "other emigrants nearly always lacked—fresh milk." Luzena Stanley Wilson dropped her unnecessary pots and kettles by the roadside, "for on bacon and flour one can ring but few changes, and it requires but few vessels to cook them." Her gentle, hornless "mulley" cow provided a reliable source of food, and she fondly recalled that the cow "followed our train across the desert, shared our food and water, and our fortunes, good or ill." The lucky bovine lived to a serene old age in California, enjoying "a paradise of green clover and golden stubble-fields, full to the last of good works."[168] Such fortunate folks put the jolting of their wagons to good use. "We have a tin churn in which the morning's milk is put," wrote Eliza Ann McAuley, "and by noon or evening we have a nice little pat of butter and some good buttermilk."[169]

For all John Tucker Scott's careful preparations, his family reached Oregon in a starving condition. His wife, Ann, died west of Fort Laramie, leaving him with nine children. The survivors crossed the Cascades with worn-out oxen and disintegrating prairie schooners. "Food for cattle was scarce and what was worse, we had *none* for ourselves, as we had been disappo[i]nted about receiving supplies," his daughter Abigail wrote in her journal. "Rations grew shorter and shorter," Catharine Scott recalled. The family boiled "an antiquated ham bone" and added "real relish" to the broth by pouring the last scrapings from "the dough pan in which the biscuit from our last measure of flour—which, by the way, was both musty and sour—had been mixed."[170] Her sister Harriet described the same meal thus: "Our provisions were exhausted by this time, and for three days we had only salal berries and some soup made by thickening water, from flour shaken from a remaining flour sack." Uncle Levi, "who was a great joker, looked at the poor mess and said to his wife, 'Why Ellen, ain't there a little bread or something.' 'Oh no,' she said, 'we are all starving together.'"[171]

---

[165]Loveland, *California Trail Herd,* 31 August 1850, 75.
[166]Shoemaker, Overland Diary, 16 July 1850, BYU Library, 105.
[167]Hardy, Journal, 15 August 1850, Beinecke Library, 201.
[168]Wilson, *Luzena Stanley Wilson,* 2.
[169]McAuley, "Iowa to the 'Land of Gold,'" 13 June 1852, 55.
[170]Scott, "Journal of a Trip to Oregon," 5:133–34n56.
[171]Palmer, *Crossing over the Great Plains,* in Holmes, *Covered Wagon Women,* 5:134n56.

SHOELESS, HATLESS, AND NEARLY CLOTHESLESS:
ATTIRE, GOGGLES, AND SUITS OF RUBBER

"In the motley crowd assembled at this point," Alonzo Delano wrote at Saint Joseph, "you see every variety of costume and arrangements for traveling according to the taste and ability of the emigrants. It seems to be a general disposition to set fashion at defiance, or rather it is fashionable to be unfashionable." Most of his Delano's companions wore "a check or woolen shirt, a Mexican broadbrim, small crown, white or brown wool hat, high boots reaching up on the knee, as uncomfortable as can be made." The "bowie-knife gentry" sang a song that described them as dressed in red shirts and buckskin pants, ready to "plow sloughs, mudholes, Indian hunting grounds, Rocky Mountains, and Sierra Nevadas."[172] Knud Knudsen's party bought extra shoes in Iowa, for "there would be plenty of walking to do before we reached our destination."[173] It probably did not help, for the march proved fatal for most footwear. Uncle Billy Holcomb recalled walking barefoot from Green River to California in 1850.[174] Mary Ellen Compton left Independence with ten pairs of shoes, wore all of them out, and finished the trek barefoot.[175]

Members of the more pretentious joint-stock companies adopted military-style uniforms. William Kelly's party wore "a uniform costume—green caps and jackets, with white trousers; and in selecting all our other appointments, we endeavoured to have them as similar as possible." Kelly thought his companions looked rather gay in their plain but handsome outfits.[176] The Washington City and California Mining Association's uniform was "a short gray frock coat, single-breasted, with gilt edge buttons; pantaloons the same color, with black stripe; glazed forage-cap, with the initials in the front: W.C.C.M.A." At Fort Leavenworth, Lucius Fairchild had fun watching a uniformed company from Virginia try to break mules "being, most of them, clerks & machanics who never had any thing to do with animals. They make awkward business of it and a good deal of sport for the by standers."[177]

After leaving the frontier, virtually everyone was reduced to the same uniform: rags. Oliver Sloane sold his trunk on the North Platte for four dollars and packed his few remaining clothes to California in a flour sack. "Clothes were of no value on the plains," he wrote. "I could of picked up a boat load of the very best clothing."[178] Solomon Litton saw a veteran of the Hastings Cutoff who "had left all that he had on the desert even to his coat, shoes, butcher knife, etc. He got so weak they

[172]Delano, *California Correspondence,* 21 April 1849, 10–11.

[173]Stabæk, "An Account of a Journey to California," 102.

[174]Holcomb, Sketch of the Life, Bancroft Library, 23.

[175]Compton, *Mary Murdock Compton,* in Mattes, *Platte River Road Narratives,* 406.

[176]Kelly, *Excursion to California,* 34, 44.

[177]Fairchild, *California Letters,* 14–15.

[178]Sloane to "Dear Friends," 14 March 1851, Mattes Library, 28.

were two heavy for him to carry. He had nothing on but his shirt and pantaloons and his feet wrapped up with rags."[179] Mothers would not know their own sons if they could see them after a day's drive, wrote Joseph Waring Berrien: "Some of us are shoeless, hatless, and nearly clothes less and we are generally so tired when we arrive at camp that we feel no inclination to mend or repair the rents our clothes sustain on our journey."[180]

Few problems tormented overlanders as persistently as dust. Debilitating clouds of pulverized grime sometimes prevented a wagon driver from seeing the ears of his wheel horses, Charles Boyle wrote, "and at night the faces of his drivers were so begrimmed that we could only recognize them by voice as that was not quite so dusty as the countenance."[181] On entering the Humboldt Valley, William Hart reported, "our Road was generally very good but dusty so much so that in some places the drivers would get so covered as to be hardly recognisable and the dust pervaded every part of our wagon and even penetrated into all our packages of provisions that were not air tight in spite of our best exertions."[182] James Tolles crossed a creek whose bottom was composed of red soil, and "the dust just rolled in perfect clouds so that we see neither the road or the front teams." The red dust ironically gave everything a green appearance: "Our wagon was painted a bright red but exactly resembled a green wagon. The cause of this we could not divine. . . . After passing these hills we much resembled the red men of the forest especially in color," he reported. "The man and cattle have been almost suffocated with dust to day. It begins to look a little Elephantish along these digins."[183]

In addition to destroying clothing, dust affected the choice of fashion accessories. "Getting my eyes pretty well filled up with dust yesterday, got up a pair of goggles last evening," said Samuel A. Lane. "Answer an admirable purpose."[184] Blinding dust and intense prairie sun made eyeshades essential equipment. "A pair of green goggles partially remedied" problems with the dust that continually made life on the trail miserable, "and I would advise every one who contemplates a journey across these sandy plains, to provide himself with several pairs before starting," Howard Stansbury suggested. "They afford great relief from the incessant glare of a bright sun, to which he may make up his mind to be constantly exposed during the whole of his weary route." On the captain's return from Utah in 1850, he met an Ogallala leader, "a noble-looking old man," who begged for something to cure his greatly afflicted and sore eyes. "I had nothing but an old pair of goggles, with very

[179]Litton to "My Dear Wife," 30 November 1850, Western Historical Manuscripts.

[180]Berrien, "Overland from St. Louis," 11 July 1849, 334–35.

[181]Boyle, Diary, 9 July 1849.

[182]Hart, Diaries, 3 September 1852, BYU Library, 1:147.

[183]Tolles, Journal of My Travels, 23 June 1849, BYU Library.

[184]Lane, Gold Rush, 15 May 1850, 29.

dark green glasses, which I gave him, and with which he was very much delighted, mounting them with great complacency, although it was then very nearly dark," Captain Stansbury wrote.[185] Dr. Thomas Galbraith thought one of his companions made a respectable mule driver, "particularly when he is mounted on a mule, goggles on his eyes."[186] After crossing the Sublette Cutoff with hundreds of dust-raising cattle, Cyrus Loveland said "the dust flew so that we could not see a cow ten feet before us, and it could not be endured without goggles on or a handkerchief over our faces."[187] Noted British adventurer Richard F. Burton later reported, "Those who suffer from sore eyes wear huge green goggles, which give a crab-like air to the physiognomy." He described how one begoggled Indian's "eyes were protected by glass and wire goggles, which gave them the appearance of being mounted on stalks like a crustacean's." Mountaineers used goggles to prevent snowblindness, and when they were not at hand, "those who can not procure them line the circumorbital region with lampblack."[188]

The great rush drove the development of technology and marketing of a surprising array of goods. "This was about the time the Goodyear rubber goods were put on the market. For the overland trip we bought full suits of rubber, long boots, overcoats, caps, gloves, canteens, drinking cups and flour bags," recalled a gold seeker who outfitted in New York. His party even bought a four-passenger rubber boat with a folding frame that served as a packsaddle.[189] The Boston Belting Company advertised "all the Different Varieties" of air mattresses, pillows, cushions, tent carpets, wading boots and pants, ponchos, caps with capes and pants with boots, horse covers, gun cases, life preservers, and even figured carpets and gold pouches—all forged of vulcanized rubber and "made expressly to stand the climate of California, being entirely unaffected by heat or cold, and perfectly adapted to the wants of Gold Diggers, Exploring Parties, Traders, emigrants, and all others going to that El Dorado."[190]

As a hard winter eased into a cold spring, it seemed half the world was bound for that El Dorado. Alonzo Delano watched "a well-dressed, clean-shaved and good-looking set of men, with civilized notions of good order and propriety," gather at the edge of the wild Indian country. They would soon share uncombed locks, ragged unmentionables, and weather-beaten, sun-burnt faces as they joined "the great unwashed and unshaved family of mankind."[191]

---

[185]Stansbury, *Exploration and Survey,* 64, 263–54. For the definitive study, see Boorn, "Goggles in the Rocky Mountain West."

[186]Galbraith, Journal, 7 August 1849, Mattes Library.

[187]Loveland, *California Trail Herd,* 15 July 1850, 77.

[188]Burton, *The City of the Saints,* 24, 146, 278.

[189]Eliot, Overland to California, Braun Library, Southwest Museum, 1.

[190]"California Outfits," *California Bulletin,* 5 April 1849, Huntington Library.

[191]Delano, *Life on the Plains,* 12 June 1849, 77.

CHAPTER 2

AVARICE SEEMS TO RULE

The Forty-niners Set Out

By chance, the 1847 Post Route bill authorized building four steam packets to carry mail to the Pacific. The first, the *California,* set sail from New York in October 1848. Her destination aroused so little interest that she carried no passengers bound for San Francisco on her maiden voyage. But when she docked at Panama in February after rounding Cape Horn, the steamer found 1,500 Americans clamoring for a passage to the new El Dorado. "The name California was in every mouth," wrote H. H. Bancroft, so "the noise of preparation" was heard in every town from Maine to Texas. Keeping their ovens hot day and night, New York bakers turned out immense quantities of hardtack, but could not keep up with demand; orders for rubber goods, rifles, pistols, and Bowie knives swamped manufacturers. The first passenger ships bound for California sailed in November. Between mid-December 1848 and mid-January 1849, some sixty ships left America's northern ports for the goldfields—and that number more than doubled in February. Soon everything with "a hull and masts was overhauled and made ready for sea."[1] Shipbuilding, particularly of revolutionary clippers, exploded. When the inspired Donald McKay launched the *Reindeer* in 1849, the ship sailed immediately for San Francisco.[2] On her maiden voyage in 1852, McKay's legendary *Flying Cloud* made it to San Francisco in eighty-nine days, twenty-one hours—a record that endured until 1989. By the end of 1849, 775 ships from all over the world had docked in California. The dusty village at San Francisco became an instant metropolis, and its bay a forest of masts rising above rotting hulks.

News of the discovery at Coloma reached the States at the perfect time to encourage Americans to head west. The country was still far from prosperous. Peace with Mexico had cast adrift a host of footloose young men with a taste for adventure. Horace Greeley of the *New-York Tribune,* long skeptical about the entire westering

---

[1]Delgado, *To California By Sea;* Bancroft, *History of California,* 6:117–22, 129–30.
[2]"The Clipper Ship Stag Hound," *Boston Atlas,* 5 June 1851.

enterprise, was bedazzled: "There is no doubt of it," he wrote. "We are on the brink of an Age of Gold!" As the cost of a sea passage to the West Coast rocketed, the advantages of a trip across the plains mounted, even in eastern seaports. The West's romantic image increased the trek's appeal, enchanting "the briefless lawyer, the starving student, the quack, the idler, the harlot, the gambler, the hen-pecked husband, the disgraced," as Bancroft wrote, giving a careful nod to the "many earnest, enterprising, honest men and devoted women."[3] Risking fate and fortune, some 30,000 speculators left behind friends, homes, and families and headed for the Platte River. They left the frontier full of bright dreams and fond illusions, but by the time they had crossed the Platte's North Fork, endured "the cholera" and the Pawnee and the Black Hills, and ascended the Sweetwater River to South Pass, those who survived were a hardy band of veterans—men and women alike. This is how they did it.

Toward That Unknown and Wonderful Country: Jumping Off

As the cold, late spring of 1849 progressed, a handful of families heading for Oregon and a vast male horde bound for the goldfields jammed towns and steamboats along the Missouri River. "The immense emigration to California" generated business at Independence, Westport, "the village of Kansas," Weston, and Saint Joseph that was "unprecedented by that of any other season," wrote a *St. Louis Republican* correspondent.[4] Saint Joseph was crowded with emigrants; one goldseeker wrote home, "Several ferries here are employed, by day and night, in crossing the Californians, yet cannot keep pace with the arrivals."[5] As Charles Kelly observed, the golden army of 1849 was "the biggest spectacle that had ever been seen on the plains."[6]

Four major trails left the Missouri River in 1849 and converged on the Platte at the head of Grand Island, near Fort Kearny. The two main branches of the Oregon Trail, the Independence Road and the Saint Joe Road, came from the south, as did a new route called the Ox-Bow Trail, which started at the original site of Fort Kearny, now Nebraska City. North of the Platte, emigrants used the Mormon Trail. Only a handful of fur traders, missionaries, and dreamers used the route until 1847, when the Mormons permanently affixed their name to the trail. Mormons called their settlement Kanesville, but after they left in 1853 it became Council Bluffs, Iowa.

"You would not credit your senses to see the vast number that are crowding the streets of every City town & village making preparation," wrote Samuel Wilson

---

[3]Bancroft, *History of California,* 5:117, 119.

[4]Ibid., 293, and Browning, *To the Golden Shore,* 188, quoting letter of 2 April 1849.

[5]T. J. to "Mr. Sosey," 10 May 1849, "From the Californians," *Missouri Whig,* ca. June 1849. Only their initials often appear in the letters of the many friends to write to Mr. J. Sosey, Esq., of Palmyra, Missouri.

[6]Kelly, "Gold Seekers on the Hastings Cutoff," 13.

aboard the steamboat *Sacramento*. "You see men of every age from the gray headed to the boy in his teens, the rich and poore though not many of the latter, men from every state in the union of every Clime Country and language." They always wore some peculiar mark to distinguish them the crowd, so their outfits were "as different and as whimsical as if they were dressed for a masquerade Ball." Men wore everything from the dress uniforms of their Mexican War volunteer companies to the undress blue frock coat of a military officer "to the red fringed Hunting shirt of the backwoods." The "almost universal slouched Sombrero" was a sure sign that the wearer was bound for El Dorado. Taken altogether, Wilson concluded, they were "the finest looking set of men I ever saw."[7] As their colorful outfits demonstrated, the young men who made up the majority of the 1849 emigration shared a sense of exhilaration. "A happier set of fellows you couldn't find out of *jail*," John Blair wrote from beside the Missouri. "We felt like birds uncaged. The canopy of heaven our covering, the beach our resting place, and a log heap our cradle."[8]

Founded in 1827, Independence and the nearby village of Westport had become the main depots for trade with Santa Fe and the Rocky Mountains. The gold mania attracted adventurers from all over the world and all parts of the United States to both towns. Chaotic social conditions accompanied the business boom. A journalist claimed five persons had been shot in the area in the last two weeks, "one of them killed in a fight at Wayne City, the others accidentally."[9] Waterloo veteran Joseph Middleton found "immense numbers of oxen, of wagons, gamblers and cut throats" filling the jumping-off towns.[10] Hundreds of ox-teams and mule-teams were departing daily for California, "besides many pack-trains, coaches and almost every kind of team or vehicle," reported Kimball Webster. "Everything here was bustle and wild confusion."[11]

Opposite Independence's public square stood a two-story building with a saloon on the ground floor and "the upper part filled with gaming tables—dice, Roulette, Faro & Monte tables in abundance which are filled to overflowing night and day every day of the week." Four "street organ girls" arrived from Saint Louis to play the squeezebox and tambourine and were soon drawing crowds. "Every one in the town who has anything to sell is getting rich for they ask double price for everything & as they know the Californians must have it they show no mercy," wrote one eyewitness.[12] Samuel Mathews heard in April that more than 10,000 emigrants had already gathered at Independence and Saint Joseph—and that number was "considered a safe

---

[7] Wilson to "Dear Mother," 17 April 1849, Western Historical Manuscripts.

[8] Blair to "Dear Morris," 25 April 1849, Mattes Library.

[9] "Frontier Sketches," 4 May 1849, *St. Louis Weekly Reveille,* Missouri Historical Society.

[10] Middleton, Diary, Typescript, Beinecke Library, iii.

[11] Webster, *Gold Seekers of '49,* 5 May 1849, 35.

[12] Tiffany, Diary and Letters, Missouri Historical Society, 5, 10.

reckoning. Some accounts state 10,000 at each place." He learned it was common for small parties to go to California, and several men had "made it their business for several years. One of them is a Mexican, who lassos mules handsomely."[13]

For the first time, entrepreneurs offered passenger service to California. Proprietors Thomas Turner and "Captain" Allen, veteran wagonmasters of the Mexican War and reportedly experienced stage coach operators, organized the Pioneer Line at Independence and offered transportation to California in fifty-five to sixty days for a mere $200. This magnificent enterprise used twenty well-built square-topped spring carriages with seats for six passengers, twenty-two large freight wagons to transport each customer's allotted hundred pounds of baggage, and an enormous herd of about three hundred "remarkably fine" mules. The promoters had actually purchased young, cheap, "soft," unbroken mules that had never seen a harness. Many were so wild and unbroken, L. H. Woolley said, that they could be found "sometimes inside the traces, sometimes outside; sometimes down, sometimes up; sometimes one end forward and sometimes the other." After a week or two, "they got sobered down so as to do very well." The company had two amphibious wagons fitted with pontoons to serve as ferries. Joseph Lamalfa, an Italian confectioner who had won fame as the "Ice Cream King" of Saint Louis, brought a four-horse wagon loaded with "an outfit for business in California." His supplies included so much pasta his companions called him "Macaroni."[14]

The owners hired Moses "Black" Harris to guide the train to the goldfields. Forty hired hands staffed the line, including "the requisite number of teamsters and herders, some of these being Mexican vaqueros skilled in throwing the riata or lasso." The teamsters painted names like Prairie Bird, Tempest, Albatross, and *Have You Saw the Elephant?*" on each wagon's canvas top. About 120 passengers—lawyers, merchants, seafarers, surveyors, clerks, gamblers, and ten doctors, "enough to kill us all" one passenger noted—eagerly paid their fares to join the "gay and festive" enterprise.[15]

The trail from Independence to the Platte River was already decades old. A fur-trade caravan's wagons and carts first broke the sod in 1830, and the first independent wagon train left Westport for the Pacific in 1841. During the next two years hundreds of wagons outfitted at Independence and set out for Oregon. Over the decade a growing number of travelers headed for a more exotic destination, the Mexican province of California. Gradually, the trace became a wagon road. Enterprising Indians and French-Americans opened ferries at the more difficult river crossings, but it was still possible to lose the trail.

---

[13]Mathews, Letters, 6 and 30 April 1849, in *Mathews Family,* 289, 295.

[14]Reid, *Overland to California,* 13–14, 37, 53n5, 198–99; Wilkins, *An Artist on the Overland Trail,* 74n13; Woolley, *California,* 4.

[15]Reid, *Overland to California,* 14, 30–31; Tiffany, Diary and Letters, 18, 26 May 1849, Missouri Historical Society, 22, 26.

Captain G. W. Paul of Saint Louis led the first known party to head west from Independence on 14 April, but it took his train of Missourians and Ohioans about two weeks to reach the Big Blue River. (The scarcity of grass forced the Sandusky City Company to stop fifty miles beyond the Kansas River and send back for corn to feed their animals.) Paul's party nailed a board to a tree beyond the junction with the Saint Joseph Road on 30 April, thus claiming to be ahead of everyone else on the trail. They reached the forks of the Platte by about 10 May, with Captain Winter's band of Southerners, several trains from Pittsburgh, and Colonel Vital Jarrot's and "Harvy's" Illinois companies not far behind.[16] Charles Lockwood left Independence on 8 May. He passed the junction of the Saint Joseph Road on the seventeenth, where "there could be seen about five hundred waggons at one view, all bound for California."[17] From a height overlooking the Little Blue, Thomas Van Dorn could "count distinctly 80 odd waggons and the road is dotted with them as far as the view extends—probably 200 teams are within the scope of 5 miles."[18] The long trains of slowly moving wagons, the horsemen prancing on the road, "the display of banners from many wagons, and the multitude of armed men, looked as if a mighty army was on its march," wrote Alonzo Delano as his party prepared to make the long dry crossing from the Little Blue to the Platte River.[19]

Attorney Pardon Dexter Tiffany wrote home to Saint Louis, "The principal part of our company are bound for California with golden visions bright before them, and their distance undoubtedly makes them more enchanting." Almost everyone he met on the streets at Independence was armed to the teeth, and the crowd, which was made up of people from every state, included "many hard cases." Tiffany's vivid letters and lively journal show that keeping such a record was no easy task. After crossing a branch of the Wakarusa River, he sat down to finish a letter to his wife. "A part of the foregoing was written in the carriage in the rain on the top of a small tin pail, part on a hat, & part on the top of a cigar box," he reported. Tiffany wrote under almost every condition imaginable. He sent his wife a "kind of Journal of my trip up to this day" written in pencil "at all times of the day & night & in all weather." Farther down the trail, he closed another letter, "hoping that you will receive all that I have written & preserve them." He scribbled this note "on a three legged stool on a tottering table in the log cabin of a French man (Papin) with about twenty persons coming & going & talking all the time."[20] As Samuel Mathews observed, "Californians must learn to write anywhere."[21]

[16] Barry, *Beginning of the West,* 807–808.

[17] Lockwood to "Respected and highly esteemed friends," 7 December 1849, Missouri Historical Society.

[18] Van Dorn, Diary, 22 May 1849, Beinecke Library, 7.

[19] Delano, *Life on the Plains,* 21 May 1849, 46.

[20] Tiffany to "My Dear Wife," 6 May 1849, Missouri Historical Society.

[21] Mathews, *Mathews Family,* 288.

Born in Massachusetts in 1812, P. Dexter Tiffany was no ordinary frontier lawyer. A graduate of Brown University and Harvard Law School, he was a member of the elite American Antiquarian Society. By 1839 he had established a successful practice in Saint Louis, where he invested in real estate, much of which went up in smoke shortly after he set out for California. He married Hannah Kerr, daughter of a prominent Philadelphia businessman, and the couple eventually had seven children. He sent them vivid descriptions of the unspoiled scenery. "The air was clear & bracing and the vast prairie stretched out before us undulating in every direction & clothed with the most beautiful verdure & decorated with beautiful flowers," he rhapsodized. "The farther we went the more beautiful the scene became until the blue sky above the green earth beneath were the only visible objects." The countryside at the Kansas River "was most beautifully diversified with hill & dale. Woods & green fields looking like English lawns & parks on an extensive scale." His letters repeatedly express his love for his wife and deep affection for "our dear sweet children." Beyond a romantic desire "to win the prize which glitters in the distance to his eager eyes," Tiffany never explained why he made the risky trek across the continent.[22]

The landscape proved intoxicating. The last rays of the setting sun at Wolf Creek broke through clouds floating "Slowly in the West, as if lingering to gild their borders in his golden beams," wrote Daniel Burgert. "The full moon had just risen in the east, and poured a flood of silvery light upon the earth, still giving additional radiance to the Scene." The wet spring supported a lush growth of forage. Burgert found "excellent grass, wood & water, the three great essentials of a good campground" at the Big Blue River. For many miles "an almost unbroken train of wagons could be seen wending their way over the vast plains towards the 'Eldorado of the west,'" he reported, even before encountering the second wave of wagons on the Saint Joseph Road. "It resembled some grand procession & was calculated to suggest grave reflections on the probable result of such a vast emigration, many of whom it is to be presumed may never reach their destination." The headstones of emigrants dead of disease, gunshot wounds, and animal accidents proved Burgert right.[23]

The Immense *Rush*: Saint Joseph

The primary jumping-off place to California in 1849 was Saint Joseph, the town Joseph Robidoux had founded six years earlier on the Missouri River's eastern shore to take advantage of the overland trade. The boomtown already boasted "a fine spacious courthouse, two or three churches, a population of two thousand souls,

[22]Tiffany, Diary and Letters, 6, 16, 20 May 1849, Missouri Historical Society.
[23]Burgert and Rudy, Diary, 8, 17, 18 May 1849, Mattes Library, 14, 18, 19–20

twenty-one mercantile stores, mechanics in proportion, three steam flouring mills," plus three sawmills, Alonzo Delano reported. Since fall the citizens had slaughtered 12,000 hogs and erected fifty-four brick and ninety frame houses.[24] The population did "not appear to be composed of very church-going people. There are but few women comparatively to be seen here, nothing but men, mules and tents. The town is six year old and contains 1,500 to 1,800 inhabitants, and lots of California adventurers. Deliver me from a constant residence in a border town," Dr. Charles Boyle prayed.[25] Saint Joseph was still "an unfinished town," wrote a Danish sailor, "but swarming with people who were raging with the gold fever."[26] Peter Decker told his sisters the place had "about 2000 inhabitants and but one church. Some of the people seem very kind but many are of the 'baser sort.' I think ladies are scarce here"—and the two or three he had seen held no charm for him. The town was all bustle and business; one store was selling $900 worth of goods every day. Decker, who had eaten only fowl and fish for ten years, took up red meat again.[27]

Most of the gold rushers were greenhorns, so when they purchased unbroken mules the result was usually chaotic. "At last the word was given to start & such starting & stopping, such bucking & backing & plunging, such swearing & yelling, that it looked like pandemonium had broke loose," recalled Dr. Solon Martin.[28] Dr. Samuel Mathews arrived "after floating just a week on the prolonged mud puddle, the Missouri river" to find camps and wagons scattered for miles in every direction. He accused the town's livestock traders of sharp practice: his company bought sixteen yoke of oxen at Saint Joseph—"little fellows, mostly unbroken"—but the animals had been "broken before we got there, broken to death almost."[29]

The parade of humanity astonished observers at Saint Joseph. "Over five thousand persons will cross the plain from this place—old men and young—married men with their wives and children, some at the breast, some just large enough to walk, some half grown and now and then a maid of sweet sixteen," wrote Frederick Barnard. "I never saw such a [strange] looking crowd before—Yankees from the east, and *planters* from the south—suckers from the west, and Frenchmen from the Canadas—some wear long hair and some wear short—some have whiskers and no mustachios, and some have mustachios and no whiskers—some have military pants and homespun coats with one peak; and others have one boot and one shoe—no two are dressed alike."[30] The native dress of the Iowas and Wyandottes struck John

[24]Delano, *California Correspondence,* 8.

[25]Boyle, Diary, 1849, 22 April 1849.

[26]Hansen, Diary, 25 April 1849, LDS Archives.

[27]Decker to "Dear Sisters," 27 April 1849; and Decker, *The Diaries,* 19 April 1849, 14, 55.

[28]Martin, Reminiscences, Mattes Library.

[29]Mathews to Gray, 14 April 1849; "By Wagon Train," in *Mathews Family,* 23, 292–93.

[30]Barnard to "Dear Larry," 6 May 1849, Beinecke Library.

McCarty's band of Hoosiers as a "strange sight to many of us, who never saw an Indian until our arrival here." He told the folks back home, "A white man has no mercy on the Indians, they seem to have a natural antipathy for them."[31]

"There is some very respectable people on the road, but I must say that there is a set of the worst characters—profane blagards [blackguards] I ever seen," wrote Joshua Sullivan. He found at least two hundred wagons and a thousand men crowding the town's ferries, "quarelling and swearing and shooting." The spectacle gave him pause: "I think this is the worst operation I ever went into."[32] William Murray called Saint Joseph "a large stirring town"; the crowd of California emigrants caused the stir: "some [were] selling out and backing out, some going out and buying out, auctioneering off, buying horses, mules, ponies, and oxen; some for packs, some for teams, some . . . full of sickness, bad road, etc. Indian murders, and some any way to get on not knowing, hearing or caring anything about one or the other." He and his companions had "found everything better than was represented to us thus far and so we prefer going on to see the balance and the Elephant." The next day his party marched four miles north to the upper ferry "and could not get across till afternoon."[33] The ferry at Saint Joseph was running two weeks behind when John Hudgins arrived, and "people there were dying like hogs from the cholera." Conditions at the trailhead were so grim that his party abandoned its plans to go by South Pass and headed for Santa Fe.[34] Thomas Van Dorn went three miles north to the upper ferry, "hoping to cross early as at the lower ferry at town there was little hope for a week, the rush being now to get across the river." He found fifty teams waiting there, "sufficient for 2 days work."[35]

Passengers came "from almost every State North and some South," wrote James A. Gooding. "Nothing can equal—no one can hardly form an idea of the immense *rush* to California. Every boat is loaded down to the *waters edge*." One of the "*Gentlemen black-legs*" he met was the notorious Captain Howard, whose wife had stabbed and killed his mistress in Cincinnati. Howard was "a *very* handsome, genteel, fine appearing man—alias desperado," Gooding observed. At Independence he had "pointed out another man by the name of Freeman as a counterfeiter, whereupon the latter drew a pistol & threatened to fire at Howard who is a Gambler." Freeman confronted Howard, who shot him through the body. Dexter Tiffany commented on this escapade, "He is not dead yet and may not die though badly wounded. This is one of the fruits of Gaming. Howard is about the streets and will probably be examined tomorrow if the people can get time to attend to

[31]McCarty, Correspondence to the *Indiana American*, 3 May 1849, 1.
[32]Sullivan to "Dear Wife," 8 May 1849, Oregon Historical Society.
[33]Murray, Diary, 22, 23 May 1849, Mattes Library.
[34]Hudgins, California in 1849, Western Historical Manuscripts.
[35]Van Dorn, Diary, 2 May 1849, Beinecke Library, 2.

it." The next day Howard was acquitted on the grounds of self-defense, but he quickly left Independence for the greener fields of Saint Joseph.[36]

The wagons assembling along the river were almost as colorful as their owners. Charles T. Harker left Independence in "a large dashing red wagon, covered with Indian rubber cloth, drawn by four fiery mules."[37] Kickapoos "wrapped in colored blankets" but otherwise almost naked greeted Wilhelm Hoffmann as he rolled west from Saint Joseph in a blue wagon with red wheels and a yellow top.[38] Alonzo Delano described "the quaint names and devices on some of the wagons: the 'Lone Star,' would be seen rising over a hill; the 'Live Hoosier' rolled along; the 'Wild Yankee,' the 'Rough and Ready,' the 'Enterprise,' the 'Dowdle Family,' were moving with slow and steady pace, with a 'right smart sprinkle' of 'Elephants,' 'Buffaloes,' and 'Gold Hunters,' painted on the canvass of the wagons, together with many other quite amusing devices."[39] William Lorton saw one wagon labeled "Traveling Edition of Pilgrim's Progress" and wagon tops painted with elephants and buffaloes "on their way to California in caricature."[40]

As the magnitude of the migration made clear, the advance guard and their animals would sweep the trail clean of forage for those who followed. A few veterans bought grain for their teams and set out before grass grew on the prairie, slogging through mud to seize the advantage over those who followed. Vital Jarrot's Illinois company, the first party to set out from Saint Joseph, left its camp on 19 April. Colonel Jarrot was a colorful frontiersman who had served in the Black Hawk War as Governor John Reynold's adjutant. With him Jarrot built Illinois's first railroad and started Cahokia's first newspaper, *American Bottom.* Like his friend Abe Lincoln, Jarrot was a prominent Whig, but in 1845 he tangled with Senator Lyman Trumbull, losing a slave in a landmark legal case that ended slavery in Illinois. Jarrott's train set out under unpropitious but common circumstances, for its "mules were mostly young and wild, which caused us considerable trouble," Lewis Tremble reported. "We had purchased corn for our animals to last until we reached the Big Blue River, for the grass was quite scarce at the time of our parting." Tremble complained, "the whole time we were on Platte River we never had a clear day or night—nothing but rain, hail and wind, and bad roads," but Jarrot's well-run train stayed at the head of the race.[41]

---

[36]Gooding to "my dear wife," 12 April 1849; Tiffany, Diary and Letters, 6 May 1849, both Missouri Historical Society, 7, 9. This was perhaps Captain Howard of the San Francisco police, who had $5,100 stolen from a trunk in his sleeping room in 1851. See Delano, *Life on the Plains,* 362,366.

[37]Harker to "Dear Reveille," in Mattes, *Platte River Road Narratives,* 165.

[38]Hoffmann, Reise Skitzen, in Ibid., 171.

[39]Delano, *Life on the Plains,* 8 June 1849, 71–72.

[40]Lorton, Diary, 8 May 1849, Bancroft Library.

[41]Tremble to Miles, 6 August 1849, *Illinois Republican,* 1 January 1850, Mattes Library; Anonymous, *St. Clair County History,* 299.

"As far as we could see, over a great extent of vallies & hills, the country was speckled with the white tents and wagon-covers for the emmigrants," wrote J. Goldsborough Bruff. Saint Joseph's main street "was one dense mass of wagons, oxen, and people, and as soon as a wagon entered the scow, the next moved down to the water's edge, and the mass in the rear closed up to the front." Ferries operated "from earliest day till midnight, every day; had been so for weeks, and from the mass here, would continue for several weeks more." Fighting for a place in line was common.[42] After crossing the river, Solon Martin "could see a great number of wagons ahead of us winding their slow & tedious way along the ridge to the west. Here we looked back for the last time into Missouri and civilization & set our faces towards that unknown & wonderful country."[43]

Savannah Landing, Old Fort Kearny, and the Council Bluffs Road

Lewis and Clark named Council Bluffs in August 1804 when they camped on the Missouri's west bank fifteen miles north of today's Omaha. Fur trade caravans and missionaries, notably Marcus Whitman, had headed west from the bluffs, as did the first train to get wagons over the Sierra Nevada in 1844. After the Mormons established refuge camps on both sides of the river in 1846, their fearsome reputation had scared off most travelers, so until 1849 Latter-day Saints dominated traffic on the Mormon Trail, the shorter (and arguably better) road up the Platte River's north side. The great rush for gold changed all that. Thousands of wagons soon transformed the Mormon Trail into what many called the Council Bluffs Road. In addition to gold seekers, some five hundred wagons and 1,400 Mormons joined five church-sponsored trains headed for Great Salt Lake City in 1849. The Mormon trains typically left weeks after parties bound for Oregon or California, and a Welsh company did not leave the Missouri River until 14 July. At South Pass in October, "west of the rocky ridge, they were overtaken by a furious wind and snow storm." A cost of leaving the frontier too late in the season, the storm lasted thirty-six hours.[44]

Council Bluffs was the most westerly of the jumping-off points, which gave parties following the Platte's "north coast" a natural head start. They had to ascend the Loup Fork and cross the river's treacherous quicksand bottom, but they had fewer streams to ford than companies coming from the south. Eventually Council Bluffs and Omaha became the preeminent jumping-off points to the West.[45] The immense

---

[42]Bruff, *Gold Rush*, 7 May 1849, 7.

[43]Martin, Reminiscences, Mattes Library.

[44]Roberts, *Comprehensive History*, 3:338 and 338n19.

[45]In "Potholes in the Great Platte River Road," 6–14, eminent trail scholar Merrill Mattes argued that after 1849 the term "Mormon Trail" was a misnomer for the road up the north side of the Platte. Emigrant journals using the name Council Bluffs Road include James Evans, John Wier, H. C. St. Clair, Francis Hardy, and Edmund Cavileer Hinde.

crowds pressing to cross the wide Missouri accelerated this shift and led to the opening of ferries north of Saint Joseph. Two thousand wagons crossed at Duncan Ferry,
Boston, Savannah Landing, and "ferries as far up as the bluffs" that season, observers
calculated. The *St. Joseph Gazette* estimated 4,193 wagons and 17,000 emigrants had
gone west from ferries between Saint Joseph and Council Bluffs.[46] "America with
one heave throws her life toward Sacramento," wrote Charles Benjamin Darwin.[47]

The first westbound company did not take their twenty-four wagons across the
Missouri to the future site of Omaha until 4 May 1849. Gold seekers found several
thousand Mormons who had "started for the Salt Lake and could not get any fa[r]
ther on the a count of their fundes failed them," Randall Fuller noted. Most of these
stranded refugees had settled in Iowa. Some 12,000 "of these poor creatures" still
lived in the area, Fuller estimated. They were the poorest souls he had ever seen,
"and the people in this place is a hard set." Locals had already killed a Californian
who got drunk and "out of his head." Fuller was able to reach Fort Laramie at the
forefront of the emigration on 6 June, beating teams that had started from Independence on 17 April, almost three weeks before his train left the Missouri. A party
of Latter-day Saints under Samuel Gully was already on the trail, along with "some
40 or 50 tons of merchandise" belonging to Saint Louis merchants Livingston and
Kinkead. Fuller followed a few days later in a company of forty wagons and about
120 men that crossed the Elkhorn River and struck the north bank of the Platte
River at the "liberty pole" campground where the Mormons traditionally organized
their trains.[48] Behind him the rising river complicated crossing the Missouri. The
spring freshet—the June rise—compelled many gold rushers who had followed
the Mormon Trail across Iowa to Council Bluffs to go downriver and cross below
the mouth of the Platte. Those like Fuller who arrived early in May managed to
get their outfits over, but the river's spring flood left later arrivals trapped on the
Iowa shore. Cephas Arms had to leave eighteen yoke of oxen on the left bank and
wait days for the high water to subside.[49]

Bringing up the rear of the migration in late May, the blue wagons of the Washington City and California Mining Association marched north from Saint Joseph
to the crossing from Savannah Landing, Missouri, to Indian Point, several miles
south of Old Fort Kearny. "The two men I sent ahead returned, informing me
that the June freshet of the Mo. had set in, and was running fuller, and with more
drift in it, than has been known for several years," wrote Captain J. Goldsborough
Bruff. The ferry had already been suspended for a week because of the dangerous

[46]Bruff, *Gold Rush*, 446n48.

[47]Darwin, "1,000 Miles From Home," 26 May 1849, 77.

[48]Fuller, "The Diary," 7, 18 May and 6 June 1849, 5, 7, 8–9, 30n8; Hyde, Private Journal, Spring 1849, LDS
Archives.

[49]Arms, *The Long Road to California*, 23 May 1849, 1.

BRUFF'S PERILOUS FERRIAGE

J. Goldsborough Bruff's 1849 sketch of ferrying the Missouri River at Indian Point during the June rise conveys the perilous nature of crossing a wild river in the spring. Courtesy Huntington Library.

conditions, and a Mexican told Bruff it would be impossible to cross south of Council Bluffs—"and even there it would be very bad."[50] Not to be deterred by mere floodwaters, the company spent four days ferrying the Missouri. "River still rising rapidly, much confusion, the bottom already flooded, men labouring their utmost to make their escape in fear of its being flooded before the wagons & mules could be removed," John Bates recorded.[51] The Washingtonians finally started west on 4 June.[52]

Sarah and Josiah Royce arrived at Council Bluffs in late May to find "a city of wagons, some of which had been there many days waiting their turn to cross the great river." After ferrying the turbid and unfriendly Missouri at Traders Point, they started west on 10 June, ignoring "Indians, by hundreds" who lined the road to demand a toll. A month later the Royces finally left Fort Laramie. For the rest of the journey, they would fall farther and farther behind the other wagons.[53]

This Scourge of God: The Cholera Epidemic, 1849

As he sailed up the Missouri aboard the steamboat *Embassy* in April 1849, Alonzo Delano heard news that "struck with alarm the stoutest heart—'the cholera is on board!'" His silent companions "each looked in another's face in mute inquiry, expecting, perhaps, to see a victim in his neighbor. 'The cholera? Gracious Heaven! How?—where? Who has got it?'—and from that moment anxiety prevailed—for who could tell that he might not become a victim?" The first casualty, a young gentleman from Virginia, was dead by ten o'clock the next morning. His companions buried him in a gorge on the riverbank.[54]

Invisible, deadly, and relentless, cholera was especially terrifying because no one knew its cause. "This scourge" was the bacterium *Vibrio cholerae,* usually transmitted by waterborne fecal contamination due to poor sanitation. European ships had carried what was already a worldwide epidemic to New York and New Orleans. As emigrants crowded into filthy camps along the Missouri frontier in 1849, the disease swept up the Mississippi Valley, killing at least forty-five hundred—some 6 percent of the population—in Saint Louis alone. This acute intestinal infection began with increasingly intense and copious diarrhea; violent vomiting soon followed. The combination produced pain in the arms and legs, stomach, and abdomen, profound thirst, and debilitating dehydration. The victim's skin eventually took on a pallid bluish-grey hue. If its symptoms were terrifying, the disease's course was horrific.

---

[50]Bruff, *Gold Rush,* 31 May 1849, 14.
[51]Bates, Diary, 3 June 1849, Mattes Library.
[52]Barry, *Beginning of the West,* 806.
[53]Royce, *Across the Plains,* 33–35, 43.
[54]Delano, *Life on the Plains,* 14–15.

Victims could be healthy in the morning and dead by evening. Small wonder cholera spread panic. Samuel Wilson left Saint Louis "as soon as possible on account of the Cholera which is prevailing there brought by steamboats from New Orleans."[55]

The epidemic reached Independence with the gold seekers, where the demoralizing disease made the already chaotic scene even more violent. "The colary rages here. The emigrants are dying like sheep," reported Joshua Sullivan. "More or less dies every day, as high as ten a day, and they are a-killing one another, thieving and robbing."[56] As May ended, "the cholera was raging fearfully," wrote Samuel Breck. "The strongest hearts were made to tremble in fear of the fearful scourge."[57] The disease killed James K. Polk at Nashville on 15 June: his successor declared 3 August 1849 a national day of fasting, humiliation, and prayer to seek divine mercy for this "visitation of a fearful Pestilence."[58] A year later cholera killed President Taylor after his doctors treated him with ipecac, calomel, opium, and quinine.

Basic challenges, notably the primitive state of medical knowledge, contributed to the rapid spread of cholera. Dehydration was one of the disease's most lethal consequences, but several popular "cures" denied sufferers the water that would have saved them. Common conditions made the trail a breeding ground for disease and complicated dealing with illnesses when they struck. Standard medical theory attributed "bilious intermittent fevers" not to mosquitoes or polluted water, but to "febrifacient causes" and "the noxious miasmatic effluvia" produced by "low, marshy regions."[59] The lack of latrines or any sanitation standards combined with the common reliance on easily contaminated wells spread the infection. The emigrants "suffered desperately with the Cholera," and a string of graves reached thirty-five miles west from the Missouri, wrote George Davidson. "We have become so used to see Cholera that its not noticed half as much as fever is," he observed. "The whole of the route thus far is full of old waggons deserted, some broke down. Others lost their stock others their friends and have become so sick of the trip that they [are] willing to sell everything they have if they can only get home once more." Davidson had seen trouble in his life, he said, "but nothing like what I have seen thus far on the trip."[60]

Those who departed early or traveled on the Platte's north side usually avoided the epidemic. Otherwise the indiscriminate affliction struck down gold seekers and religious pilgrims, trail veterans, and Indians—and young and old alike. Cholera killed many Mormons on the way to Saint Joseph and even more Californians, wrote Charles Bush—"but that is easily accounted for, for they laid drunk in the

---

[55]Wilson to "Dear Mother," 17 April 1849, Western Historical Manuscripts. For studies of cholera on the trail, see Milikien, " 'Dead of the Bloody Flux'," 6–11; Blair, "The Doctor Gets Some Practice," 54–66.

[56]Sullivan to "Dear Wife," 8 May 1849, Oregon Historical Society.

[57]Breck, "A Letter from California," 23 November 1849, 1.

[58]"The Pestilence," *American National Preacher*, September 1849, 199.

[59]Hastings, *The Emigrants' Guide*, 85.

[60]Davidson to Lewin Davidson, 12 May 1849, Beinecke Library.

streets for days at a time."[61] Panic and alcohol consumption intensified as casualties mounted. "On one Boat forty have died, and on an other nearly double that
number—but few Boats arrive that have not lost more, or less," Gordon Cone
wrote at Saint Joseph. "It is a great misfortune to many of extreem nervousness,
and those that are adicted to drinking, that they are out on this journey, as the
Cholera is sure to find them, and it generaly goes hard with them."[62]

Death hardened many emigrants. Richard Owen Hickman, after finding an
unburied corpse on the Sweetwater, wrote, "Men on the plains have less feeling for
each other than dumb brutes."[63] Most parties did their best to support sick members, but some barbarously abandoned them "without water, provisions, covering or
medicines, to die!" Alonzo Delano asked, "What misery has not California brought
on individuals?"[64] Not far from the forks of the Santa Fe and Oregon trails, the
Pioneer Line's doctor told the train that two of their comrades were now buried in
one grave. "They died within three minutes of one another," wrote Dexter Tiffany.
"How sad must be the thoughts of death out here, to be attacked by this 'scourge
of God' on such a journey with no more comforts than a tent or a waggon afford
& no more nursing than mere strangers." Near Ash Hollow he passed two men
whose train had left them behind to dig a grave for a young man who appeared
doomed. "Instead of trying to save him, they were impatient to see him die when we
passed," Tiffany wrote. "This is the state of feeling here." Despite the crowded trail
and the rising death toll, the emigration rolled on to Fort Laramie. Californians
"look for gold and nothing deters them," he observed.[65] "Hundreds that have left
their homes with the brightest anticipations are now mouldering upon the plains,"
wrote Elmon S. Camp. "Were there no other marks, to guide the emigrant upon
his way, the graves upon either side of the trail would be sufficient to direct him
with unerring certainty for hundreds of miles."[66] Cholera had slain emigrants by
the hundreds, Henry E. Wiman reported. The road to Fort Laramie was "allmost
a continual grave yard and sometimes as high as 20 or 25 buried in one place."[67]

West of Laramie, the epidemic virtually stopped, largely because emigrants
quit drinking from stagnant wells and other easily contaminated water sources.
Having entered the eternal sage plains, overlanders left the *Vibrio cholerae* behind
but encountered a mysterious tick-borne infection they called "mountain fever."
Emigrants applied the diagnosis to almost every fever they encountered in the high

---

[61]Bush, Letters, 21 May 1849, Bancroft Library.

[62]Cone, Journal of Travels, 16 May 1849, BYU Library, 11.

[63]Hickman, "Dick's Works," 18 June 1852, 168–69.

[64]Delano, *Life on the Plains*, 163–65. Delano thought the victim was guidebook-author Joseph Ware, but Dale
Morgan identified him as Thomas Waring. See Wheat, *Mapping the Transmississippi West*, 3:89n21.

[65]Tiffany, Diary and Letters, 6, 17 May 1849, 21 June 1849, Missouri Historical Society, 8, 9, 68.

[66]Camp to "Dear Brother," 8 July 1849, in Cumming, *Gold Rush*, 48.

[67]Wiman to "Dear Parents," 25 October 1849, Missouri Historical Society.

country, but the disease was most probably Colorado tick fever, a virus transmitted by the ticks infesting the sea of sagebrush the trail had to cross. After a sudden onset of chills and aches, symptoms included intermittent fever, headache, backache, nausea, vomiting, and an excruciating pain behind the eyes. Mountain fever was quite prevalent, Lewis Shutterly wrote after falling ill at Green River along with his father and a friend. "Near one half the emigrants is and have been afflicted with it."[68] Most survived the unpleasant experience, but it could be fatal.

Cholera, the "king of terror," would haunt the trail with increasing intensity for two more years, sparing no one, including seasoned mountain men who had made survival an art form. All the perils of thirty years in the West could not kill Moses "Black" Harris, but cholera did on 6 May 1849. Harris had signed on as a scout for the "Pioneer Line" passenger service, but his despite his experience as a trapper, his path-finding talents were overrated. "The cholera has raged at this place for several days, but is now apparently subsiding as emigration ceases," the *St. Louis Weekly Reveille* reported, but "the famous 'Black Harris,' the guide, was one of its victims; he had just returned from Santa Fe, was somewhat unwell, and died within six hours after he was attacked on Sunday last."[69] "The Guide of the Pioneer train (the one I go with) was taken with Cholera about four o'clock this morning and died about twelve at noon," wrote Dexter Tiffany, noting that Harris had "been a guide for twenty two years. He was old [and] had been with many parties to the Rocky Mountains and returned but recently. He has had a drunken revel from the effects of which he was about recovering when he was attacked but the prostration by the disease was such that he could not recover."[70]

James Clyman wrote a poetic tribute to his old friend:

> Here lies the bones of old Black Harris
> who often traveled beyond the far west
> and for the freedom of Equal rights
> He crossed the snowy mountain Hights
> was [a] free and easy kind of soul
> Especially with a Belly full.[71]

A MIGHTY ARMY WAS ON ITS MARCH: FORT KEARNY

Throughout May an unbroken parade of wagons crowded every trail to the West Coast. "It was a grand sight—grand beyond description, a continuous line of covered wagons for miles and miles to the westward; one team was pressing onto

---

[68]Aldous and Nicholes, "What Is Mountain Fever?" 22–23; Shutterly, *Diary,* 27 June 1849, 26.

[69]"The Pacific March," 28 May 1849, *St. Louis Weekly Reveille,* in Gold Rush Letters, Missouri Historical Society.

[70]Tiffany to "My Dear Wife," 7 May 1849, Missouri Historical Society.

[71]Clyman, *James Clyman, Frontiersman,* 64.

the rear wagon of the train next ahead," wrote Jasper Hixson.[72] As far as the eye could see, trains wended their way to the Platte where their tracks converged at Fort Kearny. "Here all the roads south of the Platte river leading to Oregon and on the Northern route to California centre," wrote one diarist, who praised the fort's beautiful location a mile from the river, "commanding a view of a country entirely level for miles in every direction."[73] The first specimen of a California-bound gold digger arrived in early May "with a pick axe over his shoulder, his long rifle in his hand, and two revolvers and a Bowie knife stuck in his belt," a soldier reported.[74] "The road here is the junction of all the roads on the northern rout[e] to California," John Bates wrote at the fort. "It is a plain road showing evidence of immense travel." Six thousand wagons had passed by mid-June. No one could guess how many more were still coming.[75]

The Telegraph Company of Saint Louis led the way. Hagan Z. Ludington hoped they would have time to bridge the roads and save his party the delay. Many called the cattle, wagons, and "outfit throughout" of his own Star Brilliant Company the best on the road—"and the road is completely lined from St. Joseph to this fort," he noted after learning the fundamentals of ox driving. "We have had a pretty hard time coming up from St. Joseph—the country was hilly, the hollows very soft, so that wagons would sink in up to the hub in mud." Yet the experience was exhilarating: "I have drove hard all day through mud and water over the top of [my] California boots—sup on hard biscuit and flitch bacon, then lay down on my robes, sleep better and wake up as happy as I ever did in my life," Ludington wrote.[76] At Fort Kearny, veteran frontiersman Miles Goodyear reported a good many of "the adventurers and navigators have arrived at this point, on their way to the 'Happy land.'" He estimated some three hundred wagons had already passed the post, including Captain Paul's "go ahead boys from St. Louis." The mountaineer hoped to be within hailing distance of them by the time he crossed the Rocky Mountains. "There is every variety of conveyance—ox, mule, and horse trains, foot travelers," Goodyear observed: they included a sixty-year-old stalwart who had trudged on foot from Maine with his faithful dog.[77]

Fort Kearny was barely a year old when the Forty-niners swept past. Two companies of dragoons and one of infantry manned the post, but the foot soldiers were sent to Fort Laramie, so most Forty-niners found few troops at the fort. It consisted

---

[72]Hixson, "A Gold Hunter," 7 May 1849.

[73]Anonymous, Tour to California Overland, 1849, BYU Library.

[74]*Missouri Republican*, 4 June 1849, in Pritchard, *The Overland Diary*, 21n11.

[75]Bates, Diary, 16 June 1849, Mattes Library. Goldsborough Bruff, captain of Bates's train, had breakfast with the new post commander, his friend Benjamin Bonneville, whose fur trade ventures had been instrumental in opening the California Trail. See Bruff, *Gold Rush*, 460n98.

[76]Ludington to "My Dear Father," 4 May 1849, California State Library.

[77]Goodyear, 17 May 1849, *St. Louis Missouri Republican*, 6 July 1849, in Morgan, "Miles Goodyear," 322–23.

"of nothing but a few houses built of turf while having walls some two feet thick," wrote Dexter Tiffany. "There are several turf stables, a turf outhouse, suttlers store, officers quarters &c all built of turf." The officers' quarters had wood floors and fire places, but in a heavy shower, rain poured through the sod roofs "as if through a sift." Many buildings did not seem fit to live in, but the fort's garrison "appear however to enjoy themselves and keep them as clean & neat as possible."[78] The outpost stood on a low, flat bottom about fifteen miles from where the Oregon Trail entered the Platte River Valley. Rifleman George Gibbs thought the army could hardly have chosen a worse spot: "Entirely unprotected by trees or high ground, its climate is excessively severe in winter and in the spring the plain is rendered a marsh by the heavy rains." Major Osborne Cross, however, considered the site "very well located to keep in check the Pawnee and Sioux nations and . . . also a great protection to the emigrants who travel this route to California and Oregon."[79] John Markle concluded ten men with shotguns could take the fort "and blow it to thunder."[80]

As the emigration swarmed past, storms and the heavy traffic chewed up the trail west of the fort. "The Roads at this point," reported Charles Lockwood, "are extremely bad." His opinion did not change when he survived a thunderstorm that "beggars all descriptions." The tempest flattened some thirty tents and flooded the handful that withstood the storm with four to six inches of water—"2 wagons capsized & smashed, distributing their contents in various directions." Many shared Lockwood's perspective. After a terrible thunderstorm, Alexander Ramsay found the deluge "and the immense number of heavy loaded wagons passing over them" cut up the already bad roads. Solon Martin saw a great many wagons completely stuck in the mud within sight of Fort Kearny. "We learned the fact here that all the wagons on the road were too heavily loaded, & here they learned the truth of it." Four thousand wagons had passed the fort by 29 May 1849, estimated George Gibbs. "The condition of many of the emigrants," he wrote, "already for[e]bodes the disasters that await them." Some had already abandoned their wagons or cut them up to make packsaddles—but the disasters awaiting the Forty-niners had hardly begun.[81]

The Little-Known Indian Country: The Plains Tribes

As they moved up the roads from Independence, Saint Joseph, and Council Bluffs, sojourners crossed the traditional homelands of the Iowa, Kanza, Oto, Omaha, and

---

[78] Tiffany, Diary and Letters, 7 June 1849, Missouri Historical Society, 49.

[79] Settle, *March of the Mounted Riflemen,* 55–56, 299.

[80] Markle, "A Letter from California," 26 January 1850, 4.

[81] Lockwood to "Respected and highly esteemed friends," 7 December 1849, Missouri Historical Society; Ramsay, "Gold Rush Diary," 22 May 1849, 445; Martin, Reminiscences, Mattes Library; Settle, *March of the Mounted Riflemen,* 299, 301.

Pawnee peoples, now settled by the displaced Delaware, Sac and Fox, Kickapoo, Miami, Pottawatomie, Seneca, Shawnee, Stockbridge, Winnebago, and Wyandotte nations. Overlanders passed Baptist, Presbyterian, Methodist, Catholic, Moravian, and Friends missions—all dedicated to bringing the blessings of Christianity and civilization to the tribes. Indians owned and ran many of the trading stations, ferries, and bridges travelers relied upon. Many Forty-niners met not a single Indian, but what they saw when they did mattered little in the face of their preconceived notions. Dexter Tiffany found a Shawnee running a ferry at the Kansas River. "These are the Indians, Kaws & Pottawattomies they all appear alike," he wrote a few days later, expressing a widely held view.[82]

Despite occasional flashes of violence, bad weather and incessant intertribal warfare so preoccupied the Pawnee and Lakota that they caused the Forty-niners few problems. The Plains Indians were extremely vulnerable to blizzards, and the bitter winter of 1849 hit them hard. The unusually severe cold drove the game south, Major Charles Ruff told visitors to Fort Kearny, and prevented the Pawnees from hunting successfully, which forced them to kill their horses for food. Hundreds had died of starvation "and many of the bands came into the fort in midwinter, some so weak as to be unable to walk." Between February and May Ruff gave the tribes 5,000 pounds of flour.[83] Once spring provided more resources, the long struggle between the Lakota and Pawnee became the focus of most Natives travelers met on the road west. "These tribes are *always* at war," noted Silas Newcomb, "and hate each other to the utmost degree."[84] The two nations were "actively employed in taking each other's scalps, running off horses, and other amusements incidental to Indian life," a soldier wrote blandly from Fort Kearny late in 1848. "This is a war of twenty-five years standing between these two tribes, and in all probability will continue until one is exterminated." He thought, "the Sioux are the best warriors, but the Pawnees are decidedly the best thieves."[85]

Its location at an ancient crossroads made Fort Kearny a flashpoint for conflict. "I became acquainted with a Negro interpreter, who was born in St. Louis but had been raised among the Indians," wrote Charles Boyle. "He spoke English, French and several other Indian languages, and had been in Paris. He told me that he received a pension from the government for the share he had in perpetrating an Indian treaty and was also appointed interpreter at a salary of $300 per year. After this who dares say that Republicans are ungrateful!" The interpreter had helped Captain Walker's dragoons rescue a twelve-year-old Pawnee boy from his Cheyenne captors, whose booty included the scalps of the boy's father, mother,

[82]Tiffany, Diary and Letters, 23 May 1849, Missouri Historical Society.

[83]Muscott to Robbins, 10 June 1849, California State Library.

[84]Newcomb, Overland Journey, 1 June 1850, Beinecke Library, 64.

[85]"From Nebraska Territory," 6 October 1848, *Missouri Republican,* 31 October 1848, in Watkins, "Notes," 187.

brother, and sister. The Cheyenne refused to give him up until Walker ordered his men to ride in among them, cut the boy loose, and "cut down any of the Indians who resisted. Their respect for the Long Knives was so great they offered no resistance." The interpreter, Boyle wrote, taught him a great many curious things about Indian trading customs and superstitions.[86]

Although they seldom encountered violence themselves, Forty-niners entered a war zone in the hills along the Platte River. Many diarists reported meeting large and heavily armed parties from both tribes. "We were overtaken today by about three-hundred Sioux Indian warriors returning from a fight with the Pawnees," Thomas Galbraith wrote in May. "Their weapons were the bow and arrow, lances, and a few muskets. They were all mounted on ponies and mules, and all our efforts to trade for either were ineffectual." A few warriors traded moccasins and lariats for baked goods. "They appeared to be in a starving condition and were pressing rapidly up the river."[87] One gold seeker reported the Lakota "were friendly and wished to express it by shaking hands with us all."[88]

Journals often described meeting large war parties on the approaches to the Platte River—three hundred was a favorite if unlikely number. On the Little Blue in early June, "about three hundred 'Pawnee' Indians came down upon" Gordon Cone's train with "a most threatning attitude," demanding knives, whiskey, and food. The tribes practiced "robbing the emigrants if they can find small parties, or those that they can intimidate." After much posturing on both sides—some of Cone's men "expected to fight at any rate, and were anxious to have the first shot"—he persuaded the Pawnees to let them pass for twenty papers of tobacco. The next day, his company met a Cheyenne war party looking for the Pawnees. "Their line extended nearly half a mile in length," Cone wrote. He estimated they "numbered some three hundred, and our numbers all told amounted to only forty three men, and one women." After much posing, the encounter ended peacefully, this time in a trading session with "the men cheating the Indians all they could, and the Indians in turn stealling whatever they could find that was not guarded," Cone wrote. "Thus ended the whole affair without violence."[89]

Emigrant expectations and apprehension caused more violence than did skulking Indians. If both parties were lucky, a potentially disastrous encounter resulted only in a close call. A nearby company raised "the Alarm of Indians" shortly after

---

[86]Boyle, Diary, 14 May 1849, *Columbus Dispatch*. Anthropologist Lilah Morton Pengra has identified David Desiré (or Dezery in the 1870 federal census) as the most likely candidate for Boyle's talented linguist. Born in Missouri and sometimes known as "Black Dave," Desiré was a civilian employee with the 1855 Harney expedition and post interpreter at Fort Randall by 1865. He married an Ihanktonwan Dakota woman. Their descendants are members of the Yankton Sioux Tribe in South Dakota. Personal communication, 11 January 2012.

[87]Galbraith, Journal, 19 May 1849, Mattes Library.

[88]Anonymous, Overland Diary, 14 June 1849, in John T. Mason Diaries, Beinecke Library.

[89]Cone, Journal of Travels, 6, 7 June 1849, BYU Library, 21–25.

Jasper Hixson's train reached the Platte: "Our mules were soon secured to the wheels of our wagons, and guns in hand we marched out in front of our wagons for battle." The fifty-four men "thought this would be rare sport. But at looking down the prairie we saw the whole bottom lined with them nearly 1,000." Almost immediately two men opened fire without orders but fortunately did no damage. The hotheads retreated to the safety of the wagons as a scout identified the Indians as friendly Lakotas, not hostile Pawnee. The trigger-happy train placated the band with gifts, "though doubtless if those shots had taken effect we would have had trouble, and 54 men against 1000 was right fearful odds," Hixson realized. Still, "some were for firing even after they found out they were friendly."[90]

Which tribes emigrants encountered depended on which route they used and when they passed. "We have had no difficulty with the Indians as yet and I do not think we will have any. We have seen but few Indians in the road," John Hunter wrote at Fort Laramie. "They seem all to be run or scared off."[91] "We are all surprised at seeing so few Indians, for we have not seen 20 all along our whole route," wrote Old Boone at Chimney Rock. "They seem to be terror stricken at the multitude of whites swarming through their solitary plains and do not annoy us one particle."[92] It was not white numbers but their terrifying diseases that led tribes to avoid the trail: "All the Indians have left for the settlements on account of the Cholera & have locked up their houses," Dexter Tiffany wrote at the forks of the Santa Fe and Oregon trails. The Native village on the Black Vermillion was "all deserted, through fear of the cholera."[93] At Salt Creek, a Gentile who had joined Samuel Gifford's Mormon party "was nearly dead with the Small Pox. This word was soon conveyed to the redmen who disappeared like dew before the searching rays of the sun."[94]

Others recalled being besieged by Natives who wanted to trade or who asked for food, which emigrants usually described as begging. "Indians seem to be hungry at all times," Lorenzo Dow Stephens remembered. One of his companions with false teeth devised a way to discourage such visitors. He flashed a smile to show off his beautiful white teeth, removed them, and would then "turn around, grin at them again, this time showing his gums. He had only to repeat this several times when the Indians would back away, walk off, and in a few moments start into a trot until they were out of sight." Perhaps they thought the man was an evil spirit, but Stephens "often wondered just what they did think."[95]

---

[90]Hixson to Miller, 20 May 1849, Missouri Historical Society.
[91]Hunter, "The Letters of a Missourian in the Gold Rush," 18 June 1849, 42.
[92]"Old Boone," 3 June 1849, in Wyman, *California Emigrant Letters,* 57.
[93]Tiffany, Diary and Letters, 17, 26 May 1849, Missouri Historical Society.
[94]Gifford, Journal Book, LDS Archives, 13.
[95]Stephens, *Life Sketches of a Jayhawker,* 7–8.

Charles Turner described a more typical experience: "We passed through the Indian Territory with comparatively little trouble, experiencing none from the Indians, and in fact seeing very few, and these without exception very friendly."[96] The failure to encounter any Indians did not prevent imaginary terrors. The Pioneer Line heard one hundred Indians were lurking near the junction of the Independence and Saint Joseph roads. "Every horse was mounted & all went to see the Indians, but they soon returned & though they had not exactly seen the Indians they had seen a plenty of Indian traces, so there must be a double guard & every man armed to the teeth for all the mules were to be stolen this night and about half a dozen tribes of Indians were to be killed and scalped," Dexter Tiffany reported. "Well the night passed off quietly and not an Indian had been killed nor an animal stolen. The fact was that not an Indian had been within twenty miles of us perhaps not within an hundred, but our men are so scary that every stump is about 5 Indians and every clump of bush is a whole tribe." The passing hordes inflicted far more damage on the Indians than the Indians did to passing wagon trains. To cross the Vermillion, a Kentucky train "made a bridge by falling trees across & into the stream and then covering them with rails" they stole from Indian fences.[97]

Men desecrated Native graves without a thought. Joseph Warren Wood saw a corpse that "had been pulled down from a tree by someone who was reckless enough to do it." The body was covered with beautiful and costly buckskin, beads, and porcupine quillwork. "He had everything which an Indian could desire in this world or the next," Wood wrote. The body "smelt so bad that I soon quit him without obtaining a relic."[98]

The few gold seekers who reported encountering a hostile reception in 1849 usually tangled with the Pawnee. "At the Loup Fork of the Platte River, in what is now Nebraska, but was then a portion of the little known Indian country, our train was stopped by Indians," recalled deaf Forty-niner Edmund Booth. A dozen warriors blocked the road and demanded ten dollars to cross their lands, while some two hundred members of the band watched from nearby hills. (Like most reports of Indian numbers, Booth's appear wildly inflated). His captain, West Pointer William Hamilton, ordered his company of some sixty men and three women to ready their arms and resume their march. "The Indians moved and stood in line by the road as we drove by. There was no further trouble from the Indians. They seemed to have left the way clear, it was said, from fear of cholera."[99]

Forty-niners occasionally reported meeting Cheyenne and Lakota bands on the Platte, but few encountered Plains Indians once they had left Pawnee country,

[96]Turner to "Dear Bro. & Sister," 23 August 1849, in Mathews, *Mathews Family,* 307.

[97]Tiffany, Diary and Letters, 27, 31 May 1849, Missouri Historical Society, 36, 42–43.

[98]Wood, Diary, 14 June 1849, Huntington Library.

[99]Booth, *Edmund Booth (1810–1905), Forty-niner,* 7.

partly due to the Natives' fear of cholera and partly as a result of the army's efforts. Despite its limited manpower, the U.S. military managed to keep the tribes away from travelers. "We have not seen an Indian since we left the Civilized tribes," Cyrus Sumner wrote on reaching the Platte. "They seem to all have deserted the track."[100] Dexter Tiffany heard that 150 Cheyenne who "intended to follow up the emigrants but [Colonel Benjamin] Bonneville ordered them off to the South & they left in the morning about 9 o'clock."[101] Trains bringing up the rear of the migration found large numbers of Lakotas camped at the forks of the Platte, their traditional spot to wait for bison. The Absaroka, popularly known as the Crows, challenged the generally peaceful reputation of the Plains Indians. Many trains met two eastbound Mormon mail carriers, Thomas Williams and Levi Merrill, whom the Crows had robbed.[102] The Absaroka, whose country touched the trail for hundreds of miles, "were a fierce, cruel, and powerful tribe, whose vigilance we could not hope to elude," the commander at Fort Laramie warned William Kelly. On the Sweetwater, Kelly claimed his pack train scuffled with thirty-seven warriors, "all nobly mounted," leaving one Crow dead and several wounded.[103]

By the time they met the gold rushers, Indians had standard greetings for white travelers. Many had studied ox and mule drivers and "learned to swear as a friendly salutation at meeting," David Shaw recalled. "With a friendly shake of the hand it would be, 'Whoa, haw, G—d—n you; haw, gee.' "[104] Indians had picked up a few words of English listening to teamsters. They greeted the Hudspeth train "in the most cordial manner with, 'How de do—whoa haw! G—d d—n you!' " When the party asked about a campground, the Indians said there was "plenty of grass for the *whoa haws,* but no water for the G—d d—ns!"[105] Some of Alexander B. Nixon's companions took "some Tincture of Cayenne, to prevent them from taking cold" after crossing the Platte. When a "big Indian rode up and asked for some 'whisk,' " Nixon's friends poured a draft of the fiery pepper concoction into a tin cup and handed it to the man. "He drank it off at a quaff—let the cup fall to the ground—stood a moment with both hands up showing signs of utter amazement apparently holding his breath, when all at once he gave a hard *blow* and started for the river," Nixon reported. The man left his horse behind, "and never stopped until he plunged himself into the water. No doubt he thought that he was literally on fire. Our inference was he would be careful how he beg[g]ed *Whiskey* again."[106]

---

[100]Sumner, Letters from Uncle Cyrus, 29 May 1849, Bancroft Library.

[101]Tiffany, Diary and Letters, 11 June 1849, Missouri Historical Society, 57.

[102]Hansen, Diary, 9 June 1849, LDS Archives.

[103]Kelly, *Excursion to California,* 157, 180–82.

[104]Shaw, *Eldorado,* 24.

[105]Stewart, *California Trail,* 251, 256.

[106]Nixon, Diary, 26 May 1849, California State Library.

How the tribes viewed this invasion of gold-crazed madmen is not clear. "The Indians are generally dissatisfied with the appearance of so many whites in their territory," a newspaper correspondent speculated, "but the overwhelming numbers of the intruders prevent a very marked expression of dissatisfaction, and hostile demonstrations."[107] Yet the consequences of this contact are clear. At Council Bluffs, 1,234 Pawnees—one quarter of the tribe—died in 1849. The Kiowa pictograph for the year showed a man howling in agony, his knees drawn up to his chest. To the Southern Cheyenne, this was "When the Big Cramps Take Place," a year of disease so devastating that entire bands ceased to exist. The Flexed Leg Band of the Cheyenne vanished, George Bent recalled, and the tribe absorbed the few survivors. Wagon trains found deserted Lakota camps inhabited by no one but the dead. On the Fourth of July, "the total absence of any living or moving thing" around five Lakota lodges prompted Captain Howard Stansbury to wade across the Platte River to investigate. The lodges held the bodies of nine cholera victims, including a young woman dressed in her funeral finery—she was apparently abandoned alive when her people fled this "novel and terrible" disease in terror.[108]

After the emigration had passed and peace returned to the plains, Captain L. C. Easton found the prominent Ogallala chief Whirlwind's band camped at Horse Creek. As an act of friendships, the Lakotas helped the soldiers pull a mired wagon out of a stream. But the passing troops left a legacy in their wake that was killing Whirlwind's people, who were well known at Fort Laramie. "I regretted to learn that the cholera was raging in this village," Easton reported, "and had carried off a large number of the tribe."[109] For the peoples of the Great Plains, the legacy of the highway they called the Medicine Road was bad medicine.

The Long but Beautiful Road up the Platte

Beyond Fort Kearny, wagons and emigrants surged up both sides of the Platte. The broad but shallow river intrigued prairie travelers. "The Platte is a majestic looking stream in some places nearly a mile wide but very shallow and running very swift, filled with inumerable small islands covered with trees clothed in the most luxuriant foliage," wrote William Z. Walker. "This is more remarkable as there are no trees of any description on the shores thus far," a phenomenon attributed to either the bison or the Indians, who were reputed to burn the old grass off the

---

[107]"Latest from the Emigrants," *St. Louis Weekly Reveille*, 9 July 1849, in Gold Rush Letters, Missouri Historical Society.

[108]Powers and Leiker, "Cholera among the Plains Indians," 322; West, *Contested Plains*, 88–89; Stansbury, *Exploration and Survey*, 42–43.

[109]Easton, "Report," 12 October 1849, 399. Francis Parkman met Whirlwind in 1846, and Loren Hastings found him collecting tolls near Laramie in 1847.

plains every spring.[110] The unpredictable Platte was ever changing: "a strange river, filled to the brim today and tomorrow its mass of water has disappeared beneath the sand which forms its bed," it swelled to four miles wide in May 1849.[111] The river's nature evoked a number of jokes: it "looks as if it might float a man-of-war," one wag later observed, "but in reality it is only navigable for small catfish."[112]

Upon reaching "the long but beautiful road up the Platte," Daniel Burgert fell in love with the landscape. The Platte valley "is one of the most beautiful in the known world, extending from each side of the River for Several Miles in an unbroken plain, Covered at this Season with a rich gro[w]th of Prairie grass," he wrote. "A Slight bluff ridge rises Some Miles from the River, beyond which it again becomes level. The River is nearly as wide as the Mississippi & would appear navigable from Sight but it is quite Shallow & has no regular Channel, the bottom being sand, principally, & the whole body of the River dotted with Small Islands which afford the Timber & brush that is to be Seen along its green and fertile Banks." Looking more like "a grand Canal through Some level Country than a River," the Platte's muddy waters abounded with fish.[113]

The vanguard of the rush now resembled a horserace. "Our teams are amongst the best & we are all stout able bodied men, capable of undergoing hardships. We are trying to [be] the first company through," wrote Jasper Hixson. "All are anxious to get there first and are pushing their teams."[114] The Platte River Road was now a highway that carried traffic in both directions: westbound travelers met Mormon mail carriers heading east and mountaineers from Fort Laramie using wagons, carts, or canvas boats to haul piles of buckskins and buffalo robes, "taking their skins to the states to sell." William Knox noted, "they were hard looking customers I tell you."[115]

At the forks of the Platte, wrote John Bates, the country "began to assume a different appearance from the plain, level & monotonous country to that of the wild, interesting & picturesque."[116] Hidden among the hills along the river were the "most lovely valleys covered with the richest verdure & running up from the valleys into the hills are beautiful glens & grottos," Dexter Tiffany discovered. "These valleys & glens or ravines are the most quiet retired spot I was ever in & at this time look lovely." Few travelers could identify where the mighty river divided, but from an elevation Tiffany beheld "the two forks of the Platte mingling their

---

[110]Walker, Diary, 7 June 1849, BYU Library, 34.

[111]Van Dorn, Diary, 22 May 1849, Beinecke Library, 8.

[112]Richardson, "Letters on the Pike's Peak Gold Region," 23.

[113]Burgert and Rudy, Diary, 28, 29 May and 1 June 1849, Mattes Library, 31–32, 34.

[114]Hixson to Miller, 20 May 1849, Missouri Historical Society, 5.

[115]Knox to "Dear Father," 25 May 1849, Mattes Library; Boyle, Diary, 19 June 1849.

[116]Bates, Diary, 25 June 1849, Mattes Library.

waters, each marked by a few trees which here line their sides. Behind & all around you is nothing but hill after hill, range after range."[117]

Emigrants usually crossed the lower Platte without much trouble, but quicksand and deep holes made the broad and sluggish watercourse dangerous. Wagons forded from both shores of the Platte, apparently believing the grass was greener on the other side, but to reach Fort Laramie every train had to cross the river at some point. Some crossed near Fort Kearny, but most south-side trains used fords located above the forks of the Platte. The main crossing below California Hill attracted the most traffic in 1849, but Thomas Van Dorn found a newly opened ford about twenty-five miles above the forks that "from indications may be preferable to any above of which there are 3."[118] Once across the South Fork, a waterless stretch of some twenty-five miles of high plains brought wagons to the head of a steep canyon. "You enter the valley at the Ash hollow by a descent of about 400 feet in two miles, the road running down a ravine bounded on each side by cliffs between 3 and 400 feet high from the crevices of which grow Cedar, Pine and a little evergreen shrub name unknown, giving to the valley a romantic and picturesque appearance," wrote Dabney Carr. "On emerging from the hollow, the scene changes, the valley of the Platte spreads itself out before you from one to two miles wide, the river rushing along with a velocity that is almost incredible in such a level country."[119]

"The scenery is more wild and picturesque while some of the bluffs we climb are so steep that nothing but California interprize would drive us over," wrote Edward Jackson, noting his surprise at finding "currants, and, to make it more sweet, wild roses and columbine!" Ash Hollow was "one of the grandest places I ever saw. We descended into the valley into a long winding road for not less than 500 ft when we came to the boiling spring," which Edwin Bryant had called the finest water on the route. "On one side are the beautiful ash trees, on the other rise the stupendous bluffs not less than 300 feet, pile upon pile of chalky rock partly with overgrown with woodvines and savins clinging and growing in the crevices." Atop a cliff Jackson saw "a natural monument which resembles very much the fancy chymneys on the houses at home."[120]

Daniel Burgert's party "descended into a deep Ravine that Soon gave unmistakable proof from the Ash Trees Scattered Along its Course that we were in 'Ash Hollow' a point well known to all travellers on this Route, it being marked on all the charts." The oasis was graced with large, beautiful ash trees, a good spring of

---

[117]Tiffany, Diary and Letters, 14 June 1849, Missouri Historical Society, 60, 61. These hidden canyons, which provided critical winter shelter to the Plains Indians, did not fare well during the gold rush.

[118]Van Dorn, Diary, 2 June 1849, Beinecke Library.

[119]Carr to "My Dear Cousin," 31 May 1850, Missouri Historical Society.

[120]Jackson, Journal, 18 June 1849, BYU Library, 34–35.

cold water, and wildflowers in bloom. "Wild roses we found here in abundance, also quite a variety of other flowers decorated the face of the valley with their richest & gayest Colors and lent their sweetest perfume to the Clear and purling stream which flowed from a deep recess at the base of the bluff that overlooked the green little valley below," Burgert rhapsodized. "We traveled leisurely through this attractive & fascinating little vale & nearly felt pained while emerging from its plesant shades & enchanting Sceneries & again found ourselves pursuing our course up the monotonous valey of North fork of the Platte."[121]

West of Ash Hollow, the trail passed the string of landmarks called the Wildcat Hills, where the scenery was anything but monotonous. The first of these striking formations originally was known by various names—the Mansion, the Solitary Tower, the Church, the Capitol, and Castle Rock—until a perceived resemblance to the Saint Louis Courthouse settled the matter—although Alphonse Day of the Badger State imagined it "looked just like the Capitol at Madison." "We passed the court house or church, a tremendous remnant bluff, composed of sand stone. It is very irregular in form, elongated from the level surrounding it is about two hundred feet," wrote Thomas Galbraith. "In front the prairie is rolling. In the rear it is level and traversed by a beautiful stream of water." Galbraith climbed the north side of the bluff using handholds cut in the sandstone. Next to the formation stood "an immense pillar of the same material, its base separated from the former by the deep fissure," which emigrants called the Jail or the Jail House before it acquired its modern name, Jail Rock.[122] On every hand immense bluffs rose "to the height of 1 to 5 hundred feet, at the distance of five to ten miles; and they exhibit every conceivable outline of figure, and assume every shape that fancy or imagination could invest," said J. M. Muscott. "The 'Court House' has a regular architectural appearance and the top of it looks like the dome of the Capitol at Washington or St. Paul's church, London."[123]

As Chimney Rock loomed steadily on the horizon, it reminded William G. Johnston "of pictures often seen of the great Egyptian obelisks, towering high above the vast deserts which surround them."[124] An unknown diarist thought this curious work of nature "seemed as one of those monuments of great dimensions which nature in her solitude cuts to mock the puny works of man."[125] Amasa Morgan climbed the Chimney "by a steep and circulour route" and found hundreds of names cut into the rock above a shelf. Like many early observers, he thought

[121]Burgert and Rudy, Diary, 8 June 1849, 41–42.

[122]Mattes, *Great Platte River Road,* 339–49; Day, Journal, 15 June 1849, BYU Library; Galbraith, Journal, 6 June 1849, Mattes Library.

[123]Muscott to Robbins, 10 June 1849, California State Library.

[124]Johnston, *Experiences of a Forty-niner,* 26 May 1849.

[125]Anonymous, Overland Diary, 18 June 1849, in Mason Diaries, Beinecke Library.

the decaying landmark was doomed: "the top is split and looks as though it would soon fall." Morgan fired his revolver, and the echo was louder than the gunshot.[126] "The 'Chimney Rock' has its chimney, or spire, 100 feet high and 30 or 40 broad, almost square in shape, [and] the base on which it stands is some 200 feet in height," wrote J. M. Muscott.[127] Edward Jackson called it "that wonder of wonders Chimney rock rearing its head 250 ft into the air. The base covers I should judge an acre of ground the cone is a hundred ft & the shaft 150 more making 250 ft high—It is composed of a chalky kind of stone." Jackson made a rude sketch of the rock and described the "smooth green lawn" that stretched below it for two miles. Behind the rock was a fifty-foot deep ravine "at the bottom of which was a beautiful spring gurgling from a hole in the rock and pure cold as a Californian emigrant could wish." Beyond the Chimney, Jackson wrote, "commences a combination of high ground and bluffs some appearing like Forts & others like ruined castles but all wonderful to me."[128]

"The singular sublimity, beauty and grandeur of this scenery" around Scotts Bluff inspired the poet in Mr. Muscott, who wrote a letter from the site. "Now a fort with its bastions and walls, regular in outline, with port holes, its out-houses and barracks, now a Castle with its towers and gates, anon a Turkish Mosque with its white minuets and spires, with windows and doors, burst upon the view, then a 'City upon the Hill,' with its churches, public edifices, ornamental shaped trees, groves and valleys at another turn in the road reach you. In addition to this a soft mellow light, a partially clouded day, with light and shade alternate, light up the entire bluffs with an almost unearthly splendor." Muscott admitted his bones complained with every step, which tempered "any fanciful embellishments he might be disposed to throw around natural scenery." Despite the adversity, "the admiration extorted from every man in our company, from the ignorant alike with the intelligent, proves that the wild and beautiful, the grave and the sublime in nature arouses similar emotions in every bosom."[129]

Amid the beauty, observed Stillman Churchill, "the mosquitoes bit like scissors." The road over Scotts Bluff was "first sandy, then muddy, then sandy again," Charles Boyle complained. About halfway up the hill stood a surprising island of civilization, "the blacksmith shop kept by Robidous, a Frenchman, of St. Joseph, who has a Sioux wife. He keeps tinware to trade to the Indians and here 500 miles from any place, I found Webster's dictionary and other books to match, besides some French devotional and historical works." Churchill discovered "a spring of

---

[126]Morgan, Diary, 31 May 1849, Bancroft Library.
[127]Muscott to Robbins, 10 June 1849, California State Library.
[128]Jackson, Journal, 21 June 1849, BYU Library.
[129]Muscott to Robbins, 10 June 1849, California State Library.

pure cold water on the right directly below. Near a small stream is a blacks[mith] shop, store and dwelling house, all owned by a trapper from Missouri" and "all under one roof built of cedar the only kind of wood in this vicinity."[130]

Several members of the sprawling Robidoux clan maintained this "country residence" for years, apparently as a cooperative effort by the entire family. Emigrant diaries listed the names of six different Robidouxs associated with the post, historian Merrill J. Mattes noted. Late in June 1849, Charles Darwin had dinner with Antoine Robidoux, who told him he had spent thirteen years among the Sioux "tho only last spring came to Scotts Bluffs." Darwin found him living with two Lakota women, but he could not divine the blacksmith's confusing marital status. William Kelly reported he had taken "unto himself a Sioux spouse, a perfect queen of the wilderness." Several overlanders said Charles Robidoux had two wives, and one claimed he had three. All sources agree he "had several children and they seemed to enjoy life as well as the best of us."[131]

Looking west from the summit of Robidoux Pass on a clear day, Forty-niners could see Laramie Peak, "snow-capped, dim and indistinct like a faint cloud or haze in the atmosphere," rising to the west—their "first view of a spur of the Rocky Mountains."[132] The massive blue mountain loomed larger as the trains marched the fifty miles from Scotts Bluff to Fort Laramie. For virtually all the prospective gold hunters, it was the biggest mountain they had ever seen—and it marked only the beginning of the Great Stony Mountains.

ALL THEY WANTED WAS TO GET BACK ALIVE: ON THE BACK TRACK

The fearful toll of cholera, the loss of teams and supplies, and the hardship of the trek persuaded many gold seekers and Oregon dreamers to abandon their quest. "We frequently met men who had given up the struggle, who had lost their teams, abandoned their wagons, and, with their blankets on their back, were tramping home," Luzena Wilson recalled after meeting some of these discouraged pilgrims.[133] Eventually there were names for such reformed overlanders: go-backs and back-outs.[134] "Many are turning back with their teams, having become discouraged in anticipation of the long and tedious journey before them; large numbers are dying daily of cholera and other fatal diseases," wrote Kimball Webster. Ten

---

[130]Churchill, Journal, 27 and 29 June 1849, BYU Library; Boyle, Diary, 31 May 1849.

[131]Darwin, "1,000 Miles From Home," 26 June 1849, 105; Boyle, Diary, 31 May 1849; Kelly, *Excursion to California,* 154; BYU Library; Mattes, *Great Platte River Road,* 438–40; 446–53 and "Joseph Robidoux's Family," 5.

[132]Boyle, Diary, 31 May 1849.

[133]Stanley, *Luzena Stanley Wilson,* 5.

[134]Richardson, "Letters on the Pike's Peak Gold Region," 25.

days later he admitted his own prospects of reaching California were somewhat discouraging, while reports that there was no grass ahead and fear of Indians and Mormons combined "to frighten many and cause them to banish the bright, golden visions which allured them from their homes, with the bright anticipations of soon becoming wealthy." The eastbound throng Webster encountered wanted nothing more than to escape the trail's trials as soon as possible. "To meet so many who have been farther westward on the trail, and who have turned backward, and are now seeking their former homes, has its influence upon a large number that would otherwise proceed and causes them to also reverse their course." But Webster was resolved "not to return until I have seen the place I set out to reach."[135]

There were good reasons to give up. "It is no uncommon occurrence for us to meet return parties, who have become discouraged, homesick [or] affrighted at the difficulties of the way," wrote one Wolverine Ranger. "Every return party we have met, has told us of the difficulties ahead, and could you see their long and doleful faces you would think them almost insurmountable."[136] Most who quit did so before reaching Fort Laramie, but as Niles Searls noted, "We frequently meet with emigrants returning home, even after having reached nearly South Pass. Some are deterred by sickness or accident from proceeding farther, others by reports of the poor feed for stock in the mountains."[137] As with most gold-rush statistics, how many took what Alonzo Delano called "the back track for the settlements" is a guess, but in 1849 alone they probably numbered in the thousands.[138] A packer who had left Saint Joseph on 2 May told Thomas Van Dorn at Ice Springs "he had passed over 4000 teams and one thousand turned backwards."[139] John H. Benson met a Missourian one night who "said out of his company of thirty-three wagons, thirty wagons had gone back."[140] In the face of death and disaster, most pressed on. "Even our cattle," Samuel Mathews wrote, "long before we got through, had learned that the best course was ahead; and the loose ones, at morning, invariably pointed their heads to the west, before the company had prepared to start."[141]

Reports of families that gave up the trek after losing a husband or father are among the most moving of all trail sagas. "This evening we met a widow of an emigrant whose husband died of cholera at Kan[sas] River & she [was] returning with her waggon & five yoke of oxen to her friends in Warren County Mo. She had in her arms a small child not more than six months old and appeared to be in

---

[135]Webster, *Gold Seekers of '49,* 31 May, 10 June 1849, 39, 44–45.

[136]Camp to "Dear Brother," 8 July 1849, in Cumming, *Gold Rush,* 46–47.

[137]Searls, in Reid, *Overland to California,* 71.

[138]Delano, *Life on the Plains,* 29.

[139]Van Dorn, Diary, 29 June 1849, Beinecke Library, 20.

[140]Benson, From St. Joseph to Sacramento, 14 August 1849, Nebraska State Historical Society, 51.

[141]Mathews to "Friend Gray," 7 October 1849, in Mathews, *Mathews Family,* 312.

LARAMIE PEAK

Overland emigrants got their first look at the Rocky Mountains when Laramie Peak came into view west of Scotts Bluff. Frederick Hawkins Piercy sketched the peak in 1853 as the trail followed the arc of the North Platte River west from Fort Laramie. From *Route From Liverpool to Great Salt Lake Valley.* Author's collection.

good health & spirits," wrote Dexter Tiffany. "She had been able to keep her waggon & team & hire a driver to return with her."[142] "We met some people on the
road today comeing back; haveing lost some of their company, they have became
discouraged, have given up 'the journey,' and are going back to lament that they
ever started for California," Gordon Cone wrote east of the Big Blue. "One Woman
with her husband and four children started for California, the husband was taken
with the Cholera and died, and the mother with her little children are on their
way back, solitary, and alone."[143]

A POOR, MISERABLE, OLD DELAPIDATED MUD FORT:
FORT LARAMIE

The first wagons, probably G. W. Paul's Saint Louis train, reached Fort John—the
official name of the American Fur Company's post on Laramie Fork—on 22 May.
The crumbling adobe ruin seldom impressed visitors. William Kelly envisioned "a
bold fortress, perched, in stern solitary grandeur, on a beetling crag, with corbled
battlements bristling with cannon, encircled by chasms." Wretched reality instead
revealed "a miserable, cracked, dilapidated, adobe, quadrangular enclosure, with
a wall about twelve feet high." The mud citadel was only eight years old, but its
already dissolving walls had to be propped up with beams, "which an enemy had
only to kick away and down would come the whole structure."[144] The fort was "of
considerable dimensions and constructed of sun burnt brick," T. J. Van Dorn noted,
showing "it had experienced a little hard weather, tho once of quite respectable
appearance."[145] Elijah Allen Spooner was "much disappointed in the place," and
many felt no differently about the grizzled fur traders who ran the post.[146] "At
Fort Laramie, we found a poor, miserable, old delapidated mud fort, tenanted by
a lot of lazy, lounging, loafing renegade Indian-French, all drunken and swollen,"
wrote Samuel Sufferins. "It gave us the dolefuls to look at them."[147] Except for a
few women and their children, "there were no Indians about, they having gone to
war with the Crows," Vincent Geiger reported. He found nothing enticing about
the post, which had nothing to trade except jerked buffalo meat. Geiger noted
the presence of a number of Mexicans. As Joseph Hackney observed, the outpost
was built after the fashion of a Mexican ranch.[148]

[142]Tiffany, Diary and Letters, 18 May 1849, Missouri Historical Society.
[143]Cone, Journal of Travels, 28 May 1849, BYU Library, 15–16.
[144]Kelly, *Excursion to California,* 154.
[145]Van Dorn, Diary, 13 June 1849, Beinecke Library.
[146]Spooner, Letters and Diary, 13 June 1849, BYU Library.
[147]Sufferins, 4 August 1849, *Richmond Palladium,* 31 October 1849.
[148]Potter, *Trail to California,* 14 June 1849, 107; Hackney, 13 June 1849, *Wagons West,* 143.

FORT LARAMIE, 1849

The Stansbury Expedition's artist, Franklin Richard Grist, sketched Fort Laramie in July 1849, shortly after the army purchased the outpost from John Jacob Astor's American Fur Company. From Howard Stansbury, *Exploration and Survey of the Valley of the Great Salt Lake,* 1852. Author's collection.

As throngs of gold seekers paraded by, the government turned its attention to the most famous fort on the trail. The first Mounted Riflemen reached Laramie Fork on 16 June 1849 with orders either to establish a new post or to purchase the old one. During the next ten days Major Winslow Sanderson and Lieutenant Daniel Woodbury considered sites some distance from the old fort. After a thorough reconnaissance examining both the "Ridge or Mountain road" and the river road, the officers concluded Fort John was the best location for a military station. Woodbury purchased the fort on 26 June 1849 for $4,000 from agent Bruce Husband of the American Fur Company. Sanderson hoped to buy the land it stood on from its rightful owners, the Lakota, the next spring.[149] When the regiment resumed its march, Sanderson was left in command of a company of Riflemen and two companies of infantry. By 10 July, the troops were building a mill, a house for the commander, and barracks. In August Colonel Loring left two companies on the Snake River to found Cantonment Loring near Fort Hall, and the rest of the Riflemen marched to Oregon. After a trek plagued by desertions, the regiment arrived at Fort Vancouver.[150]

[149]Sanderson to Adjutant-General, 27 June 1847, in Watkins, "Notes," 201.
[150]Settle, *March of the Mounted Riflemen,* 52, 97–98, 170n185, 324. Supply problems led the army to abandon Cantonment Loring on 1 May 1850.

Administering justice and tracking down deserters who had committed vicious assaults on vulnerable emigrants became one of the army's top priorities. Most overlanders "were law abiding to the last degree beyond law and churches," but "the outer if not the inner nature of men changed as they left civilization, law and courts behind them," a frontier veteran told William Manly. Some men "seemed to change their characters entirely out on these wild wastes. When anything excited their displeasure their blood boiled over." Amid such conditions, women received special consideration, and homicide was justified to defend their honor. Near Fort Kearny, a man from Illinois "attempted some improper liberties" with another man's wife. After a warning, he again grossly insulted the woman. "In a country where there was no law—where redress could not be had by a legal process," wrote Alonzo Delano, the husband "determined to protect his own honor, and raising his rifle, shot the scoundrel down." (John Muscott said the husband killed the man with an axe.) The killer was either arrested or returned voluntarily to the fort, "where an investigation into the circumstances was made, and he was honorably acquitted."[151]

Throughout the gold rush, the U.S. Army lost more men to desertion than it did to Indians. "To serve as a check to desertion," Congress doubled the pay of enlisted men serving in Oregon and California. The Mounted Riflemen's officers had ample proof that many of their men "had enlisted for no other purpose than to get the means of reaching California." The regiment lost forty men before it reached Fort Laramie. Joseph Middleton heard "about 100 dragoons departed from Fort Laramie, and set out for California," while others returned to the States. The problem continued, so Loring "issued a proclamation at Independence Rock, offering a reward of two hundred dollars for every deserter that might be brought back." The bounty did not stop desertion, Osborne Cross noted, but "it had a tendency to decrease the number," especially after trappers turned in five men at Fort Bridger.[152]

A particularly brutal robbery and gang rape had a revealing aftermath. Captain Thomas Duncan left Fort Laramie on 19 July 1849 with a sergeant and one man "in hot pursuit of four deserters, who had decamped with an equal number of the best horses belonging to the command." The deserters—William Aloysius, William Hyslop, George W. Herman, and Asa Young—"went to a camp, where they found a woman, they compelled her to open her trunk or box, and they took all the money which was $115. Then they *ravished her,* one after the other,

[151]Manly, *Death Valley in '49,* 48, 104–105; Delano, *Life on the Plains,* 23 May 1849, 50; Muscott to Robbins, 10 June 1849, California State Library.

[152]Fillmore, "Message of the President," House Exec. Doc. 1 (33-2), Part 2, 115; Settle, *March of the Mounted Riflemen,* 128–29; Middleton, Diary, 18 July 1849, Beinecke Library, 24.

in immed[i]ate succession—then they left," Joseph Middleton reported. Duncan recruited emigrants to help track down the culprits, paying some $100 to "go and assist him to take the 4 wretches." Duncan's horse was nearly worn out when he camped with the Boston-Newton Company on 25 July. Two nights later the Knox County Company entertained the captain and his six armed men with "hot biscuit and good bacon." Duncan offered to pay, but the emigrants said they did not "keep tavern." The posse set out for Green River about dusk "to travel in the night and take them asleep." About midnight as 27 July began, they discovered the fugitives "fast asleep on the ground, and no guard out." After silently disarming the criminals, Duncan "called them up and said it was time to relieve the guard. They were much frightened and made no resistance," wrote William Lorton. "Two of them cried." Charles Gould saw Duncan at the Mormon Ferry with the four deserters, whom "he intended to take back to Fort Larimie, making them perform the whole journey on foot." "Poor fools," observed David Staples, "they are to be pitied."[153]

Howard Stansbury met Duncan heading east with five prisoners (he had captured an additional deserter) on 3 August. "The pursuit was one of great hardship, privation, and fatigue," Stansbury wrote, "and the energy and perseverance with which it had been continued was the subject of admiration with all." The men were handcuffed and on foot, Stansbury noted, "& will doubtless pay dearly for their frolic."[154] Duncan had hired a man from the Boston Company who told Joseph Middleton the captain had caught three of the men and was "supposed to have shot the fourth one."[155] Whatever happened, Duncan delivered four men to confinement at Fort Laramie, where Asa Young died on 20 November 1849. Aloysius and Hyslop were court-martialed and drummed out of the service in 1850, but by August George Herman was back on the payroll and herding the quartermaster's cattle. His last assignment was "Waiter to Captain Duncan."[156]

Fort Laramie was the end of the road for many joint-stock operations, where many companies "split all to pieces, and every man was 'for himself,' " as Henry Cox wrote. Forage was getting scarce, "and by the time we got there almost the entire emigration became panic struck, so much so that many feared they could not get through and cast away everything they thought they could do without." Spurred on by a burning desire to get to California as quickly as possible, many swapped their exhausted animals and the safety and convenience of their wagons for faster pack animals, usually at a steep loss. Like thousands of others, Cox left his wagon

---

[153]Stansbury, *Exploration and Survey,* 55; Lorton, Diary, 27–28 July 1849, Bancroft Library; Gould and Staples, in Hannon, ed., *The Boston-Newton Company,* 25, 26, 19 July 1849, 143–44, 151–52.

[154]Stansbury, *Exploration and Survey,* 69; and Madsen, *Exploring the Great Salt Lake,* 118.

[155]Middleton, Diary, 24 July, 4 August 1849, Beinecke Library, 59, 123.

[156]Lowery to Bagley, personal communication, 16 August 2004. I am deeply indebted to Sandra Lowery, librarian at Fort Laramie National Historic Site, for this information.

and packed west with a few companions.[157] "We found parts of several disbanded California companies here," wrote Charles Boyle. "Some of them were abandoning their wagons and everything else except the most absolutely necessary articles of provisions and clothing," having "overloaded and over driven their teams."[158] Isaac Wistar saw a large number of dilapidated wagons standing forlornly outside the "rough and primitive-looking" fort: "whatever their value at home, [they are] quite worthless here. Many have been broken up for material for pack saddles."[159]

The strategy was not always successful—especially not for greenhorns. "The science of packing animals ranks amongst the learned professions," William Kelly concluded. He and his comrades found that rigging a packsaddle with cruppers, britchings, lash ropes, and apichments while mastering a plunging and kicking mule firmly bent on resistance was "by far the most bothersome and temper-testing job we encountered yet."[160] Mr. Esterbrooks gave Amasa Morgan's wagon train a little history of his party's troubles. Being "green at packing," Esterbrooks's companions had not buckled the bands on their packs properly, making them bulky and not "scientifantly balanced." A jackass led the way, "but not far before the packs began to turn and the mules to run [and] the packs ware soon all turned and swung under their bellys, the mules breighing kicking and running." The animals scattered the packer's flour, sugar, coffee, bacon, and hard bread all along the road as "some of the men laughed and some cursed the poor honest mules."[161]

ANVILS, FEATHER BEDS, ROCKING CHAIRS, GOLD WASHERS: LIGHTEN THE LOAD!

"Our success depended upon our early start and cracking ahead which gave us the advantage of pasture and that of being out of the dust," wrote John M. Blair, among the first to reach California. "I would not take $500 for what I have seen and learned, but if any one comes tell them to start with good teams and light loads and early in the spring."[162] Forty-niners who loaded their wagons with mining equipment, blacksmith tools, and even a diving bell lacked the common sense to follow such good advice. "As a rule, the emigrants, when making up their outfits, had but little idea what they needed," G. W. Thissell recalled. "Hence, everything that a man's wife or a boy's mother could think of was piled in the wagons." Much

---

[157]Cox, "Letter from California," 26 September 1849, 1/2.
[158]Boyle, Diary, 2 June 1849.
[159]Wistar, *Autobiography,* 15 June 1849, 84.
[160]Kelly, *Excursion to California,* 160–61.
[161]Morgan, Diary, 9 June 1849, Bancroft Library.
[162]Blair to "Dear Brothers and Sisters," 19 August 1849, Mattes Library.

of it proved about as useful "as two tails to a dog."[163] Wagons set out for California that spring crammed with useless sawmills, anvils, feather beds, rocking chairs, gold washers, and even gold vases—and began dumping the excess baggage almost immediately. Forty-niners were "profoundly ignorant of what was before them," wrote the supply officer at Fort Kearny. He feared the abandoned provisions would be "sadly wanted by those who threw them away, before they reach the Pacific."[164]

Bernard Reid saw a "Bonfire of wagons" at Fort Laramie. "Wagons are being burnt or sold at prices varying from twenty-five cents to thirty dollars," noted Niles Searls, but by early July the market had totally collapsed.[165] "Scores of wagons are lying in all directions and are worth nothing, provisions are the same," wrote Stillman Churchill.[166] "All the camp grounds near the fort are literally covered with wagon irons, clothing, beans, bacon, pork and provisions of almost all kinds, which have been left by the advance immigration to lighten their loads and facilitate their speed," Kimball Webster reported.[167] Even those who kept their wagons often jettisoned provisions, tools, and goods. Thomas Galbraith's party used a typical strategy to lighten the load "by throwing out all our boxes or duds, packing our bread in sacks."[168] Few Forty-niners regretted leaving their slow wagons behind, but the memory of the piles of food they cast aside would haunt them.

Despite the strain overloaded wagons put upon teams, gold seekers often held onto their possessions as long as possible. Forsaken treasures littered the trail up the Platte River and stacked up all the way to the Sierra Nevada. "The road on either side for the last hundred miles has been literally strewn with broken waggons and even those that are sound and good: with stoves, trunks, cooking utensils, Iron, steel, barrels, boxes, black smith tools of almost all kinds, broken chains and provisions," Elmon Camp wrote in the Black Hills. "Yesterday we passed several piles of most beautiful bacon, which had been thrown away by companies preceding us, to lighten their loads. If any of the companies fail to reach their destination it will be those who have thrown away their provisions to make greater speed," he predicted.[169] "The bacon was piled like cordwood, and some of the men poured turpentine on the provisions and set fire to them, so the Indians couldn't eat them," Lorenzo Dow Stephens recalled. "Some men seem to be born mean."[170]

---

[163]Thissell, *Crossing the Plains*, 64–65.

[164]"Pawnee," *Missouri Republican*, 16 June 1849. Dale Morgan identified "Pawnee" as Captain Stewart Van Vliet. See Pritchard, *The Overland Diary*, 22n13.

[165]Reid, *Overland to California*, 67–68.

[166]Churchill, Journal, 2 July 1849, BYU Library, 53.

[167]Webster, *Gold Seekers of '49*, 11 July 1849, 58.

[168]Galbraith, Journal, 11 May 1849, Mattes Library.

[169]Camp to "Dear Brother," 8 July 1849, in Cumming, *Gold Rush*, 47–48.

[170]Stephens, *Life Sketches of a Jayhawker*, 12.

Luxury goods were worth no more than rubbish. "A fine walnut book case found, new, of gothic pattern, broke it up for fuel—fine doors & drawers boiled our coffee," J. Goldsborough Bruff wrote at the Platte Ferry. The riverbottom was "strew'd with clothes, boots, shoes, hats, lead, iron, tin-ware, trunks, meat, wheels, wagon beds, mining tools, &c—& dead oxen."[171] Half a million dollars would not purchase the property thrown away between Forts Laramie and Hall, J. M. Muscott estimated. The road to El Dorado "looked more like the route of a vanquished army flying before a host of Goths and Vandals, than the road of citizens engaged in the peaceful pursuits of civilized life."[172]

Joseph Middleton cataloged the odd and expensive items he found scattered along three-quarters of a mile of road in the Sweetwater Valley, including "a pile of hub hoops and wagon boxes, an old shirt with fine plaited bosom, a leather portmanteau, wagon wheels, axle trees, half a wagon sawed through the middle, a wagon cover, a fine carriage back-band with silver plated mounting for the reins, a large clothes basket, a carriage spring, carriage traces, an ox-chain, and a sprinkling of cast off rags strewn about—no longer fit to wear. On again, a similar wreck: a fine chair, hub hoops, old pants and coats, piles of beans, and of salt, a large keg, old rag carpet, wagon tires and hoops, coupling bolts, a tar kit, and more old clothes." At Smiths Fork he listed "carts, stoves, irons, chains, a tent, a window sash and old clothes," and on the Lassen Trail he found "log chains, gun barrels, stoves, tires, hub hoops, wagon boxes, and every kind of iron, ox-yoke, lead ladles, hat boxes, clothes, &c." Back at the Big Sandy one discovery topped them all: "Saw a piece of real brick, with several broken pieces. Who would have thought that any person would have hauled a brick so far over such horrible roads?"

Not everyone was content to give up hope of recovering his possessions. Middleton noted the grave of "a coloured man." He soon learned that Daniel Wheeler's grave was "what in the wilderness is called a 'cache.' It contains hidden articles of an entire wagon taken to pieces and carefully packed away." He concluded, "Many large graves we have lately passed are doubtless *caches*." A Wolverine told him the three graves he had seen at the South Platte crossing marked the spot where "the Pioneer Train had hid 3 casks of brandy in these graves instead of dead bodies." Overlanders learned a hard lesson: "Life is dearer than the treasures of the world," wrote Middleton on the Humboldt. "A few weeks ago not a man in the crowd would have parted with many things they now leave with the most perfect indifference, and pass by on the road things that they would have grabbed at as if they had found a lump of gold."[173]

---

[171]Bruff, *Gold Rush,* 22 July 1849, 124.
[172]Muscott to Robbins, 14 October 1849, California State Library.
[173]Middleton, Diary, 8 September 1849, Beinecke Library, 39, 54, 75, 115–16, 141, 148–50.

Rough and Rocky and Flinty: The Black Hills

The Black Hills, the mountain range the Lakota called *Pahá Sápa* and the Cheyenne *Mo'öhta-vo'honáaeva,* stretch from South Dakota to northeastern Wyoming. The range is geologically distinct from the Laramie Range that dominates southwestern Wyoming, but to the overland travelers who crossed the range's foothills, they were the Black Hills. The hills were "so thickly covered with pine that at a distance they look perfectly black," noted Alonzo Reynolds.[174] Here wagon trains left the plains and entered the difficult terrain of the arid West. The crowds that had ascended both sides of the Platte came together on "the same road over which all emigrants have passed," as Dexter Tiffany wrote. The advantages the advance parties had became clearer as their teams swept away the forage. For those in their wake, the trail was soon as "worn, plain, and bare of grass" as the main street of Saint Louis. "The prospect for the poor emigrant began to look bad," he observed. As the trail arced around the looming mass of Laramie Peak, the country became increasingly "rough Sterile & broken. The black hills on the right hand are dotted all over with red cedar & pitch pine trees which are very black & spare," Tiffany said. "The country looks desolate enough and as you extend your view the more hilly & mountainous it appears."[175]

"Soon after we left Laramie hard times commenced," wrote John L. Martin. "Great God what suffering and misery."[176] Elijah Spooner called the Black Hills a sandy waste, "with wild sage its chief product."[177] The road "became very rough & rocky & flinty," Solon Martin recalled. "Everything showed evidence of a Volcanic nature: the road was covered with sharp flinty rocks, & lava or pumice stone" that lacerated the feet of his mules.[178] The copperas soil created "clouds of dust with which we are enveloped left our skins our clothes and even our oxen tinged with a greenish hue," complained one Forty-niner as a strong wind drove the dust "in our faces and down our throats."[179] Alonzo Delano spent five days toiling over the rugged roads, with "the naked Black Hills peering down upon us, like goblins, laughing at our way-worn wretchedness, and apparently deriding our search for gold."[180] Some faced the challenge of the gloomy Black Hills more stoically. One evening Dr. Joseph Middleton "saw a woman walking through the deep sand by the side of a wagon drawn by 8 oxen and driven by two men. She seemed to have tranquility and resolution depicted in her fair, though sunburnt face."[181]

---

[174]Reynolds to "My Dear Parents," 6 July 1849, 2/2
[175]Tiffany, Diary and Letters, 2 July 1849, Missouri Historical Society, 75.
[176]Martin to "Dear & much beloved wife," 22 December 1849, Typescript, Mattes Library.
[177]Spooner, Letters and Diary, 28 June 1849, BYU Library.
[178]Martin, Reminiscences, Mattes Library.
[179]Anonymous, Overland Diary, 25 June 1849, in Mason Diaries, Beinecke Library.
[180]Delano, *Life on the Plains,* 17 June 1849, 84.
[181]Middleton, Diary, 17 June 1849, Beinecke Library, 14–15.

After traversing the Black Hills, travelers lined up to cross the North Platte at fords and ferries from Deer Creek to the Mormon Ferry at today's Casper, Wyoming. In early June, Brigham Young sent Latter-day Saints from Salt Lake to reopen the lucrative business he had founded in 1847. Their boat was "made of two canvasses, fastened together about six feet apart by means of planks so that a wagon can stand upon them," wrote Charles Boyle. "The mules were forced to swim the river, which is 150 to 200 yards in width."[182] Other entrepreneurs, drawn largely from the ranks of fur-trade veterans of French descent, quickly set up competing operations. In early June, Amasa Morgan found a hundred teams already waiting to cross the river, and his train had to send their mules a mile away to graze.[183] As the crowds swelled, so did competition for grass and ferry services. Randall Fuller saw "such a rush" of Californians that the ferries could not cross them as fast as they came up. Already eight or nine men had drowned.[184] The rapid river was ten to fifteen feet deep and "a great crowd [was] trying to pass over on some rafts, others in wagon beds made tight." By late June, John Edwin Banks thought the chaos at the North Platte ferries looked "a little like a battlefield." He found "scarcely enough grass for one ox, much less thousands." In places grasshoppers and a "vast number of astonishingly large crickets" covered the baked earth, further depleting the range.[185] When Sarah Royce camped under the shade of the cottonwood trees at Deer Creek, far behind almost everyone else, the "ground was entirely destitute of vegetation." The Royces had to drive their animals fifteen miles upstream to "a very rich valley, in which the poor animals luxuriated and rested for two days."[186]

Not everyone happily handed over cash to the enterprising ferrymen. Impatient gold seekers turned to "digging out canoos and crossing them selves."[187] Alonzo Reynolds found the river, some forty rods wide with a swift current, too deep to ford. His train "took three wagon-beds, corked and pitched them, and commenced crossing in the morning, and by evening we were all over."[188] Luzena Wilson recalled her party felled several huge sycamore trees and built a "semblance of a raft" to cross the "boiling, seething, turbulent stream, which foamed and whirled as if enraged at the imprisoning banks."[189] To cut off as many teams as possible, Benjamin Hoffman's Charleston Mining Company used "our sheet iron wagon-bed

[182]Boyle, Diary, 8 June 1849.

[183]Morgan, Diary, 8, 9 June 1849, Bancroft Library.

[184]Fuller, "The Diary," 12 June 1849.

[185]Armstrong and Banks, *The Buckeye Rovers*, 22, 24 June 1849, 24.

[186]Royce, *Across the Plains*, 43–44.

[187]Fuller, "The Diary," 12 June 1849.

[188]Reynolds to "My Dear Parents," 6 July 1849, 2/2.

[189]Wilson, *Luzena Stanley Wilson*, 4.

to ferry our goods and wagons over. We crossed at the mouth of Deer Creek, about 30 miles below the regular Mormon ferry."[190] The party planned to cut up their two big boat-shaped iron wagons when they reached California "to make rockers and tongs to wash the gold," Edward McIlhany recalled. The Charlestonians also bought a small cannon "in case we needed one" for protection against Indians.[191]

Edward Jackson's party took "seven air beds and lashed them together and hitched all our ropes we use for the mules together and made a line across the stream." The current was so swift that "it took eight men on the raft and four on either side to hold the rope so you can judge how rapid it was," he wrote. "We found that this would not work well, so we concluded to take the load off and float them across."[192] Apparently imitating this approach, another company tried "to make a rope fast to the opposite shore by the means of men floating themselves over on air tight India rubber beds." The next day their hastily built raft sank one hundred feet from shore. "So much for this days crossing," one member noted caustically, although the party had saved most of the supplies in their provision wagon. They finally paid the toll and began crossing at 5:00 P.M. on the Fourth of July, a task they did not complete until 1:30 the next morning.[193]

Fording the North Platte at high water sometimes proved fatal. During two days in June 1849, while he waited "five hundred miles from no place," J. W. Crane saw two men drown. "We have had a long and tedious journey so far and the prospects is no better for the future," Crane wrote. "No man knows any thing of the trip until he trys it. It is attended with so much phatigue and danger that a man knows not of until he has had some experience."[194] Young and vital, Daniel Burgert enjoyed his trip up the Platte. "I'm heartier than I've been in 5 years with an appetite like a sawmill," he wrote near Fort Laramie. "This trip agrees with me very well." At the upper crossing early on 25 June 1849, Burgert and A. D. Starr decided to swim their horses across the river. Manlius Stone Rudy, Bergert's "partickular friend, messmate and partner," looked on in horror as Bergert "by some means got off his horse and the stream carried him down. He swam for a considerable distance very well" until he reached a sand bar. Bergert waded for a short distance and "then appeared to stop & squar off into deep water, after which from the view of those on shore he swam again. But sunk and arose giving a number of moans and the third time he sunk to rise no more. The stream ran so swift that no assistance could be rendered him." The Ashland Company searched

[190]Hoffman, "West Virginia Forty-niners," 20 June 1849, 64.

[191]McIlhany, Recollections, 16.

[192]Jackson, Journal, 1 July 1849, BYU Library, 45.

[193]Anonymous, Overland Diary, 2, 4 July 1849, in Mason Diaries, Beinecke Library.

[194]Crane to Howe, 12 June 1849, Mattes Library.

in vain for his body. Late in the afternoon the party pushed off and made camp at dark. "[We] went to bed without supper mourning our loss," Rudy wrote. "Never did I feel So perfectly horible."[195]

Growing desperation inspired confrontations. Charles Tinker met the Oquawka Company under William R. Findley, a veteran of at least two overland treks to Oregon, who had built the first ferryboat on the North Platte. "We tried to get the use of their boats to cross in," Tinker wrote, but the Oquawkas "said they made them for their own use and calculated to destroy them as soon as they got over so as to prevent others from crowding them so hard." To no avail, Tinker's party offered fifty dollars for use of the ferry and began building their boat when they heard cries of panic. Two of Findley's men had tried to cross the river on horseback "but floated down and lodged on a bar in water up to their waists and would have drowned in a few minutes if we had not saved their lives." The accident "turned things in our favor," wrote James Haines, who nearly drowned himself but managed to save the men. Haines and Charles Davis swam a rope to the sandbar, tied it around one man, and hauled him ashore. By this time, Findley's company had rescued the second man with a canoe. "We took them to camp and nursed them up and kept them until morning when they were able to go to their own camp." The Oquawkas "felt so grateful to us for our kindness and assistance that it seemed that they could not do too much for us. They offered us the use of their boats & men to help us over." By noon Tinker's party had crossed, which put them ahead of some two hundred wagons. Their benefactors "made us pledge ourselves to destroy the boats as they intended to do," Tinker wrote, but a company of Pennsylvanians threatened to seize them by force. Findley's train armed seventy men "to the teeth" and marched to the ferry to make sure the boats were destroyed.[196] Some Forty-niners threw together poorly made boats, but "the current was so swift that they would swamp them." Three men drowned due to Findley's callousness, Randall Fuller charged, but he dismantled his wagon and crossed safely.[197]

THE GREAT AMERICAN DESERT:
UP THE SWEETWATER AND OVER SOUTH PASS

"We left the Platt at six o'clock, and do not expect to see it again," Gordon Cone wrote after crossing the river's North Fork. "We part with the Platt as from an old friend—haveing received many comforts from its water, and enjoyed much of the varying prospects that a journey of some eight hundred miles along its valley,

[195]Burgert and Rudy, Diary, 25 June 1849, Mattes Library, 55–56.

[196]Tinker, "Journal," 11 June 1849; Haines to "Dear Father," 13 August 1849, in Mathews, *Mathews Family,* 304.

[197]Fuller, "The Diary," 13 June 1849, 9, 31n25

has afforded."[198] He had reason to be sentimental, for he left behind a reliable if murky source of water. Over the next thirty miles, the trail entered the truly arid West. "The water is very strong of alkali, and where it has dried away there is a white scum over the ground, sometimes an inch thick. This water is very poisonous; half a dozen swallows will kill an ox," noted Alonzo Reynolds. "I have not seen one acre of land in seven hundred miles that would raise white beans. It is all hard, barren sand; even the creek bottoms are good for nothing."[199] Feed for livestock grew as scarce as it was essential. "We enter what is called the great American desert," wrote John L. Martin. "Here commenced the cry, drive on, drive on, let no one pass us, or they will eat the little grass that is left, and our animals will die, and we must perish."[200]

By late June the dry passage between the Platte and the Sweetwater was so devastated that some simply gave up and turned back, even after having come so far. "The whole earth appears filled with alkali," gasped Israel Hale.[201] The dismal region between the Platte and the Sweetwater disgusted many diarists. "Nothing but hills sand alkalie & rocks," complained Dexter Tiffany, who counted thirty-five dead oxen as he passed Alkali Springs. He thought the region "must always be a perfect blank in creation."[202] "We are on a desert without water or grass for our cattle and this hard drive has only brought us to a meager stopping place late in the afternoon," wrote Elijah Spooner, whose train spent two dry nights camping on the trail to Willow Springs. "Numbers of cattle have given out during this days drive and have been left to die either from drinking alkaline water or over exertion."[203]

With all the traffic funneled onto a single road, crowding became intense. "Dead oxen to be seen all along the road at every few rods," George Davidson recorded.[204] "Saw many dead cattle today," agreed Andrew Murphy. "A whole team of 4 yoke oxen lying near in one place having been killed by lightning in the yoke."[205] Between Mineral (or Poisoned) and Willow springs, "the road seems to be well beaten and traveled as the turnpike between London and Edinburgh," Joseph Middleton remarked. He saw twenty-two dead oxen plus discarded "lanterns, candlesticks, stoves, iron hasps, water buckets, coffee pots, tea kettles and many other notions . . . [and a] side saddle, wagon trees, bolts, wheels, burnt wagons, a jack screw, boots, shoes &c. Many encampments exhibit the appearance of an extensive Rag-fair."[206]

---

[198]Cone, Journal of Travels, 13 July 1849, BYU Library, 50.
[199]Reynolds to "My Dear Parents," 6 July 1849, 2/2.
[200]Martin to "Dear & much beloved wife," 22 December 1849, Mattes Library.
[201]Hale, "Diary of a Trip to California in 1849," 27 June 1849, 86.
[202]Tiffany, Diary and Letters, 7 July 1849, Missouri Historical Society, 80.
[203]Spooner, Letters and Diary, 24 June 1849, BYU Library.
[204]Davidson, Diary, 2 July 1849, Beinecke Library.
[205]Murphy, Diary, 1 July 1849, Western Historical Manuscripts.
[206]Middleton, Diary, 19 July 1849, Beinecke Library, 19–21.

The trail over South Pass

Historian Charles Kelly captured what the "trail over South Pass, used by the western emigrants and the Gold Rush trains" looked like about 1930, before surplus Jeeps began the transformation of the trail after World War II. Courtesy Utah State Historical Society. All rights reserved.

The aridity left "the lips clammy and parched, and the eyes much inflamed from the drifting dust," Howard Stansbury observed. Thousands of wagons and animals pulverized the fragile western soil, raising clouds of inescapable grit. Dexter Tiffany complained the alkaline dust was "blowing continually in our face, frequently so thick that we could not catch our breath without turning round."[207] The tide of emigration devastated favored campsites such as Willow Springs. "This must be a beautiful place in any other season but now so many camping here makes it a waste," wrote Edward Jackson. The grass was gone and the willows cut down; and broken wagons, trash, and thirty dead cattle made it a loathsome place: he "hurried away and pressed on to the Sweetwater." At 6:00 P.M. he reached the river, "which was named," Jackson supposed, "by some traveller like myself who had been all day without water and come upon this stream."[208]

After quenching his parched throat, Joseph Middleton climbed Independence Rock and watched "the Sweetwater coming down through the green valley winding like a silver serpent." By mid-July 1849 the normally lush valley's grass was "eaten bare, and what remains looks rather brown. The roadside is almost red with so much camping." Pockets of range survived even as the elevation and aridity increased, but Dexter Tiffany found the country becoming "more Sandy & barren. In many places nothing grows but sagewood & greasewood," although two days later he found the finest grass he had seen for a dozen days. He nooned at Ice Slough, where "by digging six or 8 inches we found a cake of ice about six inches thick as clear & pure as any I ever saw. The soil above the ice is one mass of grass roots & as fast as you dig out the soil & ice the water comes to the top of the ground & fills the hole." Tiffany had dinner with a Missouri merchant, and "by the way of des[s]ert asked us to his camp & gave us a glass of iced champaigne. Think of that to dig ice out of the ground in cakes 8 inches thick clear & good when the mercury is 85 & 90." Edward Harrow also found the ice "perfectly clear and good. The water you dig it from is muddy and alkaline in its nature, but I never saw or ate better than that I dug today, and it went down with a perfect relish, strangely in contrast with the scorching over head, and burning and blistering sand under our feet." The presence of snow in July astonished the gold seekers as much the buried ice. "I was picking ripe strawberries & directly before me in 40 rods was a bank of snow," Tiffany marveled.[209]

Cyrus Sumner's party "discovered some small particles of shining substance" near Devils Gate. They laid over for a day and decided to "go up the river toward

---

[207] Tiffany, Diary and Letters, 7 July 1849, Missouri Historical Society, 80.

[208] Jackson, Journal, 5 July 1849, BYU Library, 47–48.

[209] Middleton, Diary, 21 July 1849, Beinecke Library, 24–25; Tiffany, Diary, 13–19 July 1849, Missouri Historical Society; Harrow, Gold Rush Overland Journal, 31. Subterranean ice was not restricted to a single spot: Thomas Galbraith found ice at Pacific Springs.

the *south pass*—to trace them to their source, as there is no doubt they are washed down the river from some Mine in the Rocky Mountains." The gold dust proved "to be a failure as the farther we go up the sweet water the less appearance there is of it—in all probability the little scales we saw were washed down from the rocks about the Devils gate—and you know the old fellows coin is always counterfeit."[210]

After travelers crossed the Sweetwater five times, the Wind River Mountains and the crest of the Rocky Mountains came into view. "They were almost entirely covered with snow and as the sun arose we could see what appeared to be a large city (caused by rocks &c on which the snow had melted) we could temples, arches, churches," wrote William Z. Walker.[211] The climb up the twenty-mile-wide valley of South Pass was "more like journeying over some vast plain or prairie, than crossing a vast mountain range," wrote Gordon Cone. "This pass through one of the greatest mountain ranges that our country affords, presents nothing that I had expected to find." The ascent was so gradual "that it would require some more visable sign than the mountain affords, to know where you are at the culminating point."[212] Forty-niners sometimes repeated Frémont's mistake and believed the Twin Mounds marked the spot. A few like William Clarke correctly located "Twin Mounds, two and a half miles south east of Rocky Mountain south pass."[213] "If you were not told this was the pass you would not know it," Dexter Tiffany wrote after crossing South Pass. "By examining the ground you can perceive that the water would run west from the top of a small hill. And in about 2 or 3 miles you find the Pacific creek & springs whose water flow west."[214] Many companies missed the spot entirely. "To my disappointment it seems that we have passed the culminating point without realizing it," Joseph Middleton wrote. "No 'Rocky Mountain' appearance here. It just looks as if you were in the middle of the Missouri plains."[215]

West of South Pass the trail entered a new land. "We were now in Oregon—the ridge of the Rocky Mountains being its eastern boundary—and fifteen hundred miles from our homes," wrote Alonzo Delano, capturing the anticipation and dread shared by many of his companions. After two months of steady toil on their weary journey, they were "but little more than half way to our point of destination; and although thus far, no serious mishap had befallen us, no one could tell what trials awaited us."[216]

---

[210]Sumner, Letters from Uncle Cyrus, 5, 7 July 1849, Bancroft Library, 89–90.
[211]Walker, Diary, 7 July 1849, BYU Library.
[212]Cone, Journal of Travels, 24 July 1849, BYU Library, 58
[213]Clarke, Journey to the El Dorado, 28 May 1850, Idaho State Historical Society, 17.
[214]Tiffany, Diary and Letters, 19 July 1849, Missouri Historical Society, 89.
[215]Middleton, Diary, 29 July 1849, Beinecke Library, 92.
[216]Delano, *Life on the Plains,* 29 June 1849, 116.

CHAPTER 3

WHICH ROAD TO TAKE?

South Pass to City of Rocks

Gold seekers had virtually no reliable information when they had to pick the best and shortest way to get to the Sacramento River in 1849. Forty-niners tried to guess which one of the many forks in the road would take them to California as quickly as possible. Beyond South Pass, their hard choices multiplied, for over the next three hundred miles, the trail divided into a half dozen cutoffs and shortcuts. Eighteen miles west of the pass, between the Dry Sandy and the Little Sandy, the single trail from Fort Laramie unraveled at the Parting of the Ways. Travelers now had to decide, "Which road to take," Edward Jackson wrote. "We could scarcely choose." Here the old Oregon Trail turned south to follow the Little and Big Sandy rivers to Green River and Fort Bridger. The north fork led to the Sublette Cutoff's fifty parched and barren miles across the Little Colorado Desert, a shorter but much harder path to Fort Hall. Overlanders usually named roads for their destination, so they called the Sublette Cutoff the California route or the Fort Hall Road, while the trail to Fort Bridger became "the Oregon and Mormon or Salt Lake roads."[1] The trails, cutoffs, and roads they followed—and the comedies and tragedies that played out on them—created the thousand and one tales they told about the California Trail.

Beyond the Parting of the Ways, overlanders crossed the worst fifty dry miles they had encountered. Travelers who took the easier trail to the south had to choose between visiting the City of the Saints or turning north at Fort Bridger to Bear River and Fort Hall. Most Forty-niners used the tried-if-torturous Sublette Cutoff, but about a third of the trains visited Salt Lake—where they then had two and later three choices, about which they knew nothing and could learn little more. Gold seekers could follow the Hastings Cutoff to the Humboldt or take the new Salt Lake Cutoff to City of Rocks. Some latecomers to the City of the Saints,

---

[1]Jackson, Journal, 11 July 1849, BYU Library, 50.

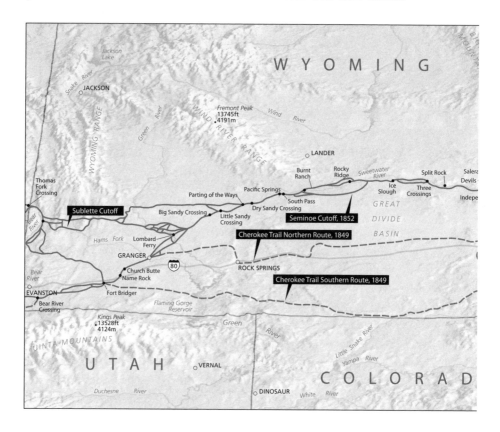

fearing the snows in the Sierra, headed south to the Spanish Trail, the Mexican trace across the Mojave Desert to Los Angeles.

The first parties to reach South Pass found veteran mountaineer Louis Vasquez waiting for them, "dressed in fantastic fringed buckskin clothes," among a sharp set of traders and bands of Shoshones on their way to hunt buffalo.[2] The gentlemanly proprietor's companion was Narcissa Burdette Land Coldwell Ashcraft, "a rather pretty and well dressed American woman, with an easy, pleasant address." She shared Vasquez's carpeted lodge—complete with a camp bed, a cushioned rocker, and several books.[3] Vasquez had come "on a speculation with a number of horses, hoping to find good customers in the emigrants." He persuaded many trains to take the Salt Lake Road, which passed the trading post on Blacks Fork he owned with Jim Bridger.[4] One of the Hudspeth brothers had advised James Stewart "by all

---

[2]Decker, *The Diaries*, 15 June 1849, 97.
[3]Delano, *Life on the Plains*, 28 June 1849, 109–10.
[4]Kelly, *Excursion to California*, 194.

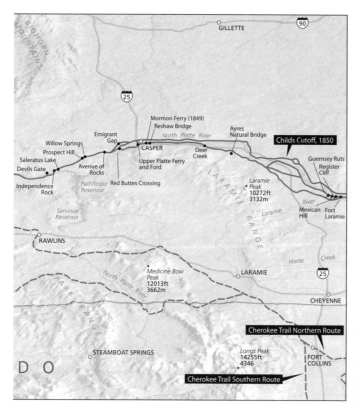

WAGON ROADS OVER
SOUTH PASS, 1852
The gold rush led to
the opening of Childs
Cutoff up the North
Platte while west of
South Pass the Sublette
Cutoff and Oregon
Trail developed a host of
variations. Based on the
National Park Service's
map of the California
National Historic Trail.

means" to take the Sublette Cutoff. William Johnston recalled that Vasquez warned
Stewart it would be a grave mistake: the route crossed a "desert of considerable
length, destitute of water and feed." He assured them the Salt Lake Road was free
from such difficulties, but Johnston later complained about this "misdirection" and
charged that the shrewd mountaineer plotted "to direct the tide of emigration in
the direction of Fort Bridger."[5] Vasquez did advise a few early arrivals to try the
untested shortcut, but his boosterism was not entirely successful and probably had
little overall impact. Curiosity, dire reports about the Sublette Cutoff, a lack of
provisions, or simply the chance to see something resembling civilization persuaded
many sojourners to visit the new settlement in the Great Basin.[6]

The Continental Divide marked the federal border between Indian Country

---

[5]Johnston, *Experiences of a Forty-niner,* 146–47, 200, 234.

[6]The best studies of Utah and the Mormons in the gold rush are Morgan, "Letters by Forty-niners," 98–116;
Madsen, *Gold Rush Sojourners;* "The Mormon 'Half-Way House,'" in Unruh, *The Plains Across,* 302–37; Goodell, *A
Winter with the Mormons.*

NARCISSA BURDETTE VASQUEZ
Heinrich Lienhard claimed the emigration abandoned this "skinny widow with two children" at Fort Laramie in 1846. According to another tradition, Louis Vasquez needed a cook and Narcissa accompanied him to Fort Bridger, where the couple had a daughter in July 1849. By this account, there was "considerable trouble between Mrs. Vasquez and Mrs. Bridger." She liked "Old Gabe," but Narcissa Vasquez "was extremely prejudiced against Bridger's squaw and did not care to have her around." They became friends in later years, "and Mrs. Vasquez was with Mrs. Bridger when she died." Sketch courtesy Colorado Historical Society.

and the Oregon Country. "The gate of the Rocky Mountains" did not impress deaf Forty-niner Edmund Booth when he crossed South Pass on 1 August; nor did the surrounding country prove any more inspiring: it was "the same barren desert we had been traveling for nearly a month—no grass—nothing but sand, pebbles, and wild sage."[7] Alexander Ramsay thought Pacific Spring did not deserve its name, "for its waters never reach the ocean but are absorbed by the desert sands," yet the small oasis of west-flowing water and bright green meadows extending along Pacific Creek gave comfort to beleaguered travelers and their battered livestock.[8] Teams grazed the meadow and drank the clear and cold water rising from "the middle of a swamp in almost any part of which ice could be found by digging to a depth of two feet," Thomas Galbraith wrote.[9] Alphonse Day considered the springs "a curiosity being a lake covered with muck & grass, cattle feeds on it & the Sod bends everry step from 4 to 6 inches & sometimes break through." In early July he counted at least a hundred teams camped there.[10] "Here we were obliged to throw away everything not actually nessessary to take and cut our wagon down in consequence of loseing our cattle," wrote Lucius Fairchild.[11]

The road west crossed three creeks called Dry, Little, and Big Sandy. The first of the Forty-niners found them all flowing to the top of their banks. Edward Jackson camped beside a small creek at the Dry Sandy. Thomas Galbraith found the usually

[7]Booth, *Edmund Booth (1810–1905), Forty-niner*, 9.
[8]Ramsay, "Gold Rush Diary," 28 June 1849.
[9]Galbraith, Journal, 10 July 1849, Mattes Library.
[10]Day, Journal, 6 July 1849, BYU Library.
[11]Fairchild, *California Letters*, 17 July 1849, 32.

dusty wash "proved to be Wet Sandy, for it was a running stream. We watered our mules from it, passed on to and crossed Little Sandy ten miles, thence to Big Sandy six miles."[12] The Big Sandy, William Kelly reported, was "a largish river, running between very high and steep sandbanks, fringed in places with willow."[13] Here trains prepared to cross the dusty road to Green River. "It reminded us of some large publick place," wrote an unknown diarist. "The people were camped up and down the River."[14]

John D. Lee, a Mormon who came from Salt Lake to recruit visitors and collect iron, told him the trail west of South Pass was strewn with so many dead animals "that if they were strung in a row a person could walk along on them without touching the ground."[15] The migration's size created a host of problems. Westbound hordes stripped the arid plains of grass and campsites of wood. West of South Pass, Joseph Middleton found wormwood, sand, and nothing else all the way to the Little Sandy. Thousands of narrow iron tires pulverized the soil and generated choking clouds of dust. The crowds left behind a legacy of waste, for their overcrowded campsites and unsanitary habits poisoned standing water sources and spread dysentery and diarrhea, diseases emigrants often identified as cholera. Middleton described a spot on the Big Sandy as "a nasty dirty place where many have camped before and left all their filth and offals." The wreckage of a Missouri family Dexter Tiffany met between the Big and Little Sandy put a human face on the cost of gold fever. Equipped with two wagons, a horse, and nine yoke of oxen, the Reverend Robert Gilmore had left home with his wife, three sons, and a daughter. Gilmore, his wife, and oldest son all died within three days of each other in mid-July: "the youngest son is now very sick desponding & probably will die. The remaining son 18 years old has gone to look for 9 oxen which run away this morning & the girl of 14 is taking care of the sick brother of 16 & they are all alone in this desert." Tiffany got medicine for the boy and stayed with the devastated family for two hours.[16]

The Right-hand Fork: The Sublette Cutoff

A day's wagon drive west of South Pass the trail divided; the traditional, safer Oregon Trail turned left and the shorter but drier Sublette route veered to the right. "We halted at noon at the forks of the road," Amasa Morgan wrote at the Parting of

---

[12]Galbraith, Journal, 11 July 1849, Mattes Library; Jackson, Journal, 10 July 1849, BYU Library, 58.

[13]Kelly, *Excursion to California*, 198.

[14]Anonymous, Diary from Michigan in California in 1849, 11 July 1849, Mattes Library.

[15]Middleton, Diary, 28–31 July 1849, Beinecke Library. John D. Lee was later executed for his role in the Mountain Meadows massacre of 1857. Lee, *A Mormon Chronicle*, 1:111.

[16]Tiffany, Diary and Letters, 20 July 1849, Missouri Historical Society, 89–90.

the Ways. "We took a vote to see wether we should go Subletts cut off or by Fort Bridger." The men lined up along the route of their choice. "The majority being for the cut off we all moved that way," he reported.[17] Gold rush trains often held a vote at the same spot and sometimes split up when they could not agree. When Lorenzo Dow Stephens's party came to the fork, the men "argued the advantages and disadvantages, and the result was a natural one, a disagreement," he recalled. "We parted company, each man choosing his company to travel in, so all were entirely satisfied."[18]

Misinformation and an increasing anxiety to get to El Dorado before all its riches disappeared led most gold seekers to risk the direct route across the Little Colorado Desert. T. J. Van Dorn estimated at least two-thirds of the emigration took the cutoff. "It is call'd by the emmigrants, very improperly, 'Soublette's Cut-Off,' but was discovered by another mountaineer,—Greenwood; and should be called 'Greenwood's Cut-Off,'" Goldsborough Bruff observed, for Old Caleb Greenwood had opened it in 1844. Sublette "had discovered a short cut higher up, from near the base of 'Fremont's Peak' to Fort Hall," Goldsborough Bruff deduced correctly, "which is only practicable for mules, and now probably nearly obliterated." When Bruff's Washingtonians voted at the forks of the road on 3 August, all but two ox wagons chose the cutoff and turned to the right. "A great many wagons have already preceded us on this route," Bruff noted, and it was now a "broad and well beaten trail."[19]

Journal keepers complained that their guide books—notably Joseph Ware's *Emigrants' Guide to California,* which Joseph Middleton denounced as "Ware's lying book"—deceived them into believing the waterless passage was only thirty-five miles long, whereas the route they took was forty-five to fifty miles from the Big Sandy to Green River. Dale Morgan concluded Solomon Sublette had described his brother William's 1836 trail to the Big Sandy to Ware, but Ware's description did not "in any particular conform to what was ever known as the Sublette Cutoff." Ware's itinerary apparently described an old trapper's trace to Piney Creek. Only fur-trade veteran Joseph Thing, now piloting the Granite State and Mount Washington companies, tried to follow Ware's directions—and Thing got profoundly lost.[20]

The Oregon/Mormon Trail to Fort Bridger followed relatively flat rivers, but the maze of trails attributed to Greenwood and Sublette crossed what journals

[17]Morgan, Diary, 16 June 1849, Bancroft Library.

[18]Stephens, *Life Sketches of a Jayhawker,* 12.

[19]Van Dorn, Diary, 8 July 1849, Beinecke Library, 22; Bruff, *Gold Rush,* 2, 3 August 1849, 64, 68.

[20]Middleton, Diary, 13 August 1849, Beinecke Library, 77; Morgan, "Ferries on the Sublette Cutoff," 32:2, 167–68. After wandering in the mountains for twelve days following Ware's directions, Kimball Webster recalled Thing's train "lost all confidence in his knowledge as a guide in the Rocky Mountain country." Webster, *Gold Seekers of '49,* 12 August 1849, 21, 70–71.

called valleys, washouts, ravines, gorges; climbed hills and summits so steep they earned nicknames like the Devil's Gangway; and came to pitches, precipices, and cliffs so sheer emigrants had to dismantle their wagons or use ropes to lower them. One trail over Dempsey Ridge rose to 8,400 feet in elevation—a thousand feet higher than South Pass.[21]

Parties with odometers gave varying distances for the waterless crossing. "After taking on board thirteen gallons of water, we took up our line of march across the desert," Thomas Galbraith reported in mid-July. Twenty-six hours later his party reached Green River, five miles below the old crossing. "The road after midnight was very hilly and rough, but we were favored by the light of the moon. The distance as measured by roadometer was forty-five miles," he wrote.[22] Joseph Warren Wood found the exceedingly dusty cutoff "a hard long stretch." It took twenty-eight hours of steady driving to make the crossing, which measured fifty-two miles.[23] On reaching Green River, one Forty-niner "learned that the distance was 43 miles as measured by roadodometer."[24] The conflicting reports were not due to problems with the primitive odometers; they indicate that different trains used different routes to cross the dusty, flinty cutoff. "The Sublette Cutoff is most confusing," noted historian Greg Franzwa, since the cutoff is "more a corridor than a single road." The confusion this maze of trails created persists: "Everyone has a different idea of where the trail actually goes. Even those living in this area don't agree," observed Wyoming rancher Karen Buck Rennells. "But each in his own way is right." Crossing "from the Sandy to the Green in the dark isn't the easiest thing to do," she notes. "You can get lost out there in the daylight."[25]

After fording the Big Sandy, the cutoff passed Haystack Butte, "a singular little mountain" that "looked in the distance just like a farmers hay stack," Amasa Morgan said. With the point of his Bowie knife, Goldsborough Bruff dug a fossil from this "singular clay mount, of buff colored clay and soft sandstone."[26] The road branched north and south around the forty-foot tall formation and came out on "very fine and easy travelling" across the Sublette Flats. Beyond Buckhorn Canyon, the "hilly & heavy" country was "cut up very much by deep ravines" for the cutoff's last fifteen miles. The trail passed through hills and canyons and was "up & down hill, some of them very steep, it being necessary to let the heavy wagons down with ropes to prevent their utter destruction," Wakeman Bryarly reported. Before reaching the

---

[21]Larsen, "The Devil's Gangway," 5–23.

[22]Galbraith, Journal, 12 July 1849, Mattes Library.

[23]Wood, Diary, 21 July 1849, Huntington Library.

[24]Anonymous, Overland Diary, 23 July 1849, Beinecke Library. Other roadometers measured the waterless drive as being 32.5 miles long. See Tate, Diary, 6 July 1849, Western Historical Manuscripts.

[25]Franzwa, *Maps of the Oregon Trail* 166, 170.

[26]Morgan, Diary, 16 June 1849, Bancroft Library; Bruff, *Gold Rush,* 4 August 1849, 71.

Green, travelers had to negotiate "the last but not least of the hills": it was almost three miles to the bottom of a "precipitous and difficult de[s]cent from the top of a very high bluff" before reaching the river and relief for parched oxen a few miles south of today's LaBarge, Wyoming.[27]

Forty-niners often waited until late afternoon or nightfall to make the dry passage. "We started after sunset to take the desert," Joseph Middleton wrote as he set out under a fine moon. As a passenger, Middleton slept in a wagon for most of the first twenty miles. On awaking, he found his train on a dusty road that soon reached "an immense tract of ocean-like plains." When the company unyoked its teams at midnight for a short rest, two-thirds of the overtaxed oxen collapsed. After a ninety-minute morning break, the exhausted, hungry cattle trudged on, having drunk a gallon of water and eaten whatever "spindly straws" they might find. Three oxen and two mules collapsed several miles short of the river. They struggled up and down barren hills and across deep gullies, and the first wagon reached Green River at 10:00 P.M., having completed a twenty-seven-hour drive with only four hours' rest. His party should have given their animals more time to recruit before facing the ordeal, Middleton concluded. The next morning a French-Canadian mountaineer said the cutoff saved sixty-five miles, "but that more was lost by the injury done to the oxen by the bad road." The train had to hitch eight yoke of oxen and beat the used-up animals to pull a single wagon out of the valley. "Our cattle have been ruined by bad drivers, who whip and abuse them without either humanity or judgment," Middleton wrote.[28]

From the sandy bottoms of the Green, the cutoff followed the river south for a few miles, passing Names Hill and making "a half retrograde movement of three miles" around Holden Hill. It then climbed a narrow ridge, "just wide enough for a good road, from which we had a view of the bottom and river which we had just left, and the broad bottom of a beautiful creek on the left, along which the road ran," Alonzo Delano wrote. From Fontenelle Creek the trail headed southwest to Rocky Gap and Hams Fork over broken, barren terrain. The wet year made the cutoff less arduous. A mountaineer told Delano "that the season was unusual, and that there were more and later rains than he had ever known, and more grass," so that usually barren hillsides were now covered with abundant forage.[29] The trail forded Hams Fork north of today's Kemmerer; climbed up and down more steep hills, including one Delano considered the worst he ever saw a wagon cross; and turned west-northwest to strike Bear River and rejoin the old Oregon Trail at today's Cokeville, Wyoming.

---

[27]Bryarly in Potter, *Trail to California,* 2 July 1849, 132; Pritchard, *The Overland Diary,* 20, 21 June 1849, 95–96.
[28]Middleton, Diary, 31 July, 1–3, 8 August 1849, Beinecke Library, 55–61, 70.
[29]Delano, *Life on the Plains,* 128–29; Franzwa, *Maps of the Oregon Trail,* 161–75.

The Sublette Cutoff saved several days' travel, but the barren passage was a risky ordeal over challenging terrain. A range of variants—the Kinney, Slate Creek, Dempsey, and Hockaday cutoffs—evolved over the next decade as emigrants tried to find the best route across the desert barrier. The rough trek across a harsh landscape that still challenges four-wheel-drive vehicles proved devastating for oxen and the men driving them. "Our thirst was almost intolerable & the dust in our mouth was so great, that it could be rolled up and spit out in lumps," recalled Solon Martin.[30] Livestock suffered more than their masters, and the ordeal doomed many already broken-down teams. Many who risked their lives and livestock on the right-hand fork found that the Sublette Cutoff, like almost every overland shortcut, was a bad bet.[31]

The Left-hand Fork: The Road to Fort Bridger

The Sublette Cutoff suffered the worst wear and tear the massive migration could offer, which persuaded many parties to visit Fort Bridger. James Tolles and his companions spent half an hour at "the forks of the Oregon & Salt Lake roads" trying to decide which route to take. All but one man "voted to go via Salt Lake as most of the travel had gone the other road." Two days later, Mormon John D. Lee told them, "The cattle on the other road were starving by hundreds and that many were turning down Green River to this road." Captain J. Bodley headed to Fort Bridger and was glad he did, for he "had an excellent road, grass, wood, and water." It took ten days and 140 miles to reach the fort, where he found a beautiful stream "with grass enough to feed a whole creation of cattle."[32]

Despite the strong preference for the Sublette Cutoff, several advance parties chose the road to Fort Bridger and the new Mormon settlements. There was no ferry when William Kelly reached Green River in mid-June, so crossing the swift and swollen torrent proved "one of the longest and most trying jobs of the entire journey." Kelly's companions tried using a caulked wagon, but eventually built a ferry out of cottonwood trunks. It barely floated when launched, but after sixteen or more trips they got their wagons across. Beyond Green River, the trail crossed sixteen dry miles before fording Blacks Fork, Hams Fork, and then Blacks Fork again—passing the badlands surrounding the conspicuous Church Butte, whose immense proportions towered "aloft like the dome of some mighty temple."[33]

---

[30]Martin, Reminiscences, Mattes Library.

[31]For maps and explanations of these trails, see Franzwa, *Maps of the Oregon Trail* 160–74.

[32]Tolles, Journal of My Travels, 11 July 1849, BYU Library; Bodley to "Dear Ristine," 22 July 1849, *People's Friend* (Covington, Indiana), 20 October 1849, 2/2.

[33]Kelly, *Excursion to California,* 193, 199–204.

Fifty miles beyond Green River, the trail came to the lush meadows surrounding Fort Bridger, founded in 1842 in the shadow of the Uinta Mountains. "The fort is in a most beautiful valley surrounded on three sides by high hills & on the other by mountains covered even now with snow & from these a large stream enters the valley but in passing through the land descends so rapidly that the stream divides into seven rushing brooks & all unite again about 2 miles below the fort," wrote Dexter Tiffany.[34] William Z. Walker was effusive: "The deep green foliage on the banks of the numerous streams, the level prairie along the banks of the rivers covered with roses and wild flowers the Bear river mountains covered with snow to the South gave the whole the appearance of a second Eden."[35] James Wilkins found twenty or thirty families living in skin lodges, "principally Canadian French married to Indian women," and a store offering a few goods "at most exorbitant prices." Twenty-five cents would buy a cold or thirsty gold seeker only a small box of matches or a drink of whiskey.[36] Bridger and Vasquez lived with their families in two of the four cabins. The third served as a store and the fourth was a black-smith's forge and rude carpenter's shop. "The fort is made of logs, or rather, the cabins form the fort, and the yard is the middle, [with] a large plank gateway to the entrance," William Lorton noted. "On the north end is the store containing goods for traffic"; on the east end Indian women did the cooking, and the other rooms held provisions or served as sleeping quarters. "The roof of the fort and chimneys are made of sod, while on the north is the 'caral' made of logs stood endways." The gold rush was transforming the old mountaineer into a rancher, Lorton observed, for Bridger was heavily engaged in trading cattle and horses, and had "lots of young ones he had brought up."[37]

Like his fort, "Old Gabe" got mixed reviews. Bridger "had been a very athletic active man though now he is bent & looks like a man of 55," wrote Dexter Tiffany. "He is very thin in consequence of a wound in the back by an arrow which had to be cut out." His life had "been full of adventure & spent among hostile Indians," but he complained his work had only enriched Missouri fur magnates.[38] Bridger was only in his mid-forties but appeared to be "an elderly man with a skin as red as one of his Indian servants or slaves," wrote Edward Harrow. "I think like most of these old traders he is pretty wealthy but from appearance he does not appear to be worth ten dollars."[39]

[34]Tiffany, Diary, 28 July 1849, Missouri Historical Society.

[35]Walker, Diary, 16 July 1849, 76, BYU Library.

[36]Wilkins, *An Artist on the Overland Trail*, 25 July 1849, 57.

[37]Lorton, Diary, 31 July 1849, Bancroft Library.

[38]Tiffany, Diary, 28 July 1849, Missouri Historical Society. Dr. Marcus Whitman extracted a three-inch iron arrowhead from Bridger's back in 1835.

[39]Harrow, *Gold Rush Overland Journal*, 38.

The Fort Hall Road

At Fort Bridger a handful of Forty-niners turned north to follow the old Oregon Trail to Bear River on a well-watered, well-worn wagon road. Occasionally challenging, the trail was refreshingly beautiful and provided bountiful grass for teams badly weakened by the rigors of the high desert. Hearing it was only forty miles longer than the Sublette route but better supplied with water and forage, Colonel William Loring led the first divisions of the Mounted Riflemen down the Oregon Trail. From Blacks Fork, the trail went eighteen miles over "several hills somewhat precipitous and dangerous for wagons" to the steep ravine of Muddy Creek near today's Carter, Wyoming. The next day, after following the Muddy to its source, the trail crossed the Hogsbacks through the evocatively named Cumberland Gap and climbed the Bear River Divide west of Oyster Ridge. Loring considered the ascent gradual and the descent easy, but much of the road was circuitous and dangerous.[40]

"Here is plenty of excellent grass, which has scarcely been touched, as very little emigration has gone this way," wrote James Wilkins on a smoky day in late July. "So we have it our own way, our cattle now being in fine condition." The three- to five-mile-wide Bear River Valley lay between steep bluffs, "they may almost be called mountains they are so very high." The peaks were "the finest I have ever seen, rich in color oweing to a kind of red clay." Wilkins viewed the scenery with an artist's eye: "The country seemed a succession of ridges or high hills generally barren of vegetation on the crowns, with short brown bunch grass on the sides while valleys meandering here and there between the hills had a line of more brilliant green."[41] When Wakeman Bryarly "struck the old road, the Fort Bridger road" in early July, it had seen little travel. "We could see but three tracks of wagons along it."[42] Dexter Tiffany commented on the popularity of the Sublette shortcut. Despite the savings in miles, Tiffany thought the Pioneer Line had "missed the mark in going the cut off because everybody has gone the same way & the grass is all eaten up."[43] In contrast, Major Osborne Cross of the Mounted Riflemen claimed the cutoff was worth the wear and tear on the livestock. Had Loring's companies taken the shortcut, Cross reasoned, he could have rested his horses and mules for a week on Bear River, "one of the few spots on the route where a temporary repose may be had."[44]

Travelers waxed eloquent over the scenery. "The Bear River Valley is clothed in the finest grass and would make fine hay. Wild rye and flax grows very luxuriantly," wrote Samuel Murray Stover, who had noticed the universal gloom among his

[40]Loring, in Settle, *March of the Mounted Riflemen,* 129n140, 335–36.
[41]Wilkins, *An Artist on the Overland Trail,* 29 July 1849, 60.
[42]Bryarly, *Trail to California,* 8 July 1849, 140.
[43]Tiffany, Diary, 21 July 1849, Missouri Historical Society.
[44]Settle, *March of the Mounted Riflemen,* 151, 336.

comrades after crossing the Green River barrens. "The immigrants seem to have bright hopes and are more jovial."[45] John Bates praised "the beautiful mountain country which is lovely beyond description—Its mountains the most graceful & lofty we have yet seen with fertile vallies which we alternately crossed presenting many beautiful garden spots sparkling here & there with christal springs & myriads of flowers of varied hue."[46] Early arrivals like Amasa Morgan found the river valley "covered with flowers and good grass." A mountaineer said that the previous spring's rains had raised the most grass he had ever seen. "The view of the valley with its green grass along the river bottom revived our spirits," Alonzo Delano wrote, "and upon the hills we found flax and wild oats growing thriftily."[47] After a thousand miles of timberless monotony, David Leeper praised the valley's "comely trees and shrubs; bright foliage; refreshing shade; fragrant flowers; pure, cold springs; sparkling rivulets; luxuriant grasses; the chirp and chatter of many birds,—such was the scene as my memory now recalls it. It seemed indeed like a precious gem plucked from fairy land."[48]

After the Sublette Cutoff rejoined the older trail, the massive migration pressed on down both sides of Bear River. Those who stayed on the west bank had to ford Smiths Fork and then Thomas Fork, where the river valley "was walled by mountains for about ten miles." Sojourners had to make several hard climbs, notably up the Big Hill, "the steepest and longest ascent we have made on the route."[49] John Evans Brown called Big Hill "decidedly the hilliest and most difficult" climb on the entire trail.[50] The half-mile ascent was "desperately steep," wrote Joseph Middleton, and the view was "of contorted brick-dust hilltops before us, amongst which the windings of the road is lost to view. It ascends to the west, then sweeps around to the south, and makes a deep dive into a ravine where there is a large block of rock of many tons weight in the middle of the gorge with only room for one wagon to pass." Getting back to the Bear required "a tremendous plunge."[51]

Most travelers struck the river again near Pegleg Smith's trading post, a cluster of log buildings called Fort Smith.[52] Like Jim Bridger, his quarter century in the fur trade had made Thomas L. Smith a western legend. After falling out with Bridger in 1842, Smith became an independent HBC agent. Over the years he operated several stations, including one about four miles above the mouth of Smiths Fork and another at what he called Big Timbers. "Whilst leading the life of a mountaineer,

[45]Stover, *Diary,* 21 July 1849, 25–26.
[46]Bates, Diary, 10 August 1849, Mattes Library.
[47]Morgan, Diary, 21 June 1849, Bancroft Library; Delano, *Life on the Plains,* 7, 11 July 1849, 129, 133.
[48]Leeper, *Argonauts of 'Forty-nine,* 42.
[49]Wilkins, *An Artist on the Overland Trail,* 1 August 1849, 60.
[50]Brown, "Memoirs of an American Gold Seeker," 146.
[51]Middleton, Diary, 13 August 1849, Beinecke Library, 77–78.
[52]Webster, *Gold Seekers of '49,* 14 August 1849; Boyle, Diary, 24 June 1849.

he visited nearly every portion of the country lying between the Mississippi river and the Pacific Ocean, and the Red River of the North and Mexico on the South," his obituary reported accurately. However, its claim that Smith had been "a chief in the Utah tribe" and could speak Ute, Sioux, Shoshone, Pawnee, Crow, Blackfeet, Navajo, plus the languages of a few other tribes probably stretched the truth.[53]

That spring Smith informed Brigham Young he had been "laid up with my leg all winter" but had $200 or $300 on hand if the Mormon leader needed hard cash. The first wagons arrived at Smith's Bear River outpost by mid-June 1849. "There has one company of 9 or 10 men pass With waggons for california and we expect some more to day," Smith wrote. "They told me that they thought that there was 20 thousand people on the road for california with the gold fevor. About the 26 of this month I look for plenty here."[54] During the long, snowbound winter, Pegleg had "fed a great many Indians on his beef and horses and saved them from starvation," reported William Chamberlain. Smith was "a man of about 50 or 55 years of age, rather portly, round headed"— and quite rich, he concluded.[55]

No one ever nailed down exactly where Smith's main post was located, but he probably had several stations around today's Dingle, Idaho. Smith's home in 1849 was a fourteen-by-twenty foot adobe "hovell" furnished with nothing but a stone fireplace, buffalo hides, and deerskins, recalled Reuben Shaw. Shaw thought Pegleg's scanty buckskins, long hair, and "smoke cured-face gave him the appearance of being as good an Indian as any of them, but I failed to see that he was any better." Smith had announced in 1848 that he would soon have a large farm in operation, but Shaw thought the rich bottoms of Bear River "had never been polluted by hand of a white Indian."[56] He was wrong. Smith "conceived the idea in the spring of '48 of raising vegetables and grains, and packed a plough, tools and seed from Salt Lake, bringing a Mormon to assist him," Israel Lord reported. Conditions conspired to thwart Pegleg's plans. His wheat was eighteen inches tall "when from the hills a swarm of fierce black crickets, rushing down, Swept it away." Smith failed at everything, Lord noted, including his relationship with his Mormon assistant, Isaac Brown.[57] Brown had talked "pretty hard" about him, Smith knew, and he complained to Brigham Young. "I want [to] let you know something about those hard feelings," Smith wrote, claiming he had fed not only Brown and his family but also his hired man and hired girl. "That is all I have to say About Mr Brown. He is a verry bad trader," Pegleg wrote, "and A verry ungrateful man."[58]

---

[53]"'Peg Leg' Smith," *San Francisco Call*, in *Salt Lake Semi-Weekly Telegraph*, 15 November 1866, 1/3, courtesy Ardis Parshall.

[54]Smith to Young, 26 May, 15 June 1849, Brigham Young Collection, LDS Archives.

[55]Chamberlain, Diary, 8 July 1849, Bancroft Library.

[56]Shaw, *Across the Plains*, 102–104; Templeton, *The Lame Captain*, 183.

[57]Lord, *"At the Extremity of Civilization,"* 3 August 1849, 67.

[58]Smith to Young, 15 June 1849, LDS Archives.

Charles Boyle got a bowl of bread and milk from Isaac Brown's wife at Smith's Fort. "It was quite good," he noted, and he sold the "jolly but one-legged man commonly known as Peg-legged Smith" a pint of brandy for four dollars.[59] "This Old Smith who lives here has a cork leg—a rough looking man he is too. The place is better known as Smith's trading post. A Salt Lake Mormon & wife were here for the purpose of trading with the Emmegrants, & several Frenchmen," noted James A. Pritchard.[60] Smith was "a fleshy, shrewd looking man, about 50 years old, and as rough as the tawny customers with which he is surrounded," Amos Batchelder reported.[61] The hospitable, honest mountaineer had money in abundance and an Indian wife "who he calls Mary & who he appears to love," Hugh Brown Heiskell observed. "He has some peculiar ideas about some things, of course, owing to his habits from so long a residence among savages."[62] Smith had "a comfortable house, cooking stoves, hogs, cattle, cats and also a churn," and he was "fond of company and treats them on the best he has and in great abundance almost to wastefulness," Israel Hale recalled. He guessed Smith's Shoshone wife was about sixteen years old, "rather bulky than otherwise," and claimed the couple's boy was "a spoiled child." Smith, Hale concluded, appeared as happy as a lord.[63]

Both Smith and Brown made money hand over fist. Joseph Middleton found Brown winding up his trading season on Smiths Fork, twenty miles upstream from Pegleg's post. "Mr. Brown is from the State of New York, and is going to the Mormon settlements this fall," Middleton wrote. "He said that he has been speculating with the emigrants and is worth $2000 at present. He is going to stay about 2 weeks longer before he starts for the Salt Lake."[64] Smith and his Mormon were "ready now, to shoot each other—indeed did threaten it only day before yesterday," Lord reported. Pegleg, he decided, was "a 'customer.' "[65]

Besides the established traders at Smith's Fort, French mountaineers and Shoshones opened trading operations all along the Bear. The Natives impressed most travelers: H. C. St. Clair called them "some of the handsomest & best made Indians that I ever saw."[66] The tribe's honesty was so proverbial that Alonzo Delano's train did not stand guard while traveling through their country, "a confidence which was not misplaced."[67] Charles Boyle took a long ride with several Shoshones he found "as lively and good-humored as could well be." When Boyle told one hunter

[59]Boyle, Diary, 24 June 1849.

[60]Pritchard, *The Overland Diary,* 27 June 1849.

[61]Batchelder, Journal, 14 August 1849, Bancroft Library.

[62]Heiskell, *A Forty-niner from Tennessee,* 20 August 1849, 13.

[63]Hale, "Diary of a Trip to California," 16 July 1849, 92.

[64]Middleton, Diary, 12 August 1849, Beinecke Library, 75–76.

[65]Lord, *"At the Extremity of Civilization,"* 3 August 1849, 67.

[66]St. Clair, Journal, 18 July 1849, Beinecke Library.

[67]Delano, *Life on the Plains,* 18 July 1849, 141.

that his short, sinew-backed, sheephorn bow was fit only to shoot mosquitoes, the man assured him it would drive an arrow through a buffalo.[68]

THE PASSING SWARMS: SODA SPRINGS AND FORT HALL

Thirty-five miles down the Bear from the Big Timbers, travelers came to the cluster of hot and carbonated "soda fountains" at today's Soda Springs, Idaho, one of the trail's superlative natural wonders. "The water oozes out at the top of a rock of a mineral substance about 15 feet high," wrote Amasa Morgan, one of the first of the Forty-niners to see the conical limestone formation emigrants called the Beer Spring. It tasted, he observed, something like sour beer. About a mile west, over ground strewn with cinders he came to *the* Soda Springs, "near the road in a pleasant grove," where carbonated water bubbled out of the ground. His companions sounded the depth of one spring with a long pole, "but could not touch the bottom." Two hundred yards away on the bank of Bear River was Steamboat Spring. "If I had it at home," Morgan noted wistfully, it would be "fortune Enough with out going to California."[69]

Wakeman Bryarly found carbonated springs shooting up all over the delightful spot. Boiling Springs alone covered a quarter acre and steamed "up from crevices in the rocks in a thousand different places, making the surface foam & hiss, as boiling water" that came "bursting out from every crevice & hole that you can find." The greatest curiosity was the "foaming, whizzing, sizzling, blowing, splashing & spraying" Steamboat Spring. The valley's "many different freaks, irregularities, & the remains of departed times," Bryarly said, made it "a grand field for the geologist, minerologist, naturalist, & any other kind of 'ist' that you can conceive."[70] Joseph Middleton complained that drinking from Soda Springs "made my stomach sick, and sometime after I had a dull headache and retched."[71] Elisha Perkins found the taste unpleasant, like "soda water without any syrup or flavoring, slightly acid, also a very distinct metallic taste, & a foetid old swamp like flavor combined."[72] Benjamin Hoffman thought that with a little sugar and vinegar, the taste was equal to the best soda, but he believed there were several poisonous springs, "which are said to be instant death to anything that drinks them."[73]

---

[68]Boyle, Diary, 23 June 1849.

[69]Morgan, Diary, 24 June 1849, Bancroft Library.

[70]Bryarly, *Trail to California*, 11 July 1849, 144–47.

[71]Middleton, Diary, 17 August 1849, Beinecke Library, 83. A power-generating reservoir has flooded Steamboat Springs, but several of the other historic springs survive at city parks and at the Oregon Trail Golf Club, which preserves Oregon Trail ruts on its fairways.

[72]Perkins, *Gold Rush Diary*, 91.

[73]Hoffman, "West Virginia Forty-niners," 11 July 1849, 68–69. Residents of Soda Springs still prefer carbonated drinks they make themselves to store-bought soft drinks.

After leaving the fountains of Soda Springs, the first Forty-niners crossed fifty miles of bad road to Fort Hall, the Hudson's Bay Company station on Snake River. Wagon parties often camped at a spring six miles to the east because the post was "surrounded by a vast plain, cut through and through with Rivers, creeks, branches & Sloughs running in every direction" and was constantly under siege by mosquitoes.[74] The trading post was not quite as large as Fort Laramie, Joseph Warren Wood wrote, but had a neater appearance.[75] Others thought it looked well built, despite the timbers propping up the dilapidated adobe citadel's northwest wall.

Goldsborough Bruff visited the fort in late August. After entering the "Great Portal," he climbed a set of stairs to the apartment of Chief Trader Richard Grant, the Snake Country's senior officer since 1841 and a forgotten giant of the early West. "Grant is a Scotchman, from Canada, a fine looking portly old man, and quite courteous, for an old mountaineer," Bruff wrote. He found the captain "very English, and anti-Yankee." His Native clients loved the proud old trader, which made him the most powerful man between the Bear River and the Cascades. "He is 6 ft., 2 or 3 inches, high & made in proportion, with a handsome figure. His face is perfectly English, fat round, chubby, & red. His hair is now getting in the sere & yellow leaf & his whiskers are also turning grey," Wakeman Bryarly observed, calling him "a most remarkable looking man." His fort's courtyard had a fine fountain of water in the middle surrounded by small shops and storage rooms. When Bruff asked if there was a good wagon road to Oregon, Grant said it was tolerable despite some bad places. But, said he, "There is no place where you Yankees cannot carry a wagon that I ever saw!" Grant's wife made Bruff a pitcher of lemonade, which he found most refreshing. Grant "said that his whisky was out, and apologized for the deficiency."[76]

The settlement of the Oregon question reduced the HBC's influence, but Grant still ruled a virtual kingdom, which historian Peter Boag called "a multi-cultural, multi-ethnic, multi-racial middle ground" where visitors met Shoshone, Bannock, English, Scottish, Canadian, French, Spanish, Mexican, Hawaiian, Chinook, Nez Perces, Iroquois, Kiowa, and Mormon peoples.[77] Emigrants commented on the notably diverse community gathered around the fort. "There are several families living here—some French, some English, and some Americans," James Pritchard observed. "It was quite a pleasant sight to see White women & children."[78] Bannock and Shoshone Indians "were plenty here," Charles Boyle wrote. He shared a

---

[74]Pritchard, *The Overland Diary*, 2 July 1849, 104–105.

[75]Wood, Diary, 21 July 1849. Huntington Library.

[76]Bryarly, *Trail to California*, 14 July 1849, 151–53; Bruff, *Gold Rush*, 24 August 1849, 102, 105–107.

[77]Boag, "Idaho's Fort Hall as a Western Crossroads," 24.

[78]Pritchard, *The Overland Diary*, 2 July 1849, 105.

pipe with Salish Indians and met Mexicans and French Canadians who had Indian wives.[79]

The first wagon reached Fort Hall on 22 June. Within a month about 1,300 overlanders stopped at the outpost.[80] Grant was absent early in the season and his men did not count the emigrants' wagons, "but the number that passed by this and the New Road and what was supposed to have gone past previous to my return cannot be far below ten thousand," he calculated. Grant "managed to pick up a few Dollars"—nearly $3,500 by his own estimate—advancing cash to the Mounted Riflemen and trading with "the passing swarms." Otherwise the fort's trade was "anything but flattering. I have done I may almost say nothing." Like his colleagues, Grant believed the big money still lay in the fur trade, which was much reduced with the Indians "being now so amply supplied with all their wants by the passing Emigrants."[81] His repeated pleas to the HBC to stock his post with goods for the emigrant trade went unheeded. Alonzo Delano had hoped to resupply at the fort but was disappointed—Grant was himself buying bacon and flour from overloaded emigrants.[82]

Visitors commented on the number and quality of Grant's cattle and horses, and the old Scot was already finding new ways to profit from his long experience as a frontier entrepreneur. "I saw some of the very best cattle here that I ever saw," wrote Palmer Tiffany, but the store had "a poor assortment of goods."[83] Large numbers of Indians and traders, generally Frenchmen, surrounded the fort, where Latter-day Saint women had opened a restaurant. "A Mormon had rented a room in the fort where he kept a kind of tavern, in which some of our men procured a meal of bread, butter, and milk, for which they paid three bits," B. R. Biddle reported.[84] Wakeman Bryarly and his friends were able to get "some nice milk & also a fried chicken, which carried us so far back 'to days that's past.'"[85] A family from Salt Lake "had bought a very large number of cows. Butter was very scarce as they sold it as fast as they could make it"; cheese and milk were equally popular. "We halted at the fort for a couple of hours to regale ourselves on bread and milk as these articles could be had here in great abundance," Charles Boyle noted.[86] "We had dinner at the fort which consisted of milk cheese and warm light bread, and after being confined so long upon strong coffee crackers slapjacks and fat bacon it

[79]Boyle, Diary, 29 June 1849.

[80]Wood, Diary, 22 July 1849, Huntington Library.

[81]Grant to Simpson, 22 February 1850, HBC Archives, D.5/27, 335–37.

[82]Delano, Life on the Plains, 18 July 1849, 141–42.

[83]Tiffany, Overland Journey, 10 July 1849, Beinecke Library, 77.

[84]Biddle, "Journey to California," 16 July 1849. A "bit" was worth 12.5 cents.

[85]Bryarly, Trail to California, 14 July 1849, 151–53.

[86]Boyle, Diary, 29 June 1849.

was just the thing which our apetite craved and invalids and all did ample justice to the dinner, giving our English hostess most unmistakable evidence of our satisfaction in regard to her dinner," wrote Alexander Nixon, adding that the pioneer dairy was trading a lot of cheese to the Indians.[87] One of their first customers, Lewis Tremble, bought milk, cheese, butter, and fresh beef. "I made myself sick drinking milk, which satisfied me with luxuries."[88]

Few Forty-niners paused for long. Alarming tales about the road to California persuaded many to cut down their wagons or abandon them altogether and turn to "the last hope of the adventurer, namely, packs."[89] James Pritchard saw a New York train trade two good wagons for a horse, and a band of his fellow Kentuckians swapped their wagon and spare provisions for an unbroken animal. "The traders knew that the men were bound to sell at those prices or leave the wagons," he noted. "And therefore they would give them no more."[90] Joseph Warren Wood saw several deserted wagons, but "most of them have been burnt up for fuel." Indian women picked up the articles the gold seekers had abandoned. "I presume they visit the spot every day and scrape up the plunder which is continually left," Wood noted.[91] Along Snake River, abandoned wagons were "plenty at short distances on this part of the road & furnish good material for camp fires," wrote Alexander Nixon. Their greasy hubs blazed "like pine knots, making a cheerful fire."[92]

The trail down the Snake River was "very dusty; grass scarce, wild sage very thick; mosquitoes very bad."[93] Three miles from the fort, the trail crossed the Portneuf River, "a beautiful mountain stream about 30 yards in width."[94] In another three miles it came to the slightly wider Bannock Creek, "a very bold & beautiful stream."[95] Below the ford, the wagon road climbed a steep hill to "a barren, sandy plain, where nothing but the interminable sage and greasewood grew," wrote Alonzo Delano, who drove on until nightfall under "the sultry sun, and through suffocating clouds of dust."[96]

Charles Tinker found the sixty miles between Fort Hall and the Raft River "a sandy barren track of land covered with not much but wild sage."[97] After about twenty miles of tedious travel "through burning sand, and in dense clouds of dust" travelers

---

[87]Nixon, Diary, 6 July 1849, California State Library.

[88]Tremble to Miles, 6 August 1849, *Illinois Republican*, 1 January 1850, Mattes Library.

[89]Harrow, *Gold Rush Overland Journal*, 30 June 1849, 32.

[90]Pritchard, *The Overland Diary*, 3 July 1849, 107.

[91]Wood, Diary, 21 July 1849, Huntington Library.

[92]Nixon, Diary, 7 July 1849, California State Library.

[93]Watson, *Journal of an Overland Journey to Oregon*, 19 July 1849, 29.

[94]Nixon, Diary, 7 July 1849, California State Library.

[95]Clark, "A Journey," 10 July 1849, 27.

[96]Delano, *Life on the Plains*, 18 July 1849, 143.

[97]Tinker, "Journal," 80.

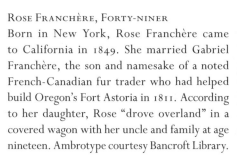

ROSE FRANCHÈRE, FORTY-NINER
Born in New York, Rose Franchère came to California in 1849. She married Gabriel Franchère, the son and namesake of a noted French-Canadian fur trader who had helped build Oregon's Fort Astoria in 1811. According to her daughter, Rose "drove overland" in a covered wagon with her uncle and family at age nineteen. Ambrotype courtesy Bancroft Library.

came to the diverting scenery at American Falls. "We heard the sound of their dashing before reaching them, and none could conjecture what it was," wrote Lewis Tremble. "We had seen the 'elephant' yet such a sight could not but make one halt and view the sublime work of nature." Some two hundred yards wide, the Snake "fell some hundred and fifty feet, over a bed of rocks causing a loud roar, very much like a violent storm. The reflection of the storm upon the falling waters caused rainbows of great beauty. After feasting our eyes for some time, we left this spot, all satisfied, and felt fully repaid for the hardships we had undergone since leaving home."[98] The falls were formed by "a dyke of black trap-rock, extending across the river in a horseshoe form, making nearly a perpendicular fall," Alonzo Delano noted. "Near this are scattered on the ground, black volcanic *debris,* resembling somewhat anthracite coal, but which is merely melted matter, thrown to the surface."[99] "The de[s]cent is about 50 feet in a very short distance," wrote James Tate, "dashing and foaming in wild confusion presenting a sublime view of beauty wildness and Horror."[100]

Forty-niners had a universal complaint about the road between the Bear and Raft rivers: the "most devilish bad" mosquitoes.[101] Wakeman Bryarly had spent

[98]Tremble to Miles, 6 August 1849, *Illinois Republican,* 1 January 1850, Mattes Library.
[99]Delano, *Life on the Plains,* 19 July 1849, 14.
[100]Tate, Diary, 27 July 1849, Western Historical Manuscripts, 23.
[101]Clarke, Journey to the El Dorado, 10 June 1849, Idaho State Historical Society, 18.

much time in mosquito country, but he had never seen them in their glory until he camped near Fort Hall. "They were so thick you could reach out & get your handfuls."[102] The "countless hoards of mosquitoes which for ravenousness and perseverance I never saw equaled" drove Joseph Warren Wood from his camp-ground. They were "troublesome beyond everything I have ever conceived. There are clouds of them. Smoke is no protection though they fall in it by myriads."[103]

James Pritchard could hear the roaring waters of American Falls for miles and called them "a most wonderful & beautiful sight," but on the Fourth of July, the pests were so bad "they nearly ran Our mules crazy. They would break & run & lay down & roll, jirk up their picket pins or break Lorrietts."[104] "This camp beats all the places I ever saw for Musketoes," Alexander Nixon reported. "The air is litterly alive with them and they appear to be determined on having our last drop blood, but we are not going to let them have it without an effort on our part to prevent them." Nixon's train kept "our camp fires blazing high and they don't like the looks of fire."[105] Others felt they defied any countermeasures. Dr. Samuel Mathews recalled "our 'mosquito night'": the predatory insects were so thick he had to eat with one hand and fight them off with the other. "These were the remnants of Lewis & Clarke's mosquitoes—they would go through the thickest blanket," he wrote.[106] J. M. Muscott summed up his memorable trip down the Snake: "I never suffered so much misery from the bite of insects as I suffered in 3 or 4 days on the river from the gnats and Musquetoes."[107]

THE RUINS OF THE DESERT:
RAFT RIVER AND THE CITY OF ROCKS

Eight miles below the Quaternary formations that created the cascades of Fall Creek, which many travelers mistook for petrified beaver dams, the road reached a critical fork at Raft River, "a small stream with a smooth strong current and gravely bed," wrote James Pritchard. "It is at the crossing of this stream that the Oregon & California roads seperate." Here travelers had to decide whether they would go to Oregon or California—and it was not until David Pease's train came to the crossroads in mid-July that anyone headed to Oregon. Virtually every Forty-niner who came to the last parting of the Oregon and California trails, even those who had initially set out for the Pacific Northwest, turned and marched south. The

---

[102]Bryarly, *Trail to California,* 14 July 1849, 151.
[103]Wood, Diary, 21 July 1849, Huntington Library.
[104]Pritchard, *The Overland Diary,* 4, 5 July 1849, 109.
[105]Nixon, Diary, 5 July 1849, California State Library.
[106]Mathews, "By Wagon Train to California, 1849: A Narrative," 25.
[107]Muscott to Robbins, 14 October 1849, California State Library.

Raft River Valley was a level, barren plain, but it was blessed with ample forage along its bottoms and at the wetlands surrounding springs: Pritchard found an "Oasis in the dessert" at a spring a mile off the road that had excellent grass up to his waist. "The grass is abundant and the water excellent," John Bates wrote as his mules luxuriated on the good feed. Friends from Lexington overtook Dr. William L. Thomas near the crossroads. "We had quite a friendly meeting, found and tapped a bottle of old Bourbon and had great jollification—the boys dined with us today," he recorded. The Kentuckians "got up spedily and in good stile a most excellent dinner. Indeed the boys were surprised and astonished at finding such comforts and luxuries here in the mountains." Lemuel Herbert, upon reaching the site a year later, was not so impressed. To him Raft River looked like "John Bunyan's Slough of dispond."[108]

One type of wagon train preferred the Oregon Trail. Henry Tappan met "quite a train taking the Oregon Trail, mostly families."[109] "The oregon road turnes off hear," Joseph Hackney wrote on 24 July, and many of those camped on Raft River intended to go to Oregon: "They are all family wagons." Before the Oregonians parted ways with the gold seekers, some Pike County boys paid Hackney's party a visit and brought a fiddler along to stage a sociable dance.[110] Two days later at the mouth of Raft River, Joseph Warren Wood found a company "beating up recruits" for Oregon. "A great many are turning off for Oregon on account of the prospects for scarce food in California, especially family wagons."[111] "This morning we had a separation: two wagons for California, five for Oregon," wrote William Watson, who turned to the northwest and made a nineteen-mile waterless trek "over a very rocky road, covered with wild sage." The Oregon Trail was not as dusty as the California road, he noted.[112]

After climbing fifteen miles and fording the Raft River three times, the trail crossed five miles to Cassia Creek, a fine trout stream. Gold seekers ascended the creek and crossed swampy ground to a narrow passage through the Albion Mountains, "through a gorge or ravine on either side of which are ridges several hundred ft high, very rocky in the gorge, the rockiest & most difficult road we have passed requiring great care with wagons," Peter Decker reported. "Here are rocks jutting out near the road of peculiar shapes from 5 to 100 ft high. Some are hollow—this is a romantic spot."[113] This scenic wonder was "the city of the rocks, a noted place

[108]Pritchard, *The Overland Diary*, 6 July 1849, 110; Bates, Diary, 26 July 1849, Mattes Library; Herbert, Personal Diary, 9 July 1850, Delaware County Historical Society, 40; Thomas, Diary, 6 July 1849, Bancroft Library.

[109]Tappan, "The Gold Rush Diary," 22 July 1849, 131–32.

[110]Hackney, Journal, 24 July 1849, *Wagons West*, 175.

[111]Wood, Diary, 24 July 1849, Huntington Library.

[112]Watson, *Journal of an Overland Journey to Oregon*, 22 July 1849, 30.

[113]Decker, *The Diaries*, 4 July 1849, 112.

from the granite rocks rising abruptly out of the ground," wrote James Wilkins. "They are in a romantic valley clustered together which gives them the appearance of a city."[114] A young geological formation thrusting up through some of the oldest granite in the lower forty-eight states created the Silent City of Rocks, as a 1918 Conoco highway map called it.[115] Emigrants gave the place fanciful names, such as Steeple Rocks, Castle City, the Grey Granite Rocks, Granite City, City of Castles, Pyramid City, Pyramid Pass, the Three Towers, the Valley of Rocks, Monumental Rocks, and the Ruins of the Desert. Pioneers even named individual rocks—Napoleon's Castle, Sarcophagus Rock, Novelty Pass, Temple or Recorder's Rock, Castle Rock Hotel, the Deity of the Spring, and the Rock Gemini.[116]

A few diarists managed to ignore these wonders completely, but most commented on the spectacular landforms looming above the trail as it wandered more than four miles through the formations. "Our place of encampment last night had more of grandeur and picturesque beauty than any yet seen—high conical, or I might say comical shaped peaks present on all sides making a circuit of some 6 miles," wrote T. J. Van Dorn, reflecting how Castle City fascinated his fellow Forty-niners. "Once in, we see no passage out. Entry and passing out through deep canyons. The little valley was filled with teams and the cattle over the plains gave quite a home like appearance to the place. The road leading out over a slight elevation, our road led us through a kind of gate way, of which there are several, as if designed by nature as a passage way to our route," he concluded.[117] "To day the scenery was more beautifully interesting & romantic than I had yet seen it—the mountain being composed of granite & beautiful white marble of the first quality & representing figures from the grotesque to the most sublime & magnifficent," wrote John Bates.[118] Wakeman Bryarly saw a perfect face on the highest cliff and thought "with a little imagination one could see church domes, spires, and pyramids" amid the massive piles, and with a little fancying one could see anything "from the Capitol at Washington to a lovely thatched cottage."[119]

The landforms seemed entirely whimsical. "After travelling a mile we enter a gorge which brings us into a large elevated amphitheatre surrounded with rocks of every kind of fanciful character. A spring of fine water comes from the west

[114]Wilkins, *An Artist on the Overland Trail,* 13 August 1849, 63. Wilkins appears to have conjured up the name City of Rocks himself, but Edward Smith made the first known use of the name in his Journal of Scenes and Incidents, 16 August 1848, California State Library.

[115]Martin, "Geology of Silent City of Rocks," 24–27; Photo 19598, Utah State Historical Society.

[116]These names, from Bruff, Burbank, Hutchings, Johnston, Loveland, Pratt, Steele, Wayman, and Woodhams, can be found in "City of Rocks (California Trail)," Idaho State Historical Society Reference Series No. 924; Hunt, "Silent City of Rocks," 13–23.

[117]Van Dorn, Diary, 27 July 1849, 1849, Beinecke Library, 29.

[118]Bates, Diary, 27 August 1849, Mattes Library.

[119]Bryarly, *Trail to California,* 19 July 1849, 160–61.

but is lost before reaching the gorge," Joseph Middleton observed. "On passing through this amphitheatre you see Domes, Turrets, Monuments, Urns, Pyramids, Columns, Idols, and astonishing grandeur. In advancing through the gorge the insulated blocks of stone rise up before you in succession spearing up into the sky in pyramids of all kinds in an astonishing manner of sublime desolation. The rock is white micacious granite of a soft character which moulders away by throwing off thin crusts." The Ruins of the Desert extended three miles to "the south gate from the Ruins," where there was a singular double cone Middleton called the "Twin Pyramids," the towering monoliths now known as the Twin Sisters.[120] Awestruck by "the most beautiful mountain scenery that I have seen on the road," Gordon Cone wrote that "these rocks present a singular appearance—riseing from the base of the mountain in a pyramidal form" and giving the impression "of a Hottontot village."[121]

Much more than its spectacular scenery, its geography made City of Rocks one of the most important crossroads on the California Trail. "We are now in the great thorofare, w[h]ere all the wagons by the different routes come together and it is now one continued string," James Wilkins observed. Beyond the narrow granite gate at the backdoor of the City of Rocks, the Salt Lake Cutoff reunited with the main road to California. Looming dust clouds helped travelers on both trails spot the wagon tops of trains across the Raft River Valley. After the two trails met beneath the Twin Sisters, the strands of the California Trail that had unraveled beyond South Pass—the Sublette, Hudspeth, and Salt Lake cutoffs and the Fort Hall Road—united again. When the Hastings Cutoff rejoined the road at the Humboldt River's South Fork, the dispersed migration again became one mighty army. At City of Rocks Wilkins already saw the impact of this reunion: "Every bit of grass any w[h]ere near water is eaten off close, and we have to drive the cattle from 1 to 2 miles off [the trail] to grass."[122]

Travelers who had detoured to Fort Bridger usually missed the wonders of the silent city. About noon on 2 July William Johnston's party arrived from Salt Lake after a morning's march through a cold, pitiless rain. Beneath the Twin Sisters, they met three scouts from a train that had been far behind them when Johnston's party left the main track at the Parting of the Ways. "From this fact it was easy to realize that still others left in our rear might also be in advance of us, whilst we had been flattering ourselves that with the exception of Captain Paul's pack train—and even this a matter of doubt—we were in the lead of all emigrants," Johnston recalled. He railed at Louis Vasquez for the deception "the wily Spaniard"

[120]Middleton, Diary, 6 August 1849, Diary, Beinecke Library.
[121]Cone, Journal of Travels , 23 August 1849, BYU Library, 91.
[122]Wilkins, *An Artist on the Overland Trail,* 13 August 1849, 63.

had practiced at South Pass to turn emigrants to Salt Lake—and Fort Bridger. James Stewart, Johnston's guide, was so outraged at the innumerable difficulties of the Salt Lake Road that in his fury he "talked of returning to the South Pass to punish the author of this deception." Instead, Stewart "announced it as his determination once again to be in the lead of every wagon train."[123]

OVER THE RIM:
GRANITE PASS, GOOSE CREEK,
AND THE ROAD TO THE HUMBOLDT

When William Z. Walker "struck the Old road again" at City of Rocks in early August, the trail was densely crowded: he found himself "once more among Ox teams dust and noise, which we have been free from since we took the Salt Lake road."[124] From the junction, the trail climbed ten miles through several pleasant, wooded valleys to Granite Springs. Here at the top of Granite Pass, Gordon Cone said the grand and beautiful mountains seemed to increase in magnitude "as they rise one above another, in the succession of their ranges."[125] From a summit above "the wild, strange valley of Goose Creek," Alonzo Delano thought the peculiarly interesting view looked like the scene of a violent commotion, "as if there had been a breaking up of the world. Far as the eye could reach, cones, tables, and nebulæ, peculiar to the country, extended in a confused mass, with many hills apparently white with lime and melted quartz." The lime and sandstone of the broken hills exhibited "the varied colors of the rainbow" in parallel lines of "white, red, brown, pink, green and yellow."[126]

Granite Pass was one of the roughest roads between the Missouri and the Sierra, but almost everyone commented on the beauty and difficulty of the descent to Goose Creek. "Here we got to the top of the hill and an extensive view to the west is spread before me," Joseph Middleton wrote upon taking in the spectacle. "A congeries of small conical hills, all nearly the same height, is ahead of us. After descending the west side say 5 miles over a contorted road, up some steeps, but more commonly down very steep and twisting places, we come to a small stream of pure water" at Birch Creek. Middleton's driver said the last hill "was so steep and bad it was the worst since Independence."[127] "The trail to day has led through a wild & picturesque country," Amasa Morgan wrote as the first wagons made

<hr>

[123]Johnston, *Experiences of a Forty-niner*, 2 July 1849. In point of fact, Pierre Louis Vasquez was an American born in Saint Louis to a Spanish father and French-Canadian mother.

[124]Walker, Diary, 9 August 1849, BYU Library.

[125]Cone, Journal of Travels, 23 August 1849, BYU Library, 91.

[126]Delano, *Life on the Plains*, 24 July 1849, 152–53.

[127]Middleton, Diary, 27 August 1849, Beinecke Library, 95.

the tricky passage down Granite Pass. "A part of the way to day the road has been over rocks and mountains," he deadpanned. His hard-pushing companions made it all the way to Goose Creek by 4:00 P.M., weary and tired out.[128]

After a sharp climb and the difficult crossing of Birch Creek, the trail struck Goose Creek, the last watercourse on the California Trail draining into the Columbia. "For about 10 miles it was nothing but up and down steep hills," Walker complained.[129] "We had some very stoney road this afternoon and one place we had to let our wagons down by hand (with a rope)," Abel Lewis wrote. "Found one place very sideling whare 3 waggons had turned over."[130] Edward Jackson reached Goose Creek after his most fatiguing day's journey yet. From atop one of the highest peaks overlooking the pass, he "could see for miles and miles, and here and there espy our road in the far off distance." For seventeen miles the "steep, rugged, and difficult" trail was stripped of every scrap of vegetation except sagebrush. That night Jackson lay down "in the dust and dirt" amid two hundred people camped within a half mile. He heard twenty men were digging for gold within fifteen miles of Goose Creek.[131]

Since early July, Forty-niners had heard stories of miners prospecting near what Joseph Ware called Rattlesnake River. "All hands have been looking anxiously for Goose Creek—a little stream where gold is said to be deposited," Charles Boyle wrote. "It has been just 12 miles ahead for several days and has not yet been discovered."[132] Tales of gold on Goose Creek reached Alonzo Delano, who concluded, "it is far from improbable that gold, or valuable mineral, exists in those seared and scarified hills."[133] A multitude of huzzahs greeted William Kelly at the creek, and "on looking into the limpid water, seeing the bottom speckled with shining yellow particles, the very image of gold," he almost let out a cheer himself. " 'But all is not gold that glistens,' nor was it gold that glistened in the sands of Goose Creek," as Kelly discovered.[134] James Pritchard heard reports that a Mormon had discovered gold there the previous fall. Veterans of the first big strikes in the Sierra foothills had found mica—a form of fool's gold—on their way to Salt Lake in 1848, Dale Morgan concluded, which sparked these golden rumors and the delusion that Goose Creek was paved with the shiny metal.[135]

About where the trail turned up Little Goose Creek, David DeWolf "passed a singular rock composed of sand stone the outside being hard & inside quite soft,

---

[128]Morgan, Diary, 1 July 1849, Bancroft Library.

[129]Walker, Diary, 10 August 1849, BYU Library.

[130]Lewis, An Account of the Expedition, 7 August 1849, Bancroft Library.

[131]Jackson, Journal, 7, 8 August 1849, BYU Library, 71–72.

[132]Boyle, Diary, 7 July 1849.

[133]Delano, Life on the Plains, 24 July 1849, 153. Ironically, several active gold mines surround Granite Pass today, including one named after Pegleg Smith.

[134]Kelly, Excursion to California, 258.

[135]Pritchard, The Overland Diary, 8 July 1849, 111, 162n69.

THE RAVEN CLIFF GARGOYLE

Charles Kelly photographed the famous "gargoyle" along Nevada's Little Goose Creek in 1941. Although long said to be "carved on the top of Raven Cliff by some Forty-Niner," no one knows who created it or when it appeared. A Bannock, Western Shoshone, or even a "Kanaka"—a Hawaiian— employed at Fort Hall might have been the real sculptor. A similar petroglyph, Tsagaglalal (She Who Watches), overlooks the Columbia Gorge at Columbia Hills State Park. Courtesy Utah State Historical Society. All rights reserved.

so soft one can cut it with a knife"—the intriguing formation later called Record Bluff. "It was singular shaped with some large cavities in it & in the different cavities were a large number of names."[136] DeWolf's singular rock was covered with inscriptions, and perhaps the gargoyles that still overlook the valley. "Near where we nooned is a curiousity in the shape of a sandstone cliff. There is places that is cut in the rock in the shape of an urn large enough for a man to stand," wrote Henry St. Clair. "There is thousands of names engraved here."[137]

Emigrants rated the road up Goose Creek "smooth & excellent," although forage was spotty. By August, Dr. Caldwell observed the "grass has been good, but much graz'd off, so that those behind will have short pickings."[138] James Wilkins soon found the grass eaten off to the last blade. Goose Creek proved to be a fine trout stream, which Wilkins considered a great luxury. His companions gathered "a lot of fresh clams, which at any other time nobody would eat they are so tough and tasteless, but by the addition of plenty of pepper and salt they went down very well."[139] By the end of the month, Joseph Middleton reported, "The grass along the creek is all dried up. I have been wondering how our cattle could subsist, let alone work, for the last few weeks." After about twenty-two miles climbing Goose Creek and the stony, narrow, crooked, "rough & rocky" left fork of Little Goose Creek, the trail made a dry, fifteen-mile *jornada*. The dust got worse, as Middleton learned climbing the canyon. "We are getting into a country the like of which I never saw before. In ½ mile we enter a rough rocky gorge, through which a small creek passes and which we follow. It is very windy and the dust flies from the wagon as smoke from a furnace, darkening the air, and at times like to suffocate you." The trail descended Rock Creek along a series of springs before crossing the rim of the Great Basin and the divide over what Middleton called Cinder Hill to enter the "forlorn and horrid desolation" of Hot Springs Valley. "The road has been occasionally so deep with fine dust that it could be compared to nothing but travelling through deep beds of dry wood ashes," Middleton wrote.[140] At the foot of the valley at the Hot and Cold Springs, Joseph Hackney expressed the general amazement at finding a spring "hot enough to boil an egg in a short time [and] within fifty yards of them was an other spring of water as cold as ice."[141]

On the Fourth of July, the first wagons reached these springs, about twenty miles from the Humboldt River's headwaters. Beyond that spot the arduous road

---

[136]DeWolf, "Diary of the Overland Trail," 4 September 1849, 208.

[137]St. Clair, Journal, 1 August 1849, Beinecke Library. For the first known use of the name "Record Bluff," see Woodworth, *Diary,* Lane County Historical Society.

[138]Caldwell, "Notes of a Journey," in Bruff, *Gold Rush,* 8 August 1849, 1261.

[139]Wilkins, *An Artist on the Overland Trail,* 17 August 1849, 64. Wilkins crossed out "went down" and replaced it with "relished."

[140]Middleton, Diary, 28, 29, 31 August 1849, Beinecke Library, 98–99, 103.

[141]Hackney, Journal, 2 August 1849, *Wagons West,* 178–79.

would become even more difficult and unforgiving—and the elephant was still waiting for the unwary in the Sierra Nevada, almost four hundred miles away.

THE GLORIOUS FOURTH

Forty-niners celebrated the birthday of the United States scattered along the overland trail all the way from the Michigan and Illinois Enterprise Company, which was bringing up the rear on Nebraska's Loup Fork, to the foremost parties camped in Nevada's Thousand Springs Valley.[142] The common wisdom of a decade held that to avoid trouble, wagon trains must reach Independence Rock by the Fourth, but so far only about half of the Forty-niners had passed the landmark.[143] Some gold seekers were too absorbed in the trials of the trail even to mention the holiday, and not every celebration was memorable or even pleasant. After two members of his mess, one an Englishman, almost killed each other at a North Platte ferry, artist James Wilkins's holiday dinner "consisted of a piece of hard sea bread and a tin cup of indifferent water."[144]

For a thousand miles, the Glorious Fourth dawned with a bang. Jake, a teamster, awakened Lucius Fairchild by "yelling 'Hurrah for Hail Columbia' & firing his pistols & musket," but his party traveled all day looking for grass along Poison Creek.[145] Edward Jackson had hoped to celebrate at Independence Rock, but his party was delayed at the North Platte, so instead he fired a few guns at dawn and spent the day "in a hot, sandy, march" looking for water. When he stopped at a camp for a bite of dinner, his hosts gave him "some ship bread and cold boiled pork with a little warm water (what a man will eat) and it tasted nice," Jackson wrote. "This is my 4th of July, did you have a better one?"[146] James Pritchard wrote at American Falls, "Our Fourth of July was spent in travelling in the dust and fighting off Musketoes."[147]

Most Forty-niners did their best to salute the day with the speeches, feasts, and fireworks they had loved in the States. At dawn, Kimball Webster and his companions "fired several rounds, and made as much noise as possible in honor of the day of Independence." The Star-Spangled Banner floated in a cool breeze as they marched past trains camped at Court House Rock.[148] Prominent among them was the Washington City and California Mining Association, whose uniformed dandies welcomed the nearby Colony Guards and formed a banquet hall

---

142 Hecox, The Way I Went to California, 4 July 1849.
143 See the table in Martin and Martin, "The Fourth of July," 16.
144 Wilkins, An Artist on the Overland Trail, 4 July 1849, 52.
145 Fairchild, California Letters, 31.
146 Jackson, Journal, 4 July 1849, BYU Library, 46–47.
147 Pritchard, The Overland Diary, 4 July 1849, 108.
148 Webster, Gold Seekers of '49, 4 July 1849, 55–56.

using four wagons: "2 on each side, and parallel, about 8 feet apart—covered over with tent cloths." Old Glory floated above the impromptu pavilion's roof. Gum tent liners carpeted the ground, and at 3:00 P.M. the men sat down for a feast, with tin platters and iron spoons for the men, and "Knives & forks for the ladies. Down the center, the *luxuries of the season* were placed, at convenient distances, in tin pans,—viz:—boiled beans and salt pork, bean broth, middling bacon, ship bread, and *hot rolls of wheat bread*," Captain Bruff reported. Buffalo steaks formed part of the sumptuous repast. When a large rattlesnake appeared near the dining tent, volunteers quickly "turned out to receive his snakeship by fir[ing] a few vollies into his head," wrote Henry Austin. "He had scarcely ceased to breathe when he was cut up and fried and eaten by some of our men." Austin did not partake of the delicacy, "being of a fastidious taste to such luxuries." In honor of the two women with the party, the gentlemen improvised a sofa out of flour sacks and red blankets opposite the rostrum, where Bruff gave the oration of the day. Thirteen regular and more volunteer toasts used up the train's supply of port and medicinal brandy.[149]

After a debate about whether the anniversary was too sacred "to be desecrated by travelling," as James D. Lyon insisted, the Wolverine Rangers stayed in camp eight miles below Fort Laramie and "celebrated the day with as much patriotism as we could have in the States." At dawn they fired a thirteen-gun salute. "A large majority of the company were anxious to have a Fourth of July celebration, so we concluded to remain camped and have a grand 'blow out,'" recalled Oliver Goldsmith. "All the mess chests were removed from the wagons and converted into tables, and the finest dinner we could get up, by drawing liberally on the commissary department, was prepared." Herman Camp described the elaborate arrangements in detail: "The wagons were hauled in two rows about 15 feet apart, and their covers stretched across to form an awning—under which a table was set 100 feet long, and also with seats for 100 men, that being the number in our train." Rev. Mr. Hobart opened the festivities with prayer at 11:30 A.M., and James Pratt read the Declaration of Independence. The band played "Hail Columbia" and William T. Sexton gave the oration.

Food formed the heart of any proper Fourth of July celebration. The Wolverines "marched to the banquet of fat and luxurious things": sweet cake, vinegar, pepper sauce and mustard, sugar, "boiled ham, excellent; boiled and baked beans, buffalo meat cooked in different ways, good bread and biscuit, fried cakes sweetened and unsweetened, various kinds of baked cakes, and ginger-bread, apple pies, peach pies and plumb pies, assorted pickles put up in jars, corn bread, johnnycake, dried beef, buffalo meat, apple sauce, peach sauce and plumb sauce, rice and bread and

---

[149]Bruff, *Gold Rush*, 4 July 1849, 30, 1180–81; Austin, Diary, 4 July 1849, Bancroft Library, 54–55. Bruff's appendix 3 provides the text of his speech, the Programme, and the Regular Toasts.

Indian puddings, good coffee, lemonade and spirits—all of which were greedily partaken of," Camp recounted, presenting his sketch as an example of "how we poor fellows do suffer out here on the plains." It was "all well cooked, although done by rude men," James Lyon wrote. "All enjoyed it well," William Swain noted, but he was not pleased with the results of the hour of toasts that followed the rich repast. "The boys had raked and scraped together all the brandy they could," Swain wrote that evening, "and they toasted, hurrayed, and drank till reason was out and brandy was in." Disgusted, Swain went to his tent and wrote a letter to his wife while his companions were "drinking, carousing, and hallooing all around the camp." Oliver Goldsmith recalled the speeches, songs, games, and general hilarity, but mostly he complained that "two good days were thus lost, which only Captain Potts and myself seemed to realize might be very valuable before our journey's end was reached."[150]

On the far side of the Black Hills, the Knox County Company followed the "tremendous dusty up hill and down dale" road. Vast piles of manure gave the dust "a curious and obnoxious smell," William Lorton wrote. They found a beautiful campsite at Deer Creek, near present Glenrock, Wyoming, amid the many sojourners, white tents, and "others without number" camped along the North Platte. As evening fell, he heard the Pioneer Line's passengers "blazing away for dear life." Lorton gave a sample of the day's trail toasts: "Washington! It shall be a password even in the wilderness"; "Three cheers for Old Zach, President of the United States"; "For our sweethearts and wives." The boys fired a gun for every state in the union, Lorton wrote, "and a volley for California and the gold diggings." Peter P. Acker of the Fayette Rovers shot off his thumb when his gun fired prematurely. "The firing kept up till a late hour, and then the violin was brought out and a cotillion commenced on the green." Not to be outdone, the Knox County boys mustered with their firearms and listened to an orator. "You have heard of the elephant, you may see it on your journey to California, but when he throws out his trunk," Lorton joked, "tell him you have thrown out a great many trunks since you started." The whole company fired "a feu de joie"—a rapid-fire sequential volley—listened to another very eloquent speech, gave three cheers, and fired another fusillade while the surrounding camps rang with the sound of musketry. They reloaded and fired yet another volley. The Iowa Rangers marched up, "and turning an angle near us, fired as they turned separately. We were then collected in a circle and saluted them with three hearty cheers and fired a salute." A committee of the whole invited the Rangers to join the fun. Three deafening cheers

---

[150]The Wolverines' celebration is described in Lyon, "Ten Miles East of Fort Laramie," 4 July 1849, *Detroit Advertiser,* 10 September 1849, in Bruff, *Gold Rush,* 479n135; Goldsmith, *Overland in Forty-Nine,* 41–43; Camp to "Dear Mary, Edna, and Others," 8 July 1849, in Cumming, *Gold Rush,* 54; Swain, *The World Rushed In,* 4 July 1849, 167–70.

and swinging hats followed another speech, and the company's bugle "sounded forth with spirit, when we all formed in one line and fired." After enlisting the Oscaloosa and Batavia companies, "we had several hundred in our lines, firing round after round, with a sentiment in between." Lorton, a teetotaler, drank lemon syrup, smoked a cigar, and ate antelope meat.[151]

The Pioneer Line spent Independence Day and night ferrying the North Platte at Deer Creek—"A sorry way to celebrate the Glorious Fourth," Bernard Reid lamented after almost drowning. Charles Mulford prepared a fresh fish dinner and peach pie. After the line's carriages were finally across the river, twenty passengers "got up a jollification" and the "welkin rang till midnight with their volleys, cheers, songs, toasts and carousels."[152] Dexter Tiffany swam the last mule and horse across and, like Reid, barely escaped drowning. He joined Reid's jollification—or indulged in one like it—by loading a revolver and two pistols while others fired them. "The boys got some brandy in a dish out of which they all drank but me & I gave them the toasts," he wrote. "The moon was beautiful, the air fine without any dew & we sat down by the fire & told stories untill sunrise."[153]

Crowds camped between Independence Rock and Devils Gate. There was already "considerable shooting going on" when James Tolles stopped just above Devils Gate on the third. After dark Tolles and his friends climbed a high rock overlooking Devils Gate "and built a large bonfire which made a grand appearance in the valley below." At dawn the camp formed a line and fired a couple of rounds, "and then we fired off a couple of wagon wheel hubs filled with powder and pluged up tight." The improvised artillery made a report equal to two six-pounder cannons. "We heard that there was to be a couple of weddings to day at Independence rock," Tolles reported.[154] A young lawyer who had gallantly defended David Leeper for sleeping on guard gave the oration.[155]

Emigrants camped around South Pass awoke to find what Elijah Spooner called "a curiosity to us for the season of the year: Water was frozen in pails and other vessels a fourth of an inch in thickness this morning; and water exposed was immediately frozen over, even after sunrise."[156] Charles Parke laid over for the afternoon ten miles above the last crossing of the Sweetwater, camping virtually on the Continental Divide. "This being the nation's birthday and our clothing not as clean as we could wish, we commenced our celebration by 'washing dirty linen' or rather woolens, as we all wore woolen shirts. Washing done and shirts hung out to dry—we

[151]Lorton, Diary, 4 July 1849, Bancroft Library.

[152]Reid, *Overland to California*, 4 July 1849, 76.

[153]Tiffany, Journals and Letters, 4 July 1849, 11–12, Missouri Historical Society.

[154]Tolles, Journal of My Travels, 3, 4 July 1849, BYU Library, 39–40.

[155]Leeper, *Argonauts of 'Forty-nine*, 35–36.

[156]Spooner, Letters and Diary, 4 July 1849, BYU Library, 38–39.

never iron—all hands set about enjoying themselves as best they could." After such a prosaic beginning, Parke provided his lucky companions with a unique treat: "Having plenty of milk from the cows we had with us," he wrote, "I determined to [do] something no other living man ever did in this place and on this sacred day of the year, and that was to make *Ice Cream at the South Pass of the Rockies*." Parke found a two-quart tin pail, sweetened and flavored the cream with peppermint—he had nothing else—put the pail "inside a wooden bucket or 'Yankee Pale' and the top put on." Nature provided a huge bank of coarse snow, "which was just the thing for this new factory. With alternate layers of this and salt between the two buckets and with the aid of a *clean* stick to stir with, I soon produced the most delicious ice cream tasted in this place." His delighted companions "as a compliment drew up in front of our tent and fired a salute, bursting one gun but injuring no one."[157]

After a cold night at Pacific Spring, Joseph Warren Wood slept until noon. He greeted the Fourth "in a manner which though simple, suited me. I fired 3 rounds with my rifle—one for liberty one for home & one for success." The gold seekers at the spring examined and honorably acquitted a man suspected of murdering an emigrant named Reed. Wood's party all partook heartily of a few homespun extras for dinner—fried cakes, fried apple pie, and applesauce, and drank a basin of soda mingled with waters destined for the Atlantic and Pacific. "The celebration began in earnest in the pass at evening. Fire works were displayed and many large guns were fired. Companies of men would discharge their guns in rapid succession & among the hills they sounded very loud," Wood wrote. As night fell, his train decided to "steal a march on the crowd" by moving on. "The moon shone bright and we journeyed on, with the rattle of firearms about us for a while, man and animals felt a strange exhileration of spirits—After a while all signs died away save that of the wolves as they howled their oregies over the body of some dead Ox."[158] Elijah Spooner's train nooned at Pacific Spring: "Here we took a glass of lemon punch, which we drank to the Health and Happiness of those Dearly Beloved ones that we had left far behind." Like Wood, Spooner commented on the hundreds of dead animals he had passed: "Every mile still bears witness to the destruction of stock."[159]

On the evening of 3 July, a good many trains camped around Henry Wiman along Big Sandy River. "We serenaded all the camps, we had an excellent band of music. On the morning of the fourth at the rising of the sun we fired 13 salutes then we killed the fatted calf and barbecued it." Eight or ten women "baked bread and pies and sweet cakes, stewed fruit, made coffee and tea. We had molasses and brandy all fixed off in style, a better dinner I thought I never ate any where." Someone read the

---

[157]Parke, *Dreams to Dust,* 4 July 1849, 46.

[158]Wood, Diary, 4 July 1849, Huntington Library, 54.

[159]Spooner, Letters and Diary, 4 July 1849, BYU Library, 38–39.

Declaration of Independence, and J. C. Morris made a speech and gave the toasts. After the feast the ladies joined in the music and dancing, but by "four o'clock we were all on the desert moving through a cloud of dust."[160] The day filled "every American patriot's heart with gratitude and love to our forefathers for the noble and daring deeds which they put into execution on this day," William J. Watson wrote. West of Big Sandy, his train "took all the extra powder that we had and put it in a keg, and wrapped it with two table cloths and three log chains, which we found at the creek and taking it up on the hill we sunk it two feet deep, put a slow match to it (and firing a national salute three times, with twenty rifles besides our pistols) when our magazine exploded seeming to make the neighboring mountains shake."[161]

On the Fourth perhaps the largest crowd of Forty-niners clustered along the Green River, where the Charleston Company ushered in the first dawn with a blast from their previously unfired six-pounder, "which reverberated, echoed & reechoed from hillock to hill, until the very earth itself seemed to tremble in fear at such strange noises," wrote Wakeman Bryarly.[162] The Virginians spent the day cooking, sewing, and washing. "Being the Fourth of July, our quartermaster issued whisky rations," Edward Washington McIlhany recalled. "Some had more or less, and some didn't have any." The orator of the day, Tom Moore, "felt pretty good, feeling the effects of his whisky, and every time that he would say anything patriotic would touch the little cannon off, and the echo would bellow up and down the valley." Some of the company's more practical men "concluded that they would steal the cannon and throw it into the river, so that they would not haul it any further." Their comrades frustrated their plans, and the train hauled the cannon all the way to Sacramento, where their committee on disposition sold it for one dollar.[163]

"This is the Great day of American Independence and on which our nation will meet in crowds and do honors to the day and to offer thanks to God for the gift," Alexander Ramsay wrote while waiting to cross the "shockling and dangerous" Green River ferry on the Sublette Cutoff. The holiday turned Ramsay's thoughts to "distant friends and relatives whilst we cannot suppress a secret wish that we could spend this day with them." He estimated there were two or three hundred men crowded around his campsite, which was covered with a two-inch coat of dust. "We are much weried by the toils & fatigues of the long journey and the immense numbers of emigrants who are upon the road makes it doubly tiresome from the fact that they are constantly in each others way," particularly at river crossings and at tight spots in the road.[164]

---

[160] Wiman to "Dear Parents," 25 October 1849, Missouri Historical Society.

[161] Watson, *Journal of an Overland Journey to Oregon* 4 July 1849, 24–25.

[162] Bryarly, *Trail to California,* 4 July 1849, 134.

[163] McIlhany, *Recollections,* 23–24, 34–35.

[164] Ramsay, "Gold Rush Diary," 3, 4 July 1849, 451–52.

Ramsay witnessed one of the oddest events of the holiday, an impromptu murder trial. A few days earlier a "reckless villain" named Brown had stabbed a man in the back for refusing to fetch him a piece of soap, a crime regarded as "a cruel and fiendish murder." The emigrants met and resolved "to arrest the villain, give him a fair trial, and if found guilty, to execute him on the spot." Major John S. Simonson ordered the Mounted Riflemen to track down the killer with the help of a dozen volunteers. "Several murders had been committed on the road, and all felt the necessity of doing something to protect themselves, where there was no other law but brute force," Alonzo Delano observed. The men could not find Brown, but they did find a Hoosier named Williams who had killed "a perfect desperado" in self-defense at Devils Gate two weeks earlier. One killer seemed as good as another, and having resolved to hold a trial, the posse hauled Williams back to Green River.[165]

"This is the glorious Fourth of July," B. R. Biddle wrote at the ferry. "Many banners were floating in the breeze." His party "intended to have a fine time of it" while the authorities were out hunting for Brown, "but the heat and dust are so annoying, and the bustle is so great that we do not enjoy it so well as we would otherwise. However, we had a good dinner," he noted. Among other delicacies, the cooks conjured up a dainty known as a black dog: a concoction of stewed apples and dried cherries rolled in thin dough, "boiled and served up with sauce. All partook freely." Black dog was not the only treat being partaken of freely, for by the time the authorities convened their Independence Day court at 4:00 P.M. under a fine clump of willows, "the officers and lawyers had been celebrating it to the full, and a spirit other than that of '76 was apparent." Major Simonson was "as drunk as Bacchus."[166]

"The evening concluded with one of the greatest farces I have ever witnessed," Biddle complained. With Alexander Ramsay, Biddle was called upon "to serve as a jury in a case of murder." Williams voluntarily returned to stand trial, but lacking witnesses from his own party, he engaged B. F. Washington to defend him. "The Major and officers and men, being drunk, had a good deal to say," Biddle noted. Delano said Mr. Washington gave "a somewhat lengthy and occasionally flighty speech," denying that the court had any right to try the case. "The major insulted the lawyer, and the officers insulted the Major. Each party swearing and calling the other hard names, and each threatening the other with arrest," juror Biddle wrote in disgust. "The whole thing broke up in a row. The prisoner escaped and thus ended the affair. Thus it is that these officers and men protect the interests of the emigrants by getting drunk."[167]

West of Green River, the parties in the lead were more interested in pressing

---

[165]Delano, *Life on the Plains,* 23 June, 3 July 1849, 124.

[166]Biddle, "Journey to California," 4 July 1849; Delano, *Life on the Plains,* 4 July 1849, 126.

[167]Accounts of the trail appear in Morgan, "Ferries on the Sublette Cutoff," 32:2, 178–82.

ahead than in celebrating their country's birth, and the Mormons deliberately ignored the holiday. "Is not this a funny place to be spending the 4th of July, in an isolated settlement of fanatics of the 19th century persecuted pilgrims?" Thomas Evershed asked at Salt Lake City. "The people here feel rather sore towards the U.S. for not protecting them at Nauvoo," he observed. The Mormons "did not keep the 4th but intend to keep the 24 July the anniversary of the arrival of the pioneers," which they did in grand style.[168] Palmer C. Tiffany's company took a long noontime break on Bear River, and he cut the cake his wife had prepared for the occasion and passed it around.[169] No one mentioned any festivities at Fort Hall. "Some of the boys made great noise & fired pistols &c at 3 o'clock in honor of the 4th, all the celebration we can have today," Peter Decker wrote at City of Rocks.[170]

Not far away on the Salt Lake Cutoff, William Kelly's Yankee companions "concocted a bucket of capital punch" on the evening of the third, ushered in the holiday "with a peppery salvo of revolvers and rifles" at midnight, and tested British loyalties "through the insinuating agency of whisky-toddy." Some grew tried of songs and oratorical displays, and insisted on investigating a nearby fire that resulted in a drunken raid on a small Indian encampment, "breaking in upon their slumbers with a wild hurra! that made the poor savages jump up in terror, and run off." The festivities only ended when the morning star appeared. Even the mules "got a regular blow out."[171]

What does this extraordinary commemoration reveal about the people who spent America's seventy-third birthday along the trails to Oregon and California? "The Indians, when they heard that cannon, would not come anywhere near us. They got out of the way," recalled Washington McIlhany.[172] No Forty-niner described any Indian joining the celebrations, so the largest part of the population avoided the happy event entirely. Perhaps the massive barrages that began at dawn convinced all the Natives within earshot that the crazed *Wasichus* had started slaughtering each other. For the patriots firing the salutes, did this communal festival and its grandiloquent evocation of the great Washington and the nation's noble and daring forefathers reflect a shared belief in an imperial destiny? Did this jingoistic bacchanal and blowout express a common commitment to subdue and subject those who had long occupied the American West, or a naïve belief that the blessings of civilization and "the glory, wisdom and majesty of our beloved republic" would liberate and enlighten the savages?[173] For some it probably did. A few of these hardy

[168]Evershed, "The Gold Rush Journal," 4 July 1849, 23, 26.

[169]Tiffany, Overland Journey, 4 July 1849, Beinecke Library, 73.

[170]Decker, *The Diaries,* 4 July 1849, 112.

[171]Kelly, *Excursion to California,* 255–56.

[172]McIlhany, *Recollections,* 23.

[173]Patterson, Diary, 4 July 1850, Mattes Library.

adventurers no doubt harbored dreams of building a glorious Anglo-Saxon empire that would eventually embrace the entire Western Hemisphere, but this glorious and remote Fourth of July was first and foremost a festival, a party celebrating the youth, vitality and exuberance of both the Forty-niners and their idealistic and expanding nation. The Plains Indians would happily have traded every bison robe they owned for the gunpowder converted to smoke and fire along the trail that day, but this quintessentially American celebration represented an impulse more than it did a national policy.

When the smoke of the last volley dissipated that night, Forty-niners were scatted along the Oregon-California Trail for more than a thousand miles, with the great swollen center of the year's migration still on the wrong side of South Pass. All were increasingly aware that time was short and the devil might literally take the hindmost. Those in the rear guard continually jockeyed to press ahead of the crowd or get a slight edge over their closest competitors. "They have become foolishly alarmed, and are now rushing ahead like mad men," wrote Elmon Camp. " 'Push on! push on!!' seemed to be the motto of every one," an Illinois newspaper reported. Now "the journey seemed to have become a race, as to who shall get there first."[174]

---

[174]Camp to "Dear Brother," 8 July 1849, in Cumming, *Gold Rush,* 47–48; West to Thomas James, 17 June 1849, "From the California Emigrants," *Belleville Weekly Advocate,* 7 August 1849.

CHAPTER 4

FIRST FLIGHT OF FORTY-NINERS

The Race to the Goldfields

The men leading the way in 1849 fared the best by far of anyone on the road to California. "We have had plenty of game, lots of fun, and our whole journey so far has been a pleasure trip," Gus Blair wrote from Salt Lake in early July. "We have not seen the Elephant at all yet, not even his tail."[1] The fastest parties spent Independence Day traveling down Thousand Springs Valley and celebrating the Great National Day camped at the Hot and Cold Springs near the Humboldt River's headwaters. They included Vital Jarrot's outfit from East Saint Louis; two pack mule trains; and James Gooding's Banner Company from Wisconsin, including "two Sucker trains" from Illinois and Captain Hendrickson's wagons. According to Lewis Tremble, 170 men assembled at the springs.[2] "We are Brothers," wrote Amasa Morgan. Some of the men hailed from France, England, Ireland, Scotland, or Canada, but all were "now bound together by the Bonds of our national Union." After a good shortcake supper, the men drank soda water—and more potent beverages. "After drinking all around," J. Murray Morrison addressed the assembled multitudes, wrote Tremble, who had to spend most of the night guarding the mules. "A large fire was made, a fiddler provided, and the dance commenced." The mountains echoed the folksy sound of violins until midnight. It was a scene worth beholding, "surrounded by the wild woodman with mountains all around us," far from country, families, and friends. "In the wildness of the scene and its excitement," Morgan said, "we forgot temporally all things Else." But, as Lewis Tremble noted, "early next morning we were under way—all anxious to reach Humbolt River."[3]

Thousands of men and women camped along the trail shared similar anxieties. What the first Forty-niners found when they reached the Humboldt River Valley

[1]Blair to "Dr. Sir," 13 July 1849, *Fort Des Moines Star,* 2 November 1849, 2/2.

[2]Tremble to Miles, 6 August 1849, *Illinois Republican,* 1 January 1850, Mattes Library.

[3]Morgan, Diary, 4 July 1849, Bancroft Library; Tremble to Miles, 6 August 1849, *Illinois Republican,* 1 January 1850, Mattes Library.

that night was troubling: "after traveling about twenty miles through a poor country [with] scarcely any grass and no water," Amasa Morgan's party camped at the Humboldt Wells. The next morning, the Banner Company expected to find the best grass on the route—but they spent the day traveling through a "dry barron country" and made camp that night "all covered with a Saleratus dust." "The grass is poor, but there is an abundance of currants, yellow, red, black," wrote Charles Boyle, accentuating the positive. "The yellow are many of them very sweet and palatable." A few days later, packers overtook Boyle's party and described the many trains they had passed. The question they asked was this: 'Where will they find grass for their mules when in this region of country?'" The overland guides proved full of falsehoods: "Books represented the valley of this river as a place where all the comforts the emigrant required, could be obtained—plenty of grass for our animals, [and] a good level road for three hundred miles," Lewis Tremble complained. The distance was accurate, but everything else was false—the valley was nothing but a desert. His animals often did not get a mouthful of grass for three days running, "and instead of the road being level, it was over mountains."[4] And what Tremble found had yet to be trampled by thousands of desperate people and animals.

Many happy emigrants farther back along the overland road did not wake happily with the sunrise on the fifth of July. "Arose with a bursting head-ache," moaned survivor Joseph Hamelin, who was moved to quote Robert Burns: "'Inspiring, bold John Barleycorn / What dangers thou dost make us scorn &c.' O! for a glass of soda water." His party stayed in camp for the day.[5]

Depressed diarists contemplated their grim prospects in the wake of the Fourth. "The lone & inhospitable country which surrounded me presented a scene of indescribable solemnity & grandiour," wrote John Bates near Chimney Rock, "& when compared with the land of my home & its dear scenes I thought no spot in the world could produce a picture of more perfect contrast."[6] William Z. Walker spent the day at Devils Gate and "engraved my name here among thousands of others who have visited the place." The intensely hot weather kept his party in camp until sundown, after which the party traveled until midnight. "We noticed along on the road fires burning in the mountains, whether made by the indians or kept alive by some internal process we did not ascertain."[7] James Tolles praised the beautiful morning as his party marched west from Devils Gate past twelve dead cattle. J. D. Manlove had to abandon his largest oxen. The next day, Tolles's father was too sick to ride in his wagon, and their train broke up.[8]

[4]Ibid.; Morgan, Diary, 5, 6 July 1849, Bancroft Library; Boyle, Diary, 12, 17 July 1849.
[5]Hamelin, Journal, 5 July 1849, Beinecke Library.
[6]Bates, Diary, 5 July 1849, Mattes Library.
[7]Walker, Diary, 5 July 1849, BYU Library, 64–65.
[8]Tolles, Journal of My Travels, 5, 6 July 1849, BYU Library.

After crossing the North Platte, the Pioneer Line began to disintegrate. Even before the carriage passengers and their overloaded baggage wagons reached Fort Kearny, "a strong feeling of discontent prevailed throughout the entire company." The clerks, doctors, divines, gentlemen of leisure, and speculators "were loud in denouncing all fast lines, and the Pioneer Line in particular," the quartermaster reported. "The devil himself would find it impossible to give satisfaction to [such] an incongruous crowd of one hundred and twenty persons drawn from all over the world and thrown together for the first time."[9] By the time the train's advance division dragged into camp at Independence Rock on 11 July, "the passengers had got discouraged, thought they could not get through & intended to take steps to lighten up their baggage," Dexter Tiffany wrote. The company called a mass meeting at one o'clock. "Speeches were made[;] some got mad & others got drunk," and the passengers voted to dump a quarter of their baggage. A few, like Tiffany, decided to press ahead on their own.[10]

A. H. Houston explained the dilemma facing the migration: "The immense crowd that was on the road made the trip much more difficult and disagreeable than usual. If you tried to pass other trains, you were breaking down your team in doing so. If you laid by to recruit, hundreds of teams were passing daily, making it more difficult to procure grass," he wrote. "The great mania of every one, as they got farther on the road, was to get through as fast as possible, at no matter what sacrifice."[11] The trek down the Humboldt intensified the mania. Supplies were plentiful in California and "gold is found in great abundance," eastbound Mormon miners assured Elisha Lewis. But ahead feed was very scarce, and "likewise we had got the Elephant yet to see before we had accomplished our journy."[12] The armada of wagons spilling over the rim of the Great Basin was bound to see that elephant.

THE FIRST FLIGHT OF THE GREAT OVERLAND EMIGRATION

Irish swashbuckler William Kelly liked to claim he traveled with "the first flight of the great overland emigration," but in truth, wagons and pack trains began leaving the Mormon Zion months before Kelly reached the Great Basin in early July. "There are some people here who are about to leave for the gold mines. Some for other places, but most of them have the yellow fever," Patty Sessions noted in March. Joseph Hackney heard that sixty Mormon teams left Salt Lake for California that spring. Before the end of 1849, several hundred Latter-day Saints decamped

[9]"Pawnee," 19 June 1849, in Wyman, *California Emigrant Letters,* 54–55.
[10]Tiffany, Diary, 11 July 1849, Missouri Historical Society, 37.
[11]Houston, "From California," 16 October 1849; *Indiana American* (Brookville), 4 January 1850.
[12]Lewis, Overland to California, 27 August 1849, Beinecke Library.

for El Dorado. "We are shut of the most [miserable] part of our community, they are not fit for the society of good men, they are hardly fit for the cellar kitchens of hell," growled Brigham Young. "If you Elders of Isreal want to go to the gold mines, go and be damned."[13]

The first Mormon trains left Great Salt Lake City for the gold mines on 21 and 22 March, despite Brigham Young's vociferous opposition. Already a seasoned trail veteran at age twenty-two, Abner Blackburn "joined a pack train for the gold mines" with the first westbound party to try the Salt Lake Cutoff, the trail Samuel Hensley and two Salt Lake–bound trains had opened the previous fall. "We had the usual amount of quarreling and swearing that all such companys have in crossing the plains," he recalled, and the packers took the "new rout to California [that] goes by way of Carson River." Fellow veterans of the Mormon Battalion had blazed the road, now officially known as the Mormon-Carson Emigrant Trail, by taking two wagon trains over the route the previous summer. Blackburn's party camped for two days on the Carson River to recruit their animals and he did some desultory prospecting, finding color at the mouth of Gold Canyon, but they soon pressed on across the Sierra. "Our horses nearly starved and some of our party were snow blind," Blackburn remembered, but they somehow found their way to Weberville and bought provisions, tobacco, and whiskey.[14]

"The first Pioneers of '49" to leave City of Rocks found evidence of the Mormons' passing. "On our arrival at the Humboldt, we found fresh wagon tracks made a short time before and were informed that some Mormons had been sent to California to found a settlement," recalled Edmund Green, who was traveling so rapidly that he and six companions left the fast-moving Captain Paul behind at Green River. "We had no trouble in following their track all the way down the Humboldt and, in fact, into California." (Green eventually caught up with these trail-blazing Mormons in Pleasant Valley, ten miles short of Hangtown.)[15] At Goose Creek, Amasa Morgan estimated there were about forty-five wagons ahead of his party, which so far had "passed every Train of waggons that we have come up with." Men who had tried it told him "the road by Salt Lake is not as good as it is by fort Hall." Time rolled on, Morgan wrote, "and we roll towards California."[16]

By July most gold seekers were rolling very slowly. A random sample of sixty-three 1849 journals shows that on the Fourth of July, forty-nine of the writers were still east of Green River.[17] The men in the lead knew they had a tremendous

[13]Kelly, *Excursion to California,* 3, 4 July 1849, 254–55; Hackney, Journal, 28 July 1849, *Wagons West,* 176–77; Journal History, 17 March 1849; Young, 8 July 1849, in Owens, *Gold Rush Saints,* 211.

[14]Blackburn, *Frontiersman,* 132, 139–41.

[15]Green, "Recollections," 8–9.

[16]Morgan, Diary, 2 July 1849, Bancroft Library.

[17]Martin and Martin, "The Fourth of July," 16.

advantage and zealously protected it. Travelers in early July calculated their position in the great race. "Several trains are in sight. Some are behind, some before," noted Charles Boyle after reaching the Humboldt. "For several days we have heard frequent mention made of Captain Russell, Lewis and others who took the Ft. Bridger Rd. and so lost several days."[18] Joseph Ledlie Moody's party had taken the Salt Lake Road and were now infected with a desire to recapture the lead and pushed hard to do so.[19]

The almost three hundred primary sources describing the 1849 trek down the Humboldt paint a colorful but confusing picture. Estimates of distances, accounts of the quality of the grass or water, descriptions of the scenery and the river, and reports of encounters with Natives vary wildly and often contradict each other. Some of these disagreements reflect the different traces individual travelers followed and how dramatically and quickly conditions changed, but the accounts often seem to describe entirely different experiences, even for people passing the same spot at about the same time. At least part of the confusion reflects how unfamiliar and strange these woodland people found the arid and alien world of the Great Basin. The harsh landscape left travelers utterly bewildered, puzzled and perplexed, and more than a little scared. Few of them could appreciate the Great Basin: "This is I think one of the most detestable countries God ever made, to say nothing of its sterility and barrenness," wrote James Wilkins.[20]

Geographic ignorance and illusions hampered all the Forty-niners. "Not a man in company knows anything about the road nor are there any directions or descriptions of the route given by anyone so that we have to go by guess altogether," Joshua D. Breyfogle wrote while on the Salt Lake Cutoff.[21] "Where we are traveling we do not know. We suppose, however, on the Humboldt, but the distance to the Sink we have no way of finding out at present," lamented Israel E. Hale, at that point halfway down the river. "No marks are laid down in any of our guide books and we have no person along familiar with the route."[22] Most Forty-niners knew that the wagon trace followed the Humboldt for three hundred miles before it disappeared in the sand, but as the increasingly dismal river wandered southwest and then northwest and southwest again, the trek seemed never ending. Even William H. Russell, who had made the trip in 1846, found the geography deceptive. Russell overtook Charles Boyle one night and told him they were only three miles from the river's sink, "but this has been his story every day for a week," Boyle complained after traveling twenty-eight miles the next day. "No one here has any

---

[18]Boyle, Diary, 10, 11 July 1849.
[19]Moody to "My Dear Father," 7 August 1849, 84.
[20]Wilkins, *An Artist on the Overland Trail,* 20 August 1849, 65.
[21]Breyfogle, Diary, 2 July 1849, 14–15.
[22]Hale, "Diary of a Trip to California," 18 August 1849, 111.

very clear notion of where the sink really is," he concluded.[23] This mix of naïveté and misinformation profoundly affected the decisions of these exhausted, hungry, and terrified sojourners.

WILD SAGE AND GREASE WOOD: THE HUMBOLDT RIVER

West of Salt Lake and south of Granite Pass, the Forty-niners' prospects looked grim. "There was not enough grass to support the increased emigration beyond Salt Lake," an old plainsman told John Hudgins, warning him "that only the advance guard would get through, the balance would starve."[24] Joseph Berrien estimated there were only about 110 teams ahead him, but even "their transit over the valley has been very much like the descent of the locusts in Egypt which ate up every green thing."[25]

After climbing West Brush Creek from Thousand Springs Valley, two trails led to the headwaters of the Humboldt: the original track down Bishop Creek Canyon, a scenic but difficult road James Tate called "rocky, crooked, and sideling"; and the trail Old Greenwood had opened in 1845 to the deep pools known as the Wells.[26] Since it lacked the dramatic scenery of Bishop Creek, few diarists described the barren road to the Humboldt Wells. "After traveling about twenty miles through a poor country [with] scarcely any grass and no water we came to some wells that appears to be at the source of Marys or Humbolts River," wrote Amasa Morgan. The marshy valley was full of curlews, which Morgan thought resembled the snipe at home. "The water in these wells is good," he commented. "No Bottom to them as I could discover."[27] John Bates's party nooned "at pivital springs denominated by Emigrants as Mary's Springs or wells varying in size & depth many of them to[o] deep to be fanthomed by any thing we had & measuring from 10 to 50 ft in circumference. This water is the extreme head of Mary's river—a point we had most anxiously looked for."[28]

"We nooned at a spring at the foot of the ridge we have to cross to strike the head waters of humbolt river," wrote Joseph Hackney at Brush Creek. Here the road forked; the right-hand road to Bishop Creek led to water in only four miles, but the road to the Humboldt Wells was a fifteen- or twenty-mile dry passage. His companions chose the rough road down the creek because no wagons had used it "since last spring as all the other emigrants have gone the other road." They found a

---

[23]Boyle, Diary, 19 July 1849.
[24]Hudgins, California in 1849, Western Historical Manuscripts.
[25]Berrien, "Overland from St. Louis," 11 July 1849, 334.
[26]Tate, Diary, 6 August 1849, Western Historical Manuscripts, 26.
[27]Morgan, Diary, 5 July 1849, Bancroft Library.
[28]Bates, Diary, 3 September 1849, Mattes Library.

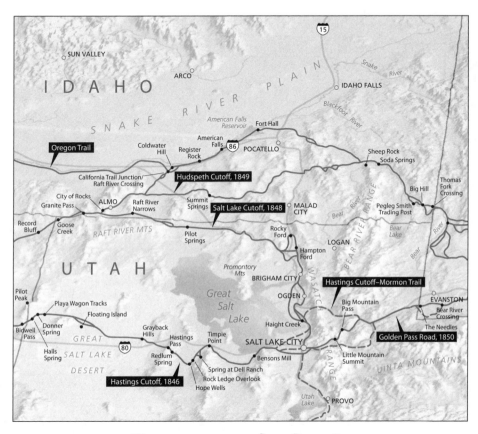

WAGON ROADS INTO THE GREAT BASIN, 1852

After the Donner tragedy of 1846 and the arrival of the Mormons at Great Salt Lake in 1847, a variety of alternatives into and across the Great Basin became available to overland travelers. Based on the National Park Service's map of the California National Historic Trail.

fine camping ground in a valley alive with sage grouse. "About half of the road was good the rest was awful," he learned the next day. "The road in places was piled full of rock that had rolled down from the side of the canon and appeared impossible to take a wagon over but we pushed her through." He emerged in a beautiful valley thickly covered with grass and acres of wild flax. Despite the route's difficulty, his party saved about twenty miles by coming through the canyon and had good water and fine grass the whole way. Hackney heard several oxen were poisoned at the Humboldt Wells and felt "in luck in not going around."[29]

The narrow road required crossing Bishop Creek eight or nine times, and as Israel Hale observed, "some of the crossings were bad. A portion of the road through the canyon was very rocky, so taking it all together it was far from being a good carriage road," but Hale thought the canyon's crystal-clear warm spring was the handsomest he had ever seen.[30] In contrast, James Wilkins believed the longer route to the Wells gave him much the best of it, since those who took the canyon road described it as the worst road they had ever traveled.[31]

The range in the upper valley proved resilient, and many trains found good grass between the Humboldt Wells and the Palisades. Forty-niners reaching the river in early August apparently had better feed than the parties that preceded them, perhaps due to thunderstorms. After emerging from "the stoney narrow road" down Bishop Creek Canyon, M. Phillips reported an "abundance of grass knee high." But a week later he warned, "No trains can pass with safety in two weeks hence [down] this valley if the present dry weather continues. We have had to make long marches already because we could not find grass."[32] The valley grew more desolate with every mile the trail twisted west and south. "Avarice seems to rule the action of too many of the men, who are disposed to rush every thing, and especially our poor ox-teams beyond the power of their endurance," noted Thomas Van Dorn.[33]

Many Forty-niners commented on the snowcapped peaks of the East Humboldt Range rising abruptly south of the Wells, but—even amid spectacular scenery—disappointment was the most common emotion emigrants expressed upon reaching the fabled river's relatively hospitable upper valley. "Nothing in the shape of vegetation can be found except Wild Sage and Grease Wood—except on the margin of the stream where a coarse grass is occasionally found which furnishes the only food for our animals and this is rapidly drying up under the influence of a blistering sun," wrote Joseph Berrien. "I cannot help fearing that those who come after us will

---

[29]Hackney, Journal, 2, 3 August 1849, *Wagons West,* 179.

[30]Hale, "Diary of a Trip to California," 6 August 1849, 101.

[31]Wilkins, *An Artist on the Overland Trail,* 20 August 1849, 65.

[32]Phillips, Diary to California, 6, 13 August 1849, Bancroft Library, 18, 19.

[33]Van Dorn, Diary, 14 August 1849, 1849, Beinecke Library, 34.

experience great distress and suffering and perhaps lose their lives in this desert valley."[34] The river was "not as large a stream as I expected to see but increases rapidly,
on account of its numerous branches from the snow capped range of Mountains in
the east. Mountain Peaks are visible on every side & at all distances," wrote Joseph
Wood.[35] "The grass has been good since we came into this valley," commented Israel
E. Hale, who described in detail the quality of the feed found along the river. "It
is wild rye and several kinds of coarse grass. Our cattle eat it well, but it is not as
good for them as finer grasses. I see a large quantity of wild flax but the cattle do
not appear to like it." Within days his cattle began wasting away: "The grass does
not possess sufficient nourishment for teams that have so much work to perform or
hardships to endure." The upper valley's range had been fresh and good, but "the
grass began to diminish by degrees" and soon became "very scarce and of an inferior
quality." Hales had to track his half-famished cattle as they foraged from midnight
until dawn "in search of grass. I am astonished they hold up as well as they do. The
grass is so dry that it will break if you step on it."[36]

The willows and sagebrush lining the Humboldt made poor firewood—but, as
the season advanced, hundreds of abandoned wagons solved the problem. "Many
horses, cattle and mules and good and broken down wagons now literally line the
road, and I believe there are now hundreds of men footing it to the mines with
their provisions on their own backs," commented Edward Harrow. "I pity them,
but I expect in a few days to have to do the same."[37] The trail was now nothing
like the broad, flat road up the Platte. "The whole country appears to be composed
of mountains and ravines, except in the immediate vicinity of the river," wrote
Amos Batchelder. "Bushes, and sand, a sluggish stream of turbid, muddy water,
dry bunches of grass—few and far between—lofty mountains here and there, and
barren hills, make up the landscape."[38] "This is the crookedest river I ever saw,"
J. D. Breyfogle complained, "and once in a while it takes a shoot into the mountains
while we have to climb over hills a mile or two when we meet again on the plain."[39]

The twisting wagon road sought to avoid narrow canyons, swamps, cattle-killing
alkali springs, and sandhills. From the Wells, the trail headed west-southwest
some one hundred miles to Gravelly Ford, then west twenty miles to present-
day Battle Mountain, where it turned west-northwest for another fifty miles to
today's Winnemucca and the meadows at the mouth of the Little Humboldt.
Here the desert river bent south-southwest for some fifty-five miles to Lassens

[34]Berrien, "Overland from St. Louis," 11 July 1849, 334.
[35]Wood, Diary, 3 August 1849, Huntington Library.
[36]Hale, "Diary of a Trip to California," 7, 11, 12, 14 August 1849, 102, 106–107.
[37]Harrow, *Gold Rush Overland Journal,* 28 July 1849, 48.
[38]Batchelder, Diary/Journal, September 1849, Bancroft Library, 89.
[39]Breyfogle, Diary, 10 July 1849, 16.

Meadows, then pursued the same course to the sink of the Humboldt, where the fetid, sludge-laden waters collected in a great marsh known as Humboldt Lake. "It is the most serpentine of all rivers I ever saw being made up of one unbroken succession of bends," groused Jerome B. Howard. "If some power could get hold of it and straighten it out, it would reach to the Pacific."[40]

Until the arrival of the gold seekers, the trail usually ran along only one side of the river, but with the great press of travelers, wagons broke new roads down both banks. Charles C. Brady's party crossed the Humboldt several times, "keeping on the best roadway side."[41] William Z. Walker described one of the dynamics that drove the evolution of the trail over three decades: "We left the river and travelled about 6 miles through the wild sage. The road was thronged with emigrants. and we avoided the dust by making a cut off."[42] A series of meadows made it barely possible to get an ox wagon down the lower river. They began with the "large swamp or a series of swamps and sloughs" that Edmund Booth found at the Little Humboldt. "Grass tall and thick and the sloughs filled with tall reeds with which the Indians construct arrows," he wrote.[43] These marshy sloughs were "grown up with bullrushes and cat-tails flags 8 or 10 feet high." Even in late August, Andrew Murphy found good grass growing on an island "as thick as it can stand from 3 to 4 feet high. Thousands of acres of it surpassing most of the cultivated meadows in the States." He spent all day cutting and curing enough grass to sustain his teams during the trek across the desert. "Our camp this morning has more the appearance of a farmyard than an emigrant camp," he noted. "All hands busy rigging up scythes and other hay making implements. All contend to be the best mower etc. In about 2 hours time we had laid to the land about a ton of as good hay as any farm in the U.S. could produce."[44]

Below its big bend, the river became increasingly narrow, polluted, and locked up in tight canyons, but emigrants could still find occasional pockets of grass hidden in its many twists and turns. As Israel Hale trudged south in August, he noted, "the grass and willows in the valley were on fire, but we soon discovered that it had not burned to any extent. Grass and willows are the main support of our teams, consequently we were very thankful that the burning was not a general thing." The last oasis before the sink, Lassens Meadows, now Rye Patch Reservoir, was at the end of thirty-five dry, dusty miles. Few Forty-niners had much to say about the forage: Hale found only "tolerable grass and some willows."[45]

[40]Howard, "California Correspondence," 25 April 1850, in Perkins, *Gold Rush Diary,* 180.

[41]Brady, "Hannibal to the Gold Fields in 1849," 7.

[42]Walker, Diary, 29 August 1849, BYU Library.

[43]Booth, *Edmund Booth (1810–1905), Forty-niner,* 16 September 1849.

[44]Murphy, Diary, 31 August, 1 September 1849, Western Historical Manuscripts, 44–45.

[45]Hale, "Diary of a Trip to California," 19, 21 August 1849, 112, 114.

"Feed grew scarcer & water poorer & the weather hotter" as the fortune hunters marched down the river valley, wrote Charles Tinker.[46] Now their contempt for the dwindling alkaline river knew no bounds. "I must agree with the majority of the Emigrants in nicknaming it 'Humbug River.' The stream itself does not deserve the name of river being only a good sized creek," snarled Elisha Perkins. The grass at the head of the river was splendid, but "then the valley begins to narrow and feed to get poorer and less of it all the rest of its course," till at its end "we could hardly get enough for our mules to eat and water barely drinkable from saline and sulphurous impregnation and having a milky color. I think Baron Humboldt would feel but little honored by his name being affixed to a stream of so little pretension. It is far inferior in every respect to either Bear River, Green River, or Big Sandy. We leave it without any feelings for it at the foot of the Sink," Perkins recounted.[47]

Dust lay on the road six to ten inches deep, Joseph Bates reported. "Today we were almost smothered with dust, the pulverised clay was so very light & deep that a south wester which blew strong during the evening raised it in clouds around us."[48] William Z. Walker agreed: "The dust along the stream is intolerable, filling our eyes so that we can hardly see our animals. We were visited by such [a] hurricane of dust during the forenoon that we were obliged to turn out of the road and stop till the wind subsided."[49] Samuel Mathews wrote, "We had dust in any quantity, from an inch to a foot deep, but almost always dust, fine as flour, and having something like the odor of a mixture of Ipecac and ashes and brick dust, in equal proportions."[50]

"This Mary River Valley, with some occasional exceptions, is an inhospitable desert," Joseph Middleton concluded. "Pasture and feed for cattle is precarious, scanty, and meagre, and in many places there is none of any kind." He was astonished the cattle could live, much less work, on no apparent grass. "Our poor faded, and exhausted cattle! It harrowed up my soul that I could render them no relief—that we must rush on to save our lives at the expense of others. Poor obedient creatures, what hellish cruelties I have witnessed inflicted on them by hard-hearted, worthless men."[51] The desolation took its toll on men, teams, and equipment. "The grass was poor and [too] many poor cattle to eat it," wrote Edward Jackson. "The aspect of the valley changes a little; growing narrower; which of course, is no advantage to feed, and the poor animals are obliged to fill up with any green shrubs that chance to come in their way."[52] Wagon wheels were constantly immersed in hot sand, and "the felloes and naves shrunk, the tyres loosened, and

[46]Tinker, "Journal," 81.

[47]Perkins, *Gold Rush Diary,* 7 September 1849, 120.

[48]Bates, Diary, 9, 12 September 1849, Mattes Library.

[49]Walker, Diary, 16 August 1849, BYU Library, 109.

[50]Mathews to "Friend Gray," 7 October 1849, in Mathews, *Mathews Family,* 312.

[51]Middleton, Diary, 10, 12, 21 September 1849, Beinecke Library, 117, 119, 127.

[52]Jackson, Journal, 21, 22 August 1849, BYU Library, 78.

the spokes rattled like a bag of bones."[53] Cut off from the world and society, Amasa Morgan thought the trip was the hardest time of his life. "I would give One Dollar for a newspaper, Five for a letter and Fifty to see our friends."[54] "We shall be glad to leave the valley of the Humboldt," wrote Joseph Wood.[55]

At least one Forty-niner developed a strange affection for the desert river. "After haveing travelled along its Banks four hundred miles, and enjoyed so many refreshing draugh[t]s from its limped stream," Gordon Cone wrote as he left the Humboldt, "it is not without some little emotion that we see it in its final resting place, in the midst of a Desert."[56] In contrast, Cherokee Forty-niner and poet John Ridge denounced the Humboldt as the River of Death. He did not mourn the Stygian stream's disappearance "into the jaws of thy Hell."[57]

CRACKED INTO CHASMS: HUMBOLDT LAKE AND THE SINK

Near today's Lovelock, Nevada, the depleted river spread out into a vast intermittent swamp somewhat carelessly named Humboldt Lake. At Lucius Fairchild's "Grand Marsh," gold seekers had one last chance to prepare their exhausted livestock to cross the Forty-mile Desert.[58] The stark scenery and haunting mirages made the desert country seem unearthly. "In this valley Whirlwinds frequently raise mighty columns of dust, which form pillars reaching from the earth to the heavens," wrote Joseph Wood. "In the distance they look like mighty giants fleeing over the mountains to avoid our presence." Before reaching Humboldt Lake, Wood crossed a dry slough many miles wide; it had once been covered with vegetation but was now "cracked into chasms." The playa's crust was made of peat, "which was on fire & in some places had been burnt off from acres of the surface."[59] Thomas Evershed came in sight of "a beautiful sheet of water seemingly about a mile across it with the reflections of the mountains in it," but because the wagons passing through it raised dust, he concluded "the sink was not yet and that it was a mirage, the first we had seen. Soon it disappeared, leaving not a trace behind" except the carcass of an old ox. "The sink is some 4 miles long & spreading over nearly the whole valley which extends on about the same as usual as though the river might have gone on as usual had the bottom not fallen out," Evershed wrote. "Oh! For a drink of good ice water."[60]

[53]Kelly, *Excursion to California,* 278.

[54]Morgan, Diary, 10 July 1849, Bancroft Library.

[55]Wood, Diary, 18 August 1849, Huntington Library, 82.

[56]Cone, Journal of Travels, 22 September 1849, BYU Library, 118.

[57]Ridge, *Poems,* 4.

[58]Fairchild, *California Letters,* 33.

[59]Wood, Diary, 15, 18 August 1849, Huntington Library, 78, 83.

[60]Evershed, "The Gold Rush Journal," 30 July 1849, 36.

" 'How far to the Sink?' has been a question *often* asked & *often* answered, & *often* heard in the last month," wrote Wakeman Bryarly. A friend thought the sooner the "Hellboldt River" disappeared into the lower regions, the better. Here the Humbug met its ignominious end at "the Sink, the desideratum," where "the desert finally overcomes and destroys it" as it radiated into an extensive swamp renowned as "the far famed sink of Humboldt river." There was "considerable dispute among Emigrants as to what the Sink is," noted Elisha Perkins. Isaac Wistar provided a telling description: "The Sink is a pond several hundred yards in diameter with [a] stagnant surface looking as if it had received several coats of lead-colored paint, and with indefinite, shallow, marshy borders, where the water eternally contends with the enveloping sands."[61]

The playa's geography baffled overland travelers and has confused historians. The sink was half of two barely separated basins where the waters of the Humboldt and Carson rivers filled the immense Lake Lahontan during the Ice Age. For gold seekers, the sink began with "a great marsh or meadow" where the river's alkaline-laden waters collected behind a natural dam known as Humboldt Bar. Geographers today distinguish between Humboldt Lake—which created a broad, if miry, grazing ground—and the sink, where waters of the desert river vanished into a salt plain. Forty-niners tended to see them as one dismal unit spreading over twenty-five or thirty miles.[62] At its heart in the summer, wetlands covered more than a thousand acres with coarse grass. "The Sink is a vast plain Over which the water spreads & gradually sink or looses its self in the sand. It is a vast Quagmire or Marsh of Stagnant Saline and Alkali water mixed, and emits a most offensive and nauseating effluvia," wrote James Pritchard. "There is nothing of the appearance of Lake about it, as you can only see the water about in spots. It therefore has more the appearance of Ponds than of a Lake. Takeing it all in all, it is one of the most disagreeable and loathsome looking places on the face of the earth." His "weary thirsty and hungary" company "failed to so much as find a bunch of wild Sage, which before had never failed, to cook a bite of supper." The resilient Kentuckian, however, waded into the marsh and collected enough dry bulrushes to heat "a *good* cup of tea."[63]

"Before reaching the Sink the road leaves the River on account of the marshes & swampy ground in its vicinity & passed through the plain covered with swamp grass, & saline crustations," wrote Perkins, in what was one of the best descriptions of 1849. "Some 10 miles travel brings you to what we called the 'first Wells' & here I take it you get a view of the Sink proper being a vast marsh some 4 or 5

---

[61]Perkins, *Gold Rush Diary*, 13 September 1849, 126; Bryarly, *Trail to California*, 11 August 1849, 189, 191. Wistar, *Autobiography*, 13 August 1849, 106.

[62]More precisely, geographers identify two lakes: Toulon Lake, which lies close to the east side of Interstate 80; and Humboldt Lake, about a mile farther east.

[63]Pritchard, *The Overland Diary*, 25 July 1849, 122.

miles across with a lake or lakes in the middle—the ground white with sulphurous & saline deposits & the water milky for the same reasons." The lake was a natural wildlife refuge: "The ponds of the Sink were covered with all kinds of wild fowl, geese, ducks, curlews, snipes, cranes, &c," Perkins observed. The "perfect mire in every direction" made the birds feel perfectly secure from man or beast. When a companion fired a heavily loaded shotgun over the lake, "the noise made by the wings of the frightened birds was like thunder, & we could hear it continuing up the plain as flock after flock take the alarm like the rumbling of thunder after the first heavy roll."[64]

Throughout August the meadow was jammed with gold seekers. Thomas Van Dorn "found a constant stretch of encampments," which reminded him of camp meetings or great political celebrations, sprawling across the edge of the Big Meadow for six miles. The "handsomest grass in the world" extended for twelve miles; he estimated yields of at least two tons of hay to the acre. "Without this grass here, this route would be abandoned but it forms a natural recruiting point in this vast desert region." Van Dorn's weary party passed the evening "with a grand musical entertainment, the Pike Co. Ill. boys having joined ours and brought in their artillery of music, which [they] accompanied by darkie extravaganzas. Concluded the exercises and at a pretty late hour. From actions tonight I should judge our men show the days rest as virtually as our cattle."[65]

Travelers had a hard time determining where the sink began. "It is 20 miles yet to the point designated as the 'sink,'" Joseph Wood wrote, "but the water sinks all around here." During wet years like 1849 and 1850, the grasses covering Humboldt Lake created essential pasturage for draft animals: without it, the California Trail would have been impassible. Joseph Wood spent several days cutting grass and letting his cattle recuperate in preparation for the crossing of the Forty-mile Desert. "There are a great many teams congregated here & it is a very smart business village"; it was so busy Wood found it impossible to sleep.[66] "We sent men on with sythes and have got our grass all cut," Joseph Hackney wrote a few days later. "It is the best grass we have seen on the river." He watched his cattle "laying into it finely and they need it bad enough as they have not had a good feed for the last four days and will not have any more four [sic] the next three but what we can haul on the wagons." But the water was not very good and there was scarcely any wood.[67] Others denounced the sink as a fetid, miserable place: "Water in it is about the color of what comes from a stable manure field, so that neither man nor

[64]Perkins, *Gold Rush Diary,* 13 September 1849, 126–27.
[65]Van Dorn, Diary, 21, 22 August 1849, Beinecke Library, 37.
[66]Wood, Diary, 18 August 1849, Huntington Library, 81.
[67]Hackney, Journal, 22 August 1849, *Wagons West,* 184–85.

beast can take a mouthful of it," Felix Negley wrote while at its lower end in late July. "The grass on this edge is so meager that a mule eating all day could not fill his belly. Water worse than none!"[68]

From the slough it took about four hours to reach the stark desolation of the sink of the Humboldt. "This river wich forces its way 290 miles through narrow Kanyans sandy Deserts and around many a mountain here is lost in the earth," wrote Amasa Morgan, "and whare its waters go to no one knows."[69] The sink was "a pool of black, stagnant water; and to the east, south and west, we beheld a barren waste upon which the stillness of death was resting," David Hindman remembered. "The desolation which surrounded us, the gloom in which the sun descended below the western horizon and the coming darkness of night, will never be obliterated from my memory."[70]

Hoping to find better water, the first trains to reach the lake began digging wells. At a popular campsite, William Johnston's company dug one about four feet wide and a little less deep that "furnished an abundant supply of water, but intensely brackish, bitter with salt and sulpher." There were several such wells, and they tended to filter out a few of the chlorides that poisoned the open waters of the lake. The last semi-potable water was at the Sulphur Wells, dug near the last slough before travelers entered the playa that was the sink proper. By late July there was no grass left at the wells, but it was the last water this side of the desert, wrote Joseph Berrien: "The Water itself was very unpleasant both to taste and smell and of a greenish color, but was cool and the cattle drank it eagerly."[71]

About ten miles farther on was a miserable salt creek that early in the season provided some feed for livestock, but half a cup of the creek's briny water made Joseph Wood sick. "At this point the waters of the river entirely disappear," Henry Tappan wrote. He observed, "wells have been dug by the Emigrants in advance but the water is so highly impregnated with Sulphur that but few teams will drink of it. Within a mile or two of the springs or wells the road diverges. The left leading to Carson River & the right to the Truckee."[72] A mile beyond this parting of the ways, the diverging trails ran into the Humboldt Bar, a natural dike that separated Humboldt Lake from the true sink—a vast, salt-encrusted pan. "An embankment some twenty feet high extends across the bed of the river, extending from mountain to mountain, perhaps one and a half miles wide," wrote John Banks in a particularly apt description of this strange landform. "Mountaineers say that in

[68]Negley, "Gold Fever," 25 July 1849, 28.

[69]Morgan, Diary, 16 July 1849, Bancroft Library.

[70]Hindman, "California Gold Rush Experiences," chapter 4 in *The Way To My Golden Wedding*.

[71]Berrien, "Overland from St. Louis," 24 July 1849, 339.

[72]Tappan, "The Gold Rush Diary," 24 August 1849, 135.

the spring when the snow is melting the river forms a large lake that is many miles long, which is confirmed by its present appearance, being completely level and destitute of vegetation." Overlanders such as Banks were sometimes surprised to find water on the downstream side of the dike: "The barrier has all the regularity of art, and what is remarkably strange, it has a large slough on the opposite side in the corner next [to] the river."[73] During wet years, the swampy area was the result of seepage that produced what James Pritchard called a "salt creek" where the "dregs of the Humboldt" flowed from a break in the Humboldt Bar as "a small creek or slough of putrid poisonous water" onto Carson Sink. Here, Dale Morgan noted, "its waters mingled with those of the decaying Carson River."[74] The far side of the dike marked the start of the most notorious passage on the California Trail: the Forty-mile Desert.

This was the swamp where hope died. "Sink—sink of everything that is human and humanizing," Niles Searls, a survivor of the Pioneer Line, wrote in despair. "We have absolutely used up a good sized river! Have run it in the ground! It is gone!" In mid-August, Searls claimed, the thermometer "indicates 140 on this arid plain. I never felt the heat till now," as he looked "out over the arid, burning waste." Beneath the merciless sun, "the whole atmosphere glows like an oven. The water is bitter and nauseous. Off to the southwest, as far as the eye can extend, nothing appears but a level desert. And this we must cross!"[75] William Johnston felt he had reached the valley of the shadow of death: "Over its portals might be inscribed: 'Who enters here, leaves hope behind.'"[76]

Their Nods and Smiles:
Western Shoshones and Northern Paiutes

At the forefront of the 1849 emigration, William Kelly's party was among the first to reach Humboldt Lake. After staking their horses, the men looked up to see some thirty Paiutes sitting quietly and watching. "Our first impulse was to run to our rifles; but the pacific posture of our visitors, and their nods and smiles, forbade the apprehension of danger." Using signs, the Native leader offered to cut grass if the travelers would give him a knife, and when Kelly handed him one, "at it he went like a good workman, laughing immoderately at the idea of his new employment." His companions joined him and soon the "sable mowers" had made considerable hay in exchange for a worn-out red flannel shirt. Despite such benign encounters,

---

[73]Armstrong and Banks, *The Buckeye Rovers*, 31 August 1849, 76.

[74]Pritchard, *The Overland Diary*, 25 July 1849, 166n84.

[75]Searls, 9 September 1849, in Reid, *Overland to California*, 128.

[76]Johnston, *Experiences of a Forty-niner*, 15 July 1849.

Forty-niners usually described the peoples of the Great Basin in brutally racist terms. Kelly considered them "the most degraded and debased of all the Indian race, the refuse and dregs of savage society," and argued, "the Digger Indian is very few degrees removed from the orang-outang." He thought they had "the instinctive cunning of the monkey, without a scintilla of energy," and labeled them "a terrible pest and nuisance." Kelly denounced their stealthy tactics and implicitly praised the trappers and travelers who shot them down "without hesitation or remorse wherever they meet them."[77]

The gold rush escalated the level of violence between emigrants and Indians in the Great Basin, where the tactics of the Northern Paiutes, Bannocks, and Western Shoshones outraged the exhausted sojourners. "The Diggers are a nation of Indians who have some other name but are called 'diggers' because their chief food is from roots which they dig out of the ground," Joseph Middleton wrote. They had won "the reputation of being the greatest thieves of all the North American Indians," but the British Army veteran had his doubts. The scarcity of grass forced the cattle "to spread out and stroll to great distances and prowl into the labyrinths of willows on the river banks and bottoms." This made it very difficult to find them, and when they could not be found, "the 'white man' immediately says that the 'Diggers' have stolen them. This may be true or it may not, but is asserted," Middleton observed.[78] Gordon Cone described their "mode of opperateing" precisely: they "watch their opportunity, and drive off the cattle, or horses of the emigrants into these mountains, or by shooting them with arrows, so that they become lame, and have to be left, thus enabling them to accomplish their object, which is to kill and eat them."[79]

John A. Markle called the "tetorally naked" Paiutes and Shoshones "the most degraded beings I ever saw." They ate snakes, lizards, grasshoppers—"everything of the flesh kind"—and "killed a great many mules and oxen at night and when the train would pass on they could come and carry them away," but he did not believe the widespread reports of their killing emigrants. He found the notion "that if a man left the road 2 or 3 miles he was sure to be killd" completely incredible, and declared that such stories "must have been got up by some tarnal Bragedocious, and if there was any body killed I think it was their own fault." Markle often ranged five or six miles away from the road, "alone in search of game, and have frequently come to where they were camped and also met them while they were hunting." They "were always friendly and reach out there hand to shake hands and mut[t]er a kind of grunting how do you do."[80] The Indians had not molested the

---

[77]Kelly, *Excursion to California,* 253–54, 290–91.

[78]Middleton, Diary, 7 September 1849, Diary, Beinecke Library, 4–15.

[79]Cone, Journal of Travels, 1 September 1849, BYU Library, 98–99.

[80]Markle "A Letter from California," 26 January 1850, 6–7.

emigrants themselves, John Muscott observed, even though "on the Humboldt River immense numbers of oxen and mules were stolen and slaughtered by them." He, too, described the raiders' highly effective tactics: "They would frequently crawl up to the cattle in the darkness of the night, and so wound them by shooting arrows into them, that emigrants are compelled to leave them behind, and the Indians thus secure them for food."[81]

Lumped together under the Digger epithet and condemned as "the most hostile of all the tribes," the three nations suffered an onslaught of savagery from the desperate fortune hunters. "The Indians are treacherous rascals," wrote Edward Jackson. "One came into our camp last night and the watchman drove him off. To day, one stole a steer and drove him off. A man followed and found him. He had killed the steer, & was roasting part. The man immediately shot him." The carnage continued after raiders stole nine cattle and four horses on the very crooked Humboldt River, and Jackson's train sent four or five men to search for them. "After a tramp of 25 miles, they came upon 4 indians, cooking and drying their meat. The men thought to take them by surprize, but as soon as they got within 15 feet of them they shot a volley of arrows which wounded three of the men," Jackson reported. "A desperate fight ensued and the whites succeeded in killing all the Indians."[82]

Gordon Cone found the "Par Utah" Indians at Humboldt Lake "filthy in their habits," but, unlike most of his companions, he had kind words for them. They were "harmless, simple, and not disposed to steal, or meddle with things that do not belong to them—They are small in stature, well formed, with regular and rather hansome features, and appear quite cheerful and hapy." Much to his discomfort, Cone watched one Paiute eat a raw duck "entrails and all" and the "heads, scales, inwards and every part" of some lightly cooked fish "except the back bone—Thus much for Indian cookery."[83] Elisha B. Lewis found the "Utes" (probably Northern Paiutes) at Great Meadows dressed in well-tanned antelope robes and considered them "very athletic and quite inteligent."[84]

A vast bird sanctuary, the sink of the Humboldt River was a natural gathering spot for Shoshones and Paiutes eager to exploit its enormous bounty, which included protein-rich cattails. "The 'Sink' appears to be a kind of convention ground for all the feathered tribes of North America," wrote Alexander Nixon. "Their number at this time is legion."[85] The California Trail cut a white man's road directly through the heart of such natural resources, and the abandoned property

---

[81]Muscott to Robbins, 14 October 1849, California State Library.
[82]Jackson, Journal, 14–15 1849, BYU Library.
[83]Cone, Journal of Travels, 19, 20 September 1849, BYU Library, 114, 116.
[84]Lewis, Overland to California, 4 September 1849, Beinecke Library, 53.
[85]Nixon, Diary, 27 July 1849, California State Library.

littering the emigrant corridor became an irresistible magnet for Indians far and wide. Wagon trains offered staggering temptations to the region's Natives, who were accustomed to exploiting the slender resources of a hard land to their absolute limits. An ox, after all, could feed many more people than a rabbit. Overlanders scattered unimaginable treasures for Native peoples—cast-off clothing, wagons, iron tools, cookware, and weapons—in their wake. This windfall came at a high price, since so many encounters between Paiutes and Forty-niners ended with lethal violence.

As Edmund Booth's party ate breakfast near the Humboldt Sink, four Northern Paiutes came into camp. They gave them bread, meat, and coffee, but the train's animals were in desperate need of feed. One of the Indians, Booth reported, "undertook to guide us to grass. In a half hour we came to a good running stream 2 or 3 yards wide with abundance of tall fine grass—the best I have seen on the river yet." Booth found six wagons camped with "the famous Indian chief Truckee. He understands English enough to be understood and let us know we were already near the sink and gave directions for the route to the Truckee river," named when he first showed a wagon train the trail in 1844. The twenty tribesmen struck Booth as "the most civilized Indians I ever met. It is evident they are familiar with the whites"—so familiar they had "lumps of gold among them." Five of Truckee's men accompanied Booth's train to the sink, where he heard that Indians had killed two men on the Forty-mile Desert.[86]

No record survives of what the Northern Paiutes made of their bizarre and powerful visitors. An encounter at Truckee Meadows when a Captain Dobbins hailed a few Indians in Spanish may reflect the Natives' best hope: "They understood him and answered him in the same language, telling him to go and mind his own business."[87]

FOUR PASSES OVER THE SIERRA

After reaching Sacramento, a perceptive sojourner, John M. Muscott, identified four ways to cross the Sierra in 1849. From north to south, he described Fandango, Donner, Carson, and Sonora passes, which summed up the geographical knowledge of the best-informed Forty-niners.[88] No matter where they crested the North American Cordillera, travelers on the California Trail thought the passes ranging from Fandango Pass in the north to Cajon Pass in the south crossed the Sierra Nevada. They did not. The last barricade between the Great Basin and the

---

[86]Booth, *Edmund Booth (1810–1905), Forty-niner,* 23 September 1849, 14.

[87]Jackson, Journal, 3 September 1849, BYU Library, 85.

[88]Muscott to Robbins, 14 October 1849, California State Library. Subsequent quotations are from this letter.

Pacific actually confronted overland travelers with a maze of mountains—the Cascade, Warner, Siskiyou, Panamint, San Bernardino, San Gabriel, and Sierra ranges, to name a few.

The Cascade Range posed the Oregon Trail's greatest challenge. To reach the Willamette Valley, emigrants could float down the Columbia, clamber over Mount Hood on the Barlow Road, or use the southern road from the Humboldt to approach today's Klamath Falls, Oregon, and then cross a divide to Ashland and the Rogue River Valley along the line of what is now Green Springs Highway. Far to the south, Nobles Trail later crossed the northern flank of Lassen Peak using the Cascades' southernmost pass over its southernmost volcano. Muscott's "Northern" pass was the Lassen Trail, which diverged "from the old route on Humboldt River, about 60 miles above what is called the 'Sink' of that river." Oregon's South Road Expedition first explored what is now called the Applegate Trail in 1846. Peter Lassen used it in 1848 to take about six wagons to Rancho Bosquejo, his massive Mexican land grant near the confluence of Deer Creek and the Sacramento River. The Lassen Trail was no cutoff. The desperate souls who began pouring over it in early August 1849 soon learned, as Muscott put it, that the Lassen Trail was "worse, and some 250 or 300 miles longer than on the old route."

The complex of mountain ranges along the Oregon-California border made building wagon roads difficult and describing how they navigated the terrain a challenge. The Lassen Trail escaped the Great Basin over the Warner Mountains, not the Sierra, crossing the 6,135-foot Fandango Pass. To the north and west, lava flows and isolated buttes bordered the Goose Lake Basin, where the Lassen Trail went south across the Modoc Plateau; the Applegate Trail headed east across a hundred miles of open plain and broken country to pass between two peaks in the Cascades. Here the Cascades met the Siskiyou Mountains (technically part of the Klamath Range) and bent southeast to Mounts Shasta and Lassen. Multiple wagon roads eventually crossed the Sierra Nevada from Sonora Pass in the south to the gap between the Cascades and the Sierra at Fredonyer Pass. Most gold seekers crossed the central Sierra Nevada using Donner or Carson passes, where they faced the range's most formidable challenges. North of Donner Pass, the Sierra's high, rugged, and plutonic granite ridges gradually tapered off beneath volcanic layers. Its steep-sided peaks declined, giving way to mountains whose lower passes and less difficult terrain made later wagon roads such as the Henness Pass Road and the Beckwourth Trail easier to navigate.

Muscott called the classic California Trail over Donner Pass "the first or old route down the Humboldt River to the Sink and via Truckie's River, over the Sierra and down the headwaters of Bear River." The Northern Paiute leader whom emigrants called Truckee helped open the wagon road in 1844. Disaster imprinted the Donner

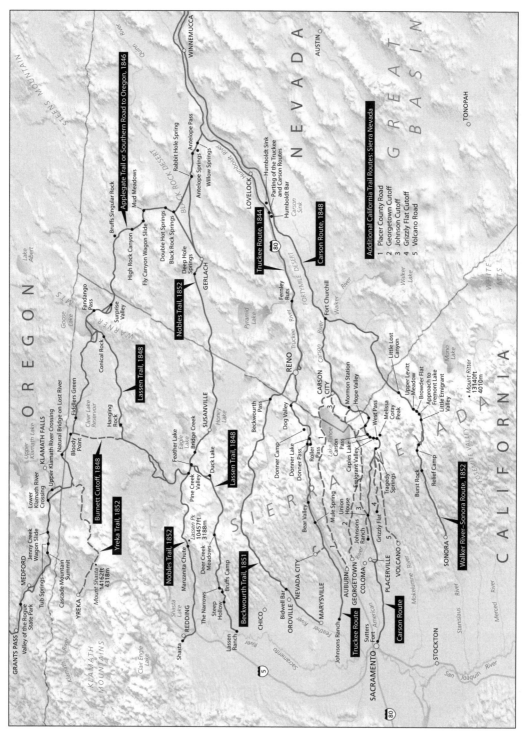

WAGON ROADS OVER THE PACIFIC CORDILLERA, 1852

As a gateway to the goldfields, Forty-niners could cross Fandango, Donner, or Carson Pass, but by 1852 speculators and boomtown promoters had created a network of new wagon roads over Henness, Daggett, Beckwourth, Johnson, Nobles, party's name on local sites two years later and gave the route its lethal reputation. The trail Muscott called the "route between the Childs route and the old route" up the Truckee River was the new road over Carson Pass, which became the first choice of the Forty-niners and for years remained the most popular gateway to the goldfields. Muscott ambiguously called the southernmost of his four passes the "Child's route, south and west of the Carson River." The name referred to Joseph B. Chiles and could apply to either Sonora or Walker pass, since Chiles had packed across the Sierra near Sonora Pass with the Bidwell-Bartleson party in 1841—and, two years later, Joseph R. Walker himself got a few wagons as far as Walker Pass while hauling a sawmill for Chiles. No gold seekers crossed Sonora Pass until 1852, and only a few of the Mississippi boys who wandered into Death Valley attempted the route in 1849. Forty-niners coming from Salt Lake used Cajon Pass to squeeze between the San Bernardino and San Gabriel mountains.

For those on the northern route, "The rush was so great this year as to drive many companies off their road, from half to two miles from the road in some places, to procure grass, and this alarmed them so much that when they arrived on the Humboldt River they separated, taking different routes," John Muscott wrote. His final observation was unarguable: "Much suffering has been experienced by emigrants this year on all the routes."[89]

HEAVY SAND: THE FORTY-MILE DESERT

The Forty-mile Desert began at the Humboldt Bar. The trail divided just short of the bar, forming a wishbone where Forty-niners had to choose between the old Truckee road and or the new trail over Carson Pass. Diarists estimated that both *journadas* were longer than the desert's name implied. Today, Interstate 80 slices through the twists and turns of the original California Trail to the Truckee, crossing the White Plains salt playa and the forty-two miles of desert between the Truckee Range and the Hot Springs Mountains. At the halfway point, the famous Boiling Springs overlooked Hot Springs Flat, now the site of a thermal energy plant. Highway 95 traces the left-hand branch of the trail to the Carson River, the route James Clyman, Joseph B. Chiles, and Joseph R. Walker opened in 1848 to provide a direct connection to the road Mormon Battalion veterans had blazed over Carson Pass.

A strange dynamic helped determine which road emigrants chose. As was true at any fork in the overland road, a powerful compulsion to follow the most heavily traveled trace led all the foremost trains to pick the trail to the Carson River.

---

[89]Johnson and Johnson, *Escape from Death Valley*, 185n169. I am indebted to Stafford Hazelett, Don Buck, and LeRoy Johnson for repeatedly correcting my grasp of this complex mountainology.

On the evening of 17 July, the Banner Company came "to the place or fork whare the old route by Trucky river makes off to the right or more westward," Amasa Morgan wrote. "But thare being no track that way it gave us some reason to hope that what some call the Morman new road would prove to be better than the old one."[90] Reports of disastrous conditions on the Carson road in late July turned most trains onto the Truckee route: on 26 August, Henry Mann wrote that no one had taken the Truckee road for two weeks—"all the teams having gone the Southern road for some time past"—but now they had begun to head for the Truckee again.[91] The shift was temporary. By early September, William Z. Walker complained that trying to buy provisions on the older trail seemed impossible because "teams are getting scarcer since the road forked and most of the emigration have gone the Carson river route."[92] To complicate matters, a few Forty-niners crossed to the Truckee and then turned south to the Carson River, following the tracks of the first Mormon wagons over Carson Pass, now the route of U.S. Alternate 50. "Having heard from a man who was returning to meet his train, that the route by the way of Truckee was nearly impassable, we changed our course and took a twenty-six mile desert, arriving at Carson river six miles above Dayton," Mary Caples recalled.[93] Thomas Van Dorn found that "the emigration had divided at the bend of the Truckee," and crossed twenty-five arid miles to the Carson River.[94]

Whichever route they chose, travelers did their best to prepare their exhausted and starving livestock for the coming ordeal. Charles Boyle's train filled everything that would hold water—kegs, boilers, kettles, coffee pots, India rubber boots and blankets—"with the life-preserver—water to their utmost capacity," he wrote. "We also packed the grass we had cut and dried in our wagons and upon the backs of our mule and horses."[95] Aretas Blackman thought the suffering men endured crossing the desert and the spectacle of animals dying of dehydration was the best remedy for the thirst for gold. The "thirst for fresh water, & traveling in the heat of the day over the blazing hot sand without a shrub or tree to rest under for a moment" made the remedy all the more effective. Wracked with fever at the foot of the Humboldt Sink, Blackman contemplated the desert. "The heat here is almost suffocating. It not only glimmered but almost blazed from the barren and encrusted ground and rolled like the plain from Prairie grass on fire. I had quite a fever now and felt in quite a poor condition for the trip across the desert but there

[90]Morgan, Diary, 7 July 1849, Bancroft Library.

[91]Mann, Diary, 26 August 1849, in Pritchard, *The Overland Diary,* 167n87.

[92]Walker, Diary, 4 September 1849, BYU Library, 125.

[93]Caples, Overland Journey to California, California State Library, 4–5. The Caples family settled along the Carson Pass trail and gave their name to Caples Lake.

[94]Van Dorn, Diary, 28 August 1849, Beinecke Library, 40.

[95]Boyle, Diary, 23 July 1849.

was no alternative." By torchlight he read the notice James Gooding had posted on the edge of the desolation: "Imagine to yourself the worst desert you can and you will find it worse than you have imagined."[96] Joseph Berrien reported his own version of Gooding's conspicuous warning: "We have crossd the Desert and find it 45 miles long, 15 heavy sand—Be careful to drive in the night. Expect to find the worst desert you ever saw and you will find it worse than you expected."[97]

THIS DESERT WILL TRY MEN AND MULES: THE ROAD TO CARSON VALLEY

The parties at the very forefront of the emigration suffered from an astonishing ignorance about the challenge they faced after the Humboldt disappeared. Edmund Green failed to recognize the Forty-mile Desert when he reached it early in July 1849. "We had no guide and knew nothing about the country beyond us but as we had had no trouble finding water, we did not provide an extra supply," he recalled. After traveling all day and making a waterless camp, Green and a companion went ahead to find water, "and just before night we came to a clear, cool, beautiful stream of water, the Carson River." After refreshing their worn-out horses, "we took all that we could carry and returned to meet our companions. About five miles out we found them completely exhausted. Some of them could not speak their tongues were so swollen." The packers spent several days on the river recuperating.[98] Few parties were better informed: "We were all ignorant of the extent of the desert, so that we were taken completely by surprise, and suffered extremely from heat and thirst," reported one gold seeker. "I saw several with their tongues so much swollen that they could neither speak nor shut their mouths."[99]

Compared to those who followed the "left-hand road" to the Carson in the heat of summer, Green's experience was a cakewalk. Even the lead parties found it a demoralizing ordeal. Unaware of what lay ahead, Colonel Jarrot's wagons left the Sulphur Wells having already traveled twenty-five miles. "The sun was intensely hot, and not a breath of air stirring," said Louis Tremble of the poisonous slough. "We harnessed our jaded animals, and again moved off, the whole company being under the impression that we had only some ten miles further to go before reaching the river. We were all out of water, and the weather was extremely hot, which made our thirst ten times worse." Ten miles later, "we found a notice stuck-up

---

[96]Blackman to "Brother John," 19 August 1849; Blackman, Journal, 26–27 July 1849, Bancroft Library.

[97]Berrien, "Overland from St. Louis," 24 July 1849, 339. Other diarists saw Gooding's poster: see Boyle, Diary, 22 July 1849.

[98]Green, "Recollections," 8–9.

[99]Anonymous, "From California," 24 August 1849, *Missouri Whig,* 8 November 1849.

stating that it was twenty five miles to the river. We could not believe it, and sup-posed that some wag had stuck it up for the purpose of humbugging folks." Jarrot used his best mules to pull two of his wagons to the river. Tremble spent the most miserable night of his life watching over another wagon as Louis Bayette walked for sixty hours without a rest to rescue the guards with five canteens of water. Tremble found it "impossible to imagine how much suffering will be experienced here by the thousands behind us."[100]

Amasa Morgan's animals and companions were "parched up creatures of mis-ery" even before leaving the sink on 17 July 1849 to face heat Morgan described as "more intense than any I have ever experienced." Abandoned wagons and dead animals littered the next forty miles, while clusters of men and wagons waited for relief from the river. Paiutes arrived to harass the teams and butcher dying oxen. "Digger Indians, quite numerous, sought to shoot mules and oxen," Morgan wrote. "The emigrants returning fire kept the Indians away, for the guns seemed continuous in operation!" Sent ahead, Morgan made the crossing in about sixteen hours. The next day his company brought in all their wagons and animals without a loss—but he said laconically of his trek, "This Desert will try men and mules."[101]

The "wonderful illusory spectacle of mirage" tormented desperate gold seek-ers, but these watery illusions never deceived "dumb brutes." "While crossing this desert we could see the prettiest lakes of water that ever was seen, but as we approached them they disappeared, then they would mak[e] their appearance behind us," wrote Henry Wiman. "Some men would not believe but what they were real and followed them up but never could reach them."[102] Over the desert's first seven miles, Gordon Cone counted twenty-six abandoned wagons. "These scenes and sacrifices are among the variety that go to make up the experience of those that cross these plains, mountains, and desarts," he commented. His train stayed in camp all day—"the most unhapy Sabath that I have experienced on the trip"—and then traveled all night, hoping to reach the river before dawn. Early the next morning Cone guessed, "[we have] eighteen miles yet to go before we find water, and water is what our cattle are suffering for—The heat of the Sun is almost unendurable." The air was impregnated with salt, which made the thirst of both man and beast intolerable. The last twenty miles lay "over an ocean of deep heavy sand that takes the cattle and wagons in from six, to twelve inches deep." For 140 miles these animals "had nothing to eat but a few willows, and for the last thirty six hours not a drop of water to drink." His cattle began to fail before

[100]Tremble to Miles, 6 August 1849, *Illinois Republican*, 1 January 1850, Mattes Library.

[101]Morgan, Diary, 17–18 July 1849, Bancroft Library.

[102]Kelly, *Excursion to California*, 291, 296–302; Wiman to "Dear Parents," 25 October 1849, Missouri Historical Society.

SCENE ON THE DESERT

George Baker's 1853 sketch captured the horrific carnage that many overland veterans described so vividly in their letters and journals. From "Hutchings Panoramic Scenes—Crossing the Plains," a pictorial letter sheet. Author's collection.

midnight. An hour later a faithful ox lay down and died. Six more soon gave out. Cone hitched his last six oxen to his large wagon and left a smaller one twelve miles from the river. He hauled the big wagon another six miles and then drove what cattle could still walk to the river, "where they find water plenty, and grass to some extent." His teams reached the river about 8:00 A.M., "nearly as much broken down as our cattle." Every wagon in his train lost animals: "The road for thirty miles back is literally strewed with dead cattle, and horses." Packers counted two hundred abandoned wagons and over four hundred dead animals.[103]

By mid-August, the route had to be changed "on account of the stench."[104] The fourteenth was extremely warm, wrote John Kincade: "The road is desolate. There are occasional signs of volcanic action. As the rays of sunshine strike the bleached sand of the desert, a reflection may be seen on all sides. It presents in the distance, the appearance of water. During the day, our supply of water became exhausted. The teams began to fail. The roadside was almost covered with the carcasses of animals that could not make further progress and lay there." The dead animals created "an unsupportable stench, while the moans and creaky teeth of the yet living was enough to move a dragon to pity. Wagons, abandoned by their owners, are to be seen in every direction."[105] Luzena Wilson recalled, "It was a hard march over the desert. The men were tired out goading on the poor oxen which seemed ready to drop at every step. They were covered with a thick coating of dust, even to the

[103]Cone, Journal of Travels," 22, 23, 24 September 1849, BYU Library, 118–23.

[104]Anonymous, "From California," 24 August 1849, *Missouri Whig,* 8 November 1849.

[105]Kincade, Saga of Pioneer John Thompson Kincade, 14 August 1849, Mattes Library.

red tongues which hung from their mouths swollen with thirst and heat." Five miles from the Carson River, "the miserable beasts seemed to scent the freshness in the air, and they raised their heads and traveled briskly." When within a half mile of the river, "every animal seemed spurred by an invisible imp. They broke into a run, a perfect stampede, and refused to be stopped until they had plunged neck deep in the refreshing flood; and when they were unyoked, they snorted, tossed their heads, and rolled over and over in the water in their dumb delight. It would have been pathetic had it not been so funny, to see those poor, patient, overworked, hard-driven beasts, after a journey of two thousand miles, raise heads and tails and gallop at full speed, an emigrant wagon with flapping sides jolting at their heels."[106]

As it came to its end, Forty-mile Desert grew more difficult, and the tortured livestock made the last dozen miles of the waterless trek through loose sand. Aretas J. Blackman collapsed from exhaustion as a streak of daylight appeared in the east, and staggered another dozen miles before he hit the heavy sand, "the sun blazing hot and the sand getting hotter, which before getting to the river would almost blister ones feet in boots (yet I walked but little after daylight) and the reflection from the sand really burned ones face."[107] Joseph Berrien thought driving his pony and mule through the deep sand was "the hardest work I had ever attempted. The sand was very deep. The sun shone very hot." The obstinate mules pulled him from one side of the road to the other, "anxious to bite at every bunch of Grease Wood."[108] By that point overlanders had experienced every form of extreme weather, but when most emigrants crossed the Nevada barrens, temperatures could hit 115° F. Amasa Morgan found it was "hot enough to cook Eggs in the sand."[109]

Many trains foundered during this arduous passage, and many who had struggled to bring their wagons so far finally left them on the desert. The wreckage increased as the summer wore on. "The road up and across the desert is strewed with carcasses of oxen, horses, mules and abandoned wagons almost numberless," wrote Edmund Booth.[110] What was left of the Pioneer Line—fourteen wagons, 150 mules, and about thirty of the original 120 passengers—abandoned their wagons and crossed the desert in late September. With much trouble, they managed to get their best animals to the river.[111] The surviving livestock were often useless. "Coming across this infernal desert hit our mules more than any three weeks of travel since we started," said Felix Negley.[112] After Indians put an arrow

[106]Wilson, *Luzena Stanley Wilson,* 8.

[107]Blackman to "Brother John," 19 August 1849; Blackman, Journal, 26–27 July 1849, Bancroft Library.

[108]Berrien, "Overland from St. Louis," 24 July 1849, 338.

[109]Morgan, Diary, 14 July 1849, Bancroft Library.

[110]Booth, *Edmund Booth (1810–1905), Forty-niner,* 27 September 1849, 15.

[111]Cone, Journal of Travels," 27 September 1849, BYU Library, 125.

[112]Negley, "Gold Fever," 27 July 1849, 28.

into a bell mare on the approach to Carson River and his party killed two Indians, William Kelly reflected, "the hurrying of two unfortunate souls into eternity for hunting a dumb beast, came, I must say, with sad concern upon my conscience." But he argued the end justified the means, for otherwise "the lives and properties of hundreds of emigrants might be sacrificed."[113]

The trail at last reached the Carson River about seven miles northwest of today's Fallon. "I am nearly exhausted, not haveing had any rest for the last three days and nights; anxiety seems to keep up a kind of excitement in my mind, or I should give out entirely," wrote Gordon Cone. Few made it across the desert in one trek. Virtually every outfit had to abandon its wagons, forge ahead to the river, and either return and retrieve them or abandon their property altogether. After spending twenty hours crossing "the most gloomy looking country I ever saw," J. D. Breyfogle's train left him and several companions to guard two wagons while the others took their horses and a buckboard to the river. The men waited for four long days "on the broad desert surrounded by mountains in the distance, not a soul near us, [and] no water within 17 miles." Their friends, wrote Breyfogle, finally returned on "the most horrid night I ever passed. The road was strewn with dead mules, horses and cattle."[114]

Carson River was "a lively mountain stream of pure water, about sixty feet wide, with banks twelve, to eighteen feet high," and not more than one to three feet deep in the dry season. "Some trains have been as long as seven days getting their wagons in after leaveing them back only eight, and ten miles," Gordon Cone observed. "Our road runs up this river," he wrote, "but how far I do not know, as I have no guide of this part of the rout." Overlanders were still two deserts and almost ninety miles from the narrow canyon where the west fork of the Carson entered the Sierra Nevada—and another hundred mountainous miles lay between the gold seekers and the gold. By late September, camps spread out for miles along the river, giving the appearance of a busy town with emigrants engaged in hauling wagons off the desert, lightening their loads, or tending teams that had "to be recruited before they can be worked at all, and then recruited again before they can start on their journey." Some were packing their oxen, Cone reported, "and some a packing themselves and pressing on." He saw many families. "This portion of this strange population are extreemly unfortunate in this respect; for their wives and children must go on whether their teams are able or not."[115]

Only a year old, the wagon road followed Carson River west around the Dead Camel Mountains before striking across a twelve-mile desert from the point where today's U.S. 50 touches Lahontan Reservoir. The trace "passed over half a mile of

---

[113]Kelly, *Excursion to California,* 312.

[114]Breyfogle, Diary, 23 July 1849, 19–20.

[115]Cone, Journal of Travels," 25, 27 September 1849, BYU Library, 125–26.

beautiful smooth white level basin," which struck Bernard Reid as "looking like a fairy lake surrounded by steep rough hills." The trail returned to the river near present-day Silver Springs, where it cut west across the Big Bend of the Carson over the Twenty-six Mile Desert. By mid-September, P. W. Thurston, "a philantropic Kentuckian," had posted a large placard advertising a new road along the river, which was longer but eliminated the desert crossing. It circled south around Churchill Butte to the spot on the Carson where the army built Fort Churchill in 1860. James Wilkins went this way and found the best grass he had seen for several hundred miles.[116]

From the high ground of the Twenty-six Mile Desert, emigrants got their first glimpse of "the snowy peaks of the Sierra Nevada."[117] Trail-weary Forty-niners reached good campsites along the creeks draining the Virginia Range, beneath whose barren slopes lay the greatest deposit of silver ore on earth. After climbing a dozen miles over the mountain spur containing the Comstock Lode, the trail turned south, generally staying about a mile from the river as it crossed Eagle Valley, near the future site of Carson City. Leaving the sandhills and sagebrush behind at last, emigrants reached the fertile pastures of Carson Valley, which David R. Hindman recalled were "clothed with a thick growth of grass from eighteen inches to two feet high."[118] Amasa Morgan called it the finest valley he had seen on the road, praising its fine clover and grass, forested hillsides, and wild peaches, and the hot springs that boiled up at the eastern foot of "the everlasting chain of the Sierra Nevada."[119] "There are thousands upon thousands of acres of the best grass I ever saw," wrote Palmer C. Tiffany. "This Carson Valley can beat all the world for grass."[120] Here most travelers rested, giving their teams the opportunity "to pluck up for the last great task—the crossing of the Sierra," while their masters feasted on the valley's abundant trout and deer.[121] Even though it was perilously late in the season and his own foot was badly injured, James Hutchings decided to stay behind when his best and favorite mare, Kit, dropped her foal. Hutchings apparently got Kit over the Sierra.[122]

THE WILDEST WRECK OF DESTRUCTION: THE ROAD TO TRUCKEE MEADOWS

No Forty-niner took the old road across the Forty-mile Desert until about 25 July, when Edwin Bryant led his pack train to the Truckee River over the trail he had

---

[116]Wilkins, *An Artist on the Overland Trail*, 20 September 1849, 74; Reid, *Overland to California*, 13 September 1849, 137.

[117]Booth, *Edmund Booth (1810–1905), Forty-niner*, 1 October 1849, 15.

[118]Hindman, "California Gold Rush Experiences," in *The Way To My Golden Wedding*.

[119]Morgan, Diary, 23 July 1849, Bancroft Library.

[120]Tiffany, Overland Journey, 15 August 1849, Beinecke Library, 102.

[121]Kelly, *Excursion to California*, 305.

[122]Hutchings, *Seeking the Elephant*, 8 October 1849, 178, 182.

used coming to California in 1846 and leaving in 1847. Joseph Buffum made the first documented passage, having reached the river on 2 August.[123] The same day, companies at the Humboldt Sink heard of the disastrous conditions now common on the road to the Carson River. A scout who had surveyed the trail for his train "returned to advise them to take the old road." He gave Bennett Clark "a wretched description of the state of things" on the Carson route, describing the deserted wagons and failed teams that lined the trail. "What water there was, was saline & unwholesome," the man said. He met a woman and her child left "alone in a wagon on the desert, her husband having gone ahead to get water. Like the good Samaritan he supplied her necessities & went on his way." Two days later, at the Sulphur Wells, he was waiting to start across the desert with hundreds of wagons when another eyewitness warned him about the Carson route. "A general panic now seized upon all & doubt & fear prevailed every where," Clark wrote. Soon every party chose to take the right fork to Truckee Meadows and Donner Pass.[124]

Joseph Warren Wood described the great destruction of property between Sulphur and Boiling springs. He counted fifty-two dead animals, twenty-one wagons, and ten gun barrels—and that did not include what darkness had hidden. "The Hot springs are a great natural curiosity, about an acre of surface is dotted with them & many are incessantly Boiling—one of them throws the water & spray 4 & 5 feet high so violent is its ebullition," Wood observed. "Others are calm—the largest spring is 40 yards in circumference & from 4 to 8 feet deep." The thermal springs had stained the nearby rocks white, and its outflow disappeared into "some subterranean outlet."[125] "The water boils up in one large pool and several smaller ones, and so hot was it that some made tea of it, which proved tolerably palatable," wrote J. E. H. He "never want to be nearer to His Satanic Majesty's dominion than I was at that time."[126] Many complained that "this hell of boiling liquid," which tastes remarkably like Alka-Seltzer, was undrinkable. "We found no feed here & the water boiling hot," said Charles Tinker. "We cooled some for our cattle but they hated to drink it. The water is full of mineral & a little brackish—this place is a perfect hell upon earth."[127] A dog with Samuel Mathews's party stepped to the edge of one of the steaming pots, burned his paws, jumped, and then toppled into the scorching water—a common accident at Boiling Springs. The dog, Mathews recalled, "cooked to death in a few seconds."[128] The thermal feature could be equally dangerous for humans: "Mr. Greenabum fell in it up to his knees and the

[123]Dale Morgan, in Pritchard, *The Overland Diary,* 167n87.

[124]Clark, "A Journey," 2, 4 August 1849, 38.

[125]Wood, Diary, 23 August 1849, Huntington Library.

[126]Anonymous (J. E. H.), "Letter from California," 12 August 1849, 4/1–2.

[127]Tinker, "Journal," 3 August 1849.

[128]Mathews, *Mathews Family,* 27. James Clyman, Henry Bigler, and Charles Tinker, who saw a person "scaled to death in an instant," reported similar disasters.

water instantly took all the skin off," wrote B. F. Dowell. "He will be a cripple for life."[129] For all its dangers, the springs offered rest and refreshment for animals and emigrants and made the Truckee route a bit more bearable than the Carson road.

By the time trains began turning to the Truckee, the first companies had swept the foliage from along the lower Humboldt. "Dead and dying teams line the road and there is one continuous stench which is almost unbearable," wrote Edward Harrow, stumbling through the darkness as howling wolves serenaded him. At dawn, "the wildest wreck of destruction" greeted him at Boiling Springs. He had to hide his horror on learning the water was undrinkable until made into coffee.[130] "This is the most dreary desolate looking place we ever saw," Bennett Clark said. His mules "were so hungry that they ate dust & gravel & chewed up whatever came in their way—gearing, wagon covers or any thing they could reach."[131] As he approached the Truckee in September, Elisha Lewis's starving cattle tried to eat his whip stalk while he was driving them.[132]

Edward Jackson's train started across the great sand desert early one evening under a fine moon. He reached Boiling Springs not long before dawn. "When the daylight had fairly come—what a sight! Some dozen oxen lay dead on the plain; waggons were broken, and all descriptions of emigrants truck, strown over the ground." A footsore old dog, "left behind to starve and die," lay under a wagon, whining piteously. "There are nine springs here. All of them hot," Jackson wrote. "One particularly worthy of notice, gushed up from a round hole, with a noise like a steam-engine and throwing scalding water 6 feet into the air. This is a great curiosity." He made what he considered very good tea with the water. At sunset Jackson started again for the river.[133]

Before reaching the Truckee near present-day Wadsworth, Nevada, animals and emigrants had to slog through ten miles of deep sand. "I would travel a little and lay down on the sand and rest and the sun shining on me," wrote Andrew Orvis. "I thought I never would get through and laide down to kick the bucket; but I thought of home and it gave me a little more grit and I would get up and stagger along. I was so thirsty my tonge and lips cracked and bled but I was able to get to water."[134] By the time they got to the river, many were nearly delirious. "Water was all my wants," wrote Charles Tinker. "I would have given all I possessed for a drink of cold water. My tongue and lips was parched and furred over so it took one hour to soak it off." Tinker lay down in the "stream of pure soft water from

---

[129]Dowell, Journal, 3 September 1850, Beinecke Library, 30.
[130]Harrow, Gold Rush Overland Journal, 14 August 1849, 57.
[131]Clark, "A Journey," 4 August 1849, 39.
[132]Lewis, Overland to California, 7 September 1849, Beinecke Library, 56.
[133]Jackson, Journal, 29–30 August 1849, BYU Library, 81–82.
[134]Orvis, Overland Journey, in Fey, King, and Lepisto, Emigrant Shadows, 47.

the Sierra Nevada" and admired the first trees he had seen for 460 miles. "You cant imagine our joy on our arrival here."[135] Thomas Van Dorn crossed the desert in three days—without sleep or rest—and lost only one animal: "Never did my eyes meet anything more welcome than the green scattering forest which lines the border of Truckee river," he wrote after crossing the "*grand* barren waste."[136]

Lucius Fairchild found the desert "lined with dead cattle, horses & mules with piles of provisions burned & whole wagons left for want of cattle to pull them through." He was thankful to get through safely. "That desert is truly the great Elephant of the route and God knows I never want to see it again," he wrote.[137] "All along the desert road from the very start even the way side was strewed with the dead bodies of oxen, mules & horses & the stench was horrible. All our traveling experience furnishes no parallel for all this," remarked Bennett Clark. "Many persons suffered greatly for water during the last 8 or 10 miles, and many instances of noble generosity were developed on these occasions. Some trains that got over before us sent water back in kegs & left them on the road marked for the benefit of the feeble." Upon reaching the Truckee, Clark "found grass very abundant and the water very fine" and slept for the first time in four nights.[138] "I would not beleave that an ox could stand the hardship that ours have without seeing it with my own eyes," Joseph Hackney said after driving his cattle five miles upriver to good grass. "The water is splendid and the luxeary of laying under the shade of a tree no one knows but one that has traveled a thousend miles through the hot sun and not seen a tree large enough to shelter a dog."[139]

Fourteen-year-old Sallie Hester's family spent four days crossing the desert and had to abandon an ox. At dawn, they glimpsed the line of trees marking the Truckee River "and with it the feeling, Saved at last!" The poor cattle kept bellowing even after they reached the stream and stood knee deep in water. "The weary journey last night, the mooing of the cattle for water, their exhausted condition, with the cry of 'Another ox down,' the stopping of the train to unyoke the poor dying brute, to let him follow at will or stop by the wayside and die, and the weary, weary tramp of men and beasts, worn out with heat and famished for water, will never be erased from my memory." But like many who had survived the ordeal, she felt inspired. "The dreaded long desert has been crossed and we are all safe and well."[140]

Gold seekers expressed universal relief upon tasting the clear and deep water flowing from the backside of the Sierra Nevada. Truckee River was "a splendid

---

[135]Tinker, "Journal," 3 August 1849, 81–82. Spelling corrected.
[136]Van Dorn, Diary, 26 August 1849, Beinecke Library, 38, 40.
[137]Fairchild, *California Letters,* 34.
[138]Clark, "A Journey," 5 August 1849, 39–40.
[139]Hackney, Journal, 26 August 1849, *Wagons West,* 187.
[140]Hester, "The Diary of a Pioneer Girl," 4 September 1849, 1:240–241.

stream," wrote Joseph Wood. "There are willows and cottonwood trees on its bank, and to see a tree seems like a glorious sight now. I am tired, sick and worn out, and so are all the company. But a drink from this cool, clear stream has almost cured me"[141] The Truckee, which John C. Frémont had christened the Salmon Trout River, delighted weary Forty-niners. Edward Jackson called it a fine little stream that flowed "clear as crystal. It is well appreciated by the thirsty traveller, after a journey of 45 miles over a desert."[142] William Z. Walker described it as a "fine stream about 30 yds wide and about 3 ft in depth," swift running and tough to cross. "We were obliged to ford it getting our clothes thoroughly soaked by the operation."[143]

Overlanders loved the river, but they hated its narrow, twisting canyon and its seemingly endless fords. In fifty miles, the river's rocky and sandy road required fording the turbulent stream some twenty-seven times "before crossing the first mountain, after which we crossed it once or twice," noted Thomas Galbraith.[144] "The road between the crossings was sandy in some places, rocky in others, & very steep both going up & coming down in others," wrote Wakeman Bryarly.[145] The swift-moving current carried away animals and men, drowning both, and by mid-September, livestock had stripped the canyon of grass. Edward Harrow described the third ford as "one of the worst crossings I ever saw." Rocks made it "not only a difficult but dangerous crossing for man and beast": Harrow almost lost a mule when it stumbled. The animal rolled three or four times before striking a of rock ledge "over which the current madly sweeps. In this position he lay kicking until we got to him." Harrow did lose one of his last two shoes in the disaster.[146]

Edward Jackson had to ford the Truckee seven times in a single morning: "The bottom is rocky and bad to cross, and our mules floundered about badly. I found it very difficult to keep my footing, as the stream is very rapid." (That afternoon he found a path over the hills that bypassed five additional crossings.)[147] William Z. Walker crossed the Truckee seventeen times one Sunday. "The water runs so rapidly that it was almost impossible for men or animals to keep their footing," he wrote. "The water in some places was breast high and the bottom being covered with slippery black rocks we had the greatest difficulty in crossing." Walker slipped and was swept downstream several yards but "by the Aid of a long pole I got ashore with only a ducking." His party had to abandon a horse after it stumbled

---

[141]Wood, Diary, 24 August 1849, Huntington Library.
[142]Jackson, Journal, 1 September 1849, BYU Library, 82–83.
[143]Walker, Diary, 31 August 1849, BYU Library, 119–20.
[144]Galbraith, Journal, August 1849, Mattes Library.
[145]Bryarly, Trail to California, 17 August 1849, 197.
[146]Harrow, Gold Rush Overland Journal, 16 August 1849, 58.
[147]Jackson, Journal, 2 September 1849, BYU Library, 83.

in the rapids; Walker later spotted a watchful Indian leading the rescued animal up a mountainside.[148]

After days battling the twisting river canyon, emigrants emerged into what Elisha Perkins called Mist Valley, the oasis where Reno now stands. It was "a beautiful level plain covered with fine grass, some 10 miles across & formed by the widening of the mountain ranges. Through this valley the river winds after leaving the gorge on the other side, its course marked by a line of cotton woods & willows." Perkins's party took what they thought would be a cutoff, but it led to an Indian fishing camp and an "entirely uncrossable" marsh that proved "a perfect quagmire."[149] Mist Valley was better known as Truckee Meadows, "a very extensive plain, 5 by 10 miles, covered by a luxuriant growth of grass," wrote Edward Jackson, "and walled in on all sides by the lofty Sierra Nevada."[150] Wakeman Bryarly's company "fixed & bridged" the slough, which had made the "beautiful, green, velvety valley" almost impassable. His party crossed the swamp and camped in bluegrass that reached the horses' knees.[151]

HELL-GATE AND THE KING OF MOUNTAINS:
WEST CARSON CANYON AND CARSON PASS

The hard truth about the California Trail was that it never got easier. The farther west it went, the more challenging it became. "We thought we had seen the elephant but were mistaken," wrote one Forty-niner after crossing the Forty-mile Desert. "But at the mountain, we saw him, good!"[152] One last obstacle separated the gold seekers gathered at Truckee Meadows and in Carson Valley from their golden dreams: the Sierra Nevada. They had never seen the like. "The Rocky mountains are very high and steep, and some of them look as though they were one solid mass of rock; however, they are nothing when compared with the California mountains," Edward Murphy said. "These mountains are majestic, awful, and at the same time picturesque."[153]

As pines displaced the cottonwoods that had lined its banks, the Carson River forked near an enormous hot springs. The trail climbed the West Fork by what Forty-niners called Pass Creek Canyon, a name derived from guidebooks handwritten by the Mormons whose twenty-nine wagons had scratched out a primitive road through the high-walled gorge in 1848. The six-mile-long canyon was

---

[148]Walker, Diary, 2 September 1849, BYU Library, 120–21.

[149]Perkins, *Gold Rush Diary,* 12 September 1849, 124–25.

[150]Jackson, Journal, 3 September 1849, BYU Library, 84.

[151]Bryarly, *Trail to California,* 17 August 1849, 197.

[152]Wyman, *California Emigrant Letters,* 73.

[153]Murphy, letter, 2 September 1849, in "Letters from California," *Missouri Whig,* 29 November 1849.

the gateway to the Sierra. "Here begins a cañon, of which the first mile or two is pretty and shady, with a good road—but presto, what a change!" wrote Bernard Reid. "Steep pitches up and down—appalling rocks,—stumps and logs,—sudden bends—all make the worst piece of road I ever saw or dreamed of." Reid asked the question that haunted every teamster who faced the crevice: "How will our wagon get through such a hell-gate?"[154]

"It is absolutely impossible for any man to give such a description of this frightful chasm," wrote Palmer C. Tiffany, but he and others tried to picture this "serpentine gap through a lofty range of mountains composed almost entirely of solid rock" and the "Wagon Bone Yard" he found at the bottom of a hill.[155] The constricted, twisting path up the canyon required three river crossings, two with rude bridges. It was "the most desperate road I ever saw, even for pack horses and for wagons you would think it impossible," wrote George Lawson.[156] Amasa Morgan found the "Canyon of the Mountains" choked with "rocks so large we found difficulty in driving our wagons through."[157] "As the cañon narrowed, its rocky walls towered nearly perpendicular, hundreds of feet," recalled Sarah Royce, "and seemed in some places almost to meet above our heads."[158] Lell Hawley Woolley considered the six miles of Carson Canyon "the roughest piece of road that we found between Missouri and California. There were great boulders from the size of a barrel to that of a stage coach, promiscuously piled in the bed of this tributary to the Carson, and over which we were obliged to haul our wagons. It took us two days to make the six miles."[159]

"The road (or rather where we go) is along a mad, and rushing stream, that leaps and tumbles among the most hetrogenious mass of rocks that I ever set eyes upon, much more attempted to drive a team over—This passage is not only rough, and difficult, but extreemly dangerous," Gordon Cone wrote. "In many places the mountain is steep, which with the rocks that have to be passed over, make it almost impossible to get along." Cone's train entered the canyon at half past two o'clock "and intended to get through before dark." They made it halfway through the very narrow canyon, where "in many places the rocks on each side rise one, and two thousand feet, makeing it one of the most frightful looking places on earth." His companions chained their cattle to small trees by the creek "and setting ourselves down by a large fire of pine logs, find it quite comfortable—The reflection of the light from our fire upon the massive piles of rock that hang nearly over our heads,

[154]Reid, *Overland to California*, 17 September 1849, 139–40.
[155]Tiffany, Overland Journey, 15, 16 August 1849, Beinecke Library, 103–104.
[156]Lawson to "Dear Parents," 26 September 1850, Huntington Library.
[157]Morgan, Diary, 24 July 1849, Bancroft Library.
[158]Royce, *Across the Plains*, 69.
[159]Woolley, *California*, 7.

presents the most wild, yet beautiful prospect I ever beheld." Cone's train made it through the canyon without losing an ox or breaking a wagon, but it was the worst road he ever saw. "To give a description of this road is out of the question here, as it beggars all description—The dead cattle and horses, the smashed wagons that we find every few rods, are proofs that this is a dangerous pass through the mountain."[160] Thomas Evershed said simply, "Poor McAdam would have wept to see such a road."[161] "If wagons had not gone over this road," wrote Alexander Nixon, "I would have thought it impossible for them to do so."[162]

Beyond the hell-gate, more than one hundred miles of rugged terrain lay between gold seekers and the first diggings at Weber Creek.[163] The Mormon-Carson Emigrant Trail, which is what most gold seekers called the Carson route, "emerged from the cut into a valley quite handsome," Palmer Tiffany wrote. This was the alpine vale the Mormon pioneers had named Hope Valley the year before. High mountain walls, notably the slump-shouldered Elephants Back, which rose a thousand feet above the pass, encircled the head of the valley above Red Lake, "a beautiful lake covering a few hundred acres of land; the mountains which surround this lake are of a reddish cast, the reflection of which gives the water a reddish colour." Red Lake lay at the foot of the precipitous slope leading to Carson Pass. By mid-August the campground was jammed with emigrants. Tiffany found "the entrance to the pass wedged up with trains, both mule and ox"; their teamsters, "whooping and yelling at the top of their voices," covered the infamous slope leading to Carson Pass.[164] The climb was called by some the Devils Ladder and was "the steepest hill for a wagon road I ever saw," Aretas J. Blackman observed.[165]

While camped at Red Lake, William Kelly found the approach to Carson Pass to be as hard on his horse as "climbing a good wall." A companion surveyed the ascent and said, "It was not only right up and down, but leant a little over." The next day, Kelly's company made four difficult climbs up to the pass, first packing over baggage and then hauling their wagons. "We had infinite trouble with the horses here before we could get them to try it, and many of them would have turned back if they dared," he wrote. The animals had good reason to be fearful: a toppled wagon injured a pair of mules, "causing them such torture that death was a relief," and a falling rock killed one of the company's horses.[166]

---

[160]Cone, Journal of Travels, 6, 7 October 1849, BYU Library, 135–37.

[161]Evershed, "The Gold Rush Journal," 5 August 1849, 39.

[162]Nixon, Diary, 6 August 1846, California State Library.

[163]Giles S. Isham's Guide to California and the Mines, 45–47, gave the distance from Pass Creek Canyon to Weber Creek and the Dry Gold Diggins as 105 miles.

[164]Tiffany, Overland Journey, 17 and 18 August 1849, Beinecke Library, 105–106.

[165]Blackman, Journal, 1 August 1849, Bancroft Library. "Here we helped a man up the hill and also eat a first rate cheese," Blackman continued.

[166]Kelly, Excursion to California, 327, 328–29.

"We were half the day at least in getting our waggons the two miles over the mountains, using eight yoke of oxen to do it," wrote Elijah Spooner.[167] "We have to lift our wagons round frequently and make a square tact to the right or left. Many of the places have such perpendicular falls, that, if a mule were thrown off or wagon & team they would fall from 50 to 100 feet without touching anything," reported James Pritchard after climbing Devils Ladder. He watched as a companion sent a wagon wheel rolling down the mountain. "It leaped from one large pile of stone to another," and when the wheel hit the last rock "its velocity was so great, that it bounded with such force that it touched nothing for several hundred yards and in its [a]erial flight it cleared the tops of some of the tallest Pine trees that grow upon the mountains."[168]

"The Mountain itself was sufficient to damp the courage of almost anyone wishing to cross it with a waggon, for the road up its side was so steep and rocky, that it was with difficulty foot men could ascend much less loaded waggons with their teams," wrote Joseph Berrien. A day behind Pritchard, he found wrecked wagons, trunks, axes, gold washers, two sawmill blades, and "articles too numerous to mention" scattered in all directions. "No description I can give would fully portray the difficulty of ascending this mountain or give other than a faint idea of the horrid road up its side," he said. "There were so many stones, rocks, short turns, and trees in the way, that teams could not draw to advantage but were continually falling down and slipping from one side of the road to the other.[169] The hard-driving Banner Company traveled twelve miles over the 8,573-foot Carson Pass, "working our selves and mules almost to Death," wrote Amasa Morgan. No one could appreciate the difficulty of surmounting the Sierra Nevada without trying it. "Eight or ten mules are from one to three hours in ascending it with an emty wagon." He expected to see more of the elephant the next day.[170]

There was a campsite half a mile west of Carson Pass, but most trains descended to Twin Lakes, now dammed to create Caples Lake. Over the brow of the mountain "a scene presented itself to our eyes which was the most lovely and picturesque that a mortal eye ever beheld," wrote Charles Boyle after surmounting the pass. "Before us far down between the mountains, lay a beautiful green valley surrounded by high mountains of bare solid granite of which the lower part was covered by a growth of pine trees while the summits were lightly capped with snow."[171] Parties camped in Lake Valley on 6 August met Lansford W. Hastings, "the same who wrote a book about Cal. and Oregon some years ago. He had come out to meet a

[167]Spooner, Letters and Diary, 19 September 1849, BYU Library, 53.

[168]Pritchard, *The Overland Diary*, 5 August 1849, 132.

[169]Berrien, "Overland from St. Louis," 5 August 1849, 346.

[170]Morgan, Diary, 25 July 1849, Bancroft Library.

[171]Boyle, Diary, 4 August 1849.

brother who was crossing the Plains."[172] James Pritchard's companions told the "very communicative" Hastings they had passed his brother twenty miles above the sink and learned "he would take the Truckey rout."[173] Peter Decker met Hastings and a "Mexican Indian" west of Tragedy Spring. Hastings gave him a flattering account of the mines, saying there was "gold enough for 1000 years in California."[174]

Forty-niners had to cross not only Carson Pass but West Pass, at 9,550 feet the highest elevation any wagon crossed in 1849.[175] From Lake Valley, Amasa Morgan looked up at "one of the grandest mountains we had yet seen whare human beings could think of ascending with wagons." He watched four wagons snaking up the side of Thimble Peak: "It was really a great sight to see these waggons a way up almost in the clouds on this snow at this time in the year." By one o'clock, "we found our selves really perched up on the King of Mountains as tired as ever men was," Morgan wrote. "Now we had no doubt of our being on the Back of elephant. We could see as much as the Devel could in old times."[176]

Some found the second ascent—part of it traversing a glacial snowfield—worse than climbing Devils Ladder. "Eight miles today brot us to the top of the highest mountain and a rocky, sidling, steep hard road it was," commented Elijah Spooner. "We capsized our wagon once, though without much injury."[177] "To describe the difficulties, and dangers of this passage, would consume more time than I have to spare," wrote Gordon Cone, who awoke to six inches of snow in Lake Valley and crossed West Pass during the season's first heavy storm. His party had to double-team most of the way, but a few wagons required twelve yoke of oxen to reach the summit. "Some have smashed their wagons, and others have killed some of their cattle," Cone wrote. "One wagon was overset with a family of children in it, but fortunately none of them were hurt."[178] Joseph Berrien remarked that he had never worked so hard in his life: "From the summit of this mountain we had a very extensive view of the surrounding country to the westward which as far as the eye could reach seemed to be nothing more than a succession of rugged rocky barren looking mountains covered with pine trees and by their appearance discouraging us in a great degree when we brought to mind that our road lay over them."[179]

"Nearly exhausted (men & animals) we reached the top—the highest point of the Sierra Nevada mountains, called the Backbone," Peter Decker wrote after crossing West Pass. "Stopping we looked around & here is a view too magnificently grand &

[172]Nixon, Diary, 7 August 1849, California State Library.
[173]Pritchard, *The Overland Diary*, 6 August 1849, 133–34.
[174]Decker, *The Diaries*, 6 August 1849, 148.
[175]Owens, *Gold Rush Saints*, 159.
[176]Morgan, Diary, 26 July 1849, Bancroft Library.
[177]Spooner, Letters and Diary, 21 September 1849, BYU Library, 53.
[178]Cone, Journal of Travels, 10 October 1849, BYU Library, 141.
[179]Berrien, "Overland from St. Louis," 6 August 1849, 347.

wildly romantic for me to attempt to describe."[180] The artist James Wilkins thought "the scenery is sublime, *vastness* being the great feature to express in a picture of it. Here on the very summit of the back bone of the American continent (and back bone of the Elephant as the emigrants call it) we were favored with a storm of hail, rain, and sleet. The wind blew icy cold." The wild weather was not the most dramatic event Wilkins's companions experienced on the roof of the Sierra: "To add to our difficulties the lady in our company was taken with the pangs of labour, and we had to descend as quickly as possible over a most rocky road, to the first grass, which we did not reach till an hour after dark." The wagon almost pitched over several times—Wilkins could not understand how the woman stood the jolting. He hastily pitched his tent to shelter her, and "before morning she was delivered of a little girl, without any of those little luxuries, nay without the common necessities usually had on such occasions by the very poorest classes." The new mother was an Englishwoman, "just from London, and moving in a pretty good sphere of life, but through the improvidence of her husband now reduced and penniless," Wilkins reported. Two days later, after the company rested briefly and moved on, the woman was "doing *as well as could be expected* under the circumstances."[181]

Today Stonebreaker Grade and the Mormon-Carson Emigrant Trail Road follow the trail along Iron Mountain Ridge, and Highway 88 crosses Carson Pass through one of the most magnificent landscapes in the United States. The trail beyond West Pass followed the hogback of "a long ridge that commanded a fine view of these American Alps." It crossed the gorge of Rock Valley and made a steep climb to Tragedy Spring, where the road-blazing Mormons had discovered the bodies of three murdered scouts. Wagons then headed west and northwest, tracing the crest of Iron Mountain Ridge, the divide between the American and Cosumnes River drainages, to campsites at Leek Spring, Camp Creek, Sly Park, and on to the trail's end at Pleasant Valley, Weberville, and Hangtown (now Placerville). "In a word," wrote Peter Decker as he crossed the ridge during a long afternoon, "the scenery was varied & beautiful."[182] A few gold seekers were too tired to appreciate the view. "The road presented the same dreary monotony of Stony Hillsides and Rocky Ridges covered with Emmense Pine tress (some of them 10 feet in diameter and at least 200 feet high) through which we were obliged to thread our tedious way," said Joseph Berrien. "Our road generally lay along the top of a ridge and beneath us on each side we could look down in immense rocky chasms rugged desolate and bare of everything in the shape of vegetation except the tall pines before mentioned which looked like reeds so great was their distance beneath us."[183]

---

[180]Decker, *The Diaries,* 5 August 1849, 146.

[181]Wilkins, *An Artist on the Overland Trail,* 28 September 1849, 76–77.

[182]Decker, *The Diaries,* 5 and 6 August 1849, 146, 149; Owens, "The Mormon-Carson Emigrant Trail," 16–17.

[183]Berrien, "Overland from St. Louis," 7 August 1849, 347.

"The grass here is exceedingly scanty," James Wilkins complained, "not picking enough for a mountain goat."[184] As William Kelly reported, the first companies turned up occasional "tufts of grass growing in the chinks of the rock," along with hidden pockets of lush grass and clover that were "fitter for the scythe than browsing." But the forested slopes of the eastern Sierra foothills were already "so parched and burned up" they were picked clean of forage.[185] Peter Decker went three miles from the road "over hill & through narrow defiles winding among bushes &c difficult passes even for packed animals" to find "a fine piece of grass like a meadow where we found hundreds of animals."[186] In August Palmer Tiffany found excellent grass near the passes, but when the last companies passed a month later, it was gone. "Tall timber, tall mountains, and large rocks have been the order of the day," Tiffany wrote near Tragedy Spring. "Indeed everything has been too tall except the grass, which by the by has been a little too short for our cattle."[187] Lake Valley was the only place in the high country "where grass has ever grown," wrote Gordon Cone, "but at this time there is none of any account, so our cattle are doomed to fare hard." After crossing West Pass late in the season, Cone recounted, "[we] chained up our cattle to spend another night without anything to eat, after a hard days work—This is hard fare, but it cannot be avoided, as there is no grass, nor anything on which they can browse." The next day, he turned his oxen loose to browse on willows in Rock Valley and made camp early after finding grass on the side of the mountain. As he descended to the foothills, Cone found "some grass in spots, thinly scattered over the sides of some of the hills," but on reaching the mines he learned there was "no grass along through this region, and report says that we shall not find any for eighty miles"; the Central Valley's hot and arid summer, combined with the starving animals flooding over the Sierra, had consumed all the range.[188] "Grass scarce since crossing the mountains," wrote Edmund Booth late in the season. "Tonight cut down oak trees for the animals to feed on the leaves."[189]

"We are now in the gold region, and beyond all danger from snows on the mountains," Cone wrote near Pleasant Valley. "The climate is warm, and the atmosphere is balmy—The weather is fine, clear, and the prospect around us very beautiful."[190] From their last camp on the trail, Charles Boyle and the survivors of the Columbus and California Industrial Association could see the "light of the numerous watch fires, visible all around the valley—the frequent firing of guns

---

[184]Wilkins, *An Artist on the Overland Trail,* 28 September 1849, 77.

[185]Kelly, *Excursion to California,* 330, 336.

[186]Decker, *The Diaries,* 6 August 1849, 149.

[187]Tiffany, Overland Journey, 20 August 1849, Beinecke Library, 108.

[188]Cone, Journal of Travels, 9–11, 13 October 1849, BYU Library, 140, 143, 145, 151.

[189]Booth, *Edmund Booth (1810–1905), Forty-niner,* 12 October 1849, 16.

[190]Cone, Journal of Travels, 16 October 1849, BYU Library, 155.

and the whooping of the persons engaged in herding the animals all combined, made quite a wild, strange and romantic scene." Two carts and four wagons, all that remained of ten wagons that had left Ohio, got an early start, and at noon the party stopped to hunt for gold. At the Weber Creek diggings, "we met Mexicans, Chileans, Peruvians, Indians and a few Americans," Boyle noted. "We did not stay long but proceeded on to the next dry diggings, four or five miles, where we landed before dark." Boyle and his friends camped under the spreading branches of a beautiful oak tree, where a few houses marked the beginnings of a settlement. "We soon learned that this was the gallows tree as three men were hanged upon it six months before for robbery and murder after a fair trial by a jury of miners, as has been the custom in this country." Boyle had landed at Hangtown, where Tommy Davis found two specks of gold. "We lay down under the tree thinking of our homes and our present situation and the thousand other things which would naturally crowd upon the mind," wrote Dr. Boyle, "and fell asleep."[191]

Our Last Tremendous Summit: Donner Pass

Having crossed the last desert on their journey, Forty-niners who took the old California Trail faced Truckee Pass, now Donner Pass. After navigating the river's twisting canyon and its twenty-seven crossings, they had to avoid the swamps of Truckee Meadows, cross a barren plain, and ford the river again. They used what Isaac Wistar called "a rough and rocky, but at first not very steep ravine" to climb out of the valley that now shelters Reno.[192] It was a long, difficult trek for either man or mule, about forty miles from Truckee Meadows to Donner Pass and another eighty-three miles to Johnsons Ranch, the traditional end of the California Trail. After fording the Truckee for the last time near today's Verdi, the trail "commenced the ascent of the first summit of the mountain." Joseph Wood and a partner found the hill was "long and steep and we labored to get up. Our packs began to feel quite heavy and we frequently stopped to rest." From the top, the splendid prospect of Dog Valley was almost worth the trouble of the ascent of what others called "the first mountain."[193] Ansel McCall thought the trail crossed "the sweetest valley mortal eye ever rested upon. It was four and a half miles in width, as level as a floor, and completely embosomed by green hills sweeping up from their base a thousand feet, densely covered with pines, cyprus, and cedars." Wagons climbed out of Dog Valley over a second summit, forded Prosser Creek,

---

[191]Boyle, Diary, 11 August 1849.

[192]Wistar, *Autobiography*, 18 August 1849, 110.

[193]Wood, Diary, 27 August 1849, Huntington Library; Howard, "California Correspondence," 25 April 1850, in Perkins, *Gold Rush Diary*, 180.

"a beautiful mountain stream," and dropped into Stampede Valley "over a very good road for a mountain road." After the desolation of the Great Basin's deserts, the evergreens and plentiful game delighted Augustus Burbank: "The country over which we have passed is clothed with a heavy forest & is highly elevated, with occasionally a valley. Some grass & small streams."[194]

Another hard pull brought travelers to "the foot of Truckee Lake. I went up this evening to view the lake—it's a romantic sheet, lined on all sides by the highest mountains in America, apparently deep and remarkably clear, with a pebbly shore, except a strip on the south side," wrote Thomas Van Dorn. "The mountains surrounding it heavily timbered with pine and the dark green reflected from them—gave to this water a deeper hue than any I have seen. Near the foot, or within half a mile, are the remains of the fated Donner party."[195] A surprising number of gold seekers described visiting what they often called the cannibal camp, the ruins of the shanties on Alder Creek and Donner Lake. They told grotesque tales: Edward McIlhany "stopped at the cabins at the foot of the Sierra Nevada mountains where the Donovan party perished in '46. There were several cabins. The roofs had rotted and fallen in and the stumps were twenty feet high where they stood on the snow to get wood to make a fire to keep them from freezing. The ground was covered with human bones, still there."[196]

"We saw many stumps of trees which were cut by this party from eight to twelve feet from the ground to the place where they were cut on the snows," James Abell reported.[197] Nothing remained standing at the lake camp "but the square enclosures with patches of newspaper hanging to the logs on the inside" to keep out the cold. Scattered shreds of dresses, scraps of jeans, and "bones of all descriptions, human & other" surrounded the ruins. "Twas a most melancholy & gloomy spot," Elisha Perkins wrote, "& the imagination could find full scope in the indications of human suffering scattered around. I gathered some relics as curiosities & left, thankful that late as my journey had been prolonged, I was still safe from any such catastrophe as befell these unfortunates."[198] Elisha Lewis found the ruins "an affecting sight. Around the cabins were strune the bones of the once living man or woman which had been boiled the flesh of which to serve for the sustenance of those living. Childrens shoes and fragments of garments were also scatered around the Mountainous primices." The next day Lewis discovered a pair of roughly made snowshoes and "the bones of some one who had perished

---

[194]McCall, *The Great California Trail,* in Fey, King, and Lepisto, *Emigrant Shadows,* 83; Burbank, Diary, 10 September 1849, Bancroft Library.

[195]Van Dorn, Diary, 3 September 1849, Beinecke Library, 42.

[196]McIlhany, *Recollections,* 27.

[197]Abell, Journal, 31 August 1849, Minnesota Historical Society.

[198]Perkins, *Gold Rush Diary,* 15 September 1849, 130.

in the mountains"—perhaps the heroic Charles Stanton. "We took the scull and continued our march toward the summit."[199]

For William Graves of the Pittsburgh and California Enterprise Company, the valley where he had spent the winter in 1846 evoked hard memories. Graves, a Donner party survivor, avoided "any conversation about his misfortune" when he spoke to Wakeman Bryarly. "Graves started off without saying anything to them, & did not [re]join them until after they had passed. He preferred viewing the place of his unprecedented suffering alone, not wishing that the eye of unsympathising man should be a witness to his harrowed feelings."[200] Bryarly was wrong: Graves had actually gone hunting with John Markle and had shown him around the two camps. The Graves and Foster cabins, noted Markle, "[are] the only ones that are standing yet and they present a gloomy appearance."[201]

Edward Jackson called the granite ramparts of the Sierra Nevada "our last tremendous summit."[202] The approach to Donner Pass was "over the worst road we have seen yet, and Commenced ascending the dividing ridge of the California Mountains. The road was filled with large rocks which seemed impossible for wagons to pass over," William Z. Walker wrote. "The emigrants now all double their teams which make slow progress over a road almost perpendicular in ascent."[203] The road took John T. McCarty "over rocks, rugged mountains, down precipices and long steep hills, where ninety-nine out of every hundred in the states would swear a wagon could never go." The ascent was "extremely difficult—took twelve or fifteen yoke of cattle to draw up the lightest loaded wagon."[204]

Forty-niners used two roads to scramble over the crest of the Sierra—Donner Pass, which Elisha Stephens's party opened in 1844; and Roller Pass, first used in 1846. "These mountains are mountains in good earnest, and very difficult to pass over, being very steep in ascent and descent and many places so near perpendicular and so rocky that we were compelled to take the teams from the wagons and let them down by ropes," John Prichet reported.[205] Thomas Van Dorn's party set out to cross Roller Pass, "the hog-back of Creation, being a wall of granite near 1000 feet above the surrounding region." It was evident "a great deal of work has been done by the emigrants in ascending the great ridge. Where the old track went up, it would have been impossible to get a waggon up with all the oxen in the train, for it would be quite all they could do to get themselves," he wrote. "The road is

[199]Lewis, Overland to California, 16–18 September 1849, Beinecke Library.

[200]Bryarly, Trail to California, 21 August 1849, 201–202.

[201]Markle, Diary, 20 August 1849, Bancroft Library.

[202]Jackson, Journal, 6 September 1849, BYU Library, 87.

[203]Walker, Diary, 6 September 1849, BYU Library, 129–30.

[204]McCarty, "A Letter from John T. M'Carty," 30 November 1849, Indiana American, 8 February 1850, Bieber Collection.

[205]Pritchet, "A Letter from California," 17 January 1850, Mattes Library.

now improved and takes a slanting shute up the ridge, so that with 8 or 12 yoke on each waggon, we made the summit with safety and without difficulty and not taking out any part of our loading, tho this is now but little exertion." Van Dorn's train felt as if they "had achieved a victory, having today completed the great work of making the pass over the Sierra Nevadas."[206]

Having surmounted the backbone, many thought their troubles were over. While his mules rested, Isaac Wistar climbed to the top of a nearby peak. "It was bitterly cold, but from the almost pointed summit, the grandeur and wild, confused desolation of the prospect was sublime indeed. North, east and south, peak rose beyond peak in endless succession while in the west the eye looked far down into a chasm where every ravine and gorge shone and glistened with the spotless white of vast snow fields," he recalled. "Beyond, instead of the expected Sacramento Valley, nothing broke the magnificent expanse of the mountain chains."[207]

To make matters worse, the High Sierra was an arsonist's paradise. "We amused our selves this evening, by setting dead trees on fire, which are from 75 to 100 ft high and the fire streamed far above their tops. The sight is magnificent and the fire roars like a tempest," Edward Jackson wrote. "Three of them burnt all night."[208] Others failed to enjoy the spectacle: "I am sorry to see the careless destruction of timber in this noble forest," railed Edward Harrow. "The fools, whoever they are, fire the roots or bottoms of the largest trees they can find. The fire when once applied will burn for days, probably weeks or months until all within its reach is consumed." Harrow had scarcely passed a large burning pine tree "when it fell with an awful crash across my very path, the public road," he said. "This practice not only makes the road dangerous, it delays wagon trains considerable, and that too when time is precious."[209]

Getting down proved to be even more difficult than making the hard climb to the summit. "The western descent of these mountains is the most rugged and difficult portion of the whole journey," warned T. H. Jefferson.[210] "The western slope of the Sierra is rough beyond description. The mountain breaks off in immense granite ridges from the main summit," wrote D. B. Wood. "Streams heading in near the main divide, plunge down impassable Kanyons" and made "fierce and terrific descents you would not deem it possible for wagons to pass. This rough country continues some 10 miles from the summit."[211] The trail to the pass was bad, Lucius Fairchild wrote, but the rest was "the most *damnable* road on the face of the earth," filled with rocks "from the size of a teakettle up to that of a hogshead,

[206]Van Dorn, Diary, 4 September 1849, Beinecke Library, 42.

[207]Wistar, *Autobiography,* 19 August 1849, 112–13.

[208]Jackson, Journal, 7 September 1849, BYU Library, 90.

[209]Harrow, *Gold Rush Overland Journal,* 20 August 1849, 62.

[210]Jefferson, *Map of the Emigrant Road,* Part 4.

[211]Wood to "Dear Judge," 13 September 1849; "From California," *Indiana American,* 7 December 1849.

over which we were obliged to drive, or rather lift the wagons." All in all, Fairchild considered it "the most miserable, gloomy road on earth" and was a little surprised to survive the trek: "one would swear that a wagon could not be driven over and God only knows how we did get through—but we did."[212] Having crossed the summit, Isaac Wistar's party expected "a short, easy down-hill road, but we were rudely disappointed, finding ourselves involved in a wild labyrinth of mountains and chasms, with no visible way out." His train spent an entire day "in the hardest labor, dragging the wagons over rocky ledges, and hoisting and lowering them over 'jump-offs' by 'Spanish windlasses' and other mechanical means." At dark they looked into "a deep, rocky gorge with impassable precipices on either hand. Without knowing what might be at the bottom, we undertook to get the wagons down over the huge boulders which choked the gorge."[213]

The trail crossed Summit Valley, studded with small alpine lakes and a thick forest. "My mistake was that I said I had seen 'The Elephant' when getting over the first mountain," wrote Wakeman Bryarly. "I had only seen the tail. This evening I think I saw him in toto." He concluded, "no Elephant upon this route can be so large that another cannot be larger. If I had not seen wagon tracks marked upon the rocks, I should not have known where the road was, nor could I have imagined that any wagon and team could possibly pass over in safety."[214] The trail traced a granite ridge past the lakes and dropped from the valley's southwest corner through a narrow ravine to the canyon of the Yuba River. From Cold Springs the road followed a route John Markle called "indescribable, but it was the damn-dest, roughest and rockyest road I ever saw." He recalled, "We had to take out our mules and let our wagons down with ropes and it was off of one rock onto another all day."[215] The roads were precipitous, up and down, crooked and rocky beyond description, Joseph Wood wrote. He saw trees "worn half down where wagons had been let down by a rope wound around them."[216] To reach the Yuba, Thomas Van Dorn used roads "such as would hardly be believed possible for waggons to have passed over." One morning his company "found the elephant, or at least others thought so and left the animal figured out on a board in fair style. This point was a descent over a ledge of rock some 30 feet—*not quite perpendicular*—our cattle taken around by a narrow passage and our waggons let down by ropes."[217]

The road through Bear Valley was dreadful: "It looks as if some ugly rascal had been heaping up stones on purpose to pitch the wagon of the New Yorkers and

[212]Fairchild, *California Letters*, 26 September and 13 October 1849, 34, 36.
[213]Wistar, *Autobiography*, 21 August 1849, 113.
[214]Bryarly, *Trail to California*, 24 August 1849, 205.
[215]Markle, Diary, 23 August 1849, Bancroft Library.
[216]Wood, Diary, 29 August 1849, Huntington Library.
[217]Van Dorn, Diary, 7 September 1849, Beinecke Library, 43, 44.

Virginians & jerk their oxen out fits," Cyrus Sumner reported.[218] The trail left the Yuba River near Cisco Butte, crossed Carpenter Flat past Crystal Lake, and after winding along a narrow hogback made a sharp decent into Bear Valley at Emigrant Gap, where wagons again had to slide down a precipitous slope. "Sometimes, to get the waggons down, we cut a tree and tie it to the back part of a waggon & ease it down, sometimes, we tie a rope to the back and give it a turn or two around a tree then all take hold and ease it down as slowly as possible," wrote Edward Jackson. To reach Bear River, he "came to the Father of all hills," which "required all sort of manouvering to get the waggons down. The log chain to one of them, broke, and it rolled over three times, smashing every thing to pieces." To make matters worse, as Jackson made camp, a mule stepped on a hornet's nest.[219]

Whichever way his party went, Henry Tappan said, "at the foot of almost every Steep we find the remains of broken Yankee Wagons."[220] Beyond Emigrant Gap, one leg of the trail briefly touched the north fork of the American River while the main branch climbed Lowell Hill Ridge to Deadmans Flat. Now the road faced its last great challenge, Steep Hollow Creek. "One place was a quarter of a mile de[s]cent," Abner Blackburn found in 1847. "The waggons that proceded us were rough locked and [had] young pine trees tied behind the waggons and then slid down to the bottom."[221] When John Banks saw the hollow, the trees stacked at the bottom resembled a woodyard.[222] Samuel Mathews saw wrecked wagons at Steep Hollow smashed against the woodpile at the foot of "that dreaded descent": "Sometimes they rested against that tree, sometimes they turned from the track and capsized, and when a wagon performed that motion on that hill, it performed it thoroughly. It did not stop till it came down on the bows and cover, with the wheels whirling in 'mid air.'" Mathews "saw one ox literally torn to pieces."[223]

Besides the Truckee route's bone-crushing physical challenges, "There was no grass in the mountains and canons," recalled Edward McIlhany. "We had to cut down trees for the mules to get food from the leaves and bark." Men picked up their axes and began felling trees as soon as they reached camp, while others unharnessed the teams. The starving mules immediately ran to the trees "and commence[d] stripping them of their bark ravenously." The mules soon associated the sound

---

[218]Sumner, Letters from Uncle Cyrus, Bancroft Library. Trail markers laid out in the 1920s led generations of historians (including this one) to believe a third trail crossed Coldstream Pass between Donner and Roller passes. After surveying General Land Office maps and notes, all known primary sources, and the terrain itself, trails sleuth Don Wiggins found no evidence emigrants ever used the route. Roller Pass was the main road "from its opening in September of 1846 until at least 1855." See Buck, Where Did Emigrants Surmount the Sierra Nevada on the Truckee Trail?

[219]Jackson, Journal, 7, 8 September 1849, BYU Library, 89–91.

[220]Tappan, "The Gold Rush Diary," 5 September 1849, 137.

[221]Blackburn, Frontiersman, 103.

[222]Armstrong and Banks, The Buckeye Rovers, 90.

[223]Mathews to "Friend Gray," 7 October 1849, in Mathews, Mathews Family, 312–13.

of an ax with such rough forage, "and they commenced braying for their food all through the herd."[224] Edward Jackson stopped one night on Bear River with "no grass and hardly a spot free from rocks and large enough to camp upon."[225] Joseph Hackney complained his cattle were "getting very weak as they have had nothing to eat but oak leaves for the last two days and traveled over the worst roads that ever a wagon came over." Below Steep Hollow, the road followed the Bear River through rolling foothills to the trail's end at Johnsons Ranch in the Sacramento Valley, near today's Wheatland. On the way, Hackney saw "the prosess of gold working a going on" as miners washed dirt from a rich stream. Hackney and his friends "got out our pans and went at it and washed out half a dollars worth in [no] time, the first money I ever made out of the land."[226] He had found El Dorado.

WE BROKE THE WAY:
THE FIRST FORTY-NINERS REACH THE GOLDFIELDS

After surviving a hard crossing of Carson Pass, Edmund Green's pack train met a party of Indians "quite well dressed in new clothes" who showed them a pouch of gold. The Natives pointed to the valley and told the newcomers, perhaps the first overlanders to reach the goldfields, that they would find "plenty oro and plenty white man" there. Ten miles down the road on 21 July 1849, the packers heard a cowbell: "Never did we hear a more welcome sound," Green remembered, "for we realized we were nearing civilization." Needing supplies and longing for mail, the men headed for Sutters Fort, "the Mecca of all Americans." Green found the city of Sacramento consisted of two buildings—both stores; the rest "was composed of tents. I continued on through the town until I came to the bank of the Sacramento, being the first emigrant in '49 to stand on tidewater."[227]

Many claimed to have brought the first wagon over the Sierra and into Sacramento in 1849, but the titleholder will never be identified with certainty. "Emigrants from Missouri, over the mountains, are now arriving daily," a 24 July letter said. "The first party of packers has been here five or six days, and reports four wagons in Pleasant Valley, about 100 miles above, and five or six thousand wagons on the way and not far behind."[228] Miles Goodyear's "first company of adventurers" was in Sacramento by about 21 July. When David Cosad arrived at the dry diggings

---

[224]McIlhany, *Recollections*, 29–30.

[225]Jackson, Journal, 7 September 1849, BYU Library, 90.

[226]Hackney, Journal, 11 September 1849, *Wagons West*, 191.

[227]Green, "Recollections," 9According to the *Placer Times*, 21 July 1849, 2/2, seven men "arrived at the Dry Diggings on the 14th [of July] having left the Missouri on the 5th of May. Among them are Dr. J. H. Dickson of Pa. and E. Green of Michigan."

[228]*Missouri Republican*, 24 September 1849, in Morgan, "Miles Goodyear," 329n47.

(soon to be Placerville) on 25 July, he became the first overland journal keeper to reach the mines in 1849. All these men, except perhaps Goodyear, had come over Carson Pass. Edwin Bryant's pack train would not reach Johnsons Ranch from the Truckee until 3 August, "after a long & very fatiguing journey of about 85 days."[229]

William Johnston maintained his wagons arrived on 24 July 1849, "in the lead of the overland emigration of this memorable year," due to the determination, "superior judgment and never tiring energy" of his captain, Jim Stewart, "to place our train in the lead of all others."[230] A letter from another Pittsburgh boy shows the train actually reached Sacramento five days later: "We arrived here all safe on Sunday morning 29 July in exactly three months from Independence," wrote Joseph Moody from that "flourishing place of some 300 Canvass Houses." When his party "left the Regular trail" at the Sublette Cutoff, "there were but three trains a head of us; having passed all we came in sight of, some 800 Wagons or more." At City of Rocks, "we found some 70 wagons a head of us." Like Johnston, Moody blamed the long detour for his loss of the race. "We had the trouble of again passing the trains a head of us and succeeded in getting the 10th Wagon in to the Valley of Sacramento. Since then they have been coming in daily." Moody said "a great many left their wagons and packed through." He did "not know of one mess that came across here the Same as they left the States."[231]

James Gooding's Banner Company broke up near the diggings on 28 July, having heard there were only twenty wagons ahead of them. "Our actual traveling time is 68 Days and laid bye 12," wrote Amasa Morgan, who thought the eighty-day crossing was probably better "than any will be able to make the journey with wagons this year."[232] John Blair apparently traveled with Morgan. "We arrived last of July in good health with out the loss of much property or any of our company. Our trip was a short one considering the distance, [and] to me a pleasant one. To many I fear it is the reverse," he wrote home. Blair credited his party's success to their early start and to "cracking ahead," which gave them the advantage of the best grass and the least dust: "From Green River to Ft. Hall we broke the way, after which a few mule teams overtook us and then there was racing and chacing o'er the Sierra Nevada. The most of them 'caved in,' a few however lightened their loads and beat us by a day or two. Our company which left St. Jo together stuck together till the end of the journey."[233]

William Kelly claimed his party reached a large encampment of Chilean, Mexican, and American miners near Weber Creek on 26 July—"at least four days too

[229]See Dale L. Morgan's analysis in Pritchard, *The Overland Diary,* 25–26, 163n71.

[230]Johnston, *Experiences of a Forty-niner,* 234–35.

[231]Moody to "My Dear Father," 7 August 1849, "An 1849 Letter from California," 84–85.

[232]Morgan, Diary, 28 July 1849, Bancroft Library.

[233]Blair to "Dear Brothers and Sisters," 19 August 1849, Mattes Library.

WILLIAM P. COLEMAN OF THE
"TELEGRAPH TRAIN," CIRCA 1854
Kentuckian William P. Coleman came to California in
1849 as a teamster with Harry Brolaski's "Telegraph
Train," which made the trek in ninety days—"an
unusually rapid and prosperous journey." He started an
outfitting company in Sacramento, and as a banker and
merchant prince, Coleman became one of the richest
men in California. (W. P. should not be confused with
fellow Forty-niner William Tell Coleman, leader of the
1856 vigilante movement.) Courtesy California History
Room, California State Library, Sacramento.

early," as Dale Morgan noted. Whatever the engaging Irishman lacked in precision
he made up for with great storytelling. "Although not absolutely in the Valley of
Sacramento, we now regarded our great journey as accomplished," he wrote, having taken 102 days, "including stoppages," to cross 2,043 miles. Kelly marveled that
a company made up of strangers of different nationalities and religions could take
wagons over such barren and trackless wastes, through "tribes of savage Indians,"
across swollen rivers, burning deserts, and over the giddy heights of frightful precipices without a serious misunderstanding. What had been a mere trail was now a
great thoroughfare. The vanguard companies had "to make corduroy roads across
morasses, dig away river banks, cut down and remove obstacles, construct rude
bridges, force paths through craggy canons, smooth the ascent of escalades, ford
and ferry over broad and rapid rivers, where ferries have since been established, and
carry provisions for the whole route," Kelly proclaimed, ignoring the key advantage
the advance companies enjoyed—an abundance of feed for their animals. "What
to us was a journey of perpetual doubt, difficulty, toil, and danger," he wrote, "can
now be only properly designated as one of weariness and occasional privation."[234]

Having arrived at the forefront of the Forty-niners, Vital Jarrot trembled after
using a pick and shovel all day but picked up his pen to write to the man caring
for his wife. The wagons of his Saint Clair Mining Company were among the
first to reach the Sacramento Valley. "Men are arriving daily in squads, wretched
in their appearance from the hardships of the trip," he reported. Only eighteen
wagons were ahead of his party, and most of their owners had abandoned three
or four wagons on the way. The mysterious G. W. Paul's carriage arrived in July

---

[234]Kelly, *Excursion to California,* 339–41; Pritchard, *The Overland Diary,* 190.

1849—perhaps as early as the twentieth of July, but probably not until a few days later—making it the first wheeled vehicle to reach Sutters Fort. Paul may have been first, but he started with three or four wagons and "left them all and arrived here in a lone Buggy," Jarrot wrote, adding that all five of *his* wagons had completed the journey. Having reached the mines on 1 August with all his freight, he predicted no one else would equal his accomplishment: "Now the grass is so eaten off that I do not believe one waggon out of 50 will reach here and not one half of the animals; and I fear that hundreds of persons will perish on the deserts." Reports of the desperate straits of many overland Argonauts poured in from all points. Jarrot was perfectly satisfied with his prospects of acquiring wealth in "the long looked for California mines," but the death of a young friend within days of reaching El Dorado poisoned the promise of his accumulating fortune. "I sometimes wish I had never come to California," he wrote. "It is no trouble to make money here, but it is work to keep it."[235]

For some, the wondrous spectacle of the gold country proved disappointing. "There is plenty of gold here but it is not near what we expected," wrote Joshua D. Breyfogle. "A great many are troubled with the blues and talk of going home."[236] One of Jarrot's youngest companions agreed. "Had I but known the half I have endured before starting, not all the gold in California would have make me undertake it," said Louis Tremble. "We were the first to cross the desert this summer, and it is impossible to imagine how much suffering will be experienced here by the thousands behind us." He reached the gold diggings on 1 August after 104 days on the road. "It is a wonder to me that people get along as smoothly as they do, for not having established rules to go by, everything goes off in a hurry, yet peacefully," he remarked. Yet every other house in Sacramento was "a drinking house—and to each of such are connected one or two monte banks, a roulette, a faro bank too. Gaming of every description and on the most expensive scale is going on in every part of this young and thriving city. Men bet thousands upon a single card, and as coolly lose or win it as if it were a dime." Despite his feeble health, Tremble found work and board with a San Francisco newspaper at fifty dollars a week, but 104 days after reaching the mines, this respected and gifted young writer died of dysentery.[237]

---

[235]Jarrot to Charles Tillman, 23 August 1849, Missouri Historical Society.

[236]Breyfogle, Diary, 12 August 1849, 23.

[237]Tremble to Miles, 6, 18 August 1849, *Illinois Republican,* 1 and 23 January 1850, Mattes Library.

CHAPTER 5

Shortcuts to Death

Cutoffs, Detours, and Delusion in 1849

By the first of September 1849, no more than a third of the emigrants who had set out for California had reached the goldfields. Those who fell behind faced grim prospects. "There are fearful apprehensions by many persons here about the emigrants, who are some distance back; it is believed that at least one third of the wagons can't possibly get here in consequence of grass being bad in many places," wrote D. H. Moss from Sacramento.[1] "If the emigrants do not get this side of the California mountains before the last of October," Edward Murphy predicted, "it is very doubtful whether they will be able to get through this winter."[2] The grass was gone, "and God only knows how the last trains can get along," Alonzo Delano observed. "Many with families of little children are suffering, and those behind on the Humboldt must suffer severely if not perish."[3] On the despised river, "men were left dead & dying, uncared for, for nearly all were weak and starving and all fearing to share the same fate," Edmund Booth told his wife.[4]

As the human tide reached the Black Rock Desert in mid-August, a strange dynamic drew most of the emigration onto the Lassen Trail and its imagined shortcut to the mines. This was a costly mistake for a third of the Forty-niners, but it relieved pressure on the routes across the Forty-mile Desert. Similar forces inspired other alternatives, as when fear of meeting the fate of the Donner party encouraged perhaps a thousand adventurous folk to try a southwestern trace from the City of the Saints to the City of the Angels. Only a single wagon had tried the trail in 1848, but the following year's experiment left behind a wagon road and gave Death Valley its name. Even the Hastings Cutoff, whose evil reputation after the Donner debacle should have ended its use, saw its heaviest travel in 1849 and

---

[1]Moss, 14 October 1849, in Wyman, *California Emigrant Letters*, 65.
[2]Murphy, letter, 2 September 1849, "Letters from California," *Missouri Whig*, 29 November 1849.
[3]Delano, *California Correspondence*, 13 September 1849, 18.
[4]Booth to "Dear Mary Ann," 3 November 1850, in *Edmund Booth (1810–1905), Forty-niner*, 31.

1850, after which no wagon ever used it again. These variants had few advantages, and none saved distance or time, but they all provided choices that reduced the devastating impact emigrants and their animals had on western grasslands.

At Goose Creek in early August, Edward Jackson found "the valley would be beautiful, were it not that the immense emigration that has gone before us has camped on every foot of ground which gives it the appearance of a Boston common after a 4th of July." Ironically, Peter Lassen's terrible road attracted enough travelers to make the old road a better choice. By the time Jackson reached Truckee River and the old California Trail, the detours to Lassens Ranch and Carson River had absorbed most of the traffic on the road. "The two cut-offs which so many have taken had made the grass on the regular road very good," Jackson noted. "My motto is, 'Never forsake an old for a new.'"[5]

The revolution of 1849 remade the road west, but the transformation of the trail in that extraordinary year was part of an ongoing, organic evolution. The trail grew as relentlessly as cheatgrass, developing entirely new trunk lines like the Cherokee Trail, which connected Fort Bridger with Fort Smith, Arkansas. Wagon travelers sought out new paths around apparently insurmountable obstacles such as the trackless deserts of the Great Basin or the ramparts of the Sierra Nevada. It is a dramatic story, an adventure that exacted a telling cost from anyone who answered the Siren's call of a cutoff to El Dorado. In the face of what looked like an inevitable catastrophe, a remarkable effort by the military government and the people of California—an astonishing example of frontier compassion toward those who had dallied too long or had taken too many purported shortcuts—averted total disaster. Singular acts of benevolence saved hundreds, perhaps thousands, including the most rugged of the individualists who owed their lives to the generosity and cooperative effort of a newborn community, from starving in the desert or freezing in the mountain passes.

To Apprise the Prairie Traveler of a New Road:
The Cherokee Trail

Forty-niners who reached Fort Bridger at the end of July met one of the most notable wagon trains ever to cross the plains. On 24 April 1849, some 130 Arkansans and Cherokees calling themselves the Washington County Gold Mining Company left the salt works on the Grand Saline in the Cherokee Nation with forty wagons to join the scramble to California. A few of its members were veterans of the 1828 rush to the mines of northern Georgia, whose discovery precipitated the removal

---

[5]Jackson, Journal, 8 August, 3 September 1849, BYU Library.

of the Cherokee Nation from the Great Smoky Mountains to today's Oklahoma along a path of suffering now known as the Trail of Tears. The party included five slaves and about ten free blacks. Under the leadership of Lewis Evans, the company blazed a trail north across what became Oklahoma to the Santa Fe Trail east of today's McPherson, Kansas. Here Hiram Davis reported the train "obtained a large stone and planted it in the fork of the road; and one of our cunning workmen cut these letters upon it, 'To Fayetteville, Arkansas, three hundred miles—Captain Evans' California Company, May 12, 1849,' to appraise the prairie traveler of a new road."[6] Later travelers called the trail the Evans Road, partly because an 1850 party had a copy of his journal, but also due to the California Company's memorialization of its trailblazing.

The train climbed the Arkansas River to the trapper's post at Pueblo to join the Trappers Trail, an "indistinct Waggon trail, made by some Traders," that already connected Fort Laramie with New Mexico. About 150 miles north of Pueblo, the company built a ferry "large enough to carry the largest of our wagons without unloading them" to cross the Platte below the mouth of the Cache la Poudre River. The party had to "make our own road, without road, trail or guide through the plains" of today's northwest Colorado and southwest Wyoming. They followed the Cache la Poudre "thro' the mountains to Laramie Plains; thence crossed Laramie river near the mountains, crossed Medicine Bow river, crossed Medicine Bow Mountains; crossed the North Park and North Platt, Green river, south of the South Pass, and intersected the Independence road on Blacks Fork, about 14 miles west of Green River," as New Yorker Oliver Wack Lipe described the route for the *Cherokee Advocate*. Probably following Frémont's map of his 1843 trek, thirty wagons blazed a road to the North Platte River near present Rawlins, Wyoming, crossing the Continental Divide Basin and the Red Desert along the general line of Interstate 80 in southern Wyoming. Evans's train joined the Oregon-California Trail near today's Granger, thirty-six miles east of Fort Bridger.[7]

The Cherokee wagons were the first to cross the Continental Divide by any route other than South Pass. The knowledge that such an alternative existed was not new. William Ashley's fur trade packers used much of it in 1824, and three years later, an anonymous mountaineer—perhaps Jim Bridger himself—suggested leaving the South Platte at Lodgepole Creek to cross the Rockies. Heading directly east from Green River, this route would ascend "the valley of the Bitter Creek, thence crossing the north fork of the Platte near the Medicine Bow mountain, and the Laramie River in Laramie plains. It would cross the Sherman Hills country, and

---

[6] Bieber, *Southern Trails to California,* 333–39. For best collection of Cherokee Trail sources, see Fletcher, Fletcher, and Whitely, *Cherokee Trail Diaries.*

[7] Easton, "Report," 400; Bieber, *Southern Trails to California,* 341–48; Whiteley, *The Cherokee Trail,* 15–16.

the southern part of the Black Hills, and probably descend the Lodge Pole Creek to its junction with the South Platte."[8] This was precisely the path the Transcontinental Railroad followed in 1868.

Blacksmith John Rankin Pyeatt wrote from Salt Lake, "This Bridgers Fort is 48 miles from green river and 440 miles from the South Fork of the Platte. 36 miles of this distance we had a road and the balance we had to make our own road, without trail or guide through mountains and plains," reporting mileage derived from the odometer attached to one of the party's wagons. "Thus you will see why we have bin so long gitten hear." The Evans company spent "one month coming from Pueblo to this place, a distance of about 400 miles over one of the worst roads in the west with several rivers to cross; we had to swim and raft," George Keys reported. A man named Garvin drowned crossing the Green River and some of the Cherokees lost their guns, provisions, money, and saddles.[9]

Like many gold rush trains, the Washington County Gold Mining Company splintered at Great Salt Lake City. Twelve wagons joined a party of packers that left Salt Lake in late July and probably took Hensley's Salt Lake Cutoff to the main California Trail. At Lassens Meadows, the majority of them headed west toward Rabbit Hole Spring. The Cherokee companies suffered their share of hardship on Lassen's "death route."[10] Part of Evans's train followed the Hastings Cutoff, which no wheel had crossed since 1846. Twenty-one members of his party set out across the cutoff with fourteen wagons in late August, James Pearce recalled years later. In Skull Valley, he wrote, "we filled our water barrels, one for each wagon, and started across the desert, which our odometer showed to be ninety miles in width." They spent three days and two nights crossing the Great Salt Lake Desert, abandoning ten wagons on the second day. "Each man was allowed to put on his blankets, one change of clothes and his gun, and in addition enough food was selected as the company thought to carry us through," Pearce wrote, "but all the rest of our supplies, tools, camp equipage and ten wagons were left on the desert to be destroyed by the elements." The train ran out of provisions and slaughtered several oxen for food. They crossed Carson Pass in a snowstorm, fearing they would meet "the same fate which overtook the Donner party." Pearce's companions reached the goldfields on 26 October 1849, "hungry, weary, footsore and nearly naked."[11]

Even more wagons—and three talented diarists—gathered along the Verdigris River in 1850. About eight trains made up of Cherokees, whites, and their slaves

---

[8]*Niles' Weekly Register*, 6 October 1827.

[9]Whiteley, *The Cherokee Trail*, 15–16; Bieber, *Southern Trails to California*, 342.

[10]Fletcher, Fletcher, and Whitely, *Cherokee Trail Diaries*, 135–37, 173–81.

[11]James Pearce, in "The Find on the Desert," *Salt Lake Tribune*, 11 May 1902, 31:4–7. Archeologists attributed some of the artifacts they located in 1986 to the Reed family wagon. Robert Hoshide concluded the wagon probably belonged to the Cherokee company. See Hoshide, "Salt Desert Trails Revisited," 5–9.

headed for the West Coast. The Cane Hill Emigrating California Company led the way, almost three weeks ahead of the Cherokee Emigrating California Company, which organized on Elk Creek and drafted a constitution on 29 April 1850. The party elected Thomas Fox Taylor captain; Clement Vann McNair and John Wolfe led other trains. As was customary, the companies changed leaders and expanded and contracted as members came and went. Traveling with Clem McNair on 9 May, diarist John Lowery Brown noted that twenty-one men joined his party, bringing its total number to 105, including "15 negroes and 12 females."[12]

Hardly anyone noticed, but Lewis Ralston found gold near the South Platte on 22 June 1850. The *Cherokee Advocate* reported the discovery "of a full placer of gold" at the foot of the Rocky Mountains that September, commenting, "We do not believe this report, until we hear something more confirmatory." The surprising strike did not prevent the trains from moving on, and it was almost a decade before the gold in Ralston Creek would make its own dramatic impact on overland trails and emigration.[13]

Except for a few shortcuts, the 1850 trains followed the previous year's "Evans Trace" to the Cache la Poudre River at today's Fort Collins, where they took a more southerly course along the present Wyoming border to the North Platte. Their Native guide, veteran mountaineer Ben Simon, took them across the Continental Divide south of present-day Saratoga at Twin Groves, and headed west over what became the Cherokee Trail's south branch to rejoin the main trail at Fort Bridger. On his return from the Great Salt Lake in 1850, topographical engineer Howard Stansbury followed Jim Bridger over the Cherokee Trail's northern trace.[14] For the rest of the decade, the route became the highroad from Arkansas, Indian Territory, and Texas to the Great Basin. "The road to California will be filled with cattle from Arkansas for many miles," the *Fort Smith Herald* reported in April 1854. "We have no doubt but 100,000 head will go from our State."[15] Thousands more emigrants and trail herds were to follow.

Many veterans of the Cherokee gold rush trains settled in California's Butte County at a camp known as Cherokee Flat, about twelve miles north of Oroville. After the placers gave out, a large hydraulic mine yielded an estimated $15 million and several hundred small diamonds. Today a desolate landscape resembling the red-rock country of southern Utah surrounds the country town of Cherokee, a testament to the Indian Forty-niners and the consequences of hydraulic mining in the Sierra Nevada foothills.[16]

---

[12]Brown, "Journal," 178, 183.

[13]Fletcher, Fletcher, and Whitely, *Cherokee Trail Diaries*, 2:193–204, 310.

[14]Madsen, *Exploring the Great Salt Lake*, 618–81.

[15]Barry, *Beginning of the West*, 1197.

[16]Clark, *Gold Districts of California*, 36–39.

A decade after its opening, the Overland Stage Line followed the general path of the 1849 Cherokee Trail, as did the Transcontinental Railroad and Interstate 80. But of all the major wagon roads to the West, the Cherokee Trail may be the least remembered. Although it was the subject of a 1960s television series and a Louis L'Amour novel, the trail has only recently received serious scholarly attention.

THE DEVIL'S PASSAGE: HUDSPETH CUTOFF

Five Hudspeth brothers—Benoni Morgan, Robert Nicholas, George Washington, Thomas Jefferson, and Silas Bourke—left Jackson County, Missouri, in 1849 with their slaves and a train of wagons freighted with playing cards, silk handkerchiefs, whiskey, brandy, wine, belts, scabbards, boots, spades, picks, ropes, coffee, and blankets. "Dave and Ben Headspeth's train was ahead of us," black Forty-niner Alvin A. Coffey recalled. "They had fourteen or fifteen wagons in the train and three to five men to a wagon."[17] Benoni Hudspeth was a veteran of John C. Frémont's 1845 filibustering expedition and had served as an officer in the California Battalion in 1846. Guiding the Hudspeths was John J. Myers, "a man of that peculiar build and stature that can endure untold physical hardships without fatigue," who had first explored northern California in 1843 with Joseph B. Chiles.[18]

Benoni Hudspeth and Myers took the first wagons due west from Bear River on 19 July 1849, but such a route had been speculated about for years. A shortcut could be found between the end of the Sublette Cutoff and the head of Raft River that would "cut off 100 miles of travel," Levi Scott suggested in October 1847. Next spring, Scott's "Way Bill From Fort Hall to Willamette Valley," published under Jesse Applegate's name, claimed mountaineers knew about a direct route from Bear River to the Raft River. "I would advise emigrants to examine, and if practicable, to make this cut-off, it will avoid some bad roads and some seven or eight days travel," the article promised.[19] When Goldsborough Bruff asked Richard Grant about the "Emmigrants' Cut-Off," Grant replied that he had heard its discovery attributed "to certain mountaineers," notably Caleb Greenwood and Hudspeth. But "a gentleman, from the States, on his way to California," had actually found it early in 1848 after showing Grant letters of introduction "from the most prominent men in the country" and securing a loan of $250, which Grant said was still unpaid.[20]

The large Hudspeth-Myers train left the Oregon Trail at Soda Point, where the Bear River turns south toward the Great Salt Lake. "Not a wagon had been

---

[17]Coffey, Recollection of 1849, California Society of Pioneers.
[18]Stewart, *California Trail,* 233; McCoy, *Historic Sketches of the Cattle Trade,* 145–47.
[19]See the *Oregon Spectator,* 11 November 1847, 3/1–2; and 6 April 1848, 1/5–2/1.
[20]Bates, Diary, 18 August 1849; Bruff, *Gold Rush,* 24 August 1849, 105.

on [it] before that time," wrote Elijah Farnham, who took the cutoff the day after it opened, but it already had traffic enough "so it looks like an old road of a great deal of travel."[21] Five days later, the trailblazers escaped from the tangled hill country on the northern rim of the Great Basin into the Raft River Valley—not, as they hoped, at the head of the Humboldt River. "We bade a last farewell to the Bear River and we left the trail and took a new cut off explored by Myers who has been 40 years a mountaineer—it was opened the day before," wrote emigrant M. Phillips, "and a card was left to inform the trains that the new route would save [between] 80 miles and 60 miles of bad road the other side of Fort Hall." Had Hudspeth and Myers actually found a direct road to the Humboldt, Henry Mann noted on 24 July, they might have shaved hundreds of miles off the old road, "but not understanding their true latitude have struck the old road before it crosses the dividing ridge to the Basin. They would have made some 200 miles on the old road had they succeeded, but as it is they have made nothing."[22] Once again Lansford Hastings's dream of a shortcut to Mary's River that would eliminate the Oregon-California Trail's long detour to Fort Hall had proven a fantasy.

Three days behind the Hudspeth train, H. C. St. Clair reached the new fork in the road, where "one goes by Fort Hall the other a new one is a cut off that saves 80 miles & a better road so it is said but we risk a greatdeal [sic] by taking it," for the rough track was said to be full of Indians. Despite St. Clair's skepticism, "the majority was in favor of taking it so the minority had to give in." His party thought the foremost wagons on the new route were only two days ahead. The leading train, he wrote, "numbers 133 wagons. They have a guide as pilot, behind Hedspeth. There is about 30 wagons that are before us so there is not more than 163 wagons ahead of us on this road and the foremost ones have to do some work on the road before they can cross some places. The grass is not all killed in the road & in some places it is quite dusty." St. Clair reported, "the distance across the cut off as near as I can make it by having the road-ameter most of the way is 117 miles so the difference is onely 48 miles." The actual savings were even less, but St. Clair accurately predicted "that the cut off will be alltogether traveled now with the exception of those that have some business at Fort Hall or [are] going to Oregon."[23]

Joseph Warren Wood's party reached the end of the cutoff on 25 July, only two hours after the Hudspeth train. Six days earlier he had watched Hudspeth's sixty

---

[21]Farnham, "From Ohio to California," 20 July 1849. No diarist accompanied the Hudspeth party, but when T. J. Van Dorn overtook the train on Raft River, it consisted of sixty wagons. See Van Dorn, Diary, 27 July 1849, Beinecke Library, 29.

[22]Phillips, Diary to California, 20 July 1849, Bancroft Library; Pritchard, *The Overland Diary,* 27, 144n7, 159n59.

[23]St. Clair, Journal, 22, 29 July, Beinecke Library. Elison, *Hudspeth Cutoff Field Guide,* estimated the length of the cutoff was 132 miles. Thomas Galbraith gave a shorter distance on 26 July: "The whole distance through Myer's cut-off being, according to roadometer, 112 miles."

wagons leave "the old road at Bear River to strike west across the hills and make a cut-off," but Wood's train stayed on the road to Fort Hall. Hudspeth "undoubtedly saved two days drive in distance but lost it in time on account of breaking a road. Some future trains may be benefited by the cut-off."[24] D. Hoyt considered the new cutoff much better than the trail by Fort Hall "and as near or nearer."[25] The new trail acquired several names. Lucius Fairchild set out on the "hilly but otherwise good" route on 1 August, calling it Lee's Cut-off.[26]

Although it was not yet denuded of grass, the trail that would soon be named after the Hudspeths was only about twenty-five miles shorter than the Fort Hall Road, but it had "a stretch of 25 miles without water . . . over much bad road." The cutoff had to cross four (some said five) mountain ranges and divides, but "the ascent and descent of the ridges [was] very gradual and in no place steep or difficult," wrote Andrew Murphy.[27] It took wagons about the same time to travel either route, but livestock generally fared better on the old bell-shaped trail to Fort Hall. The cutoff had one major, if seldom noted, advantage: it was virtually free of the mosquitoes that tortured travelers at Fort Hall.

One 1857 emigrant called the trail "the Devil's passage."[28] Despite its rough terrain, virtually every wagon on the Oregon-California Trail used the Hudspeth Cutoff for the duration of the gold rush. The shortcut was not much of an improvement, but as Dale Morgan noted, "small though the savings in distance was, the opening pinched off travel via Fort Hall, instantly and almost completely." Before the creation of what Richard Grant called "the New Road," every wagon that did not go to Salt Lake went by Fort Hall. After 19 July 1849, virtually none did for another ten years. An old Indian advised Margaret Frink's party in 1850 to take the right-hand road to Fort Hall at Soda Springs. "He raised up the bail of a bucket to signify a high mountain, and passing his hand over the top, said, 'This is Myer's Cut-off,'" Frink recalled. The old man put the handle down, made a level motion with his hand, and said, "This is the Fort Hall road." She had to endure the route's pestiferous mosquitoes, which "were as thick as flakes in a snow-storm," but Frink complimented Captain Grant on his hospitality and admired his wife, "an Indian woman, of middle age, quite good-looking, and dressed in true American s[t]yle."[29]

Thomas Van Dorn barely missed accompanying the trail-blazing Hudspeth expedition. He found Fort Hall "gave quite an animated and business like appearance from the rush of emigrants and the soldier's encampment" at Cantonment Loring,

---

[24]Wood, Diary, 25 July 1849, Huntington Library.

[25]Hoyt to "Mr. Sosey," 20 January 1850, *Missouri Whig.*

[26]Fairchild, *California Letters,* 34.

[27]Murphy, Diary, 30 July 1849, Western Historical Manuscripts.

[28]Menefee, "Travels across the Plains," 22, referring to a "very deep and long canyon" on the Hudspeth Cutoff.

[29]Frink, "Adventures of a Party of Gold Seekers," 9–12 July 1850, 2:114–15, 117–18.

the post that the Mounted Rifleman founded in 1849. One of the first emigrants to use the trail told him it was about forty miles shorter than the Fort Hall road. "This cutoff route will be the one travelled in the main hereafter I think," Van Dorn observed.[30] The options now available to California emigrants meant anyone wanting "to carry on trade with them should be stationed where the different roads fork off," Richard Grant realized.[31] Pacific Military District commander Persifor Smith abandoned Cantonment Loring in October 1849, since it was "nearly useless, because [emigrants] follow a new route more to the southward."[32] Ironically, the opening of the Pacific Wagon Road's Lander Cutoff in 1859 again put Fort Hall close the main road to the Pacific and ended the glory days of the Hudspeth Cutoff.

Thomas Jefferson Hudspeth made it to California "with my waggon 4 yoak of good cattle and 1 odd ox [but] a great many had to Throw a way the principle part of there Loading," he wrote home to Missouri. "A man that has Family ort never to think of coming [on] the trip." He hoped to make enough money to last the balance of his life, "and that is plenty," he wrote. "But if I was in Missouri and I new [sic] as much about the hardships of the Jorney as I now Do I would not [have] made the trip for all the gold in California."[33] Hudspeth had more to regret than he knew—he would be dead of typhus within a month. Benoni Morgan Hudspeth, his trailblazing brother, died 16 November 1850—exactly one year later.[34]

THE ROAD TO ZION: THE SALT LAKE CUTOFF

After founding Great Salt Lake City, Brigham Young returned to the Missouri to lead a second wave of some 2,400 Mormon emigrants to the Great Basin in 1848. A harsh season "like a severe New England winter" left the settlement close to starvation. Spring brought little relief: a heavy snowfall blanketed Salt Lake Valley on 23 May 1849. "Most of the early crops were destroyed in the month of May by crickets, and frost, which continued occasionally till June," reported Mormon leaders.[35] Despite the adverse conditions, Apostle Heber C. Kimball prophesied in April that clothing in Great Salt Lake would soon be as cheap as it was in New York City and everything else at less than Saint Louis prices. It was an audacious forecast that "astonished the people. One of his brethren said to him after meeting that he did not believe it. 'Neither did I,' said Brother Kimball, 'but I said it. It will have to go.' "[36]

---

[30]Van Dorn, Diary, 20, 27 July 1849, Beinecke Library, 26, 29.

[31]Grant to Simpson, Fort Hall, 31 January 1851, HBC Archives, D.5/30, 85.

[32]Bruff, Gold Rush, 529.

[33]Hudspeth to Cynthia Hudspeth, 23 October 1849, Jackson County Historical Society Archives.

[34]Ford, Through the Years with the Hudspeths, 1:4–5.

[35]White, News of the Plains, 3:201, 212.

[36]Jenson, Latter-day Saint Biographical Encyclopedia, 1:32.

Kimball "felt scared almost out of his wits that he had predicted such as unlikely thing as that." A fellow apostle assured him, "Brother Kimball, you have burst your boiler this time for sure."[37]

The thousands of Forty-niners who visited Great Salt Lake City made Elder Kimball's prophecy come true. "There has been 4 or 5000 Emigrants to this place this summer & Enroute for the gold regions," wrote George Withers in August.[38] Perhaps a third of the emigration took the trail to Great Salt Lake City, often believing it was a shortcut. It was not. Both Mormons and mountaineers promoted the Salt Lake route, perhaps unaware that it was longer than the traditional trail via Fort Hall. Jim Bridger himself told Edwin Hillyer, "this route by Salt Lake is about 160 miles shorter than the other and a better road." When he rejoined the old road at City of Rocks, Hillyer's former company was about five days ahead of him.[39] Even using the shortest roads it was almost forty miles "farther by way of Salt Lake" from South Pass than by the Fort Hall road.[40] Nor was it easy, since the primitive trail over the Wasatch Mountains crossed the roughest terrain between the Missouri and the Sierra. "Our road was by far the most precipitous and the scenery the wildest, we had yet seen," Sarah Royce recalled.[41] Mormons told Charles Glass Gray the forty miles between Echo Canyon and the valley was "the *worst piece of road on the whole route*."[42] The Latter-day Saints had used the trail since the Donner party blazed it in 1846, but it was still 113 miles of bad road from Fort Bridger to Great Salt Lake.

"On the 16th of June, the gold diggers began to arrive here on their way to the gold regions," Mormon leaders wrote in July. G. W. Paul's pack train from Independence led the way. Wagons had reached the valley by 22 June, and soon the emigrant trade was booming. Thousands of weary Forty-niners found respite and relief at Great Salt Lake, and in turn provided financial salvation for the remote but strategically located colony. The lure of California gold challenged Brigham Young's efforts to keep his followers building up the kingdom. Mormon leaders feared California's "golden inducements . . . might empty the valley of its population," observed William Kelly. "If you Elders of Israel want to go to the gold mines, go and be damned," the prophet said in July. Those who left, he warned, would "black boots and sweep chimneys for others in hell." At the same time, Young had already collected thousands in tithing from Mormon miners and could not resist

---

[37]Madsen, *Gold Rush Sojourners*, 53.

[38]Withers to "Mr. Miller," 12 August 1849, Missouri Historical Society.

[39]Hillyer, "From Waupun to Sacramento," 4 July 1849, 237, 239.

[40]Platt and Slater's 1852 *Travelers' Guide across the Plains*, 35–36, measured the distance from the Parting of the Ways to City of Rocks via the Sublette Cutoff as 339.75 miles, while it was 379 by way of Salt Lake. The Golden Pass toll road added 5 miles, while using the best ford of Malad Creek added 18 more.

[41]Royce, *Across the Plains*, 46.

[42]Gray, *Off at Sunrise*, 12 July 1849, 60–61.

California gold dust as a source of capital and currency. He started a mint and secretly dispatched about fifty "gold missionaries" to mine on shares. Mormon miners poured over $80,000 in gold into the church's mint between 1848 and 1851, and trade brought in thousands more. The Forty-niners helped keep the infant economy afloat and even brought a season of prosperity to Great Salt Lake.[43]

The Latter-day Saints, as they liked to be known, had acquired such a dreadful national reputation by 1849 that many gold seekers arrived expecting to find fire-breathing zealots or wild-eyed deviants. A visit to their orderly settlement in its spectacular mountain valley and contact with these hardworking and entirely ordinary families quickly dispelled many prejudices. The general friendliness of the Mormon people and their willingness to deal fairly with visitors dramatically improved the image of the young religious movement, whose stock had fallen so low during its turbulent and often violent stay in the Midwest. "The prices [we] paid the Mormons were reasonable, much to our surprise, as we dreaded the Mormons as much as the Indians and did not expect fair treatment from them. The tales told of the Mormons in those days were worse than those of the Indians," recalled Pauline Wonderly.[44] "Men may say what they please about the Mormons but I think they are a first rate set of men mostly from the eastern states and I am sure the amount of work they have done since they have been here is very great," wrote Thomas Evershed. "There must have been fault on both sides in Illinois & I should think they were full as much sinned against as sinning."[45]

Early arrivals were especially pleased with their reception. "We are living off the fat of the land, such as milk, butter, cheese and eggs," observed Joshua Breyfogle in June. "We have been treated with great kindness and hospitality as far as it was in their power from their destitute condition. We recruited ourselves and our horses finely," he wrote upon leaving "the great Mormon City." Breyfogle's Delaware Mining Company even signed an affidavit stating that on the Platte River Jacques Rouvel Brunnette had said the Mormons were bad men who "had instigated the Indians to be unfriendly to all emigrants." The party "found the Indians friendly, and we firmly believed his statement to be false." They testified they had "received universal kind treatment" from the Latter-day Saints.[46]

Visitors appreciated the variety of useful services available in the new settlement. "There were tradesmen and artisans of all descriptions," wrote William Kelly, "and from the shoeing of a waggon to the mending of a watch, there was

[43]Kelly, *Excursion to California,* 231–32; Arrington, *Great Basin Kingdom,* 74; Davies and Hansen, *Mormon Gold,* xix. For Young's long campaign to discourage mining, see Owens, *Gold Rush Saints,* 211–44.

[44]Wonderly, *Reminiscences of a Pioneer,* 3–4.

[45]Evershed, "The Gold Rush Journal," 26.

[46]Breyfogle, *Diary,* 25, 26 June 1849, 13; Roberts, *Comprehensive History,* 3:356.

no difficulty experienced in getting it done, as cheap and as well put out of hand as in any other city in America."[47] They especially welcomed the chance to eat "garden sauce"—fresh vegetables—and welcomed any change from beans and bacon and bacon and beans. "We had during our stay at the City, plenty of green peas radishes, beans, turnips and other garden sauce. Also an abundance of good buttermilk, sweet milk and fresh butter. Which was quite a luxury for us after coming over 1500 miles on bread meat & coffee," wrote James Tolles.[48] Charles Glass Gray hired a woman to cook a grand dinner of "fresh fish, pot cheese, butter green peas, rye bread & milk & buckwheat cakes, which to an appetite of 75 days continuance seemed perfectly delicious."[49]

The twenty-fourth of July marked "the anniversary day of the entrance of the Mormons into the valley," wrote William Z. Walker. For the trail-weary, it was a spectacular event. "We sat down to one of the best dinners we had enjoyed for many a day. The tables were loaded with every delicacy." But before joining the feast, Walker and his friends had to listen to Mormon leaders' two hours of hard talking, consisting of "inflammatory speeches and threats against their enemies in Missouri."[50] John Benson crossed Big Mountain, descended Emigration Canyon, and arrived in time for the feast. "An immense amount of work and energy had been expended in preparing for the celebration," he noted. "It was estimated that 6,000 to 8,000 took dinner. I think 200 emigrants took dinner with them. All were urged to sit in. I hesitated but did so after two urgent invitations." The function was held in "a large shed open on all sides which they call a bower. It is a roof supported on posts" covered with boughs to provide shade. "The dinner went off admirably and was followed by toasts songs recitations &c and we left highly pleased with our first day among the Mormons," he wrote. "The tables were spread with the greatest plenty and in taste and quantity not to be excelled," Benson noted. "I have seen tables set for probably 100 or more, but here were tables for thousands." This act of generosity impressed him deeply: "As I walked away from the bower, I turned and looked back. There were more people (except emigrants and Indians) 200 to 1 than I had seen since I left the Missouri River. Where did they come from? How did they get here? I pinched myself to make sure that I was not dreaming," he said,

> But the greatest marvel is how they could, in so short a time, produce in a desert, the
> variety of food stuffs with which the tables were spread. Men do not gather vegetables

[47]Kelly, *Excursion to California,* 226.
[48]Tolles, Journal of My Travels, 26 July 1849, BYU Library, 44.
[49]Gray, *Off at Sunrise,* 14 July 1849, 62–63.
[50]Walker, Diary, 24 July 1849, BYU Library, 89. The anniversary actually marked the day Brigham Young reached the valley; advance parties had arrived two days earlier.

from sage brushes or cereals from cactus. The seeds, the tubers, the roots, the fouls, the pigs, the sheep, the cows, everything from which this abundance was produced had to all be transported a thousand miles or more over such roads as we have traveled. Even then, how could they in so short a time with so small a beginning, have produced so much. It seems incredible. I take off my hat to those who planned and executed it.[51]

The trading fair at Great Salt Lake City lasted all summer. The Mormons "were glad to see emigrants for they were short of rations and had been since they first got to the valley," Mark D. Manlove recalled.[52] Before the harvest, "there is a great call for bacon, and every kind of food, and articles for clothing," Edward Jackson observed.[53] The sojourners brought desperately needed provisions, clothing, stoves, tools, medicines, and wagons that they were ready to trade for a fraction of their original cost—or else they simply abandoned these items along the trail and the Mormons retrieved them on what one called "a Picking up Expedition."[54] By the time they reached Great Salt Lake, gold seekers felt pressed to get to California as quickly as possible, so the focus of trading quickly became livestock. "Most of the emigrants here are leaving their waggons and packing fearing they will not get through on account of the scarcity of feed," wrote William Walker.[55]

George Morris recalled the Forty-niners were "perfectly frantic with excitement and were very eager to trade off their footsore cattle for fresh ones"; they sometimes traded four to six oxen for a single fresh yoke. Horses, mules, and packsaddles fetched fabulous prices, although it was soon impossible to get more than $25 for a wagon or $30 for a carriage. Many Mormons—even those like Morris, who "never was one to trade"—exchanged healthy animals for worn-out livestock, let them graze for a few days in the valley's lush river bottoms, and then repeated the operation. Morris started with a team of steers. By summer's end he had five yoke of oxen, four cows, a $110 wagon, plus enough clothing, footwear, and provisions "to make us more comfortable than we had ever been before."[56]

Traders such as Dimick Huntington acted as middlemen between Indians and emigrants. Huntington represented the Ute warrior Wakara as his "agent in the disposition of the horses," Jerome Howard reported. "Many of the emigrants got fresh animals of Walker [Wakara], Huntington receiving a per cent for his services. I witnessed some of these bargains."[57] Horse thievery and accusations of theft became common: "Some of the emigrants said that the Mormon boys sold their lariats in the

---

[51]Benson, From St. Joseph to Sacramento, 24 July 1849, Nebraska State Historical Society, 48–51. Dexter Tiffany, Diary, 12 August 1849, Missouri Historical Society, described the Bowery.

[52]Manlove, An Overland Trip, California State Library.

[53]Jackson, Journal, BYU Library, 9 August 1849, 75.

[54]Lee, A Mormon Chronicle, 1:111.

[55]Walker, Diary, 29 July 1849, BYU Library, 91.

[56]Madsen, Gold Rush Sojourners, 55–56, 59.

[57]Howard, "California Correspondence," 18 April 1850, in Perkins, Gold Rush Diary, 177.

day and stole them back in the night," Mark Manlove recalled. But, he admitted, "I think there are some other boys that would do the same."[58]

Not every sojourner had a pleasant visit, especially as the summer wore on. Many Forty-niners went away with mixed or simply bad opinions of their hosts: "As a general thing they are not a very intelligent looking Community," wrote David DeWolf.[59] "The city is built of unburnt bricks or adobes as they are called here and is not much more than a grain field at present. The people are superstitious industrious & this year money making, that is they are shaving the emigration devilishly," Charles W. Haze complained. The contempt Mormon leaders openly expressed for the U.S. government, which they felt had failed to protect their religious liberties, entertained some Forty-niners and discomforted others. "They boast of their strength and set at defiance all authority," Haze wrote.[60] Even James Tolles, who had complimented the "grand and sublime view of the great Mormon Valley," complained he had "had to give large boot" to trade for cattle and charged that the Saints falsely accused his party of stealing Indian ponies.[61] Edward Harrow called the Mormons "a bigoted and skinning people (this is my opinion) from the way they trade with the unfortunate emigrants, giving them about ⅛ the worth for what he has to sell, and charging him about 4 times the worth for what he wants to buy." At City of Rocks, Harrow complained, "we had been the dupes of those lying Mormons," who had claimed the detour through Salt Lake "was at least from 150 to 200 miles the nearest, [and] also the best road."[62] "Both the prophets and elders speeches were rantings malignant and hostile to our government and administration and the people in the West," Edward Jackson observed, "but altogether this has been one of the happiest days of my journey."[63]

"The Mormons were living peacefully and in comparative contentment, although suffering many hardships and privations, having, according to their own account, subsisted a considerable portion of the time on milk and roots," J. B. Witt wrote home. He attended a local church service, heard the Mormon creed dispensed, and learned about plans to celebrate the anniversary of President Young's entrance into the Promised Land. "There were many singular features in this performance, such as three groans for Martin Van Buren, three groans for the United States and sundry rejoiceings at its wished-for downfall." Witt called Great Salt Lake "this city of groans and enthusiasms."[64] "The people are sociable, intelligent & pleasant,"

[58]Manlove, An Overland Trip, California State Library.

[59]DeWolf, "Diary of the Overland Trail," 17 August 1849, 205.

[60]Haze to "Dear friends . . . ," 6 January 1850, Bentley Historical Library.

[61]Tolles, Journal of My Travels, 26, 28 July 1849, BYU Library, 44.

[62]Harrow, Gold Rush Overland Journal, 41, 46.

[63]Jackson, Journal, 24 July 1849, BYU Library, 62, 63.

[64]Witt, "Correspondence," 27 August 1849, Chicago Journal, 30 November 1849, 3/3.

Charles Glass Gray observed, "in fact part & parcel of that great human family." But he thought there was something slightly off-balance about the Mormon settlement and its people: "there *appears to be a tinge of fanaticism as it were about all their actions, their looks & manners.*"[65]

The gold seekers enjoyed the Mormons' bounty much more than their politics. "We came upon a patch of water melons, had some to eat, then called for bread, butter and milk," James Hutchings wrote upon reaching Great Salt Lake; "And then came the greatest luxury of all. We saw some ladies." Upon leaving, he mourned, "Tomorrow we leave civilization, pretty girls, and pleasant memories."[66] Forty-niners commented on the surprising number of attractive young women they saw in Great Salt Lake, but the practice the Mormons called "Celestial Marriage" intrigued, scandalized, and fascinated the visitors. The Mormons finally gave up trying to deny the practice in 1852, but it was already an open secret in 1849. "Polygamy is here practiced and tolerated by Law! the same was practiced by some in the States, but they denied that it was tolerated by their rules, or sanctioned by their faith," wrote Gordon Cone. "They openly avow it here."[67] Indeed, they did. "You will hardly believe me when I tell you that Polygamy is a part of their religious creed & universal here. The two first presidents have about 40 wives each—& so on down," wrote Franklin Grist. "The man who refuses more than one is considered weak in the faith." He reported that "the presidents haram" included "several young & pretty odalisques."[68] The practice struck many visitors as an odd anachronism: "One strange peculiarity prevails here for modern times. Every man is allowed as many wives as he can support," wrote Elijah Spooner. "Bah! rather have the undivided affections of my one than share it with more."[69]

In late August, the arrival of the Stansbury Expedition and Indian agent John Wilson brought the federal government to Salt Lake Valley. Both studiously ignored local marriage customs and won over nervous local leaders. Brigham Young agreed to assist Stansbury's exploration, and Wilson conveyed Zachary Taylor's promise of support and friendship. The Latter-day Saints had tired of Congress's failure to organize a civil government, so in March 1849 they initiated "a free and independent government, by the name of the State of Deseret." Under a territorial government, the Mormons feared "the President might appoint some whippersnappers, or broken down politicians, who would not be acceptable to us, to rule over us." Statehood would allow the Mormons to elect their own officials. The question of

[65]Gray, *Off at Sunrise,* 14 July 1849, 63.

[66]Hutchings, *Seeking the Elephant,* 30 August, 5 September 1849, 154, 156.

[67]Cone, Journal of Travels, 11 August 1849, BYU Library, 78.

[68]Grist to "Dearest Mother," 15 February 1850, University of North Carolina.

[69]Spooner to "Affectionate Companion," 19 July 1849, BYU Library, 3.

slavery in the new territories already had Congress tied in knots, and many feared the issue would have a "tendency to break up the Union." The president proposed creating one state out of the entire Mexican conquest, "leaving it to the power of the people to say whether it shall be a slave or a free State, and thus taking the bone from the Congress," Wilson informed Mormon leaders. They agreed to Wilson's proposal, on condition that the arrangement would end in 1851 and create two "free, sovereign, independent" states. Like many of Zachary Taylor's frontier policies, his one-big-state solution had unintended consequences. Wilson found an already-functioning provisional state when he reached California, and it soundly rejected his proposal, which aggravated Brigham Young, who felt double-crossed when Congress gave California statehood and created Utah Territory a year later.[70]

Visitors to the Salt Lake Valley could take the Hastings Cutoff across the Great Salt Lake Desert, but most wisely chose to follow the 167-mile-long trail Samuel Hensley had blazed in 1848 up the east side of the Great Salt Lake and over the Hansel and Raft River mountains to City of Rocks.[71] Before leaving the city, many gold seekers took advantage of the hot springs that lined the Wasatch Front. William Walker visited the Warm Spring and "found several persons in the basin enjoying the luxury of a warm bath." The pool almost scalded him, but he soon found it about the right temperature for bathing: "The water in the basin was about 3 feet deep and of density enough to buoy a person up. I remained in the water nearly an hour."[72] Edward Jackson saw a dozen emigrants bathing at Warm Spring and in a few miles noted the hot springs—"hot enough to boil eggs." Neither Jackson nor any of his fourteen companions tried the waters, but "one of the mules got in here; but she was soon out."[73]

Joseph Moody wrote, upon reaching California, "After getting a 'guide' we left the mud city." James Sly, a veteran of the Mexican-American War and the gold mines, led Jim Stewart's Diamond K Company north to City of Rocks, where they met the Fort Hall Road. Stewart's party apparently drove the first wagons over the Salt Lake Cutoff with little trouble in eight days. The trek required fording or ferrying the Weber and Bear rivers again, fighting mosquitoes, bad water (James Hutchings complained about "the sulphurous unpleasantness of the water all the way from Salt Lake City") and several dry drives, but the trail initially passed through Mormon farmsteads set in what Joshua Breyfogle called "a great country for a lazy man." The new road had few ups and downs, plenty of grass, and—in

---

[70]Bernhisel to Young, 21 March 1850, Brigham Young Collection, LDS Archives; Morgan, "The State of Deseret," 92–96, 156; Tullidge, "Utah and California," 88–90.

[71]Fleming and Standing, "The Road to 'Fortune,'" 248–71. Derived from Hensley, the name "Hansel" first appeared in 1851 as "Hensell's Spring," in Cain and Brower, *Mormon Way-bill*.

[72]Walker, Diary, 29 July 1849, BYU Library, 91–92.

[73]Jackson, Journal, 31 July 1849, BYU Library, 66–67.

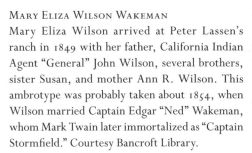

MARY ELIZA WILSON WAKEMAN
Mary Eliza Wilson arrived at Peter Lassen's ranch in 1849 with her father, California Indian Agent "General" John Wilson, several brothers, sister Susan, and mother Ann R. Wilson. This ambrotype was probably taken about 1854, when Wilson married Captain Edgar "Ned" Wakeman, whom Mark Twain later immortalized as "Captain Stormfield." Courtesy Bancroft Library.

places—spectacular scenery. "The road was good and hot springs numerous," Mark Manlove remembered. "We had a fine view of the lake."[74]

The detour to Great Salt Lake relieved overgrazing on the main trail, and the community provided a vital way station for the crowd bound for the goldfields. In return, the Forty-niners and the gold dust flooding in from California provided economic salvation for the struggling religious utopia. This materiel and capital support ensured the survival of the first American settlement in the Great Basin. But the uncontrolled influx of outsiders made Mormon leaders nervous. "Our peaceful valley has appeared like the half-way house of the pilgrims to Mecca," they wrote in July 1849, "and still they come and go, and probably will continue to do so till fall." The precise number of Forty-niners who visited Great Salt Lake in 1849 will never be known, but it totaled at least ten thousand. The number was large enough to make Brigham Young uneasy about the approaching winter. After mid-August he encouraged late arrivals to avoid the northern Sierra passes by using the trail to southern California. Even after these adventurers left Great Salt Lake, several hundred emigrants "arrived too late in the season to continue their journey on the north route, and many of them contemplated wintering with us." These uninvited guests, known as "Winter Mormons," were not entirely welcome. "So

---

[74]Moody to "My Dear Father," 7 August 1849, 84; Johnston, *Experiences of a Forty-niner*, 25 June to 2 July 1849, 192–99; Hutchings, *Seeking the Elephant*, 14 September 1849, 161; Breyfogle, *Diary*, 28 June 1849, 14; Manlove, An Overland Trip, California State Library.

large an accession of mouths, in addition to those of our own emigration," Young wrote, "threatened almost a famine for bread."[75]

Those who took the Salt Lake Cutoff had mixed reactions about the quality of the road and the nature of their reception, but the Mormon lion's encounter with the Forty-niners was generally a happy experience for both sides. Some who stayed on the main trail regretted not visiting civilization. "We are lamenting very much that we did not go by the way of Salt Lake and pay a visit to the *Mormons* as those who went that way enjoyed themselves so well," wrote Cyrus Sumner. "It would be worth 10 dollars to see a human habitation again and some ladies—they say there are 3 women for every man at Salt Lake—and that the Ladies are very clever and sociable and will not let the poor Emigrants want for anything."[76]

Seem Like Crazy Men: The Hastings Cutoff

Not a single wagon had ventured over Lansford Hastings's road across the Salt Desert since the Donner party disaster in 1846. The size of the emigration, and the popularity of Edwin Bryant's book and T. H. Jefferson's *Map of the Emigrant Road,* helped revive this dry and difficult route. The hectic summer of 1849 made men "so anxious to reach the diggings in the shortest possible time that they chanced any and every reported cutoff which might be supposed to shorten the distance," Charles Kelly observed. When he published his study of the Hastings Cutoff in 1952, the only information about the road in 1849 was from secondhand reports recorded by diarists "who themselves remained on the regular California Trail but whose friends took the cutoff."[77]

The redoubtable Saint Louis attorney P. Dexter Tiffany once again fills a gap in the historical record. After abandoning the Pioneer Line near South Pass, Tiffany headed west on the Hastings Cutoff on the morning of 20 August 1849 with six companions who were "packing it" to El Dorado. "For the first time in my life I packed a mule without instruction or assistance & succeeded so well that my packs never came loose," he observed proudly. After a dip in the Great Salt Lake, his party camped "on a small brook some 2 miles beyond Hastings Wells," near today's Grantsville. Following Jefferson's map, about fifteen men spent a day taking advantage of the excellent forage at Hope Wells to prepare for the march across the Salt Flats, with Tiffany "mowing grass & sewing up my India rubber overpants to put water in for my stock." After grazing their mules on the fine bunch grass

---

[75]Brigham Young, 8 October 1849, in Roberts, *Comprehensive History,* 3:338–39.

[76]Sumner, Letters from Uncle Cyrus, 15 August 1849, Bancroft Library. For the political evolution of this relationship, see Bigler, "The Elephant Meets the Lion."

[77]Kelly, "Gold Seekers on the Hastings Cutoff," 9–10.

at Spring Dell, at 5:00 P.M. the packers and fifteen more men from the Ithaca and California Mining Company began "the 'Long drive.'" They climbed "some six or 7 miles to the top of the ridge, the last two miles of which was up some very steep hills" to Hastings Pass, where Tiffany took in the expansive view from Scorpion Mountain in today's Stansbury Mountains. He "saw nothing of the dreariness & felt none of the horror" Edwin Bryant had experienced in 1846.

Tiffany noted at the edge of the Great Salt Lake Desert, "Our route was nearly West & as far as I could judge, it appeared to be a succession of plains separated by low ridges of 10 or 20 feet high. Some appeared to curve around so as to form the rim of an immense basin." Part of the playa was "entirely destitute of all vegetation as much so as your parlor carpet & perfectly white," and "most of these plains are hard & afford fine roads although the ridges are mostly of sand as white as snow." As he approached Silver Island, Tiffany found "the surface of which is not broken by any vegetation & as smooth as water about the colour & consistency of wet mortar into which the feet of our horses & mules sank in some few places just over the hoof." Wagon wheels sank "some six or 8 inches though these places are not long though frequent." As Samuel Hensley had learned in 1848, after a rainstorm neither man nor beast could cross the playa. Not long before dawn, "down this valley swept a very strong current of air so cold that it immediately compelled me to button up my coat to my chin, tie 2 handkerchiefs around my throat then put on gloves & my blanket coat & still was very cold."

With the coming of daylight, Tiffany found six wagons "apparently abandoned though as I came up I found men in them, some of whom arose as I came up." The men had loaned their oxen to their companions "to help them out expecting the like favour after they should cross this long drive. It was the most dreary desolate discouraging sight I have seen on the way." Exhausted oxen littered the trail's next twenty miles. He finally reached the "fine springs & fine grass" at Pilot Spring at 3:00 P.M., "my horses in good condition, myself not very tired, having been out some 22 hours & having been about 18 in motion." The not-very-tired Tiffany collapsed and slept till sundown. His friends had fared much worse, losing two horses and a mule. The debilitated livestock "had been driven from Missouri this year & was broken down & the same was the case with the ox teams." Unlike many others who had crossed the Salt Desert, he thought that "with fresh animals or those in good condition I should have no hesitation in making the trip whether with waggons or packs. It has been represented as being much more difficult than it really is to cross this place for to a resolute man there are none." Tiffany did note, however, "What the effect of a heavy rain might be on the 12 miles [of] *mud* I know not."

Like all who survived the crossing, Tiffany's company lay over the next day and only set out again in the evening after a second day's rest. "I felt sick & weak & slept

& dozed all day & thought I should have a return of the fever & could not go on but
I did," he wrote. His party traveled until 1:00 A.M., rested, and did not make camp
until almost noon the next day. After visiting the "warm sulphurous" Mound Spring,
where "the water boiling up has thrown up a mound some ten or 15 feet high"
and as big as a square in Saint Louis, the packers crossed Ruby Valley. Their maps
showed that the Hastings road meandered 120 miles to get only thirty miles west,
so the Ithacans "determined to make a cut-off over the mountain." The guide was
soon hopelessly lost among the canyons of the Ruby Mountains. In disgust, Tiffany
"told the men I would go not a step further as I would not risk my horses over such
steeps." Backtracking alone, he encountered five Shoshones, who fortunately greeted
him with "How do" and "Swop." He fell in with some of his old friends "within five
rods of an old camping ground" on the main trail down the Humboldt: "A pretty
good guess for a Yankee," Tiffany wrote proudly. His friends had found their way
over Secret Pass and they all camped together once again on 2 September.[78]

Most who risked the purported shortcut found the "roads dusty and hard wheel-
ing," wrote O. J. Hall. Those who took Hastings Cutoff "went 60 miles without
grass or water, many died—some that reached water were past speaking, with
black tongue, blood ran from mouth. When they revived they carried water back to
others. It must have been a horrible scene. Wagons lay in piles, and property, along
the trail," Hall said. The "very thievish" Indians had stolen eleven head of cattle in
one place: "Some lost their whole train by death or theft and have to take pack on
back and seem like crazy men."[79] A pack train from the Colony Guards and other
cutoff veterans told Goldsborough Bruff about their "great sufferings on the long
desert of 'Utaria.'" Hastings Cutoff was "82 miles perfect arid waste," Captain John
McNulty complained. "They suffered much—reduced to the necessity of drinking
their mules' urine, &c.," Bruff reported. McNulty then made a dire prediction.
The rest of the Guard proposed taking a southern road from Great Salt Lake to
California, "a route in my humble opinion, which will consign many emigrants and
their animals to the wolves, and the rest to much suffering."[80] McNulty was right.

GREAT CHAINS OF MOUNTAINS: FORGOTTEN CORRIDORS

As he painfully made his way up Carson Valley in late September, Gordon Cone
was overtaken "by a 'pack' train from the south that started to go the 'Fort Smith'
rout." Everyone who "started on that trail, found that it was utterly impossible to get
through, have come north to the Santefee rout, and finding this also impractable,

---

[78]Tiffany, Diary, 20 August to 3 September 1849, Missouri Historical Society.
[79]Hall, Diary of a Forty-Niner, 23 September 1849, Utah State Historical Society, 7.
[80]Bruff, *Gold Rush,* 17 September 1849, 560, 176.

have been obleiged to come still farther north to this road, as the only one on which
the emigrant can pass the great chains of mountains that are found in the way."
Cone had met many men who had taken the Santa Fe Trail and had "not found their
mistake until it was to[o] late to retrace their steps without considerable loss, and
hardship." He blamed predatory promoters for trying to attract "as much of the
buisness of the country as possible that way, that they may reap some bennefit!"[81]

Cone's packers were not alone. Adventurers wandered far and wide in 1849,
creating little-known and surprising variations of the California Trail. Some Forty-
niners took the Santa Fe Trail to Bents Fort and then turned north to reach Fort
Bridger by a variety of routes, either going up the Front Range or directly over the
Rockies. At Green River, several men took a bold speculation and left the main trail.
"Two Dutchmen & a Yankee from Boston by the name of Quensby took 20 days
provision & embarked in a skiff that was left by some emigrants at Green river for
California," Hugh Heiskell reported.[82] Teamster William Manly and seven friends
also tried to float to California. "It looked as if we were taking the most sensible
way to get to the Pacific," he recalled, "and almost wondered that everybody was so
blind as not to see it as we did." Desolation Canyon's cataracts and a lucky encounter
with Wakara, the great Ute freebooter, convinced the bold adventurers that the
unexplored Colorado River system was not the royal road to the Pacific. Manly and
his companions gave up near today's Green River, Utah, where the Spanish Trail
from New Mexico forded the Green. They made their way to the Mormon settlements before striking out through Southern Utah to find Death Valley.[83]

Oregon Trail veteran William Gilpin—the promoter who said "Progress is
God" during the Pikes Peak gold rush—offered one pack-mule train perfectly
wretched advice. The Ithaca and California Mining Company included the noted
Dr. Elijah White, organizer of the 1842 emigration to Oregon, who had already
crossed the plains twice and should have known better. Gilpin told them to go up
the Arkansas River, "thence directly over the mountains" to Utah Lake and Great
Salt Lake City, across Hastings Cutoff to the Humboldt, "and down it, taking
the usual route over the Sierra Nevada," Jerome Howard reported. This, Gilpin
promised, would let them "make an unparalleled quick trip to El Dorado." When

[81]Cone, Journal of Travels," 2 October 1849, BYU Library, 132–33. This pack train may have been the one Hosea
Stout noted on 6 August at Salt Lake: "Emegrants arrived here direct from Santa Fe over the mountains." See Stout,
On the Mormon Frontier, 355. A wealth of new information has come to light, such as M. G. D.'s report that he "came
through from Santa Fe on pack mules, via Salt Lake. Our company numbered 80 odd men for defence, but only had
one skirmish with Indians (Eutahs), in which there was no damage done on either side." See M. G. D., 23 February
1850, "Letters from California," Arkansas State Gazette, 19 April 1850. The question of whether anyone used the Spanish
Trail to get to California in 1849 is no closer to an answer than when Dale Morgan posed it in 1959. See Pritchard,
The Overland Diary, 139, 171n104.

[82]Heiskell, A Forty-niner from Tennessee, 23 August 1849, 17.

[83]Manly, Death Valley in '49, 74–101. Manly found evidence that others, perhaps including "Quensby," also tried
to float to California. See ibid., 84.

they reached the Rockies, fur-trade veteran Charles Kinney assured the packers Gilpin's itinerary was sheer lunacy. The Ithacans hired Kinney to take them to Salt Lake, but nothing could persuade him "to go the route recommended by Colonel Gilpen [sic], as it lay through the country of the Utah Indians, who were then at war with the whites." Kinney led the party up the Cherokee Trail and over the Laramie Plains to Browns Hole. "Thence our final course was south of west to the Utah Lake, our company deciding to go there rather than Fort Bridger." Entering Utah Valley by way of Spanish Fork Canyon, the men turned north and arrived at Great Salt Lake City on 30 July.[84] They basically followed the "verry rough road" Frémont's third expedition had taken from Utah Lake to the Cache la Poudre River, which George Withers called "the Worst road certainly that ever White Men packed over."[85] The Ithaca joint-stock company dissolved in what Howard called the "City of Gardens." On 25 August, fifteen Ithacans headed west with Dexter Tiffany on the Hastings Cutoff, but some stayed in Great Salt Lake till October and went "through by a southern route" to Los Angeles. Some of those who followed the tracks of their supply wagon would find Death Valley. Jerome Howard made the best choice; he and a companion joined a new company and took the Salt Lake Cutoff north to the main California Trail.[86]

Others tried even more divergent paths to the goldfields. "Some packers over-took us to day, that had started to go by way of Santa fee," wrote James Wilkins near Lassens Meadows.[87] Lieutenant Alfred Pleasanton, ordered to California to serve as General Persifor Smith's aide-de-camp, left Santa Fe on 9 June with an escort of ten dragoons and mountain man Dick Owens as guide. They crossed the Rockies via Browns Hole—a pack trail sometimes called the Cherokee Trail's south branch—to Utah Lake, reaching Great Salt Lake in July, where they took Hensley's Salt Lake Cutoff to the main California Trail. Their train helped fill Thousand Springs Valley with teams and pack mules on August 1, noted Thomas Van Dorn.[88] Pleasanton "passed by the 'Grosventre' pass in the Rocky mountains about latitude 38 N. and represents that as not only practicable for a rail-road, but as scarcely requiring any work," reported General Smith.[89]

---

[84]Howard to "Friend Gates," 18 April 1850, in Perkins, Gold Rush Diary, 175–76. Augustus Heslep used the Ithaca Company's "miserable plight" at Greenhorn in July 1849 to support his "facts and arguments against the pack mule mode of transit." See Bieber, Southern Trails to California, 364–67.

[85]Withers to "Mr. Miller," 12 August 1849, Missouri Historical Society.

[86]Howard to "Friend Gates," 18 April 1850, in Perkins, Gold Rush Diary, 175–92.

[87]Wilkins, An Artist on the Overland Trail, 30 August 1849, 67.

[88]Van Dorn, Diary, 27 July 1849, Bienecke Library; Fletcher, Fletcher, and Whitely, Cherokee Trail Diaries, 135–37.

[89]Smith, "Correspondence," Serial 561, 86. On the Truckee River, John Markle wrote, "About 9 o'clock a.m. Kit Carson passed our camp with a pack train." He said Carson had started at Fort Smith, but "had to steer his way through the mountains and strike the road by way of Fort Bridger, about 500 miles out of his way." Whoever Markle met, it was not Carson, who was ranching in New Mexico in 1849. Markle, Diary, Bancroft Library, 2; Carter, "Kit Carson," in Hafen, Mountain Men, 6:121–24.

William Doty told his mother in November, "We arrived in California October 15, after a long and tedious trip, having travelled one thousand miles farther to this country than any other immigrants." He was probably correct. After losing their physician to cholera at Independence, his wagon train decided to take the Gila River route across the Southwest. "As we had started in search of gold, we heard golden stories," wrote Samuel Breck. At Bents Fort those rumors told of gold mines in New Mexico. The party visited the trappers' settlement at Green Horn and sent a delegation "fifty miles to the Taos gold mines" to investigate. They returned three weeks later and "poured forth their golden treasures, to the amount of *six long bits*. O what a bumper!" mourned Breck. Having visited Green Horn, they all felt sensible "of proving ourselves green horns, in fact, to all sensible persons." Nor were they alone. Breck said hundreds faced the same dilemma and "old trappers discouraged the Gila route, with hundreds of objections." The greenhorns were learning, and "a part of us made up our minds that the Gila route to California was a great humbug." Fifteen of the men abandoned their wagons, elected Doty captain, and "turned our faces direct for the Rocky Mountains, aiming to reach the main California road at Ft. Bridger." Doty "engaged a Delaware chief, named John Swannie, to guide us." (The guide was probably Jim Swannock, son of the Delaware leader Shawanock, or the old warrior himself—only a bold man would venture to lead such a risky expedition through the heart of Ute country.) They joined forces with fifteen Arkansans under a Captain Park "until they heard the route we were going." Park's company "backed out, and said it was madness to undertake it. We then left him he took one route, and we another," Doty recalled. "Our trusty Indian led directly into the mountains; at one time our faithful mules were climbing over the most lofty mountains along side of snow in the midst of July," wrote Breck. "This part of our journey was truly grand; our path was through hostile tribes of Indians." Over the next thirty-five days, Park and Doty traveled eight hundred miles to Fort Bridger, "and singular as it may seem, arrived there the same day—our party with every mule we started with, and in good health—they on foot, and half starved," Doty wrote.

"Part of the way our road was before never traveled by white men, and this part of the trip entirely pays me for all fatigues and hardships experienced since leaving the States," Samuel Breck reported. At Bridger's they "found we were nearly the last of the tremendous emigration on their way to California." They visited Great Salt Lake and tried the Lassen Trail, on which Indians killed one of their guards. Like most parties, this one adopted an every-man-for-himself philosophy. Captain Doty arrived in California with four men and six horses. "We had but fifteen pounds of provisions, and the clothes on our backs," he reported at the end of seven months' journey. "We raised a loud shout when the Sacramento Valley first opened to our view," Breck wrote after reaching the settlements on 15 October. Despite the trouble, he was "glad I have come, perfectly contented, crossed mountains, plains, deserts, watched Indians and arrived at last in California, seen the elephant all over, and am resolved, if health is permitted, to fight him the best I know how."[90]

A CENTRAL SOUTHERN ROUTE:
GREAT SALT LAKE TO LOS ANGELES—AND DEATH VALLEY

For Forty-niners arriving in the Great Basin too late to risk crossing the Sierra Nevada, a new southern route to Los Angeles offered an attractive alternative to wintering over in the Mormon settlements, which had little work and no food to share with outsiders. There was not a single non-Indian habitation between Utah Valley and the Lugo Ranch at San Bernardino, but a faint trace had connected them since 1846, when Solomon Sublette returned from Los Angeles via Fort Bridger.[91] Mormon Battalion veteran Captain Jefferson Hunt led a pack train down the route in 1847 and back again in 1848. That spring Captain Daniel Davis and his wife, Susan, hauled a small buckboard up the trail. They "arrived at the old Fort Salt Lake Valley on the 5th of June 1848 all Safe & well, bringing through with us the first wagon that ever passed that rout." The majority of the men were packers, John J. Riser recalled, "but this wagon that we took was the first wagon that ever traveled the route, and this wagon route afterwards proved to be the only feasible wagon road from southern Utah in winter to California."[92]

Travelers pouring into Great Salt Lake City heard reports claiming the northern trails were "so obstructed with dead cattle as to admit no passage for wagons." The grass "was entirely consumed, so that no animal could live." An eyewitness told Cephas Arms, "the road was thronged with men, women and children with packs on their backs and their feet bleeding from the roughness of the road—and all this 700 miles from their destination. What the suffering will be after the two roads come together, which they do 300 miles this side of the Sierra Nevada, God only knows." Late arrivals knew snow would block the northern passes by November, and "the Mormons, better acquainted with the road, pronounced it madness" to take the Humboldt River trail. They also questioned their ability to feed so many visitors. As noted, Brigham Young feared the many sojourners who wanted to winter over in Great Salt Lake would eat the Mormons out of house and home. Young probably saw an opportunity to have these unwanted guests pioneer a wagon

---

[90]Doty to "Dear Mother," 22 November 1849, "W. Doty's Letter from California," *Chicago Commercial Advertiser,* 7 February 1850; Breck to "Dear Father," 23 November 1849, *Chicago Commercial Advertiser,* 13 February 1850.

[91]Morgan, *Overland in 1846,* 62.

[92]Bigler and Bagley, *Army of Israel,* 397, 399.

road across the southern Great Basin at no expense to the Latter-day Saints: as one Forty-niner charged, "Brigham and the church wanted a short route to the Pacific Coast, and here was the opportunity of having that route prospected."[93] Cephas Arms heard that someone had offered to guide the emigrants "through the southern route for $20 per wagon." At the Bowery, the Mormons' makeshift brush tabernacle, on the afternoon of 12 August, Jefferson Hunt "proposed to the Emigrants to lead them for $1000 to the City of the Angels Oct. 1 & explained the route & succeeded in forming a company," wrote Dexter Tiffany.[94] By October, more than a hundred wagons and about five hundred people had decided to follow Hunt to California.

The passage of a single wagon proved the trip could be done, but it did not establish a wagon road. The first large expedition over what historian Leo Lyman called "the most difficult wagon road in American history" became an ordeal of legendary proportions. The next spring, Mary E. Neal wrote the only surviving contemporaneous account of the miseries of the Gruwell-Derr Company, the train that broke the trail. Her party, expecting plenty of grass and water and warm weather, left Utah Valley on 21 September with twenty-two wagons and provisions for six weeks. "But instead of that we had no grass, no water, got out of provisions, had cold weather, accompanied with snow, [and] our cattle died for want of nourishment." When their provisions ran out, the party ate their weaker oxen, "it being against the rules to kill any thing that could work." On one of the many arid stretches someone offered her ten cents for half of her last quart of water. "You may be sure we did not take it—ten dollars would have been no temptation, as we could not eat nor drink money." She did not grumble, "for I thought I had to die, and there was no need of complaining."[95]

Packers had picked up a map from mountaineer Barney Ward that purported to show a cutoff to the goldfields, but more than a hundred wagons fell in behind Jefferson Hunt. The trek began well enough, but the farther south the wagons rolled, the harder and drier the trail became, and their guide made some unfortunate attempts at finding a shortcut. Frustrated with Hunt's slow pace and sketchy knowledge of the country, all but seven wagons headed west in early November from near today's Newcastle, Utah, to seek Ward's fantasy shortcut. "Cut offs in an unknown country are very dangerous," wrote diarist Vincent Hoover, "and too often result disastrously."[96] Most of the emigrants recognized their mistake upon reaching the precipitous canyon at Headwaters Wash, and "at Mount Misery

---

[93]Stephens, *Life Sketches of a Jayhawker*, 19.

[94]Arms, *The Long Road to California*, xi, 81–85; Tiffany, Diary, 12 August 1849, Missouri Historical Society, 33.

[95]Neal to "Dear Parents," 26 May 1850, "Extracts from Mr. Day's Letter," *Western Democrat,* 7 June 1850, Huntington Library, 2/1–2.

[96]Hoover, Diary, 3 December 1849, Huntington Library.

the ranks were broken." The majority backtracked or followed Beaver Dam Wash down to the Spanish Trail, but more than one hundred people headed west over the basin and range country of southern Nevada. Two months later these desperate adventurers reached the "great desert sink," where their hard experiences gave Death Valley its name. Those who made the fortunate decision to stick with the main road reached the green valleys of southern California by early 1850, but their trip was only somewhat less of an ordeal. "Some of them that packed in, eat one horse, a dog, and one wolf and several ravens, and some of them had not a mouthful of bread for more than five weeks," noted one survivor. "So there are various ways of getting to the gold mine, and all hard to accomplish."[97]

Washington Peck followed the Forty-niners' tracks down the southern trail in 1850, leading "29 wagons and two carts, 92 men, 9 women and 28 children." West of Las Vegas, Peck said the country lacked "sufficient vegetation to feed a grasshopper." The party's weakened animals began to drop as the Mojave Desert took on a terrifying aspect. "It appears as if the godess of desolation and barrenness has erected her throne and reigns without rival."[98] Such experiences did little to encourage use of this difficult trail, but in 1851 the Mormons established a large colony at San Bernardino that quickly became the second largest city in California. During the 1850s the trail served as a mail route and benefited from federally subsidized construction work. Military parties occasionally surveyed the trail and a few emigrant companies used it until 1857, when the brutal massacre at Mountain Meadows stopped most wagon travel until the 1860s, when travelers and freighters again traversed it sporadically. The wagon road to Los Angeles provided another road to California, but after the harrowing experience of the Death Valley Forty-niners, it practically vanished from historical awareness.[99]

Except for the trains that blazed the Cherokee Trail in 1849, none of the wanderers seeking a shortcut to the goldfields had much impact on the evolution of the road across the plains. Yet their experiences reveal the intense, widespread desire to find a better way to the Pacific and the dynamics that drove the process. The Americans caught up in the rush to California demonstrated a taste for adventure and a lust for quick riches, along with a relentless determination to realize their dreams—no matter the cost.

---

[97]"Letter from J. Fish," 1 March 1849, *Democratic Enquirer* (Muscatine, Iowa), 1 June 1850, 1/2.

[98]Peck, *On the Western Trails*, 9 October, 27 and 28 November 1850, 113, 128–29.

[99]The central southern route is not yet part of the California National Historic Trail. Edward Leo Lyman's *The Overland Journey from Utah to California* is the best history of this overlooked link in the overland trail system.

CHAPTER 6

A New and Shorter Route

Lassen's Horn

T he vanguard of the emigration marched down the Humboldt in June and July 1849, but most gold seekers and their exhausted teams reached the devastated river valley in August, and the rearguard trailed behind in September and October. With mounting dread, their trains confronted the California Trail's most arduous challenges—the Forty-mile Desert and the Sierra Nevada, whose grim reputations were dreadfully renowned. As the Humboldt Valley grew more desolate and their supplies shorter, desperate emigrants sought a better way to reach the land of gold: shortcuts real or imagined became irresistible. The leading candidate, the Lassen Trail or the "Oregon Road," promised "a new and shorter route to Feather River where we will cross the Sierra Nevada," wrote Joseph Middleton. "By doing so they will avoid the tremendous mountains, so difficult to pass, on the route by Salmon [Truckee] River, and Mary River sink."[1]

The road across the Black Rock Desert, which Oregon's South Road Expedition had blazed in 1846, already had a history. The possibility of using a northern pass to outflank the Sierra Nevada had long intrigued western travelers. Frémont's second expedition turned south from the Columbia at The Dalles in 1843 to look for the mythical Buenaventura River, visited Klamath Marsh, and climbed over the Warner Mountains to enter the Great Basin. He crossed the Black Rock Desert to the Great Boiling Spring near present-day Gerlach, Nevada, but the Pathfinder's cursory survey of northern California's complicated geography meant the maps his expedition produced proved woefully inaccurate. In October 1843, Joseph Chiles led John Jacob Myers, Milton McGee, Pierson Reading, Samuel Hensley, and thirteen others west from Fort Boise to look for the Sacramento River. After battling Indians and nearly starving to death in the "high and rugged" mountains, they reached Sutters Fort in November. "Starvation and fatigue were our constant

---

[1]Middleton, Diary, 20 September 1849, Beinecke Library, 125–26.

companions and as a last resource to sustain sinking nature we were forced to eat our horses and mules," Reading reported the following spring. "Mountain after mountain rose to our view, seeming to offer barriers sufficient to discourage the stoutest heart," while hostile Indians dogged their every step. Crossing California's northern mountains was not an easy way to reach its interior.[2]

Late in August 1848, Peter Lassen set out with ten wagons on the South Road's difficult trace from the Humboldt River meadow that would soon bear his name. The "wily Dane," as John Unruh called him, never expressed his exact intent, but at Goose Lake he turned south to blaze a wagon road to his ranch on the Upper Sacramento River. Wily he was not, but Lassen knew that whoever controlled trade at the end of a trail should quickly get rich. Lassen was indeed dedicated to making money from the trails, but he proved no more financially adept than John Sutter. As a way to get to the gold mines, his cutoff had many disadvantages, the worst being that it was at least two hundred miles longer than the roads over Donner and Carson passes.

Milton McGee and J. J. Myers had been in California since 1843 and probably knew as much about its geography as anyone. Before heading west again from Missouri in 1849, Myers wrote the army's adjutant general, offering his services as a guide to any military expeditions bound for the Sierra. "It is a well known fact that whare the Waggon Road crosses the California Mountain it is both Difficult and Dangerous," he noted. During his five years in the country trapping beaver Myers had "examined every stream South of the San Joaquin to the head of the Sacramento." He was familiar with several Sierra passes, "and from what I have seen the Head of the Sacramento is by far the best Rout through the Mountain and can be passed at any Season." Myers crossed Truckee Pass on his way to the States with Commodore Stockton in 1847, but he had not actually seen Fandango Pass, which the Applegate and Lassen routes used. Despite this, Myers recommended "leaving Marys River about one hundred miles above its sink whare the Suthern road to Oregon now leaves it." He was confident that "with very little work a good waggon road can be maid Down the Sacramento" with "but one small mountain to cross not exceeding ten miles over it which can be passed any time during the Winter." An examination would confirm his report, Myers claimed. In a few years it would be "the only Rout traveled by land from that Country."[3]

The army ignored Myers's offer, but his letter got results, for Goldsborough Bruff made a copy and carried it west. Charles Reed, Bruff's colleague in the Washington City Association, speculated about the new northern crossing while still on the Platte River. Bruff's train planned to "strike somewhere near the head of the

---

[2]Reading, Letter, 7 February 1844, in Bekeart, "A Biography"; and 143; Reading, "Journal," 16 September, 1 October, 10 November 1843, 176, 181, 195.

[3]Myers to Jones, "Myers' Letter," 13 February 1849, in Bruff, *Gold Rush,* 1201–1202.

Sacramento River and go down the valley after looking around the mountains for a spell," Reed wrote at Fort Kearny. "I cannot tell how long exactly it will take us to go but we shall make as short a trip as possible and not infirm our mules, for we depend on them to carry us through."[4] Easterners had another seemingly reliable report about the road, which was first released in San Francisco and was reprinted in the *New York Herald* on 12 February 1849. Packers who came from Oregon with Peter Burnett in 1848 said they considered "the pass discovered by Capt. Lawson, one of the finest in the world." With very little labor a road over it would "prove of lasting benefit to parties travelling to and from Oregon and California, and from the United States," they claimed. The Oregonians had not actually "seen any evidence of any work having been bestowed upon the road by the emigrants" and had rescued Lassen's demoralized train, but they praised "the energy and decision displayed by him in surveying the route" and tendered the captain a vote of thanks.[5]

By late summer, Austin J. Howard said the Upper Humboldt River had been reduced to "the most dry and arid region I have ever seen in my life, and the water almost sickening, being very warm, and tinctured with saltpeter and alkali, and the dust continually rising in dense clouds from the feet of the immense crowd that thronged the road, seemed as if it would smother every thing that had life."[6] When trains reached the overgrazed fields at Lassens Meadows, they heard rumors about the desolate state of the trails to the south. After crossing fifteen waterless miles at night, B. R. Biddle's train reached the meadow early on 11 August. Milton McGee headed west that morning with eleven teams; more wagons followed during the day. "As I am writing this I hear little else discussed around me but the merits and demerits of this new route," reported Biddle. Many wanted to take the new trace "on account of their being more water and grass along it than on the usual route to Sutter's Fort, and not increasing the distance to that point." He believed "this cut-off, as it is called," would lead directly to the headwaters of the Feather or Sacramento rivers in seven or eight days. Except for his illusions about the distance, the remarkably well informed Biddle knew of Lassen's trek the previous fall: the Dane himself allegedly gave McGee and Myers, "two mountain traders," a description of the road, perhaps when the three returned to the States with Stockton in 1847. Biddle's party recruited at the meadows for two days and then voted 14 to 6 to take the new trail. "We have discouraging news about the grass on the old route," he wrote, "and our mules, if they are to take us through, must have grass."[7]

---

[4]Reed to "Dear Sister Abby," St. Joseph, 13 May 1849, Newberry Library.

[5]"Meeting of Emigrants—The New Road," *California Star & Californian,* 18 November 1848, 2/3-4. For a brilliant analysis of what Forty-niners knew about Lassen's road, see Stillson, *Spreading the Word,* 109–19.

[6]Howard, "California Letter," 25 November 1849, *Iowa Star* (Des Moines), 31 May 1850?

[7]Biddle, "Journey to California," 11, 13 August 1849. The *Illinois Journal,* 15 December 1849, read Biddle's reference as "Clareson," probably a misreading of "Clawson."

The cutoff soon diverted hundreds of sojourners. Before the season ended, nearly ten thousand of them gambled on the new road. "Came to another rout called Applegates rout to oragon," Abram Minges reported. "We take this route on account of Scarsity of feed on the old ro[a]d," even though his party knew it was two hundred miles longer than the old trail.[8] "There is a good deal of exciting debate in camp today as to the propriety of leaving this river and road at this point and taking a reported new route," Alexander Ramsay wrote, "but we have no reliable source of information and it will be a hazardous adventure if we try it." The next day, after the train's "spies" reported finding a good road with water at fifteen miles, "three out of the five companies decided to risk the new route." Before they were out of sight, the two others decided to join them.[9] Amos Josselyn left the Great Meadows the same day as Minges and Ramsay, noting, "There was 8 wagons started in yesterday led by Magee."[10]

The first Forty-niners on the illusory shortcut found sterility and volcanic desolation prevailed everywhere; B. R. Biddle complained, "nearly everything we eat or drink has salt in it, and nearly everything is hot." He estimated the desert was seventy-five miles across and thought there were only fourteen teams ahead of his train.[11] While going down the Humboldt, "a report began to be accredited among the emigrants that there was a new road that led to Feather River, or the Sacramento, or [to] somewhere, that it was an hundred miles nearer to the mines, a better route, no difficulty in crossing the mountains (Sierra Nevada), and plenty of grass and water all the way," wrote Alonzo Delano, whose train was among the first to take the trail. The conflicting reports meant, he observed, "we did not know what to believe. In fact nobody knew certain whether there was a road leading to California that way, though there was one to Oregon. In much doubt we finally came to the turning-off point and our company determined to take it anyhow." Delano had heard there was grass and water at short intervals and good forage only thirty-five miles away. "We took it—there was no grass for sixty-five miles and but one spring, a mile off the road, where water could be had for the cattle; in short, we were on the desert and drove the whole distance without feeding our cattle, and no water except at the commencement." He counted fifty dead oxen scattered along the thirty parched miles to Black Rock Springs and calculated the desert extended for 105 miles.[12]

---

[8]Minges, Journal, 13 August 1849, Bentley Historical Library, 20.

[9]Ramsay, "Gold Rush Diary," 12, 13 August 1849, 458–59.

[10]Josselyn, The Overland Journal, 13 August 1849, 42. Dale Morgan correctly dated Milton McGee's departure to 11 August. See Pritchard, The Overland Diary, 27.

[11]Biddle, "Journey to California," 14–16 August 1849.

[12]Delano, California Correspondence, 16.

Still guiding the Hudspeth train, John J. Myers did not leave Lassens Meadows until about a week after McGee's first train. Many of those behind him had followed Myers over the Hudspeth Cutoff and were willing to gamble on another shortcut. "Some speculation exists as to the practicability of a new shute—to avoid the desert across the sink," wrote T. J. Van Dorn after hearing that six hundred dead cattle lined the road to the south. "We learn today that Jack Myers, in charge of Headspeth's train, decide[s] by a vote today whether they take the new route. Myers has been over it twice with packs, but it has never been travelled with wagons."[13] Ten days later Philip Badman came to the camp of a train from California "& talked with the man concerning the Roads & Gold. They gave me a hard Story about the Roads but Sufficiently good about the Gold to Overbalance the Roads." While camped that night a mile from the "Hedsbtys Cut off," his party determined to lay by for a day, "Cut Rushes or grass—& take it"—it being Lassen's, not Hudspeth's, trail.[14]

The promised cutoff developed a wishful mythology as thousands of weary sojourners pinned their hopes on it, attributing its discovery to mountaineers, Cherokees, or legendary pioneers. "We passed Myers company and camped at the forks of the road, that is the South Oregon Road. There was what we term a Post Office, that is a board set up with papers of information nailed on it," noted H. C. St. Clair. "Myers, McGee, Adams and other mountaineers have taken the new road. Myers intends (so he says) to take a road or make a cutoff that will take him to the gold diggings in ten days. But there is no grass for 60 miles and but little water."[15] A man who had scouted ahead advised Israel Hale to risk the new route, with the assurance "that by doing so we would cross the mountain at a lower gap and would find better grass" and get to the Sacramento River in nine days. Having heard "that Myers and Hudspeth, two old mountaineers," had taken it, Hale followed. Conflict on the Humboldt encouraged others to try the trail. Hale told of a train that sent thirty men in pursuit of lost cattle: four of them tried to capture four Natives, "but when they got within bow shot of the Indians they shot their arrows at them and wounded three of the white men; one in the shoulder, one in the forehead, and the other in the wrist." The whites killed three men, but the warrior who had inflicted all the damage ran away. The man "had two wounds himself and when he found that the white men would catch him, as he had shot all his arrows, he stopped and told the man to shoot him in the head, which he did." The emigrants found their cattle dead.[16]

---

[13]Van Dorn, Diary, 14, 15 August 1849, Beinecke Library, 35.
[14]Badman, Diary, 24 August 1849, Beinecke Library.
[15]St. Clair, Journal, 19 August 1849, Beinecke Library.
[16]Hale, "Diary of a Trip to California," 20–21 August 1849.

Dexter Tiffany "came to where the new road branches off to the right & found here a general Post office that is a great many letters & notices [by] the trains who had passed struck in split sticks written on slips of paper, cards, & boards." Many of the messages informed travelers which way their friends and loved ones had gone. "I advised the leader not to go but he urged us," Tiffany wrote after his companions voted to take the new road. To accommodate them, he agreed to go along. Two days earlier, in a broad meadow at today's Winnemucca, he had "learned that a Cherokee had come through from California to guide a train of Cherokees & had given the distance on an entirely new route which shortened the road very much [and] avoided the desert at the sink of Mary's River & went through a pass in the mountains without any steep hills to go over, with fine grass & water all the way."[17] Israel Lord heard the same story, and several diarists mentioned "the guide book of the Cherokees." Goldsborough Bruff copied several "Cherokee waybills" into his journals, but they were actually Levi Scott's description of the southern road, printed in the *Oregon Spectator* in April 1848. Historians Georgia Willis Read and Ruth Gaines suggested a Cherokee carried a version the waybill to Lassens Meadows in 1849, but the actual origin of the name "Cherokee Cutoff" remains a mystery.[18]

Edmund Booth said the purported shortcut was "more fitly called of late 'The Greenhorns' Route,'" so not everyone was easily fooled. All his companions wanted to try the "Cherokee Trail," believing it was only 160 miles to the gold mines. Booth used Frémont's map to show "that the distance, even in an air line, was much greater and the story therefore was entitled to little credit." When his train reached the barrel post office at the start of the road, "without saying anything or taking a vote, one old fellow took up his whip and drove on, another followed and another. So we all kept on the old route, and well we did so."[19]

Such common sense was uncommon among the desperate gold seekers. Strangely, many of the very best (and presumably most intelligent) 1849 diarists—Biddle, Bruff, Delano, Goldsmith, Gray, Hale, Lord, Middleton, Pierce, Swain, and Tiffany—chronicled Greenhorn Cutoff, the Cherokee or Applegate route, or the Oregon road, as they variously called the trace. Perhaps their slower-traveling trains gave these resilient writers time to create their extraordinary documents under such difficult conditions. Then again, this phenomenon might simply reflect how heavily the trail was used. Kimball Webster guessed, "Probably nearly one-half of the immigrants came by this route," but the number was closer to one-third.[20]

---

[17]Tiffany, Diary, 12, 14 September 1849, Missouri Historical Society, 113–14, 117–19.

[18]Lord, *"At the Extremity of Civilization,"* 9 September 1849, 108; Bruff, *Gold Rush,* 621–24, 1209–11.

[19]Booth to "My Dear Wife," 18 August 1850, in *Edmund Booth (1810–1905), Forty-niner,* 27.

[20]Webster, *Gold Seekers of '49,* 17 September 1849, 95.

By the time her family reached Lassens Meadows in September 1849, twenty-five-year-old Mary E. Brush had already endured more than most of her contemporaries would experience in a lifetime. Three hundred miles west of South Pass, she watched as her treasured wardrobe was split up for firewood. Albert and Mary Brush may have been among the few—Dexter Tiffany being the only other such unfortunate—who crossed both the Hastings and Lassen cutoffs. On the last night of August, her train "encamped and sent out the oxen with a guard of four men. My husband was one of them." After dark, cries of "help," "Indians," "murder," "I am shot," and "the cattle are gone" reached the campfire, and "every man sprang for his gun. Albert was unarmed. I sent him his rifle, and in less than five minutes there was not a man in camp. You may imagine what a night we women spent." Now she and her three-year-old daughter Emily faced another unknown desert crossing.[21]

THE WRONG ROAD:
APPLEGATE'S SOUTHERN ROAD TO OREGON

As the earliest accounts indicate, the first parties to head west on the Lassen Trail had accurate information, but wildly optimistic rumors, probably encouraged by a dose of wishful thinking, distorted estimates of the distance to the goldfields. Their misconceptions reflected the desperate hopes of the gold seekers and their ignorance about the geography of northern California. No one on the trail in 1849 understood that the Lassen Trail crossed hundreds of miles of challenging terrain, often heading in the wrong direction. Northwest of today's Imlay, Nevada, at the head of Rye Patch Reservoir, the trail went directly west for twelve miles across a sage plain to small seeps at Willow and Antelope springs. Neither spring provided enough water for the thousands of men, women, and children and the tens of thousands of animals that surged through in 1849. The trace climbed Imlay Summit and the Antelope Mountains, ran through Rosebud Canyon, crossed another nineteen miles to Kamma Pass, and descended Painted Canyon to Rabbit Hole Spring, which was on a mountainside "and very difficult to get at," Alexander Ramsay complained.[22] "We have not seen fifty spears of grass since we took this road," Israel Hale wrote at Rabbit Hole in mid-August. Soon there was no grass at all for seventy miles on the desert road.[23]

The presumed shortcut became a graveyard of emaciated and exhausted livestock. The carnage was horrific even on the initial dry passage. "Where we started from this morning there was a lot of dead oxen, broken wagons, wheels & lots of iron

[21]Brush to "Dear Parents," 27 January 1850, "Letter from California," 1.
[22]Ramsay, "Gold Rush Diary," 13 August 1849, 459.
[23]Hale, "Diary of a Trip to California," 22 August 1849, 114.

fixtures scatter'd in every direction," wrote Charles Glass Gray after his second day on the road. "I counted 160 oxen, dead & dying & wandering about scarce able to stand up—being left here to die!"[24] "While some of us tried to sleep," wrote one unknown diarist, who had counted fifty dead animals to the mile, "the moans of the cattle some of whome were actually dying with hunger and thirst were truly distressing."[25] Near Rabbit Hole Spring, Alvin Coffey found a downed ox that was unable to get back up. "The ox commenced bawling pitifully. Some of the boys had gone to bed. I said, 'Let us go out and kill the ox for it is too bad to hear him bawl.' The wolves were eating him alive." No one would help, but Coffey ended the animal's misery.[26] "The day was very warm & dusty & the men almost exhausted with fatigue & sickened by the constant smell of carcasses on the road," wrote John Bates.[27] "Most of the oxen I saw were shot in the head as they had given out unable to travel," Dexter Tiffany observed. "Their owners in kindness had ended their sufferings quickly rather than leave them to the slower & severer pangs of hunger."[28]

Beyond Rabbit Hole Spring, the trail took an alarming swing to the northwest over the Black Rock Desert's glistening playa. Dust, heat, hunger, and the decimation of their cattle made the dry *journada* torturous. "We have discovered that we are on the wrong road," Joseph Middleton wrote after traveling about thirty-six miles west from the Humboldt and still fifty desert miles from good grass. His party loaded their provisions and worldly goods onto a cart and decided to "abandon all the rest and go ahead." In two and one-half miles he passed forty-one dead oxen.

"This has been the saddest day of my journey," wrote Dexter Tiffany. There was a greater loss of teams on that day's march than on any he had yet made: "I counted on this days drive 367 dead oxen, includeing 3 or 4 mules & horses."[29] Emigrants at last found water and grass at Black Rock's Great Boiling Spring. Its funnel, about twenty-five feet in diameter, was "a deep circular pit like what I would suppose the shape of the mouth of a small volcano," Middleton said. "I can see about 10 feet down but no further; the water looks green, and constantly sends up bubbles that are incessantly rising over an oval surface of 2 by 3 feet." The spring formed a shallow pond some one hundred feet long and almost as wide, which drained into a broad meadow to the west. He camped two miles beyond the great spring and "counted the steam rising from 10 hot springs and wells close bye." Wells one or two yards deep produced drinkable cold water. Middleton took the opportunity to shave and launder three shirts. The water, he said, did "a famous job of washing."

[24]Gray, *Off at Sunrise,* 22 August 1849, 84.

[25]Anonymous, Overland Diary, 18 September 1849, Mason Diaries, Beinecke Library.

[26]Coffey, Recollection of 1849, California Society of Pioneers.

[27]Bates, Diary, 20 September 1849, Mattes Library.

[28]Tiffany, Diary, 14 September 1849, Missouri Historical Society, 120.

[29]Ibid., 119.

Extreme heat compounded the suffering. "Half an hour before sunset thermometer in the sun 105°," he noted. At Black Rock, "a volcanic crater, rough and reefy, towering high in the air . . . the heat was 109° in the sun in the afternoon." In the midst of this ordeal Middleton paused to ponder the rewards of his adventure: "My greatest pleasure in travelling through the country is derived from the knowledge that it has seldom been traversed, or at least never been described by any hackneyed tourist, that everything I see or look upon has been seen by me before it has become common by the vulgar gaze or description of others."[30]

Beyond the spring, thousands of Forty-niners found themselves heading northwest over a hundred miles of the barren Black Rock Desert on a trail that took them away from Sacramento. "The route through here was strewn with the wrecks of waggons, and the carcasses of cattle; the stench arising from them was horrible," wrote Thomas E. Cook. After losing twenty head of cattle and abandoning three wagons, Cook at last reached water and grass at Black Rock Spring, "an immense boiling spring some eight rods in length and four in breadth, the water strongly impregnated with sulpher, salts, and alkalie." There his company "ascertained that we were on Lawson's route, and some 300 miles further from the diggings than we would have been on the old route; but we had gone too far to turn back; our only alternative was to go ahead."[31]

Forty miles more of desert and mud flats lay northwest of Black Rock, past thermal features including Double Hot Springs, to Salt Valley, also known as Mud Lake or Meadows, where emigrants finally found abundant water and grass. "We are now at what is cald mud Lake," complained Philip Badman, "but still there is no lake at this place." The lake, David Leeper explained, was "simply an extensive group of springs whose waters here came to the surface and radiated in rivulets in such manner as to form a sort of morass containing several hundred acres." After sliding into Fly Canyon down a slope so steep "it would seem as if it would be difficult to prevent the hind wheels from turning a somersault over the fore ones," wagons climbed out and entered "the jaws of a rent hill of black-red rock, which seems to have opened as if to swallow one up," whose rocks Middleton thought looked "very much like enormous knots in mahogany wood." High Rock Canyon cut "through a range of lava that is some twenty miles in width and as bare of vegetation as if it had cooled but the day before," Leeper recalled. "The fissure or gorge that afforded us passage is about the width of a common road, and is inclosed by high walls that are carved in irregular outline, as if by the action of an ancient ice-river."[32]

---

[30]Middleton, Diary, 24–27 September 1849, Beinecke Library.

[31]Cook to "Dear Mother," 11 February 1850, in Mathews, *Mathews Family*, 326.

[32]Leeper, *Argonauts of 'Forty-nine*, 63–64; Badman, Diary, 29 August 1849, Beinecke Library, 44; Middleton, Diary, 30 September to 2 October 1849, Beinecke Library, 143, 145, especially the mileage table on page 136. As Don Buck noted, emigrants soon opened a trail that bypassed Fly Canyon. See Howell, *1849 California Trail Diaries*, 113n170.

BLACK ROCK DESERT

Daniel A. Jenks sketched a wagon train approaching the edge of the Black Rock Desert in August 1859. These springs on Nobles Trail had been developed as part of the Fort Kearney, South Pass, and Honey Lake Wagon Road. Courtesy Library of Congress.

The colorful canyon was a "narrow, rocky pass through the mountains, just wide enough for a smooth, level road, with intervals of space occasionally, to afford grass and water. On each side were walls of perpendicular rock, four or five hundred feet high, or mountains so steep that the ascent was either impossible, or extremely difficult," Alonzo Delano noted. "Without this singular avenue, a passage across the mountains in this vicinity would have been impossible, and it seemed as if Providence, foreseeing the wants of his creatures, had in mercy opened this strange path, by which they could extricate themselves from destruction and death." The canyon ran through the Calico Mountains to Painted Point, where the trail turned west up Long Valley and over Forty-nine Pass to Surprise Valley, inside today's California border. "We have traveled through the wildest region the imagination can depict," B. R. Biddle wrote in High Rock Canyon. "Solitude claims this region as its dominion." Beyond the canyon, Joseph Middleton found an immense playa "as smooth & level as a lake full of water." He stepped off the Mud Pond "across its middle and it is 1157 good yards wide" and "perhaps 3 times or more wide than it is broad; and about the same width from one end to the other." From Surprise Valley, emigrants saw "proudly glittering afar, the snowy peaks of the Nevada," their first view of what soon became the Warner Mountains, a Great Basin range not part of the Sierra Nevada.[33]

Wagons now climbed 1,600 feet to an elevation of 6,100 feet in a little over two miles to reach Fandango Pass; the steepest rise occurred in the last mile. "The ascent was easy generally, but occasionally there were benches which were to be overcome," wrote Delano. "Still the passage was far from difficult—indeed not as bad as many hills which we had already climbed." Not everyone found climbing out of the Great Basin easy. "We are at the foot of the highest ridge which is half a mile long & steeper than the roof of a house," noted Dexter Tiffany as he approached the pass, where the tall pines reminded him of Maine. "Walked to the top of the ridge leading horses and had a fine view of the region beyond. It took 11 yoke of oxen to pull up an almost empty wagon." B. R. Biddle remarked, "the atmosphere is so filled with smoke that we can see little that surrounds us." Many believed it was manmade: "The immigrants have set the grass on fire and have destroyed a quantity of it," Samuel Stover wrote on Pit River, and Alonzo Delano thought Indians had set the blazes. Jonas Hittle persuasively attributed the damage to emigrants: "There has Been a great Quantity of Grass Burnt it is Said By a train from Indiana" known as the Wild Hoosiers, reputed to be "a very hartless Set of Beasts who try to distress the Emigrants Behind Them," he charged. "They are

---

[33]Delano, *Life on the Plains,* 21 August, 193–94, Biddle, "Journey to California," 20 August 1849; Middleton, Diary, 6 October 1849, Beinecke Library.

a disgrace to their State." The Hoosiers had destroyed the grass on the Pit River Divide: "they have tried to Burn all the Gras that would Burn," Hittle said. Like their compatriots on the Truckee route, travelers set trees on fire as the weather grew cold. "Large fires are burning all through the forest," Tiffany wrote on a fork of Feather River. Wolverine Ranger James Pratt blamed his fellow Forty-niners for the conflagrations: "Evidences of a large emigration though here are seen in the blackened trees which have been set on fire, many of which we see burning every day, as well as in the condition of the road and the camping grounds."[34]

Due to "the weak state of our mules & the immense hight we had to attain," the Washington City Association set out before sunrise to cross Fandango Pass. John Bates was with the first men to struggle to the top. His wagons double-teamed up the steep mountain but still had to stop and rest twenty or thirty times before the first wagon hoisted a flag on the summit—and when the weakest team caught up almost four hours later, members "gave a general Hurrah!" From the pass, the men could look down on Goose Lake and the difficult terrain that lay ahead. They descended "into a beautiful valley where we camped on the bourder of a splendid pine timbered region." The forested valley "was quite a relief to eyes wearied by looking for months on nothing but barron hills & dull & monotinous plains of volcanic rock & ashes," Bates wrote.[35]

After crossing Fandango Pass, William Swain noted, "We bid a long and hearty goodbye to this team-killing, back-breaking, leg-soring mountain." Government relief trains "got up" dancing parties for the families camped at the foot of the mountain, "which gave a lasting name to the valley," James Pratt reported. A large and less credible body of lore explains how the pass got its name: legends tell how a wagon train danced all night to keep warm or, more outrageously, how one company danced the fandango to celebrate crossing the pass before Modoc warriors swept down upon the festivities and wiped out the train. Years later, Oliver Goldsmith recalled hearing this story: "After camping one night the weather grew so terribly cold that the men had to dance to keep warm, and named their wild camping place 'Fandango Valley.'" But the evening after the Wolverine Rangers crossed the pass, they "joined with the Smith girls and had a tall time in the way of a fandango, which lasted till ten o'clock," Swain wrote on the spot.[36]

---

[34]Delano, *Life on the Plains,* 204, 208; Tiffany, Diary, 26 September, 3 October 1849, Missouri Historical Society; Biddle, "Journey to California," 29 August 1849; Stover, *Diary,* 4 September 1849, 37; Hittle, Diary, 2, 3, and 5 September 1849, Illinois State Historical Library; Pratt, 25 October 1849, in Cumming, *The Gold Rush,* 281.

[35]Bates, Diary, 3 October 1849, Mattes Library.

[36]Swain, 12, 13 October 1849, *The World Rushed In,* 276–77; Pratt, 24 October 1849, in Cumming, *The Gold Rush,* 103–104; Hughey, "Peter Lassen and the Fandango Pass"; Goldsmith, *Overland in Forty-Nine,* 88; Swain, 13 October 1849, *The World Rushed In,* 277.

A WILD SPECULATION: GOVERNMENT TRAINS

Westbound gold seekers encountered government expeditions on the Applegate and Lassen trails, including Mounted Riflemen from Oregon bound for Fort Hall with supplies for the regiment's troops at Cantonment Loring. Author and 1845 trail veteran Joel Palmer, who had served as commissary general in Oregon's Cayuse War, was the train's wagon master, and Southern Road trailblazer Levi Scott was its guide. They met resistance. Indians in Salt Valley had filled a pack train's livestock with arrows, Abram Minges noted—"the first attack that has bin Since we Started."[37] Eight days later, Palmer's train was embroiled in a much rougher fight. "General Palmer reports having had a serious battle with the Digger Indians at Mud Lake, where he lost one man killed and had two or three wounded," wrote Kimball Webster.[38]

Jonas Hittle almost witnessed the fight when he camped with the supply train at Salt Valley. Scott and three scouts, looking for a shorter route to the Humboldt River, returned to camp not long after daylight, with Scott slightly wounded and a dead Phinney Garretson tied on his horse. "Scott and Garretson were in advance of the other two men and Came to two indians who had a grey mare with Shoes on and they knew they had Stolen her," Hittle wrote. Scott spoke to the Indians in their own language, but Garretson ordered one of them to surrender his bow, threatened him with his rifle, and received a flight of arrows in return. A second Indian "seized hold on Scotts gun and a Scuffle ensued and Garretson fired at the indian and missed him then turnd and Struck at the indian who was Scufling with Scott but Slipt on a Rock and Come near falling and missed the indian." A Native "shot an arrow through" Garretson as he struggled to his feet, while Scott wrested the rifle "out of the hands of the indian and Garretson told Scott to kill them that he was mortally wounded." Both Indians turned their bows on Scott, "and he Shot one of them and the other Run away" after they "had hit Scott in four places none of the wounds mortal." Scott had warned, "if we got into an indian fight to face them and not turn our back and the indians would Seldom hit us and he faced them and they missed him," Hittle wrote, "all but four arrows." The train buried Garretson in the road "and drove their teams over the grave to hide it from the Indians."[39] The dead man "brought on the encounter by his own imprudence, by first firing on the Indian because he refused to give up his bows and arrows," wrote J. M. Muscott, who camped with the "intelligent, affable and sensible" Joel Palmer on 25 August and "obtained much valuable information touching our route." Scott said he fired in self-defense and "shot the same Indian and the other fled."[40]

---

[37]Minges, Journal, 17 August 1849, 54, 21.
[38]Webster, *Gold Seekers of '49*, 7 September 1849, 82.
[39]Hittle, Diary, 24, 25 August 1849, Illinois State Historical Library, 78–82.
[40]Muscott to Robbins, 14 October 1849, California State Library.

On the Humboldt, the supply train advised everyone it met to take the "old Oregon route, which, owing to the lateness of the season, was considered the safest." At Goose Creek in mid-September, the eastbound Riflemen met the westbound Riflemen escorting John Wilson's ponderous baggage train. The imperious Indian agent hired trail veteran Joel Palmer, "perhaps the most efficient guide that has travelled the plains," at Palmer's lowest rate—"being $2000 for the trip." Captain Robert Morris had discharged the train's mutinous teamsters after reaching the Humboldt; the next day Wilson "dispensed with my escorting farther," wrote the captain. "I did all that my means would allow me to do, so I felt Satisfied with my conduct and let him take his own course." Morris was in no position to comply when the "rascally attorney" sent a note asking for additional mules and provisions for his teamsters. Now far behind schedule, Morris kept to the main trail, provided aid to the last emigrants on the Carson Pass trail, and on 27 October led his "considerably way-worn" but healthy troopers into Weberville, having abandoned "most of his wagons on the desert, as many of his mules were broken down and unable to travel any further."[41]

West of Fandango Pass, Abram Minges met a government pack train on 5 September under the command of topographical engineer William Warner, one of the most talented officers in the service. Captain Warner and Lieutenant Robert Williamson left Sacramento in August with orders to find the best railroad pass in northern California. Warner had two guides: Minges incorrectly identified François Bercier as a Mexican, but "old Lawson" was Peter Lassen himself, who accompanied the expedition for a reported fee of $1,000 a month. "They told us they ware exploring a railroad rout through to the humbolt river," Minges wrote, "but I think they are going to the head of feather rivr to hunt gold."[42] B. R. Biddle, who met Warner the next day, was less skeptical. "It savors rather of a wild speculation to talk of a railroad through this part of the world," he wrote, "but they may do it. Uncle Sam can accomplish much." Biddle found the officers to be gentlemen, and they gave him much information.[43]

Warner hired emigrants as he headed north, paying $300 per month for a man and his horse: he had some thirty men with him in late September. Bad luck and ill health plagued the expedition, which left its sick and its surgeon behind at Deer Creek. "They had among them several invalids and I sold them one ounce of quinine for twenty dollars," wrote Dr. Israel Hale.[44] Dexter Tiffany dined with Warner at

[41]Culmer, " 'General' John Wilson," 328; Morris and Haynes journals, 17, 25, 26 September, 27 October 1849, Beinecke Library; Smith, "Correspondence," Serial 561, 111, 113.

[42]Minges, Journal, 5 September 1849, 64, 66, Bentley Historical Library, 25.

[43]Biddle, "Journey to California," 6 September 1849.

[44]Hale, "Diary of a Trip to California," 12 September 1849, 129.

Goose Lake on California beef and stewed wild plums. Weeks later Tiffany found the invalids still camped at Deer Creek. Every man was sick.[45] A grizzly bear dug up a dead soldier, dragged him a few yards, and gnawed one leg off, Abram Minges reported grimly.[46] The expedition's hard luck soon got worse. Between Goose Lake and Pit River, John Bates fell in with the advance elements of the expedition, which "reported the Indians to be very troublesome in this part of the country." A band had followed the soldiers for several days, "but attributing their motives more to curiosity than mischief, they treated the matter with indifference." Then some thirty or forty warriors ambushed the party in a canyon, killing Warner and wounding two men. "The first they knew of their being so near the Captain had recd 15 arrows in his body."[47]

Confusion shrouds the details of Warner's death, including where he died and who killed him. According to the official report, he divided his company at Goose Lake. About thirty miles north of Fandango Pass, "a party of about twenty-five Indians, who had been lying in ambush behind some large rocks near the summit, suddenly sprang up and shot a volley of arrows into the party," wrote Warner's second-in-command. Most of the arrows hit Warner and Bercier. "The Captain's mule turned with him, and plunged down the hill; and having been carried about two hundred yards, he fell from the animal dead." Thrown into confusion, the men fled. Bercier died the next morning, and a second casualty did not make it back to the settlements.[48] The army sent a punitive expedition to track down Warner's attackers the following summer, but no one could say which tribe killed the promising young officer. Today, the Warner Mountains bear the brave captain's name.

Long Drives over Bad Roads: The Lassen Trail

Peter Lassen's trail left the southern route to Oregon and turned south at Goose Lake. Twelve miles west of Fandango Pass, Goose Lake was "so called from the immense numbers of wild geese that inhabited it," wrote John Muscott, who found the landscape enchanting. "A flock of swans was sailing over the Lake and the whole picture was one of freshness, beauty and grandeur that thrilled, warmed and electrified my spirits to an unusual degree, and it needed only the addition of farm houses or villages on the plain or on the gentle declivities to have completed

---

[45]Tiffany, Diary, Missouri Historical Society, 27 September, 7 October 1849, 36–37, 49. Tiffany's diary is misdated in places.

[46]Minges, Journal, 9 September 1849, 66, Bentley Historical Library, 26.

[47]Bates, Diary, 5 October 1849, Mattes Library. William Horace Warner died on 26 September 1849. He graduated from West Point in 1836, had served in the Topographical Engineers since 1838, and was breveted a captain in December 1846 for gallantry in California.

[48]Williamson, "Report," 20, in Bruff, Gold Rush, 624–25.

the loveliest landscape that imagination could paint or eye behold."[49] From the lovely lake, the trail crossed the Modoc Plateau to the Pit River's north fork, where it followed the stream through a series of open valleys to the main river's narrow canyon at Warm Springs Valley. West of Hanging Rock, the trail intersected with the 1848 wagon road from the Willamette Valley. There, at the end of August, Alexander Ramsay got discouraging news from Oregonians returning from the goldfields. The mines were still 190, not sixty, miles away. Ramsay's mules were giving out and his party, he wrote, was "heartily sorry that we had taken the new rout [with] some wishing themselves back upon the Humboldt river where we had left it and some wishing themselves farther back still."[50]

The twisting trail down Pit River was an ordeal. "The indians have dug pits along here So that it is dangerous to Ride along the Banks," Jonas Hittle observed. "They dig them about Six feet deep and Smallest at the top and Cover them Slightly and the Game Stumbles in them," a custom that gave the river its name. As if these physical obstacles were not enough, the Indians themselves were aggressive and resolute. The Achomawi, who shared Goose Lake with the Klamaths, Modocs, and Northern Paiutes, ranged far to the south, so emigrants knew them as the Pit River Indians. E. D. Pierce called the tribe "the most hostile and war like that ever infested the mountains or valleys of California." Given the dependence on their teams, emigrants felt Indians threatened their lives as well as the animals they filled with arrows in hopes of picking up the carcasses. Alonzo Delano met three packers whose train broke up after Indians stole all their horses and mules in the Salt Valley: "They were getting through in the only way which was left"—on foot. Desperate conditions evoked desperate responses; "Here we could see emigrants travelling in all manners of style, some were reduced to a cart and one yoke of oxen, or a span of horses and mules, others had become impatient and left their trains, and with their Blankets and a few pounds of provisions on their backs were taking it a foot," Pierce wrote. "So great was the anxiety of the Emigration to be the first through, that many were almost insane upon the subject."[51]

His party felt perfectly secure on Pit River, Samuel Breck recalled, "but at three o'clock in the morning we were roused by the cries of my friend Easterman, with the most agonizing shriek, exclaiming 'I am shot, I am shot.' In an instant we were all alert." Breck's esteemed friend lived ninety minutes before dying from his arrow wound. "We had to bury my friend enclosed in nothing but his blankets,

[49]Muscott to Robbins, 14 October 1849, California State Library.

[50]Ramsay, "Gold Rush Diary," 29 August 1849, 462.

[51]Hittle, Diary, 8 September 1849, Illinois State Historical Library, 97; Delano, *Life on the Plains*, 30 August 1849, 217; Pierce, *The Pierce Chronicle*, 21 August 1849, 28.

without any ceremony whatsoever."[52] Israel Lord saw the arrow's long shaft stuck in Easterman's grave, lacking its point: "The workmanship is neat, and the weapon must be an efficient one, as the man was killed instantly," Lord reported. "The Indian was probably from Oregon, judging by the length of the arrow."[53]

The arduous track went down the broken canyons of Pit River to Big Valley, where the trail split to avoid a narrow defile, with one alternate going to today's Pitville and the second to Little Valley. "We are surrounded by mountains that seem to defy our escape," wrote B. R. Biddle.[54] The trails reunited at Blacks Mountain before dividing again through Patterson and Grays valleys and reuniting at Pine Creek. The trace left the Pit River Valley "over a long hill, the precursor of a hard, rocky road," Alonzo Delano wrote. "It was twelve miles to the first water, and fourteen to the first grass." The climb was worth it, for it led to a mountain paradise where the trail followed the headwaters of the Feather River to Big Meadows, now submerged beneath Lake Almanor.[55] "We are near several lakes which some one calls Feather lake, everything being now called feather except our beds," Dexter Tiffany wrote sardonically.[56]

There Elijah Preston Howell "cut grass to do us across the desert between deer creek ahead of us and Lawson's ranch." Over the next two days trains could cut more fodder at Soldier Meadows and Deer Creek Meadows, where the trail climbed the thickly forested and grassless ridge running between Deer and Mill creeks. Most of the final sixty-nine miles to Lassen's were a desert, Joseph Middleton noted. The trace had its own Steep Hollow, whose sharp descent was littered with "ox chains & yokes & wagon bodies & fixtures, axel trees & broken wheels & tongues & enough old irons to set up a foundary."[57] Travelers were now a dozen miles from the Sacramento Valley and only a little farther from Peter Lassen's ranch near today's Vina.

Lassen's road had several advantages—the crossing of Fandango Pass was comparatively easy, and beyond the Black Rock Desert it usually offered good grass and water—but it shared the ruinous flaw that made most cutoffs a bad bet: it was not a shortcut. "Well, here are the facts, and they *are* stubborn things!" Goldsborough Bruff wrote after reading Lieutenant Williamson's accurate waybill. The route

[52]Breck, "A Letter from California," 23 November 1849, 1. Joseph Middleton said Emmerson died after catching an Indian stealing a horse tied to a wagon wheel. Middleton also saw a notice saying, "Clayton Reeve was shot 15th October by Indians, there was more than a dozen Arrows in him." Middleton, Diary, 18 October 1849, Beinecke Library. Bruff recorded this epitaph: "Mr Eastman;—The deceased was killed by an Indian arrow; Octr 4th 1849." He found an arrow "in the breast of the grave" with a card attached: "This is the fatal arrow." See Bruff, *Gold Rush,* 207.
[53]Lord, *"At the Extremity of Civilization,"* 5 October 1849, 142–43.
[54]Biddle, "Journey to California," 3 September 1849.
[55]Delano, *Life on the Plains,* 5, 10 September 1849, 219, 222.
[56]Tiffany, Diary, 4 October 1849, Missouri Historical Society, 45.
[57]Howell, *1849 California Trail Diaries,* 19 September 1849, 143n223; Middleton, Diary, 26 October 1849, Beinecke Library, 180; Gray, *Off at Sunrise,* 30 September 1849, 112.

was at least 150 miles farther from the nearest settlement than most emigrants suspected—and this did not take into account the 130 miles separating Lassen's Rancho Bosquejo from Sutters Fort. Alonzo Delano estimated the trail was about 300 miles longer than the old road. Bruff copied Dr. Caldwell's waybill, which gave the distance between Lassens Meadows and Sacramento as 477 miles. Factoring in the exhaustion plaguing emigrants and their animals, the Indians' hostile reception, and its "long drives over bad roads," the Lassen Trail proved to be a bad bargain.[58]

Acts of sacrifice and heroism illuminated the struggles of those who faced disaster on the cutoff. Men shared their last two days' bread with women and children who had eaten nothing for days. "They gave all they had left to these helpless ones," Delano wrote, "and went on without."[59] In High Rock Canyon, someone asked Dexter Tiffany if he knew an old man from Saint Louis named Bell. Tiffany discovered his family friend was "very sick & that he could not live one day longer & that his train had gone on & left him alone & that the man who was waiting on him was using very abusive language to him & damning him because he did not die or get well so that they could go ahead." A doctor who had seen the "old Gent" said the septuagenarian "was all alone & that he never had his feelings so hurt as he had in having this man talk so severely to a man so sick & old." The next morning Tiffany discovered John Bell lying on the ground beside his wagon. "By conversing with him I found his mind was gone & learned that he had been so for three days." Four physicians told Tiffany his "only chance was to try & get him forward to better quarters." He took charge of the wagon, cleaned it out, and "fixed up a swinging bed." After washing Bell and loading him in the wagon, the men set off with the train. When Bell's abuser "came to camp he was very cross & snapped me up about some tea. I settled the matter pretty quick & told him not to use one uncivil word either to Mr. Bell or myself again if he knew what was good for his health," Tiffany said.

At dawn, Bell was in his right mind. He recognized Tiffany, "though he said my beard was so long he did not know me at first." Bell had been lamed falling off a wagon tongue in June and was sensible of his situation. "He was a perfect skeleton." The next day he moved Bell "& put him in the tent and washed him all over." The sick man had suffered from diarrhea for ten days and was "too weak to move & we have no bed pan. You can judge. Worked very hard all day in fixing things up & taking care of Mr. Bell." By the morning of 22 September, Tiffany was satisfied Bell could not survive the day. "I told him if he had anything to say he must do it

<hr />

[58]Bruff, *Gold Rush,* 4 October 1849, 206, 1208, 1220; Delano, *California Correspondence,* 17; Biddle, "Journey to California," 3 September 1849. Historian J. S. Holiday estimated it was 350 miles to Sutters Fort by either Truckee or Carson Pass. Swain, *The World Rushed In,* 272.

[59]Delano, *Life on the Plains,* 237.

then as it would be his only chance. He said nothing & appeared too weak to talk." As the wagon lurched down the trail, the old man "frequently called for water & when I went to give it to him he was too weak to drink it. Before noon he began to sink & died before we reached our journey's end. He was as comfortable in motion as at rest but died without pain."

At sunrise, Tiffany and two men took spades and selected a burial spot near Warm Spring. After laying out and washing the corpse, Tiffany made a coffin from a wagon box and "laid him down in his last resting place." He printed Bell's name on a large board for a headstone. "So I have taken care of & buried the very man you desired me to go with to take care of me," Tiffany wrote his wife. "How strange are the ways of Providence."[60]

Is It Not Hard to Get to California?
The Relief of the Emigrants

The first overlanders to reach California made grim predictions. "There are some 20,000 emigrants behind us, the majority of whom, unless they turn aside and winter in Oregon, will meet with certain death," J. E. H. noted after reaching Johnsons Ranch on 10 August. "There is not a blade of grass for the last hundred miles on the Humboldt river; and upon the desert we counted no less than 50 dead animals. Every emigrant that arrives has a tale to tell more mournful than his that preceded him."[61] Of the six to eight thousand wagons that set out, not more than a quarter would ever get over the trail, predicted a Missourian. "What the others will do the Lord only knows. For when we passed the Sink of Mary's river, there was a perfect desert of a hundred miles. I have since learned that there was no grass for more than 250 miles above the Sink, making a desert utterly impassable of 350 miles."[62] Disaster awaited the thousands still on the trail, for the Humboldt Valley resembled "a bed of hot ashes, with the exception of here and there a small patch of willows; by this time there is neither grass or willows," wrote S. F. Rodmon. By mid-August heat and poisonous water had killed 1,500 oxen and mules on the Carson route, "but this is only the beginning of distress—hundreds of men, women and children will perish on these roads this winter."[63] The last trains suffered from "exhaustion, dysentery, diarrhea, mountain fever, scurvy, and poor, broken-down cattle," recalled Dr. Charles Dexter Cleveland. They "had reached

[60]Tiffany, Diary, 18–22 September 1849, Missouri Historical Society, 123–26. The epitaph read, "Jnº Bell, of St. Louis, Sep. 22. '49, aged 70." See Bruff, Gold Rush, 201, 307.

[61]Anonymous (J. E. H.), "Letter from California," 12 August 1849, 4/1–2.

[62]Anonymous, "From California," 24 August 1849, Missouri Whig, 8 November 1849.

[63]Rodmon, "From California," 17 August 1849.

a pitiful stage. Many were so afflicted with scurvy, that their limbs were swollen, and covered with purple blotches, where the morbid blood had leaked through the impoverished tissues, and when they sat down, it was difficult for them to arise."[64]

As the season wore on reports grew increasingly dire. "The general supposition was that there was between 8000 and 9000 teams on the road, about 100,000 head of stock including horses, mules and all, and about 40,000 men. It is impossible for them all to get here this season," wrote Henry Wiman. "Some have stopped at the salt lake others have gone to Oregon and some on the road yet who I am afraid will never get in. Some have come in lately badly frost biten and some say that the snow was 18 inches deep on Carson River which is beyond the Sierra Nevada or snowy mountains [with] 5 or 600 teams back yet, and a great many of them family waggons."[65] Those still on the trail in October presented a sorry spectacle: "The last part of the emigration resembled the rout of an army, with its distressed multitudes of helpless sufferers, rather than the voluntary movement of a free people," Alonzo Delano observed.[66]

The crisis did not go unheeded. The first trains brought in so many alarming reports that the military government immediately "took active measures for their relief," J. M. Muscott reported. "We met one of these relief parties on our route; just as we were entering the valley of the Sacrimento."[67] With the specter of the Donner party in mind, army officers and private citizens organized an extraordinary rescue effort. Military governor Persifor Smith directed Major Daniel Rucker to take the equivalent of $2.6 million in civil funds to send provisions and livestock to the last poor souls on the trail. San Franciscans contributed another $12,000.[68] "Many of those far in the rear are doomed to undergo many privations if not to perish in the mountains," George Murrell predicted. "Government is doing every thing in its power to aid them in. Gen Smith has handed over $100,000 dollars for that purpose. Even the citizens are alive to their distressed situation & are making liberal donations. I think from the zeal manifested in the cause that much can and will be done."[69] Smith's orders eventually "sent men and supplies for those in need to every pass in these mountains," Joseph Middleton noted.[70]

The "the generally received opinion" was that the last trains would use the classic California Trail, so Rucker requisitioned 13,000 rations, sent three relief parties to the Truckee River, and dispatched only one under Robert Hunt to the Carson.

[64]Cleveland, Autobiography, 68.
[65]Wiman to "Dear Parents," 25 October 1849, Missouri Historical Society, 1–2.
[66]Delano, Life on the Plains, 236.
[67]Muscott to Robbins, 14 October 1849, California State Library.
[68]Lamb, "Emigrant Aid," 124–256.
[69]Murrell to "Dear Father," 17 September 1849, Mattes Library.
[70]Middleton, Diary, 11 October 1849, Beinecke Library, 159.

A GRAVE IN THE WILDERNESS

In June 1937, explorer and historian Charles Kelly discovered the grave of a man identified only as Jesse on Little Goose Creek in Elko County, Nevada. Utah State Historical Society.

John Chandler assembled thirty men and horses, 119 mules, and four wagons loaded
with provisions for the Truckee relief. Leaving his wagons at Mule Springs on 26
September, he pushed ahead with pack animals. Elisha Lewis passed "a Mule train
100 in number sent by Government for the relief of the back Emergration which it
was feared would not get over the mountains before winter set in." At Grass Valley
the rescuers gave Dr. Elijah White and the ruins of the Ithaca Company nine mules
and two horses, and sent back three men too sick to proceed. As October began,
it was clear that "all the emigrants on this route with wagons had already reached
the western side of the mountains." At the last crossing of the Truckee, Chandler
turned south to survey conditions on the Carson River but found "no signs of any
portion of the emigration having passed for several days." The scouts he sent out
onto the Forty-mile Desert located the Lamdell party on 10 October: they reported
the families behind them were also "destitute of animals of any kind." Chandler
sent men and mules to relieve them and led the twenty wagons he found at Carson
Canyon on 12 October over the mountains to the settlements. "This philanthropic
movement is timely; and will be of inestimable value to many a weary, hungry
traveller, who has been on short allowance for a long time, and perhaps destitute
for days," wrote Gordon Cone after meeting the relief at Leek Springs.[71]

Meanwhile, the single relief party sent to Carson Pass under Robert Hunt
learned that a blizzard had caught Dr. B. B. Brown on 11 October on his way up
West Pass, and the wind, snow, and hail made it "utterly impossible to proceed
any further." All Brown's animals froze to death, except for two mules tied close
to the large fire that saved Brown's family. Between Tragedy Spring and Lake Valley, Hunt gave two mules and provisions to an old man and his wife and daughter,
"who had nothing in the world but a few blankets, which they were packing on
their backs." Packer F. J. Clayton gave Hunt solid information about the parties
bringing up the rear. Charles Sackett's Saint Louis train, the last on the road, was
still "a hundred miles beyond the mountains," Clayton reported, but Sackett led the
last family on the Carson route into Weberville about 29 October 1849. By early
November the relief effort had brought in everyone on the Truckee and Carson
routes. From Sacramento, Sackett sent his whole train's thanks for Hunt's timely
and efficient aid "in overcoming the passage of the mountains." Latecomer Josiah
Royce apologized for losing a black government mule last seen with "fifteen feet
of rope on its neck."[72]

Having arrived in relatively good order, the first parties on the Lassen Trail
alerted Major Rucker that those in their wake were desperate. He dispatched

---

[71]Lewis, Overland to California, 28 September 1849, Beinecke Library, 64; Cone, Journal of Travels, 13 October
1849, 150–51; Smith, "Correspondence," Senate Exec. Doc. 52 (31–1), Serial 561, 109–11, 135.

[72]Ibid., 106, 108, 111–14; Pritchard, The Overland Diary, 27.

John H. Peoples on 14 September to buy cattle and mules, and hire men to help distribute "any other provisions you may get." Three days later, after bringing the "foremost wagons" from Lassen's Rancho Bosquejo to Sacramento, Milton McGee informed Rucker that most of those behind him were "now entirely destitute of provisions." Rucker headed north, reaching Rancho Bosquejo on 1 October. Sickness, escalating costs, exploding demand, and increasing chaos plagued the rescue. After coming down with mountain fever on 7 October, Peoples turned over command to Elisha Todd, who established a relief station at Fandango Pass, where Rucker joined him with additional supplies. The fever soon struck Rucker himself, and the recovered John Peoples returned to manage the rescue.[73]

Dexter Tiffany met the advance relief party at Pit River on 1 October "with several horses & men hired at $5 per day sent out with beef cattle to distribute among the distressed & starving Emigrants." In ten days, the rescuers "had relieved many persons," and a larger train was behind them. A week later, Tiffany found some one hundred wagons camped at Deer Creek, along with invalids from Warner's expedition and thirty-nine steers. Major Rucker and four wagons loaded with flour, rice, bread, and pork had not yet arrived. That evening Tiffany dined with the officers on "soup, birds, venison, liver of beef, rice, & molasses. Pretty good fare for the mountains," some of whose peaks were snow covered. He met an Irishman who was "so weak he could not stand having eaten nothing for 9 days being lost in the woods." He considered volunteering to help, but when Rucker appeared the next morning, Tiffany declined to join the expedition. "Almost every step you find a broken or an abandoned waggon. What will the poor weak teams do & if snow comes alas, alas," he wondered.[74]

Hermann Scharmann's family was still seventy-five miles from the Sacramento on 18 October. They "could only cover seven or eight miles a day because of the bad condition of the road," he recalled. "The oxen had soon eaten the little fodder that we had been able to carry with us, and almost fell from sheer weakness, barely sustaining them selves by nibbling at a few dry bushes." As he struggled down the trail, Scharmann spotted Captain Todd's five wagons. "We certainly were in a bad way; my wife and I were walking next to the two-wheeled cart which our three oxen, as weak as ourselves, could scarcely drag; my youngest son rode on the emaciated pony which was proceeding with careful steps, and held his little sister in front of him." The humane captain "offered to help out with a few crackers and said that if we wished to wait a while he could give us a good piece of beef," he wrote. "They were only going to travel three miles further before slaughtering a young fat ox." The emigrants declined to wait, so Todd gave them nineteen

[73]Lamb, "Emigrant Aid," 126; Smith, "Correspondence," Serial 561, 98, 106, 136.

[74]Tiffany, Diary, 1, 7, and 9 October 1849, Missouri Historical Society.

pounds of crackers and pork. Four years later, Scharmann thanked "the California Government for its humane action."[75]

It began to rain in the Northern Sierra foothills on the evening of 7 October: snow soon followed. "The rains and snow commenced much earlier than usual, and fell to an unprecedented depth," Alonzo Delano wrote. It seemed utterly impossible for the last trains to get through.[76] The deteriorating weather compounded the suffering and devastation. "Saw many of the Emigrants arriving here. They are broken down with the fatigue, young men made old & stiff, many dying with Dystentery, fever, Scurvey & Erysepelas," wrote Dexter Tiffany. "There will be an awful mortality in this valley this fall. Almost every man in the valley has had the fever this summer & fall & the fever & Scurvey in the mines is becoming worse every day."[77]

Mary Brush wrote home that it was on Lassen's track, which was "about 500 miles further, and [over] such roads as none but a Californian has ever seen," that her real troubles commenced. Trapped in the snow and rain with her daughter Emily while her husband went for help, Brush survived for a week without "a dry thread on me, and everything in the wagon was thoroughly soaked," she said. "I could have wrung the bedclothes." On the bitterly cold night of 3 November 1849, she made supper and went to bed with Emily. Brush got up three times to wring the water from her hair and found a yoke of oxen chilled to death in the morning. "Dear friends is it not hard to get to California?" she asked. "Do not let anyone come if you can hinder it, particularly overland." It was estimated "that not one tenth the number of animals that leave the States live to get through," but as she had learned, "if necessity says so, people do with very little."[78]

Reduced to five wagons, its mules collapsing from exhaustion and starvation, on 21 October 1849 the Washington City and California Mining Association's road ended at Deer Creek, still some thirty miles from the Sacramento River. Having brought his train "to this point, together, and more prosperous than any company of men in this vast emigration," Captain Goldsborough Bruff advised caching their goods and volunteered to stay behind and guard the party's still substantial property. By a spring atop a ridge, he established Bruffs Camp, and began collecting and drying out abandoned clothing, boots, and shoes. "Many a poor, wet, tired, and ragged hombre" who wandered past the mountain station benefited from such compassion. "The distress & sufferings in the rear, must be very great," he wrote. It was. The despondent Jenkins family arrived on 4 November. "The poor old man had scurvy," Bruff noted. "They were all wet, cold, tired, hungry, & disheartened." So was everyone else.[79]

---

[75]Scharmann, *Overland Journey*, 42–44.
[76]Delano, *Life on the Plains*, 237/35.
[77]Tiffany, Diary, 10 October 1849, Missouri Historical Society.
[78]Brush to "Dear Parents," 27 January 1850, "Letter from California," 1.
[79]Bruff, *Gold Rush*, 4 November 1849, 257–58, 325, 600n148.

On the last day of October snow began pounding the mountains, hitting the relief parties particularly hard. "On the Feather river road were sent about 100 mules, 92 of which perished in a storm which overtook them on their return, in one night," a Missourian reported. A Mr. Murray's daughters "had put on boots and pantaloons, and travelled through, leaving their father and mother, and the younger children behind, who I fear have perished."[80] Leading the relief at the Feather River's headwaters, John Peoples awoke on 1 November to discover the snow made it "impossible to see a spear of grass." The next day he "found all the rear of the emigration with General Wilson, family, and escort." The irascible Indian agent proved as intractable as ever. Peoples gave him two mules for his carriage, but Wilson refused to abandon his wagons, pack lightly, and get his family to safety. That night Wilson "lost all his mules in the storm, whilst mine were safely sheltered in the valley," Peoples reported.[81] Wilson was eventually compelled to cache his "extensive and valuable law library, and many valuable goods, including silks." Captain Bruff began preparing a large circular tent to make the family "a comfortable lodging place, when they come up." The Wilsons, including "3 interesting little children," arrived on 12 November, "on foot with part of our train 80 miles & part 20 miles from the settlements," through "snow 2½ feet deep, on roads with no bottom that a mule could reach," Wilson complained. His oldest son, "as uncouth as a bear," repaid Bruff's kindness with insults.[82]

Meanwhile Peoples hitched up four wagons, mounted the healthy females on mules, and left Feather River "with every woman, child, and sick man" he could find. For three more weeks, Captains Todd and Peoples battled mud and the elements, lost their best mules to the cold, issued a circular warning emigrants "that if they were awaiting relief, they had better move in at once," and made repeated trips to shepherd in the stragglers. Had the last men on the trail "thought less of their property and more of the lives of their families," Peoples reported, everyone could have reached safety in October before the snow began to fall. As it was, by 26 November the government relief had brought in all who would come.[83] "The army, out of supplies and men, could not mount another expedition," historian Blaine Lamb observed. Remarkably, Prussian emigrant Joseph Petrie mounted four independent efforts to rescue stranded emigrants, who later swore his help made the difference between life and death.[84]

---

[80]Hoyt to "Mr. Sosey," 20 January 1850, *Missouri Whig.*

[81]Smith, "Correspondence," Serial 561, 120.

[82]Bruff, *Gold Rush,* 259–60, 696, 1009n19; Wilson to Ewing, 22 December 1849, National Archives.

[83]Smith, "Correspondence," Serial 561, 51, 120, 151.

[84]Lamb, "Emigrant Aid," 127, 134n8. In 1850 the legislature appropriated $6,050 to Petrie "for Rendering Assistance to Migrants."

This Awful Tragedy

In the midst of the bleak rainstorm on All Hallows' Eve, a cry for help awakened Goldsborough Bruff. "Hallo, here! turn out and assist, a tree has fallen on a couple of tents, and killed & wounded several persons!" A hundred yards from Bruff's canvas shelter, a massive oak had crushed two tents. The rescuers found two slightly hurt little girls in the tent nearest the tree, but in the second they found an old man named Ormond Alford and his son, "their ghastly eyes turned up in death," and two boys "slowly dying in agony, with broken legs and mutillated bodies." After the disaster "a heavy snow fell, making a white winding sheet that covered the dead bodies to a depth of six or eight inches, thus adding sadness to the awful scene," recalled Henry Ferguson, whose family was camped next to their old friends. John Cameron died about daybreak, and the Alfords' son Willard died the next evening. "This awful tragedy left us in a helpless condition," wrote Ferguson.

It was too wet to dig graves. When their neighbors finally succeeded in burying the four the next day, the widowed mother asked for a last look at their faces. Bruff climbed down into the muddy hole and obliged. "Their eyes were wide open," Bruff wrote, "and she was vehement in her grief."

"*Why did He take them all at once?*" she cried, "*and not leave me one!*"[85]

Everyone I Have Seen Curses the Route

Nineteen exhausted and very hungry men staggered into Great Salt Lake on 1 December, having "wallowed through the snow sometimes over their hips." They had left the States under a man named Critcher on 24 September, the last wagon train to head for California. They had taken grave risks starting so late in the season, Dale Morgan noted, "and their arrival gave a proper dramatic flourish to the final curtain for the overland immigration of 1849."[86]

Farther west, as winter choked the mountain passes, the great overland rush to California came to an end. In late October, Hugh Heiskell met Sarah Royce, one of the last mothers on the Carson Pass road, riding a government mule.[87] Despite concern that people were still trapped in the northern mountains, by the end of November the government relief effort had rescued every willing straggler on every branch of the California Trail. "Imagine to yourself, desert plains, long drives, without grass or water, boiling springs, lofty mountains, stony roads, cattle giving out, and dying men, women and children, worn out with fatigue [and] exposure, and patience all gone, and you can have some faint idea of the scenery on the last

[85]Bruff, *Gold Rush,* 251–53, 349–51, 353; Ferguson, Reminiscences, Bancroft Library.

[86]Stout, *On the Mormon Frontier,* 358; Morgan, "Letters by Forty-Niners," 98.

[87]Heiskell, *A Forty-niner from Tennessee,* 144–47.

of our journey," wrote Austin Howard. The new route took him three hundred extra miles, but he was thankful to reach the Sacramento Valley "with all our lives and in good health, though out of money, and out of clothes, out at the heels, and out at the toes, out of provisions, and of course out of credit."[88] Like Howard, most who came over Fandango Pass would regret it, but the Lassen Trail reduced the loss of human and animal life on the California Trail. "Although the distance is much greater than by the old routes, and some of the emigrants were longer in getting in, I cannot but think it a fortunate circumstance they did so," Major Daniel Rucker reported, "for the loss of property would have been greater on the old trail, as the grass would all have been eaten off long before they could have arrived." Without the extensive public and private aid to those in desperate need at the end of the trail, the suffering that thousands experienced would have been multiplied many times over.[89]

"Colonel" Peter Davis's ranch was the first sign of "civilization" at the end of the trail, but many travelers continued on another mile to Lassen's establishment on Deer Creek, which by late October was the scene of a virtual carnival. For a mile to the south, "the plain was dotted with tents, wagons, and cattle of the emigrants and those going to the gold mines from below." A small adobe cabin "was called by courtesy a store, having a little flour, whisky, and a few groceries for sale. Around the trading post were lounging gangs of naked Indians of both sexes, drunken Mexicans, and weary emigrants, enjoying respite from excessive fatigue in the flowing bowl," wrote Alonzo Delano.[90] Besides the dilapidated buildings and an unfinished log house, there was "no lack of drink or drunkards," another visitor reported. "Quarters and parts of beef hang on the trees and lie around on logs. The whole place is surrounded with filth. Bones, rags, chips, sticks, skulls, hair entrails, blood, etc. The steep bank, down which all must go for water, is paved with this offal."[91]

Many who endured the Lassen Trail's arduous hardships assigned sinister motives to those they perceived as its promoters. Hermann B. Scharmann's German party had been living up to its slogan, "Fifteen miles a day!" until they reached Lassens Meadows. "At the crossroads many signs told us to take a new road, because it was one hundred and fifty miles nearer," Scharmann wrote. He claimed Joel Palmer told him the Oregon road was much better, but concluded bitterly, "He deceived us." During one day's travel he counted eighty-one shattered and abandoned wagons and 1,663 oxen, either dead or dying. "For the sake of a handful of gold one man will oft cause another man's misfortune. That was the case here."[92]

---

[88]Howard, "California Letter," 25 November 1849, *Des Moines Iowa Star*.
[89]Smith, "Correspondence," Serial 561, 140; Lamb, "Emigrant Aid," 126–27.
[90]Delano, *California Correspondence*, 20; and *Life on the Plains*, 232–33.
[91]Lord, *"At the Extremity of Civilization,"* 1 November 1849, 167.
[92]Scharmann, *Overland Journey*, 28.

Others blamed Jack Myers for their troubles. "Instead of continuing on the old route I left it 80 miles above the sink of Humboldt river & followed Myeres an old mountaineer who said he was going to make a cutoff & get a better road," George Murrell complained. "He did not make the cut-off. But increased the length of the road some 300 or 350 miles or else I would have been here much sooner."[93] A few diarists realized the new route was "got up" not by a conspiracy but by their own general ignorance. "I have noticed, some days since, that this was an unknown route to any person on it," wrote Israel Hale. "Myers, the pilot of Hudspeth's train, is the only man who has been in this country before. But this road was not made at that time, consequently he knows nothing of the route of the road."[94]

A few charged Peter Lassen with intentionally diverting the emigration. "At the great bend of the Humboldt or Mary's River," wrote Thomas E. Cook, "we were spirited off the regular route on a northern route by the lying misrepresentations of certain scoundrels sent out from the Sacramento Valley by the proprietors of Ranchos in that quarter." The messengers, Cook charged, wanted to lure emigrants onto the alleged cutoff so the ranchers "might strip them with greater certainty than if they went the old route by Truckie Pass."[95] Kimball Webster thought Lassen had sent an agent "to induce so much of the immigration as possible to take that route and which he called the 'Cherokee Cutoff,' and represented the distance to be but 180 miles to the Feather River mines, with a good road to travel over with many superior advantages over the old trail." Lassen, he claimed, "probably succeeded in profiting several thousand dollars by his trade with the poor immigrants, and it is currently reported that the immigrants have threatened his life, and that they have killed many of his cattle for food, without any remuneration to him."[96]

"The emigrants are generally deeply prejudiced against Lassen as believing he has been the cause of giving recommendation to this long and disastrous route," wrote Joseph Middleton. "Such roads for badness and steepness cannot be described. It is astonishing if an ox can get through alive, far less a wagon. I don't believe any man would have attempted this road if he had not been drawn into it by imperceptible degrees, and now the preservation of life compels him to go on as far as the ox can go, and when they fail, foot it as I had to do."[97] The new route "was recommended by a Mr. Lawson who has a rancho in the upper part of the valley where they would come in," Jerome Howard charged. "Many took that route and everyone I have seen curses the route and Lawson too. It was feared he would be assassinated at one time."[98] Some thought the entire scheme was concocted. "A story had been

[93]Murrell to "Dear Father," 17 September 1849, Mattes Library.
[94]Hale, "Diary of a Trip to California," 12 September 1849, 128.
[95]Cook to "Dear Mother," 11 February 1850, in Mathews, *Mathews Family,* 326.
[96]Webster, *Gold Seekers of '49,* 7 September 1849, 80.
[97]Middleton, Diary, 29 October 1849, Beinecke Library, 183–84.
[98]Howard, "California Correspondence," 25 April 1850, in Perkins, *Gold Rush Diary,* 180.

got up that a Cherokee Indian had discovered a rout across the Sierra Nevada, much nearer and less steep than the other routes," wrote Charles W. Haze. "So this story was successful in turning nearly the whole emigration ourselves among the rest for we were like drowning men catching at every straw." Haze called it "the Living death march."[99] Despite such charges, the first trains to take the cutoff clearly did so without Lassen's encouragement. Their choice reflected how dimly Americans understood northern California's geography. Even Goose Lake was "not laid down on Fremonts map which I find to be very incorrect as to this region," noted Dexter Tiffany.[100] Those who touted the route sincerely believed it was a better road.[101]

Not everyone cursed the Lassen Trail—it had its stout defenders. "We have had no reason to induce us to believe that we have come the wrong way. We had arrived near enough to the 'sink' of Mary's river and the fearful dangers of crossing the widely extended desert beyond, to warn us from that way if we could get grass and water on another route," wrote B. R. Biddle. Its increasing difficulty failed to deflate his enthusiasm. "Since we crossed the Sierra Nevada, the road is more rocky, and our wagons have been more endangered and injured than in all our previous progress," he noted a week before his Illinois Mutual Insurance Company unfurled the Star Spangled Banner on the banks of the Sacramento. "Yet we do not feel we have anything to regret in having selected this route; every body we meet confirms the wisdom of our choice."[102]

Those who found Lassen charging fifty cents for a shot of brandy might have disagreed. Hermann Scharmann reached the ranch on 1 November. The rough settlement did not impress him. Lassen had "chosen his abode with a view to the gains afforded by the emigrant traffic," he wrote. In a civilized land, the rough limestone ranch house "would not have suited the farmer even for the housing of his pigs. His grocery and general store had the same appearance, and yet Mr. Lassen piled up great riches."[103] Others accepted the high prices as a fact of life. Alonzo Delano "bought a pound of the best beef I ever saw" at the ranch. Sutter's prices might be lower, "but here they sell at any price, as emigrants come in hungry and destitute of provisions."[104] Few who met the affable Dane could resent him, especially those he treated to a drink. Lassen, after all, was just trying to do what everyone else who came to California wanted to do: get rich.

One man who came west to get rich—and did it at government expense—proved better at making money than his Danish friend. Indian agent John Wilson

[99]Haze to "Dear friends . . . ," 6 January 1850, Bentley Historical Library, 2.
[100]Tiffany, Diary, 27 September 1849, Missouri Historical Society, 127.
[101]For a defense of Lassen, see Bruff, Gold Rush, 1226.
[102]Biddle, "Journey to California," 20 August and 2, 10 September 1849.
[103]Scharmann, Overland Journey, 46.
[104]Delano, California Correspondence, 20.

resigned his post in February 1850, shortly after his costly trip across the plains. Wilson had arrived at the ranch of "Uncle Peter Lassen," on 26 November 1849, and he and Joel Palmer each bought a one-third interest in "about 18000 acres of as fine land as ever laid out of doors." Lassen had apparently known Wilson in Missouri and offered to sell Rancho Bosquejo for $15,000, with not a penny due until 1855.[105] Inconsequential in itself, two years later this odd arrangement seemed to inspire a complicated scheme involving Lassen, Wilson, and other speculators to make the ranch the last trading post on the best road over the easiest wagon pass to California.

What happened to Milton McGee and John Jacob Myers, who led the first parties over the Lassen Trail in 1849? McGee returned to Missouri and became a prominent businessman, laying out McGee's Addition in what is now downtown Kansas City. Myers had a more colorful career. He followed his family from Missouri to Texas, where he served as colonel of the Lone Star Mounted Rifles during the Civil War. After the war, he drove cattle to Salt Lake and partnered with Joseph McCoy to bring Texas cattle north to Kansas. The veteran trailblazer laid out a route from the Red River to Lockhart, Texas, extending the trail Jesse Chisholm had marked for McCoy from the Red River to the Kansas Pacific Railroad. Myers, "a man of that peculiar build and stature that can endure untold physical hardships without fatigue," led the first herd up the Chisholm Trail in 1867 and sent tens of thousands of beeves north over the next few years. Jack Myers died in Lockhart in 1874, allegedly from the lingering effects being poisoned on a cattle drive to Salt Lake City.[106]

FORTY-NINERS: HOW MANY?

Nothing quite like the gold rush of 1849 had ever happened in American history, nor would it happen again. The youthful gold seekers resembled an inexperienced army marching to battle, but neither patriotism nor dreams of martial glory inspired these adventurers—a yearning to get rich quick and an ill-considered desire to see the elephant drew them west. The gold rush migration dramatically transformed the very nature of the move west. During 1849 the number of Americans flooding over the Sierra Nevada outnumbered those who had done so during the previous eight years by ten to one, and the human tide transformed the traces and trails across the West into a national wagon road. Many questions about this phenomenon remain unanswered: most defy a definitive answer. How many people actually took the trails over South Pass in 1849? Based on their cumulative experience, what was the best route? Finally, was the game worth the candle?

---

[105]Bruff, *Gold Rush*, 1013n36, 1049n27, 1101n18.
[106]McCoy, *Historic Sketches of the Cattle Trade*, 145–47; Whitmore, "John J. Myers."

Given the challenges of the arduous road, did the trek reward those who made the long and perilous journey across the plains?

The best estimates should be those made at the time, but travelers projected wildly variable numbers, and their guesses tended to be higher than those popular today. Almon Babbitt carried the mail west to Great Salt Lake that summer, and he returned to the Mormon settlement at Kanesville, Iowa, in September 1849. The press soon published Babbitt's "count of wagons," which conjectured that slightly more than 8,000 wagons, with an average of four persons to a wagon, headed west that season. Babbitt claimed he passed 15,000 wagons on his trip to Great Salt Lake and back. "This would make about 60,000 persons." Discounting 1,200 government wagons, Babbitt's figures "would make the number of emigrants about 55,000. Mr. B. says the number of deaths has been small." Gold seeker Peter Kessler, who gave up at Fort Laramie and returned home, thought the entire emigration totaled 32,000 sojourners.[107] Samuel Gully "heard that there were near 75,000 persons crossed at & near St Joseph [but] this amount appears to be large," he informed Brigham Young.[108] "I started among the last and got here among the first, and consequently I passed nearly all out on the road, and had a pretty good chance to judge of the number," reported J. B. Witt, who guessed that between 12,000 and 14,000 wagons had started west, along with many more packers. "I do not believe that more than one tenth of the wagons and animals will ever get in," he concluded grimly. Even using his lower number of wagons, Witt projected almost 50,000 people took to the trail.[109] However many emigrants and animals made the trip, the cost in lives and suffering was enormous. "It is generally estimated that we passed from 7,000 to 10,000 dead oxen and mules on the way," an eyewitness reported. He saw eight oxen that apparently died in the yoke, chained together.[110]

Since the 1970s, estimated overland trail numbers have risen, but during the nineteenth century, historians projected a much lower total; H. H. Bancroft concluded that 25,000 gold seekers crossed South Pass in 1849.[111] By 1962, George Stewart had revised this downward, calculating "an acceptable figure for the whole migration would be 22,500."[112] Two of the best students of the gold rush, Georgia Willis Read and Dale L. Morgan, cited estimates varying from 25,000 to 35,000 emigrants to California in 1849. Morgan settled on a "golden mean" of 30,000. Later historians projected much larger numbers, but Read and Morgan hit upon

---

[107]"Late from the Plains," *Burlington Hawk-Eye,* 19 July 1849; "California Emigration," *St. Joseph Gazette,* 19 October 1849.

[108]Gully to Young, 21 May 1849, Brigham Young Collection, LDS Archives. Gully died of cholera shortly after writing this letter.

[109]Witt, "Correspondence," 27 August 1849, *Chicago Journal,* 30 November 1849, 3/3.

[110]Hoyt to "Mr. Sosey," 20 January 1850, *Missouri Whig.*

[111]Bancroft, *History of California,* 6:159.

[112]Stewart, *California Trail,* 232.

a reasonable figure.[113] With his usual precision, John Unruh counted 26,950 emigrants to Oregon, California, and Utah in 1849.[114] Given the imprecision confounding trails numerology, a range of between 26,000 and 34,000 might be a better guess of how many Forty-niners crossed South Pass.

The California gold rush is rightly seen as a mostly male movement, but there were more women on the trails between 1849 and 1851 than is generally recognized. The consensus has long been that in 1849 men outnumbered women on the trail by as much as twenty to one. Forty-niners often noted the scarcity of women. "The main regret of the emigrants seems to be that they will necessarily be for a long time deprived of the society of females," wrote John T. McCarty.[115] Benjamin Franklin Dowell's company consisted "of 10 wagons, 1 cat, 1 Dog, 1 mule, 13 horses, 25 cows, 68 oxen and 39 men & 1 woman, which is about an average proportion of animals and women to the men that are now on their way across the plains to California."[116] Parties with women and children tended to travel more slowly than single men, which contributed to undercounting the number of women who went west in 1849. "There are hundreds of women and children on the road—men who have started with their families, intending to settle down in California—and these are most all behind," Samuel R. Smith wrote not long after reaching the "Gold Diggins."[117] Yet women were present even in the forefront of the rush, as Peter Decker learned in the Sierra Nevada. He saw a woman "which was a novelty & could not help looking at her," he wrote, adding a revealing compliment: "Women seem to undergo the hardships of this journey with uncommon philosophy."[118] After crossing the Forty-mile Desert, James Pritchard witnessed a singular incident. "It was a Lady who came in 12 or 15 miles on horseback in advance of her party to procure water for her husband who was unwell himself," he wrote. "She was a stout robust looking woman about 22 years of age. Her Husband was a Dr his name I did not learn. She borrowed several canteens of men at the river & when I saw her last she had filled 4 with water & swong them over her shoulders."[119]

As Georgia Willis Read argued in one of the first scholarly articles on women, children, and the trails, the total number of people who made the trek in 1849 will forever remain mere speculation, and the proportion of female Forty-niners "is a matter of conjecture, and such conjectures vary widely." Archer Butler Hulbert

---

[113]Pritchard, *The Overland Diary*, 17n6; Read, "Women and Children," 6.

[114]Unruh, *The Plains Across*, 120.

[115]McCarty, Correspondence to the *Indiana American*, 3 May 1849, 1.

[116]Dowell, Journal, 2 June 1850, Beinecke Library, 7.

[117]Smith, 2 September 1849, "From California," *Tioga Eagle*, 11 November 1849.

[118]Decker, *The Diaries*, 6 August 1849, 148.

[119]Pritchard, *The Overland Diary*, 28 July 1849, 126.

estimated there were sixteen men to every woman and child, but Read found this figure to be too low. "Were I to hazard a conjecture, a fairer ratio would seem to be: men, eighty-five per cent, women, ten per cent, and children, five per cent; or, on the hypothetical basis of 30,000 total human beings, 25,500 men, 3000 women and 1500 children," she wrote. "Even such figures for women and children and perhaps for the total emigration, I should expect to see revised upwards, not downwards."[120] Read was half right: the estimated total number of women for 1849 has now risen dramatically, but earlier historians revised it downward. No less an authority than Dale Morgan found Read's "reasoned if questionable analysis of the sex-distribution" to be excessive.[121] The first three years of the gold rush "were so completely male and [so] few men traveled with their families" that even John Mack Faragher excluded narratives of 1849 to 1851 from his survey of overland documents.[122]

"Women—there were very few," claimed the late J. S. Holliday, whom many hailed as the leading expert on the California gold rush experience. Holliday repeatedly stressed how few women he believed went west in 1849, reporting that during May and June 29,000 men passed Fort Kearny with only "here and there a company with women and children." Holliday discounted sources showing that a significant number of women traveled with slower trains. "The rarity of women and children should be emphasized once again," he wrote, arguing that the frequent references to women and children on the Lassen Trail "reveals the sad fact that they had fallen farther and farther to the rear, so that they made up a disproportionate percentage of emigrants in September and October."[123]

Others disagree. A closer look at the evidence indicates women were more of a presence than most historians have concluded. "So many families are on the road to California that it has ceased to be a novelty to see females on the route," J. M. Muscott noted at Scotts Bluff.[124] "We have had a regular Pic-Nic for the last three weeks," wrote Cyrus Sumner. "All that we wanted is a few Ladies to make the thing go off to Perfection." On thinking about it, he wrote, "tho there is not a day we meet more or less of them. Today I saw a nice carriage with two or three ladies in it and there are a number of families in some Companies."[125] A member of William Muldrow's Missouri train noted, "There are quite a number of respectable families on their way to the far west."[126]

---

[120]Read, "Women and Children," 1, 6.

[121]Pritchard, *The Overland Diary,* 29, 126. Pritchard mentioned a single "stout robust looking woman about 22 years of age" bringing her ailing husband four canteens from the Carson River "swong across her sholders."

[122]Faragher, *Women and Men on the Overland Trail,* 198.

[123]Swain, *The World Rushed In,* 143, 204, 240, 354. Holliday cited the 1850 Fort Laramie count of 39,560 men and 2,421 women with 609 children.

[124]Muscott to Robbins, 10 June 1849, California State Library.

[125]Sumner to My Dear Helen, 24 May 1849, Bancroft Library.

[126]"From the Plains," 17 June 1849, Gold Rush Letters in the *Missouri Whig* (Palmyra).

New sources support Georgia Read's conclusion that approximately 15 per-cent of the Forty-niners were women and children, as do colorful, well-known accounts. On the road to Fort Kearny in May 1849, Charles Benjamin Darwin passed "perhaps 200 wagons of all kinds" and "some pack horses & some pack men—all sexes—the stout strong man & the big brawny woman." The proces-sion consisted "mostly [of] youth in bright hope of a golden harvest—[but] many families—women in wagons & women on foot & women on horse aside & astride pistoled & knifed & belted & rifled—some in mens garb some old & haggard & some young & beautiful going for the vilest purposes & some who will give birth to the load living in their wombs ere they get 100 miles while some will hear their infants first cry wher mountain cats & bears can give an answer."[127]

Few gold rushers planned to stay in California, but those who fell in love with her charms often returned to the States and brought their families west. Not surprisingly, Oregon consistently attracted more families than did California. The trail to the land of gold was "crowded with white topped wagons, containing men, women and children," James Addison Bushnell recalled. "Most of the families being bound for Oregon with their cattle and other stock while the single men were nearly all bound for California."[128]

Compared to the proportion of women who helped open the trail in the 1840s, fewer females crossed the plains in 1849 and 1850, a phenomenon repeated dur-ing the Pikes Peak craze of 1859. But in 1852 they again headed west in force. "A marked feature of the emigration this year is the number of women who are going the land route," the *Missouri Republican* observed.[129] "Although the precise number of women heading west in 1849, 1850 and 1851 is not discoverable, nearly every trail diary mentions their presence," Jo Ann Levy observed. "For 1852, the Fort Kearny register offers hard data." By 13 July the post's clerks "tallied the passing by of 7,021 women and 8,270 children." The almost exclusively male gold rush, she concluded, is a western myth. "Even in 1849 when the most impetuous rushed west first, nearly every trail diary records the presence of families—wives, moth-ers, sisters and daughters."[130] John Unruh calculated that a total of only 14,247 men, women, and children went overland to the Pacific before 1849, so the 15,291 women and children who crossed the plains in 1852 exceeded the total number of people who made the trek during the trails' first eight years. Five years later, it was common to find wagon parties made up largely of women and children.[131]

[127]Darwin, "1,000 Miles From Home," 20 May 1849, 65.

[128]Bushnell, The Narrative.

[129]Editorial, *Missouri Republican,* 15 April 1852, in Watkins, "Notes," 238.

[130]Levy, "We Were Forty-niners, Too!" 29; Levy, *They Saw the Elephant,* xvi–xvii.

[131]Mattes, *Great Platte River Road,* 62; Myres, *Ho for California!* 36n3. For the 1857 ratio, see Maxwell, *Crossing the Plains,* 1.

Women who went overland during the gold rush did so at no small cost. "There is every discription of men cross the plains, & a Lady unprotected would be exposed to the insults of the vulger & Licensuous," William Dulany reported from Sacramento in July 1850. Most of the women who crossed the plains that spring, he claimed, were "public prostitutes from the different [cities] in the United States & such would be her ascociates on the plains—the fact is this is no place for wimin."[132] Many women agreed. "If any of my friends or acquaintances are coming," wrote Mrs. John Wilson, whose cantankerous husband brought her to California in relative luxury, "tell them not to bring females and to come as lightly loaded as possible."[133] Even those who admired the women they met along the trail often believed they did not belong there. At the South Platte, George Willis Read "saw many women and children; the little fellows appear to stand it as well as their sires." The ladies, he thought, felt their many privations keenly: "I wish they were all at their homes they have so recently deserted. They will all respond Amen to that wish, before they see the golden land, I entertain not so much as a shadow of the least doubt."[134]

What was the best route to the goldfields? The answer depended on a sojourner's priorities. The shortest and quickest route could kill both animals and adventurers and often took longer than the tried and true path. The most efficient way to cross the plains was to take pack animals up the Council Bluffs Road from Iowa and at the Parting of the Ways follow the right-hand fork to Fort Hall. Once the Hudspeth Cutoff opened at Soda Springs in July, travelers could save a few miles by avoiding the swing north to Fort Hall. The most difficult decision was whether to cross the Sierra by going up the Truckee River, over Carson Pass, or across the Lassen Trail. The consensus was that the Carson Pass road was the best choice. "Should you or any of your friends determine to come to this country, and by the overland route, take the left hand road at the Sink of Mary's river, (or the Carson route, which is the same)," advised George Lane. "This is the best and nearest route; but they are all bad enough."[135] The teams on the Truckee were "all broke-down, the road being so bad," and the Carson trail was "much the best rout," government rescuers told Gordon Cone.[136]

Which gateway to California was used most heavily in 1849? Dale L. Morgan surveyed the 110 trail journals available in 1959 that identified how their authors got to the gold mines. He found that forty-one had taken the Lassen Trail, thirty-seven chose Carson Pass, and thirty-two used the Truckee River.[137] The explosion

---

[132]Dulany to Col. D. M. Dulany, 26 July 1850, Dulany Papers, Missouri Historical Society.
[133]Read, "Women and Children," 7.
[134]Read, *Pioneer of 1850,* 113–14. Read's granddaughter, Georgia Willis Read, edited his narrative.
[135]Lane to "Dear Press," 25 December 1849, *Missouri Whig,* 21 March 1850.
[136]Cone, Journal of Travels, 13 October 1849, 151.
[137]Pritchard, *The Overland Diary,* 31.

of known 1849 accounts over the last fifty years produces a different result: of the 297 narratives now available, 107 of them described the Carson route, 105 the Lassen Trail, and eighty-five the road up the Truckee. So approximately 36 percent of the Forty-niners used Carson Pass, 35 percent took the Lassen Trail, and 29 percent chose the route over Donner Pass.

It Is the Journey to Learn Human Nature

Frontier California evoked reactions as varied as the colorful crowd that crossed the plains in 1849. "Our journey is done, and we hardly know what to do with ourselves, and whether to be glad or sorry," wrote Isaac Wistar. He was dressed in rags, almost barefoot, and without provisions, but still happy: "There will be no more Indian alarms, no more stampedes, no more pulling, carrying and hauling at wagons. Notwithstanding ragged clothes and empty stomachs, we are all in an exhilarant and joyous mood."[138] For most of the Forty-niners, the thrill of completing the journey did not last long.

"What a wonderful place was Sacramento then, made up of Mexicans, South Americans, Islanders, Negroes, Spaniards, Chinamen, Indians, and Americans," Lewis Cass Wittenmyer recalled more than a half century after he first saw the canvas town. "All busy; all bent on getting gold by the shortest route, and none apparently intending to make California their home."[139] He was right: virtually everyone who had struggled so hard to reach El Dorado wanted to get rich and get out as quickly as possible. Many would have happily forsaken all their riches to have been magically transported back to the states. "Had there been a vessel lying out upon the river bound for New Orleans," Alexander Ramsay wrote from Sacramento, "there was not one of us who would not rather have steped on board it than to have gone one step farther in search of gold." The closer his party got to the mines, the more obvious it became that the fabulous tales of abundant gold were false. Almost every man he met was "wishing himself out of the country."[140] This was an often-repeated theme. "I want to get away from here as soon as possible," A. H. Houston wrote from Coloma. "I am tired of sleeping on the ground, cooking, eating salt provisions and living a life of constant exposure and hardship."[141] Every steamer berth was booked for the next three months, D. B. Wood heard in September. "Thousands are returning home," he wrote.[142] Only a handful of Forty-niners chose to go back across the plains.

Much of the letdown came from learning the realities of placer mining.

---

[138] Wistar, *Autobiography*, 26 August 1849, 113.

[139] Wittenmyer, Autobiography and Reminiscence, 6:142.

[140] Ramsay, "Gold Rush Diary," 13 September 1849, 464.

[141] Houston, "From California," 16 October 1849; *Indiana American*, 4 January 1850.

[142] Wood, "From California," 13 September 1849, *Indiana American*, 7 December 1849.

Immediately after reaching the mines, Edward Harrow and three friends spent a day chasing the glittering prize. That night they "found we had got perhaps five dollars worth of gold dust. This was hard to get. It looked rather small to our expectations, which were reasonably large," he wrote. Two days later, fortune smiled and he made about six dollars and went to bed with an aching back: "This gold mining is back-breaking work, and no mistake."[143]

Not a few overlanders despised the golden land they had struggled so hard to reach. "I regret to say that California is not the country that it has been represented to be; and by no means the Italy of America, of fine climes, luxuriant soil, possessing all the requisites to make a great and flourishing state," John T. McCarty wrote home. "It has a deadly climate, unhealthy water, from the large amount of mica that exists in it; it rains here almost constantly for five or six months of every year, consequently the seasons are unfit for agriculture."[144] "We underwent everything but death," Joshua Sullivan reported from "the hollow of dispare" near Feather River. "The whole route is lined with suffering." California was "a poor, miserable country—nothing but rock and mountains."[145] The land was "so poor that snakes cannot live on it," complained D. Hoyt. "I have not seen a tree here off of which you could get a rail cut of common length." Many of those who survived the arduous journey did not survive life in the mines. "The land route is exceedingly mountainous, hard, toilsome, and in many places difficult," Hoyt wrote. "The stoutest men get through very much jaded, and not a few entirely sink under the fatigue and exposure of the trip. Scurvy and mountain fever are attendant to the land route." To make matters worse, mining was "a perfect lottery."[146]

Others prospered in the land of gold. Dexter Tiffany put his financial genius to good use in San Francisco. "Mr. Tiffany is entirely restored [in] mind and body," wrote Dr. Reuben Knox, a Saint Louis colleague who met him in September 1850. Tiffany was heading home after making about $100,000 "in speculation" during his year in California. He was in fine spirits, and his legal practice was "worth at least $1,000 per week."[147] Tiffany rejoined his wife and beloved children in Missouri. He moved the family to Worcester, Massachusetts, but continued to do business in Saint Louis. In 1860, the family traveled to Europe. When he returned to Missouri in February 1861, Tiffany complained to his wife that the secession crisis had hobbled the local economy. Four days later, P. Dexter Tiffany committed suicide. His estate was valued at $1,000,000.[148]

---

[143]Harrow, *Gold Rush Overland Journal,* 26, 28 August 1849, 66, 67.

[144]McCarty, A Letter from John T. M'Carty, 30 November 1849.

[145]Sullivan to "Dear Wife," 21 October 1849, Oregon Historical Society.

[146]Hoyt to "Mr. Sosey," 20 January 1850, *Missouri Whig.*

[147]Knox, *A Medic Fortyniner,* 20 September 1850, 59.

[148]Biographical sketch, Dexter P. Tiffany Collection, Missouri Historical Society.

"Now my advice to you is, stay where you are," Tom Hart wrote his brother. "The trip across the plains is very hard. I would rather remain here all my life, than cross them again. Woodruff Lee says he would swim around Cape Horn on a log before he would cross them again."[149] Lucius Fairchild advised his friends never to go to California, "but above all, never come the land route *for God's sake*." Notwithstanding, he did not regret the trip and would not take $10,000 for what he had learned. The journey had added years to his life, but more important were the lessons it had taught him. "It is the journey to learn human nature, a man shows just what he is at heart, every feeling, every passion, is brought into action," Fairchild wrote. "I know those with whom I have travelled by heart,—their inmost feelings—& they know me as well, for I have shown what I am at heart—Would to God I knew myself as well."[150]

Remembering his colorful youth, David Leeper recalled the gold miner's plaintive ditty, which often crossed his mind:

> They told us of the heaps of dust,
> And the lumps so mighty big;
> But they never said a single word
> How hard it was to dig.[151]

[149]Hart to Hatcher, 20 and 27 February 1850, *Missouri Whig.*
[150]Fairchild, *California Letters,* 13 October 1849, 36.
[151]Leeper, *Argonauts of 'Forty-nine,* 57.

CHAPTER 7

PASSING SWARMS

The Trails in 1850

"T he Gods of the world are fast dying out, and one deity alone is worshipped—wealth," Boston congressman Horace Mann complained in 1849. If news spread that the River Jordan was filled with gold, ships would sail for Palestine instead of San Francisco, he observed.[1] Given what was happening the world over, Mann's comment was astute. Gold seekers from Britain, France, Germany, Chile, Bolivia, Peru, China, and even Australia were flooding into California. A "grain of gold" discovered in 1851 soon inspired 370,000 people to rush to New South Wales, so gold in Palestine would surely have attracted many more fortune hunters.

Rather than diminish, gold fever raged more wildly in America during 1850 and inspired even larger passing swarms than it had the year before; some 50,000 pilgrims prepared to head west. Newspapers from Maine to Georgia carried extravagant eyewitness reports from El Dorado that helped fuel the boom. "The whole slope of the Sierra Nevada, on the eastern side, for a length of more than 400 miles, and in a belt of at least 40, contains [gold] in greater or smaller quantities, and it may extend still further, as further research is made," military governor Persifor F. Smith wrote privately, adding that anyone who dug for gold or brought goods to sell to the diggers would make money. "There must be something in gold digging when men can get $22 a day for their labor," noted S. S. Osgood. "Clothes are thrown away when once worn. No one thinks of washing them or paying for having them washed."[2] Repeated warnings that expenses were impossibly high and mining was hard work that depended on pluck and luck went unheeded.

The second season of mass emigration bore all the anarchic characteristics of the previous year's race to El Dorado—this time with more people, more animals,

---

[1]"Horac Man [*sic*]," *Indiana American,* 7 December 1849, 1/2.
[2]Smith, "California—Letter from Gov. Smith"; and Osgood, "From the Gold Diggings," both *Whig and Courier* (Bangor, Maine), 26 June 1849.

more conflict, more crime, and more distress, disease, and death—more of every-thing except Indians, who generally avoided the chaotic cavalcade except when they had to cross the trails to hunt or engage their traditional foes. "Since we left the civilized Indians," wrote Dr. Samuel Matthias Ayres, "we have not seen a single Indian and I apprehend we will not, as the emigrants are now so numerous they have scared them off."[3] Benjamin Franklin Dowell did not see an Indian between Saint Joseph and the Blue River. Traders from Fort Laramie told him the tribes "were not allowed to go on the roads by orders from their chiefs for fear they would do something to cause the great number of whites to kill the whole indian race."[4] They were mistaken: the white man's diseases, not his numbers, drove away the Natives. "Many of the Indians died of Cholera the preceding year and they were told by the Officers that if they did not keep off the Trail the pale faces would give it to them again and they would all die of it," Lewis Kilbourn learned at Fort Laramie, "which was probably the reason we saw so few of them."[5] At his Scotts Bluff outpost, Joseph Robidoux said the Lakota had "all gone over to White river, afraid that the white men would bring cholera among them this year as they had last."[6] Every other statistic about the trek ballooned: even the ranks of those who gave up not long after leaving the frontier. The cost in property, human life, and suffering was enormous—a toll so great that it appeared to trigger a brief respite in 1851 as the nation paused to catch its breath. But as 1850 began, tens of thousands of Americans joined the great move west.

This vast migration expanded and refined trails opened the previous year and created important alternates to the roads up the Platte, over the Rockies, and across the Great Basin. As fortune hunters overtaxed the trail's fragile resources, some of these cutoffs helped reduce pressure and worked quite well. The army blazed a new road from Fort Leavenworth to the Saint Joseph Road, and it may have been soldiers who improved the narrow river road at Scotts Bluff, latter known as "General Mitchell's Pass," diverting traffic from Joseph Robidoux's trading station to what emigrants called Devils Gap or simply "the Gap."[7] Despite stern warnings not to try it, travelers on the Council Bluffs Road at Fort Laramie discovered a trail up the North Platte's north side that eliminated the need to ferry the river twice, often at great risk. East of Great Salt Lake, a Mormon apostle with a tal-ent for marketing opened the Golden Pass, a toll road over the last mountainous miles leading to the valley. Far to the west, packers found a trail to the new gold camp at Georgetown, while the ever-colorful Jim Beckwith (later James Pierson

---

[3]Ayres to "My dear Frances," 25 May 1850, Western Historical Manuscripts.

[4]Dowell, Journal, 31 May 1850, Beinecke Library, 5.

[5]Kilbourn, Journal, 1850, Oregon Historical Society Library, 14.

[6]Campbell, 7 July 1850, "Interesting News from the Plains," *Frontier Guardian,* 24 July 1850, 1–2.

[7]Mattes, *Great Platte River Road,* 454–58.

Beckworth) discovered a "new and important route" over the Sierra. At long last, 1850 saw the end of the Hastings Cutoff, but the unrelenting evolution of the road across the plains led to the creation of other purported shortcuts, not all of them improvements. East of Great Salt Lake, Costmor Clark's party "lost our way in consequence of taking one of Herriman's cut *offs*," but even after suffering over the arduous Hastings detour, his companion remained "perfectly mad on Cut-off's." On the Humboldt Herriman insisted on trying the well-named Greenhorn Cutoff.[8]

Even in the wake of the failure of the Pioneer Line, trusting gold seekers like John Bailhache, Henry A. Stine, and Dr. Reuben Knox boarded the "elliptic spring carriages" and "handsome strong Barrouches" of a variety of passenger lines. Outfits such as McPike and Strother, J. C. Faine and Co., Chadwick, Laveille and Co., Wiles and Bennett's California Train, and Jerome, Hanson and Smith's Mississippi and Pacific Line promised swift and comfortable transportation to the mines at fares ranging from $125 to $300. These trains carried about one thousand passengers, including a few women, at least part of the way west in 1850. Franklin Langworthy, a discerning critic, enviously noted the "fine train of sixteen splendid carriages" sweeping past him at South Pass.[9] Two returning Forty-niners organized the Alexander and Hall line, and Captain Hall reached Sacramento by mid-September with sixteen wagons and two-thirds of his animals. All his competition disintegrated on the Sweetwater, at Great Salt Lake City, during the arduous crossings of the Great Basin's deserts, or amid the Sierra Nevada's peaks.[10] "Great dissatisfaction among the passengers, a number of them walk in order to get a head of the ox teams, the mules fail and the Ox teams take the lead," Stine wrote not long before the Glenn and Co. express fell apart at South Pass. "*Deliver me* from a *passenger Train*."[11] Fortunately, circus owners Sands and Howes failed to leave Independence with their promised camel caravan, even though the operators landed eleven Syrian camels at Baltimore in May and claimed to have fifty-three more on the way to the frontier.[12] Speculators would offer overland passenger services for years, but as S. M. E. Goheen concluded, "Passenger trains have proved a humbug to the passengers and proprietors."[13]

Much of what happened in 1850 was a replay of 1849, but the trail witnessed significant changes. Having heard of the piles of abandoned goods that lined the trail in 1849, at least some travelers packed fewer heavy and unnecessary items, and for several reasons horses became more popular than oxen as draft animals. In a surprising

[8]Clark, "Trail of Hardship," 16 July, 10 August 1850, 149, 152.

[9]Langworthy, *Scenery of the Plains, Mountains and Mines*, 29 June 1850, 62.

[10]Barry, *Beginning of the West*, 926–27.

[11]Stine, Journal and Letters, 27 June 1850, Missouri Historical Society.

[12]"Novel Enterprise," *Cherokee Advocate*, 13 May 1850, 4, in Fletcher, Fletcher, and Whitely, *Cherokee Trail Diaries*, 2:195.

[13]Unruh, *The Plains Across*, 104–105, 437n70.

development, veterans of 1849, including the redoubtable Amasa Morgan, returned next spring to capitalize on their experience as guides for express lines or wagon trains. Bridges and trading posts sprang up from one end of the trail to the other. Ambitious stockmen driving cattle herds numbering up to eight hundred animals made the most profound, enduring, and forgotten innovation of 1850. Emigrants had been trailing large droves of cattle to Oregon since 1843, but now stockmen would turn the California Trail into the longest and least remembered cattle drive in the American West. This and much more changed in 1850 as the trails to California and Oregon continued their dynamic, relentless, and astonishing evolution.

SUCH AN IMMENSE SIGHT OF PEOPLE: THE FRONTIER

The human tide bound for California reached previously unimaginable levels in 1850. Crowds swept through Saint Louis and flooded the frontier from Independence to Council Bluffs. "St Louis is ahead in everything in business. There were 100 steam boats at the levy, [and] for lying stealing robing and murdering it beats all I ever heard of," wrote Oliver Sloane. "There is going to be some hard times this year on the plains because there is such an immense sight of people going."[14] Robert Chalmers thought the throng fitting out at Independence made it quite a stirring place, but teams could still be purchased for a reasonable price, perhaps because so many emigrants had chosen to depart farther to the north.[15] "This is a great place, a beautiful place but not nearly so full of Californians as I expected to find here," wrote Henry Stine. Many had "gone out on the prairies to camp where they can live cheap."[16]

"Some towns in Missouri are nearly depopulated by the 'yellow fever.' Many who are not able to purchase animals are starting on foot, packing their provisions on their backs," Adam Brown wrote at Saint Joseph. "One stout-hearted Missourian started, several days since, with a *wheelbarrow*."[17] The young men jamming the rough-and-tumble frontier towns came from all over the country. "Hoosiers, Pukes, Corncrackers and Buckeyes were most numerous and noisy, but every state in the Union had its representatives," wrote an eyewitness using popular slang to refer to citizens of Indiana, Missouri, Kentucky, and Ohio. (Suckers came from Illinois.) Brown thought three-fourths of the emigrants started from Saint Joseph, where "noise, confusion, and excitement reigned triumphant everywhere."[18] The town was "a very busy place on account of the California emigration which seems to centre here," wrote Silas Newcomb. "Hills and dales are white with their camps,"

---

[14]Sloane to "Dear Mother," April 1850, Mattes Library, 26, 28.
[15]Chalmers, "Journal," 4 May 1850, 35.
[16]Stine to "Dearest Mother," 8 May 1850, Missouri Historical Society.
[17]Brown, "Over Barren Plains," 18.
[18]H., "Pencillings by the Way," *Alta California,* 21 September 1850, 2/2.

and he found both sides of the river crowded with impatient gold seekers. Newcomb visited a "gambling house or rather hole and saw enough to sicken any decent man," including a drunk sprawled on the barroom floor "while others were in the act of drinking, some to drown trouble for losses at gaming, others in exaltation at their sudden rise from a few rusty dollars to thousands. Every species of liquor was to be found at the bar." Three gaming rooms "were filled to overflowing [with] every game Known on the West." Some prospective Californians "deposited" their entire bankroll and were obliged to turn back without a cent, while others were forced to sell their outfit. Auctions ran from dawn till dark every day but Sunday. "Everything in the shape of feed for cattle and horses demands enormous prices," Newcomb wrote.[19] Despite the hard realities at Saint Joseph, Margaret Frink heard that Californians "kept flour-scoops to scoop the gold out of the barrels that they kept it in, and that you could soon get all that you needed for the rest of your life."[20]

The wagons clustered around Saint Joseph in 1850 were "nearly all painted on their covers with the names of their owners [and] with various devices and mottoes, quaint, odd, and appropriate," an anonymous journalist reported. Mottoes included "Gold or a Grave," "Lucky Trip or Long Absence," "Never Say Die," and "Root Hog or Die." Covers sported paintings of "a sprawling eagle, a huge elephant, a tall giraffe, a rampant lion, or a stately ox," images that were "bold and striking, if not elegant and accurate."[21] Commerce boomed. "St. Joseph is quite a village, and doing a great deal of business at this time. But the way they fleece California emigrants is worth noticing," wrote Eleazar Ingalls. "The markets are filled with broken down horses jockeyed up for the occasion, and unbroken mules, which they assure you are handy as sheep. It is the greatest place for gambling, and all over rascality that I was ever in."[22] "Californians are as plenty as apples in the trees," wrote George Washington Brouster. "If you was here you would think the world was on its edge and the people all falling here." The settlement had almost doubled in size in two years. It still had fewer than 3,000 inhabitants, but it was "a flourishing little town and there is a great business carried on." Some friends said that "if they get home they never intend to take another trip but get married and stay at home." The trials of camp life discouraged Brouster. "Tell Absalom if he want[s] to go to California to try camping out one or two nights in the rain and he will be satisfied."[23]

Only two steamboats had reached Council Bluffs by 25 April, but there was already a great rush to the northernmost jumping-off point. Four nights later, the abandoned Mormon refugee camp at Winter Quarters caught fire. "The wind blew

[19]Newcomb, Overland Journey, 19, 22 April 1850, Beinecke Library, 14–17.

[20]Frink, "Adventures of a Party of Gold Seekers," 18 April 1850, 2:73.

[21]H., "Pencillings by the Way," Alta California, 21 September 1850, 2/2.

[22]Ingalls, Journal of a Trip to California, 30 April 1850.

[23]Brouster to "Dear Parents," 12 and 16 April 1850, Western Historical Manuscripts.

a perfect herricane" and stirred the conflagration into a firestorm. William Kilgore watched six hundred abandoned log cabins blaze until rain extinguished the fire.[24] Emigrants spent time "corn hunting," and Edwin Patterson thought goods were reasonably low, "but grain—as Webster says—'get out.'" Word was that cholera had struck at Saint Joe and Independence. Patterson preferred to "take the Northern route and escape disease, even if grain should cost a little more here—health is everything on this trip."[25]

Less scrupulous merchants outfitting greenhorn gold rushers often took advantage of their customer's lack of experience and sold them more supplies and equipment than they could haul. Sharp operators soon learned they could collect goods discarded not far from the jumping-off towns and resell them. "The whole of the route thus far is full of old waggons deserted, some broke down, others lost their stock, others their friends and have become so sick of the trip that they [are] willing to sell everything they have if they can only get home once more," George Davidson observed thirty miles west of the Missouri River. "I thought I had seen some little distress in my life but nothing like what I have seen thus far on the trip."[26]

An odd development was a surge in the use of horse teams instead of the highly recommended oxen. "Horses had suddenly become popular," George Stewart noted. Reports indicate that more than half of the earliest emigrants used horses in 1850—only about one in five of the first teams were oxen. This may have been because trail veterans had learned to buy good horses, start early, and pack grain to last until enough grass grew to provide forage, Stewart speculated. In contrast, the *St. Joseph Gazette* presumed half of them used horses "owing to the scarcity of mules and oxen in Michigan, Iowa, Wisconsin, Illinois, and Indiana, where a large majority of emigrants are from." (*The St. Louis Intelligencer* estimated that at least 17,500 people would leave Missouri for California that year.) "The larger portion of the emigration go this year with horses," the *New York Tribune*'s correspondent wrote from Saint Joseph. "How the experiment will succeed is doubtful." He was right.[27] Many of the large American horses he saw at Fort Laramie in mid-May 1850, Robert James reported, "can not get through and is even now reduced to mere skeletons."[28] Down the trail, the toll would be horrific: "About 500 horses in less then a week died at the sink," George Bonniwell wrote in August.[29]

The surprising throng of 1850 included English aristocrats, notably Henry John Coke and Lord Julius Brenchley, who left Council Bluffs "with only a few

[24]Kilgore, *The Kilgore Journal*, 24, 29 April 1850.

[25]Patterson, Diary, 15, 17 April 1850, Mattes Library.

[26]George to Lewin Davidson, 12 May 1849, Beinecke Library.

[27]Stewart, *California Trail*, 298; Barry, *Beginning of the West*, 920–21.

[28]James, "From the Clay Emigrants," 18 May 1850, *Liberty Tribune*, 21 June 1850, 1:4.

[29]Bonniwell, Gold Rush Diary, 4 August 1850.

servants for his escort." As teamsters Coke hired a Métis, two French Canadians, a Pennsylvania-Dutch auctioneer, and two Americans—one of them a former acrobat for a traveling circus. The gentry set out with overloaded baggage wagons, which fared poorly on the rough roads. Before a fortnight ended, Coke recalled, "both wagons were shattered, wheels smashed, and axles irreparable." He ordered heroic measures: "The wagons were broken up and converted into packsaddles. Both tents, masses of provisions, 100 lbs. of lead for bullets, kegs of powder, warm clothing, mackintoshes, waterproof sheeting, tarpaulins, medicine chest, and bags of sugar, were flung aside to waste their sweetness on the desert soil." On the Platte River, Brenchley had trouble with his servants and wagons—he had to worry perpetually about his employees, and the wagons constantly broke down. Brenchley simply fired most of his servants and left the wagons on the road, "reserving only two saddle-horses and some pack-mules. Thus lightened, he went cheerily on his course." Coke's trip involved more combat than cheer, since not one of his men had ever packed a saddle and none of his mules had ever carried a pack. "It was a fight between man and beast every day—twice a day indeed, for we halted to rest and feed, and had to unpack and repack."[30]

Thousands tried to make an early start. The frontier filled to overflowing weeks before it was safe to take animals onto the grassless prairies. "All the papers of Missouri, Iowa, Wisconsin, Illinois, Indiana and Ohio come to us filled with accounts of preparations by companies, in all towns and counties, for California," wrote the *St. Louis Reveille* in March, predicting emigration would double from 1849—a "moderate," but perceptive, estimate. Once again, the wretchedly wet weather failed to cooperate with those who wanted to get ahead of the crowd—an inch of ice coated the Missouri at Saint Joseph on the first of May, and steamboats and ferries had to dodge large blocks of ice at Council Bluffs.[31] At Independence Landing in mid-April, "the river had risen seven and a half feet since the rains, and still rising," Silas Newcomb noted.[32] "The Missouri River rose about eight feet last night, and is full of drift and floating ice," James Abbey wrote after a rainstorm left him soaking wet but happy to be on the west side of the torrent. "We would not be in St. Jo. to-day with our teams, for the prettiest two hundred dollars [you] ever looked at."[33] On 6 May snow fell at Saint Joseph. The optimists always found in the emigration felt that the weather boded well for overlanders, since it meant there would be "plenty of Grass to travel on."[34] Despite the cold, the migration got off early, with its vanguard pressing west almost a month earlier than the first Forty-niners.

---

[30]Remy and Brenchley, *A Journey to Great-Salt-Lake City,* 2:499–500; Coke, *Tracks of a Rolling Stone,* 142.

[31]Barry, *Beginning of the West,* 918, 921.

[32]Newcomb, Overland Journey, 17 April 1850, Beinecke Library, 11.

[33]Abbey, *California,* 18 April 1850, 108.

[34]Jefferson Drake to Abigail Drake, 8 May 1850, Oregon-California Papers, Missouri Historical Society.

The First Gold Diggers on the Road

Carrying the mail east from Great Salt Lake City in mid-May 1850, Robert Campbell met party S. B. Craw's Illinois train, already eleven miles west South Pass. "They were well and hearty; their animals were in good travelling order, much to our astonishment," he reported. "But they had fed them grain and when that was exhausted they had fed their flour, depending on supplies at Salt Lake, which no doubt they would receive, being the first gold diggers on the road." The next night the mail couriers camped at the last crossing of the Sweetwater and "found Captain Denison, from Ohio, with a company of two hundred, who had just encamped; and in a few minutes a small company rolls up, crosses the river and encamps on the other side," Campbell wrote. "The animals in Denison's company were much used up and not to be at all compared with those in Craw's company." These fast-traveling overlanders were far ahead of the handful of ox teams the eastbound Mormons met on 21 May that had wintered at Fort Laramie—and most surprising of all, they found "a man with a wheelbarrow (said to be a Scotchman)" who said several companies had invited him to join them and haul his provisions and bedding. The hard-charging Scot "thanked them kindly, but wished to be excused, as he could not wait on the tardy movements of a camp. He never was afraid of the Indians stealing his horses, and he never lost any rest dreading a stampede."[35]

By the time the eastbound Mormons reached the Upper Platte Ferry on 25 May, the road "was completely covered with wagons and emigrants for the Diggins." They found abandoned harness, casks, axes, augers, and stoves littering the campgrounds, "but nothing at all in comparison to the amount of articles left and thrown away by the emigrants last season." Campbell concluded they "had learned wisdom by the things their friends last year had suffered, and come on in quite a different style. Light wagons, first rate horses and mules; in short; light loads and good teams, without any surplus property or clothing to leave for destruction on the plains." All the way to Fort Laramie, the Mormons met "a continual train of emigration." The post clerk had recorded the passage of 16,915 men, 235 women, 242 children; 4,672 wagons, 14,974 horses, 4,641 mules, 7,475 oxen, and 1,653 cows by 10 June. All along the road, Campbell saw much better feed than he had expected. "Having been on the route now for three successive years, I feel safe in saying it was much better than the two previous seasons; though the emigrants could hardly be made to believe they were on good feed, not being acquainted with mountain grasses."[36]

The 1850 emigration began early and ended late. As the first pack trains reached the goldfields in June, westbound wagons were still arriving at the Missouri.

---

[35] Campbell, 7 July 1850, "Interesting News," *Frontier Guardian*, 24 July 1850, 1–2.
[36] Ibid.

Among the late arrivals, Washington Peck found the crowd undiminished as he took in the view at Council Bluffs in early June. "The scenery is grand. The bottoms is 4 to 5 miles broad, as livel as a floor, surrounded on the north East side with Bluffs, 2 or 3 hundred feet high and very broken," he wrote. As far as the eye could see, the bottom was "dotted with groups of covered waggons, several hundred being in sight." Kanesville did not impress Peck. The settlement was situated in a deep ravine, its cabins "mostly made of hewed logs and covered with a kind of long split oak shingles, if they can be called shingles, and some is shingled with straw. Others has a layer of straw or something els[e] and is covered with old mother Earth," he wrote. "We saw one man hoeing on his house."[37]

B. F. Dowell found the grass on the Little Blue River was "almost all eatten out on its banks by the numerous herds of stock belonging to the present active, energetic emigration." The road was jammed with travelers, who were "from almost every state in the Union and are descendents of English, Irish, Dutch & French." He had seen them "with their knapsacks on their backs, others with wheelbarrows, others with packed mules and horses, some in buggies & carriages & thousands with wagons and teams all in one conglomerate mass marching on towards the golden region of the west."[38] The victims of gold fever were astonishingly diverse. At Saint Joseph, William Warren's relatives took in "a Hongarian by the name of John Cowen."[39]

The crowded trail worried Margaret Frink. "It was a grand spectacle when we came, for the first time, in view of the vast emigration, slowly winding its way westward over the broad plain," she wrote at the junction of the Savannah and Saint Joseph roads, where the country was so level she could see long trains of white-topped wagons for miles. "It seemed to me that I had never seen so many human beings in all my life before. And, when we drew nearer to the vast multitude, and saw them in all manner of vehicles and conveyances, on horseback and on foot, all eagerly driving and hurrying forward." The scene was "perfectly astonishing. In travelling hours the wagons block the road as far as eye can see." It was impossible to camp near the road without being surrounded by a dozen or more trains. The throng made Frink fear "that if one-tenth of these teams and these people got ahead of us, there would be nothing left for us in California worth picking up."[40]

The parade up the Little Blue River was made up of "all kinds of people under the sun from the man of money down to the begger from the man of honor down to the lowest thief on earth," William Bedford Temple told his wife. After three steers disappeared from his party, Temple set out with Alexander Fancher to find

[37]Peck, *On the Western Trails,* 2, 4 June 1850, 59–60.

[38]Dowell, Journal, 1 June 1850, Beinecke Library, 6.

[39]Warren to "Dear Father," 13 October 1850, California State Library.

[40]Frink, "Adventures of a Party of Gold Seekers," 20 May 1850, 85–86; W. W. R. to Col. Switzler, 21 May 1850, in Wyman, *California Emigrant Letters,* 100–101.

them. They "discovered our cattle brushed in a thickett herded by a Whiteman."
Before Temple could rally men to shoot him, the rustler disappeared and avoided
becoming "feede for Wolves. I would here remark near all the stealing and killing is
done by the Whites following the Trains." Most of "these mean white men" would
shoot a man for his provisions, Temple observed. "There is a tribe of white Indians
upon these plains at this time that are more dangerous than Pawnees," another
traveler reported. "They carry on horse and mule stealing pretty extensively and
even oxen do not escape their attention." One had been caught and tried.[41] The
crowd inspired other crimes. Believing he "was beyond the reach of law and civilization" and excited by the beautiful daughter of a "respectable old gentleman" from
Arkansas, a seventeen-year-old "adventurer" named Wilkerson "concluded to gratify
his propensities," wrote Samuel Ayres. "Accordingly, he crept to the wagon where
slept the fair one in the silence of the night, when her vigilant father discovered
the scoundrel and shot him to the heart." The train denied the killing, but Fleming
G. Hearn "saw his shirt with the blood upon it also a tinpan filled with blood."[42]

The first train reached Fort Kearny on 13 April 1850 with its stock in miserable
condition, having had no grass and not much grain.[43] As the first pack trains swept
into Fort Laramie, the mountain traders gathered at the post were prepared. They
were not yet rich but had "a fine prospect of accumulating fortunes. They are as
keen on a trade as any Yankee wooden-nutmeg or clock pedlar you may meet with
in the States," James Abbey said. Sugar sold for twenty-five cents per pound, bread
for fifty cents per loaf, flour at eighteen dollars for one hundred pounds, whiskey
for a dollar per quart and brandy at eighteen dollars a gallon.[44] The adobe outpost
was slowly disintegrating, but some thought the military had greatly improved the
property. "The old fort stands upon a bank twenty feet high. This bank is composed
of gravel and large stone," Hearn wrote. "The walls are three feet thick with watch
towers on the corners. It has large folding gates on the north side or front, and on
the South side near the center of the fort which is divided off into rooms, which
are occupied by a portion of the Officers of this Command." There was even a
large icehouse filled with ice taken from the Laramie River.[45]

Ten miles above the forks of the Platte, the Estes brothers "saw a great many turn
back but we dont blame them mutch for they have seen the elephant all over."[46]
Hardship, danger, and disease led many to give up and take "the backtrack." Calvin
Taylor saw "the large number of emigrants who returned from different points

---

[41]Temple to "Dear Wife and littleones," 2 June 1850, Oregon Historical Society.
[42]Ayres to "My dear Fanny," 19 May 1850, Western Historical Manuscripts; Hearn, Journal, 21 May 1850, Oregon Historical Society.
[43]Watkins, "Notes," 221.
[44]Abbey, California, 1 June 1850, 27.
[45]Hearn, Journal, Oregon Historical Society, 57–58.
[46]Estes Brothers to "Mother," 16 June 1850, Mattes Library.

along the road in consequence of the severe sickness." Some were "panic stricken and making the best of their way towards home." By the time he reached Salt Lake, Taylor had seen hundreds of his fellow sojourners "cut down by the ruthless hand of death, far from their homes and kindred." He had abundant proof "from persons of veracity" that the number of dead "to this point, a distance of between 1100 and 1200 miles from Missouri, would be equal to one for every mile, which is certainly not far from the actual number." Yet Taylor pressed on and considered it "far more dangerous to return than to go forward."[47]

Reasons for giving up varied from year to year, but an early start often proved self-defeating. "We have passed many emigrants who left the States in March, and early in April. There was no grass and they were obliged to give their provisions to their animals to keep them alive," wrote Dabney T. Carr. "We met several going back, some on foot, some with one yoke of oxen or a horse, who said that all their animals had died, and all that they wanted was to get back alive; poor men, they reckoned without their host. They made no preparation for the exit of the stormy Orion, they knew not what a March storm on the prairies was; sadly they have paid for their knowledge." Grass along the Platte was so depleted that Carr saw teams eating bacon. Despite the hardships, Carr himself found the trip delightful. "The river in the distance, a broad prairie around you, plenty of provisions, and good company—who would wish to be elsewhere?"[48]

No Joke: Wheelbarrow Men

Orin O. Wright described the chaotic crowd gathering at Saint Joseph in April 1850: "There are a great many emigrants at this place men from every State and Nation under the sun—old men young men one legged men and some that dont happen to be men." They were going with horses, cattle, mules and jackasses, and twenty-five men had "started afoot and to bring up the rear one fellow has started with a wheelbarrow."[49] William Temple described the astonishing parade as tens of thousands of gold-crazed Argonauts swept west using "all kinds of ways of going, some in carts, some a foot." Perhaps the oddest sight was "three large stout men with a wheel barrow, no joke."[50] The first overlander to try to cross the plains on a single wheel left Saint Joseph with "a bushel of parched corn, his blankets, and nothing else," Forty-niner Charles Ferguson recalled. He wheeled it manfully for several days but could not keep up with the wagons. He gave up and found a job at

---

[47]Taylor, "Overland to the Gold Fields," 6 August 1850, 327–28. Taylor's estimate of some 1,200 deaths was probably not far off the mark.

[48]Carr to "My Dear Cousin," 31 May 1850, Missouri Historical Society.

[49]Wright to "Dear Sister," 22 April 1850, Missouri Historical Society.

[50]Temple to "Dear Wife and littleones," 2 June 1850, Oregon Historical Society.

CHARLES FERGUSON'S ONE-MAN "WHEELBARROW TRAIN"

The morning Ferguson left Saint Joseph in 1849, "a man started with a wheelbarrow to cross the plains. He had a bushel of parched corn, his blankets, and nothing else." Ferguson did not believe anyone ever crossed the entire trail with a wheelbarrow. "This man, I am sure, could have performed the feat if any one could. He had all the advantages of youth, strength, courage and will, but I think the enterprise beyond human endurance." From Ferguson, *The Experiences of a Forty-niner,* 33. Author's collection.

Fort Kearny.[51] Like this hardy innovator, tales of these pushcart pioneers—there were at least ten of them in 1850 alone—indicate most gave up not long after they started. A few brave souls pressed on, sometimes with astonishing speed. The "Man with the Wheelbarrow" achieved legendary status.

Chroniclers met cartsmen from the Missouri River to the Wasatch Range in 1850. "An Irishman passed on a few days since actually carrying his clothing provisions &c on a Wheel barrow with nobody in company but himself. He is now going he said to the 'Gould diggings,'" wrote William Rothwell. "It is reported that the Indians were so kind as to relieve him of his loading about 40 miles out."[52] "While taking our dinner a man with his outfit in a *wheelbarrow* rolled up big as life. We asked this gallant son of Massachusetts if he wanted any supplies. 'Sugar' he said was all he wanted," noted Finley McDiarmid. "Mr. Truitt gave him half a loaf, for which he returned many thanks [and] placed it in his wheelbarrow, bid us a friendly good bye and rolled on." The next day his train passed "our wheelbarrow man."[53] John Gunnison believed it was a sturdy German who almost achieved

---

[51]Ferguson, *Experiences of a Forty-niner,* 32–34.
[52]Rothwell, Notes of a Journey, 4 May 1850, Beinecke Library, 20–21.
[53]McDiarmid, *Letters to My Wife,* 12, 13 June 1850, 24.

immortality as the "wheelbarrow man," but reports mention sojourners from Ireland, Scotland, Missouri, and Massachusetts pushing carts. The German "trundled his wheelbarrow along as rapidly as the teams advanced, and had the prospect of reaching the end of his two thousand miles in safety," but he made the mistake of ferrying the swollen Weber River. "The raft foundered in the swift current, and the wheelbarrow, with 'his all,' was swept down into the boiling kanyon below, and lost beyond redemption," Gunnison wrote.[54]

Perhaps the most intriguing of the wheelbarrow men was a hard-charging "Scotchman," who made other travelers eat his dust. Well armed and about thirty-five years old, he passed Fort Kearny on 29 April 1850 "with a wheelbarrow, refusing to join any company, saying in his own particular dialect, 'Na, na, mun, I ken ye'll all break doon in the mountains, an I'll gang along mysel'." He appeared not to be the least fatigued. Two weeks later he might have reached Fort Laramie—at least "the most distinguished character" who appeared at the fort was identified as the "wheel barrow man." He had left Saint Joseph about twenty-five days previously and was "carrying his all in a light wheel barrow" that had "out-stripped almost everything on the road." He was in high spirits and confident he would be the first man in the diggings. "He enquired how the *grass* was ahead, but reckoned his animals wouldn't want much. He pushed on to the tune of Yankee Doodle towards the setting sun—such a man must succeed."[55] Others were equally impressed. "One man is going through with a wheel barrow, who out travels our mule teams," wrote Robert James from Fort Laramie. (A preacher, James had left his young sons named Frank and Jesse behind in Missouri.)[56] At the end of May the Scot apparently pushed west from Fort Bridger, for D. A. Millington said a man had rolled his wheelbarrow all the way to Yellow Creek on today's Utah-Wyoming border. "Here he had broken it and left it having got in with a wagon and we sacrilegiously made fire of the wheelbarrow to cook our supper."[57]

No one reported wheelbarrow men in 1851, but they returned in force in 1852 when Fort Kearny's post record listed fifteen persons traveling with "hand carts."[58] Besides an old man packing a cow and three men "with their bread and dinner on their shoulders," Richard Hickman saw five Irishmen on the Little Blue with wheelbarrows.[59] "There is every description of teams & waggons; from the hand cart & wheelbarrow, to a fine six horse carriage and buggie," Lodisa Frizzell

[54]Gunnison, *The Mormons,* 66.

[55]Observer, "Scenes at Fort Kearney," 21 May 1850; Cheyenne, "Description of Emigration Seen at Fort Laramie," 14 May 1850, in Wyman, *California Emigrant Letters,* 108, 112.

[56]James, "From the Clay Emigrants," 18 May 1850, *Liberty Tribune,* 21 June 1850, 1:3.

[57]Millington, Diary, 30 May 1850, Mattes Library.

[58]Barry, *Beginning of the West,* 1,084.

[59]Hickman, "Dick's Works," 21 May 1852, 164.

reported at Saint Joseph on May Day.[60] Near the Little Blue River, a man passed Francis Hardy "bare-foot with his outfit on his back—some have left St Joseph this season with wheel barrows," he wrote. "There is almost every conceivable style of outfit to be seen."[61]

West of Fort Kearny, William Wagner "overtook an enterprising individual traveling across the plains with a wheelbarrow." This was, he thought, "A Novel way of crossing the Plains." He expressed his admiration for a man who would "start out on a journey of 2000 miles with all his effects, Grub, Clothing, Kitchin, Tent & other necessaries packed on a wheelbarrow," he wrote. "A man that will push such a load across the deep sand on the plains & the steeps of the Rocky Mountains, across innumerable small streams & large Rivers, is certainly deserving of the realization of all his hopes & anticipations, & such is actually the case with some men." Wagner admired characters who would "push through all the barriers of opposition, surmount every difficulty that comes in their way."[62] Near South Pass, Solomon Kingery noted, "A Jentleman passed us today making his way to California with a wheelbarrow. The road was a little Descending. He past us on a full trot Shouting hurrah for Cal."[63] Another company found a wheelbarrowing Kentucky printer "completely prostrated" by the roadside but helped him to the goldfields, where he prospered.[64]

"There were some with hand-carts, others with wheelbarrows trudging along and making good time. Occasionally we would see a man with a pack like a knapsack on his back and a canteen strapped on to him and a long cane in either hand. These men would just walk away from everybody," Gilbert Cole recalled.[65] Norwegian overlander Tosten Stabæk saw two men from Illinois who had a handcart "calculated to carry two hundred pounds. One of the men pulled it, and the other pushed from behind," traveling as far and as fast as the rest of the emigrants. The men hired a wagon at Fort Laramie to haul their goods "and left their hand cart standing by the roadside."[66]

The wheelbarrow tradition did not thrive after 1852, but the practice did not die. Not far from the Missouri, "a man come to our camp that has come two thousand miles on foot and fecht a wheelbarrow all the way," Mary Stone Smith wrote in 1854. "He is going to California."[67] The example inspired Brigham Young to launch an experiment that had catastrophic results in 1856.

---

[60]Frizzell, *Across the Plains,* 1 May 1852, 10.

[61]Hardy, Journal, 22 May 1850, Beinecke Library, 44.

[62]Wagner, Journal of an Ox Team Driver, 22 May 1852, 76.

[63]Kingery, Overland Letters, 18 June 1852, Beinecke Library, 10.

[64]Unruh, *The Plains Across,* 107.

[65]Cole, *In the Early Days* , 45.

[66]Stabæk, "An Account of a Journey to California," 107–108.

[67]Smith, Diary, 5 May 1854, Western Historical Manuscripts.

With the rush to Pike's Peak in 1859, handcarts saw a brief revival. "I have several times heard of a man crossing the continent with a wheelbarrow," wrote Charles Ferguson, "but I don't believe it was ever accomplished. There are so many sand dunes, so many rivers to cross, besides deep and terrible gorges to traverse, and two ranges of mighty mountains to ascend and descend, that it seems to me impossible." He was right about how tough it was to get to California, but Ferguson was wrong about the failure of transcontinental wheelbarrowing. Apparently the Irish "wheelbarrow train" made it to California in 1852 after "a relatively fast four-month trip."[68]

Far and away the most successful wheelbarrow man was the only one whose name survives, James Gordon Brookmire, an Ulster Scot who came to America in 1831. At age forty, he sold fifty acres to raise cash and set out for the goldfields in 1850, leaving six children behind in Pennsylvania, reportedly "in very indigent circumstances." Brookmire "started out with a band of Kentuckians but switched to a wheelbarrow at Fort Kearny." He and his faithful dog survived being struck by Rocky Mountain lightning. He lost his wheelbarrow and almost drowned in Utah's Weber River but Brookmire reached Hangtown that fall. Many gold rushers died broke, but early in 1852 he "returned with about fifteen thousand dollars of the 'dust,' all of which he has dug up and washed with his own hands. And as it is very apt to pour when it rains, his wife received legacies during his absence to the amount of ten thousand dollars, falling to her upon the death of some relations in Scotland."[69] Back home, Brookmire invested his fortune, educated his children, and lived "in more than comfortable circumstances, which he and his wife are worthy to enjoy." The wheelbarrow man died at age ninety, still hearty.[70]

The Drovers

Walter Crow, Alexander Fancher, and cattlemen named Thompson, Brown, and Waddle began a revolution in the trans-Mississippi livestock trade when they drove beef on the hoof over the northern road to El Dorado in 1850. Other cattle herds that year took the southern routes from Texas and Arkansas. About eight hundred California-bound cows crossed the Missouri at Saint Joseph in mid-May, while William Bedford Temple found "not less than 3000 cattle on the ground" at the Big Blue in early June.[71] Near the Little Blue in May 1849, Alphonse B. Day said

---

[68]Unruh, *The Plains Across,* 107, citing *Alta California,* 29 August 1852.

[69]"The Wheel-Barrow Emigrant Returned," *Liberty Weekly Tribune,* 26 March 1852, 2/4.

[70]Schenck and Rann, *History of Warren County,* 1887, 431–32; *Alta California,* Steamer edition, 16 April 1852, 3/4. Much of this section was derived from John D. Unruh and Morris W. Werner's essay, "Wheelbarrow Emigrant of 1850."

[71]Barry, *Beginning of the West,* 932; Temple to "Dear Wife," 2 June 1850, Oregon Historical Society.

there were five hundred head of loose cattle behind his train that could "keep pace with any teams on the road but pack mules."[72]

Cyrus Loveland had served in California during the war with Mexico and made $18,000 during the seven months he spent in the California goldfields in 1848. Eager to return west, he hired on with Walter Crow as a drover—the term "cowboy" did not come into fashion until after the Civil War. Loveland's lively diary is one of the few surviving accounts of the cattle trail to California. The evening Crow's outfit "left the line that divides us from the land of civilization and launched out on the broad prairie of the Indian Nations," his son William Crow "came up with about sixty head of cattle which swelled the number to seven hundred and twenty-one head of loose cattle and sixty-four head of work steers." Near the Little Blue River Loveland met a cattleman named Packwood who had nine wagons and about 400 head of loose cattle, having already lost sixty cows. Crow lost sixteen cattle and "several head dead from drinking the alkali" at Green River. "Tarry not on Green River but leave it is as soon as possible if you would save your cattle from death!" Loveland warned. It is not clear how many of Crow's cattle wandered off, disappeared in Indian raids, or died of hardship on the trek—or how much they were worth in the goldfields—but in 1851 Charles Coil sold 350 choice animals for between $75 and $200 a head.[73]

During the second half of June, "the renowned Kit Carson" arrived at Fort Laramie from his ranch in New Mexico with a herd of sheep, along with several men apparently posing as the legendary frontiersman. "He is the picture of a hardy Mountaineer, as he is represented, about 35 years old, 5 feet 10 inches high, dark hair, blue eyes with much of the dare devil in them," wrote Dr. Carmi P. Garlick, adding about five inches to the actual height and darkening the sandy hair of the real "dear old Kit." "He is rather taciturn. Wishes to pass unknown." The real Carson brought about fifty horses and mules to trade at the fort and may have been involved in an ambitious project to bridge the North Platte River at Deer Creek. The span was sometimes called the Trappers Bridge, but it "was poorly constructed and failed in the high waters of the following spring." William Bent, whose famous Arkansas River fort had burned in 1849, apparently accompanied Carson. "Kit Carson & Bill Bent have just left," wrote John Tutt in July.[74] West of Devils Gate, Lord Julius Brenchley fell in with "the celebrated Kit Carson, at the head of a company of miners with their pack-mules laden with gold, on their way to the United States."[75] (The authentic Carson was driving his sheep in the opposite direction.)

---

[72]Day, Journal, 25 May 1849, BYU Library.

[73]Loveland, *California Trail Herd,* 43, 46, 56, 59, 79–80. This 1961 Richard H. Dillon book remains the best overview of cattle drives over the California Trail.

[74]Garlick, "A Trip Overland to California," 15 June 1850, 23; Tutt to John Dougherty, 1 July 1850, Missouri Historical Society; Unruh, *The Plains Across,* 273; Glass, "Crossing the North Platte River," 26.

[75]Remy and Brenchley, *A Journey to Great-Salt-Lake City,* 2:502.

David Shaw fondly recalled meeting "the noted hunter, trapper, Indian fighter and chief guide to Gen. John C. Fremont." Shaw claimed he learned how to make a packsaddle while watching Carson mend his at Fort Laramie. Carson's shepherding must have been profitable, for Shaw met him again on the Humboldt in 1853 when the famed mountaineer "with his wife and several Spaniards in his employ" were on their way from Taos to California "with 400 sheep intended for that market."[76]

Throughout the gold rush, the cattle crowding the California Trail proved immensely profitable and became a major business, with large herds driven from Missouri, Illinois, Arkansas, and the Indian Territory. California Trail cattle herds were smaller than the preferred size of about 2,500 head that became popular after the Civil War during the golden age of Texas-Kansas cattle drives, but in 1852, 90,000 head of loose cattle passed Fort Kearny on their way to the goldfields.[77]

The Devil Himself Could Not Get Through:
Childs Cutoff, 1850

Travel on the Council Bluff Road up the Platte River's north shore increased dramatically in 1850. *Horn's Overland Guide* called this country the "Indian Enchanted Ground" for its exotic landmarks, fossils, and "petrafactions of every description." Those who traversed it faced dangerous crossings of the North Platte at Fort Laramie and again at the river's upper ferries clustered around today's Casper, Wyoming. A continuous road up the river's north bank, which the best experts deemed impossible, would eliminate two dangerous river crossings—if such a route could be found. Almost by accident, spring floods and drunken vandals inspired the Upper Mississippi Ox Company to blaze a new road up the north side of the Platte's north fork.

William Rothwell found "the Mormon route, which runs very close to the North side of the stream," offered better grass, a considerable savings in distance, and proved "of the greatest advantage to us" after his party crossed to the Platte's north side shortly after reaching the river. But at Fort Laramie, the North Fork was 130 yards wide and "deep and extremely swift. The only chance for crossing is an old worn out flatboat pulled by means of a rope stretched from bank to bank," which was "certainly a dangerous concern." He had supposed—and so had almost everyone else—"that by taking the Council Bluff or Mormon route we should altogether avoid crossing the North Platte, but instead of this, we have this rapid and dangerous mountain stream to cross twice—once here and again at the Upper Ferry, 130 miles above." Rothwell complained, "A great many will not believe but that there is a road leading up the North side of the river. A number of trains have

---

[76]Shaw, *Eldorado*, 35, 75.
[77]*Los Angeles Star*, 18 September 1852, in Loveland, *California Trail Herd*, 18, 36.

tried it and after winding about among almost insurmountable hills have had to retrace their steps & Ferry here." Jerome Dutton had planned to cross over to the fort, but "it could not be forded and the ferry boat was sunk the other day by some Californians who were on a spree." With the ferry out of commission, "we either had to go up on this side or ferry ourselves on a float, and no timber to build it of. We therefore concluded to keep up the north side."[78] When Rothwell arrived at the North Platte Ferry a week later, he learned the wagons that had "continued up the North side have made a road and got along, where Major Sanderson of Fort Laramie assured the emigrants a mountain goat could not make his way." As Rothwell observed, "Californians never stop to calculate obstacles."[79]

Wisconsin's Upper Mississippi Ox Company pioneered this alternative to the long, dusty trek over the Black Hills of Wyoming. A member of the party, Andrew Child, published a trail guide in 1852 describing an overland route that let travelers stay on *"the north side of the Platte River, for the whole of the distance, lying near that stream."*[80] The train that opened the road defied the advice of the best experts. The officers at Fort Laramie "were very anxious to prevent anyone from being so fool hardy as to 'risk his life' up the N. side," Byron McKinstry charged. "They said it was their duty to warn us, that they were disinterested, &c." One authority claimed the train would have to go eighty miles out of its way around a mountain. Their cattle would die "for want of food & drink, for it would be impossible to come at the Platte, for it was shut in among perpendicular hills 300 ft high." Kit Carson told some of the Upper Mississippians the Devil himself could not get through on the north side. "We have made up our minds to try it," wrote McKinstry.[81]

Skeptics charged that "Uncle Sams Epauleted Gentry" were profiting from the ferry at Fort Laramie and were in league with David Hickman, an upper crossing ferryman who charged $5 (about $100 today) per wagon.[82] Thomas Durban's party decided "to follow up on the North side of the Platte river, and not cross at all," but officers at Fort Laramie warned "it was very probable the Indians would steal our horses, and that they thought the route was impassible on account of the high water and some very high mountains that we should be compelled to cross." His company felt "we could travel where anyone else could, and were resolved to try it"—and they reached the upper ferry "without seeing an Indian or meeting with any misfortune, and on the way found plenty of good grass and water." Part of the trail was mountainous and rocky, "but patience and perseverance will accomplish

---

[78]Dutton, 13, 15 June 1850, "Across the Plains," 462, 465.

[79]Rothwell, Notes of a Journey, 25 and 26 May and 7, 9, and 16 June 1850, Beinecke Library.

[80]Child, *Overland Route to California,* title page. No one called it Childs Cutoff in trail times. Modern historians adopted the name based on Child's first published account of the alternate.

[81]McKinstry, *California Gold Rush Overland Diary,* 22 June 1850, 131–32.

[82]Langworthy, *Scenery of the Plains, Mountains and Mines,* 21 June 1850, 56.

ANDREW CHILD
The guidebook author who gave his name to
the Childs Cutoff had this daguerreotype taken
after he arrived in California in 1850. Child's
New Guide for the Overland Route described how
wagons could stay on "the north side of the
Platte River, for the whole of the distance"
from today's Council Bluffs, Iowa, to Casper,
Wyoming. Courtesy Bancroft Library.

almost any thing." Finding so much less trouble than they expected to encounter,
they kept expecting more until the trail ended. Durban was "fully satisfied it is
the nearest and best route."[83]

Those who tried the new alternate were universally delighted with the results
of their gamble. "We have gained about two days on most of those that took the
South side, had as good a road, better grass, and kept clear of the sickness of
which there is a great deal on the S. side," McKinstry concluded upon reaching
the Upper Ferry. Additionally, he had saved "the trouble and expense of crossing
the river twice."[84] Noting how many had drowned at the ferries, James E. Gale
said, "the new Road we took was A Luckey one to us. We had the Best road Best
grass and saved the Crossing [of] plat River twice."[85] By summer's end, the myth
of the North Platte's impassible north bank was debunked. "We have solved the
problem respecting the new route. It is a better road than the old one that runs on
the south side of the river. There is no serious obstacle in the way," wrote Franklin
Langworthy. "We are now of the opinion that those who own the ferries have
their agents about the Fort, to keep in circulation those false and alarming tales
in reference to the difficulties of the new route."[86]

[83]Durban to "Dear Mother," 20 July 1850, "The Route to California," *Zanesville Courier,* 7 November 1850, 2/3–4.
[84]McKinstry, *California Gold Rush Overland Diary,* 29 June 1850, 147.
[85]Gale to "Dear Wife," 1 July 1850, Beinecke Library.
[86]Langworthy, *Scenery of the Plains, Mountains and Mines,* 21 June 1850, 56.

Conspiracy or no, the man who gave the cutoff its name with his guidebook gave an excellent summary of this previously "untraveled and unknown" trace. Andrew Child said his pioneering party encountered no serious obstacles and gained two days over those who crossed to the south side, "as nearly all of the emigration did. By this route we avoided twice crossing the Platte, and also the dreaded Black Hills of the south side." Deep creeks might make the trail impractical in a very wet season, Child conceded. Otherwise, he said, "I believe it to be incomparably better than via the Black Hills of the south side."[87] Childs Cutoff turned out to be the most effective and useful cutoff opened anywhere on the California Trail during the gold rush. "By taking this route of keeping the north side the entire route will save at least an expensive ferriage of the Platte at the Upper Crossing; from five to ten dollars is usually charged each team," Joseph E. Johnson reported in September 1850 after leading a Mormon party east from the Salt Lake Valley to the Missouri River. "There is also a far greater amount of fuel and a larger number of small pure streams from the mountains or Bluffs, to be found on the North, than on the South side."[88] Among the route's many advantages, its pure streams were free of the *Vibrio cholerae*.

No Want of Dead Yankees: Cholera Rages On

"The cholerra, measles and dysentary being among the Emigration in the early part of their Journey and I believe the scarcity of grass, and the rush to get on [a]head of one another, has caused a good deal of mortality in both the men and beasts," Richard Grant reported from Fort Hall. "If reports be true there is no want of dead Yankees, Oxen and Mules on their route."[89] The disease and chaos that was the scourge of life on the trail in 1849 increased dramatically a year later when the great terror Grant mentioned—cholera—returned with a vengeance.

On the Platte Oregon emigrants told Robert Campbell of the disease, including "a woman who said she had just seen her father, mother, and sister interred within a few days. We saw a wagon alone on the river bank—mess all reported to have died." Emigrants called this the valley of death, Campbell wrote. "Graves by the wayside were reckoned at an average of one per mile," and no one could guess the number at campsites along the river.[90] Again and again, emigrant journals gave grim reports of deaths witnessed and graves counted. "We passed 13 fresh dug graves,"

---

[87]Child, *Overland Route to California,* 20–21.

[88]Johnson, "Return from the Valley," 2 February 1851, *Frontier Guardian,* 21 March 1851, 1. This was probably the first party to travel the new route from west to east.

[89]Grant to Simpson, 22 February 1850, HBC Archives, D.5/27, 335–37d.

[90]Campbell, 7 July 1850, "Interesting News," *Frontier Guardian,* 24 July 1850, 1–2.

Benjamin Franklin Dowell wrote one Sunday. "Seven of the epitaphs stated they died of cholera." Two days later, he passed twenty-five freshly dug graves whose victims had all died within five days.[91] "I cannot attempt to give you an Idea of the amount of suffering on the road from sickness & starvation. When I think of it I feel an involuntary shudder," Dr. Philip Hines wrote home. "I have seen stout men lay down at night well & in the morning their bodies wrapt in a blanket & thrown into a hole scarce 1 foot deep, & a few shovels of dirt thrown over them, so that the wolves might have a little harder work to get the body."[92]

Acts of quiet heroism mitigated the terror the mysterious epidemic generated. As one train gathered for breakfast, a small boy approached and asked for help burying two men who had died during the night not a hundred yards away. "This seemed to strike our camp with terror and many of our boys made a strong protest against any one of our company going, as they said, right into the camp of death," recalled John D. Ferrill. A young Dr. Hocker reasoned there was no more danger in the camp, since the atmospheric miasma was the same in both locations, so he and Ferrill stayed behind. "With the help of the women in camp we laid the stranger in his last resting place in that lonely spot." Hocker revived one man who had been given up for dead, and neither he nor Ferrill fell victim to the disease.[93]

Many believed doctors caused more problems than they solved. Given the state of scientific knowledge and medical practice, they might have been right. "Out of about 50,000 who have crossed the Plains, I believe that at least 1,000 have died," wrote Asa C. Call. "I am fully convinced that the mass of these deaths were caused by fear and over doctoring." He had seen men "swallow about half a pint of laudanum, get worse, double the dose, and die. I have known a man to take opium enough in one night to kill three well men, and as his comrades placed him under the sod, in the morning, you might have seen them, every now and then, pass round a bottle of laudanum and a bottle of brandy to prevent cholera." Anyone with "good sense, and a good outfit, and no medicine, may rely upon good health and a pleasant journey in crossing the Plains," Call concluded.[94] Edmund Booth swallowed twenty Mandrake Pills, thinking, "I might as well die of pills as of cholera." He reassured his wife he only used Moffatt's Pills "in severe cases and they are no more dangerous than arsenic, nightshade and henbane which the doctors use."[95] Perhaps. Given the state of knowledge, good luck was more useful than medical care. Physicians' reports make clear that they dealt with the disaster as best they could.

---

[91]Dowell, Journal, 9, 11 June 1850, 9.
[92]Hines, "An Ohioan's Letter," 161–62.
[93]Ferrill, "Early Days," 26 June 1892.
[94]Call, "From Utah," *The National Era*, 23 January 1851, 13.
[95]Booth, *Edmund Booth (1810–1905), Forty-niner*, 7, 60.

Astute medical observers and overland captains deduced the likely cause of the disease. Three doctors traveling with Henry Stine warned their companions "to be careful in drinking out of pools as they believed that if there was any sickness ahead it was occasioned by that."[96] If they followed his advice about drinking water, "I will promise you that there shall not more than five die in this camp with Cholera," Thomas Johnson told his Mormon train. He warned his people not to go near the shallow wells along the Platte, "but get the water out of the river and drink none without boiling, and fill their churns, tea kettles, and everything that they had that would hold water, with boiled water to use while traveling." They did as directed, and "just five and no more died, while the goldseekers ahead of us and the Saints behind us were dying at a fearful rate." Eastbound missionaries told Samuel Gifford they had met gold emigration companies "driving twelve abreast, hurrying to get away from the Cholera."[97]

Dr. Samuel Ayres did not believe the affliction was "the genuine Asiatic cholera and other physicians concur with me in the same opinion," but emigrants suffered indescribable distress. "Husbands have been deprived of their wives, wifes have lost their only protectors on earth, children have been made orphans and all have been left to mourn the loss of some of their traveling companions in this wild region." One Oregon-bound family train had lost so many men "that three ladies had to shoulder their whips and assume the place of drivers." After cholera struck one couple, their company abandoned them. "The man died and the woman being unable to do anything for herself, could not attend to her husband. Thus they remained for three days," Ayres wrote. Finally, a curious emigrant found the woman and buried her husband, whose remains "became quite offensive before they were interred."[98]

How many people died on the trail in 1850 was a matter of widespread speculation. "It has been estimated that not less than five thousand perished on the plains out of the sixty thousand who started for California this last season," wrote Horace Belknap, who found the trail's "difficulties and dangers truly horrible to contemplate."[99] Dr. William Allen calculated "the fell destroyer, Asiatic cholera" killed two or three thousand overland emigrants in 1850. He had attended over seven hundred patients and "was in the thick of the fight all the time. Strange to say," he recalled next spring, "while other doctors lost nearly every case I lost none that I got to in a reasonable time after the attack." (Allen's success suggests his treatment involved some form of hydration.)[100]

---

[96]Stine, Journal and Letters, 17 June 1850, Missouri Historical Society.
[97]Gifford, Journal Book, LDS Archives, 13.
[98]Ayres, 25 May, 15 June 1850, Western Historical Manuscripts.
[99]Belknap to "Esqr. McClary," 2 February 1851, "An Iowan in California, 1850," 462.
[100]Allen to "My Brother," 4 May 1851, Oregon Historical Society.

Recent mortality figures based on documented deaths indicate that the actual number was much lower than eyewitnesses thought. Richard L. Rieck, the best expert on death on the trail, accounted for about four hundred cholera deaths in 1850. He suggests the horror of witnessing such carnage inflated contemporary estimates.[101] Calvin Taylor captured that terror: "Many thousands who started full of hope and bright anticipation of the future found an untimely grave in a strange land among strangers and beyond the search of kind friends and relatives." The ruthless hand of death had "no respect of persons, age, or sex, or conditions of life." The road west became a charnel house "literally lined for hundreds of miles with not only the bodies of men, but of vast multitudes of horses, oxen, and mules, with innumerable wrecks of wagons, baggage, clothing, etc., property to the amount of hundreds of thousands of dollars totally lost to the use of man." It was all, Taylor concluded, "an immense sacrifice to avarice and the love of gold."[102]

South Pass: The Destruction of Property Is Amazing

Beyond Fort Kearny, the whole country was "poor, barren, mountainous, rocky, ashy and mean," wrote Benjamin Van Houten. Except along the creeks, from Laramie to the upper ferry the grass had been "eaten off by the tens of thousands of stock that were before us." He saw a friend die trying to get his cattle across the North Platte. "I did all I could to save him but in vain. He drowned, and I was with difficulty saved." Beyond the ferry the country grew even worse—"barren, poisonous, covered with wild sage, greasewood and salaratus. Poisonous lakes, ponds, springs and streams abound." Grass and good water was scarce, but "dead cattle line the way, and sick men are plenty. From the Pass to Green river no grass of any consequence, plenty of sage and mean greasewood [on] a desert of fifty miles without water." On Green River he watched four more men drown, while west of that ugly ferry lay rough roads and mountains. "Barrenness prevails on the last end of the stretch. From the head of Humbolt to the sink of the same is about 295 miles, but owing to the high water and deep sloughs the distance is 350 miles this year, and such a 350 miles. Oh! Gracious," Van Houten exclaimed.[103]

Henry Wellenkamp saw a thousand derelict wagons at Fort Laramie. At every subsequent campsite he found "the ruins of abandoned wagons, and articles of every description." Beyond the North Platte, the trail entered "the ante-chamber of Hell; no wood, no water, no grass, but myriad millions of departed souls in the shape of crickets." Here the urge to push forward at any cost led travelers to

---

[101]Rieck, "A Geography of Death," 14; "The Geography of Death and Graves."

[102]Taylor, "Overland to the Gold Fields," 28, 29 September 1850, 348–49.

[103]Van Houten to "My dear Wife," 8 September 1850, Typescript, Mattes Library, 1–2.

forsake even more property and provisions.[104] As livestock gave out, half the emigrants took to packing by shank's mare, "carrying their luggage on our backs." The property lining the trail was astonishing, and the junk increased as the trail got harder. Clothing of every sort was scattered along the Sweetwater—"there was towels, gowns and hairpins all along the road from the time we struck the river, and books of every sort and size from Fannie Hill to the Bible," Richard Hickman noted.[105] The stress led to countless quarrels. "Dugan and Duhner not being able to agree, made a division, sawing their wagon in two and making each a cart," wrote Samuel Lane.[106] "There was one of the waggons sawed in t[w]o and made two carts of it," George Burke said at Horse Creek, noting how the simple design of the wagon's running gear expedited the conversion.[107]

Failing teams and the desire to rush ahead again led many to put their trust in packing. "We now find our team so fairly give out that we are going to leave our wagon," James Payne wrote. He and his companions spent the day making packsaddles out of a wagon wheel "using the spokes for cross pieces and knocked a board out of the side of the body for side pieces; the balance of the body we used for firewood; this was all the benefit we got out of our wagon after getting it this far." The men left their tent and took nothing but provisions, a blanket apiece, and their best clothes. "I have one new suit, besides the one I have on; this I have worn for weeks and expect to wear it in to California. Then I can get into the river, and make an entirely new man of myself," Payne wrote.[108]

After Childs Cutoff rejoined "the main road over which all emigrants must pass, whether bound for Oregon or California," this nearly "continuous, unbroken procession of emigrants" faced more challenges. Franklin Langworthy left the North Platte early to avoid the Poison Spring but found the bleak and barren desert littered with dead animals and forsaken possessions. Cooking fires consumed thousands of fine books, boxes, barrels, and trunks. Property that cost $100 in the States went up in smoke to make one fire. At South Pass the road was so crowded Langworthy found it hard to realize he was far from civilization. "On all sides I see multitudes of people, wagons, cattle and horses at all times throng the way. The road, from morning till night, is crowded like Pearl Street or Broadway" in New York City. After sunset, fires gleamed amidst a city of white tents stretching in all directions. "We hear on all sides the lowing of cattle, the neighing of horses, the braying of mules, and barking of dogs, mingled with the clack of human voices. To this is added the sound of the viol, bugle, tamborine and clarionette. To fill

[104]Wellenkamp, Travel Diary, 8, 16, 20 June 1850, Western Historical Manuscripts.

[105]Hickman, "Dick's Works," 23 June 1852, 170.

[106]Lane, Gold Rush, 26 May 1850, 32.

[107]Burke to "Dear Sir," 3 June 1850, Western Historical Manuscripts.

[108]Payne, Saint Louis to San Francisco, 17 July 1850, California State Library, 75–76.

up the chorus, rifles and pistols are almost constantly cracking, responsive to the rumbling, grinding music of carriage-wheels still passing along."[109]

"The destruction of property is amazing. There is not a single camping ground upon the whole road from Laramie onward that is not marked by the iron remains of one or more wagons. Thousands of harness, chains, clothes, saddles, guns, in short everything but provisions are scattered along the road," said William Rothwell. "I verily believe that there is enough wagon tires to make a railway to California."[110] At South Pass James Gale wrote, "I have not seen A nuff trees to make 1 hundred Rails for 5 hundred miles But we have plentey good wagons for to Cook."[111] A few found creative ways to dispose of surplus goods. "While throwing away today, we had a keg of powder," wrote James Payne, and he decided to have some fun with it. After breaking camp, he set the keg under a deserted wagon and "put a slow match to it; you can imagine how much fun there was in it. Our troubles in camp were so great that no one took so much notice of the matter as to know or care what I was doing, but it made a big report."[112]

South of the main road across South Pass, forsaken property already littered the recently blazed Cherokee Trail. O. W. Lipe saw "the immense number of carcasses of cattle which have died along the road," so tons of iron could be picked up from burned and abandoned wagons.[113] "It is astonishing the amount of plunder that has been wasted on the road between Laramie and the valley," Riley Senter wrote from Great Salt Lake. "If I had what has been wasted on the road I would not need to go to the California gold mines."[114]

By the time the massive migration reached South Pass, rumor and reality made travelers desperate to find the shortest, fastest road to the goldfields. "We are told that thousands have taken the back track fearing to come on, that great numbers in consequence of the sickness and scarcity of provisions who Started for California, had taken the route to Oregon for safety, and that much distress had prevailed," wrote Silas Newcomb. As conditions deteriorated, overlanders grew increasingly susceptible to seductive and self-serving promises of a shortcut. The single main tail across South Pass shattered eighteen miles beyond the Continental Divide at the Parting of the Ways, "the junction of Sublette's cut off, and the Fort Bridger road." Travelers often felt they made the wrong choices: "This route proved much the worst and longest," J. D. Mason wrote after taking the left-hand road to Great Salt Lake. "It seemed as if the mountains of New Hampshire and the mud holes

---

[109]Langworthy, *Scenery of the Plains, Mountains and Mines*, 21, 28, 29 June 1850, 56, 59, 62.

[110]Rothwell, Notes of a Journey, 2 August 1850, Beinecke Library, 172.

[111]Gale to "Dear Wife," 1 July 1850, Beinecke Library.

[112]Payne, Saint Louis to San Francisco, 18 July 1850, California State Library, 76.

[113]Lipe, 27 May 1849, *Cherokee Advocate*, 30 July 1849, 2, in Bieber, *Southern Trails to California*, 345–46.

[114]Senter, *Crossing the Continent*, [13].

of Indiana had been combined together to make this road." When Newcomb rejoined the main road at City of Rocks, he estimated that "at least nine tenths of the travel came the 'cut off' and Fort Hall roads." Virtually everyone now used the Hudspeth Cutoff, even though the traders at Soda Spring strongly advised going to Fort Hall.[115]

As always, the majority sought the shortest and quickest road to their destination, in this case the Sublette and Hudspeth cutoffs. "The Emigration in Summer 1849 was considered very large," Chief Trader Richard Grant reported at the beginning of his last season at Fort Hall, "but the Emigration of Summer 1850 was immensely so, it is considered that at least 40 to 50 Thousands went on to California by the different routes."[116] Fort Hall did little in the way of trade, Fleming Hearn observed in late July, while Cyrus Loveland later found only five or six men at the fort.[117] British aristocrat Henry Coke found Grant "basking on the shafts of a wagon in front of his portals. His grey head and beard, portly frame and jovial dignity were a ready-made representation of Falstaff, and would have done justice to that character on the boards of any theatre." The old frontiersman shook Coke's hand as if he had known him for half a century, but letters of introduction from Grant's boss ensured a warm welcome. Grant conducted him "to the sanctum of his castle" and fed him. Coke feared his prairie appetite would alarm the trader's family, "for I ate new-laid eggs and drank new milk until I almost astonished even myself; but when the second course appeared, and I was expected to keep pace with my worthy host in demolishing hot rolls and duck-pies, I felt quite ashamed of my own incapacity." He could only venerate an example he could not imitate. "It was indeed a rest and a luxury to spend a couple of idle days here," Coke recalled years later, "and revive one's dim recollection of fresh eggs and milk."[118]

Beyond Bear River, fur trade veterans, Mormons, and Indians created a series of impromptu stations, notably at Soda Springs, where French traders assembled between eight hundred to a thousand horses and mules for the overland trade.[119] Thomas Turnbull found a large camp of Shoshone lodges between Soda and Beer springs next to "one Log House a Northwest trader or traders French & Americans, every thing mostly for sale," including hundreds of ponies of "all colours & kinds pretty near as good as the Montreal Ponies," along with a blacksmith's shop offering services to emigrants and Indians alike.[120] Gilbert Cole saw a thousand Shoshones camped at the spring and did some horse trading with a man named

[115]Newcomb, Overland Journey, 25 July 1850, Beinecke Library, 131; Mason, "Letter from California," August 1850.
[116]Grant to Simpson, Fort Hall, 31 January 1851, HBC Archives, D.5/30, 183–85.
[117]Hearn, Journal, 29 July 1850, Oregon Historical Society; Loveland, California Trail Herd, 30 August 1850, 90.
[118]Coke, A Ride over the Rocky Mountains, 218; Coke, Tracks of a Rolling Stone, 170.
[119]Lewis, Journal, 29 June 1852, in Unruh, The Plains Across, 487n62.
[120]Turnbull, "Travels," 30 June 1852, 185.

McClelland, "who was buying or trading for broken-down stock." The mule Cole bought "proved to be the toughest and easiest riding animal in the bunch." He later saw the horse he had traded to McClelland hitched to a dray in Sacramento, where his new owner valued him at $400.[121]

STEEP, TORTUOUS, AND WINDY:
THE GOLDEN PASS AND SALT LAKE CUTOFF

Perhaps a quarter of the migration visited Great Salt Lake City in 1850, but getting there was not easy. The trail over Big Mountain Pass was now four years old, but it crossed some of the most challenging terrain in the entire trail system and waves of Mormons and gold seekers had done little to improve it. The road from the Weber River and over Big Mountain was still "a difficult, not to say desperate, proposition," observed Dale Morgan. "It required the crossing of two steep and dangerous heights, and travel in the narrow, crooked canyon bottoms was almost as hard on wagons and animals as the ascent and descent of the two mountains." Between East Canyon Creek and the valley, the road forded streams forty-four times, and the twelve over Mountain Dell Creek were "all bad crossing places." The trail's "stiff grades and serpentine canyons" traversed the highest elevations and worst gorges east of the Sierra Nevada.[122] When Dexter Tiffany crossed on horseback in August 1849, the view from Big Mountain was magnificent, but the trail was miserable: the descent "was steep as the roof of a house for half a mile." In many places Emigration Canyon was "so narrow & with such short turns in it that the middle one of three waggons travelling closely together could not see the one before or behind. Beside this you have to cross the creek 19 times in 5 miles every one so cut by the waggons as to [be] exceedingly dangerous." The trail was so bad "it was with the greatest difficulty that I could get my horses through."[123]

Mormon apostle Parley P. Pratt began looking for a better route through the Wasatch Mountains in 1848. He found an easier, but longer, passage, and his discoveries left his name scattered across the countryside. From the Weber River at the mouth of Echo Canyon, his proposed toll road turned "up the river about ten miles, then up a canyon about eight miles into a beautiful valley in the tops of the mountains," which was soon named Parleys Park. Silver Creek, now the route of today's Interstate 80, proved too rugged. When the topographical engineers surveyed the canyon in 1859, it was "scarcely admissible for packs, & is entirely out of the question as a wagon route." Pratt's road went up Weber River fifteen

---

[121]Cole, *In the Early Days,* 3 July 1852, 78–79.
[122]Korns and Morgan, *West from Fort Bridger,* 251.
[123]Tiffany, Diary, 5 August 1849, Missouri Historical Society, 99.

miles and crossed the West Hills "through a dry hollow, and over an abrupt range" via Threemile Canyon. After traversing the "well watered, grassy, and beautiful plains and meadows" below today's Park City, the trail climbed two miles "through meadows, and table lands of pine, fir, and aspen forests, to the summit of a mountain," now Parleys Summit.

Pratt began developing his "more southern and less rugged route than the pioneer entrance to the valley" too late for Forty-niners to use it. He built enough road to extract a large amount of timber and fuel from the lower canyon, and next March began "obtaining much building and fencing timber and a large quantity of poles" from the rest of the trace. In July 1850 his road opened for the California emigration. The Mormon apostle touted his "New Road Through the Mountains" as "The Golden Pass!"—a golden-colored outcropping at the mouth of Parleys Canyon perhaps provided the happy inspiration for the name, which was sure to intrigue gold seekers, as Dale Morgan suggested. "If a road worked by the most persevering industry, an open country, good feed and fuel, beautifully romantic and sublime scenery, are any inducement, take the new road," Pratt advertised. He raked in about $1,500 in tolls the first season. Since the average toll was about $1 per wagon, between five to eight thousand emigrants probably used it during its single year of operation. A few travelers praised the new route, but it was nine miles longer than the trail over Big Mountain that cost nothing, so about two-thirds of those going to Great Salt Lake chose the free road.[124]

Costmor Clark took Pratt's Golden Pass on 10 July after emerging from Echo Canyon's "purpendicular ledges of rocks perhaps five thousand feet high." At sunset he reached the Weber River, finding himself at "the junction of the old and new roads to the city." The new trace was a toll road "turning to the left up the stream. This is recommended by a notice posted upon the guide board to be a nearer and better route—improved and subjected to toll by 'authority' of the 'State of Deseret.'" The new road was an example of Mormon enterprise, while Deseret was its odd manifestation of "theodemocracy." Its appointed legislature parceled out ferry, timber, and road concessions to powerful men like Apostle Pratt, who made the most of the opportunity. As one of his first customers, Clark found good wood and grass on the Weber River, "a cold pure mountain stream." After crossing Parleys Park and climbing "a most tremendous hill" to Parleys Summit, Clark's train faced hard traveling down Parleys Canyon. "The continual crossing of the creek where in many instances the wheels were over [their] hubs in mud and water. The sideling roads and stumps and roots proved a smasher to many waggons and a hard pull to all the teams," he observed.[125]

---

[124]Korns and Morgan, *West from Fort Bridger,* 251–61, 263.
[125]Clark, "Trail of Hardship," 10–12 July 1850, 148.

The Golden Pass avoided the arduous climb and perilous descent of Big Mountain, but the toll road was "new and so far perfectly horrible," Fleury F. Keith wrote after negotiating the narrows of Threemile Canyon. The next day his train hauled their wagons across a bad slough by hand. The trail down Pratt's "Great Kanyon" was awful: Keith "drove 14 miles to day, over the worst Road that we have had on the whole trip."[126] Even Latter-day Saints complained about it. On the Sweetwater in 1850, Nelson Whipple met fellow Mormon Anson Call, who told him to take the new route "up the Weber river from the mouth of Echo Canyon." Whipple wondered why Call recommended it, since "the road was almost impassable, much worse we were told than the other way but notwithstanding we got over." He was soaked to his hips from leading his party's heifers across the creeks in Parleys Canyon, "which was not a few," and was too tired to join his comrades at a dance. Early the next morning he walked up a bluff overlooking the valley. He saw the Great Salt Lake and its islands, "which all looked barren, dreary and desolate and the whole view had the most lonely and isolated appearance that could be." Whipple described his singular feelings as he reflected "on the condition of a handfull of people here located at least one thousand miles from all civilization in this sterile and desolate region of the Rocky mountains, to sustain themselves and become an independent nation, which I knew they had to do somewhere in these mountains."[127]

Brigham Young sent Pratt, never his favorite colleague, to proselytize in Chile in 1851. He sold his interest in the road to finance the mission, and despite its moneymaking potential and for reasons not explained in Mormon annals, the Golden Pass was seldom used as an emigrant trail for the next ten years. "At this point a road turns to the left to salt Lake," an 1852 emigrant wrote at the mouth of Echo Canyon, where the road began. "It is five miles further than the old one, & is no better and toll is charged for traveling it, it was prepared by one Perley P. Pratt, a mormon."[128] Dale Morgan thought the high cost of maintaining the toll road meant it could not compete with a shorter, free alternative. "From some combination of these causes," he concluded, "the Golden Pass Road fell into desuetude."[129] Historian Harold Schindler suggested another reason the Mormons abandoned the road. Brigham Young regarded the long trail to Zion as a test of faith, and if the bad road over Big Mountain Pass wore down California emigrants and their livestock, that was not his concern. As life in Utah became harder during the droughts and grasshopper plagues of the 1850s, the difficult trail made it as hard for disgruntled

[126]Keith, Journal of Crossing the Plains, 4, 5 July 1850, 8.

[127]Whipple, "Journal of a Pioneer," 13 September 1850, 124.

[128]Bradley and Bradley, Daily Journal, 19 June 1852, Beinecke Library, 59–60.

[129]Korns and Morgan, West from Fort Bridger, 264.

Mormons to get out of Zion as it had been to get in. Brigham Young did not want leaving the Salt Lake Valley to be easy.[130]

Eventually, the benefits of the route became too great to ignore. The Overland Stage came down Parleys Canyon in 1862, and that same year a new toll road up Silver Creek Canyon shortened the route. Mormon trains began using the Golden Pass, and it soon became the preferred road into the Salt Lake Valley, even thought it still had its problems. "The road through this kanyon again was very bad," William Ajax reported in 1862, "and it was a source of wonder to me why it was let in such a wretched condition, as the bestowal of a little sum, even where the price of labour is as high as it is in this country, would make it a good one."[131]

The Story Was Not True:
The End of the Hastings Cutoff

Exactly why anyone used the Hastings Cutoff in 1850 is a mystery. The notorious reputation of the road across the Salt Desert was no secret—and, as William Waldo observed, "All remember the fate of the Donner party."[132] Forty-niners who revived the trail had nothing good to say about it. Yet in 1850 someone was making the same false claims used in 1846 to lure travelers onto *Hastings Longtripp,*" and hundreds of gullible emigrants began "fixing to get a short cutt off in fifteen days to save twenty days travel, and we thought it best to go the nearest road," wrote Robert Chalmers.[133] "We calculate to take Hasting's cut-off, which is said to be the nearest route," Samuel Ayres told his wife.[134] At Great Salt Lake that July, "great excitement prevailed among the emigrants in relation to this Cut-off. Several old mountaineers proffered, for a considerable sum of money, to be paid in advance, to conduct companies by a new route across the Great Basin Desert to the 'Gold Diggings,' in eighteen or twenty days," wrote Adam Brown. "Many companies accepted these proposals, and others followed the trail of the proceeding companies."[135] To prepare for the "Morman Cut Off," Costmor Clark's party made pack saddles and "disposed of all our provisions excepting rations for 25 days, which we hope will last us through,"—a costly mistake.[136] "We were told of a much shorter route than that taken by wagons, through which we might 'swiftly glide' on horseback, with pack animals," William Bennett recalled. "We believed in this cutoff."[137]

---

[130]Ibid.; and author's conversations with Harold Schindler.
[131]Ajax, Journal, 5 October 1862, BYU Library.
[132]"News from the Plains," 12 September 1850, *The Gazette* (Davenport, Iowa), 28 November 1850, 2/5.
[133]Chalmers, "Journal," 20 July 1850, 47.
[134]Ayres to "My dear girl," 27 July 1850, Western Historical Manuscripts.
[135]Brown, "Over Barren Plains," 12 August 1850, 25.
[136]Clark, "Trail of Hardship," 17, 18 July 1850, 149.
[137]Bennett, *The Sky-Sifter,* 278–79.

Mormons offered their services as guides across the cutoff, but the route's main promoter was Auguste Archambault, who had crossed the Salt Desert in 1846 with John C. Frémont and now served as Captain Howard Stansbury's chief guide. Neither the local citizens nor the government explorer recommended the route to overlanders, and Archambault admitted Frémont had lost ten mules and several horses crossing the Salt Desert. Joseph Pike was worried enough about the purported shortcut to call on the topographical engineer "and found out what information I could about Hastings cut off." Stansbury, who had crossed the Salt Desert's moonlike landscape the previous autumn, was well aware of the trail's problems: "The whole plain is as desolate barren & dreary as can well be imagined," he wrote the night his expedition camped amid the wreckage of abandoned wagons. But whatever Stansbury told him, Pike took the cutoff immediately after speaking with the captain.[138]

Silas Newcomb's friends made the year's first recorded crossing of the cutoff and left behind the grim route's only known humorous anecdote. Newcomb met Allyn, Vedder, Marsh, and their pack train on the Humboldt, at the end of their arid and arduous trek. The men advised "all to Keep the old road as being safest and best—They are nearly out of eatibles and provisions being generally scarce. They look with foreboding to the future." Carlisle Abbott recalled that as the three men struggled through the desert, one of them prayed, "O Lord Almighty, send us just one drop of rain!" Soon a few clouds appeared and rain began to fall. The desperate men spread out a rubber blanket, but no more than a scattering of drops fell. "The damnphool," cursed Marsh, "might just as well have prayed for a barrel of water as for a drop, for he got ten times as much as he asked for."[139]

The largest party ever to cross the Salt Desert, consisting of no fewer than three hundred men, left Great Salt Lake City on 22 July "to take the much-lauded cutoff, under the guidance of a Frenchman who said he had traveled that way two or three times with Fremont and others." This was, of course, Archambault. Robert Chalmers set out a day earlier after meeting the renowned guide. "We started from S. L. City with 20 days provisions but expected to be in California in 15 days, as we heard others had gone there in that time; but we found that the story was not true," he wrote. His delusion was widely shared, and William Bennett recalled the guide who told this unlikely story. Archambault caught up with Chalmers at Donner Springs "with his company of two or three hundred, which gave him $300, to pilot them this far. They had lost some of their animals and had found one man dead on the plains," who had died of fatigue. This was not the only

---

[138]Pike, Diary, 20 July 1850, California State Library, 15; Chalmers, "Journal," 49n23; Stansbury, *Exploration and Survey,* 111, 114.

[139]Newcomb, Overland Journey, 4 August 1850, Beinecke Library, 143; Abbott, *Recollections,* 53–56.

casualty of the Hastings Cutoff: Finley McDiarmid attributed a death at Willow Creek to cholera. John Lowery Brown, with one of the two Cherokee companies that used the route in 1850, reported four deaths due to "the Sickness pervading in the company" between today's Grantsville and Skull Valley. Four more men died of "diarear" at Pilot Peak.[140]

On the edge of the Great Salt Lake, Costmor Clark went to bed "expecting if I sleep to dream of salt—of swimming in salt and breathing sulphurretted hydrogen and every other stink on earth." In late July, Clark found hundreds waiting at Redlum Spring, competing for a trickle of the very bad water "found by digging holes at the bottom of a ravine" as they tried "to recruit their animals and prepare for crossing the great '90 mile desert.' "[141] Finley McDiarmid admitted he was "taking Hastings cut off, the lefthand road from the city contrary to the advice of the Mormons and Captain Stansbury. Thus we intend to risk the alkalie swamp or desert." Like the thousands of others who took that gamble, McDiarmid came to regret it. The wagon road crossed the Cedar Mountains over Hastings Pass, "about 5 miles north of where Frémont crossed" in 1846 and "by far the most perpendicular of any we have found upon the whole route," he complained. He gave a graphic account of the dangerous muck lurking below the thin crust of the Salt Flats. "Captain H. Stanbury told me this is a very dangerous desert," McDiarmid wrote. "An ordinary rain would make the road altogether impassible for footmen, [to] say nothing about stock and wagons. Out of the roads there is no *bottom* to this ashy, sticky, stuff." Joseph Pike endured "a terable storm of wind and rain" on 23 July. Three days later on the Salt Desert, "It began to rain finely and continued to rain for an hour or more which mad[e] a plenty of mud." He broke his wagon tongue but somehow pulled through the mire.[142]

Previously unknown 1850 narratives provide surprising detail on the Hastings Cutoff's precise route across the Salt Desert playa, a subject of much controversy. A. S. Davies gave a short but powerful description of his crossing in mid-August. After taking on sixty-five gallons of water at Hope Wells, he "rolled out 12 miles to the last spring" at Redlum Spring, where "we watered our teams rest &c til 4 pm, then went out 4 miles to the summit of the mountain" and found "plenty of bunch grass." Davies stopped at sunrise, ate breakfast, and drove five miles to

[140]Bennett, *The Sky-Sifter,* 287; Chalmers, "Journal," 28 July, 5 August 1850, 48–49, 55; Kelly, "Gold Seekers on the Hastings Cutoff," 16, 25; McDiarmid, *Letters to My Wife,* 4 August 1850, 50; Brown, "Journal," 7 August 1850, 201.

[141]Clark, "Trail of Hardship," 27 July 1850, 150. Redlum Spring apparently derived its odd name from Return Jackson Redden (1817–1891), a bodyguard to Joseph Smith and scout for Brigham Young in 1847. During the 1850s Redden acquired a notorious reputation along the Humboldt as a "white Indian" but ended his days in Utah as a justice of the peace.

[142]Madsen, *Exploring the Great Salt Lake,* 186; McDiarmid, *Letters to My Wife,* 2, 6, 8 August 1850, 49, 50; Pike, Diary, 23, 26 July 1850, California State Library, 17. The relentlessly positive Pike concluded the rain "was a benefit to us in the end so we had no reason to complain."

Grayback Ridge. After pushing on another eight miles he stopped, "gave the cattle 4 gallons of water each [and] rested 4 hours." Next came the "big salt flat thence 7 miles *to a bend in the road to the north west* thence 8 miles to a point of mountain" at Floating Island. "Here we saw men and beasts suffering for water [and] men offering $5 a pint for water." He crossed Silver Island by 9:00 A.M. and called the ten-mile playa to Pilot or Donner Spring, "a welcome sight. I must say that I saw the most suffering here than I ever saw with man and beast. We was told it was only 60 miles accrost but it is 90 miles measured."[143]

Like most parties, Costmor Clark's pack train started the fearful long drive across the Salt Desert in late afternoon. Beyond Grayback the harsh terrain, "seemingly composed of sand ashes and salt mixed with cobble stones into which we sunk almost knee deep," nearly crippled his moccasin-clad feet, while "the dust raised by the travel ahead and blown into our faces by a strong wind was almost beyond endurance," he wrote. "It was the greatest difficulty we could either see or breath." The desert playa was "a perfect level, resembling a lake covered with ice—the salt on the surface white and glittering in the sun like snow," which made for pleasant traveling. Clark passed the sand-covered ruins of "the bones of animals, waggons and various other articals of property"—probably forsaken in 1846 or 1849, and which he thought belonged to "a company of Mormans, who, while attempting to cross the desert were overtaken by a rain which so softened the crust which covers the surface of the plain that it would not bear up their teams, they were obliged to abandon them to their fate." Now "in many places the crust will scarcely bear up a waggon however no one has broken through as yet." Learning Silver Island was still twenty-five miles from water, Clark's relentless optimism gave way to despair: "All around us were animals dying of hunger thirst and fatigue and many men as well as women in nearly the same condition." His party met a young man carrying two canteens; he invited them to drink as much as they pleased and told them about "a waggon load of water sent back by parties" only a half-mile ahead. "The 'water man' informed us that he was hired to meet the emigrants," a humane arrangement funded by contributions. Clark finally reached Pilot Springs about noon: "The place has quite the appearance of a town. Tents are pitched on every side and men and women are moving about in every direction."[144]

John Ferrill was with the rearguard of the emigration. Like those before him, his party found the cutoff to be twice as long as advertised. They managed to cross without much trouble but found desperate families strung out for miles. "Such a

---

[143]Davies, Journal to California, 15–17 August 1850, Idaho State Historical Society, emphasis added. The best experts, Rush Spedden and Roy D. Tea, have made significant contributions to our understanding of the Hastings Cutoff but disagree on important details. Davies's short account helps resolve the controversy. See Spedden, "The Fearful Long Drive," 2–16; Tea, "The Salt Lake Desert Treadmill"; "The Limitless Plain," 20–38, and 61–89.

[144]Clark, "Trail of Hardship," 28–30 July 1850, 150–51.

distressing sight I had never seen," Ferrill recalled. "We found some of them with their tongues swelled out of their mouths, and one poor fellow who attempted to bleed himself and drink his own blood." Opportunists were selling water at $10 a pint. On reaching Donner Springs, Ferrill and his friends borrowed two wagons, loaded them with water, and returned to the desert to relieve the suffering families. "After using our water, we loaded our two wagons with human freight, which so lightened the loads that all arrived safely and rested for two days," he remembered. John Wood confirmed Ferrill's recollection. "Emigrants are arriving here all the time from the desert, almost famished for water; they say men, women and children are dying with thirst and fatigue. All start in ignorance of the distance across, and many take but little water and they must perish," he wrote. "Our company rigged out a team loaded with water and have gone back on the desert to relieve the suffering, without money and without price. They found many at the point of death, and saved them, many suffering extremely." This relief work had been underway for a month. Joseph Pike met men returning to the desert, "sending out water by the wagon load and many were packing it in there canteens" as he struggled over the last miles to water. "A more benovelent set of men I never saw. The next morning the emigrants raised a $100 dollars to send out water to the perishing."[145]

The worst of Hastings Cutoff ended at Pilot Peak, but the ordeal was not yet half over. Two mountain ranges and sixty more miles of sagebrush and greasewood separated travelers from the refuge at "Fountain Valley," where John Wood passed hundreds of springs that created what he called "the most beautiful stream in the world," Ruby Valley's Franklin River. Here Wood saw a dead Shoshone with "a whip in one hand and an arrow in the other," apparently shot off his horse. "The most intense excitement now prevails among the emigrants; all are in a dread and fear of the Indians." Rumor said five packers had been "barbarously murdered by the Indians" while crossing Secret Pass, "and this intelligence has excited the revenge of all the emigrants, and every Indian is shot that can be seen." Wood's party almost shot two old traveling companions, having mistaken them for Indians. The emigrants "were in an enemy's land, in the midst of a host of blood-thirsty and revengeful savages, expecting their vengeance to be wreaked on us this night." In Huntington Valley, Wood heard guns firing almost constantly, accompanied by the "most desperate yelling, as if death was being dealt out by wholesale." He thought he was hearing emigrant cries, but on reaching camp J. H. Robinson said his company had assaulted a Western Shoshone band "and it was the effect of this lead that made the Indians scream so terrific." His men "killed eight or ten of

[145]Ferrill, "Early Days," 26 June 1892; Wood, "The Journal," 7 August 1850; Pike, Diary, 27 July 1850, California State Library, 17–18.

them in the willows," Robinson guessed. Upon reaching the Humboldt, Wood's party "felt like we ought to have satisfaction from the Indians so we rallied a force of 35 men" who attacked a Native village "and fought them four hours, and thank fortune, killed fifteen of the rebels."[146]

Many had abandoned their wagons after crossing the Salt Desert, but those who kept them had to make the cutoff's long southern detour to traverse another mountain range at Overland Pass. There the trail turned north up Huntington Valley for forty miles to the trail down South Fork Canyon. Costmor Clark "crossed the stream 24 times in passing through—Waggons were obliged to keep the channel of the stream most of the way" before they emerged into the grass, clover, and wild flax fields of the Humboldt River Valley, where he found "encampments of emigrants in all directions." In fifteen miles, "we crossed it about twenty-five times, some places having to wade along in it crotch deep, for a half mile," wrote John Wood. It was the perfect ending to Hastings Cutoff, which James Reed had calculated to be 461 miles long.[147]

"All the emigrants that come that road say that it is at least one hundred miles farther than the north road besides crossing a ninety three mile desert on which they tell us there is a great deal of suffering, there being neither grass nor water for that distance," wrote Solomon Litton, who heard "the Indians are also very bad on what's called the cut-off from Salt Lake." He saw a man reduced to "begging his way that had left all that he had on the desert even to his coat, shoes, butcher knife, etc. He got so weak they were two heavy for him to carry. He had nothing on but his shirt and pantaloons and his feet wrapped up with rags." A great many "lost their animals and some lost their outfits entirely and came very near losing their lives."[148]

"I have seen a number who came by this route, and by comparing notes we ascertained that the Cut-off was a 'cut-on,'" commented Adam Brown. The comparison showed "we had made this point in three days less time than packers and teams who came by the Hastings route!" Before returning to Great Salt Lake from the edge of the Salt Desert, the cutoff's "guides" assured their trusting clients that El Dorado lay only days ahead and provided them with "full directions," but after ruining their teams, their "arrival at the Humboldt river exposed the deception." The emigrants had suffered "almost beyond endurance," Brown wrote. "Their provisions are exhausted, and they have yet nearly five hundred miles to travel."[149]

"I never suffered so much before in all my life & thousands as well as us," wrote George Lawson. "We started out that road as we heard it was one hundred & fifty

---

[146]Wood, "The Journal," 17–23 August 1850.

[147]Clark, "Trail of Hardship," 19 August 1850, 152; Wood, "The Journal," 19 August 1850; Korns and Morgan, *West from Fort Bridger,* 232–33.

[148]Litton to "My Dear Wife," 30 November 1850, Western Historical Manuscripts.

[149]Brown, "Over Barren Plains," 12 August 1850, 25.

miles shorter than the one by the north of the lake [the Salt Lake Cutoff], but we found it about fifty or a hundred miles farther."[150] On his last day on the Hastings Cutoff, Joseph Pike called it "the hardest and worst road I ever undertook to travel."[151] The only woman known to have kept a journal of the ordeal expressed relief upon reaching "land and water" after crossing the Salt Desert. "We are across the great horn valley. The men are all tired to death as well as the cattle," Sarah Davis wrote. "We [lost] no catle nor horses. We got through safe and are thankfull."[152] Despite her gratitude, Hastings Cutoff had not served its victims well. Mormon guides and couriers used it occasionally during the 1850s, but no overland emigrant ever made the long, hard drive again.

The Desert Was like the Whirlpool: The Humbug

Few 1850 travelers packed enough supplies to carry them through to California. By the time they reached the Humboldt, most were running low or already out of provisions. Supplemented by bands from outside the Great Basin, local Paiutes and Shoshones launched nightly raids on livestock that made sleep almost impossible. Few travelers died in these raids, but angry overlanders killed many more Indians as they meted out rough justice. The march down the desert river became a spectacle of violence, despair, frustration, and starvation. "Country all around to the world's end as dry as powder, no vegetation, except on the river," Henry Wellenkamp wrote at Gravelly Ford. "The river is lined with dead horses, mules and oxen, shattered wagons in every direction."[153] Was it strange that "some should become desperate, and commit suicide, rather than continue a living death?" asked Alonzo Delano. Three men and two women drowned themselves in the river, "frantic from suffering." The women could no longer witness the suffering of their children, and "chose the dreadful alternative." No one who had not experienced the ordeal could realize what depths of desperation they faced: but Delano could "readily understand their perfect despair under the circumstances."[154] The rocky and dusty roads down the river were "enough to kill the devil," complained William Hanna.[155]

The wet season of 1850 flooded the old roads, which complicated getting down the river. "The Humboldt River was very high, said by some who travelled the road last year, to be six to ten feet deeper than last year. Its waters spread wide over

---

[150]Lawson to "Dear Parents," 26 September 1850, Huntington Library. Lawson said he "had good grass & water all the way untill we struck the main road. Then it was rather scarce."

[151]Pike, Diary, 14 August 1850, California State Library, 22.

[152]Davis, "Diary from Missouri to California," 30 August 1850, 2:194.

[153]Wellenkamp, Travel Diary, 20 July 1850, Western Historical Manuscripts.

[154]Delano, Life on the Plains, 238.

[155]Hanna, Diary, 1850, Oregon Historical Society Library.

CAMP ON THE HUMBOLDT

At his Arkansas train's hundredth camp at the Humboldt River, Daniel A. Jenks sketched his companions cooking supper, hauling water, and courting on 22 July 1859. "Women are scolding, young ones squalling, girls are singing and some of the men are cursing," he wrote. Courtesy Library of Congress.

the banks drowning the grass and making it very scarce," wrote Joseph Summers. "The old road being covered with water a new one was made, being several miles from it and touching it at intervals of from ten to thirty miles. We were frequently obliged to swim the River, or wade a quarter of a mile nearly to our waists, to get a few stalks of grass for our animals. Stock was laying dead all along this River. There being so much salraetus [*sic*] ground here, hundreds of animals were poisoned by eating the grass and drinking the water." Even the river's notorious playa had changed: "The River being unusually high it did not all disappear at the sink, but ran several miles into the desert before it disappears," Summers reported.[156] "The sink extends several miles further this year than usual owing to the large quantity of snow which fell on the mountains, the past winter, (among which the Humbolt takes its rise)," Francis Hardy wrote.[157] The wet conditions helped grass grow—"In many places the grass was higher than a man's head," G. W. Thissell reported—but it created a bumper crop of mosquitoes.[158]

Travelers found some relief in expressing their contempt for the Humboldt humbug. "Oh how I begin to loathe it," said Daniel Budd. "It is so insignificantly small, & the older it grows the more filthy it becomes."[159] James Evans called it "a perfect mudhole all the way and it was 300 miles long!"[160] "From such a river good Lord deliver me!" pleaded Benjamin Van Houten. "Deep sloughs, mire without bottom, and alkaline water—scarcity of grass and wood—deep ashy dust, salaratus, lye, poison dead stock, stink, stench, sickness, death, nastiness, maggots and uncleanness, from one end to the other of this horrible, abominable stream!"—ending only at "the sink (or stink)."[161] Nimrod Waters called the Sink a "desperate part of the world & the desert is worse." When he crossed the Twenty-six Mile Desert at night, the trail was "almost illuminated with the burning of deserted wagons."[162]

With virtually the entire 1850 migration concentrated on the lower Humboldt, journal after journal repeated a litany of horror. "Being now at Big Meadow, close to the Sink of Humbolt or Marys river and having the *last grass* on this side of the *dreaded desert,* the whole emigration made a halt to recruit their animals and make hay to take along into the desert," Wellenkamp observed. "We ferried a slough, mowed grass, and carried it 1 mile to camp. A grand destruction of wagons, tents, guns, trunks *etc* is going on, many resorting to the last alternative, to wit: Pack their bundle on their back. A famine, nearly starvation, among the

[156]Summers to "Esteemed Companion," 30 October 1850, Western Historical Manuscripts.

[157]Hardy, Journal, 14 August 1850, Beinecke Library, 187.

[158]Thissell, *Crossing the Plains,* 23 August 1850, 129.

[159]Budd, Journal, 6 August 1852, Mattes Library.

[160]Evans to "Dear Brother Ellis," 27 October 1850, Western Historical Manuscripts.

[161]Van Houten to "My dear Wife," 8 September 1850, Typescript, NFTC Manuscripts, Mattes Library.

[162]Waters, California Gold Seekers Diary, 2 August 1850, Mattes Library.

emigrants—dead animals are eaten." Before dawn he started across the Forty-mile Desert. "Morning glow soon made objects visible. Objects of desolation and destruction, which no pen can describe—wagon on wagon, carcass on carcass—and property to an amount God only knows," Wellenkamp noted. "At 7 o'clock halted, fed and made coffee. *Shot pony*."[163] According to one count, 9,771 dead animals, 3,000 abandoned wagons, and 963 graves lined the Carson Road.[164]

George Bonniwell described "a little of the suffering on this road." A shocking amount of property "was throwed away, all kinds of clothing, feather beds, tools, cooking things, barrels, and any thing that was useful. I should think that there was over 100 wagons left and destroyed on this desert. And harnesses all along the road, saddles, bridles, every thing but money and food. And the amount of horses was very great. You see the poor wretches standing along the road, starving to death and not a bit of vegetation to be seen."[165] The scene evoked Hell. "The wagons on the desert are used for fuel and they afford a more abundant supply than we have had for many hundred miles travel and many bonfires are made with them which serve to enliven and lighten the weary traveler," wrote Francis Hardy.[166] "The desert through which we are passing is strewed with dead cattle, mules, and horses," James Abbey noted, counting 350 dead horses, 280 oxen, and 120 mules over fifteen miles, with "hundreds of others are left behind being unable to keep up. Such is traveling through the desert." A Missouri train shot twenty of their dying oxen, and rotting animals kept "the air scented all the way through. A tan yard or slaughter house is a flower garden in comparison." Abbey counted 362 abandoned wagons and guessed travelers had cast aside at least $100,000 in property.[167]

Skulking in the Grass and Sunflowers: Indian Encounters

When a white man killed an Indian, Pierre De Smet observed, "every brave of that tribe considers himself justified in retaliating upon the first white man he chances to meet, without regard to his country or the part of the world from which he may come."[168] Trail justice often operated on the same blind principle. An Indian lay dead on the ground near one train's camp on Humboldt, reportedly "killed by an emigrant without provocation whatever," Benjamin Franklin Dowell wrote. The vile assassin claimed Indians "had stolen his oxen on the Salt Lake Road. A poor

---

[163]Wellenkamp, Travel Diary, 3 August 1850, Western Historical Manuscripts.
[164]Stewart, *California Trail*, 301.
[165]Bonniwell, Gold Rush Diary, 4 August 1850.
[166]Hardy, Journal, 15 August 1850. Beinecke Library, 197.
[167]Abbey, *California*, 2 August 1850, 154.
[168]De Smet, *Western Missions and Missionaries*, 4 June 1849, 36–37.

pitiful excuse for taking the life of an innocent human being. A poor excuse for murder in the first degree," he said.[169]

Not all such cross-cultural encounters ended violently, and overland journals are filled with insights into Indian lifeways. The Lakotas on the North Platte struck William Dulany as "the Happiest People in the world. I think I would like to live among them." He found nine white men serving as interpreters and agents, including one who "had a very handsome white woman for a wife & she appeared entirely comfortable."[170] William Wood found an extensive Native village assembled at Humboldt Lake in August 1850. The Northern Paiutes were "employed when we passed them Making a kind of Sugar out of a Species of Cane that grows here. Thay cut & dry it in the Sun & there is a gummey Substance comes out of it. The old & young folks are employed beating the Stalk [and] thay then fan or Sift it to get the Chalf out of it," he wrote. "It looks like Sugar and has the taste of honey."[171]

Despite such positive reports and the relatively little violence emigrants encountered, few gold seekers trusted Indians. "They are a sprightly and talkative people, rather forward and troublesome and most accomplished beggars," Calvin Taylor said of the Shoshones he met at the Great Salt Lake. "They teased us for powder balls and caps which we very unceremoniously refused giving them, thinking it bad policy to lend a club to break our own heads."[172] The Shoshones were "a quiet set of chaps, very pleasant and very good to the immigrants," wrote William Dresser, but he thought the Utah bands were "the nastiest lazeyest Indians I ever saw," looking "mean, dirty, indolent shiftless & more than all that they don't know much." Dresser called the Western Shoshones and Paiutes he met on the Humboldt Diggers because "they dig & eat a kind of artichoke." They puzzled him: "these diggers beat me. I dont know what to make of them, some of them are dreadfull hostile, thievish, impudent & murderous in the extreme," but "among them on our journey we found many that were pleasant." The Miwoks digging gold in the Sierra were "always peasable, sociable & hardly ever steal." Overall he believed that "the indians helped the emigrants a great deal. When cattle & horses would get frightened & run or stray away the Indians would drive them back, sometimes when they were gone 3 or 4 days when they might just as well of kepet them as not." If he wanted to cross the plains again (which he did not), "once clear of the Diggers, I would not be afraid of the indians to go the whole way," Dresser wrote.[173]

"We had nothing more than imaginary trouble with the Indians, not so with all," wrote William P. Warren. "Some had their horses stolen some were wounded with

---

[169]Dowell, Journal, 24 August 1850, Beinecke Library, 27.

[170]Dulany to Susan Dulany, 19 May 1850, Dulany Papers, Missouri Historical Society.

[171]Wood, Journal of an Overland Trip, 30 August 1850, Beinecke Library.

[172]Taylor, "Overland to the Gold Fields," 16 August 1850, 331.

[173]Dresser to "My Dear Boyes," October 1850, Bancroft Library, 25–26.

arrows and had to be lefte behind and more than one poor fellow loste his life by the shafts of the barberous heathans."[174] A few trains conducted vigilante campaigns. Thirteen Indians ran off two oxen along the Humboldt, and William Wood's party retrieved them after an hour's running fight. When they spotted "about 100 in the grass & willows our boys got sight of them and took after them like blood houn[d]s." A fortnight later he met four men who had shot four Indians "& Skelp them. Some of our men Saw the Skelps." He passed a man with his wife and four children who had lost his six oxen to the Indians. That night Wood heard "he had found them. 3 [oxen] was killed & the other thay got. Do not know what thay will do."[175]

Other diarists described "Indian hunts" along the Humboldt. Thirty-four of Isaac Starr's comrades resolved "to rout the Indians from their lurking places," and "started in search of the depredators." Ten miles from the trail they "came in contact with about 200 warriors, 35 or 40 of which were mounted on horseback, armed with muskets and rifles," but most carried bows and poisoned arrows. Starr felt Captain Z. Walker "conducted himself & his non-disciplined, & almost unmanageable heroes with great dexterity and honor," but the Shoshone "footmen skulking in the grass & sunflowers" kept their distance. "They formed a semi-circle with our party in the center," careful not to expose themselves on open ground. "The little party of pale-faces found their number was insufficient to meet the numerous host of natives in the grass, weeds & willows, and being almost suffocated with thirst, they accordingly left the scene of action unscathed, leaving 15 or 16 Indians dead on the field," Starr claimed.[176]

H. H. Downer thought the overland trek furnished "the materials for a person to become perfect in the study of human nature."[177] Amid the brutality that often marked the desperate march across the Great Basin in 1850, one startling act of compassion stands out. "After sunrise it grew amazingly hot—our mules poked along very slow. We passed men who said they were about to famish for water," James W. Evans wrote on the Forty-mile Desert. He met a man who despite the pleas of his friends "lay down on the sand in the hot sunshine & resolved to die, and his companions had to leave him to his fate." Evans felt faint "but rode on resolved to get as far as I could." As he pressed on across the desert's last sandy miles, Evans "met a friendly Indian; those poor savages who had during the trip shot arrows at us at night—and had killed several emigrants," including a guard he watched die. "Even they were moved with sympathy—and here came the Indian nearly naked, walking barefooted in the hot sand—with a bucket—a little tin bucket—of water for the

---

[174]Warren to "Dear Father," 13 October 1850, California State Library.
[175]Wood, Journal of an Overland Trip, 3, 16 August 1850, Beinecke Library, 64.
[176]Starr, Diary, 23 August 1850, Oregon Historical Society.
[177]Downer, "Letter from Lower California," 28 July 1849, *Iowa Republican,* 3 October 1849.

famishing Emigrants!" The man, probably a Northern Paiute, offered Evans the pail, "exclaiming, 'Watty, Watty, Oh! white man—watty!' I could not help shedding a tear—but refused to drink—telling him that there were men behind who were famishing for water worse than me, to carry it to them." The Paiute held up four fingers to show Evans how many miles until he reached water—"and to show that it was plenty he walked as if he was wading, and then showed me how deep it came to his legs." The benevolent Samaritan found the famished man, gave him two or three drinks of water, "brought up an Indian poney, put the white man on him and took him on until he came to Trucky River! Oh! Such generosity!" Evans exclaimed, "Pray, why do not these Emigrants who are ahead have the same feelings of humanity?"[178]

ONLY FIT FOR MEN AND MONKEYS:
THE GEORGETOWN CUTOFF

"There is much prejudice felt against the Lawson route," a Sacramento newspaper noted, and few of the weary and hungry emigrants opted to take the now notorious Lassen Trail.[179] Stephen Fenn was near the forefront of the migration when he "came to where the Lauson Road that fooled so many last year turned to the right. Some 200 have taken it this [year] but most of them have returned after being out from 3 to 8 days and many in a starving condition."[180] "At this stage of the game the roads fork, the one Lawson Route being finely adapted to perish even in *Hell*," wrote Henry Wellenkamp.[181] The notorious "Death Route" had nothing to recommend it, but after those who had taken the Hastings Cutoff rejoined the main trail, virtually the entire mass movement was dependent on the California Trail's sparse resources. Without the Lassen Trail's safety valve, "The desert was like the whirlpool, which gathered all within its embrace."[182]

The most popular gateway to the gold country over Carson Pass was quickly stripped of forage, and increasingly desperate travelers sought to get to the mines by whatever means available. Some converted their wagons into improvised carts. Hungry and with their draft animals in miserable shape, thousands chose to abandon their wagons and set off "with their packs on their backs and shank's horses to ride," as cattle drover Cyrus Loveland put it.[183] The traders manning posts at the foot of the mountains could hardly believe their good luck. Hampton S. Beatie and Abner Blackburn sold three yoke of cattle in Sacramento; Beatie remembered,

---

[178]Evans to "Dear Brother Ellis," 27 October 1850, Western Historical Manuscripts, 2:2.
[179]"The Emigrants," *Sacramento Transcript,* 8 August 1850, 2/3.
[180]Fenn, Letter/Journal, 29 June 1850, Idaho State Historical Society.
[181]Wellenkamp, Travel Diary, 23 July 1850, Western Historical Manuscripts.
[182]Mason, "Letter from California," August 1850.
[183]Loveland, *California Trail Herd,* 23 July 1850, 83.

"with what money we raised we loaded the team with flour, dried fruit, bacon, sugar & coffee. We went through Carson Canyon & over the mountains—the old emigration route." They rejoined their comrades at today's Genoa and set up Mormon Station, the first white settlement in Nevada. Flour sold for $2 a pound, but the traders could not keep up with demand: "we used to deal it out in small quantities thereby benefitting more people." One train's captain "wanted to buy 500 lbs. of Flour @ $2.00 a lb but I refused him not having sufficient to deal out in such large amounts. There was a good deal of emigration that year & a great amount of suffering. For a few loaves of bread I could get a good horse," Beatie said. "Trade flowed in onto us," Blackburn recalled. He could have made all the money he wanted but it was hard to keep supplies on hand. "A great manny left waggons, harness[es], guns, and numerous other things and would pack over to the mines. Any thing to get there."[184]

It is not clear whether avaricious traders, desperate overlanders, or boomtown promoters opened the steep but scenic Georgetown Cutoff, "a near route to Sacramento City, being a pack route" from Mormon Station to Georgetown, also known as Growlersburg and Jumptown.[185] Located high in the mountains about ten rough miles northeast of Coloma, Georgetown had a population of five thousand by December 1849. When high water left them unemployed, miners "turned their attention to the now road which is being cut through from Coloma to Georgetown." Speculators raised $13,000 for the project and soon had some seventy men working on it at $8 per day, which opened the boomtown to freighting operations.[186]

In July 1850 Hampton Beatie and Thomas Blackburn took fifteen pack animals from Mormon Station over "what was known as the Jumptown route"; they crossed all the streams on a log. Beatie's memory was fuzzy—at least about the year, which he thought was 1849—but these Mormon traders may well have pioneered the new pack trail.[187] By early August, the *Sacramento Transcript* noted, the vast majority of emigrants flooded over Carson Pass, but "many of them pack through by way of the Georgetown Cut-off so called."[188] Packers entered the mountains about a mile below Mormon Station, skirted the southern edge of what was called the Mountain Lake (later Lake Bigler and now Lake Tahoe), and traversed terrain still lacking a paved road though the Desolation Wilderness. The cutoff followed the Rubicon River drainage to Georgetown, and was not for the faint of heart.

After crossing the "most lovely valley I ever saw," Stephen Fenn reached the cluster of hot pots south of Mormon Station later known as Walley's Hot Springs.

[184]Blackburn, *Frontiersman,* 172–73, 262–64.
[185]Taylor, "Overland to the Gold Fields," 20 September 1850, 345.
[186]"From the Mines," *Alta California,* 29 May 1850, 2/3.
[187]Blackburn, *Frontiersman,* 263.
[188]"The Emigrants," *Sacramento Transcript,* 8 August 1850, 2/3.

Fenn "passed the hot springs and camped at Georgetown Cutoff," where his party "burnt our waggons & prepared for packing."[189] This would approximate the route's opening date, which Seth Lewelling gave on 27 July, when he called the new route "a pack trail made 3 weeks ago."[190] On 20 July Edmund Cavileer Hinde met men from Georgetown promoting the cutoff who "offered to pilot us throug[h]. They say we can get through in 3 days." His company agreed to join them, but became skeptical when the erstwhile guides reported Mormon Station was ten miles away and it proved to be only six. "On looking at the road we concluded to keep to the old one," Hinde wrote.[191] Others did not like the looks of the trace but took it anyway. "We bid adieu to sage grass bush and desart and commenced asending the mountain over craggy rocks and precipetous cliffs that on any other buisenese than getting to California would think it imposable," wrote Joseph Pike. "But men are after gold, and there is no danger that can stop them or dant there courage," including a new trail "about 30 miles up and about 95 miles down on this side or up and down mountains."[192]

The trail began with a steep four-mile climb that defied description. "The first mountain was the worst mountain I think, that horse ever climbed," Abial Whitman wrote. "It is only fit for Men & Monkeys."[193] Calvin Taylor said, "The track is very narrow, a mere bridle path passing over loose stone, gravel, and sand along the steep sides of the mountain." After the initial ascent the trail became much more reasonable, and the view of Carson Valley was spectacular. The pine forests contained "the most beautiful trees I ever beheld." Taylor's pack train ascended a high mountain and followed the trail along the ridge at the top. "To the west as far as the eye could reach rose ridge after ridge until mountain and sky blended together in the distance." The men thought they could see the coast range beyond the Sacramento Valley, "making one of the grandest scenes my eyes ever rested upon. The whole country as far as we could see was densely timbered with gigantic pines, cedars, etc., their rich green foliage contrasted finely with the naked and barren region of the country we had passed over," he rhapsodized.[194]

Robert Chalmers took "the short cut off to the mines" and estimated it was 112 miles from Mormon Station to Georgetown across "a stony, hilly country" that took seven days to traverse, including one day to recruit his animals. "There was no road through here, but a packers trace has been made," he wrote. Near the crest

---

[189]Fenn, Letter/Journal, 7 July 1850, Idaho State Historical Society; David Walley established a resort at the hot springs in the early 1860s.

[190]Lewelling, Excerpts from the Journal, 27 July 1850, California State Library. Lewelling joined his brother Henderson in a running a nursery in Milwaukie, Oregon, in 1853. Seth Lewelling is credited with developing the Bing cherry.

[191]Hinde, *Overland to California*, 20 July 1850, 38.

[192]Pike, Diary, 10, 19 September 1850, California State Library, 27, 29.

[193]Whitman, Overland Journey, 6 September 1850, Beinecke Library, 80.

[194]Taylor, "Overland to the Gold Fields," 20, 24 September 1850, 345–46.

of the Sierra, Chalmers "lost the path and could not find the right one for some time. There were so many paths that we thought we had arrived at the jumping off place." Two days after crossing the summit, he reached "a rancho or herding station, 40 miles from Georgetown." The rest of the journey was relatively easy, but "there are plenty of grizzley bears here. We have not met any of them yet." Most travelers were happy to reach the end of the trail, even if the rough-and-ready mining camp hardly looked like civilization. "There are 5 or 6 hundred houses or tents here, such as they are," Chalmers noted. "Some are enclosed with cotton and some with clapboards and some with logs."[195]

Those who crossed the new shortcut had mixed reactions. "I believe this cutoff to be a humbug like everything else in California," Abial Whitman wrote in disgust.[196] "I would not advise any one to throw away their waggons to take the cut off all though it shortens the distance 45 M and the feed is better & the road not as good," concluded Stephen Fenn, "but packers I would advise to take the Cut off."[197] However rough it might be, the new trace was considerably shorter than the overwhelmed Carson route, and the boomtown's inspired exploitation of its new road proved to be a model for ambitious mining camps.

CALIFORNIA! THE LAND OF GOLDEN HOPES

The first forty travelers from Missouri crossed Carson Pass in early June 1850. "This party left Independence about the first of April, and came with pack mules," the *Sacramento Transcript* reported. "The company arrived are all in good health, and it appears that they chose the best season to perform their journey. The animals are reported in good condition, and generally have been in good grazing." The packers averaged over thirty miles per day. The paper predicted that the lessons of 1849 would prevent "much suffering this season, as those who follow the example of the former will set out, knowing the difficulties they will have to encounter and prepared to meet them." This was wishful thinking. The second great wave of overland migration played out much like the first. By late September, travelers were "destitute of all kinds of provisions; yet the period of the greatest suffering has not yet arrived, if the supposition is to be correct, that twenty-five thousand are yet back of the Sink," the *Transcript* reported. Californians rallied with a second great rescue, and a great public effort once again averted a disaster.[198]

---

[195]Chalmers, "Journal," 25, 31 August 1850, 54.

[196]Whitman, Overland Journey, 8 September 1850, Beinecke Library, 82.

[197]Fenn, Letter/Journal, 11 July 1850, Idaho State Historical Society.

[198]"Arrival of Overland Emigrants," *Sacramento Transcript,* 12 June 1850; "News from the Plains," *Sacramento Transcript,* 23 September 1850.

Amos Sweet Warren
Amos Sweet Warren headed west two
days before he turned nineteen in June
1850. A Mormon blacksmith, he settled in
Springville, Utah, where he worked as a
carpenter, Indian interpreter, and "Dealer
in All kinds of honey." Warren died in 1909,
the father of ten children and a respected
Old Pioneer. Courtesy Utah State Historical
Society.

Paradise itself would not have prevented the disappointment these exhausted
sojourners often felt upon reaching the Sacramento Valley. "*California!*" exclaimed
J. D. Mason. "The land of golden hopes and disappointed ones, too!"[199] Many shared
Mason's feelings. "Well now, about California," wrote Samuel Ayres, almost sighing
audibly. "Everybody is disappointed in this place. Hundreds are returning immediately after their arrival here, a great many of whom beg money from their friends
to take them home." Everyone, Ayres said, was "very much discouraged. The mines
are failing, property depreciating, the country full of poverty stricken people. Many
are committing suicide, and others are wishing themselves dead, while others still
are working with brilliant expectations, but very few are prospering."[200]

The doctor was too pessimistic. The massive infusion of population by the
overland route alone, not to mention the even greater numbers that came by sea,
would have kept California's economy booming. Placer gold production was still
on the rise and did not peak until 1852, at a phenomenal 3.93 million ounces.
Two years later miners at Carson Hill found a 195-pound nugget, the largest ever
discovered in North America. Speculative opportunities abounded, while various
"excitements" made mining life an adventure. Reports arrived in May 1850 of a
fantastic Gold Lake far up the Feather River, "the shores of which abounded with

---

[199]Mason, "Letter from California," August 1850.
[200]Ayres to "My very dear Fanny," 25 September 1850, Western Historical Manuscripts.

gold, and to such an extent that it lay like pebbles on the beach." The next year began with tales of Gold Bluffs at the mouth of the Klamath River, where bright and glittering gold covered an entire beach. As the last wagons struggled across the Sierra, on 18 October 1850 the steamer *Oregon* brought joyful tidings to San Francisco: Congress had ended "the useless debates of demagogues" and admitted California to the glorious Union. "Bonfires were kindled, artillery pealed, and acclamations resounded in every town throughout the length and breadth of the land," recalled Alonzo Delano. The people of California's ardent desire for the Star Spangled Banner to wave over her mountains and plains had come true.[201]

Placer miners, Delano observed, lacked any clearly established mining theory and depended on their own observations. They understood that gold dust was a product of erosion, so they followed gold-bearing sands upstream, seeking the hard-rock source. Early prospectors learned "where there are good quartz veins there are almost invariably good placer diggings." Geologists now believe the earth is made of coalesced stardust and that gold, like all of our planet's elements, was created in supernova explosions. The convergence of ancient rivers from the east, the seabed to the west, and the granite magma that created the Sierra Nevada accounts for California's considerable accumulation of the rare metal.[202]

During the gold rush, no overland journal used the old Mexican mining term "mother lode," a literal translation of *veta madre,* nor did it appear in any newspaper until the mid-1860s.[203] Journalist J. Ross Browne popularized the name, calling California's Mother Lode "in many respects the most remarkable metalliferous vein in the world." The region's miners already knew a gold-rich quartz deposit, sometimes fifty feet wide, stretched southeast for 120 miles from the Middle Fork of the American River to John C. Frémont's estate in Mariposa County. They knew erosion and time had scattered the Mother Lode's riches along the Sierra foothills, but the vein constituted the mere tip of California's glittering wealth, for the most famous mining counties—Placer, Nevada, Sierra, Yuba, Butte, and Plumas—lay to the north, "placed one on top of another like bricks in a wall," as Rodman Paul put it so well. A separate deposit extended from Shasta County into Oregon. By 1855 Californians understood that gold country encompassed hundreds of square miles, from the Merced to the Umpqua rivers. Both gold production and the population of the less-blessed southern mines collapsed: in 1866 Browne estimated 80 percent of California's gold came from the state's northern mines.[204] The spring

---

[201]Delano, *Life on the Plains,* 332, 356–58.

[202]Meldahl, *Hard Road West,* 265–71.

[203]The first verifiable appearance of the name "Mother Lode" was in the *Amador Ledger* of 24 June 1865, extracted two days later as "Mining in Amador," *Sacramento Union,* 1:7.

[204]Paul, *California Gold,* 39–42; Browne, *Resources of the Pacific Slope,* 14.

of 1850 brought reports of gold discoveries on Salmon Creek, and by year's end news from the Klamath, Shasta, and Scott rivers and Greenhorn and Humbug creeks shifted the focus of mining northward. By 1851 there was a boomtown at Yreka, so far north it was thought to be in Oregon.

Oregonians on the trail to California had long noticed the color of gold along the Rogue River, but none of it appeared worth working. On their return from a freighting expedition the new diggings at Yreka in December 1851, James Cluggage and James Poole stopped to water their mules. "After scraping out a hole to fill with water they saw a lot of placer gold," one chronicler observed. They found plenty of gold wherever they looked along Jackson Creek, and the two made "the first discovery of paying gold mines in Oregon." No fools, the men filed land claims and founded Rich Gulch—now Jacksonville, Oregon. Cluggage spread word that he and his partners had taken seventy ounces a day from their claim for ten weeks, which the *Alta California* called "certainly one of the richest claims we have heard of for a long time."[205]

Both rich strikes and humbugs contributed to a much better understanding of the complex geography of northern California. Along with Goldsborough Bruff, Peter Lassen himself searched for Gold Lake, the imagined fountainhead of the northern mines' fabulous wealth. Such geological snipe hunts made no one rich but helped unlock the region's rugged terrain. On his way west in 1850, William H. Nobles concluded that there must be a better way to reach Sacramento than over the existing trails' long waterless passages of forty to sixty miles. "I believed that these deserts could be avoided without increasing the distance," he later wrote. The steep passes of the central Sierra Nevada formed "the most formidable obstacle to overland travel"—Nobles had seen ten to twenty oxen struggle to haul a single empty wagon over Carson and West passes. A man of immense energy, Nobles was an inveterate promoter whose subsequent adventures would have an enduring, if largely forgotten and poorly understood, impact on trail history.[206] But after 1850, when more people crossed the plains than ever before, America's westering impulse came to an abrupt and mysterious halt.

---

[205]Bancroft, *History of Oregon*, 2:184–86; Gaston, *Centennial History*, 1:495; "Rich Diggings," *Alta California*, 22 May 1852, 1/3.

[206]White, *News of the Plains*, 5:239; Nobles to Thompson, 16 April 1857, National Archives. Historians Thomas H. Hunt and Donald Buck shared this invaluable source, which corrected a host of misconceptions about Nobles and his cutoff.

CHAPTER 8

The Very Windows of Heaven

The Bust of 1851

Overland emigration experienced a statistical singularity in 1851, when the frenzy that compelled perhaps 100,000 souls to make the trek overland in 1849 and 1850 momentarily dissipated. John Unruh estimated only 1,100 emigrants headed for California in 1851, less than a third of the 3,600 souls who went to Oregon. Even Merrill Mattes's generous (and optimistic) estimate that about 10,000 people went west reflects "a nose dive" of 80 percent from the previous year.[1] The puzzle has baffled trail chroniclers, who often turned to H. H. Bancroft's 1890 explanation that "reports of dread hardships during the trip and at the mines," conflicting rumors from the goldfields, and disastrous commercial speculations caused the decline.[2] Tales of suffering and disease, especially the vivid and terrifying descriptions of cholera, particularly discouraged potential gold seekers. "Obviously, the hysteria of the gold rush could not be maintained," George Stewart observed. "By this time the returned Californian—back from the mines, and stony broke—was a well known figure in every village."[3]

The problem with these explanations is what followed. Some 70,000 Americans headed to California, Oregon, and Utah in 1852, setting a record for overland travel that would endure for at least a decade. This surge makes explaining why trail numbers plunged so precipitously in 1851 especially difficult. What sparked such a dramatic change? Did the less crowded trail of 1851 persuade more people to make the perilous journey? Did more successful fortune hunters return home (and fewer stony broke ones) to inspire more people to follow their golden visions? Was the sudden drop simply an anomaly, or was it the bust of the Far West's first boom? None of these explanations adequately accounts for the phenomenon, nor does the notion that the United States had merely paused to catch its breath.

---

[1]Unruh, *The Plains Across,* 120; Mattes, *Great Platte River Road,* 16; *Platte River Road Narratives,* 2–3.
[2]Bancroft, *History of California,* 7:696n1.
[3]Stewart, *California Trail,* 301. Kenneth Holmes summarized the problem in *Covered Wagon Women,* 3:10.

Like many such historical puzzles, part of the reason for the dramatic decrease in overland travel in 1851 is simple: it rained. More than six feet of water fell on Iowa in less than five months that spring, old-timer Tacitus Hussey calculated. "The deluge began in May. For more than forty days the rain fell, not continuously but at very frequent intervals," wrote historian John Briggs. "Not until July did the skies clear and the floods subside." Throughout the Midwest, the previous two years had been wetter than usual. Almost as much rain fell in 1849 as would fall in 1851, but the cumulative effect of repeated heavy rainfall was devastating. "For three weeks it has rained almost incessantly, pouring down from the clouds as if the very windows of heaven were opened," an Iowa newspaper reported in May. "Neither the memory of the oldest settlers along the banks of the Des Moines river, nor the memory of the natives who resided here before it was settled by the whites, nor any traditionary account from the natives, furnishes any evidence of such a flood ever having occurred here, in all past time."[4]

The rains surged relatively late in the emigration season, but a particularly bitter winter throughout the eastern United States had already reduced the number of prospective overlanders. "From the best information," the *St. Joseph Gazette* suggested in early March, "but few people will emigrate to California or Oregon this year. This time last year our town literally was crowded, but now very few are in the place. A few Oregon emigrants have passed through." The *Adventure* reported the first large number of "emigrants for the plains this spring" arrived on the steamboat *Saranak* on 4 April, and the influx increased as spring wore on. "Quite a number of Oregon and California emigrants are here now," the *Gazette* stated on 23 April. By the end of the month, many parties had crossed the Missouri at Saint Joseph and emigrants were arriving daily. Companies continued to appear throughout May, but the deluge stopped them in their tracks. Many trains simply gave up.[5]

Others had a reason to press on, for after years of dallying, on 27 September 1850, Congress authorized a surveyor general for Oregon "to make Donations to Settlers" of public lands. Commonly called the Donation Land Act, the law defused the tensions Congress had created in 1848 with its "Act to Establish the Territorial Government of Oregon," which affected every acre west of South Pass between the 42nd and 49th parallels. The law extended the 1787 Northwest Ordinance to Oregon, created a territorial government to replace the improvised provisional government, and in a single stroke declared Oregon's existing land grants null and void. Now the new law imposed the grid-like boundaries of Thomas Jefferson's section-and-township system on the rolling land of Oregon, and deeds would only be issued after the land was surveyed and divided into sections. U.S. land laws typically required extinguishing

[4]Briggs, "Flood of 1851"; *Fort Des Moines Star,* 29 May 1851, in Hussey, "The Flood of 1851," 406.
[5]Barry, *Beginning of the West,* 986, 990–94.

aboriginal claims, but the Donation Land Act said nothing about Indian land titles. The federal government, whose single greatest source of revenue came from the sale of public lands, would sell them, not give them away. The act suspended the fee, but its terms were complicated: a white adult male citizen could claim a half section, 320 acres; if married by 1 December 1851, his wife could make an equal claim in her own right. After that, settlers could claim 320 acres until 1 December 1853. They had to improve and cultivate the land for four years to receive a patent, or title. As James Tompkins noted, the legislation calmed public resentment and "prevented a major revolt by pre-territorial settlers who migrated to Oregon under the belief the land was free." The long overdue resolution created a boom that boosted traffic on the Oregon Trail. As Tompkins observed, "Whenever talk was of free land in Oregon, the next year's migration were larger than any previous."[6] Between 1852 and 1854, the promise of free land lured some 28,000 new citizens over the trail to Oregon, or more than half the new state's population in 1860.

Whatever factors caused emigration to California to plunge and Oregon's to boom in 1851, the evolving trail followed the patterns established during a decade of overland emigration and reinforced with the rush that began in 1849. Trading stations proliferated, while veteran speculators began to invest in sophisticated improvements to the road. "A fine and substantial bridge has been built over the Platte 100 miles above Laramie," a correspondent reported in February. Those who saw it were not impressed with John Richards's bridge at Deer Creek. It "does not seem to be used much," wrote Robert Robe. The structure washed out by the next summer, but "Reshaw," as Richards was known to phonetic spellers, did not give up.[7] And as usual, the road across the plains sprouted new cutoffs and alternates like a tree growing new branches.

THE HALFWAY HOUSE OF THE PILGRIMS:
UTAH AND THE GOLD RUSH

The first trains bound for Oregon and California in 1851 did not set out from Independence or Council Bluffs—they left camps along the Great Salt Lake on 27 March. When their wagons crossed the rim of the Great Basin on the southern border of today's Idaho, "A shout went up from a hundred voices which made the mountains quake," wrote Jotham Goodell. "Some wept for joy," for they felt their days of bondage were at an end.[8]

---

[6]Tompkins, "The Law of the Land," 90–91, 95–96; Stewart, *California Trail,* 301. In 1853 Congress extended the deadline to 1855.

[7]Robe, "Diary," 22 June 1851, 57; Watkins, "Notes," 232–34.

[8]Goodell, *A Winter with the Mormons,* 214–15.

This event reflected a dramatic shift in Mormon overland policy. The hard history of the Latter-day Saints meant that an odd mix of hospitality and hostility greeted visitors to Deseret, as shown when Salt Lake again staged a feast on 24 July 1850. "The whole valley comes to the city today and have a perfect jubilee. The music wagon for today is drawn by 14 horses, large and commodious," Dan Carpenter noted. But the welcome was double-edged. "The Mormons curse the d—d ragged Emigrant Sons of Bitches from Mo. & Ill. traveling through their country."[9] They treated his party well, Lewis Kilbourn reported, "but they told some of our men that if the people of the States troubled them again they would manure their land with their Carcasses."[10] The 1844 murders of two Mormon prophets in Illinois had left bitter memories. "I do not think it would be safe for anyone concerned in the death of Joseph and Hiram Smith, to be seen there," wrote J. D. Mason. "They speak of the death of these men with much feeling, and it would not take many words from their elders to kindle their displeasure to madness."[11] Not every visitor got the message. Godfrey Ingrim recalled his party traded eight oxen for two mules at Great Salt Lake City in 1852. "We named one Jo Smith and the other Brigham Young and they were a daisy pair."[12]

Asa Cyrus Call started from Wisconsin on foot for California in March 1850, and reached the Salt Lake Valley in late August. After the trek across plains, mountains, and deserts, it was astonishing to look down upon the beautiful valley with its lakes and mountains, which was "dotted all over with the little white houses, the gardens, and the farms, of these enterprising pioneers." After only three years, the Saints had "opened good farms, built houses and barns, erected mills of various kinds, made bridges across the rivers, built school-houses, and established schools, built a State-house, chartered a university, and, in fact, they have done more to advance the real prosperity of a State than some of the original thirteen," Call testified. In the Great Basin only "one twentieth part is arable land," he estimated—the largest fertile tract lying along the Wasatch Mountains—"but even in this valley there is much barren land, and much that requires artificial irrigation." Call praised the bountiful crops the Saints had produced in 1850 and their liberal social policies. "Having felt the yoke themselves, *Liberty,* with them, is something more than a *word;* and, in organizing their infant State, their first care was to guaranty to every one who shall choose to settle within their borders the most perfect liberty of person and conscience."

A month after his arrival Call concluded "that no one who has witnessed the

---

[9]Carpenter, Journal, 24 July 1850, Idaho State Historical Society.

[10]Kilbourn, Journal, 1850, MSS 1508, Oregon Historical Society, 19.

[11]Mason, "Letter from California," August 1850.

[12]Ingrim, Reminiscences, Kansas State Historical Society.

ASA CYRUS CALL, 1850
Like many visitors to Utah, Asa Call found the
Mormons had established a singular community
where "consistency and inconsistency, light and
darkness, bigotry and toleration, are strangely
blended." As one of the thousand or so outsiders
who wintered in Utah during 1850–51, Call
complained that among the Mormons, "the voice
of Brigham is the voice of God." Gift of John R.
Call. Author's collection.

friendship and harmony that prevail here, and shared the hospitality of these people,
and seen their industry, and frugality, and benevolence, will quarrel with them
about their religion, however strange or absurd it may seem." His remarkable letter
captured this singular community's contradictions. The Saints respected their visitors' "natural rights and duties, and having established the largest liberty of others,
they are themselves the *veriest slaves* of the priesthood." Oddly, he noted, "profanity
is as common here as prayers are at Oberlin. Even the priests can, many of them,
utter oaths that would make an ordinary Christian man's hair stand up."[13] Jotham
Goodell explained this apparent inconsistency: "I heard Brigham say in public, that
they did not consider any language as profane, unless it was blaspheming the name
of Deity." One Forty-niner claimed he heard the Mormon leader say, "Some of you
might think I am swearing, but I am not, for when I swear I swear in the name of
the Lord, therefore this is not swearing." His flock loved Brigham Young's blunt
and belligerent eloquence, but to Joseph Hamelin the prophet's sermons sounded
like "a string of blasphemy which would put a blush on a Five-points bully. He
insulted every member of his church, cursed, swore, and used the most vulgar
language. Every decent person must have been much disgusted."[14]

---

[13]Call, "From Utah," 20 September 1850, 13.

[14]Goodell, *A Winter with the Mormons,* 70; Stephens, *Life Sketches of a Jayhawker,* 15; Hamelin, Journal, 23 September
1849, Beinecke Library. Five Points was a notorious New York City slum and vice district.

When the 1850 emigration arrived at Salt Lake, the Mormons were "making money like dirt," George Read commented, but they faced a critical shortage of skilled labor and offered high wages to millwrights, mechanics, and even common workers.[15] Local authorities "held out every encouragement to emigrants to remain amongst them during the winter," reported Asa Call, who joined the six or eight hundred late arrivals who spent the winter at Salt Lake. At first, local authorities "seemed to deal fairly by them, and in some instances, even showed kindness to persons in distress," Call wrote after reaching Sacramento, "but no sooner had cold weather set in, and cut off every avenue of escape, than they began to show the cloven foot." The Saints, as they liked to be known, refused to sell provisions to the Gentiles, "as all dissenters are called," except at exorbitant prices. As winter advanced, Mormons ran up debts to the outsiders and then refused to pay them. Those who sued the debtors in local courts "invariably came off losers. The emigrants complained of this treatment, and the Mormons bore down all the harder."[16]

The season Asa Call and other emigrants spent among the Latter-day Saints as "Winter Mormons" transformed many of them from sympathetic friends of the embattled faith into outraged critics. They witnessed the celebrations in January 1851 that greeted the news that Millard Fillmore had appointed Brigham Young as Utah Territory's first governor, but disgruntled emigrants and the territory's first non-Mormon federal officials complained mightily about the threats and hostility they encountered in Utah, creating a firestorm of bad publicity. "The liberty of speech was abridged—respectable men were arrested and mulcted in heavy fines, for expressing opinions and making remarks which were deemed disrespectful to the Church. Private letters were intercepted and opened, and those who had spoken unfavorable of the morals of the community, were boldly threatened with assassination," Call charged. The emigrants had only claimed the rights of American citizens on American soil, but he heard Brigham Young declare he was "the law and the order," and that "if any man stuck himself up above him, he would bring him down—*by the eternal Gods.*" Governor Young "was not afraid of *Mr. Justice,* nor *Uncle Sam,* nor *all Hell*"; and "if he heard another Gentile curse or abuse the Saints, he would *cut his d——d throat.*"[17]

Call's mixture of admiration and scorn became typical among future visitors to Utah, especially those who spent much time there. "It is admitted by all that the Mormons are a brave people; indeed, any people who can leave a civilized country and comfortable homes and journey hundreds of miles over an almost unknown country, overcome savages, cross deep and rapid rivers and climb the

[15]Read to Richard Long, 18 October 1850, in Read, *Pioneer of 1850,* 118.

[16]Goodell, *A Winter with the Mormons,* 214–15.

[17]Ibid.

THE VERY WINDOWS OF HEAVEN

highest mountains on the continent to have a peaceful home can honestly claim to be a brave people," wrote John Hawkins Clark in 1852. "If these people should continue to prosper as they have in the past they will soon become great. Salt Lake valley and the neighboring country will sustain an immense population. Many of these people are now comparatively wealthy—fine farms, well stocked with horses, cattle and pretty women. What more they want to make them happy would be hard to tell. Salt Lake City is the great half-way mile stone and resting place for the California pilgrim." Yet only ten days later, Clark was glad to leave "this part of the world with as little delay as possible." Visiting Salt Lake Valley "was something like taking in the Irishman's show; it cost nothing to get in, but a good deal to get out."[18]

Mormon ambitions and their dedicated millennialism would inevitably come into conflict with the American government, an earlier visitor predicted. At the crest of the Sierra, Gordon Cone paused to consider his experience in the Great Basin, "one of the wonderful curiosities that are found on our continent." The Mormons had "chosen this singular tract of country as the Fortress, from which, the influence that is to Mormonize the World is to eminate." He thought they were dupes of designing men who were "carried away by inducements held out by a system of religion based on hatred, and retaliation, and which only addresses itself to the passions." Decent people would never have anything to do with their "war upon the rest of mankind," but Cone believed "their leading propensities will prompt to rebellion, and internal strifes, and commotions will finally work their entire destruction—As mortal beaings their destruction is also sure, unless they leave this isolated place."[19] It was a grim and prejudiced prophecy, but within a decade it almost came true.

NOT MERE ADVENTURERS: THE SEASON BEGINS

The cold and wet spring of 1851 made traveling miserable. Americus Savage's company spent three weeks stranded on the Elkhorn River. "The rain poured down in torrents all day. We slept in our wagons expecting to start in the morning on our journey and le[ave] the dreadful place of thunder, lightening and rain," Savage complained. "There was a continual blast of lightening and thunder, peal after peal, that made the earth tremble, while the rain fell as though the doors of heaven were broke loose from their hinges." Lightning killed two men, one drowned, and one was accidentally shot while his stranded companies waited for the floodwaters to subside.[20]

---

[18]Clark, "Overland to the Gold Fields," 15 July 1852, 252.
[19]Cone, Journal of Travels, 11 October 1849, BYU Library, 146–47.
[20]Savage, "Americus Savage's Journal," 13 May, 3 June 1851.

Savage was not alone. A Mormon train of some 150 wagons found itself in a perilous situation at the Elkhorn River, "with several vehicles up to their axletrees in water."[21] The party included federal officials and their wives bound for Utah to assume their duties in the new territory. "In an incredibly short time a sudden storm came on, [and] the Elkhorn became a roaring torrent," Sarah Harris recalled. Mary Hawkins Snow described a very hard rain "which almost threatened a deluge" on 21 May. "The water poured in torrents under our tent and very much retarded the preparations we were making to cross the creek." The wagons forded the flooded river "and landed on a small island the only spot of visible land the rest being submerged," Snow wrote. "About 20 waggons and some cattle for Oregon were also there which made it very close quarters." The party was marooned for almost "three weeks under circumstances of the greatest discomfort. Rattlesnakes, small and large, were driven out of their haunts" and crawled around the camp, Harris remembered. "*Many were discouraged and some* had lost their lives," commented Snow. "I think five were drowned and one killed by Lightning—others turned back and sold their provisions."[22]

"The greater part of the emigration this year will be for Salt Lake and Oregon," a correspondent predicted at Fort Laramie in February 1851. On his return to Fort Leavenworth, Captain Stewart Van Vliet met the first wagons on the Independence Road at the Little Blue River on 2 May: he encountered only two trains bound for California. The "dull prospects of emigration" disheartened farmers and merchants at the jumping-off towns, though they ultimately did a fair business selling produce, groceries, and provisions to the "generally respectable" families bound for Oregon. "I have taken pains to gain correct information of the number of emigrants who have this Spring set out for the Plains, and upon the best information I cannot state the number at more than 6,000, including men, women, and children, and of these, by far the larger proportion are bound for Oregon," Thomas Jefferson Sutherland wrote at the end of May.[23]

More travelers began their trek at Council Bluffs, or Kanesville as the Mormons called the settlement, largely because the trail along the north side of the Platte River was shorter and required fewer river crossings. "Here you can get everything you want," Amelia Hadley observed.[24] The town "was our last chance to buy corn and other feed. Kanesville was strictly a Mormon town, but the people were sociable and clever. They had plenty of corn and wild grass hay as well as

---

[21]"Babbitt and Company," *Frontier Guardian,* 30 May 1851, 2.

[22]Harris, *An Unwritten Chapter of Salt Lake,* 10; Snow, Journal, 21 May, 1 June 1851, LDS Archives.

[23]Watkins, "Notes," 232–33; "Emigration," *Frontier Guardian,* 16 May 1851, 2; Sutherland, 30 May 1851, in Barry, *Beginning of the West,* 1006.

[24]Hadley, "Journal of Travails," 5 May 1851, 3:57.

other provisions to sell us," Supplina Hamilton recalled. The Mormon traders "had everything to eat and drink provided in the middle west, from corn whiskey to western reserve cheese. There was a large blacksmith shop there where you could get anything in that line from a wagon tire to an ox-bow key, but it took money." As Hamilton noted, the Mormons "were there for that purpose."[25]

Some thought the migrants of 1851 came from a better class of characters than the fortune hunters who dominated the first two years of the gold rush. "They are not mere adventurers—to try their luck for a season and then return; but have their families along generally, showing that they go to the west to find permanent homes," observed the *Frontier Guardian*. "If 'UNCLE SAM' should gain some Territory in the Moon, we believe that the Yankees would contrive some plan to emigrate to it, and hold it by actual possession."[26]

The flood inspired some intrepid but unsuccessful trail blazing. Apostle Orson Hyde, the Mormon emigration agent, ordered the church's trains to return to the Missouri and "counselled them to head the Horn instead of going the south side"—that is, to cut a new road to the Elkhorn and Loup Fork headwaters and so avoid the floods. Albert Carrington, who had managed the Stansbury Expedition's Mormon workers, accompanied Hyde on his way west and found "all the rivers and streams of the region passed over have run water in torrents from 20 to 30 feet above their present mark." Carrington concluded that "heading the Horn" was "an unknown experiment, late in the season, with ox teams, women, and children." The sandy route was a "dry track, road rough, [with] a little stagnant rain water in pools, strongly scented by the buffalo." The "outside track" proved to be "at least 150 miles further and a very bad road from the time you cross the Horn bridge until you reach the Platte." The Platte River Road was far shorter "and far better in every sense of the word."[27]

OVER THE MOUNTAINS: THE 1851 CALIFORNIA EMIGRATION

Eastbound travelers provide the best descriptions of the 1851 emigration's order of march. "Hurrah for home!" David Thomas Nichols wrote on 22 April, the day he left Sacramento bound for Illinois with ten companions, nine boxes of raisins, some silk, and two thousand copies of California newspapers. Traveling with the Salt Lake Mail over Carson Pass, the packers battled their way through the snow. They had packed hay for the mules but went nine days without grass before breaking free of the snowpack and Carson Canyon on 12 May. "Give me Spanish Mules for

[25]Hamilton to Powell, 9 January 1900, Beinecke Library, 3.
[26]"Emigration," *Frontier Guardian*, 16 May 1851, 2.
[27]Carrington, "Diary," 15–18 July 1851, 115–16.

hardships," Nichols wrote. Four days later he met John Reese's freighters hauling supplies to Mormon Station to sell to the anticipated onrushing hordes, and Nichols persuaded a woman to bake bread for him in exchange for some sugar. They got disturbing news on 22 May: "Kendrick & Hawly train of 12 Mormen attacked by the Indians some four weeks ago. Two were wounded [and] they were hemmed in for four days." Nichols's party reached the Utah settlements on 5 June, where they created quite an excitement since it was supposed to be "impossible to get over the Mountains so early."[28]

With companions named Halstead, Robb, and Irving, Nichols left Great Salt Lake City on 10 June. Two days later they met a company from Michigan that was "getting along very well—no sickness among them." They soon encountered a trickle of emigrant parties and freight trains. Forging onward, the packers found "Ely Meckins & Frenchmen" setting up a trading post on the Big Sandy and "plenty of Emigrants" at Pacific Springs on 18 June. A few days later they burned most of their newspaper to keep warm and gave "chase after a Grisley Bear but he gave good Leg bail & escaped." They began "meeting a good many for the Oregon road" and enjoyed milk and women's cooking almost every day. The party reached Scotts Bluff on the Fourth of July, and on the thirteenth spotted what proved to be a large Mormon train on the south side of the river. Four days later, Nichols met the "Munroz train for S L Valley," the last westbound company he mentioned. (James Monroe's "train of Merchandise for the Valley" was hauling goods for John Reese of Mormon Station.) On 25 July the plainsmen reached Kanesville, where the citizens could hardly believe they had come from California "so quick and so few in number." Nichols called on the friendly editor of the *Frontier Guardian,* Daniel Mackintosh, and gave him the California newspapers his party had not burned on the Sweetwater. Nichols, who had "all the appearance of a gentleman, and a good citizen," told Mackintosh "he did very well, during his brief stay in the great El Dorado of the West." On 13 August, the ragged traveler "got shaved & hair cut trying to spruce up a little cause I am going to see my *wife* & *Children*." That afternoon David Nichols arrived home near Dixon, Illinois, with his pockets full of gold dust but "just 30c left in specie."[29]

Despite the decline in numbers, emigrants heading west in 1851 faced the same challenging geography, and travelers reenacted many scenes that had played out during the boom years. There was less competition for grass, game, water, and campsites, but wagon trains faced a marked increase in Indian violence. Perhaps the most significant advantage plains travelers had in 1851 over all other gold-rush sojourners was that their lower numbers led to fewer deaths from diseases

---

[28]Nichols, Diary, Mattes Library, 1–16.

[29]Ibid., 17–45; "News from the Plains," *Frontier Guardian,* 8 August 1851, 2.

like cholera, which had reappeared at the Missouri jumping-off points in June and August; a letter from Fort Laramie claimed "there was no sickness among the Oregon and California emigrants."[30] But death on the trail was impossible to escape. "Mary was taken sick with a severe cold from which she never recovered," reported Abner Bryan. She died nine miles from South Pass. "She gave me her 2 little boys to add to my 3."[31]

In addition to bad weather and a lot of hard luck, 1851 overlanders survived a bumper crop of the most terrifying of all trail disasters—the stampede, "a sudden and unaccountable panic taken by the cattle and horses, in which they become unmanageable and run away."[32] Such calamities struck with no warning at any time of the day or night. Cephas Arms's train had not seen an Indian for three weeks and was in good spirits when it crossed South Pass but was "very much afraid of stampedes, and it is no wonder. An earthquake is scarcely more to be dreaded, or more terrible."[33] Emigrants blamed these catastrophes on bison, wolves, skulking Indians, bad weather, the smell of the blood of dead bison, their own dogs, or simply on an ox's oddity or a mare's friskiness—as did Quincy Adams Brooks. To catch up with a train, a young mare, "kicking up her heels and snorting, away she started pelmell as fast she could run," spooking the loose cattle trailing the wagons. Soon a frightful bawl "spread from wagon to wagon along the whole line with the velocity of a telegraph dispatch." Despite the ox's slow reputation, Brooks said, "in a *stampede,* I don't think I ever saw anything run so fast."[34]

After their cattle "ran off with a noise like that of a mighty rushing wind" one night, Daniel Bigelow's train caught and yoked up the oxen, supposing it would keep them from trying it again, but "they did try again causing every body to get out of the way as fast as possible."[35] Harriet Buckingham thought it wise to pay tribute to the Indians, or they would "stampede the cattle some dark night if not well treated." The sudden tramping of animals awakened her one midnight. Within moments forty men rose "like specters from under waggons tents & carriages with guns & bowie knives." They stood ready to fire at their imagined assailants as the train's cattle scattered amid "the consternation & chagrin that momentarily depicted itself upon their countenances." A guard confessed he had accidentally frightened the livestock and soon all was quiet again. The next day the party passed a dead Indian "who had been wilfully shot by some daring fellow

---

[30]Barry, *Beginning of the West,* 1010–11; Watkins, "Notes," 234.

[31]Bryan, 6 September 1851, in Mattes, *Platte River Road Narratives,* 320.

[32]Brooks, "Letter," 7 November 1851, 211.

[33]Arms, *Long Road to California,* 62.

[34]Brooks, Journal, 12 May 1851, in Belanger, *On the Oregon Trail in 1851,* 46–47. This intensive study revised many long-held assumptions about the 1851 emigration. Belanger has identified almost 5,500 participants by name, suggesting more people went west that year than is typically assumed.

[35]Bigelow, Diary, May 1851, 112.

& farther on lay the bodies of eight white men who innocently fell to revenge the blood of the redmen."[36]

Besides being terrifying, stampedes caused uncounted injuries and fatalities. After cattle trampled a man near South Pass, his friends "could only find a few shreds of his clothing & parts of his gun," wrote Solon Martin.[37] Rampaging live-stock could "kill and trample everything before them to the Earth." One night stampeding cattle stepped on the neck of a boy named Jones, who was out a-milk-ing, "and hurt him rather bad," reported Ossian Taylor. "They were a running and cutting up all night." The next morning the wild teams took fright and ran again: Ellen Kingsley "jumped out of the hind part of the wagon and before she could get out of the way, another team and wagon ran over her." After telling her sister she did not know if she was hurt, Kingsley "instantly expired, leaving her only sister without a relative in the company. It was sad to see how bitterly she wept and no wonder she could not be comforted, to have an only sister killed in so shocking a manner." A few days later the cattle trampled German Buchanan "to the earth and hurt him very much."[38]

On his way to his post in Utah, Indian agent Jacob Holeman "passed many trains of Emigrants, some for Oregon, some for California, but mostly for Utah." He found many of them "in great distress, from [depred]ations and roberies committed by the Indians." Some had been robbed of all their possessions down to the cloth-ing on their backs, and many had their stock stolen. Holeman thought the Lakota led most of the raids, while the Crows pitched in occasionally and the peaceful Shoshones had to suffer the consequences. Farther west, "the Indians on Mary's River are exceedingly troublesome to emigrants and travellers, having killed quite a number of white men the past Season," reported Utah Indian Superintendent Brigham Young. The next season, Holeman wrote, "not a train passed without murders and robberies" from the Goose Creek Mountains to Carson Valley.[39]

Once the weather dried out, westbound Californians made the trek in record time. *The El Dorado News* announced the first pack train reached Placerville on 17 July "from St. Joseph in seventy-seven days." A second party packed in four days later. The Lassen Trail experienced an unexpected revival, apparently based on the biased advice of interested parties.[40] Rumors of pending disaster played their traditional role. "Reliable news" reached San Jose "that great numbers of those who are travelling the northern land routes to this Country are suffering immensly

---

[36]Buckingham, "Crossing the Plains," 15 August 1851, 46.

[37]Martin, Reminiscences, Mattes Library.

[38]Taylor, 23 July, 5 August 1851, Marriott Library.

[39]Holeman to Lea, 21 September 1851, Young to Lea, 20 October 1851, Holeman to Lea, 30 August 1852, BIA Letters Received, Utah Superintendency, National Archives.

[40]Barry, *Beginning of the West*, 995; Mattes, *Platte River Road Narratives*, 330–331.

from the want of the common necessaries of life." Noting that "true sympathy ever prompts to benevolent action," city officials "cordially cooperate[d] with those who are engaged in the benevolent enterprise of sending relief to the starving immigrants upon the plains." Local citizens subscribed more than $1,000 and actually collected $780.50, including a $500 donation from Donner party veterans James F. and Margaret Reed.[41]

Forgotten Forty-niners:
The Road to Oregon in the Gold Rush

The California gold discovery had immediate and profound effects in Oregon, in 1848 the largest American community on the West Coast, where the extraordinary news created the most intense excitement. "Scarcely anything else was spoken of," recalled Peter Burnett. "I think that at least two thirds of the male population of Oregon, capable of bearing arms, started for California in the summer and fall of 1848."[42] More precisely, about 80 percent of the territory's male population headed south, one historian estimated.[43] By mid-October 1849 most of the men from Oregon's most productive lands "were absent in the mines of California, leaving their farms in a state of utter neglect," reported an army quartermaster. It was almost impossible to find laborers, for "all of them have gone or are going to California; and when employed they ask from five to ten dollars per day."[44]

The sheer size of the 1849 migration persuaded many to change their destination to Oregon. John Richey saw "a grate deal of Suffering among the Emigrants and I fear it is not over with yet." He said a thousand wagons changed course from California to "the Orrigon Road."[45] Down to a span of oxen when he reached Soda Springs, Alphonse Day concluded it would be impossible to get a team to California and changed course. After passing "the junction of the last California & oregon road" at Raft River, he was pleased to discover "there is but few teams on this road as yet." The Oregon Trail had plenty grass, and Day found "all the sammon you want" at Fort Boise. On the Umatilla River he met "a world of indians." Like many of the forgotten Forty-niners who went to Oregon, Day found the "roads heavy & verry dusty with many steep hills" but generally supplied with water and grass.[46] The scarcity of water on long stretches of the trek up the Snake and Burnt rivers and through central Oregon to The Dalles meant the classic route of the Oregon

---

[41]Reed, Pioneer Manuscript Collection, California State Library.
[42]Burnett, Recollections, 253–54.
[43]Tompkins, "The Law of the Land," 91.
[44]Ingalls to Vinton, 17 October 1849, in Marcy, Report of the Secretary of War, 1850, 287.
[45]Richey to "Friend Emmons," 3 October 1850, Missouri Historical Society.
[46]Day, Journal, 21, 22, 31 July, 8, 19, 31 August 1849, BYU Library.

Trail was never easy. Even on the Snake, one of the great rivers of the West, water was not always accessible. "This is one of the most singular rivers in the world being for miles enclosed by a perpendicular ledge of rocks & the thirsty animals were obliged to toil for miles together in the heat and dust with the sound of water in their ears & neither man [n]or beast able to get a drop," Polly Coon wrote.[47]

Enoch Conyers set out for El Dorado in 1852, but at South Pass he "decided to go to Oregon instead of California to avoid any trouble with the Mormons." He described how a train hired Indians to take a wagon loaded with provisions, livestock, and women across the Snake River above Shoshone Falls. In midstream "the cattle became frightened of the Indians and turned their course right down the stream." The Shoshones "left the cattle to their fate and turned their attention to the wagon and the ladies, and with great effort succeeded in landing the wagon" before it was swept over the 212-foot-high falls, which were higher than Niagara. The cattle saved themselves.[48]

The train he led to Oregon in 1851 encountered "no serious obstacles to mar our peace and quiet progress until we passed Fort Hall," recalled Americus Savage. The Lakotas had proved peaceful, and one "chief had told the emigration party they should be protected through his territory." The experts at Fort Hall warned the train to post a strong guard. Savage called a council and advised the men to keep a vigilant lookout. "Some hooted at the idea, said the proposition was a mark of cowardice." An old doctor named Simmons boasted that "he could kill all the Indians in the road with his broad sword." When Savage put the question to a vote, the equestrians refused to post guards. He warned that their horses would be stolen first but selected an easily defended campsite. That night Savage heard the horses stampeding. He roused the owners "and told them the Indians were after their horses, and if they wanted to save them they better get up and go after them and hitch them close to the wagons." Two men followed his advice and retrieved their animals, but the rest refused to leave their blankets. "False alarm as usual," said one who went back to sleep. The next day a search party set out to find the animals, while Savage led the wagons ahead. The searchers traveled five or six miles, found the trail, and demanded that the train stop and help them retrieve the horses. When Savage ignored him, Dr. Simmons "whined out, 'Captain, are you not going to stop and camp?' " Savage replied, "Simmons, go and kill your Indians with your broad sword. We are going to Oregon." That evening the train voted unanimously to post a guard.[49]

---

[47]Coon, "Journal of a Journey," 8 August 1852, 5:198.

[48]Conyers, "Diary," 11 July and 10 August 1852, 462, 482.

[49]Savage, "Americus Savage's Journal," 2 August 1851. Savage reported that Indians later killed three members of a family named Clark in another train and wounded a man named Powell from his train who tried to help track down the murderers. The panicked avengers left Powell in a thicket. "No one ever went back to bury the unfortunate man," Savage observed.

The basic motivations that drew people to Oregon remained unchanged. Fleming G. Hearn's decision to go to Oregon in 1850 sprang "from a desire to procure a restoration of Health and personally decide the veracity of the assertions which has hitherto represented California & Oregon in regard to their vast resources and beautiful Scenery."[50] As California gold fueled an economic boom in Oregon, many settlers concluded they were better off to stay put. "Times is good and brisk hear [and] propity of all kinds is high," wrote 1844 trail veteran Fielding Lewis during the gold rush. He was even "in better health than I have bin in fifteen year[s]."[51] Oregon prospered, but getting there was still not easy.

Oregon's true gold rush began when most of the men came home with "long pockets" weighted down with gold. From the territory's farms and forests, they used this capital to export lumber, wheat, and fruit to trade for much of California's gold. As the West developed, Oregon drew a different type of emigrant than did El Dorado. Rather than attracting men who came to make their "pile" and return home, the Northwest appealed to men and women who intended to stay and raise families. Over time, this distinction would profoundly influence the character of both states.[52]

Hurrying Onward: A Day on the Gold Rush Trail

Wagon trains had established the pace and pattern of life on the trail long before the rush to California began. Once they left the frontier, even the greenest of greenhorns fell into a daily routine closely resembling the schedule followed since the first fur-trade caravans headed west. "I will give you a description of one day's occupation and will suffice with but little alteration for the whole trip," James MacDonald wrote while resting for a day at Pacific Springs. "Commencing in the morning, we rise at daybreak, start a fire, wash, cook breakfast, take up our tent, fold our bedding and pack [it] in the wagon (once in two days grease the wagon), eat breakfast which consists of fried side of meat, sometimes ham, or dried beef, sugar, coffee, sometimes stewed peaches of which we have pretty plenty. Our bread is either sea biscuit, crackers or biscuits of our own baking. These are generally cold as we have not time to bake in the morning." Except for the peaches, MacDonald's party ate standard emigrant breakfast fare. "By 5 or 6 o'clock the cattle are driven in. Two of the men take up the long gad, say, 'Come haw, Taylor and Buck, come here to me.' We change drivers at noon, stop, kindle a fire, make some soup," he said. "We rest about 1½ hours, then drove on until five o'clock. Two commence

---

[50]Hearn, Journal, Oregon Historical Society, 1.
[51]Lewis to "Dear Cosin," 8 May 1852, Mattes Library.
[52]Jim Tompkins, personal communication, 25 April 2011.

cooking, two drive the cattle off to water and pasture. Two fetch wood and water, set up the tent, make down the bed. When the men return from the cattle they eat their supper, take their blankets and buffalo robe, go out and watch the cattle till they lay down, then they lay down and sleep till morning, then as before about 5–6 o'clock fetch them in, etc. Once a week we air our wagons."[53]

A day on the trail began at the crack of dawn, allowing time for livestock to graze and their owners to eat. All-male parties usually divided into groups of friends who split the cost of provisions and cooking and other chores. "Companies going this route are generally divided into messes of from four to six men each," one Forty-niner explained. "Each of these messes has their wagon and mules or oxen and their separate duties to perform as well as duties for the general interests of the company."[54] "At four o'clock in the morning, I ran the boys all out to breakfast," James Abbey wrote. "We had hot coffee, broiled ham, light bread, and dried peaches."[55] Then came the task of rounding up and hitching up the teams. For the inexperienced, looking for lost or uncooperative livestock could be a daily ordeal, but rural families with trained animals had few problems. "The steers knew their own names, as well as where they belonged in the team. In the morning, we began calling them by name, they would stop grazing, lift their heads as though listening, and start sedately toward us, their bells tinkling as they came," John Stockton recalled. "They walked to their own side of their wagon, and stood patiently [waiting] for the yoke."[56]

John Cumming, who edited the party's letters, observed, "There is no question that the Wolverine Rangers was the largest and best organized" of all the Michigan companies bound for the goldfields in 1849. One of the Wolverines left a detailed and lively account of an exciting day on the Platte River for an all-male gold-rush train. "We are very early risers on this trip," Herman Camp wrote to the folks back home after the bugle sounded at 4:00 A.M. "The cattle having been turned out of cor[r]al to feed, the herdsmen might be seen off on the plain keeping them from scattering, and in readiness to drive them in at the sound of the bugle." As soon as the men were out of their bedrolls, "you might see the smoke curling up from a dozen stoves, and every preparation in the culinary department being made by the cooks, while others were greasing the wagons for the day's march. At 5 o'clock breakfast. At half past the horn blows for the cattle to be driven into coral and yoked up and hitched to the wagons. At 6 o'clock the whole train is in motion." The party's scouts spotted five missing horses with their telescope, "some

[53]MacDonald to "Dear Mary," in *The Trek,* 3 July 1850, 134–35. A gad was a stick used to goad the oxen.
[54]Anonymous, Tour to California Overland, 17 May 1849, BYU Library, 22–23.
[55]Abbey, *California,* 8.
[56]Stockton, The Trail of the Covered Wagon, 1929.

eight miles distant, making their way back towards the States." The men sent to fetch the horses "started a large herd of buffaloes, and drove them between our train and the river Platte." The company's hunters turned the herd toward the train, and as the frenzied bison charged through the line of wagons, the men's rifles brought down five animals. The Wolverines collected the choicest cuts and moved on, halting to "noon" and eat dinner, the common name for the midday meal. "All were delighted with the sports of the day, as well as the pleasure in partaking of the luxury of the meat prepared by our most experienced cooks," Camp wrote. "At half past 1 o'clock our train was again in motion."

Clouds began to gather in the northwest. Soon "peal after peal of thunder seemed to roll around the plain, while the forked lightning was constantly darting across the thick gathering blackness—dense clouds which were fast approaching; and soon to our great surprise, we heard a deep heavy roaring sound in the direction of the storm." Hailstones hammered men and livestock as "the storm burst upon us in all its fury. In a moment all was wild confusion; a torrent of hail stones was pouring down upon us from the size of hen's eggs to at least the size of goose eggs." The teams panicked and "immediately whirled round and ran with the storm, some with and some without the wagons being attached to them." Wagons capsized, tongues broke, and some took shelter under the remaining wagons; those who could not find refuge were "knocked down by the hail; many had large holes cut in their heads; others were wounded on their arms, hands, shoulders and backs." The gale lasted only fifteen minutes, but left animals and wagons scattered over four miles: "all looked like a perfect shipwreck." At least twenty men had "blood streaming down their faces; others with their hands covered with blood, all in search of the Doctor." The men regrouped and "the clouds passed away, the sun set clear in the west, and all was tranquil." The Wolverines camped and spent the evening in the usual routine of duties, forming the wagon corral, "herding the cattle, cooking suppers, washing dishes, pitching tents, &c.; which usually takes us all till about half past 8 o'clock," Camp concluded. "Thus you see that from 4 o'clock in the morning till about 9 in the evening, we are kept busy."[57]

Camp's stirring report covered only one eventful day early in the trek and hardly reflected a typical experience, but his exuberance characterized male accounts as the journey began. While these adventure stories painted the trip as a series of daring exploits, many found crossing the plains to be "a long, tedious and toilsome journey."[58] "Nothing of startling importance happened to-day. The same old monotony—endless prairies," wrote Francis Sawyer, voicing a sentiment many

[57]Camp's description of his day on the trail is in his letter to "Dear Mary, Edna, and Others," 8 July 1849, in Cumming, *The Gold Rush,* 48–55.

[58]Kirtley to "My Dear Wife," 27 October 1849, *Missouri Whig,* January 1850.

women shared.[59] The tedium of crossing two thousand miles on foot imbued most days with a relentless sameness. "Nothing of interest occurred to-day; it was travel, travel, travel, amid the dust of a thousand teams, some before and others behind, all like ourselves hurrying onwards," said John Hawkins Clark.[60]

Overland travel, James Meikle Sharp recalled, required "a vast amount of walking."[61] After David Shaw's party abandoned their wagons at Devils Gate in 1850, he complained they had "to ride 'shank's horses' in the future, as we had mainly in the past. In fact, we had simply become human walking machines," he recalled.[62] "Company excessively tired from walking. I drive half the time & walk the other half," complained Daniel Budd. "My feet are sore & much blistered."[63] The grinding routine eventually wore down almost all who endured it. "We had now plodded our way to a wearying length. To hitch up and start on with every returning sun had long comprised the chief round of our existence. We came to wonder how we should feel when this trudging routine should be a thing of the past," recalled David Rohrer Leeper. "Thus dragging our slow lengths along, fatigued, half-hearted, nauseated with the ever-present sage odor, seeing not a single tree, and having a dreary, inhospitable solitude everywhere staring us in the face, we were often prone to ask ourselves whether this sort of life was ever to have an end."[64] Even the spectacular scenery of the Sierra Nevada and Cascades did little to relieve the bone-deep exhaustion most felt at the end of the trail. "The road presented the same dreary monotony of Stony Hillsides and Rocky Ridges covered with Emmense Pine trees (some of them 10 feet in diameter and at least 200 feet high) through which we were obliged to thread our tedious way," wrote Joseph Berrien.[65]

Making camp had become a ritual. The captain usually rode ahead to find a site with wood, grass, and water. "On arriving at camp in the evening they drive the wagons round to a circle forming a corral, the tongue of one wagon resting on the hindmost axle tree of the next," a Forty-niner wrote. "Each mess unharness their own mules and each one in the mess has his appropriate duties. As soon as the wagon stops the cook gets out bucket, frying pan, coffee pot &c preparatory to getting supper while the balance of the mess unharness the mules and turn them loose after putting on a collar or halter." Trains tried to end their day's travel by "about six or seven oclock but when good camping grounds could not be obtained at these hours we would proceed on until nine, ten or sometimes twelve o'clock

---

[59]Sawyer, "Kentucky to California," 28 May 1852, 92.
[60]Clark, "Overland to the Gold Fields," 31 May 1852, 246.
[61]Sharp, *Brief Account of the Experiences,* 3.
[62]Shaw, *Eldorado,* 45.
[63]Budd, Journal, 24 May 1852, Mattes Library.
[64]Leeper, *Argonauts of 'Forty-nine,* 55.
[65]Berrien, "Overland from St. Louis," 7 August 1849, 347.

at night." If a party could make camp early, "it was [an] advantage both to the men and mules for constant travelling from an early hour in the morning until late at night was very fatiguing both to the men and mules," he wrote. "But necessity often compelled us to go on until midnight the men worn down with fasting and fatigue And the mules with labor and then find but indifferent camp grounds, perhaps scarcity of grass, no wood for fuel, and bad water."[66]

Even after pitching camp, sending the livestock to graze, and cooking and eating, for many men the day was not over. Some considered guard duty the trail's greatest hardship. "I could walk all day driving team, through heat and dust, could live on the meanest fare and still be content," said William Hart, "but running around in the wet grass herding cattle half the night was the most exhausting of all and tried my firmness severely."[67] As Alonzo Reynolds observed, "it wants a tough, hardy man, who can stand hardships, wade streams, travel all day in hot sand and a cloud of dust, and at night go perhaps two miles and guard cattle half the night, and then wrap up in his blanket and curl down under a sage bush the other part of the night," he wrote. "All this has to be done, not one night but every night."[68]

"If there was wood enough, small camp fires would soon be burning, as the families each chose a corner of the square made by the wagons. If wood was scarce, one or two fires were used in common," remembered John Stockton.[69] "After eating a hearty supper all hands volunteered and hauled up a big pile of logs for our camp fire, around which all seated themselves to hear some music," wrote James Abbey. His talented camp included men who could play the cornet, ophicleide, trumpet, fiddle, guitar, and flute. The musicians elected Billy Reissinger leader of the band and launched into "Home Sweet Home" and "Life on the Ocean Wave," while Abbey and his homesick companions found a "gush of gentle sorrow will spring up in the bosom when we chance to hear some air that a good old mother used to sing at home years ago!"[70] Women too might relax from their never-ending camp chores. "The most pleasant part of the trip across the plains in 1849–1850 was around the campfire. Supper over, dishes and pots out of the way, we would gather around the campfire and relate the rich scenes of the day, and the spinning of long yarns. Some played the violin, others the accordion," G. W. Thissell reminisced. "A few would play cards, while the young men would sing their favorite California songs . . . 'O, Susanna, Don't you cry for me, I'm going to California, Some gold dust to see.' "[71]

[66]Anonymous, Tour to California Overland, 17 May 1849, BYU Library, 23–25.

[67]Hart, Diaries, 24 May 1852, BYU Library, 62.

[68]Reynolds to "My Dear Parents," 13 July 1849, 2/4.

[69]Stockton, The Trail of the Covered Wagon, 1929.

[70]Abbey, California, 18 April 1850. Now rare, the ophicleide (literally, "keyed serpent") was a family of bugles with nine to twelve keys.

[71]Thissell, Crossing the Plains, 168.

FIRST NIGHT ON THE PLAINS

George Baker sketched this scene on his 1853 overland trek. It appeared on a pictorial letter sheet entitled "Hutchings Panoramic Scenes—Crossing the Plains." As acclaimed bibliographer Gary Kurutz noted, these precursors of the picture postcard provide "the best visual chronicle of the California Gold Rush and the golden decades of the 1850s and 1860s." Author's collection.

Except for the best organized and managed parties, virtually every wagon train eventually encountered hardships that made a day at the end of the trail a scramble for survival. "The road has been very tedious and crooked and [crosses] one of the wildest looking countries I ever saw," George Bonniwell wrote at Goose Creek after three months on the trek. "I hope we shall soon get at our journey's end for I am quite tired of traveling on this long and dusty road, and I believe we all are."[72] As the landscape became bleaker, the hardships greater, the food scarcer and less palatable, trail's last hard miles proved to be an ordeal. The reassuring if tedious daily schedule succumbed to the demands of geography. To avoid the heat of the day, travelers crossed deserts at night and did not stop until they had endured forty or fifty miles of sand, bitterbrush, and greasewood. "Burning wagons render still more hideous the solemn march; dead horses line the road, and living ones may be constantly seen, lapping and rolling the empty water casks (which have been cast away) for a drop of water to quench their burning thirst, or standing with drooping heads, waiting for death to relieve them of their tortures, or lying on the sand half buried, unable to rise, yet still trying," wrote Eleazar Ingalls. At the Forty-mile Desert's end, "a

[72]Bonniwell, Gold Rush Diary, 9 July 1850.

scene of confusion and dismay" greeted sojourners, who saw their animals collapse and, "too weak to travel, lie and broil in the sun." Parties abandoned hundreds, if not thousands, of wagons as a single thought consumed the sojourners—reaching water before they too lay rotting in the sun. "The desert!" Ingalls exclaimed. "You must see it and feel it on an August day, when legions have crossed it before you, to realize it in all its horrors. But heaven save you from the experience."[73]

E. W. Conyers described a heartbreaking scene on the Burnt River in Oregon. "We found a family, consisting of husband, wife, and four small children, whose cattle, as we supposed, had given out and died. They were here all alone and no wagon or cattle in sight, the husband sick and scarcely able to raise his head from the pillow, lying by the roadside in the shade of some small bushes to protect them from the burning rays of the sun." The wife showed them her children's feet: "The sole of each little foot was covered with sores, and swollen to nearly twice their natural size, caused by their long and continued walk over the rocks and hot sands of the plains." The mother had wrapped her family's feet in rags "to protect them as much as possible from the sharp rocks and burning sand." Conyer's party resolved to help the desperate clan, who "would have softened even the savage heart of Dionysius, the tyrant of Sicily."[74]

Women had their own perspectives on life on the trail. Even decades later they often had more realistic memories of the trek than did men. "Nothing but actual experience will give one an idea of the plodding, unvarying monotony, the vexations, the exhaustive energy, the throbs of hope, the depths of despair, through which we lived," Luzena Wilson wrote. "Day after day, week after week, we went through the same weary routine of breaking camp at daybreak, yoking the oxen, cooking our meagre rations over a fire of sage-brush and scrub-oak; packing up again, coffeepot and camp-kettle; washing our scanty wardrobe in the little streams we crossed; striking camp again at sunset, or later if wood and water were scarce. Tired, dusty, tried in temper, worn out in patience, we had to go over the weary experience tomorrow."[75]

WOMEN ARE WORTH SOMETHING AFTER ALL: MEN MEET WOMEN'S WORK

Bachelors who hit the overland road and those who left their wives behind learned an unexpected lesson. Being forced to survive without women taught them a new respect for the "women's work" once done by their mothers, sisters, wives, and daughters. Men who traveled with their families seldom learned these lessons.

---

[73]Ingalls, *Journal of a Trip to California*, 30 April 1850.
[74]Conyers, "Diary," 23 August 1852.
[75]Wilson, *Luzena Stanley Wilson*, 3–4.

"Sometimes we would camp for several days at one place," recalled Henry O. Ferguson. "The women would do their washing and the men would fish and hunt."[76] Life on the trail imposed fewer burdens on married males than it did on their wives. Except for sporadic guard duty, a man's labor typically ended after making camp and caring for the livestock, while a woman's work was never done. Mid-nineteenth-century America strictly defined gender roles, but the trail experience often stood prevailing custom on its head. Overland narratives tell of women hunting, driving oxen, fighting disease, and negotiating with Indians.

Men who went west with other men quickly developed a new perspective on women's work, and when compelled to do work typically delegated to women, they complained mightily. "I have always been inclined to deride the vocation of ladies until now," James Lynn wrote after using a washboard for the first time, for it was the most irksome work he had ever done. If he had stayed at home, Jackson Thomason mourned, "I would not be compelled to wash my clothes." Niles Searles found a new respect for "the labors of those by whom this arduous task is performed." A few witty souls refused to be humbled. He could "wash better than my wife, for her washing lasts only one week, while mine lasts from three to six weeks," J. Robert Brown concluded.[77]

Bachelors adapted. Thomas Van Dorn thought, "the veriest housewife would be surprised to see how admirably we succeeded with some *doughnuts* which we are accustomed to prepare for noon lunch." But no housewife would be impressed when Van Dorn said he changed clothes at Fort Laramie for only "the second time since I left St. Joe."[78] Alonzo Delano observed that women in the emigrant camps were "all grinning at the thought of what a fist you will make on the bank of a puddle washing your own clothes without soap, or trying to stop up a hole in your shirt with a darning needle." As he sweated over a buffalo-chip fire, roasting coffee, he imagined his wife triumphantly exclaiming, "It's good enough for you; you might have staid at home instead of going off on a wild goose expedition. You'll find out that women are worth something after all." The single men who made up most of the gold-rush migration had to "repair all 'breaks,' wash and mend their own clothes, bake their own cakes, cook their own meat, brown and boil their own coffee, in short, be teamster, carpenter, blacksmith, shoemaker, tailor, cook and bottle-washer all in one." Few enjoyed their new chores and all avoided these tasks whenever possible. "Of all miserable work, washing is the meanest," Delano complained. "No man who has crossed the plains will ever find fault with his wife for scolding on a washing day."[79]

---

[76]Ferguson, Reminiscences, Bancroft Library.

[77]Walker, "A Woman's Work," 6–8.

[78]Van Dorn, Diary, 6 and 14 June 1849, Beinecke Library, 12, 14.

[79]Delano, *California Correspondence,* 21 April 1849, 10–11; *Life on the Plains,* 17 July 149, 141.

Not many male Forty-niners could cook anything, but a few hardy souls met the challenge. "We are now very well acquainted with camping and think we can cross the plains easy," Charles Hassenplug wrote. "We are now skilled in baking shortcakes slabjacks, potato soup."[80] On his first attempt at cooking, Warren Hafford "made some of the *best* pies that was ever eaten."[81] By the time he arrived at Independence Rock, Uncle Wash could "throw pan cakes over (not quite) his head and catch them again," wrote G. W. Brouster. "He is well and as well satisfied as if he [were] in the King's palace."[82] William Hart described how a bachelor train did its chores after finding "good grass wood and water, the three grand requisites of a camp life. We soon kindled our fires, brought water, mixd the bread, made it into biscuit, and set it to bake. We generally made biscuit in the evening and pancakes in the morning." They converted a common frying pan into an oven "by standing it up on its edge so as to face the fire and when one side was baked we turned it over in the pan and baked the other side." By this time the camp teakettle was boiling, "the bacon fried or the dried beef stewed and we gathered around our simple meal with appetites sharpened by travel and not at all dainty," Hart admitted. "Of course we had our daily accidents such as burning the bread or meat or getting too much dirt into them or having our kettles upset by the sticks being burnt away from under them but we soon got used to them."[83]

Of all trail chores, men hated doing laundry the most, and many put off the inevitable as long as possible. A day west of Fort Laramie, Henry Tappan decided to do laundry for the first time in five hundred miles. At a warm spring called the Emigrant's Washtub, he wrote, "I tried my hand in the art of washing dirty clothes. Succeeded admirabley although my fingers suffered some from the effects of very good soap."[84] "Today I am doing some washing, being the first thing of the kind I ever did," Methodist minister Lemuel Herbert wrote on the Big Sandy. "We did our washing of course without the use of wash tubs, wash boards, &c. We took one piece of clothing at the time together with a lump of soap and waded into the river above our knees and performed the work with good effect. We did not change the water at all, for the filth ran down the stream just as fast as we rub[b]ed it out."[85] On Bear River, Phillip Badman recalled, "I undertook to wash my Shirt & I let it lay till morning & I found it Frozen Stiff."[86]

Men felt the absence of women in different ways: "The most of us have had sore

---

[80]Hassenplug, Diary, 10 April 1850, Mattes Library.

[81]Hafford, Diary, 19 May 1850, Rutherford B. Hayes Presidential Center.

[82]Brouster to "Dear Parents," 10 June 1850, Western Historical Manuscripts.

[83]Hart, Diaries, 8 May 1852, BYU Library, 45–46.

[84]Tappan, "The Gold Rush Diary," 14 June 1849, 125.

[85]Herbert, Personal Diary, 24 June 1850, Delaware County Historical Society, 33.

[86]Badman, Diary, 27 July 1849, Beinecke Library, 2:15.

lips ever since we started, probably caused by the difference in the air, the hot sun and dust, and having no women to kiss," mourned Alonzo Reynolds at the Big Sandy.[87] However much they might have missed sexual companionship, men disliked having no one to do their chores even more, and the need to do what was traditionally women's work did not stop at the trail's end. Mining camp life was "rather a tedious business, taking it all round: for we have to be a man of all sorts of work, and a house maid besides," wrote Elijah Spooner, seated in a homemade armchair at his "old winter quarters." "Have to cook, wash dishes, make beds, wash our clothes, darn old stockings, patch the old pants, cut and bring wood, and then rock the cradle all day. And aint this tuff now?"[88]

Tough is better used to describe the fortitude with which women faced the challenges they met on the trail. Sitting under a fallen tree on the decent from Donner Pass, Charles Benjamin Darwin met a "distressed & worn woman of the california mountains." Her clothes were "all dust soiled & begrimed with sweat & toil," while "all her manifestations marked one of great trial & extream weariness." With her elbow on her knee and chin in hand, her attitude told a story of "exposure & suffering which each feeling observer could not fail to commiserate." She might have been the woman with "a spinal disease to whom the least motion is death," whose husband fed her half a spoon of morphine per day to soothe her suffering. "Oh the inhuman villain," Darwin wrote.[89]

Sarah Royce recalled, "If we rise *very* early tomorrow morning, we shall get there by noon, and have a half day to settle camp, and get ready for work," describing how the last party on the trail prepared for the terrifying crossing of the Forty-mile Desert. "Accordingly the first one who woke the next morning roused all the rest, and, though we found it not much past two o'clock, we agreed it was not best to sleep again." Her companions drank hot coffee beside a sagebrush fire, ate their last bit of rabbit potpie, "yoked up the oxen, and went resolutely on our way."[90]

NEW EMIGRANT ROUTES: BECKWOURTH AND NOBLES

No American ever claimed he went west to get poor, and Jim Beckwith certainly did not when he signed on with General Ashley to go to the Rocky Mountains in 1824. Born in Virginia in 1798, the son of a planter and Miss Kill, his African slave, the man renowned as a gaudy liar became James Pierson Beckwourth only when he dictated his autobiography in 1855 after surviving the fur trade, the

---

[87]Reynolds to "My Dear Parents," 7 July 1849, 2/2.

[88]Spooner to "My Dear Wife," 2 March 1850, BYU Library.

[89]Darwin, "1,000 Miles From Home," 27 August 1849, 90–91.

[90]Royce, *Across the Plains,* 40.

Second Seminole War, and alleged service as "war chief" of the Crow Nation. "Beckwourth" is now applied to the pass and trail the famous scout opened, but in June 1851, "the discoverer and projector of this new and important route," was Mr. Beckwith. As it promoted his "New Emigrant Route," the *Marysville Herald* announced Beckwith had "several men at work cutting a wagon road, by which the emigration can save 150 miles in coming to this city." The trail's reported advantages included "crossing the Truckee but once," which was only technically true, but it did have "good grass and water all the way." Most important, the gradual ascents to his northern passes avoided the sheer granite walls of the central Sierra Nevada. The *Herald* predicted the road would become "by far the most important to the emigration and valuable to our city." It encouraged local citizens to support Beckwith with subscriptions, to be "paid when he has brought the trains here."[91]

The discovery of "Beckwith's Route" heralded a sea change in the evolution of the California Trail. The previous decade's haphazard trail blazing, based on limited knowledge of the barrier the North American Cordillera posed to Alta California, gave way to attempts to win control of trade at the end of the most popular overland road to the gold mines. Occasionally based on hard information gained through actual explorations, this impulse launched a thousand schemes. Sharp-eyed entrepreneurs like Beckwith allied with ambitious boomtown promoters at Placerville, Marysville, Downieville, Columbia, and Shasta to create the best and nearest wagon road "from the other side of the mountains into the Sacramento Valley." An American rancher who Beckwith told about his pass remarked that if Jim could carry out his plan "and divert travel into that road, he thought I should be a made man for life," Beckwith recalled. The stockman drew up a subscription list and contributed $200. Marysville and Bidwells Bar offered similarly enthusiastic financial support.[92]

While prospecting in the northern Sierra in 1850, Beckwith "remarked a place far away to the southward that seemed lower than any other." On a second trip he scouted what he called "the best waggon-road" over the range. "The Pass over the Siera Nevada on this route is *extremely easy*," wrote John E. Dalton in 1852. "The ascent & descent from & to the meadows on each side are very gradual indeed, hardly any hill at all. Much like the South Pass, of the Rocky Mountains." In addition, unlike Donner and Carson passes, the new route offered "an abundance of excellent grass." With Marysville's promised backing, Beckwith began cutting a road over the route and led the first train to the city in 1851, but the town burned down the same day and he was never paid. To console himself, Beckwith established

---

[91]*Marysville Herald,* 3 June 1851, in Wilson, *Jim Beckwourth,* 134.
[92]Beckwourth, *Life and Adventures,* 514–17.

a trading post and hotel at his War Horse Ranch in Sierra Valley, where Dalton met the "*Old War Horse*" himself the next summer. Beckwith was "a dark swarthy, keen looking, shrewd old fellow; 54 years old & is of four different Nations: French, English, Indian & Nigro or Mexican." He lived in a light frame house—the first building Dalton had seen since leaving Fort Laramie—measuring about fifty by twenty feet, "the roof covered with pine boards & the sides with muslin." This frontier inn was divided into a bar, a storeroom, an eatery, and kitchen. Beckwith told Dalton he had "traveled across the mountains 14 times, and expects to live to cross them 24 times more—he gave us a diffinite discription of the route where the Rail Road would have to be located from the Atlantic to the Pacific."[93]

In one of the most colorful tales ever told about the California Trail, the state's first poet laureate, Ina Coolbrith, remembered traveling at age eleven with "the first of the covered wagons to break the trail through Beckwourth Pass into California," Her family actually arrived from Salt Lake early in 1852, but Coolbrith probably met the fabled guide, who "was rather dark and wore his hair in two long braids that gave him a picturesque appearance." For his part, when James P. Beckwourth described the families he met "without a morsel of food, and without a dollar in the world to procure any," he said he never refused anything they asked for at his ranch. He found the old folks peevish and quarrelsome, but he felt "the poor girls have suffered the most." Barefoot and dressed in improvised bloomers, their once luxuriant locks were now "frizzled and discoloured." Yet Ina recalled being the happiest little girl in the world when she and her sister crossed the pass riding bareback on the legendary mountaineer's horse. "On the boundary Jim Beckwourth stopped," Coolbrith remembered, "and pointing forward, said, 'Here is California, little girls, here is your kingdom.' "[94]

An informal survey of sources suggests the Beckwourth Trail became the most popular overland gateway into California by 1852. Beckwith again set out "to induce the emigrants to travel" his road in July 1853. He was pleased that farmers and "citizens generally" had turned out and "put the road in good order, and my advice to the emigrants would be to take that road, as they have plenty of grass and water all the way down to the valley." The first overland party passed his ranch with their livestock "in tolerable good condition." Beckwith was delighted that his valley was filling up fast. Marysville, he complained, had never bothered to pay him for his trouble, "though it is more to their advantage than to mine."[95]

---

[93]Ibid., 516; Dalton, Diary, 16, 23 August 1852, Wisconsin Historical Society. For the trail's discovery and route, see Hammond and Hammond, "Mapping the Beckwourth Trail," 10.

[94]Beckwourth, *Life and Adventures,* 523–24; Wilson, *Jim Beckwourth,* 135.

[95]Don Buck, personal communication, 19 January 2011; Beckwith to "Messrs. Editors," 27 July 1853, *Marysville Herald,* 13 August 1853.

JOSEPHINE DONNA SMITH,
"THE SAPPHO OF THE WEST"
Josephine Donna Smith, about the time she
came to California in 1852, from a copy
of a daguerreotype reportedly destroyed
in the 1906 San Francisco earthquake. As
Ina Coolbrith, she became California's
first poet laureate. Jim Beckwourth, she
recalled, was "one of the most beautiful
creatures that ever lived." Writer George
Stewart interviewed this "very handsome
and vigorous-looking old lady, strikingly
dressed in a purple dressing gown," more
than seventy years later. Courtesy Oakland
Public Library.

Due to terrain and politics, Beckwith's route declined in popularity during the
1850s and failed to endure as the dominant wagon trail into California. Its initial
crossing of the Sierra was surprisingly easy and grass filled its alpine meadows,
but 150 miles of hard road and five more summits lay between Beckwourth Pass
and Bidwells Bar. West of the War Horse Ranch, John Dalton climbed "a *mountain*
that is a *mountain*—the ascent and descent most of the way is just about as steep
as the roof of a house & in some places quite rocky. It far exceeds any hills, over
which I ever saw a road pass."[96]

As Beckwith opened his new road over the mountains, another ambitious frontier speculator, William H. Nobles, turned cutoff making into a career. By his own
account, starting in February 1851 near the southern end of the Sierra Nevada, he
followed the ridgeline and "thoroughly explored the whole range to the Columbia
River." With two men, he spent eight months exploring the Sierra, paying them
$8 a day and providing their "provisions & riding animals." His survey led to the
discovery of a pass "over which one span of horses could be able to haul from 15
to 20 hundred weight without difficulty." Between the Humboldt and Sacramento
rivers, Noble calculated the new trail over what soon became Nobles Pass would
save overland emigrants "at least 200 miles."[97]

[96]Dalton, Diary, 27 August 1852, Wisconsin Historical Society.
[97]Nobles to Thompson, 16 April 1857, National Archives.

Nobles's self-serving letter, written in 1857 to promote his talents and secure a government job, raises almost as many questions as it answers. The best authorities, Tom Hunt and Don Buck, question whether Nobles "actually ranged as far as he claimed along the backbone of the Sierra Nevada and Cascade Range," which would make him the first to traverse the approximate route of today's Pacific Crest Trail. (Nobles seems to have confused the Klamath River with the Columbia.)[98] Historians have mistakenly attributed the discovery of Nobles Pass to a search made with eighty men or Peter Lassen's hunt for the fabled Gold Lake, where, according to rumor, "one could pick up nuggets of gold on the shore of the lake without any digging."[99] The facts are far more interesting, for Nobles's exploration identified a workable alternative to the Lassen Trail that proved to be the best, easiest, and safest wagon road across the Sierra.

Nobles found this route—or at least the pass that made it practical—late in 1851, and was eager to capitalize on his hard-won knowledge. Peter Lassen had fallen on hard times: the details are murky, but it seems he and his partners used their 1849 profits to purchase a steamboat perhaps named the *Lady Washington* to deliver supplies to his ranch. Her maiden voyage, a pioneering feat of Sacramento River navigation, took five months to reach the mouth of Deer Creek, but when the *Lady Washington* hit a snag and sank, so did her owners' fortunes. According to tax records, by 1851 Lassen had assets worth $375 and no land. Broke, Lassen conveyed his remaining interest in the ranch to a German 1847 overlander, Henry Gerke. "Colonel" Charles L. Wilson, who had visions of running a railroad to the property, had already acquired General Joel Palmer's interest in Rancho Bosquejo, but neither Colonel Wilson nor General John Wilson (who apparently were not related) ever paid Lassen a dime. Lassen's financial dealings proved inept: "The truth is," Georgia Willis Read concluded, "his heart was probably better than his judgment."[100]

Late in 1851, William Nobles arrived with a sword to cut this Gordian knot. Nobles proposed forming a syndicate with Gerke and at least five others. He suggested recruiting Peter Lassen "to come in as a member of the company, equal shares with us all," which would be to everyone's advantage. Lassen was agreeable, if the partners could dispose of the Wilsons' shares in Rancho Bosquejo, although by now Lassen rejected their claims, convinced both Wilsons were crooks and livestock thieves. The partners drafted some sort of contract, which might have

[98]Buck, William Nobles Itinerary, 2; Stafford Hazelett, personal communication, 11 May 2011. Based on Craig Giffen's Pacific Coast Trail planning program and the unlikely assumption that Nobles followed the Pacific Crest Trail from Sonora Pass to the Columbia River and traveled 15.4 miles per day without a single layover, his men gained 109,865 feet in elevation over 1,088.2 miles of the national scenic trail's 2,650 miles and completed the trip in seventy-one days. Like most promoters, Don Buck noted, "Nobles was prone to exaggeration," but his improbable claim was not impossible.

[99]Potter, *Autobiography*, 110.

[100]Bruff, *Gold Rush*, 696, 1031n97, 1071–72; Hammond, "Peter Lassen and His Trail," 40.

involved establishing trading ranches along Nobles's proposed wagon road, to transfer Lassen's property to the partners. As Tom Hunt conjectured, such a company would have "a monopoly of trade with arriving emigrants over the entire length of the new route, an arrangement that could prove immensely profitable." By spring, the deal had fallen apart. "We concluded to give it up," one partner concluded, "there was no chance to win." A court later found that John and Charles Wilson had not met the terms of the original contract to buy the ranch, and in August 1852, Henry Gerke paid Peter Lassen $25,000 for all 22,206 acres of Lassen's land grant. (Needless to say, the Dane did not invest it wisely.) Meanwhile, William Nobles had taken his trail and his ambitions north.[101]

THE GREAT COUNCIL AT HORSE CREEK

"We are continually hearing of the depredations of the indians," wrote Caroline L. Richardson, "but we have not seen one yet." In the Black Hills, her party gave a Cheyenne band "something to eat after which they left us carying with them such victuals as they could not eat." The Natives put the boiled ham and cheese on a sharp stick: "they did not seem to relish their cheese very well," Richardson said. "They scrutinised it very closely before they ventured to taste it and when they did they made up a terrible wry face." Subsequent encounters convinced her that Indians were "intolerable beggars and if you give them anything to get rid of them it is sure to bait them back to you."[102]

What emigrants flooding through Indian Country perceived as begging and thievery, the residents considered compensation for the damage wagon trains inflicted on their game and grass, the resources essential to their survival. Sarah Hollister Harris thought the five Lakotas her party met 1851 "made themselves quite too familiar," but they made their purpose clear when they "spread blankets down before us, and in a lordly way demanded to have 'sucre,' whiskey, tobacco and various other things placed upon them as toll, 'for passing through their country.' "[103] Lewis Norton recalled playing the hero during a confrontation with three hundred Indians. Their leaders "said they wanted toll for going through their country," which one man paid, but a Native stopped the next wagon and said, "Me chief; me want money." Fred Parker pointed at Norton and said, "That is our chief; go to him if you want money." Knowing that "the Indians had great respect for army officers," Norton wore his officer's uniform, sword, and holstered pistols from the Mexican-American War. Drawing his sword, he ordered the Indians to

---

[101]Hunt, "William Nobles and the Origins of His Trail," 4–7.

[102]Richardson, Journal, 24 May, 13, 14 June 1852, Bancroft Library.

[103]Harris, *An Unwritten Chapter of Salt Lake,* 23.

leave the road, "when their spokesman, in fair English, told me that they had as good a right to travel the road as I had."[104]

Not far from the Missouri, Harriet Buckingham's party made a grim discovery, a field of skulls and human bones in shallow graves. After much speculation, they concluded they belonged to the large tribes "from the middle states [who] had been pushed off by our government to this frontier region to make room for white settlers, and had here perished in large numbers by starvation consequent upon removal from familiar hunting grounds." Disease rather than hunger probably accounted for the bodies she found "buried in large trenches with heads to the east." The surviving Omahas demanded a toll and her company gave a feast for the Indians, who in turn treated them to a war dance, the "young men in the glory of fine feathrs paint & skins—their war costume." She found the girls who were in the market for a husband "most grotesqely painted in vermillion & Green." They killed the calf the company gave them and ate it "even to the very entrails," then danced in front of an immense fire "that lit up the wiered hob goblin scene—their fiendish yells, as they tossed their arms about and swung the gory scalps" taken from their ancient enemies, the Lakotas. The celebration lasted until dawn, and as they prepared to leave, the emigrants noticed that the calf's mother had disappeared: they eventually found the cow tied in the brush some distance off. "The Indians were so hungry & persistent—They levy tribute on all who pass—do not always get anything." The next night, six Indians camped with the train. "We gave them supper & breakfast," wrote Buckingham. In the morning the Omahas' singing "quickly wakened" her.[105]

Such encounters contributed to the steady deterioration of relations with Native peoples during all three decades of overland emigration. "The indians are every day commiting some depredation or other, they steal and rob from every train and those dirty french put them up to it," Amelia Hadley complained on the Snake River in 1851. "I think if congress knew how bad they were they would protect the emigration." Hadley considered it cruel "for them to hold out inducements for people to settle Oregon and leave them unprotected and to fight theyr way as best they can."[106] If the government did not do something to protect overlanders and "check the further hazardous movements of these Indians, hundreds of Oregon Emigrants have said in our office that emigration will cease for that quarter after this year," announced the *Frontier Guardian*. "Already, letters have been sent back to their friends, to warn them not to proceed, until a sufficient force is placed by government on the Frontier to protect them."[107]

---

[104]Norton, *Life and Adventures*, 255–56.
[105]Buckingham, "Crossing the Plains," 4, 6, 11, 12 May 1851, 18, 20–21.
[106]Hadley, "Journal of Travails," 10 July 1851, 3:87.
[107]"Highly Important News," *Frontier Guardian*, 22 August 1851, 2.

Neither the newlywed Mrs. Hadley nor the indignant editor thought so, but the federal government was taking steps to protect the overland road. The secretary of war issued a standing order in March 1850 intended "to give confidence to the emigrants passing on the routes to New Mexico, California and Oregon." As soon as grass grew, he directed commanding officers "to patrol and examine the country along these routes" and "insure, as far as practicable, the security and protection" of passing trains "as well as to diminish the chance of attack from hostile bands of Indians."[108] More importantly, after years of neglect and lobbying by experts such as Thomas Fitzpatrick and Pierre-Jean De Smet, as summer ended in 1851 the government at last turned its attention to trying to defuse the growing tension between Indians and emigrants.

The thousands of pilgrims and their vast cattle herds wreaked havoc on grass and wood as they crossed the plains. The impact not only stripped the road west of resources, it transformed a wagon trail into a national highway. The heavy road and deep sand Peter Burnett had described in 1843 "as making his cattle's hoofs tough & their not needing shoes are things 6 years behind the times," wrote George W. Davis. "The *Sand* has all been blown out of the road by the *strong west winds*—& the *gravel* has been ground up till good McAdamised roads exist *much* of the way."[109]

In late July 1851, Father De Smet left the Upper Missouri for Fort Laramie to attend the Great Council with the tribes of the plains. In September he reached the Great Route to Oregon, which thousands of emigrants had crossed incessantly from early spring to autumn for a decade. Thousands from every country and clime had taken the long and dangerous trail to "the rich gold mines of California, or to take possession of the new lands in the fertile plains and valleys of Utah and Oregon." They had created "the broadest, longest, and most beautiful road in the whole world—from the United States to the Pacific Ocean." This magnificent highway was now "as smooth as a barn-floor swept by the winds, and not a blade of grass can shoot on it on account of the continual passing." The noble highway filled his Absaroka guides with admiration: "They conceived a high idea of the countless *White Nation*." The three young men had never seen anything wider than a hunting path, and imagined the entire White Nation must have already passed over the great road, creating an immense void "in the land of the rising sun." When the priest assured them that the departure of so many people "was in nowise perceived in *the lands of the whites,*" their "countenances testified evident incredulity." The guides filled their pouches with knives, forks, spoons, basins, coffeepots, axes, and hammers, and collected shards of decorated earthenware to decorate their necks

---

[108]Fort Laramie, Letters Received, General Orders No. 7, 14 March 1850, National Archives.

[109]Davis to Watkins, 6 December 1850, Beinecke Library.

and ears. The debris was a testament, De Smet observed, to the bold recklessness of those whose fever for gold had compelled them to "hazard everything in this enterprise which has proved fatal to thousands." A great multitude "had crossed this vast plain with a rare courage and unheard-of fatigues and difficulties," leaving the bleached bones of their animals scattered profusely along the way. Sadder monuments marked the long journey: "the rising mound hastily made over the grave of a parent or a friend," and coarse and rudely carved inscriptions on the many grave markers showed how death had thinned their ranks. Such disasters killed thousands, mocking their "flattering hope of wealth and pleasure."[110]

U.S. Commissioners Thomas Fitzpatrick and D. D. Mitchell had already drafted a document assigning territories to the tribes when they gathered the Lakota, Cheyenne, Arapaho, Arikira, Assiniboine, Absaroka, Mandan, and Gros Ventre nations at Horse Creek in September 1851 to negotiate the Treaty of Fort Laramie. The council had started when Father De Smet arrived on 10 September. To accommodate ten thousand Indians and their horses, Colonel Mitchell moved the "Great Council" thirty-five miles south to the wide meadows at Horse Creek. After eighteen days the agents came away with a document bearing the marks of twenty-one "chiefs, headmen, and braves" in which the tribes of the Great Plains agreed to end their endless warfare against each other and "make an effective and lasting peace" among themselves. The government pledged to protect Indians from American depredations, and the Indians promised to make restitution for any wrongs committed by their people. It designated the metes and boundaries of the "respective territories" the Native nations agreed to recognize and acknowledge, but it said nothing about their rights to those lands. The treaty promised to deliver an annuity of $50,000 for fifty years in return for "the right of the United States Government to establish roads, military and other posts, within their respective territories." The cash was to indemnify "the Indians for the destruction caused in their hunting-grounds, their forests, pasturages, etc., by travellers from the States who cross their lands," De Smet noted.[111]

De Smet considered the Great Council a stunning success, in part because he performed 1,586 baptisms and married several couples. But he believed the tribes had at last forgotten their "implacable hatreds, hereditary enmities, cruel and bloody encounters." The treaty marked "the commencement of a new era for the Indians—an era of peace." Now law-abiding citizens could "cross the desert unmolested, and the Indians will have little to dread from the bad white man." At Ash Hollow on his return, the priest met a German prince on a hunting expedition who was scouting a site for an agriculture colony on land recently assigned

---

[110]De Smet, *Western Missions and Missionaries*, 94, 97–102.
[111]Prucha, *Documents of United States Indian Policy*, 84–85.

to the Lakota. Any such venture, established "against the will of the numerous warlike tribes in the vicinity of those mountains, would run great dangers and meet heavy obstacles," De Smet wrote. Only religion could "prepare these parts for such a transformation,"—a transition the good priest and most of his fellow citizens regarded as inevitable.[112]

As the last battered wagons reached Oregon and California in 1852, their drivers crossed a land transformed since the first trains left the Missouri. The change was the work of more than two hundred thousand overland emigrants who had crossed South Pass since 1849. "It is really surprising to see what a vast Train of human beings are pushing forward [toward] the Three great points of attraction 'viz' Salt Lake, California, & Oregon," wrote William Wagner as he watched the cavalcade. "The young, the old, the great & small, of both sexes & colors—, from the infant a few days old, to the gray haired veteran of three score years & Ten, are alike braving the dangers, encountering the hardships, enduring the privations, of a long, tedious, & perilous Journey—through an uncultivated, uncivilized & unfriendly country." Wagner believed he was fulfilling his nation's destiny. Unlike most Americans, he could see that some people would pay dearly for the triumph of the bold pioneers: "Westward ho! The Star of empire makes its way, & the time is not far distant when the Broad & uncultivated prairies & plains, that are now the Hunting grounds of the rude Savage, will be converted into beautiful Farms & Homes for the Pale faces—'Where then will be the Red mans Home'?"[113]

From the Great Plains to the Pacific, it was a question an endless stream of wagons forced upon American Indians. During 1852 more prairie schooners than ever were to crowd the road across the plains. The "effective and lasting peace" the council hoped to achieve ended before the Senate ratified the treaty in 1853. The Treaty of Fort Laramie settled nothing.

---

[112]De Smet, *Western Missions and Missionaries*, 111–14.
[113]Wagner, Journal of an Ox Team Driver, 23 May 1852, Plumas County Museum.

CHAPTER 9

THE GREAT TIDE OF EMIGRATION

The Trails in 1852

The rush to the California goldfields reached its crescendo in 1852. "Hundreds have left the Western Reserve for California. But the stampede is not confined to this district, by any means," editorialized the *Cleveland Plain Dealer.* Michigan farmers complained the state was being depopulated: "The emigrants are mainly farmers and mechanics—the finest of stock," and now they were leaving for Oregon. The wholesale abandonment of homesteads and towns left some Hoosiers panic stricken. "In Indiana, excellent farms are offered for sale all over the State, by persons intending to seek the Gold Land. What will be the end of things?" one editor asked. "It is a grave question." The massive departures were ruining business, the *Cincinnati Gazette* complained. "Rents are falling and labor advancing, Landlords are now looking for tenants instead of tenants for farms as before," was the grim assessment. "Well-stocked farms are for sale in all parts of the country at great sacrifices, by persons who are preparing for California."[1] Augustus Linville saw some four hundred emigrants pour into Saint Joseph in a single day.[2] "From present appearances, the emigration will be larger than it was in 1849 or 1850," the *St. Joseph Gazette* reported. "We learn by a gentleman who came through Hannibal by land, that the road is crowded with teams, and hundreds are daily crossing the Mississippi at various points."[3] By mid-May, William Hart found it hard to raise an outfit at Council Bluffs. Supplies "were scarce and high as the great travel of this year had caused such a demand for them as to almost clean out the place."[4]

Disasters darkened the start of the emigration season. For pure terror, no mid-nineteenth-century American calamity could top a steamboat explosion, and none

---

[1]Eaton, *The Overland Trail to California in 1852,* 1–2.
[2]Linville, Diary, 29 March 1852, Oregon Historical Society.
[3]*St. Joseph Gazette,* 28 April 1852.
[4]Hart, Diaries, 18 May 1852, BYU Library.

matched the dramatic blasts that destroyed the *Glencoe* and the *Saluda*. The *Glencoe* was tied up at Saint Louis on 3 April when she blew three boilers, and the city watched as surviving passengers struggled to escape the burning hulk. Jacob Young estimated two hundred "Californians" perished in the catastrophe, perhaps three times the likely fatalities.[5] Six days later the northbound *Saluda* blew a boiler near Lexington, Missouri. Francis T. Belt had spent two days battling the icy, muddy, spring-swollen current, trying to round a difficult bend. On Good Friday, 9 April 1852, Captain Belt swore "he would Turn that bend just above lexington or Blow his Boat to Hell, [and] he had not more than made that expression before she did Blow indeed," eyewitness Thomas Coleman reported. "It was an awful sight. About one hundred and thirty five lives lost. Captain Bell [*sic*] was blown way upon the bank he was a dreadful sight to look at. Both pilots were Blown into the river and drowned. Such a sight I never did see before. People were thrown in every direction. Some were killed stone dead some were bruised and mangled badly. Most were mormons for Salt Lake."[6]

Casualties numbered more than ninety, and almost that many survived. Perry Gee boarded the hulk ten days after the disaster and found "a perfect wreck Blown up a few Days before we got thare with 300 passengers on bord and only three of them were saved." Gee repeated the tale that "the Captain and mate was thrown on top of the Bank 200 feet above high watter mark," twenty rods from the river.[7] As a large side-wheeler steamed past Lexington after the accident, the captain, "a big, black-bearded man, came through the crowd of passengers with a pistol in his hand," Sarah Fisher recalled. "He told us that a short time before, a boat going up the river had blown up and many people had been killed, because they had all run to one side to see the town. He threatened to shoot any of us who went over on the other side."[8]

Almost twice the population of the city of Chicago packed up and headed west in 1852. Estimating trail numbers confounded contemporary observers and underlines the treacherous guesswork involved in historical estimates. More people may have fled the Civil War over the trails in 1862 or 1863, but the "great emigration" of 1852 surpassed all the other years of antebellum wagon travel to Oregon, California, and Utah. The best guessers, John Unruh and Merle Mattes, calculated that 70,000 men, women, and children trekked overland that year. About 50,000 went to California; 10,000 traveled to Oregon; while some 10,000 Mormons set headed

---

[5]Young, letter, 26 April 1852, California State Library.
[6]Coleman to "Dear Father," 14 April 1852, Coleman-Hayter Family Letters, Western Historical Manuscripts.
[7]Gee, 19 April 1852, Journal of Travels, Beinecke Library.
[8]Fisher, Ohio to Oregon, 1852. Fisher explained what caused double-boiler steamboats to blow up: "If there is too much weight on one side the water all runs in the boiler on that side. And when it goes back in the other one again, that boiler explodes."

for the Great Basin.[9] Americans returning from the West Coast in pack trains and freighting caravans bound for the military depots and Indian agencies helped swell the tide. By one measure, California's first gold rush reached its climax in 1852 when gold production peaked at a phenomenal $81,294,700. Overland emigration went into a gradual decline for almost a decade, and El Dorado would not be so seductive until the end of World War II.

The crowding, the rough company, the awesome spectacle of massed bison, the dust, the dead oxen, and the fresh graves lining the roadside were now part and parcel of life on the trail. Yet each year had its special features. Sojourners reported fewer conflicts with Indians in 1852. Some pointed to the previous fall's treaty and believed the government's peacemaking efforts at Fort Laramie had produced positive results as far west as the Sierra, but the relative tranquility was largely due to fear of disease, which—as much as the treaty conference—persuaded the Natives to avoid the trail. Yet the treaty and the cholera epidemic did not end conflict between emigrants and Indians or reduce the endless internecine warfare among the tribes. Daniel Budd saw "Indians plenty begging by the [w]holesale" along the Council Bluffs Road: "such beggars I never saw before." Men searching for three stolen horses "saw 25 antelope in 1 flock & 2 dead Indians." He met an artillery company "with their canon going to settle an affair that occurred between the emigrants & Indians wherein 3 whites & 6 indians were killed."[10] Guernsey-man Jean Le Poidevin had heard about attacks on emigrants and had seen many Indians near Chimney Rock "who appeared to be very savage and warlike," but he had no trouble with them. They came to his camp "to say How di do, How de do, and they do not stop asking for everything that they see. They ask for things to eat, for money, for clothes, &c., &c." Their curious attire indicated the strategy worked: "One has an old hat, one has an old wesket, another a chemise, another some old handkerchiefs attached around his knees, with another one around his neck, but although most of them are only covered by buffalo skins, they are each one covered with ear rings, necklaces, medals, bells and different ornaments the like of which you have never seen."[11]

John Dalton saw "vast herds of Buffalo, Deer & Elk," but others complained the migration's size scared away the bison.[12] "I only seen one buffalow on the rout as the Emigration keep them back," Bertrand Cornell complained.[13] Killing one of the beasts was not easy: the Bradleys said hunters shot a very large one "18 times before they killed him." Even with one eye shot out, Mr. Buffalo turned his head,

[9]Unruh, Jr., *The Plains Across*, 119–12; Mattes, *Platte River Road Narratives*, 5.

[10]Budd, Journal, 19, 20 May 1852, Mattes Library.

[11]Le Poidevin to "Dear Brother," in Turk, *The Quiet Adventurers*, 35.

[12]Dalton, Diary, 7 June 1852, State Historical Society of Wisconsin.

[13]Cornell to "Dear Father," 21 November 1852, Oregon Historical Society.

spotted a hunter "& made a lunge for him & the fellow threw his gun away run," yelling for help.[14] John Hawkins Clark saw piles of buffalo chips and places where the ground was white with their bones, but he had seen not a single one of the living creatures. The "smooth, white forehead" of many a bison skull was "much used by the immigrants for transmitting news." Lost travelers would write messages on them and "set the head up on its horns in some prominent place by the roadside": for castaways, these "skull bones" functioned like messages in bottles. According to Godfrey Ingrim, "every buffalo scull along the road side was covered with the names of the emigrants." Clark deeply regretted the scarcity of live bison, but "Buffalo or no buffalo, we must make a day's work."[15]

There was always something new on the overland road, or something that seemed new, for the evolving trail constantly repeated established patterns but also invented entirely new ones. The crowd moving west in 1852 accelerated the trail's transformation into a national wagon road. Dozens if not hundreds of trading stations sprang to life with the gold rush, and by 1852 many of them had become established commercial enterprises. The westering impulse infected its victims both with a burning desire to seek out new routes and to devise new ways to profit from them. One stalwart reportedly drove a flock of two thousand turkeys from Missouri to California, while an entrepreneur named Patterson invested his profits from a Salt Lake freighting operation in chickens, loaded them onto seven wagons with custom-built decks, and sold the fowls at an enormous profit in the goldfields.[16] As competition for the emigrant trade heated up, these enterprises inspired trail development, with traders Charles "Seminoe" Lajeunesse, Jack "Cock-Eye" Johnson, and perhaps Charles Kinney opening cutoffs that would bear their names.

As Americans again flocked to the growing frontier towns and jammed the ferries to cross the Missouri in 1852, the siesta that dimmed the young nation's overland urges in 1851 had apparently reanimated the impulse to go west. "As far as the eye can reach the road is filled with an anxious crowd, all in a hurry," John Hawkins Clark wrote as he began "marching to those beautiful shores whose golden sands have set the world on fire."[17] Daniel Budd complained about Saint Joseph's "badly mixed population" and steep prices: "Old countrymen, yankies, niggors, mulattoes of all shades, horses, mules & jack asses. Perfectly teming with imigrants. Business very lively, prices for shoing horses $2.00 & everything else in proportion."[18] Thaddeus Dean called Kanesville a hard old hole and found "every hole, crack &

[14]Bradley and Bradley, A Daily Journal, 25 May 1852, Beinecke Library, 24–25.
[15]Clark, "Overland to the Gold Fields," 28, 29 May 1852, 244–45; 261n39.
[16]Eaton, The Overland Trail to California in 1852, 6.
[17]Clark, "Overland to the Gold Fields," 6 May, 1 June 1852, 12, 26.
[18]Budd, Journal, May 1852, Mattes Library.

corner is crowded full of people, horses, & cattle."[19] Overlooking the Platte River, Abigail Scott described the romantic spectacle of this living, writhing mass: "The emigrants wagons cattle and horses on the road in either direction as far as the eye could reach."[20] Atop Independence Rock, John Dalton watched two hundred wagons pass by, and from above Devils Gate he "saw them each way on the road as far as the eye could reach almost in close solid column." Fifty thousand *"poor monomaniched gold hunters"* like Dalton endured prairie downpours, the terrors of cholera, and pangs of hunger, but they kept "plodding along in fine spirits, with lighter hearts and *strong hopes,* determined, like true hearted Yankees, not to be skeared at trials but to brave all difficulties, and yet *see the Elephant* on the other side of the Siera Nevada."[21]

"We notice among the emigrants several families, who go out with the intention of making permanent settlements," the *St. Joseph Gazette* reported.[22] "A marked feature of the emigration this year is the number of women who are going out by the land route," the *Missouri Republican* editorialized in mid-April. "Boats from the Ohio, Illinois, and other rivers, come in crowded to excess, and every boat for the Missouri has more than she can accommodate."[23] For the first time since 1848, families dominated many wagon trains. "There were many travelers, a great number of them on the way to Oregon with their families," wrote Norwegian overlander Tosten Stabæk. "Few or none of the gold seekers on the way to California had their families with them."[24] The mass migration was still mostly male, with the families "bound for Oregon with their cattle and other stock while the single men were nearly all bound for California." Yet many husbands and fathers who had already make the trek returned to escort their families to El Dorado. "The trail leading to the land of gold," James Bushnell recalled, was "crowded with white topped wagons, containing men, women and children."[25]

Trail traffic increasingly ran west to east. Near South Pass, Caroline Richardson met packers from California who "offered to take letters to the frontier for us gratis." It was quite common, she noted, to encounter such parties daily.[26] Near the forks of the Platte, Chloe Ann Terry met "a number of returning packers from California. They had 2 ladies in there croud [who] wer riding on there fresch ponys as graceful as could be."[27] Elizabeth Bedwell and eight other women found a hot

---

[19]Dean, *Journey to California,* 20 May 1852, 7.

[20]Scott, "Journal of a Trip to Oregon," 3 June 1852, 5:60.

[21]Dalton, Diary, 2, 29 June 1852, State Historical Society of Wisconsin.

[22]*St. Joseph Gazette,* 28 April 1852.

[23]*Missouri Republican,* 15 April 1852, in Watkins, "Notes," 230.

[24]Stabæk, "An Account of a Journey to California."

[25]Bushnell, The Narrative, 1.

[26]Richardson, Journal, 27 June 1852, Bancroft Library, 83.

[27]Terry, Diary, 24 June 1852, Washington State Historical Society.

spring bubbling out of the bank of Salmon Falls Creek; it was too hot for dishwa-
ter, but they discovered it washed clothes very clean. "I never saw beter or softer
water to wash with in my life," she wrote."[28] Her laundry might have included
bloomers, a recent addition to western women's fashion.

BLOOMER GIRLS:

UNCONVENTIONAL WOMEN ON THE OVERLAND TRAIL

How quickly could women's fashion, a phenomenon seemingly remote from the
frontier, affect western migration? Almost immediately. Soon after the national
press first mentioned a new form of female attire, "bloomer girls" dressed "in the
bloomer style" started appearing on the road west.[29] "There is a many ladys going
through this Spring; many of them are dressed in the bloomer stile," Solomon
Kingery wrote as the 1852 emigration began. "They wore Short dresses & pantaloons & Coets & hats. They look quite handsome."[30] Daniel H. Budd camped with
an Illinois train in April 1852 with a lady dressed "in bloomer costume. Have seen
a number of the bloomers for a week past," he wrote. "Nothing new the balance
of the evening."[31]

Bloomers were more than an innovative fashion—they represented a revolution
in how women dressed. The style quickly found supporters among independent
women who felt that the conditions women encountered in the West compelled
them to replace their cumbersome traditional apparel with something more sensible. The notion that women going west should wear serviceable clothing was not
entirely new. "Side-saddles should be discarded—women should wear hunting-
frocks, loose pantaloons, men's hats and shoes, and ride the same as the men," was
T. H. Jefferson's "Brief Practical Advice" in 1849.[32] Not long after Eliza Farnham
arrived in California that year, she began building a boarding house. The "extreme
inconvenience" of wearing a long dress while doing carpentry induced this resolute
and resourceful widow "to try the suit I had worn at home in gymnastic exercises."
Her outfit matched what soon became "famous as the Bloomer," she recalled—and
once she put it on, "I could never get back into skirts during working hours."[33]
Actress Fanny Kemble was simultaneously scandalizing Bostonians with "a loose
flowing dress falling a little below the knee, and loose pantallettes or drawers,"

---

[28]Bedwell, Journal of Road to Oregon, 25 August 1852, Mattes Library.
[29]William Brown was quite taken with women "dressed in the bloomer costume"; *An Authentic Wagon Train Journal*, 15, 18, 72.
[30]Kingery to "Dear Parents & Friends," 1 May 1852, Beinecke Library. Punctuation added.
[31]Budd, Journal, 30 April 1852, Mattes Library.
[32]Jefferson, *Map of the Emigrant Road*, 1.
[33]Farnham, *California*, 108.

WOMAN'S EMANCIPATION

"The dress of the Emancipated American female is quite pretty," Theodosia Bang told London's Mr. Punch. "We have asserted our right to his garb, and especially to that part of it which invests the lower extremities." The magazine's lampoon of women wearing bloomers indicates the British satirists were not impressed. From "Woman's Emancipation," *Harper's New Monthly Magazine* (August 1851): 424.

which the press thought looked suspiciously masculine. In December 1849 woman's rights advocate Amelia Bloomer defended Kemble, who had been "ridiculed, laughed at, and condemned for being so *masculine* as to put on pantaloons."[34]

Although the pantaloon-and-skirt combination has long been associated with Amelia Jenks Bloomer, whose articles helped popularize the fashion in America, Elizabeth Smith Miller created it in 1851. Miller described the outfit as "Turkish trousers to the ankle with a skirt reaching some four inches below the knee." Miller conceived the design after garden work left her "thoroughly disgusted with the long skirt." Bloomer first saw the style when Miller visited her cousin, Elizabeth Cady Stanton, at Seneca Falls. Bloomer described the outfit in her temperance journal, *The Lily,* and bloomers quickly became a national sensation, along with the outrage and ridicule that has always greeted an insurrection in ladies' fashions.[35]

The bloomer revolution had an immediate and much-noted impact on women setting out for the Pacific. Although bloomers were often ridiculed, men and women appreciated how well the dress adapted to life on the trail. "Our clothing is light and durable," wrote Eliza Ann McAuley early in 1852. "My sister and I wear short dresses and bloomers and our foot gear includes a pair of light calf-skin

[34]Kriebl, "From Bloomers to Flappers," 36.

[35]Fischer, *Pantaloons and Power,* 82.

topboots for wading through mud and sand."[36] William Hart saw "every variety of female costume from the long flowing dress of the old style to the very opposite extreme of Bloomer, and indeed the linen pants, boots and close bodice seem admirably adapted for this mode of travelling [as] the short skirt being no hindrance to the free use of the limbs, enables the wearer to jump the gullies, travel through the grass and sage brush and climb the steep hills with as much ease as the men."[37] Women of all ages adopted the new style. "The daughter is dressed in a bloomer costume—pants, short skirt and red-top boots. I think it is a very appropriate dress for a trip like this. So many ladies wear it, that I almost wish that I was so attired myself," Francis Sawyer confessed. "The old lady wears a short skirt and pantletts. She is fifty years old."[38] The long dresses in his 1852 train "were quickly discarded and the bloomer donned," Ezra Meeker remembered. Meeker thought older women had an easier time accepting the new style. "The younger women [were] more shy of accepting the inevitable, but finally fell into the procession, and we had a community of women wearing bloomers without invidious comment, or in fact of any comment at all."[39]

Meeker's memory may have betrayed him, because the new style continually provoked invidious, not to mention rude and crude, comments. Since she was "dressed in the bloomer style," Chloe Terry wrote, "the gentlemen sayed it tuck the rag of[f] from the bush."[40] Bloomers hardly appealed to everyone. It would do you good to see the girls of Council Bluffs, Thaddeus Dean told his wife. "They are a set of squizzles all wear pants and short dresses and many of them *boots,* & occasionally a *coat*—no dress comes *below* the *knees,*" he complained. "I would love to see one and not see her a— [and] her ankles at the same time."[41] Women commented on them, too. Returning churchgoers lined both sides of the street when Clara Downes entered Great Salt Lake City in 1860. "We were [all] stared at well but the *girl in the bloomers* who led in the company drew the greatest share of *attention.*"[42]

On the road to Pikes Peak in 1858, the comments and curiosity about Julia Anna Archibald's "American costume" inspired a virtual feminist manifesto: "I wore a calico dress, reaching a little below the knee, pants of the same, Indian moccasins for my feet, and on my head a hat. However much it lacked in taste I found it to be beyond value in comfort and convenience, as it gave me freedom to roam at pleasure in search of flowers and other curiosities." Ironically, the only other woman in

---

[36]McAuley, "Iowa to the 'Land of Gold,'" 7 April 1852, 4:37.
[37]Hart, Diaries, 6 June 1852, BYU Library.
[38]Sawyer, "Kentucky to California," 22 May 1852, 4:90.
[39]Meeker, *Ox-team Days on the Oregon Trail,* 69.
[40]Terry, Diary, 24 April 1852, Washington State Historical Society.
[41]Dean to "Dearest Bell," *Journey to California,* 24 May 1852, 9.
[42]Downes, Journal across the Plains, 8 July 1860, Bancroft Library.

her train did not appreciate the new style, which "denied her the liberty to roam at pleasure." She confined herself during "the long days to feminine impotence in the hot covered wagon." With great if prickly kindness, the woman advised Ms. Holmes (Archibald did not use her husband's name) to put on a long dress, since "the men talk so much about you," saying "you look so queer with that dress on." Archibald was not intimidated. "I cannot afford to dress to please their taste," she said. She would not enjoy a moment's happiness trapped in a long skirt in a wagon, and she tried to explain "the many advantages which the reform dress possesses over the fashionable one but failed to make her appreciate my views." The woman never found her traditional garb to be at all inconvenient, for "she could walk as much in her dress as she wanted to, or as was proper for a woman among so many men." Archibald was glad she was "independent of such little views of propriety" and could exercise her right to take an interest "in any curiosities we might find on the journey as much as if I had been one of the favored lords of creation." Her train's captain, "conservative up to the eyes," refused to let her stand guard.[43]

Paris did not catch the spirit of reform, and American women still adopted styles that hardly simplified the way they dressed. Empress Eugénie revived the hoop skirt in 1856, and for all its awkwardness, the new fashion quickly swept across the United States. "There is a bride and groom in the Inmann party. The bride wears hoops," wrote Helen Carpenter. She had read about hoops, but they had not reached Kansas before she left in 1857. These were the first she had seen. "Would not recommend them for this mode of traveling. The wearer has less personal privacy than the Pawnee in his blanket. In asides the bride is called 'Miss Hoopy.' "[44] The fashion did not prosper on the overland road. "These were the days when the girls and women wore hoops and the Captain allowed us to wear them until we reached Sweetwater where we had to ferry across," Samantha Dillard recalled. There he assembled the women and told them to abandon their hoops. "On looking around we saw hundreds of these hoops hanging on trees where they had been discarded by women of previous trains."[45] Hoops had a wider appeal than one might suspect: One Sunday on the plains, Lavinia Porter "discarded a worn-out hoopskirt that I had worn thus far on my journey, and much to my amusement and amazement as well, it was almost at once donned by a huge Indian brave." The warrior proudly showed off his new togs to his comrades, who did not miss the humor. "As the skeleton hoop composed the larger part of his attire, he was a sight to behold," Porter observed. "Even the stolid squaws were provoked to mirth at the ludicrous spectacle."[46]

[43]Archibald, "To Pikes Peak and New Mexico, 1858," 7:194–96.

[44]Carpenter, "A Trip across the Plains," 22 June 1857, 110–11.

[45]Dillard, Great Grandmother Samantha Jane Emmons Dillard's Story, 1866.

[46]Porter, "By Ox Team to California," 233–34.

THE GRIM MONSTER: THE PLAGUE YEAR

The grim tales of death and dying on the overland trail in 1849 and 1850 were terrifying, but conditions in 1852 overshadowed all the previous horrors. The chief agent of death, cholera, had now spread north to the Council Bluffs Road and enlisted new allies. Gold seekers complained about and died of almost every ailment known to man—dehydration, diarrhea, dysentery, headache, smallpox, toothache, typhus, pleurisy, measles, sneezing, nasal convulsions, and constipation. A few mentioned yellow fever, but no one is known to have died of it. Their journals used traditional names for other diseases, including ague (malaria), whooping cough (diphtheria), mountain fever (probably Rocky Mountain spotted fever), consumption (tuberculosis), lung fever (pneumonia), the pox (syphilis), the clap (gonorrhea), melancholy gloom (depression), and irresipulus, irisopulus, and ursyphlus (erysipelas, an acute streptococcal bacterial infection). "Nervous affection" or prostration covered a variety of mental crises.

The international cholera epidemic that coincided with the peak years of the California gold rush attacked the 1852 migration with a vengeance. East S. Owen heard that seven thousand people died of cholera on the plains.[47] On a single day between Skunk Creek and Carrion Creek, "three died with the cholera along the road," James Akin reported. His party lost eight others on the road to Oregon. Akin's account and other "numerous sources, reasonably reliable," convinced George Himes of the Oregon Pioneer Association "that probably not less than five thousand persons died on the plains in the year 1852, principally from cholera."[48] Often cited, Himes's statistic was exaggerated. "I have heard different estimations of the number that have died, some setting it as high as 5000 but I think this is quite too high," wrote Aaron Abbott. "I think one thousand would be a low estimate, perhaps fifteen hundred would be nearer correct."[49]

Analysts now agree that the death toll was far lower, but it created a gruesome spectacle. "In some places the ground is strewed with male and female attire which indicates that the presence of the grim monster has been felt and that the last resting place of some poor mortal or mortals is near inviting the traveler to stop and read the inscription or drop a tear as the last tribute he can pay to a fellow pilgrim," Caroline Richardson reported in the Black Hills.[50] The disease appeared among the emigrants "in a virulent form, hundreds of them leaving their bones along the trail, buried in unknown graves," James Bushnell recalled.[51] "There was an epidemic

---

[47]Owen to "Dear Brother," 24 September 1853, in Journal, Beinecke Library, 7–8.

[48]Akin, "Diary," 6 June 1852, 274.

[49]Abbott to "Dear Friends," 18 September 1852, Mattes Library.

[50]Richardson, Journal, 16 June 1852, Bancroft Library. Robert Rieck found only 2,540 verifiable deaths in 415 overland sources. See Rieck, "A Geography of Death," 13.

[51]Bushnell, The Narrative.

of cholera all along the Platte River," Jane Kellogg testified. The road became "a grave yard; most any time of day you could see people burying their dead; some places five or six graves in a row, with board head signs with their names carved on them."[52] Earlier travelers had escaped the epidemic once they left the Platte, but now the disease marched west. Daniel Budd described how cholera morbus killed John Richardson seven miles east of South Pass. His friends had to go miles to find a spot where they could dig two feet into the rocky soil. "Buried him, without coffin, put his clothes into the grave. Buried him without a tear being shed, not a prayer offered, barely a general sigh as we took the last look of 1 of our number who 9 hours before walked upright, & was a man of high Scotch spirit," Budd wrote. "When sickness gets a hold in camp all appears gloomy," he observed. "Had I known there would have been so much sickness I would not have dared to start."[53]

As a waterborne disease, cholera thrived along the crowded trail, and unsanitary camping practices helped spread the contagion like a prairie fire. Emigrants such as Jane Kellogg blamed cholera on drinking standing water drawn from holes dug at campsites, and perceptive physicians deduced that contaminated water was the source of the scourge, but nonsense about miasmas and speculative explanations were more widely believed. "It was as if the infection came flying through the air," Tosten Stabæk wrote. "A warm wind blew in the night, and simultaneously over a distance of about two hundred miles people fell sick and many died."[54]

Death and disease stalked all the trails. A few travelers spread fatal afflictions such as smallpox with careless abandon. Nancy and Henry Bradley carefully tracked the progress of the "Small Pox team," who traveled "all the time among the emigration Scattering the Small pox Broad Cast, they have no sighn out, they are very careless without, always taking the side of the road next to the wind, when any one passes them," Henry complained. "A man informed us that they had the Small pox aboard, & we passed on the side next [to] the wind, but had to drive out into the Sage Brush to do it."[55]

Great Salt Lake City had a quarantine ground at the mouth of Emigration Canyon, "and here is a hospital, or what pretends to be one, established by Governor Young, where all, both great and small, Jew or Gentile, are obliged to report," noted John Hawkins Clark. "Those who are well are privileged to continue their journey, but what they do with the sick or disabled I am unable to say." The hospital was barely large enough to hold the attending physician, a barrel of whiskey, and a few decanters. The infirmary contained no sick or disabled emigrants when Clark

[52]Kellogg, "Memories," 88.
[53]Budd, Journal, 26 June, 29 July 1852, Mattes Library.
[54]Stabæk, "An Account of a Journey to California," 107.
[55]Bradley and Bradley, Daily Journal, 17 June 1852, Beinecke Library, 58.

saw it. "The doctor was busily employed in dealing out whiskey and appeared to have a good run of custom in that way, but how many sick emigrants he attended to I did not stop to inquire."[56]

Diseases other than cholera may have been more effective killers. Malaria and scurvy were probably the most deadly and debilitating of all overland ailments. Early pioneers often fled the Missouri Valley to escape "the ague," but they carried the affliction in their bloodstreams, so by 1849 malaria was endemic to the Pacific Coast. In the first clinical trial in medical history, British naval surgeon James Lind had demonstrated in 1747 that citrus juice could prevent or cure scurvy. Robert Gardner's experience a hundred years later at a Mormon refugee camp showed how poorly Lind's remedy was understood outside of elite medical and maritime circles. "Many of the older was taken with a disease called the black leg and was entirely helpless and many died with it," he recalled. "Their legs from their knees down would get as black as a coal," a symptom of scurvy, which burst blood vessels.[57]

Emigrants often knew their miserable diets caused the disease. "Soup and fresh vegetables would prevent scurvy; there are many things they could name that are 'conspicuously absent from our daily fare,'" John Clark noted, but said the boys accepted the inevitable consequences of their diet. "We have good bacon, sugar, rice, dried fruit, etc. If we had as good feed for our animals as we have for ourselves, we should be content."[58] Travelers craving fresh fruit were delighted to find "all sorts of garden Sauce done well" at Great Salt Lake City, where Lydia Atkinson "had vegetables to eat there, peas beans onions cucumbers and potatoes yea"—and chicken too.[59] As provisions ran out at the end of the trail, scurvy left many of its victims weakened and debilitated as they crossed exhausting deserts and tried to surmount the Sierra Nevada.

The dreaded black leg was only one manifestation of a gold hunter's wretched diet of beans, bacon, and bread on the trail and later in the mines. Government relief officers gave families stranded on the Lassen Trail in 1849 "pickles and sourkrout, as some of them had the scurvy." The last of those left in the snow were a "pitiable sight I had never before beheld. There were cripples from scurvy, and other diseases; women, prostrated by weakness, and children, who could not move a limb," Major Daniel Rucker reported. "In advance of the wagons were men mounted on mules, who had to be lifted on or off their animals, so entirely disabled had they become from the effect of scurvy."[60] It afflicted almost everyone. "I see chinese passing who has scurvy very bad, its a dreadful disease," Daniel Budd

[56]Clark, "Overland to the Gold Fields," 13 July 1852, 49–50.

[57]Gardner, History, BYU Library.

[58]Clark, "Overland to the Gold Fields," 13 August 1852, 283.

[59]Smith, Gold Discovery Journal, 26 August 1848, 139; Atkinson to Anna Knox, 15 October 1852, Mattes Library, 3.

[60]Hunt and Rucker, in Smith, "Correspondence," Serial 561, 52, 139.

observed.[61] Hospitals known as pest houses served as refuges and burial sites at Sacramento, Marysville, and Stockton for those afflicted with scurvy and chronic malnutrition.[62] Dr. Philip Hines found "doctors are as plenty as Grasshoppers in a Meadow" and "finally concluded to try pill pedling," but all this professional expertise had little impact on the astronomical death rate among miners debilitated by the trip across the plains.[63]

Dietary diseases such as scurvy led to irrational behavior. "For the want of vegetables or acid of some kind, I had been troubled for a week or so with an attack of scurvy in my mouth, the gums being swollen because of the alkali dust," Gilbert L. Cole recalled. "This not only caused me pain and misery, but created a strong and constant desire for something sour." When he noticed a jug of vinegar dangling from the prow of an ox wagon, he offered the owner a silver dollar for a cupful. The man refused to part with any of it, saying he might need it himself. "I was sort of crazy mad and drawing my revolver, I rode around the rear of the wagon, thinking I would kill the fellow and take his jug of vinegar," Cole wrote years later. "But when he began to run for his life around the front yoke of cattle I came to my senses and hastened away from his outfit." On reaching Ragtown on the Carson River, Cole gladly paid five dollars for a quart bottle of gherkins: "I saw in that bottle of pickles my day of deliverance and salvation, and drawing my long knife from my bootleg soon drew the cork and filled my fevered mouth with pickles. I assure my readers that I can taste those gherkins to this day." The trader brusquely informed his happy customer that his tent was not a mule stable and ordered him to get out. Fearing for the safety of his pickles, Cole beat "a hasty and complete retreat."[64]

Many lost their teams on the road to Oregon and arrived "sick ravaged & poor. There was an immense amount of sickness on the plains this season [and] the road is strewed with graves," Bertrand Cornell wrote from Portland. Many who shared his "travails" were obliged to kill their cattle and eat the miserable beef "when they were poor as snakes & needed there team," he said. "I would advise no one to come." He had slept near a man who had just heard his wife and children had died not long before setting out to join him in Oregon. "As soon as he learned of it he went crasy hollowing continuly. I am very weak and sick [myself] and have been unwell a long time," Cornell admitted. "Death seems to stare the most healthy in the face." He would be dead by New Year's Day.[65]

Others lost hope. After reaching the Platte River, William Hart met "several teams taking the back track," some having lost family members, others their cattle,

[61]Budd, Journal, 27 August 1852.

[62]Ken Owens, personal communication, 21 December 2009.

[63]Hines, "An Ohioan's Letter," 162.

[64]Cole, In the Early Days, 109–10.

[65]Cornell to "Dear Father," 30 May, 21 November 1852, Oregon Historical Society.

and they "had become discouraged and turned back." The day after burying a woman near the forks of the Platte, Hart met a widow and her children "going back to her friends. She was driving one team and her boy, about 10 years old drive[s] the other."[66] Understandably, few who turned back left a record of their reasons, but John Stockton described his own family's hard experiences on the California road. "Often, now we would meet two or three wagons, or sometimes only one, going in the opposite direction. Perhaps a woman with a baby in her arms, sat on the high, board seat, with little children beside her, going back—alone—no use to ask questions," he recalled. "We knew that somewhere on the trail ahead, she had left the husband father, in one of the nameless graves that now so thickly dotted our pathway." His father, a minister, "would read the Scripture service for the dead, say a prayer, and come back, looking more and more drawn and sad, as these incidents became more frequent," his son recalled. "Still, we pushed on—hoping against hope." His family had its own encounter with Asiatic cholera, which Stockton attributed to "bad water, the entire lack of sanitation, and the unavoidable exposure to all classes of people, from all quarters of the globe." The terrifying disease eventually infected his father, and his nine-year-old brother died by sundown. The family gave up, turned back, and settled in Iowa, but the Reverend James Stockton never recovered his health.[67]

"Death has been busy," John Hawkins Clark observed as he left the North Platte River. "There are graves at the crossing of every stream, graves at every good spring and under almost every green tree; there are graves on thy open and widespread plain and in the mountains that overlook thy swift rolling flood; in the quiet and secluded dell where the birds sing and make such beautiful music there are graves; young and old, innocent and wicked, all have found a resting place in thy lap; indeed, thou has been the 'valley and the shadow of death' to many." Clark offered excellent advice to all who set out to cross the plains. "Never get into trouble with the expectation of getting help; carry nothing but what is absolutely necessary, and mind your own business. There is but little sympathy for anyone on this road, no matter what may be his condition," he wrote. "Everyone thinks he has trouble enough and conducts himself accordingly."[68]

THE GREAT SURGE: THE OREGON TRAIL IN 1852

The lure of El Dorado bedazzled most travelers who went west in 1849 and 1850, but the appeal of Oregon as a destination rebounded during 1851, when those

---

[66]Hart, Diaries, 6 June 1852, BYU Library.

[67]Stockton, The Trail of the Covered Wagon, 1929, with the permission of J. P. Kirkpatrick.

[68]Clark, "Overland to the Gold Fields," 23 May and 23 June 1852, 240, 259.

headed for the Pacific Northwest outnumbered those going to California by more than three to one. The margin reversed the next year when Californians, as they were known, outnumbered Oregonians by five to one, but the 10,000 sojourners who headed for the Columbia River in 1852 more than matched the total number of Oregon-bound pilgrims during the previous three years of the gold rush.

The season began with acts of intimidation and violence between overlanders and the Natives. A particularly brutal conflict broke out at a bridge over Shell Creek on the Council Bluffs Road when "about 200 Pawnees assembled to make Emigrants pay them Oxen & Provisions for crossing the little Bridge, one that was made by some of the first emigrants," I. Franklin recalled. Some of his companions wanted to pay the toll, but Franklin and another hothead warned the toll keepers that if "they did not leave that we could shoot them. It made them only laugh." Angered, Franklin told his comrade "we had better commence on them." He and seven men "run up to the Bridge & opened out on them." He shot down the chief; the others "let right in on them and followed them untill they crossed the River which they did in a hurry. We kill[ed] three & wounded 4," he boasted. The Pawnees injured one emigrant, while some of the "hands acted the real cowards." Franklin claimed the Pawnees had robbed "several trains before us, but none that we could hear of afterwards. All the other tribes were perfectly friendly with us all the way through."[69]

West of the Elkhorn River, sixteen-year-old William Waters's small party came upon a large Indian camp, whose men quickly surrounded the train's teams and loose cattle. "They informed us that their wives & children were starving, and they must have a cow," he recalled exactly four years later. "We offered them provisions of every description, but they positively refused them all." Despite the odds, the nervous emigrants brandished their weapons in a failed attempt to intimidate the young warriors. "They were conscious of their superiority in numbers & strength, and seemed to laugh at our attempt to frighten them." Four or five Indians singled out an armed man, ready to kill everyone "with their arrows, & hatchets" should anyone open fire. The approach of a large train defused the confrontation: the Indians filled a cow with arrows and let the emigrants proceed. "If they had not seen the train coming up, they would have slain all of them in a short time," Waters believed. "I wished to be armed and meet each of them, in open fields, and spilled their foul blood upon the barren plain, & left their bodies to the howling wolf."[70]

Emigrants dispatched each other almost as often as they killed Indians. Near the last crossing of the North Platte, John T. Kerns saw a notice of a man who had been hanged for murder and robbery, "the fifth case of murder on the way." The grim notice read, "Dried beef for sale, wholesale or retail." At the ferry a

---

[69]Franklin to Langsdorf, 26 August 1852, in Letters, 1852–1853, Oregon State Historical Society.

[70]Waters, Private Journal, 9 May 1856, courtesy Stafford Hazelett.

man drowned while swimming horses across the swollen river. The next day his party passed six graves, and two days later, eleven more. "Two of them were close together," Kerns wrote, "one was hung for murdering the other."[71]

As usual, many trains did not decide on their final destination until they reached South Pass or the last parting of the trails at Raft River. After a general shaking of hands, William Hart's train broke up, and as the wagons bound for Oregon "moved away from us we all joined heartily in three cheers. They immediately answered us and we wound up by the single cheer that signified to them our good wishes for their safe journey." The party reached the Willamette Valley "destitute of almost everything, with only one wagon containing all the women & children and the single men had walked ahead the last 100 miles or more without provisions to procure relief for the balance," Hart wrote. "The origin of their distress was the death of their cattle from scarcity of feed & consequent inability to haul provisions."[72] The journals confirm the massive death toll among teams on the Snake River Valley's "barren, deserted, burnt-to-death waste," a country John T. Kerns called "as poor as Job's old turkey."[73] Not everyone complained of the challenges of the road, at least before reaching its end. "I never enjoyed a trip as well in all my life as has also my family," wrote Dillis V. Mason from Great Salt Lake City. "Our children are as healthy and hearty as I ever saw. Hanna particularly who was always unhealthy looks as red and fresh as if she never was sick."[74]

At the Raft River, William Thompson's company held a council and took a vote, which produced "a majority for Oregon, and association and friendship being stronger than mere individual preference, all moved out on the Oregon road." The real trials began on the Snake River. "From some cause, not then understood, our oxen began to die. The best and fattest died first, often two and three in one camp. Cows were drawn into the yoke and the journey resumed," he recalled. His train began the inevitable process of abandoning supplies and property. "Wagons loaded with stores and provisions were driven to the side of the road and an invitation written with charcoal for all to help themselves." The Indians, he charged, were surly and insolent. "Gradually a gloom settled over all. No more of laughter, of dancing and song. And faster and faster the oxen died." Dead and decaying cattle made campsites almost unbearable. "And then the terrible mountains of which we had heard so much were before us. Would we ever reach the settlements? This was a question that began to prey upon the minds of many." A few young men went ahead on foot, but many despaired of ever reaching the promised land. The

---

[71] Kerns, "Journal of Crossing the Plains," 26 June to 1 July 1852, 167–68.

[72] Hart, Diaries, 14 July 1852, BYU Library, 119–20.

[73] Kerns, "Journal of Crossing the Plains," 28 July, 13 August 1852, 174, 177.

[74] Mason to Dear Father & Mother, 27 July 1852, Mattes Library.

memory of "the wreck and desolation that lined the poisoned banks" of the Snake River haunted Thompson until the end of his days.[75]

A few trains, like Isaac Constant's, traded the frying pan for the fire and took the Southern Route (Applegate Trail) to Oregon. For most the Cascade Range remained the Oregon Trail's most daunting challenge, and it proved too much for some. At The Dalles "several women of our party who had stood the hardships of the long journey wonderfully well gave out and died almost in sight of the promised land," James Bushnell recalled.[76] Those who could afford it booked passage on sailing packets and braved the narrows of the Columbia, but many overlanders sent their livestock over the Barlow Road and built rafts to transport their wagons down the Columbia. Others tackled the road directly. "Wee struck out across the Cascade mountains and was in the mountains 10 days," wrote Philemon D. Morriss at the end of his trek. "It was a bad time but got threw safe."[77]

The rough and difficult Barlow Road had grown no smoother or easier during the six years since it opened. "The Cascade Mountain may be termed the Terror and Laurel Hill the Terror of Terrors, of the Emigrant," wrote William Byers.[78] Harriet Scott Palmer recalled how hard it was to descend Laurel Hill at the end of an exhausting overland trek. "Oh that steep road! I know it was fully a mile long. We had to chain the wagon wheels and slide the wagons down the rutty, rocky road," she remembered. "My aunt Martha lost one of her remaining shoes, it rolled down the mountainside. I can hear her now as she called out in her despair, 'Oh, me shoe, me shoe! How can I ever get along?' So she wore one shoe and one moccasin the rest of the journey." After Harriet's sister fell and rolled down the hill, Uncle Levi said, "Maggie, ain't this the damndest place you ever saw?" The Scott family heard the first sign of civilization at Philip Foster's farm—a rooster crowing on a rail fence. "Oh, how we all cried," Palmer remembered. "There we stood, a travel-worn, weary, heart and homesick group, crying over a rooster crowing."[79]

Oregon remained a land with all the promise and appeal of Eden. Nearing the end of the trail in September, Enoch Conyers looked back at his safe passage through "The Devil's Gate" and seeing "a great many of his works while reviewing his grand estate." Now, on the western slope of the Cascades, he had the pleasure of driving his team "over the old man's backbone. That is, 'The Devil's Backbone' "—the divide between the Sandy River and the Little Sandy. "Here we will leave the old man's carcass to be wet with the mists of an Oregon winter," Conyers wrote. That night his company made bread from the last of their flour and

[75]Thompson, *Reminiscences of a Pioneer,* 8–9.
[76]Bushnell, The Narrative.
[77]Morriss, Diary, 5 September 1852, End of the Oregon Trail Interpretive Center.
[78]Byers, "Oregon Odyssey," 1 October 1852, 3:23.

ate their last meat: "in fact, we are about out of everything eatable." He pondered the hungry crowd Oregonians would have to feed during the coming winter, "and the great majority of them have no money." The next morning his party reached Foster's farm, where they "engaged dinner at the house at the rate of fifty cents per meal. Our dinner consisted of hot biscuits, cold slaw, fresh beefsteak, and boiled potatoes, served with hot coffee or tea," Conyers wrote. "This meal tasted very good and sweet to us after our long trip of five months across the continent with an ox team, yet we considered it poor fare for the price."[80] Americans have always been hard to please.

ALL ALONG THE ROAD: TRADING POSTS

When the gold rush began, it was possible to count the number of trading post between the Missouri and the Pacific on two hands—the fur company forts of Laramie, Hall, and Boise; and a few scattered independent operators such as Joseph E. Robidoux at Scotts Bluff, Bridger and Vasquez on Blacks Fork, and Pegleg Smith on Bear River. Four years later small trading stations were scattered from the Platte to the Pacific offering everything from Indian goods, to blacksmith services, to what Abigail Scott called "a bottle of oh, be joyful."[81] Edmund Cavileer Hinde found trading stations "started all along the road" over the Sierra; Daniel Budd described "near a hundred trading posts" in Carson Valley alone.[82] The prospect of profiting from the overland trade made parts of the road west look like a canvas strip mall. Frontier entrepreneurs lined the trail with huts, tents, hotels, groggeries, ferries, bridges, and gambling hells from beginning to end.

The most successful overland traders, notably John Owen, Seth Ward, and William Carter, began their careers as army sutlers. Owen came west with the Mounted Riflemen to serve at Cantonment Loring. When the troops marched to Oregon in May 1850, Owen led a trading party north to the Bitterroot Valley, where he acquired seventy horses "with which he returned and met the Emigration on the route and having also a Travelling Forge and Blacksmith, and selling liquor," reported Richard Grant. Owen told Grant he cleared $15,000 that summer. He used the profits to mount an even larger commercial foray into Salish and Kootenai country, where he purchased Saint Mary's Mission from the Jesuits for $250 and established a permanent trading post.[83]

₇₉Palmer, *Crossing over the Great Plains*, 8.

₈₀Conyers, "Diary," 22, 23 September 1852.

₈₁Quoted in Holmes, *Covered Wagon Women*, 5:128n50.

₈₂Hinde, *Journal*, 22 July 1850, 39; Budd, Journal, 18 August 1852, Mattes Library.

₈₃Thrapp, *Encyclopedia of Frontier Biography*, 2:1097; Grant to Simpson, Fort Hall, 31 January 1851, HBC Archives, D.5/30, 183–85.

The gold rush drove an explosive proliferation of such enterprises. The American Fur Company sent veteran fur-trader Andrew Drips to run their new post at Scotts Bluff.[84] At the Big Blue River ferry, Cyrus Phillips was "surprised to find a store where they keep Pies Ginger Bread &C. I never liked Ginger Bread before but after being in camp so long I thought it the best of eating & there is no use talking about pies." Phillips found French traders clustered around Laramie, and other sojourners described an extensive operation at the North Platte's upper ferry. Phillips mentioned a "trading post & Blacksmiths shop on Willow creek" not far from South Pass, and about halfway down the dusty Humboldt road he "found a trading post—Flour 20¢ Malasses $1.50 of pr quart [and] other things in proportion. It seems that men from California have no hearts whatever." At Humboldt Lake "a grocery & Bakery" now serviced the emigration, while on the Forty-mile desert Phillips passed "trading posts every 2 miles where there was water for sale at 50¢ per gallon." At the first of these stations, Phillips "payed 1$ pr gallon for water which was brought 30 miles across the desert & was glad to get it at that price." At the end of the ordeal, Phillips wrote, "there is nothing that would induce me to travel down the Humbolt again with Ox teams or anything but a rail Road." That revolution, too, was on its way.[85]

By 1852 a dozen outposts associated with ferry operations lined Green River, while a flock of traders, including the Grant family, based their operations at Soda Springs. Caroline Richardson found a trading station at the middle of the Forty-mile Desert, one twenty-one miles from the sink, and a second twelve miles from Carson River. "Came out to what is called rag town," she wrote, "a very appropriate name as it is built of tents and wagon covers." She saw "a great many new graves" and entrepreneurs selling pies for six bits a pound and meals for a dollar.[86]

A closer look at this phenomenon reveals that the location of such posts would dramatically influence the evolution of the overland trail. The creation of new trading stations and trails—notably on the Seminoe, Kinney, and Nobles routes—casts light on what drove the overland trail's relentless advance and its constant generation of new tentacles.

West of Devils Gate, travelers saw a new trading station take shape right next to the trail. "We passed here a trading post, they kept quite an assortment of goods, which were all brought from St. Louis; they had enormous waggons, serving as a kind of shop, & store house," Lodisa Frizzell wrote in June. The traders had brought eight tons of freight in each wagon and recruited their teams on secret pastures not far from Devils Gate. "Some of them were fat, for here the grass was

[84]Mattes, *Platte River Road Narratives*, 275.

[85]Phillips, Diary, 15 May, 25 June, 11, 13, 15, and 18 August 1852, BYU Library.

[86]Richardson, Journal, 31 August 1852, Bancroft Library, 168–69.

excellent; they offered them for sale, one of our company bought 3 yoke," for $45 to $60 dollars per yoke, Frizzell wrote. "This is a romantic place, & a good place for a post, for there is [an] abundance of grass, & water; & some considerable pine & cedar timber on the mountains."[87]

Ten days later William Hart found "a trading shanty of brush wood and canvass belonging to a French man who had established himself here to buy furs of the Indians, and weakly and sickly stock of the emigrants and to sell provisions to those who needed." He appeared to be doing a good business and kept an Indian herding "his cattle on a little pasture that he had discovered a few miles off," which quickly restored the broken-down but valuable oxen. Hart's companions "succeeded in getting enough to buy a half gallon of brandy and two of them went to the frenchmans after it." His train celebrated the Fourth of July at a hidden grassland where "the ladies brought out a handsome flag composed of red, white, & blue stripes and patches taken from sundry garments supposed to form parts of female wearing apparel." A woman donated a sheet, another a skirt for the red stripes, while a third "ran to her tent and brought forth a blue jacket, saying: 'Here, take this, it will do for the field,'" wrote Enoch Conyers. The Stars and Stripes soon "floated in the breeze amidst the cheers and waving handkerchiefs of the entire party." They enjoyed a remarkable feast—"a fine set out of Antelope, roasted & stewed Prairie Fowl, [roasted & stewed] Smoked Beef, Bacon fried & boiled Dried apples & peaches, Rice Beans Bread & cupcakes with an ample supply of Tea & Coffee and Bean Soup," Hart wrote. Conyers said dessert included pound cake, fruit cake, jelly cake, peach pie, apple pie, strawberry pie, custard pie, what he called Sweetwater Mountain Cake, and "a fine lot of Sweetwater Mountain ice cream." The train had a little too much firewater, but it was "a Fourth of July on the plains never to be forgotten."[88]

Within a month, the traders' shanty at Devils Gate had evolved into a home. "Passed a house where a trader lived. He had everything to sell that emigrants want—two ladies here," wrote Chloe Terry.[89] By June 1853 a full-fledged trading post was under construction: "a very fine hewed log house built in a square [with] three sides being built." The fort was about 120 feet long, and as one brother noted, "quite a number of French about here."[90] Late that summer James Farmer found "about 10 houses all neatly built of wood" located a short distance west of Devils Gate.[91] Mary Burrell thought the landmark was "a Devilish Gate in earnest" when

[87]Frizzell, *Across the Plains,* 21 June 1852, 27–28.

[88]Hart, Diaries, 2 to 4 July 1852, BYU Library, 101–10; Conyers, "Diary," 2 to 4 July 1852.

[89]Terry, Diary, 4 August 1852, Washington State Historical Society. Punctuation added.

[90]Dinwiddie, "Overland from Indiana to Oregon," 23 June 1853, 8.

[91]Farmer, Journal, 4 September 1853, Collection of Mormon Diaries, Library of Congress.

she passed in June 1854 and camped near the post, which she called "a blacksmith shop quite an establishment. Hewed logs & shingled with mud."[92]

Archambault's Fort, as the *St. Joseph Gazette* called the post on 28 April 1852, was a partnership between Charles Lajeunesse, "dit Simond (Simino)," and Auguste Archambault, guide of the Stansbury Expedition and chief promoter of the Hastings Cutoff in 1850. In 1855 Mormon apostle Erastus Snow mentioned "Seminoe's Fort," the station's modern name. Enoch Conyer identified the French trader at Devils Gate as Schambau, who "was building a trading post near the Devil's Gate with timber hauled from the mountains about six miles distant." When Joseph Terrell abandoned his wagon at Devils Gate, he opened a store and sold his provisions, clothing, and gear "in opposition to Archambeaux, the trapper and trader, with Indian wife." No one mentioned his partner, whose nickname was spelled variously as Seminoe, Siminoes, Simmeno, Semineau, Semenole, Seminole, Siminoes, and Sendriose. The entire Lajeunesse clan had long experience in the fur trade and by 1823 Charles was already a skilled interpreter. His younger brother, Basil Cimineau, was said to be Frémont's favorite man. Charles won the nickname "Bad Hand" after ramming his arm down a bear's throat as a companion killed the beast. Lajeunesse was involved with overland trade at Fort Bridger as early as 1843, when he traveled up the Sweetwater with Joseph Chiles's train.[93]

No journalists mentioned Charles Lajeunesse in 1852 at Fort Seminoe, perhaps because he collected fees to guide trains to South Pass over "the track to avoid rocky ridges" now known as the Seminoe Cutoff. The trail was already in use, for Walker's lost overland guide mentioned it in 1853, when George Whitworth said the road was so "indefinite and not little used that we missed it."[94] The cutoff had several advantages, for it bypassed the last four crossings of the Sweetwater and avoided the hard climb up Rocky Ridge. Like other alternates, it might (or might not) have offered better forage, but it was notoriously dry. The forty-mile trace left the main trail about six miles beyond Ice Spring and followed Warm Springs Creek southwest to the Warm Springs, "one of the many alkaline pans which lie scattered over the face of the country," Richard Burton noted.[95] Fourteen miles west of Warm Springs, Seminoe's route crossed the Antelope Hills to Antelope Springs, passed Wagon Tire Spring and Upper Mormon Spring, touched the Sweetwater near its confluence with Rock Creek, and connected to the Sweetwater's fifth and ninth crossings or skirted Oregon Slough to rejoin the main trail about five miles east of South Pass.[96]

---

[92]Burrell, "Council Bluffs to California," 9 June 1854, 238.

[93]"Our Correspondence," *Deseret News,* 5 September 1855, 208; Conyers, "Diary," 2 July 1852; Terrell, "Overland Trip to California," 83; Unruh, *The Plains Across,* 487n62; Dale L. Morgan, in Anderson, *The Rocky Mountain Journals,* 334.

[94]Whitworth, Diary, 21 July 1853, Whitworth College Archives.

[95]Burton, *The City of the Saints,* 158, 174–75.

[96]The modern names of these springs are shown on the USGS South Pass 1:100,000 quadrangle.

Farther west, the Sublette Cutoff between the Big Sandy and Green River was many miles shorter than the road to Fort Bridger, but the suffering its fifty waterless miles inflicted on livestock cried out for a less devastating route. The metamorphosing trail created several solutions. The Kinney Cutoff—also known as the Kenney, Kinne, Kennie, McKinze, and even Kain Cutoff—appeared somewhat mysteriously in 1852. By June overlanders on the Fort Bridger Road knew about a shortcut from the bend of the Big Sandy to "Kinneys Ferry." No one identified Kinney, but Charles Kinney, an old mountaineer, is the most likely candidate.[97] When she "came on kinys cut off" in early July, Caroline Richardson found it "not a very plain road over the bluffs at the right hand," suggesting both its recent creation and greatest attraction: "This road cuts off a piece of desart and also an interval of fifty miles without water."[98] Solomon Kingery "took Kinneys cutt off," a new road "that followes the Salt Lake road 34 miles turnes to the right escapes the Desert & comes in to the fort Hall road again in 75 miles." The trail initially followed the old Oregon and Mormon trails to four or five miles beyond the Big Sandy, where it headed directly west to Green River and Kinneys Ferry, creating better way to cross the Little Colorado Desert south of the Sublette Cutoff. If Kinney's plan was to make money with his ferry operation, it worked: Kingery found "about 200 teams waiting to get across" at the rate of seven dollars each.[99]

From the big bend of the Sandy to the junction "of Kinne's Cut off with the Salt Lake road is four miles—Road Sandy Some. Kinne's Cut off Saves Crossing all of the 54 mile desert, except 12 miles, it unites with Subletts cut off at or near Greene river," the Bradleys reported in June 1852. "It is 12 miles from the above mentioned junction to Greene River, & this 12 miles is all of the Desert that the road crosses."[100] After ascending the Green, the trail crossed the river where men named Robinson, Holden, Dodge, Case, and Kinney ran ferries at what Richard Hickman called "the middle ferry on Green River."[101] The trail went up the valley of Slate Creek to join the last stretch of the Sublette at Rocky Gap. From a mile away atop a long hill with a very fine view, Origen Thomson could see "the wagons on Sublet's road, creeping along on the side of what appeared to be a perpendicular hill."[102]

West of South Pass, Enoch Conyer chose to try "Kinney's cut-off for Fort Hall." Twelve miles after crossing the Green, Conyers's train "left the river to our right and came five miles to Slate Creek, where we were obliged to water our cattle

[97]William I. Appleby to Brigham Young, 24 June 1854, Brigham Young Collection, LDS Archives.

[98]Richardson, Journal, 2 July 1852, Bancroft Library, 92.

[99]Kingery, Overland Letters, 22 June 1852, Beinecke Library.

[100]Bradley and Bradley, Daily Journal, 23 June 1852, Beinecke Library, 59–60.

[101]Hickman, "Dick's Works," 27 June 1852, 171.

[102]Thomson, *Crossing the Plains,* 13 July 1852, 64. For the route, see Decker, "Variants of the Slate Creek Cutoff," 30–35.

from our buckets. We then came on seven miles, where we struck Slate Creek again, followed it up three miles and crossed." His party camped for the night, finding "Slate Creek water is excellent" and the grass good, but "Roads today very rough and hilly." Twenty miles farther and "the Kinney and Sublett cut-offs join. Just before we arrived at Sublett's cut-off we had to descend a very steep hill about half a mile long." All in all Conyer was pleased with the route: "Grass is very good, and in fact the grass is getting much better. Plenty of sagebrush for wood. The road today has been very bad rough and narrow. Kinney's cut-off is thirty-three miles nearer than Sublett's cut-off and a much better road." Three months and 850 miles later, Conyers met an enterprising emigrant on the Barlow Road who had "sold his outfit and purchased a supply of the necessaries of life and, returning to this place, had set up a small trading post for the benefit (?) of the poor emigrant." The man complained that every trader he met on the road west "skinned us emigrants for all we were worth, and now I have come back here to skin all the balance of the emigrants."[103]

Few emigrants reached the end of the trail with a whole skin. They could buy a hundred pounds of flour for $25 at Fort Laramie, but beyond South Pass, the traditional outposts had practically nothing to offer them. Pegleg Smith had forsaken his Shoshone bride and Bear River trading stations. Enoch Conyer found a sergeant's guard at Fort Hall watching over a hundred or so rotting government wagons. Travelers "who were short of provisions purchased a few necessary articles of food at this place, but it was dealt out very sparingly." Christian Kauffman said the sole Frenchman "and a lot of Indians" he met at Fort Hall had nothing to sell but sugar at 8 cents per pound, while at Fort Boise she "found nothing but tobacco."[104] Tosten Stabæk's party bought fifty pounds of flour from a man from Salt Lake, while Francis Sawyer "traded a string of beads to an Indian boy for some fish," and ate them for supper on the Fourth of July.[105]

Besides being a bustling commercial site in 1852, Soda Springs witnessed its usual share of hijinks. Reuben Doyle wagered he could stop the flow of Steamboat Spring by sitting on it. "He waited until the water began to recede, then took off his pants and seated himself on the crevice," Enoch Conyers wrote. He did not have to wait long for the eruption and was soon "bobbing up and down like a cork." Doyle finally gave up, saying, "Boys, there is no use trying to hold the devil down. It can't be did, for the more weight you put on the more the devil churns me. I am now pounded into a beefsteak."[106]

---

[103] Conyers, "Diary," 11, 16 July, 15 September 1852.

[104] Ibid., 26 July 1852; Kauffman, "Letter," 18 November 1852, 22–23.

[105] Stabæk, "An Account of a Journey"; Sawyer, "Kentucky to California," 103.

[106] Conyers, "Diary," 22 July 1852.

ONE WOMAN'S WEST:
CHLOE ANN TERRY AND THE WONDERFUL WAY TO OREGON

Statistics, contemporary opinion, and a vast historical record shed light on the over-land experience, but nothing conveys the reality of crossing the plains as well as the story of someone who made the trek. An abstract discussion of the hardships of the journey or the trail's toll on families is one thing, but appreciating the human cost is another. To comprehend whether women perceived this life-changing journey as an ordeal, an adventure, or both, it helps to see it through one woman's eyes.

Born in upstate New York in 1827, Chloe Ann Terry left her home in Michigan for Oregon shortly after her twenty-fifth birthday. She traveled with her married sister, Caroline Phoebe Terry; and brother-in-law Dr. John Kellogg; sister-in-law Eliza Terry, wife of Chloe's brother Grove, who awaited his family in Oregon; Eliza's children, "little Marie & Florence"; her cousin Rachel; and her single brother, Charles Townsend Terry: the complexity of her extended family defies analysis. To help handle their wagon and omnibus, the family hired a teamster named Edward or Edwin. Eliza Ann Woodard was traveling with "Grand Ma Woodard," perhaps Chloe's maternal grandmother. Although Chloe used a cane all her life, "she was very active, a beautiful seamstress and also men's tailor," noted her nephew, George A. Kellogg, the Seattle history teacher who donated her journal to the University of Washington. Terry's lively diary contains ample evidence of formidable domestic skills and her astonishing capacity for work but no hint of any disability.[107]

Late one April evening, after a pleasant day save for an afternoon snow squall, Chloe Terry began her journal on the Illinois prairie. "It has commensed raining & blowing & I'm off to bed," she wrote. The family ferried the Mississippi at Fulton "& landed in Ioway" on 24 April. They headed west on a road crowded with more than one "drove of Californians," ferried the Wapsipinicon, and paused near Tipton "to get rested & get recruited" on a friend's farm. At least the men and animals rested. "But Oh I must note down what us girls has performed." The women cared for three babies, "did some sewing & washing," and baked thirty-one loaves of bread and some pastry. Her family did not intend to starve as long as they traveled where folks lived. "Would you kind reader?" Terry asked. The little band spent a week modifying its wagons and preparing for the trek. The day before they left she baked thirty-five loaves of bread. "We dry our bread after we bake it & then it will keep a long time & for my recreation to day it is ironing a lot of clothes," she said. They set out Friday, 7 May, in company with families named Olds, Wallace,

---

[107]Terry, Diary, 1852, Washington State Historical Society. This section relies on Kay Threlkeld's transcription, but for readability, I inserted punctuation and corrected obvious typos and confusing spelling.

Perkins, and Derby. "There is quite a long string of us," she wrote, "13 wagons & twice as many teems." The next day Dr. Kellogg almost died while unloading his team at the Cedar River ferry.

Despite Chloe Ann's high spirits, ill health plagued the entire company—she fell victim to various maladies herself. Over the course of the trek, she reported incidents of headache, ague, smallpox, cholera, dysentery, "dierea," toothache, headache, "billous fever," and mental breakdown. "It seems that we shall all die to gether," she mourned. The doctor had a boil, while her brother Charles was quite sick "& it is verry bad riding in the wagon & be sick," she wrote. "I have to be the teemster moste of the day. It is hard work." After crossing the Iowa River, they passed "through the country whare the Smallpox is." On 12 May Mrs. Olds "presented to the crowd with a young son. However we did our washing, baking &c. They have 5 girls & no boys so the littel fellow is a welcome guest." Two nights later it rained so hard that "we wer all wet & drownded out," Terry reported. "That was going to Oregon but it was all for the best perhaps. It give us a good colde watter sweet." On Saturday night the little band circled its eleven wagons. "The men put the ends of each wagon tonng on the back end of the next wagon to keep out intruders."

Lack of religion, especially the general disregard for the Sabbath, seemed part and parcel of an overland trek. "It is sunday once mor but it does not seem much like it, because we have traveld all day," Terry mourned. "Went 12 miles but when we are with Romans we are obliged to do as they do." Near the end of the trail she complained, "We are obliged to labor on Sunday nearly as much as any day." She never mentioned praying, and unlike many overland journals, hers contains only one reference to preaching: "Nancy A Oldes has the ague & she is out of her head. She preaches verry well but she is a universalest I think."

Terry diligently noted the wagons slogging through the cold and mud of spring. "I cannot find time to write as I would like. When I do I have to do it in a hurry, taking care of the children perhaps crying [and] knocking my elbow or worse," she observed. "I almost think it is rather of an undertaking to go to Oregon." While crossing the treeless prairies to Council Bluffs, her sister Caroline "went to jump out of the wagon. Her foot sliped & She fell. The forewheel ran over her but She was not hurt but little. We exspected she was almost killed but it lucky she was not. We pass dead horses every day & rite by the road we passed 8 newly made graves." After Cousin Rachel joined the party near Council Bluffs "us girls tride to clime one of the Bluffs but did not succead. Only got up to the first tier it being so steepe. We wanted to be on the hightest, in doing so we thought we might touch the moon." As June began the party ferried the roiling Missouri, its muddy waters covered with a scum that looked like soapsuds.

At the ferry, they saw their first Indians, who Terry thought followed the train. "They are headous loocking creatures," she wrote. "I am verry affraid of them." The train now put as many as eight men on guard duty each night. The next day Omahas, armed bows, arrows, and three rifles, appeared to collect a toll at the bridge over Papillion Creek. "Moste of the men paid them for crossing." Those who refused angered the Indians, who tried to stop the teams and showed signs of fight. Wild rumors suggested that the emigrants would have to battle five hundred angry Natives at Shell Creek, and "the women all dread it verry much," Terry reported. "We ate dinner as usual & arived at Shell Creek, about 3 oclock & how many Indians do you think we saw?" she asked. "Not one." That morning the Wallace brothers had tried to dry out a barrel of wet powder and ignited it, almost blowing themselves up, suggesting once again that an army of savages could never match the danger Christian emigrants posed to themselves. "They loocked horrid," Terry said. The party would not see another Indian until it reached Fort Laramie. "We do not see any Indians any more nor do we see the Buffalow yet," she wrote as June wore on. "The emigration bein so great keeps them fritend away over the bluffs."

They did see fresh graves, five at Loup Fork and seven new burials near Prairie Creek. As sickness swept the party, they counted thirteen graves on 16 June. The next day Chloe tallied the sick: Cousin Rachel was very ill; her brother Charles had dysentery. "Mr Olds is sick & moste all are complaining. I am afraid we are all going to be sick," she wrote. A week later they passed fifteen graves "in the most sickly part of the country." Her count reported a record on 25 June. "We have passed 23 new graves today," she recorded. "It seems lonesome to see so many." One afternoon the train came upon a party burying its dead. "It was a married lady 16 years olde," Chloe noted. "Today we have passed 20 graves. All dide this Monnth & the last of May. But thou hath all seasons for thy own, O death." Business boomed for Dr. Kellogg as travelers with sick friends or loved ones came to seek his services for all manner of troubles. As they circled the wagons one evening "a gentlemen came riding up & wanted Doct for one of his company had just been shot in the arm (a lady I believe)," she wrote. "He went but the wound was not mortal." On at least one occasion Kellogg sold a large amount of medicine. As June ended, Chloe quit counting tombstones: "We have passed quite a number of graves as usual."

The company consisted of eighteen wagons and twenty-eight men on 8 June. The men met that evening to elect new officers and, apparently, indulge in other male pastimes. "I believe they are having fun. I should think for they laught so heartily," Chloe wrote. Caroline had been very sick and Dr. Kellogg bought some medicine "to give her a spirit sweet & this afternoon she is some better." Chloe's recreation that warm day was ironing a lot of clothes, but she had fun of her own sampling the "spirit sweet" and perhaps too much of it, for she woke up the next

morning with a very bad headache. She took more medicine to get rid of it. Altogether she was reassured. "We have such a large company I feel perfectly safe on
account of Indians." Life was looking better. "I like this mode of traveling verry
well, much better than what I thout for I enjoy myself much," she concluded. "We
are all quite lively. There is 12 young gentelmen & 7 young ladies which makes it
verry plesint." Chloe Terry's episodic reports reflect how rapidly wagon parties
changed. By mid-July her train consisted of seven husbands and eleven bachelors,
ten married and seven single women from fifteen to twenty years of age, twelve
children, thirty-four head of cattle, fourteen horses, thirteen wagons, and four
tents. She would learn "small companies are the plesentest."

     After the Terry wagons passed Fort Laramie in mid-July, they met friendly and
well-dressed Lakotas and Crows eager to trade ponies, lassoes, and moccasins
for an old skirt or bed quilt. Near a North Platte ferry run by the Crow Nation,
three Indian women and two men asked permission to camp near the train. They
"pitched their tent 4 rods back of ours then staked there ponys. I do not think
any one entertained a fear as to the safety of themselfs after they had prepared
everything for the night," wrote Chloe, who stayed up late doing chores. She
occasionally took a peek at the tent. "They appeared perfectly happy while I felt
perfectly safe as to that matter." Such encounters helped dissipate the irrational
fear women like Terry brought with them. As the train approached the Umatilla
Valley "our attention was attracted by an Indian coming up the hill on horseback.
He turned out his pony to feed & then came up to our tent." This friendly, well-
dressed, and "rather an elderly loocking person" shook hands with Dr. Kellogg,
who offered him a seat on an improvised chair—a board laid across the washtub.
The man said he was sick, and after supper the doctor "gave him a bitter dose. He
took it without a murmur." The visitor described the Whitman killings of 1847.
"Said they was bad Ciouse [Cayuse] & they were hung. By his signs & motions we
could understand him very well," Chloe wrote. The Indian stayed the night.

     "I sometimes think that we will all be sick and die on the plains but my hope is
pretty large," Terry wrote in early July. "I hope always for the best." It was not to
be. Due to their continual ill health, the families traveled slowly, but it did little
good. Chloe's sister-in-law Eliza awoke on the Fourth of July and felt so much
better "she washed & dressed Maria but she overdone & brought on the fever & has
been quite sick all day." Care of the toddler, Chloe's niece Maria, fell to her young
and attentive aunt. One morning in the Black Hills, the restless child awakened
Chloe, "but as usual I sung her to sleep." She covered her up and dressed. "I was
the first up in the camp of the ladies," she wrote, "for we had our sick to take care
of besides our work & the camp was in considerable haste to get an early start."
Terry had breakfast ready when her sister Caroline told her that Maria was failing.

"I went in to see her & she appeard as if she was dieing & indeede the little sufferer was. She dide at 9 oclock, died without a strugle or a groan, mearly breathed shorter & shorter untill the last." Her aunts laid out the child's body and carried it to her mother. Eliza "said she loocked like a little doll & shurely she did. She was a pretty corps. I never saw her loock so lovely before, & by 12 oclock little Maria was sleeping in the grave with this incription at the head:

Maria R Terry
died July the 20/1852
aged 2 years 5 months & 17 days

"Eliza gave her up with great composure," Chloe observed. "Perhaps more so on account of her own lingering illness." The train set out at one o'clock, and her husband stopped the family wagon at Maria's grave to let Eliza see where the child was sleeping on a nice little rise of ground near another burial. "Eliza sat up in bed to loock at the grave. She said it was a pretty little one, that the letters wer so pretty & she said it loocked so pretty." Even in the wilderness the time's elaborate rituals of death provided some small comfort. "I could not beare to leve ltttle Maria," Chloe wrote. "It seemed so strange to come of[f] & not have her with us, but the little sufferer is better of[f], she is out of her troubels in this wourld." The wagons traveled until almost sunset and camped by a spring of cool water.

After her daughter's death, Eliza began taking quinine "to get up vitality," although Kellogg's prescription did little to ease her wracking fever. "I think it is the hardest work I ever did to take care of the sick & we have to be up so much nights," Chloe wrote. The party's hunters provided some relief the next day when they shot a young buffalo. She enjoyed a "verry fat & tender" cut of bison for breakfast. "I never ate such nice steak," Terry commented. "It was delitious." A second bison—"a monster by the tell[ing]"—became a buffalo potpie at dinner. But reality intruded on her diary's bright tone. "Eliza is no better," she wrote. "I am almost tired out & sick." During the long night Grandma said Eliza "was dying for her hands wer verry colde & feet too." The doctor agreed.

To everyone's surprise, Eliza Terry rallied, but to Chloe's despair, another dear friend named Eliza left the train when her relatives decided its slow pace would not leave enough provisions to get them through. "They started about 9 o'clock with long faces & sad countenances," Chloe wrote. She especially regretted saying goodbye to Eliza Ann Woodard. "She is so amiable so good natured. She is in every sense of the word a dear good girl. I miss her company very much indeede." Soon, Dr. Kellogg "said he would not move Eliza this time until she was perfectly able to ride but circumstances alter cases sometimes. He said if we stay here alone we are endangering all our lives & he has swung up his hammock in the wagon for Eliza." The party pressed on.

The distraught diarist did not record the death of her sister-in-law Eliza sometime toward the end of July. Instead, Chloe eloquently described the scenery. From
a high hill above the North Platte, Terry looked at the river valley and its canyons.
"The prospect was as natural as it was perfect. The undulations of the landscape
rose into hight towering bluffs & hills & sank at intervals into delightful valleys.
Far down the precipice was the Platt whose winding way dashe[d] along by the
inconstant tide, whose banks were borded with beautiful green trees. Indeede it
was a romantic place," she rhapsodized. "In the States we would of went miles to
see such choice scenery. Everything was calculated to please the eye & excite the
fancy." The view of the Blue Mountains "was delightful. It was nature's own choice
scenery, our folks observed what a beautiful scene it was, what a perfect prospect,"
as natural as it was perfect. On the plains Chloe wrote a paean to morning:

> Morning is the lovliest part of the day I think, tis then the birds carole fourth there sweet-
> est songs in the earliest hours of day; They seem to catch the loveliness of morning beauty
> & show a liveness which those beauties inspire. When the early day beams shine on the
> crystal dew drop not only that but all nature loocks gayest. Then the grass loocks greenest
> on these plains that I have heard so much about when I was in the States. Flowers [show]
> there richest colors & then they emit there sweetes fragrance. Then the air is purist, the
> thoughts most active, the mind moste clear & ready to drink in the loveliness that glows
> in the smileing fase of morning.

The party crossed South Pass on 9 August, nooned at "Specfick Springs," and
reached the Green River five days later, where Chloe Ann Terry stopped writing
for almost two months. During the interval her train climbed over the Bear River
Divide, visited Soda Springs, and made the exhausting trek down the Snake River.
By 3 October, they had overtaken the Woodards and were camped on the Powder
River in Oregon. Terry's hard labor did not let up. "I have been all around to see
the sick & then returned home to go to work as hard as ever," she wrote. "I went
to washing. Caroline to baking & we are both almost sick but the work must be
done." The men, meanwhile, went hunting in the mountains.

Two days later the train camped in the Grande Ronde Valley. A nearby trading
station offered flour, sugar, coffee, and fresh beef by the pound at stiff prices, but
the Terry family made do with "sweetend water & hard bread" until Dr. Kellogg
broke down and bought five dollars' worth of beef at twenty-five cents a pound.
He returned with good news: Chloe's brother Grove was waiting for them with
supplies. "We got in to camp about 4 oclock & shurely our brother was here,"
she wrote. It was a bittersweet reunion: "It was a happy meeting & a sad one too
for we had no Eliza nor little Maria to present to him as we had anticipated we
would. Now they are both gone the way of all the earth." The women got up a
good supper with Grove Terry's provisions. "We all appeared quite cheerful as

we came round the table but there was a vacancy, a void for no Eliza was here. I felt that the happiness would have been so great. O how happy Grove would have been." They sat up late into the night visiting. The next day, Theresa Olds died.

The train had traveled so slowly that some members of its company were "muche afraid that we all would freeze to death when crossing these mountains," Chloe reported on 9 October. But they had beautiful weather in the Blue Mountains, and their measured pace had distinct benefits. "Grove says he did not expect we would get here with more than 2 or 3 teems & one wagon," he told the family, "but instead of that we have got them all & both wagons." They all now slept in the tent, for the only wagon that still had a cover was too heavily loaded to provide shelter at night.

The families were still a long ways from the settlements, but they began to see signs of civilization, notably a large frame house at the newly established Umatilla Indian Agency. Caroline and Chloe "went into one room & sat down quite awhile in some chairs (it is not very common to find them on this road)." Chloe saw the Columbia for the first time on 25 October. Eight days later her family reached The Dalles to find "a perfect jam on account of so many passengers & a great many sick ones." They waited for four days "in the midst of wagon tents & all in a huddle" to get a passage downriver aboard the "saile boat" *North American,* which did not embark until 9 November. "The sick are no better," Terry recorded grimly. "A childe died last night & there is more that cannot survive long by all appearances." An old gentleman perished, leaving his wife with six grandchildren whose parents had died on the road. At dawn two days later, Chloe was awakened on the boat "by the most horrid groans, cries & screams. Such agony that some person was in is beyond description." It was a mother sorrowing for her lost son. "He had been sick very much deranged & crazy. He got up & went out of the tent his mother asked him if some one should not go with him. He answered her in the negative & said he was almost well & could go alone as well. So he went, however he staid longer than usual his . . ." Here this charming journal ended abruptly before describing an apparent suicide.[108]

On 23 April 1853, at Colonel Isaac Ebey's home on Whidbey Island in the newly created Washington Territory, Chloe Ann Terry married a widower with two small daughters, Reuben Lowery Doyle, former editor of the *Keokuk Gate City.* Doyle, who had tried to staunch the flow of Steamboat Spring with his posterior the previous July, had already staked a claim and built a house on the island. "Uncle Doyle was a printer by trade and the best story teller I ever heard," his niece recalled. "Aunt Chloe took in sewing, and sewed for Mrs. U.S. Grant and

---

[108]Terry, Diary, 11 November 1852, Washington State Historical Society.

others," Alice Kellogg remembered. Doyle served in the territorial legislature in 1854 but remained an eccentric. He died on a second trip to his boyhood home in 1880 while riding the rails: the "old gentleman" jumped off a Central Pacific boxcar rolling into Ogden, Utah. A long tribute indicated Doyle was living in Seattle but said nothing about a widow. Mrs. Doyle moved to Seattle about 1872, a relative recalled, but whether she and Mr. Doyle lived together is not clear. When she died in 1911, Chloe Ann Terry Doyle was laid to rest on a Whidbey Island hillside beside her mother, brothers, and sister.[109]

SAND GLISTENING IN THEIR EYES: THE CALIFORNIA ROAD IN 1852

"With water scarce and feed scarcer," gold fever transformed not only California, but also the lands and waters of the arid West. "Owing to the great overland rush in 1852, there was much difficulty in securing feed for the teams," John Barber Parkinson complained. Exceptional rainfall had blessed the first years of mass migration, but the immense numbers of animals required to power the journey west devastated "the pasture ground and paradise of the buffalo." By 1852 "it was often necessary to drive the stock back from camp one, two, and even three or four miles, to find suitable grazing," Parkinson observed.[110] At Snake River Elizabeth Bedwell's train had to drive its cattle a mile to find water and "grass up a deep ravine to the south. Grazing short, roads rough and dusty."[111] The scarcity of grass killed untold animals, while the passage of thousands of wagons pounded the trails into dust. "Our place of encampment is a bed of sand to night," Caroline Richardson wrote at the Big Sandy Swales. "Our supper was seasoned with sand our beds filled with sand, our eyes with sand, and our tents are filld with sand. In fact, it is becoming an almost indispensable item with us," she added dryly.[112]

A host of challenges confronted travelers and depleted forage, notably insect infestations by Rocky Mountain locusts and the shield-backed katydids often called grasshoppers or Mormon crickets. "Grass hoppers go in droves & sweep the grass clean as they go," wrote Daniel Budd on the Hudspeth Cutoff. A similar wingless, dark brown, two-inch-long "bug" swarmed past "in droves by countless millions, so much so that first team through them often get frightened." As usual, accidents and violence haunted the crowded trails. At the North Platte Ferry, Budd reported, a little boy "fell out of a wagon got run over & broke both legs close to his body.

[109]Kellogg, "The Life of Dr. John Coe Kellogg"; Kellogg, notes in Terry diary; and "Reuben Lowery Doyle," obituary, *Puget Sound Weekly Courier,* 27 August 1880.

[110]Parkinson, "Memories of Early Wisconsin and the Gold Mines," 12.

[111]Bedwell, Journal of Road to Oregon, 22 August 1852, Mattes Library.

[112]Richardson, Journal, 30 June 1852, Bancroft Library, 89–90.

A Physician was close by & set them immediately. Sad affair. An Irishman killed by his wife & 2 Dutchmen. She has 1 child."[113]

The Fort Laramie treaty may have reduced it but did not stop conflicts between Plains Indians and emigrants. "The Indians will steal your stock if they can," observed Bertrand Cornell, "but there is not much danger of there hurting you for they are very afraid of the whites."[114] There were no attacks on emigrant trains over the usually bloody trail from Goose Creek to Carson Valley in 1852, an agent reported. What caused this drop in bloodshed? "The vast number of emigrants, on the road, and the disposition of some, to kill the Indians, had kept the Indians from the road," Jacob Holeman concluded.[115] More accurately, violence escalated as natural resources declined. Daniel Budd met a packer who had a particularly brutal encounter with a warrior on the Upper Humboldt. The Indian shot at the man and missed, and the packer raised his rifle to return fire. The Indian "found he was discovered, uncovered his breast & presented his whole form, the man felled him, & started toward him, the indian got up on his knees & felt for another arrow, & the man put 2 pistol balls into him, scalped him & soon found the second arrow sticking in his cloths & had grazed his breast. Soon felt sick & had to call a Physician. The cause was the arrow had been poisoned." Budd considered the Paiutes the "laziest, most indolent set of creatures that ever were seen." Emigrants, he wrote, customarily "[shoot] every Indian they see, among these Diggers, for if you don't shoot them they will you if they can catch you out by yourself or in small companies. It is a common practise to kill or scare them away & take what they have, for it is all stolen."[116]

How much violence the Great Basin tribes actually committed was a matter of debate. Not long after crossing "the long and *much dreded Dessert,*" Indians "sculking about in the bushes" along the Truckee followed John Dalton and Asa Bailey. Dalton "had no fears of their hurting us; but have no doubt that if they could rob or steal any thing or everything from us, they would be certain to do so—although the many foolish, alarming & bugbear stories about their being so dangerous & bad, is all *Humbug.*"[117] Natives did not commit the few robberies that had taken place along the Humboldt, emigrants assured Indian Agent Jacob Holeman: "The *white* Indians, I apprehend, are much more dangerous than the *red,*" he observed. These renegades, deserters, thieves, and fugitives from California justice were "more savage than the Indians themselves." Their depravity "stimulated the Indians to acts of barbarity which they were never known to be guilty of before." Emigrants

---

[113]Budd, Journal, 18, 19 July 1852.

[114]Cornell, Letters, 30 May and 21 November 1852, Oregon Historical Society Library.

[115]Morgan, *Shoshonean Peoples and the Overland Trail,* 94.

[116]Budd, Journal, 28 July, 5 August 1852, Mattes Library.

[117]Dalton, Diary, 19, 21 August 1852, State Historical Society of Wisconsin.

often seemed to be at war with themselves: "companies have quarreled, killed each other, and broken up—some, from their bad conduct have been driven from their companies—many of these men are scattered over the road, without means, living or the charity of others—they, also, steal and commit other depradations, which they endeavor to lay upon the Indians." After confiscating two stolen animals from road agents, Holeman concluded such "pretended traders" were decidedly worse than the Indians and caused "nearly, if not all the troubles on the road. It is the universal opinion of the emigrants that the Indians have been quiet, and have acted friendly throughout—and that all the depradations are the acts of white men."[118]

Before reaching the "uninterrupted plain barren and perfectly dreary" Forty-mile Desert, William H. Hart found a "good road and generally abundant grass" and enough water in the Humboldt "to make a healthy running stream." In 1849 the Humboldt had been too low "and in 1850 there was a perfect flood covering the whole extent of the bottom lands or alluvials and depriving the emigration of the good road and abundant grass of this year." Sojourners seem to have lost many fewer animals along the dismal river in 1852.[119] Yet the unearthly setting and unbearable conditions provoked erratic, and sometimes violent, behavior. Gilbert Cole recalled the moonlit night he crossed the wasteland, "very bright and pleasant, but awfully still," with "no rushing of waters, no murmuring of forests no rustling of grasses. All of Nature's music-pieces had been left far behind. There was nothing but sand." The Carson Pass road "was continuously strewn with the carcasses of stock that had perished there, some of them years before." Aridity, alkali, and the crystallized soda preserved the wreckage so "the bodies of these animals remained perfect, as they had fallen. The sand glistening in their eyes gave them a very life-like appearance." Ghostly wagons lined the road, complete except for the cover, with four to eight oxen "lying dead, with the yokes on their necks, the chains still in the rings, just as they fell and died, most of them with their tongues hanging from their mouths." At the forks of the Truckee and Carson roads, Cole found men quarreling about which was better: "They finally began to shoot at each other and were still at it when we passed out of hearing, not knowing or caring how the duel might end."[120]

After crossing the Humboldt Sink, East S. Owen ascended a small hill to survey "a large scope of country with nothing on the face of Gods Earth to be seen, some rocks and sand—and now and then a withered, starved out, Dried up sage bush," along with "the scattered fragments of old wagons, the bleaching bones of animals famished and perished heretofore and fifteen or twenty lank appearing, Sunburnt, Done over, used up Emigrants with their traveling Paraphernalia wending their

[118]Morgan, *Shoshonean Peoples and the Overland Trail*, 92—95.
[119]Hart, Diaries, 6 September 1852, BYU Library.
[120]Cole, *In the Early Days*, 107—108.

way westward in search of *Gold.*" There was not a well man in his company, he wrote: three men were unable to walk and he had his feet wrapped in rags, but they all believed "two more weeks, if we live so long, will set us through." The men watered their oxen and refreshed themselves "on *Bread* and *Bacon,* the only Dainties our larder affords [and] about dark we roll ahead and travel on untill midnight and Halted again near the 'Great Boiling Spring.'" They cooled the water and gave it to their cattle to drink. About daybreak and still six miles from the Truckee he reached the "heavy sand part of the Desert." His exhausted oxen sank "nearly to the knees every step—they are weary & consequently travel exceedingly slow yet we dont urge but let them take their own time. Five out of thirty two have already failed." At ten o'clock Owen reached the river, "and we have a time of great rejoicing thinking that we will not be under the necessity of drinking any more *alkali.*"[121]

Knowlton Chandler saw trading posts at Humboldt Lake and on the Truckee placed there by government "for the benefit of the suffering Emigrants."[122] California's legislature appropriated $25,000 to aid the incoming migration in late June. Governor John Bigler quickly dispatched an "Emigrant Relief Train" of eight wagons loaded with "pilot bread, flour, pork, coffee, tea, sugar, &c," to assist "the distressed immigrants arriving from the plains" on the Carson route and a second train to the Truckee. Three wagons had orders "to proceed to some suitable point on the Humboldt river beyond the Sink, and there await the coming of the emigrants from both sides of the river, the other wagons in the meantime remaining at Carson Valley until the emigrants arrive from the Great Desert." Although hailed as "one of the most noble and benevolent" enterprises ever devised, the scheme was quickly embroiled in charges of corruption.[123] After driving an ox team from Iowa to Sacramento in ninety days, Christian Myers charged that speculators were selling the provisions at exorbitant rates and devising schemes "to 'swap' the poor immigrants out of their stock."[124] William Hart found "a collection of brush shantys, and canvass tent appropriately called Ragtown and occupied by traders in cattle horses wagons and provisions or anything else that the emigrants would be likely to want to buy or sell." California speculators told emigrants "that stock is very low in Cal. and wagons scarcely saleable and try to induce them to sell their cattle and wagons and buy horses or mules to cross the mountains." The traders were lying: draft animals and wagons were selling for a premium across the Sierra. At Mormon Station a few days later Hart sold four yoke of oxen and a wagon for $410 and bought packhorses.[125]

---

[121]Owen, Journal, 18 August 1852, Beinecke Library, 105–10.

[122]Knowlton, Diary, 10, 12 August 1852, Illinois State Historical Library, 74, 77.

[123]"The Emigrant Relief Train," *Sacramento Union,* 26 June 1852, 2/2; Unruh, *The Plains Across,* 377, 379.

[124]"The Relief Train," *Sacramento Union,* 24 August 1852, 2/2.

[125]Hart, Diaries, 8 September 1852, BYU Library, 7–9.

Overland accounts seem to verify the corruption, but political machinations and countercharges obscure much of what was going on. Governor Bigler did not cover himself in glory when he marched at the head of the "California Relief Train" as it left Sacramento. The Whig press charged James Estill and James Denver with grave offenses and mismanaging the rescue. Estill and Denver were consummate (and probably crooked) frontier politicians who in June 1850 did not endear themselves to many overland emigrants when their "Express Mail Line for the California Emigration" set up a post office, cigar store, and "doggery" at Pacific Springs.[126] Denver killed the *Alta California*'s editor, Edward Gilbert, over the corruption charges, but the legislature temporarily named Lake Tahoe after Governor Bigler, who appointed the victorious duelist secretary of state. Denver was elected to Congress in 1854, became governor of Kansas in 1857, and two years later gave his name to a promising Rocky Mountain boomtown when a gold rush began the creation of Colorado Territory.

There would be "an immense quantity of stock driven over this season," Sacramento's *Daily Union* predicted. By early June 1852, forty families, the vanguard of the overland emigration, had already arrived in Carson Valley. They were locating farms and ranches in the valley, and the newspaper was "disposed to think that the whole valley will be settled this summer."[127] By late October "the great body of the army from the Plains" had reached the Sacramento Valley, and large trains arrived almost daily. The new Carson Valley settlements offered a sanctuary where the "wagons and considerable stock in the vicinity of the Sink of Humboldt River" could safely winter without crossing the Sierra, where snow was already falling.[128] "I do not think that California will long contain the numbers that are so fast pouring in from all parts," wrote Aaron Abbott. "For every nation on earth is here represented: The Chinaman is here with his umbrella hat and loose breeches, the Chilian, the Spaniard, the German. I have seen emigrants from fifteen states while on the road. The Doctor, the Lawyer, the Merchant all have to bear their share of the fat[i]gue and the Preacher too." But, Abbott wondered, "where is the Preacher?"[129]

CUTOFF FEVER: NEW ROADS ACROSS THE MOUNTAINS

Like all western trails, the Oregon Trail was constantly mutating—and not always successfully. Five miles above Salmon Falls south of today's Hagerman Fossil Beds National Monument, enterprising mountaineers opened a ferry across the Snake River in 1852. Now known as the North Alternate Oregon Trail, the new road

[126]Starr, Diary, 10 July 1850, Oregon Historical Society.
[127]"From Carson Valley," *Sacramento Union,* 9 June 1852, 3/1.
[128]"The Overland Immigration," *Sacramento Union,* 26 October 1852, 2/1.
[129]Abbott to "Dear Friends," 18 September 1852, Mattes Library. Punctuation added.

avoided a thirty-mile desert between the falls and the traditional ford at Three
Island Crossing. The "French, Creoles and Indians" who ran the operation were
soon doing a booming business. There was no grass at Salmon Falls in 1852, but
Cecilia Adams's train "found a notice that five miles below was a ferry across the
river and plenty of grass on the other side." The operation consisted of two abandoned wagon boxes "lashed together so as to make a boat and a rope stretched
across the river to pull it across—and all they asked was $3 a wagon for ferrying."
Naturally, "the ferryman recommended the route as so much shorter and better
supplied with grass and water that we concluded to try it." Over the next three
years, some 15,000 people would use this rough, steep, rocky, and sandy road.
The trail was blessed with good forage and springs, but at Clover Creek, which
William Cornell called Grave Creek and Henry Allyn said was "a creek of poison
water," the cutoff's problems proved fatal for many. By September Adams "found
ten graves all in a row—all had died from the 28th of July to the 4th of August."
Travel mysteriously shifted back to the main trail after 1854, leaving the alternate
lined with graves. "Contaminated water caused the deaths of hundreds of cattle,"
trail sleuth Jerry Eichhorst noted, while the route's many human victims "remain
forever along this trail," their graves "lost among the sagebrush."[130]

South on the California Trail, trade boomed and cutoff fever raged in 1852.
From the Sulphur Slough to the Carson River, in late July Thomas Turnbull found
"a water & liquor station every 2 & 4 miles" and hundreds of "Bakers Butchers
Saloons traders of all kinds" who had come to sell water and liquor to a flood of
desperate customers. He found an old friend named Robert trading horses and
wagons along with companions who had built "a Wigwam & live like Indians."
A week later Turnbull met "General" Joseph Morehead's "Relief Train" from the
southern mines. They claimed to have "run a road through to Sonora—a nearer
& better route for grass & not so mountainous," besides being "some 80 miles
nearer to Sacramento," but as Turnbull noted, "deception in people here can not
be fathomed." On its circuitous path to the mining camp at Columbia, Morehead's
route went down the Walker River and over Sonora Pass to cross the highest
elevation any emigrant wagon train ever attained. "To render it at all passable, we
were compelled first to move hundreds of thousands of tons of rocks," one victim
complained. Turnbull's friend thought "the old road over the Sierrnavado was bad
enough," but Robert feared the new one would be worse.[131] It was.

At Washoe Valley, Turnbull "camp'd opposite a road leading over the Sierra
Nevada called Yankie Jims route [but] very few went it. It is hard to say what kind

---

[130]Dinwiddie, "Overland from Indiana to Oregon," 30 July 1853, 10; Adams, "Crossing the Plains in 1852," 4, 9
September 1852, 5:290, 292; Eichhorst, "Pieces to the Puzzle" 51, 64.
    [131]Turnbull, "Travels," 27 July, 5 August 1852, 205–206, 209; Davis, "The Walker River–Sonora Crossing," 19.

of a road it is." This was the Placer County Emigrant Road, a route so bad it lasted only a year. South of Mormon Station, Turnbull noted "a pack road, a little track like a foot path," which he called "Johnstones cut off." It was actually the start of the pack trail to Daggett Pass and Georgetown, which evolved into Kingsbury Grade. As it was, Turnbull wisely stuck to the old Carson Pass trail—"a regular thoroughfare coming & going," where he found "some middling good road & some terrible Sidling for some ways," with sections still "terrible to look up to ever conceive how a team could ever Scramble up straight up." At Leek Springs, he came to the Grizzly Flat Road, a "New cut out to Hangtown called some nearer. The old road goes Straight ahead up the mountain—this is bad enough & I am afraid the other is worse."[132]

He was right. As Turnbull's travels reveal, cutoff creation exploded at the end of the California Trail in 1852. Boomtowns and promoters with monikers like Jack "Cock-Eye" Johnson, Yankee Jim, and Old Daddy Dritt battled to build a better wagon road across the Sierra. Mining camps sponsored at least six shortcuts in 1852, "all of them passable and not one of them good," George Stewart noted. He listed Auburn's Placer County Emigrant Road via Squaw Valley, Shasta City's Nobles Road across the Black Rock Desert, the Henness Pass Road (or El Dorado Route) north of Donner Pass to Downieville, Columbia's Sonora Road along the Walker River, and the Johnson Cutoff to Placerville; Volcano, Grizzly Flat, and Yreka each opened their own branch roads. Some of these enterprises had been in the works for years, Stewart observed, all with the intent of "steering the migration toward a particular town." A primitive road was made passable and then "fast-talking agents were sent east along the trail to persuade people to go that way."[133]

The roads Jack Johnson and William Nobles opened were better than Stewart thought and made a lasting impact on the evolution of the California Trail. The Johnson Cutoff began as a pack trail but evolved into the most popular wagon road across the mountains. A lawyer, overland veteran, and trader, in 1850 "Colonel" John Calhoun Johnson blazed a trail from his Six Mile Ranch east of Placerville to the Carson Pass road at Junction House, now Pollock Pines. Two years later he extended the route east across the Sierra to Eagle Valley, the gateway to Carson Valley. The cutoff headed three miles southwest to today's Carson City, and then west five miles to the top of Spooner Summit and entered the Lake Tahoe basin west of Genoa Peak, following a ridgeline to avoid the marshes surrounding the lake. The cutoff climbed a 30-percent grade to Johnson Pass and the headwaters of the south fork of the American River. The trail traced Peavine Ridge for fifteen miles before descending to cross the American River, eventually over a bridge Johnson built about 1852 with William Bartlett. (After it washed out, Richard

---

[132]Turnbull, "Travels," 11, 13, 16 August 1852, 211–19.
[133]Stewart, *California Trail*, 304–306; Unruh, *Plains Across*, 356.

COCK-EYE JOHNSON
Colonel John Calhoun "Jack" Johnson.
Owner of a ranch near Placerville, in 1852
"Cock-Eye Johnson" opened the Johnson
Cutoff to Carson Valley. The California
Legislature paid Johnson substantial sums
for his militia campaigns against Indians
before Apaches killed him in Arizona in
1876. Courtesy California History Room,
California State Library, Sacramento.

Brockliss built a more enduring span a mile upstream.) From here it was only a mile to Junction House and Johnson's shortcut to Placerville.[134]

Throughout most of 1852, "Johnstones cut off," as Thomas Turnbull wrote, was nothing more than "a pack road a little track like a foot path," or "a short trail for pack animals between Carson Valley and Placerville," as William Hart called it.[135] As October began, a heavy snowfall trapped the last—and most desperate—emigrants in Carson Valley for six days. When the weather broke, William Gobin and "thirteen teams of us took the Johnsons cutt off." On the trek, "a company passed us that had not eat anything for three days": Gobin's companions shared what was left of their scant provisions. When they, too, ran out of food, they searched the wagons and stacked their provisions in a heap, which "opened the eyes of men that had no souls—so then they divided manfully." In addition to the hunger, Gobin recalled the climb to the summit, which "took fifty men of us and all the oxen we could hitch to the wagons to take thirteen wagons up in two days." It was "just like climbing a tree or worse."[136]

Despite such drawbacks, the new road was far and away the best natural path to get a wagon over the Sierra to Placerville. The Johnson Cutoff trimmed seventy-five

[134]Supernowicz, "Surmounting the Sierra," 11, 15, 19n8.
[135]Turnbull, "Travels," 213; Hart, Diary, 21 September 1852, BYU Library, 2:19.
[136]Gobin to "Dear Charley," 22 November 1852, in Supernowicz, "Surmounting the Sierra," 16–17.

of the Mormon-Carson Emigrant Trail's 175 miles, and only seven of the cutoff's miles went above 7,000 feet. The route crested at about 7,400 feet at Johnson Pass, some 2,000 feet lower than the Carson road's second summit at West Pass. The high tolls its promoters enforced insured the enduring popularity of the free road over Carson Pass, but the California Legislature picked Johnson's shortcut as its official (albeit unfunded) trans-Sierra wagon road. The overland stage, the Pony Express, the transcontinental telegraph, and the Lincoln Highway followed its path. Today's U.S. 50 follows much of Cock-Eye Johnson's cutoff.[137]

William Nobles, a more ambitious trailblazer than even Jack Johnson, appeared in April 1852 with a business proposition for the city fathers of Shasta, a boomtown north of today's Redding, California. After failing to strike a deal with Peter Lassen's partner, Nobles offered Shasta the chance to sponsor, for a fee of $2,000, a "shorter and in every respect more practicable than any other known overland immigrant route" that would led directly to their potential metropolis. "I would charge nothing for making public the proposed route, were it not for the fact that I have spent some money and much time in making its discovery," Nobles said, while offering a money-back guarantee. Waterholes were no more than eleven miles apart, grass was abundant, and the shortcut would save "the wearied immigrant" at least 250 miles "over any other known route." Citizens had raised $1,675 by mid-April, and in May 1852 Nobles set out with a pack train to survey his shortcut, which became the Nobles Trail across the Black Rock Desert, the most important wagon road opened that year.

The prospecting party reported Nobles had "fulfilled his promise to the letter, and in some respects, even more than fulfilled them." They confidently anticipated "that rich deposits of gold will be discovered on the route," which looked like "the only practicable railroad route across the Sierra Nevada." All who had crossed the plains would "readily perceive the unrivalled advantages of the Shasta Route." At the Humboldt, meanwhile, Nobles had joined twenty-two men from Yreka bound for Saint Louis. With Richard Grant's help, Nobles "devoted some fifteen days to a laborious examination of the country about the South Pass," where he found "a perfectly feasible and practicable route for a railroad the entire distance from the eastern to the western slopes of the Rocky Mountains." Back in Minnesota, the emboldened explorer launched a new career as a legislator, lobbyist, and government road builder.[138]

Back on the Humboldt, Shasta's promoters zealously recruited wagons to inaugurate their new cutoff, "but they had hard work to persuade any of them to leave

---

[137]Hughey, "Johnson's Cutoff."
[138]White, *News of the Plains,* 5:228, 239, 245.

the regular road," one chronicler recalled. "In almost every train that came along there were men who had previously crossed the plains" and among them the Lassen Trail had such a toxic reputation that they threatened "great bodily injury" to Shasta's road agents "if they did not quit trying to get people to travel their road." Part of William Dow's crowd wanted to try the new road, but most preferred to stick to the Humboldt, and the train divided. William Asbury's party "received a written description of the road" from someone at Lassens Meadows "and though it was dim, they had no trouble in following it." By late July Shasta's agents finally "succeeded in getting a small train"—about thirty wagons—"to go over their road."[139]

The "Shasta or Knobles rout[e]," wrote Solomon Kingery, who never met a cutoff he didn't like, "is a new rout across the Siera Nevada Mt & leads into the northern mines & has never been traveld before." Kingery and "three teams of us Concludet to take" the untested trail, following "another Company of 11 teams" from today's Rye Patch Reservoir. They passed the "bones of hundreds of Cattle & Blacksmith tools, saw mill Saws & Different kind[s] of machinerys" lining the Oregon road's fifty-four miles to Black Rock, where the wagons turned southwest onto Nobles's new road. After a hard day's pull across another playa, "Coverd with Salt & as Smoth & as barren as a Brick yard," they saw what Kingery called "the most beutiful sight that I ever saw," a mirage that shimmered like a great lake of water. "This would be a very beutiful Sporting ground if it was in the States." (Today's Burning Man Festival is held a few miles to the southwest.) The wagons had "to follow a packers trail from this point through." Parts of the road were so soft it was like crossing ploughed ground, while others were the "Stonyest road I ever Saw." Yet the new trail had good water and excellent grass, with clover two feet high at one campground. The trace was hardly a wagon road: a few packers had used it, Kingery noted, "but it is an Indian trail." At times his party had to rely on a Maidu guide "to Show them the right trail" to Honey Lake near today's Susanville.[140]

It had only a few shallow quartz veins in its basin, but Honey Lake may have inspired the legendary Gold Lake. Peter Lassen, its likely white discoverer, told Goldsborough Bruff in 1850 "a sweet dew distilled from some plants" gave Honey Lake its name, but Bruff also heard it came from "the sweet substance which they found exuding from the heads of wild oats in the basin." The lake supported an enormous Native population; as Kingery's journal reveals, the new wagon trail had immediate and catastrophic consequences for the Maidus. During the middle of August, as the pioneering party kept "3 & 4 men ahead of the teams to hunt & Clear the road," raiders made off with livestock, and the frustrated emigrants retaliated. After five oxen disappeared, six men "killed three of the Indians, 4 more run."

---

[139]Fairfield, *Pioneer History of Lassen County,* 19.
[140]Kingery, Overland Letters, 28 July to 10 August 1852, Beinecke Library.

When the wagons reached the Lassen Trail, "The Indians Shot 7 oxen." Only one died, but seven men from the train hid "in the Bush after the teams left to watch the Indians. After a while one come up the Creek looking & watching on every Side. When he got within about 100 yards he heard or Seen the boys. He Started & run." The bushwhackers fired, wounding the Maidu. "They followed him about one mile; he was still running. They could easey track him by the blood. We think he blead to death," Kingery wrote.[141]

Ironically, for four miles in Pine Creek Valley between today's Bogard Ranger Station and Feather Lake, travelers heading southeast on the Lassen Trail to Clover Valley met parties going northwest on the Nobles Trail. The Nobles Trail then followed Butte Creek to the foot of Lassen Peak and crossed Nobles Pass over the volcano's northern shoulder. The trail then headed west to Fort Reading and the Sacramento River, at last turning north to its destination, Shasta City. In 1854 Nobles Trail developed its own cutoff across the southern edge of the Black Rock Desert by turning directly west near Rabbit Hole Springs to Trego Hot Springs and Granite Creek, which eliminated fifteen waterless miles.

The first train to try the Nobles Trail abandoned their wagons and packed through. In response, "the Citizens of Shasta City" sent out five men to guide Solomon Kingery's party through the tangle of chaparral, manzanita, and raspberry bushes that made the last section of the "Road very hard to Brake." On 22 August 1852, the party landed in Shasta City, where the citizens sponsored a dinner at the St. Charles Hotel for the pioneers. The townspeople treated them "with great Respect as we was the first train of waggons that ever Come into Shasta" on what Kingery called "a very lucky Successful Jurny. We had provision Enough & little left."[142]

Colonel Ethan Allen Hitchcock informed Washington, "A new route of emigration, called 'Nobles Cut-off' has been opened this year, leaving the old trail on Humboldt about eighty miles above where that River sinks, thence passing 'Lassen's Butte,' through Honey Lake Valley and by Fort Reading to Shasta." Many of the passing emigrants were out of provisions and had applied for aid at the outpost. "It is said a large number will pursue that route, and there may be a considerable amount of supplies required to prevent actual suffering," he reported. "The claims of humanity are everywhere paramount," Hitchcock advised, but he ordered his officers to issue provisions, preferably local beef, only when "absolutely necessary to prevent suffering."[143]

---

[141]Bruff, *Gold Rush,* lxxxiii–iv, 1053–54n38; Kingery, Letters, 11–15 August 1852, Beinecke Library.

[142]Ibid., 15–22 August 1852. For another party that used the Nobles Trail, apparently with wagons, see J. D. Randall, Diary, 12 to 28 August 1852, Mattes Library. My thanks to Stafford Hazelett, Don Buck, and Richard Silva for helping sort this out. For the route and its evolution, see Brock and Black, *A Guide to the Nobles Trail,* 8–11, 160.

[143]Hitchcock to Jones, 14 August 1852, in Bleyhl, Indian-White Relationships, 506.

WILLIAM H. NOBLES
Minnesota blacksmith William H. Nobles, "a man of
immense vitality and energy, with a strong inventive
genius"—if perhaps "a little hasty and irritable"—came
overland in 1850. He spent the next two years seeking a
better wagon road across the deserts and mountains and
opened the Nobles Trail in 1852. It quickly became the most
popular gateway to California. Author's collection.

For gold seekers, the Nobles Trail eliminated the long northern detour the Lassen
Trail made as it followed the 1846 southern road to Oregon. It provided a much
better alternative to the last wretched deserts along the Humboldt and across the
Forty-mile Desert, especially for cattle drovers. The gradual approach to Nobles
Pass did not require an ox to do the work of a mountain goat. Soon "the greater
part of the emigration into northern California was going over it."[144] Topographical
engineer Edward Beckwith's 1853 survey reported that of the "three lines which may
be followed to the foot of the Sierra Nevada" from Lassens Meadows, the Nobles
Pass road (which actually crossed the Cascade Range) was "the most direct, and is
believed to be the best."[145] The trail acquired national significance when Congress
created the Pacific Wagon Road Office in February 1857, for it provided a destination
for the "Fort Kearney, South Pass, and Honey Lake Wagon Road" (William Nobles
used the name in March 1857, down to the misspelling of Kearny, in a "description of route for a Wagon Road from Fort Kearney to Honey Lake Valley" for the
secretary of the interior).[146] The act also authorized building the Fort Ridgeley and
South Pass Road. Nobles was appointed superintendent and had $50,000 to pursue
his dream of building "An Emigrant Route to California and Oregon through Minnesota Territory." As David A. White noted, this work "did not amount to much."[147]

---

[144] Fairfield, *Pioneer History of Lassen County,* 19.
[145] Beckwith, *Explorations and Surveys,* 2:62.
[146] Nobles to Thompson, 26 March 1857, Henderson Collection.
[147] White, *News of the Plains,* 5:227–31.

THE TRAIL TO BLOODY POINT

The first wagons to reach Yreka City, a boomtown forty miles north of Mount Shasta, arrived at the tail end of the largest migration of the overland era. Their sheer numbers made the gold seekers of 1852 eager to gamble on any trail promising a shorter or better route. A massive surge in violence accompanied the creation of the Yreka Trail, a new seventy-three-mile road to gold, and these ambushes and raids inspired a legend about the massacre of an entire wagon train at a spot called Bloody Point. The actual conflict that accompanied the opening of the trail foreshadowed the most important impact ever-expanding overland wagon roads would have on the West for decades to come.

The Yreka Trail offered an attractive if meandering shortcut to the goldfields. It left the southern road to Oregon at Willow Creek near Lower Klamath Lake, headed west to Butte Creek, followed the stream south to Orr Lake, where the road turned west, going north of Grass Lake and south of Sheep Rock before heading northwest up the Shasta Valley to Yreka.[148] As always, death and mayhem accompanied the opening of a new road to a new gold strike. William Thompson recalled how the "fierce, remorseless, cunning and treacherous" Modocs attacked a wagon train, "and of the eighty odd men, women and children, but one escaped to tell the awful tale." Other parties "consisting of men, women and children, worn and weary with the trials and hardships of the plains, were trapped and butchered." The hundreds of victims "constitute one of the saddest chapters in the annals of American pioneers"—or so Colonel Thompson claimed.[149]

The history behind the legend began late in 1851, when rangers chased stolen horses from Yreka to Lost River on the southern road to Oregon. Guided by Ben Wright, a dedicated Indian hunter, "squaw man," and veteran of the first Cayuse War, the rangers killed about thirty Modocs and blazed a pack trail from Yreka to the Applegate Trial. They even retrieved a few of the horses. Next spring twenty-two men bound for the States took the trace to reach Lassens Meadows, where William Nobles joined them. James Freaner, who had carried the Treaty of Guadalupe Hidalgo from Mexico to Washington in 1848, probably followed this route when he left Yreka City late in May 1852 to prospect "a route for the road which he is authorized to build into Oregon." Yreka was isolated on "a mule trail over a very rough country," and in July Freaner headed south to make "observations for a road" to the Sacramento Valley. When his favorite riding mule showed up in Yreka, it appeared that he and his three compatriots had fallen "victim to the fury of the Pitt River Indians." By September the town had pretty much forgotten Freaner but was "wild upon the subject of the emigration." Many citizens had

---

[148]Arnold and Arnold, "The Lonesome Rout," 4.
[149]Thompson, *Reminiscences of a Pioneer,* 74—77.

"gone to induce the emigrants" to transform the rough trace to their town into a wagon road. After reports of frightful massacres along the emigrant road poured in, Yreka sent its rangers to the rescue.[150]

As he led ten wagons on his return west in 1852, Forty-niner James Clark Tolman hoped to start a farm close to the mines, perhaps near the new diggings along the Oregon border. At the Sweetwater a man named Rollins, perhaps a member of the pack train William Nobles had joined at Lassens Meadows, told Tolman he "could go to Yreka by the old Oregon route much better than to go to the Columbia and then south from there."[151] At Lassens Meadows an agent promoting the new Nobles Trail to Shasta City warned his train that "death awaited them on the route they proposed to take." Tolman resisted the hard sell and took the new shortcut. His party reached Yreka eighty-two days after leaving Council Bluffs "without the loss of an animal, notwithstanding their journey through the hostile tribe of the Modocs."[152]

David Cartwright also recalled meeting the Yreka pack train near South Pass. They told him about a new trail where "there had never been a white man's track except theirs." After he had almost reached the Oregon border, Indians lay in wait for his train at a "narrow pass between the rocks and the lake," Cartwright recalled decades later. At this "deep projection of the land into the lake," with a half-mile reef of rocks running down its center, the Yreka party had told him their new trail started. Suspecting an ambush, his train "formed a breast-work of our wagons, fired off our guns and got everything in readiness for an attack from the Indians, having scarcely a doubt that they would come upon us." The Indians did not attack and, to the surprise of all, were gone by morning. Yreka staged a banquet when the train arrived on 7 August in honor of "the first immigrant teams that had ever been driven into the place." A few days later, the lone survivor of one of "the murderous raids of those villainous Modocs" showed up in town. Eighty men with a Native guide known as "Oregon" set out to "give the Modocs what they deserved, a thrashing with a gun-barrel for a flail." In a story incorporating virtually every element of what became the legendary annihilation of an entire wagon train, Cartwright claimed the posse killed fifty Indians, mostly women and children, and found "fourteen dead bodies, which were mangled and terribly butchered, lying near the lake." As a former Oregon Indian superintendent

---

[150] *Yreka Mountain Herald,* 24 September 1853; "Latest from Shasta," *Weekly Alta California,* 31 May 1852, 1/5; "Col. James Freaner," *Alta California,* 8 September 1852, 2/1; "Fate of Col. Freaner," *Marysville Daily Herald,* 30 October 1855, 2/3. Arnold and Silva, "Bloody Point—1852," and Hunt, "Anatomy of a Massacre," 2–25, include the essential sources on that year's violence at Tule Lake.

[151] Tolman, "Pioneer Days," 3/6.

[152] "Gen. James Clark Tolman," in Evans, *History of the Pacific Northwest,* 2:607–608.

solemnly testified, "No page in all the bloody history of Indian cruelties exceeds that of the massacre of emigrants at Bloody Point, by the Modocs."[153]

Many Bloody Point stories are patent nonsense, but elements of classic Western myths—calculated ambushes, desperate escapes, hardy pioneers in circled wagons fending off brutal assaults, and vicious murders—actually happened along the Yreka Trail in 1852. Determining exactly what transpired at Bloody Point that fall is not simple. Contemporaneous documents, which should provide the best evidence, tell a contradictory story, but they all agree that warfare between Indians and emigrants killed an extraordinary number of overland travelers, perhaps more than a dozen, and many, many more Modocs before the year ended.

The story usually begins "with a pack train consisting of nine men, eight of whom were well armed and whom they thought would come through safely," but who "were attacked by the Indians and eight out of the nine men killed." The sole survivor joined a wagon train and raised the alarm at Yreka the next day, local attorney W. A. Robertson informed Governor Bigler on 7 September. The single survivor of a massacred pack party became a standard part of the Bloody Point legend, but Sheriff Charles McDermitt mentioned no such messenger when he left Yreka with eleven men on 8 August, a day after "a train of forty packers arrived from the Plains." The packers warned that several family wagons were still days away, and unless help reached the emigrants soon, they "would undoubtedly be all murdered by the Indians." McDermitt later reported the families reached a "point of rocks" on the east side of Tule Lake "and were all murdered by the Indians" who "concealed themselves in the Tules, and would not show fight" when his posse showed up. He buried the bodies of four women and children and three men. McDermitt concluded his men could do the emigrants still on the trail "the most service by going ahead and distributing ourselves among the different trains as guides." McDermitt assigned three scouts to escort Captain Morrison's seven wagons. They rode ahead to find a nooning place, when Modocs "attacked them from a concealed position at the point of rocks, shot them full of arrows," and captured their guns and horses. Hearing gunfire, Morrison sent Felix Martin ahead "to ascertain what was going on; the report of his pistol was heard, but he did not return." The train closed up, prepared for a fight, and cautiously approached the point of rocks, where they "discovered blood in the road, but did not see an Indian till a shower of arrows came among them, wounding one man." The train drove off the Indians and "moved on briskly to a large flat, out of the reach of arrows," where they corralled their wagons about two miles from the point.[154]

---

[153]Cartwright, "A Tramp to California," 210, 220–27; Meacham, *Wigwam and War-path,* 299–300.

[154]McDermitt to Bigler, 19 December 1852, in Hunt, "Anatomy of a Massacre," 11.

On 31 August, Hinsdale Shepard wrote the only eyewitness account of the wagon fight. When the Debuke train "came up they also were attacted but suceded in passing by the bluffs but was surrounded on the flat." Apparently joining the embattled Morrison train, they "turned around formed a carrol & prepared for war." The embattled emigrants "saw A train of horseman coming" and "supposed they ware Indians [but] soon found th[ey] ware 31 packers came to our Relief." Ben Wright's Yreka rangers "shortly prepared & put after the Indians. They Surrounded them & drove them into the marsh & killed 15 or 20 of them," Shepard wrote.[155] Sheriff McDermitt reported that the Modocs besieged the emigrants for thirty-six hours "in the same place without water; and the train would undoubtedly have suffered much, and perhaps all have been murdered" but for Wright's timely arrival. McDermitt reported burying twenty-six bodies near Tule Lake, probably not counting the seventy-three Indians Wright killed.[156]

Two weeks later, Sophronia Stone found a note "tied on a stick by some willow huts" forbidding anyone from passing without an escort—otherwise "we should be killed for 300 indeans had banded to gether at a point of rocks and had killed a good maney. I think 14." Stone's train corralled its wagons, and at sundown a cloud of dust appeared. As they saw "their arms glittering in the sun," some "said it was Indians, others the rangers," she wrote. "No one can tell the feelings of that moment." The dust cloud proved to be Wright's posse, but "they looked savage." After her train camped, "a company of rogue river men come that night."[157] William Stoddard's party met the volunteers from Yreka the same day. By his account they were heading for home when they ran into rangers from Jacksonville, Oregon, and "suposed that they were Indians in force, came back much alarmed and colected quite a force of Rangers and Emigrants and started post haste for a fight." The anticipated battle "turned out very pleasantly."[158]

Word had reached Oregon in mid-September "that whole trains of immigrants had been massacred on Lost river." Twenty-two volunteers elected J. E. Ross captain and made a forced march to the lake country. "We found the bodies of fourteen immigrants and buried them. Several of them were women and children; they were much mutilated," Ross reported. At Clear Lake, Ben Wright informed him "that his men had found and buried eighteen bodies in the vicinity of Bloody Point, at Tulé lake," including two "respectable citizens of Yreka, California, who went

---

[155]Shepard, Overland Diary, 31 August 1852, California State Library.

[156]McDermitt to Bigler, 19 December 1852, 11.

[157]Stone, Diary, 16 September 1852, Tutt Library, Colorado College. An 1864 census counted only 300 men, women, and children in the entire Modoc tribe, so descriptions of hundreds of angry warriors attacking emigrant families twelve years earlier are hard to credit. See Hunt, "Anatomy of a Massacre," 13.

[158]Stoddard, Overland Diary, 16 September 1852, Society of California Pioneers. Internal evidence indicates Ezra Brown wrote this section of the journal.

BLOODY POINT

Three miles south of the Oregon border, a California State Historical Marker claims, "In 1850 one of the bloodiest massacres of emigrants ever known on the Oregon Trail occurred here when Modoc Indians killed over 90 men, women, and children in a surprise attack." It never happened, but the story was used to justify repeated assaults on the Modocs. In this June 1905 photograph, Bloody Point looms above the waters of Tule Lake, shortly before the Klamath River Project drained the lake. Bureau of Reclamation, Photo BR-49, Courtesy Klamath Waters Digital Library, Oregon Institute of Technology Library.

out to assist the immigration," along with "several more bodies of those who had been massacred by these Indians." In October, the army dispatched Captain E. H. Fitzgerald, who reported he found "a good wagon road" already leading to Yreka, and Oregon sent more mounted volunteers to escort the last of the 1852 trains to safety. The California legislature promptly "paid all expenses of Captain Wright's company, and liberally rewarded the officers and privates for their services." Law-makers appropriated $20,775, or slightly more than $200 for each of the hundred or so Natives the militia posses killed. His men, Ross complained, did arduous service for a month "and received for our services the compliments of the Oregon legislative assembly." As for the Modocs, "Wright gave them no quarter. He and his men, infuriated at the sight of the mangled bodies of the emigrants, killed men, women, and children without any discrimination—about forty in all." To finish the affair, Wright poisoned a roast ox, "gave it to the Indians, and then rode away."[159]

During another Modoc War two decades later, an Oregon newspaper told about a wagon party of "nearly 100 souls, all of whom were massacred but two. Out of the train, two young girls, sisters aged about 14 and 16 years, were taken prisoners. Their name is unknown." The younger captive died first. Her sister was murdered or fell victim to "savage jealousy" when "her ruined body could no longer administer to savage lust." In 1871, Scar-faced Charley showed a visi-tor her crumbling skeleton. "All that was discovered was a human skull, one rib, and one of the bones of the arm. Col. Bellinger gathered up the remaining relics and brought them away." He sent them to a friend in Portland, who displayed the child's bones in his cabinet of curiosities.[160]

There are always at least two sides to a story, even one like the legend of Bloody Point. Char-ka, the Handsome Boy, published his history of these events in 1914 under his white name, Jeff C. Riddle. He was the son of Frank Riddle, a Kentuckian who came overland in 1850, and Winema, the strange child who won the Modoc name meaning "woman chief" after she rescued her companions in a whitewater canoeing accident. She became famous as Tobey Riddle for her talent as an interpreter during the Modoc War of 1873. "In my work I aim to give both sides of the troubles of the Modoc Indians and the whites," her son wrote. "The Indian side has never been given to the public yet." He "tried to write as plain as I could. I use no fine language in my writing, for I lack education," Riddle admitted.

Char-ka told the story this way. When the Modoc people saw "the first emigrant wagon, with the people of a different color from themselves, they all ran for the

---

[159]Ross to Curry, 10 November 1854, in Harding, "Protection Afforded by Volunteers," Serial 1016, 15; Colvig, "Indian Wars of Southern Oregon," 232; Fitzgerald to N. H. Davis, 6 November 1852, in Arnold and Silva, "Bloody Point—1852."

[160]*Democratic Times* (Jacksonville, Oregon), 15 February 1873, courtesy Richard Silva.

hills. They thought that God had sent Evil Spirits among them to punish them in some way," he wrote, recalling the traditions of his mother's people. "But they soon learned that the white people were human, so they became friendly toward the emigrants" passing through Mowatoc, the tribe's homeland. The first white people gave the Modocs clothes, flour, coffee, tea, bacon, and blankets—a recollection perhaps written out of deference to Char-ka's father. Trouble began when the Achomawi, the Modoc's "treacherous" rivals known to whites as the Pit River tribe, "waylaid and killed quite a number of emigrants, both men and women," somewhere near today's Alturas, California. The evil Pit Rivers ambushed a sleeping militia company, which quickly exacted its vengeance on the peaceful Modocs, killing most of the Hot Creek band.

The Modocs held a tribal council to decide how to respond. "I see we cannot get along with the white people. They come along and kill my people for nothing. Not only my men, but they kill our wives and children," said an elder. If they ran, the white people would chase the Modocs from valley to mountain and mountain to valley and kill them all. "Shall we defend our wives and our children and our country?" he asked. "I am not afraid to die. If I die in war against the white people, I will die for a good cause."

When a train of wagons, looking "like a huge snake wiggling its way," camped two miles south of the Oregon border at Wa-ga-kan-na, a canyon on Tule Lake, the Modocs gathered on a hill "and there sealed the lives of the poor emigrants." Their warriors struck at dawn and killed almost half of them. But the train rallied, and "the white man's aim was good." The Modocs retreated, leaving their dead behind, and sent runners north and south; they soon returned "with many more bloodthirsty savages." The Modocs attacked at nightfall and again about midnight, but the whites routed them. When they charged the camp at daybreak, the warriors "were surprised to find that their intended victims had got away," some to Yreka, others to Oregon. The Modocs divided the loot, burned the wagons, and left the dead emigrants where they had fallen. "They all took to the mountains; some going north, some south, and others east."

The survivors reached Yreka City and raised the alarm, and the town's rangers responded. Char-ka's father was among this "strong body of hardy white men." When the rangers reached the heartbreaking scene, every man took off his hat, bowed his head, and some "shook with grief. They gathered the dead and laid them side by side" in a trench and covered them up "the best they could do under the circumstances." Frank Riddle wrapped the body of a white girl in his gray double blanket and buried her under a juniper tree. The rangers returned to Yreka without killing any Indians. After the Modocs "massacred the emigrants at Wa-ga-kan-na, they went to the mountains, and hid for almost two years." But the "massacre at

MODOC WOMEN, 1873

Winema, a Modoc translator known as Tobey Riddle, standing to the right of her husband Frank Riddle with an unidentified Indian agent and four Modoc women. Both Frank and Tobey Riddle were involved in the events at Bloody Point in 1852. Eadweard Muybridge photograph, 1873. Courtesy U.S. National Archives.

Bloody Point did not stop the white emigrants from coming through the Modoc country," Char-ka said in his history.[161]

Riddle's romance is in many ways as much a blood-and-thunder saga of his time as Colonel Thompson's florid tale. From such conflicting reports, tangled memories, and pernicious nonsense, historians try to write history. Both contain elements of the confusing and violent story of Bloody Point told in legendary recollections and the best contemporary reports, and each was written with a distinct purpose in mind—to garner political, moral, and financial support. Every source must be regarded with suspicion, for they contain conflicting descriptions of what appear to be similar events and contradict what can be established as fact. Riddle's Indian version is as problematic as any account, but it rings surprisingly true in many of its details.

The record describes neither a Bloody Point massacre nor an attack in which Indians killed every last member of a wagon party. The 1852 sources "referred to a composite of many attacks and killings," and while they reported emigrant victims of Modoc raids, they did not describe a wholesale massacre. Even the site of the murders is in dispute. During the 1930s, ditch diggers allegedly found "a number of charred wagons" at Bloody Point, "and from time to time a part of a human skeleton is still found there," but archeologists have never found a trace of evidence of the 1852 attacks. Official documents credit Wright's men with killing seventy-three Modocs that fall; the total number of Native casualties was probably higher. The sources assign names to only a handful of white casualties, many of them rangers. Hinsdale Shepard mentioned Thomas H. Coats, the only emigrant fatality identified by name. Sheriff McDermitt reported finding the bodies of "two females, two children and three men." Historians have long estimated that the Modocs killed about twenty-two nameless packers bound for Yreka and perhaps "a small train of three or four families." The number fourteen, repeated so often in so many early accounts, may be closer to the mark, but Colonel Ross of the Oregon Volunteers made a telling observation: "The precise number that were massacred in a single season by these Indians, between Klamath lake and the Sierra Nevada mountains, probably will never be known to the whites." He was right.[162]

For the next two decades, the blazing of every new road, cutoff, and trail ignited a new Indian war. The tide of humanity flowing through Native lands ran faster every year, and the peoples who had long made overland travel possible learned that the white people had come not to visit but to stay. When they did, they would do as they had done in Oregon and Utah and California and

---

[161]Riddle, *Indian History of the Modoc War*, 3, 15–27.

[162]Hunt, "Anatomy of a Massacre," 2–25; Sprague and Rodeffer, "The Bloody Point Archaeological Investigation," 26–28; Ross to Curry, 10 November 1854, 15; Murray, *The Modocs and Their War*, 24.

make the grass, game, water, and even the rocks their own. Native people had to do something. Schonchin, the Modoc leader later credited with leading the raids at Bloody Point, told an Indian agent, "I thought, if we killed all the white men we saw, that no more would come. We killed all we could; but they came more and more, like new grass in the spring."[163]

OVERFLOWED: END OF THE DELUGE

"Only twelve miles to the end of our destination," John Hawkins Clark wrote wearily at the end of his long and tiresome journey from Saint Joseph. He passed a Sacramento graveyard and an "ancient and dilapidated-looking concern," the once-glorious Sutters Fort, now "all gone, or going to decay." His party eagerly greeted "the sight and signs of civilization; from the first of May to the first of September we had been wanderers in the wilderness; everything we heard or saw appeared new. It was indeed a new world," Clark observed. His companions looked more like Hungarians than American citizens, "worn down with fatigue and looking for all the world like the remnant of a disorganized army that had just escaped destruction."[164]

Among the disasters that stalked the great emigration of 1852, Oregon's Burnt Canyon burned. "This river takes its name from the blackened & burnt appearance of the hills & mountains on either side of it, and the frequent burnings of them," wrote Esther Belle Hanna. The tinder-dry bunch grass covering the steep slopes could burn "for miles & days together." She watched the conflagration from the far side of the river. "The fire in the mountains last night was truly grand, it went to the tops of the highest of them spreading far down their sides. We were obliged to go over after our cattle at dark and bring them across the stream." The blaze raged all night, scorching several miles, but the party camped at a delightful spring branch, where they "had the joyful sight of trees for the first time" since leaving Soda Springs.[165]

Between 1849 and 1852, the lure of California gold and free land in Oregon transformed the overland trails. Where terrain and brush permitted, the overland road became a broad corridor. "The trail was nearly a quarter of a mile wide—that is, a row of wagons fifteen-hundred feet across, and extending in front and to the rear, as far as we could see," John Stockton wrote, recalling the "vast sea of white flapping wagon covers, and a seething mass of plodding animals" he saw in 1852.[166] "In many places the roads were two hundred yards wide as there was so much

---

[163]Meacham, *Wigwam and War-path,* 297.

[164]Clark, "Overland to the Gold Fields," 4 September 1852, 296.

[165]Hanna, Diary, Bancroft Library. Editor Eleanor Allen embellished the journal's text with such folderol as "throwing out great streamers of red against the night sky." See Hanna, *Canvas Caravans,* 91.

[166]Stockton, The Trail of the Covered Wagon, 1929.

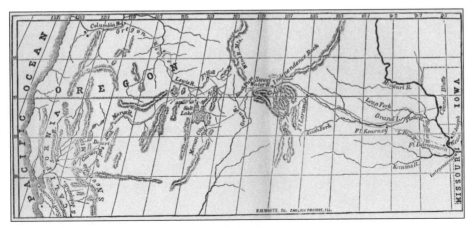

THE OVERLAND ROUTE TO CALIFORNIA, 1852

This primitive map accompanied one of the best descriptions of the overland trail to California, the *Travelers' Guide across the Plains upon the Overland Route to California* by P. L. Platt and Nelson Slater. Author's collection.

stock," Francis Hatcher recalled. "Whenever there was a good camping place a large number of trains would stop, there being so many tents it reminded one of a city."[167] Today backcountry travelers often mistake Jeep roads, known as "two tracks," for the original wagon trace, but a wide swale, an eroded depression often a hundred yards wide cut into the prairie by the passage of thousands of wagons, marks the true course of the road across the plains.

The vast migration dramatically improved the road, but the overland trek was still a long and perilous journey. "When all the Hardships, Dangers and Difficulties are considered in Crossing the Plains it is, surely, Hard at best," wrote John C. Thorniley. The "condition of Man and Beast" when a train departed the frontier and "the Same Train when it gets to its Journeys" made it "often appear as But a Wreck of its former Importance," he concluded. It was "a Journey far better Imagined than described."[168] Edward Wylie said he "went to sleep hungry and got up hungry," and his train had killed all its horses but one crossing the plains.[169] "Those who undertake this journey will find it no children's play—no 'bed of roses,'" wrote frontier editor and Oregon Trail veteran Delazon Smith. The trek was no pleasure trip, demanding plenty of "piety, patience, provisions, prudence and perseverance!

[167]Hatcher, "Crossing the Plains," in Knifong, *The Knifong Family.*
[168]Thorniley, Overland Diary, 24 August 1852, California State Library.
[169]Atkinson to Anna Knox, 15 October 1852, Mattes Library.

And unless a person has both physical and moral courage—unless he possess more or less the spirit of the age in which he lives—the spirit of go-ahead—'upward and onward'—I would advise him to stay where he is."[170]

Rain and snow greeted the last wagons to rattle over the Barlow Road or down the slopes of the Sierra in 1852 as floods up and down the West Coast confronted the exhausted travelers. The deluge destroyed Oregon City's attempt to bypass the Willamette Falls with a canal. As the year ended, Nevada settlers watched a warm downpour melt the early snowfall and drown the Carson Valley lowlands.

As the overland emigration, "destitute of all means of comfort and life," sought shelter at Sacramento, the rain king arrived amid the ruin and havoc of another devastating fire.[171] In mid-October there were still hundreds of teams between Sacramento "and the Sink, and nearly every wagon he passed contained women and children," E. C. Spring reported. Most of them "would be compelled to remain in Carson Valley until next spring."[172] O. P. Stidger gave "a deplorable account" of Marysville early in 1853, where it had rained incessantly since the first of December. The settlement was "inundated with water three different times, and now the whole of the lower part of the city, and the entire country west and south is entirely covered with water," he wrote. "The waters have been higher than at any time since the discovery of gold. All parts of the country have been either overflowed or met with some other casualty equally as disastrous." Driven by the weather from the mountains, miners turned to begging. "Thousands of persons have died, in consequence of being hemmed in by the snow—frozen to death, or died of starvation," Stidger said. "It is impossible to paint the utter destitution and ruin which pervades all parts of this country. Every wind wafts to us tidings of misery and distress. It is awful, awful! The whole Sacramento Valley is one vast sea of water."[173] Others recalled the sacrificial offerings they had left along the trail. "Cattle have died by the thousands. From Green River to the Blue Mountains dead cattle completely lined the road. I have frequently seen a dozen dead cattle lying in sight of each other," Mary Woodland wrote from Oregon. She expressed a sentiment thousands of her fellow sojourners would share: "I hope I never see another bush of wild sage as long as I live."[174]

Such experiences marked the inglorious passing of the West's first great gold rush and with it the closing of an overland era, an American adventure and an age of gold.

---

[170]Smith, "From the Oregon Times," 30 November 1852.

[171]"Sacramento Correspondence," *Alta California*, 12 November 1852, 2/3.

[172]"From the Plains," *Weekly Alta California*, 16 October 1852, 1/3.

[173]Stidger, 11 January 1853, "From California," *Ohio Repository* (Canton), 2 March 1853, 3.

[174]Woodland to "My Dear Father and Mother," October 1852.

CHAPTER 10

THIS INSATIATE THIRST FOR GOLD

The Birth of the Mining West

What do the stories told here say about the history and prospects of the American West? The answer must gauge the significance of the California gold rush and examine the impact overland wagon roads had on the people who used them and on the nation's future. Western historians usually agree with Sylvia Sun Minnick: "Beyond doubt, the California gold rush was the most momentous single episode in the development of the American West."[1] The explosive creation of the mining West was arguably second only to the Civil War in national significance during the nineteenth century. As "the republic changed in size, purpose, and values," Elliott West observed, gold reshaped how America saw itself. The great rushes "helped knit its parts into a newly imagined union—sure in its blessings, imperial in vision, blindly arrogant, naively confident of a future of untarnishable luster."[2] The experiences described in this work suggest the epoch unleashed powerful and pervasive transformative forces. But analyzing this history requires balance; as Richard White cautioned, "The Gold Rush had consequences, but specifying those consequences—and not overplaying them—that is the trick."[3]

Evaluating the impact trails had on western history also demands more caution than enthusiasm. As James Delgado noted, the California gold rush "was first and foremost a maritime event." The best expert, John Haskell Kemble, estimated 479,439 passengers reached San Francisco via Central America between 1849 and 1869, while the number of those who rounded Cape Horn declined from about 16,000 in 1849 to 3,346 in 1852. These statistics overwhelm the most generous calculations of how many people used the Platte River Road. J. S. Holliday concluded 89,000 people reached California by December 1849: 40,200 men and 800

---

[1] Minnick, "Never Far from Home," 142.
[2] West, "Golden Dreams," 3, 4.
[3] White, "The Gold Rush," 46.

women sailed to San Francisco, while 42,000 people came overland, including 10,000 over the southern routes, along with some 6,000 Sonorans. Between 1849 and 1852, using John Unruh's conservative estimate of 156,100 and Merrill Matte's liberal guess of 185,000, perhaps 175,000 sojourners crossed South Pass. We have precise documentation of 68,767 passengers crossing Panama and Nicaragua to San Francisco, while the actual number is probably closer to 100,000; 295,000 used the route to return to the United States during those four years. Between 1849 and 1859, about one-fifth of California's emigrants came across Panama. The route proved safer than crossing the plains: of the 30,000 who crossed the Isthmus in 1852, Kemble estimated "not more than a hundred died in transit." The completion of the Panama Rail Road in January 1855 reduced travel time to New Orleans to three weeks. During the 1860s, nearly half of all emigrants to California came this way, making the Panama route probably "more significant in the development of the region than the overland immigration." The origins of the state's 102 legislators in 1852 reflect how many settlers came to California as seafarers: forty-six of them crossed overland, but fifty-six came by way of Panama or Cape Horn. Census reports, travel records, and other statistics indicate that much less than half of California's 1870 population came across the plains.[4]

No matter how they arrived, "most Forty-niners went home and most Californians in the 1880s and 1890s had no experience with the Gold Rush." Reliable numbers are elusive, but overland narratives suggest that at least a third of those who followed the trail to the Pacific returned to the States as quickly as possible. "Rich or poor, there was only one way to go home: by sea," J. S. Holliday observed. As the nineteenth century drew to a close, events such as the gold discovery jubilee celebrated the Golden State's colorful mining and trails history, making it easy to overestimate the epoch's impact on the state's culture. The differences between the customs of California and the rest of the nation have more to do with its Spanish and Mexican roots than they do with gold, the overland road, or pioneer values.[5]

Even with these considerations, the revolutionary impact of the gold rush on the nation and the American West was immense. "The full and permanent effects of the California gold discovery cannot be estimated," Hubert Bancroft concluded long ago. "All over the world impulse was given to industry, values changed and commerce, social economy, and finance were revolutionized."[6] The gold rush was "a multiplier—an event that accelerated a chain of interrelated consequences, all of which accelerated economic growth," Gerald Nash observed. The mineral

---

[4]Delgado, *To California By Sea,* ix; Kemble, *The Panama Route,* 178, 206, 254, 287n20; Swain, *The World Rushed In,* 296–97; Bancroft, *History of California,* 6:159; Unruh, *The Plains Across,* 119–20; Mattes, *Platte River Road Narratives,* 2–3;
[5]White, "The Gold Rush," 46; Swain, *The World Rushed In,* 414.
[6]Bancroft, *History of California,* 6:110.

wealth cascading from the Sierra galvanized the American economy. The nation had been starved for capital since its founding: in 1840 there was not more than fifty million dollars in hard cash in the entire United States. The enormous output of California's mines doubled the amount of money in circulation and pushed up prices. This massive infusion of capital "spurred the creation of thousands of new businesses, banks, and financial institutions. It stimulated rapid agricultural expansion, quickened the volume of trade and commerce, and created demands for new forms of transportation." California gold ignited a boom in shipbuilding, manufacturing, railroad building, and the trades. This surge in demand and golden capital from the West began a national economic expansion that lasted until 1857.[7]

In ways still not fully appreciated, the California gold rush was a world event. The attractions of its Age of Gold drew miners from Central and South America, Asia, Australia, and Europe. The flood of capital created instant cities at San Francisco, Sacramento, Stockton, Portland, and Victoria. California's mines poured capital into America's cash-strapped economy, fueling a boom that underwrote much of the industrial development of the North and widened its differences with the agrarian South. Western mines did not underwrite the triumph of the Union, as many gold rush veterans claimed, but the $197,961,875 in treasure California and Nevada shipped over the Isthmus between 1861 and 1865 helped Abraham Lincoln win the costly conflict.[8] Gold transformed America, setting in motion economic, cultural, and political forces that defined the new lands. Many still endure, notably the boom-and-bust cycles of development and exploitation characteristic of the West's economy.

The golden multiplier accelerated a chain of international events. Around the Pacific's Ring of Fire, California's example inspired rushes to Australia, New Zealand, and British Columbia. The capital their mines created drove up worldwide prices and launched revolutions in trade, technology, and transportation. These in turn fueled demand for timber, wagons, boots, beef, flour, vegetables, saddles, hardware, tools, gunpowder, blue jeans, iron, paper, and alcohol and expanded markets for farms, factories, banks, and railroads. French economist Emile Levasseur put California's gold rush on his 1858 list of the fourteen great revolutions in world history. The impact of the California and Australia gold discoveries led philosopher Karl Marx to resume his study of economics in 1859. And by 1852, the rush had drawn 35,000 Chinese to San Francisco and the land they called Gold Mountain.[9]

---

[7]Nash, "A Veritable Revolution," 276; West, *Contested Plains,* 7. For more, see West, "Golden Dreams," 3–11; and Ridge, "Legacy of the Gold Rush," 58–63.

[8]Kemble, *The Panama Route,* 255.

[9]Nash, "A Veritable Revolution," 276, 286, 288.

THE GOLDEN WEST

Abe Lee, an aging Forty-niner who was prospecting an icy stream on the Arkansas River headwaters in April 1860, started serious mining in Colorado. Astonished by the color glittering before his eyes, Lee shouted, "By God, I've got California in this here pan." Within days the site of the strike was part of a mining district and named California Gulch, a tribute to the Golden State's enduring impact on the creation of the mining West. "California was more than the Mother Lode country," observed Duane Smith, dean of hard-rock historians. It "was the mother of western and to a lesser degree, world mining." The state earned the title "Mother Lode for the West" from the ubiquitous veterans of the Sierra mines, for "the 'old Californians,' went everywhere carrying with them their craft of mining," recreating the state's "materialistic, boisterous, transient" ways in mining camps across the Far West.[10]

A new American vagabond, the prospector, led the way. Cut from the same cloth in the California gold country as Abe Lee, they had known the thrill of discovery, that singular moment when a flash of auriferous color in a pan or the dull glint of a silver vein in a rocky ledge called down visions of instant wealth. They became hopelessly addicted to the ecstasy of standing atop a new fortune, and when it was squandered there was always a new one to be found just over the next ridge in an unexplored creek. As much as the gold-rush trail and the eternal quest to get rich quick changed the American West, the exhaustion and exhilaration of such singular experiences transformed the men and women who struggled to cross a continent in search of a better life. They had seen the elephant and stared him down. These often-harrowing adventures, which many recognized as the most intense experiences of their lives, made those who survived unshakably confident and physically tough, with constitutions that bordered on indestructible.

The chaotic culture of the gold camps had its own profound impact. Many families never heard again from husbands, fathers, and brothers. Men like Robert James probably vanished as one of the uncounted casualties of the poor sanitation and wretched diet common in the mining camps, but others made the choice to disappear from old friends and families. "The old California miners had long since shaken off the shackles of an effete civilization, and had been living for many years free from the trammels and restraints of Sunday-school influences," recalled William Goulder, an Oregon pioneer of 1845 who had spent years in the mines of the new El Dorado and joined the rush to Idaho in 1861. These transformed souls were devoted to "the larger liberty that comes from a wild, free life lived so far away in remote mountain regions."[11]

---

[10] Smith, *Trail of Gold and Silver,* 50; Smith, "Mother Lode for the West," 149, 169.

[11] Goulder, *Reminiscences,* 206–207.

Once they exhausted the placers of El Dorado, thousands of gold diggers had no reason to return to the East, while bad habits acquired in the West exiled thousands more from civilization. With their hard-won practical knowledge of mining and geology, these seasoned frontiersmen chased rumors to the Gold Bluffs and searched for Gold Lake, sailed to Australia and New Zealand and back, rushed to the Rogue, the Trinity, the Frasier, and to the Kern River Humbug. As California's golden wealth became harder to get at, many veterans turned back to the country they had already walked across. Some had actually found gold in the Rockies and Great Basin on their way west, but never in sufficient quantity to convince them they had gone far enough or distract them from seeking the end of the California rainbow. But as they drifted back over the trail during the next two decades, they ironically ignited rushes to the very rivers they had crossed on their way west—the Carson, the South Platte, the Boise, and the Sweetwater, where in 1867 crafty Mormon speculators ignited the trail era's last frenzy of mining and mockery at, of all places, South Pass.

By the late 1850s, industrial operations based on hard-rock mines and increasingly sophisticated smelters located in San Francisco or Nevada County had replaced placer mining as the source of California's mineral wealth. According to legend, a Carson Valley settler wanted to know what composed the mysterious "blasted blue stuff" that had frustrated local miners at a promising gold prospect on Sun Mountain. (The denizens of Gold Canyon more probably called the muck the "cursed black stuff" or, more likely still, the "damned black shit.") He carted a sack of the blue-gray quartz over the Sierra to assayers in Nevada City. Their report arrived late one evening: the quartz contained extraordinary amounts of silver. The news was supposed to be "a profound secret," but before dawn two leading citizens were in the saddle heading east, and by morning the news had set California's most prosperous mining community abuzz.[12] The 1859 rush to Washoe and the opening of the fabulous Comstock Lode led to the creation of Nevada Territory in 1861 and its admission as a state three years later, in time to vote for Abraham Lincoln.

Many tales are told about what started the rush to Pikes Peak: some of them are true. Late in 1858 rumors began to seep eastward about a discovery along Cherry Creek, where Lewis Ralston, a Cherokee miner on his way to California, had found gold near today's Denver in June 1850. The *Cherokee Advocate* reported the discovery "of a full placer of gold" along the Front Range of the Rocky Mountains that fall, but Ralston's find aroused little interest.[13] Indians came to Fort Laramie in 1857 "with a lot of gold dust and nuggets to trade for such articles as they wanted: and this was not the first time they had done it," Charles Morehead recalled. The

---

[12]Paul and West, *Mining Frontiers,* 59–60.
[13]Fletcher, Fletcher, and Whitely, *Cherokee Trail Diaries,* 310.

Cheyennes had always refused to say where they got the gold, but this time someone sweetened the pot. After demanding ponies, sugar, coffee, flour, tobacco, and
blankets, the Natives struck a deal. They took their client up the South Platte, and
when he returned, Moorhead recalled, "there was a great rush to Pikes Peak."[14]
A year later the news of the discovery attracted 60,000 fortune seekers to the
mines, Merle Mattes estimated, and the serious settlement of Colorado began.[15]

Prospectors repeated the process throughout the West. The always-restless
Elias D. Pierce could never shake the lingering effects of the Gold Bug's bite. He
rushed to California in 1849, worked as a prospector and peddler, and served in
the 1852 legislature before settling at the end of the Yreka Trail. He made the
first recorded ascent of Mount Shasta and joined the desultory rush to the Fraser
River diggings in 1858. Like most of the 30,000 men drawn to what soon became
British Columbia, Pierce concluded the strike was a humbug. Drifting south, he
explored the dusty rivers along the Oregon Trail: the Malheur, Burnt, Powder, and
Grande Ronde. Pierce "reported finding an extensive gold-field on those streams,
with room for thousands of miners, who could each make from three to fifteen
dollars a day." Some say he discovered prospector paradise on a hunt with the Nez
Perces, but Pierce never said exactly where his bonanza might be found, probably
because whatever he had seen was in Indian country.[16]

Pierre-Jean De Smet had learned of gold deposits along the Snake River tribu-
taries in today's Idaho during the early 1840s. In 1860 Pierce led ten men to the
mouth of the Clearwater River, where the Nez Perces confronted them. Ignoring
the warning, the prospectors spent a month searching for color without success,
until Wilbur Bassett turned up a shovelful of fine gold at Canal Gulch. The party
returned to Walla Walla with barely $100 in dust, but Pierce recruited thirty-three
men and evaded the troops sent to stop his return. They organized the Oro Fino
Mining District at Pierce City in December and staked seventy-one claims. After
two men snowshoed back to Walla Walla in early March with $800 in gold, the
boom was on. "Very soon every locality was converted into a scene of confusion,
bustle, and activity," recalled William Goulder. Spring 1861 witnessed a "mad
rush up the Columbia, simultaneously with the booming of cannon on the coast of
South Carolina," he wrote. "The Civil War was on in the East, and a new golden
era had opened in the west."[17]

Ten thousand gold seekers poured into the Snake River country in June 1862.
Prospectors who had initially headed for central Oregon in search of the legendary

[14]Morehead, "Personal Recollections," 606.
[15]Mattes, *Platte River Road Narratives*, 4,
[16]Thrapp, *Encyclopedia of Frontier Biography*, 4:410–11.
[17]Greever, *Bonanza West*, 257–61; Goulder, *Reminiscences*, 203–204.

Blue Bucket Mine prospected the Boise Basin and found what a local paper later touted as "the most extensive gold fields on the Continent." Located forty miles north of the Oregon Trail, the basin became the territory's richest mining district. Within a year of its founding in October 1862, Idaho City had a population of 6,167 souls, making it the largest city in the Pacific Northwest. When Congress created Idaho Territory on 3 March 1863, it boasted a population of some twenty thousand. More than a third of them were Chinese.[18]

The human saga is replete with examples of the fondness of Clio, muse of history, for irony. Hundreds of thousands of Americans crossed the scene of the era's last gold rush, South Pass, on their way to gold strikes in California, Nevada, Idaho, and Montana. The existence of gold near South Pass was not a secret: a fur trader reportedly made the first discovery in 1842, but Indians killed him.[19] Forty-niner James Godfrey's companions "found, as they imagined, large quantities of the glittering ore and brought up a large quantity of it." They decided it could not be gold, but it was "in fine scales and found in black sand on the bank of the river and would have been very rich had it been gold," Godfrey wrote.[20] Richard Burton saw "a quill full of large gold-grains from a new digging" in the Wind River Mountains in 1860. He observed, "Probably all the primitive masses of the Rocky Mountains will be found to contain the precious metal."[21]

On 27 June 1867, Lewis Robison, a grizzled veteran of twenty years in the Mormon West, rode into Great Salt Lake City with two men who claimed to have crushed the gold dust in their saddlebags from quartz rock in two days. The assayers turned the forty ounces into a $740.06 gold bar, which on 27 January 2012 would have been worth $69,240. All the discoverers would say was that "the mines are about 200 miles from here and are rich," but everyone knew Robison ran the Green River ferry. "Let there be no rush until something more definite will be ascertained," the press warned, but with the gold bar on display at the National Bank, this was like advising a prairie fire not to burn so quickly through tinder-dry grass. Within a week, the road to Green River was jammed. "THE NEW GOLD MINES" had "set the people wild." There definitely was gold at South Pass, the *Union Vedette* proclaimed that fall, "Slathers of It."[22] The region attracted several thousand fortune hunters in 1867, but this restless population ebbed and flowed. By April 1868, rumors of a strike in the Big Horn Mountains almost depopulated

---

[18]Arrington, *History of Idaho,* 1:190–97, 254.

[19]Chisholm, *South Pass,* 216.

[20]Delano, *Life on the Plains,* 109; Lorton, Diary, 24 July 1849, Bancroft Library, 176; Godfrey, "The Overland Diary," 20 June 1849.

[21]Burton, *City of the Saints,* 10 August 1859, 165/186.

[22]"Rich Gold Discovery!" 1 July 1867, 2/2; "The New Gold Mines," 11 July 1867, 3/1; "Gold, Slathers of It," 17 October 1867, 3/1, all *Union Vedette.*

South Pass City. Minor booms came and went at South Pass, and dredging operations and hydraulic mining squeezed money out of Rock Creek until the 1930s. Marginal mines generated some six million dollars over the course of a century, but they seldom did better than break even.[23]

Mining historians cannot resist telling colorful stories of the moment enterprising Americans discovered gold, even (or especially) when the discoverer was James Marshall (an embittered failure), James Finney (a drunk), or Henry Comstock (an insane charlatan). Such narratives discount the powerful influence the belief "in the supremacy of the United States, in the vital importance of commerce for national greatness, and in the legitimacy of using any means necessary to remove obstacles to that vision" had on the creation of the mining frontier. The West's legendary gold rushes all have much in common. Kent Curtis's insight that mineral rushes began with the convergence of cultural forces, not with a sudden discovery "in the raw, unmediated fact of gold in nature" reveals patterns and connections in stories historians have retold for generations. Using the 1862 rush to Montana as a prototype, Curtis noted how gold rush histories traditionally begin with an accidental discovery when "unsuspecting men happen upon an unexpected (although usually hoped for) lode of treasure." The big strike starts an epidemic of gold fever and leads to the swift creation of a new mining district. Two common factors made western mining booms possible: "acts of violence and legal agreements between the United States and the people who lived in these regions." It was no accident that Marshall's discovery took place in the last days of the Mexican-American War, nor a coincidence that rushes to the Comstock and Colorado began after Mormon retreat from Carson Valley and the Cheyenne defeat on the Solomon River in 1857. Gold was consistently "discovered" along an established or newly opened wagon road in a region or even creek where the presence of gold was well known, as happened in Montana.[24]

In 1852 near today's Dillon, Montana, veteran California horse trader François Finlay, known as Benetsee, exchanged dust panned in a local creek at a Hudson's Bay Company post for mining tools and provisions. To protect to the company's fur trade, the agent told Finlay to keep his find quiet. The gold was already an open secret, but Finlay's discovery had little impact until after the army defeated the Northwest's "most powerful tribes,—the Spokans, Coeur d'Alenes, Pelouzes and Yakimas, with a portion of the Nez Percés" who "became everywhere bold, defiant, and insulting" after the government failed to honor its treaty obligations. Weeks after miners again "discovered" gold at Benetsee Creek in 1862, topographical

---

[23]Chisolm, *South Pass,* 217–19.
[24]Curtis, "Producing a Gold Rush," 275–76.

engineer John Mullan found them "taking out about ten dollars per day to the hand, and with fair prospects of extensive digging." The captain, who had recently opened a government wagon road from Washington Territory to Fort Benton at the federally subsidized head of navigation on the Missouri River, renamed the spot "Gold Creek" and spread the news. "Mullan's completion of his wagon road represented not the beginning but a critical turning point in a much longer story about remapping the region with a new set of cultural goals," Curtis observed. The West's culture, "not nature, led the way to the gold rushes."[25]

History may not repeat itself, but the patterns and cycles of the California gold rush endure to this day. Trails played a central role in every new gold excitement and humbug. Each mining explosion began with a trail that led to a boom in population and commerce, while strike after strike created new branches and offshoots of the Oregon-California Trail. Each new frenzy changed the nature of overland travel in some subtle or dramatic way. Mining booms led to the creation of major freighting roads across the Sierra to the Comstock; to the opening of the Smoky Hills Trail up the Republican River that cut through the last isolated wintering ground of the Cheyenne; to the Simpson route across the last Paiute refuge in the central Great Basin; and to the contentious blazing of the Bozeman and Bridger trails to Montana. Each transformation of the overland road followed an Indian war and started a new one.

OUTRAGEOUS ACTS: INDIANS, TRAILS, AND THE GOLD RUSH

The West's heroic mythology ignores a basic fact: "The entire United States westward movement has been a process of dispossessing the original Indian nations and then converting public lands to private ownership."[26] Since settlers believed they put natural resources to better use than shiftless nomads, Americans had long justified their seizure of Indian lands, often in defiance of treaty obligations and federal land policy. "The day is not far distant, when what is now a 'barren waste,' on which a few miserable Indians are starving, will be occupied by an intelligent, industrious agricultural population, that can appreciate the beauties of the prospect, and enjoy the blessings that so rich a country is capable of produceing," wrote Gordon Cone on the Blue River.[27] The perception that Native peoples were a doomed race became an article of faith in the American West. The unburied bodies of Indian victims of diseases against which they had no natural resistance lining the roads to northern California in 1851 led a newspaper to conclude, "The ranks of the aborigines are

---

[25]Ibid., 84, 290, 296.

[26]Tompkins, "The Law of the Land," 83.

[27]Cone, Journal of Travels, 31 May 1849, BYU Library, 17.

rapidly wasting before the onward march of the pale face; and very soon, the last son of the forest will have been summoned to the presence of 'The Great Father.' "[28]

Between 1841 and 1860, John Unruh estimated overland emigrants killed 426 Indians, while Indians killed 362 whites; 90 percent of these deaths took place west of South Pass. Historians have relied on his numbers for a generation, but using only emigrants identified by name and excluding anonymous victims found along the trail, Richard Rieck has revised Unruh's analysis based on his much broader range of sources. He counted 105 emigrants killed by Indians east of South Pass, 226 emigrants killed west of South Pass, and twenty-two killed at unidentified locations. Rieck's total of 353 is a lower but more reliable number. Since emigrant reports of how many Indians they fought or killed are as demonstrably untrustworthy as official Vietnam War body counts, Rieck did not attempt to estimate Natives deaths.[29]

Trails had played a central role in the war on California's Indians since the days of the trailblazers. On Ewing Young's 1837 cattle drive to Oregon, Philip Edwards dismissed his companions' boasting of their plans to murder Indians as idle braggadocio. The party met friendly Indians on the Shasta River, and a man and boy about ten years old followed the drovers to camp. While unpacking, Edwards heard a shot. He turned to see the older Indian rise to flee from the man who tried to kill him, probably George Gay. A second shot rang out: the "Indian ran about 20 paces and fell dead, down the hill. Some of the scoundrels now hallooed, 'Shoot the boy! Shoot the boy!' The little fellow, however, turned, plunged in the brush, and escaped." (The murderers claimed they shot at the boy "to prevent his spreading the news.") When Edwards denounced it as "a mean, base, dastardly act," one man said coldly, "We are not missionaries, we will avenge the death of Americans." Vengeance worked both ways: four days later, Gay took an arrow in the back.[30] When Levi Scott, the Applegate brothers, and Peter Lassen opened trails through the lands of the Modoc, Klamath, and Achomawi peoples, they ignited some of the worst violence in western history.

Better assessments of the fate of California's oldest inhabitants are available elsewhere, but Alta California's long tradition of Indian bondage contributed to the brutal nature of white-Indian relations during the gold rush. Hastings Cutoff pioneer Frances Cooper recalled the slavocracy she found operating during the Mexican province's last days. "All the Spanish families had Indian slaves. They never permitted them to walk, but made them go about on the trot all the time. Those Indians made good slaves, excellent." Vaqueros would "ride in among the

---

[28]"Mortality among the Indians," *Sacramento Union,* 5 November 1851, 2/1.
[29]Unruh, *The Plains Across,* 185; Rieck, personal communication, 3 June 2011.
[30]Edwards, *The Diary of Philip Leget Edwards,* 42, 46.

Indian rancherias and drive out the boys and girls, leaving the mothers behind and killing the bucks if they offered any resistance." After she bought a female child for $100, wrote Cooper, three young Natives "came to my house of their own accord and explained that they had no home and wanted to work." These children did all her washing, ironing, cooking, and housecleaning, and one of the girls was a splendid nurse. Cooper settled at Salmon Bend near "a big rancheria of Indians right in what is now the heart of the town of Colusa, hundreds and hundreds of them," with another large rancheria five miles up the Sacramento.[31]

The story of the Kelsey clan's Indian wars illustrates the part trail veterans played in California's Indian history. In 1848 Ben and Samuel Kelsey, veterans of the first party to come overland to California in 1841, made money hand over fist trading in the mines. Using Native labor, they "made as high as $100 per day to the Indian," Nancy Kelsey recalled.[32] During 1850, the Kelseys and their "Sonomian hounds" perpetrated "outrageous acts of lawlessness and cruelty" against peaceful Natives. The newspapers and their neighbors, who depended on Indian labor, denounced the "damning deeds of the desperado gang," which upset the bonds of friendship with an Indian workforce long "employed on the farms of the white man with success." The white gang's avowed purpose was "exterminating the Indians in this valley and burning the ranches and lodges where this innocent and laboring people lived." In response to this challenge to the local labor supply's "undisturbed peaceful relations with the white settlers," Judge Stephen Cooper, a veteran of the Hastings Cutoff, ordered the arrest of fifteen lawless Americans, including the Kelseys. Who did Judge Cooper send to apprehend them? Joel P. Walker, who in 1840 brought the "first American born white family to migrate across the plains as a family."[33]

Long subjected to "the most abject servitude," California Indians supplied both Mexicans and Americans with a cheap workforce they treated as livestock, to be sold "as cattle, and the purchaser has the right to work them on the rancho, or take them into the mines." Exploiting Indian peonage was an obvious solution to the mining frontier's chronic labor shortage. After the initial rush, Native backs provided about half the labor required to pry the precious metal out of mountain streams and hillsides.[34] Combined with trading operations, the system could generate enormous fortunes, as 1846 overlander Benjamin Lippincott learned. With five partners, including John C. Frémont, Lippincott built a trading post in April

---

[31]Cooper, "Foremothers Tell of Olden Times," *San Francisco Chronicle*, 9 September 1900. Some seventy-seven members of the Cachil Dehe Band of Wintun Indians now live as the Colusa Indian Community on the Cachildehe Rancheria, a 573-acre federal reservation created in 1907. See Pritzker, *Native American Encyclopedia*, 152–54.

[32]Kelsey, "Nancy (Roberts) Kelsey's Own Story," 10–11.

[33]"Recent Outrages," *Alta California*, 16 March 1850, 2/2; "Indian Outrages," *Alta California*, 19 March 1850, 2/1; *Sacramento Bee*, 20 October 1956.

[34]Rawls, *California Indians*, 120–21; Bancroft, *History of California*, 6:90.

1849 that gave him control of "all the Indians between the Tuolumne and Merced river by which a lucrative business has been done." His Indians "gathered in one day 38 pounds of gold," he wrote in September.[35]

During 1848 almost everyone in California—Anglo, Mexican, Native, Polynesian, or Chinese—was obsessively seeking gold, but it was not a mystical golden age of peace. In a single week in July, four white men and a hundred Indians pulled $17,000 dollars in gold from a hundred-yard trench on Weber Creek for English sailor-turned-rancher William Daylor.[36] Daylor hired more Native miners in April 1849, but whites attacked his camp and beat two Indians to death. The killers continued their rampage, slaughtering fourteen Natives on the road to Daylor's ranch on the Cosumnes River, capturing the women and children, "for what purposes, I am unable to say." Daylor and his servants buried fifteen of the victims, while his father-in-law, Thomas Rhoads, buried two more. The marauders boasted of killing twenty-seven Indians. Twenty-two men and thirty-four women and children were "yet missing from the rancheria," Daylor reported.[37]

As violence spread in 1850, the federal government dispatched three commissioners to negotiate with California's tribes and settle them on reservations. "As there is *no further west,* to which they *can* be removed," one commissioner concluded, Californians had two choices "in relation to the remnants of once numerous and powerful tribes, viz: *extermination or domestication.*" That December Indians attacked an agent's trading post on the Fresno, killing the commissioner's clerk and two others. The Mariposa War against the Miwoks and the Yokuts led to the discovery of Yosemite and the conquest of one of the state's largest Indian populations. It raged until the commissioners signed a treaty with six tribes at Camp Fremont on 19 March 1851. After more than a year's work, the agents had negotiated eighteen treaties with some 25,000 Indians. They proposed creating reservations totaling 7,488,000 acres, or 7.5 percent of the state. "Congress, to no one's surprise, refused to ratify the reservation treaties," Robert Chandler noted, but agents established four insignificant reservations. Californians hated the policy and, lacking anyplace farther west to drive Native peoples, sought to ship them over the Sierra to Utah Territory. In the mountains, "we are hunted like wild beasts," said Pasqual, a Yokuts tribal leader. On the Kings River Reservation, "we are shot down like cattle."[38]

This life-and-death struggle in El Dorado troubled many overland veterans. When Natives visited the mining camps, "they evince the most timid and friendly

---

[35]Lippincott to Stephens, 25 September 1849, Bancroft Library.
[36]Taylor, "California and New Mexico," 530–31.
[37]"Correct Detail of the Massacre of Indians," *Placer Times,* 12 May 1849, 1/1–2.
[38]Rawls, *California Indians,* 141–43; Chandler, "An Uncertain Influence," 232.

nature," wrote William Swain, but the miners were "sometimes guilty of the most brutal acts with the Indians, such as killing the squaws and papooses. Such incidents have fallen under my notice that would make humanity weep and men disown their race."[39] Alonzo Delano recouped his battered fortunes in 1850 drawing crayon portraits "of the long-bearded miners, at an ounce a head" and invested in real estate next to a village he named Oleepa, after the Maidus who owned the land. Treating a widespread skin disease won Delano their goodwill, and he came to admire his neighbors during his three months among them. "The Indians of California are regarded as being treacherous, revengeful, and dishonest," he wrote, but they were "governed by their own sense of propriety and justice, and are probably less likely to break the laws which they recognize as right, than are the whites to break theirs." He blamed renegade miners for stirring up violence. "I never saw a quarrel," Delano said of his stay at Oleepa, "and I firmly believe that nine-tenths of the troubles between the whites and Indians, can be traced to imprudence in the former."[40]

Among the grim results of the California gold rush, nothing surpasses the populist campaign to exterminate Indians. Violence against Indians in Oregon and California "was not warfare; it was Indian hunting—the stalking and killing of human beings as if they were animals," wrote Richard White. Despite its brutal nature, "Genocide was never the official policy of the U.S. government, but it was the wish of many, though hardly all, Anglo American settlers. When left to their own devices, they could on occasion put it into practice."[41] Only the federal government's refusal to endorse a campaign of extermination made such brutal aggression stop short of being official policy, but historians increasingly view this as a fine distinction. "Genocide is a new word for an old crime," Huppa-Cherokee scholar Jack Norton wrote. "It means the deliberate destruction of national, racial, religious or ethnic groups."[42] Over the course of thirty years a few Californians accomplished the virtual genocide of the state's Native peoples. Although never totally dispossessed, the survivors faced a long, hard struggle. "There is a sort of predatory warfare almost constantly kept up between the whites and Indians in the mountains," former wagon train captain David Willock wrote in 1850. Indians had attacked two men near Coloma, including an intimate acquaintance of his, killing one and badly wounding the other. "The Indians have paid the debt with heavy usury," Willock noted, "which is uniformly the case."[43]

---

[39] Swain to George Swain, 16 January 1850, in Swain, *The World Rushed In,* 328.

[40] Delano, *Life on the Plains,* 292, 309–10.

[41] White, *It's Your Misfortune,* 337, 340.

[42] Norton, *When Our Worlds Cried,* 137; Madley, "California's Yuki Indians," 303–32.

[43] Willock to Sosey, 24 June 1850, *Missouri Whig,* September 1850.

Congress appropriated $924,295.65 in 1854 to pay for past California militia campaigns aimed almost exclusively at Indians. "We have an Indian hunt here in our neighborhood about once every two weeks," a miner wrote in 1850. The Americans who dominated the new state's population arrived "with generations of hatred for Indians on older frontiers." Overlanders and Argonauts committed atrocities with equal enthusiasm, driving Native Californians from their homes by the thousands, and starving, beating, raping, and murdering them with impunity. The devastation "was literally incredible," observed biologist Sherburne Cook: population figures reveal the extent of the havoc. Estimates of the number of Native Californians before the American conquest range from Stephen Powers's 1875 calculation of 705,000 (down from a pre-contact high of 1,520,000), to Alfred Kroeber's 1925 guess of 133,000 in 1770, to Cook's 1976 estimate of 310,000 in 1769, to fewer than 30,000 by 1865.[44]

The perception that trails encouraged a campaign of extermination is not new. "The tribes regarded emigrants as a white tribe infringing upon their rights," recalled Carlisle Abbott, who crossed the plains in 1850 and 1852. The Indians' fate resembled "the massacre of the whole nation of Armenians by the Turks, but no pen can describe the misery and despair of a Pawnee village,—of men, women and children dying of hunger,—while the white tribe was killing, or scaring their game off," he wrote. "I say that our Government here caused as much misery by negligence as the Turks have by savagery." The indiscriminate slaughter of the bison, "killing them and cutting out choice pieces and leaving the rest to rot, while the Indians and their wives and children were starving" constituted "the most flagrant injustice this Government ever permitted its people to practice." Abbott would not blame the Indians "if they had cleaned out the whole white tribe within their borders, for they had owned and occupied these lands long before Uncle Sam was born."[45]

Historian Albert Hurtado described the political, social, economic, and environmental revolutions the gold rush ignited in California, but in human terms, nothing matched the demographic revolution gold began, he concluded. In 1848 Indians outnumbered all whites by more than ten to one, and Native peoples controlled the headwaters of the major rivers and virtually all of California gold country, including much of its richest grazing, farm, and timberlands. "In 1860 Indians retained legal rights to none of this land." The United States did not grant them the citizenship the Treaty of Guadalupe Hidalgo had promised. Those who survived the gold rush were "marginalized and, for the most part, grievously impoverished," their lives "at the mercy of a dominant, mostly uncaring population of Euro-American invaders." Historians still speak of the long siege of violence

---

[44]Madley, "California's Yuki Indians," 322; Chandler, "An Uncertain Influence," 232; Hurtado, "Clouded Legacy," 95–96; Cook, *Population of the California Indians,* 200; Powers, "California Indian Characteristics," 308–309.
[45]Abbott, *Recollections,* 26–27.

against indigenous Californians in apocalyptic terms, but a new generation of Indian enterprises proliferating across the Golden State reveals that the region's Native population was not destroyed. Even during the worst of times, Indians "made choices about their futures based on their sense of history and their standards of justice," wrote Hurtado. "Accommodating, working, fighting, hiding out—in a word, surviving—they were the seed for today's California Indians."[46]

Every Body is Crazy: Life in the Mines

After reaching the Sacramento River in 1849, James S. Tolles thanked his great protector for sparing him many dangers and privations and bringing him to a civilized land in good health and spirits, but the long and worrisome task was "one which I would not undertake again for all the gold in this region." Tolles had traveled 2,670 miles, "and all the way but a few miles on foot. Driving ox teams, through water, mud, dust, heat, cold, and snow. And over Mountains, through hollows and deserts, first one then another but never getting discourage[d]."[47] Seventeen weeks after leaving Missouri in 1850, Henry Wellenkamp ended his "hard, dangerous and toilsome journey." The trail's natural curiosities and fine romantic passages gave it a great many pleasant scenes, he wrote, "yet the immense emigration—50 to 70,000 persons, constantly crowding, making clouds of dust, grazing away the grass—obstructing many passes by their dead animals and impregnating the air with stench, made it on the whole—unpleasant and toilsome."[48]

Those who survived the perils of the road expressed relief, joy, and exhaustion upon reaching El Dorado, but most sojourners quickly realized that their dreams of instant wealth were illusions. Even when gold was available in astonishing abundance, it required arduous work under desperate and debilitating conditions to accumulate a pile. It became harder as more and more people flooded into the mines and skimmed off the easily accessible gold. Impressions of the mines were as varied as the Argonauts themselves, but after 1849 everyone found profitable diggings elusive, health conditions perilous, supplies expensive, women scarce, violence universal, and vigilante action swift and brutal. "California is not the country that it has been represented to be; and by no means the Italy of America," wrote John McCarty. It had a deadly climate, unhealthy water, and almost constant rain for five or six months, so "consequently the seasons are unfit for agriculture." The discouraged miners John Cobbey met on Weber Creek all told him, "It is a hard old country."[49]

---

[46]Hurtado, "Clouded Legacy," 94–98; Hurtado, *Indian Survival,* 124.

[47]Tolles, Journal of My Travels, 17 October 1849, BYU Library, 51–52.

[48]Wellenkamp, Travel Diary, 21 August 1850, Western Historical Manuscripts.

[49]McCarty, Correspondence to the *Indiana American,* 3 May 1849, 1; Cobbey, Journal, 29 July 1850, BYU Library, 188.

The golden visions of the quarter million people who came to California by 1852 proved hard to shake. Fantastic tales of golden lakes or auriferous beaches lured swarms of prospectors deep into the mountains and up the rugged, rain-bound coast. Men often abandoned profitable diggings to go "looking for those 50 thousand dollar strikes," Elijah Spooner observed.[50] For all but a lucky few, the big payday was always just over the next mountain or down the next stream. "We hear about great diggins," wrote John M. Blair, "but have never got to the place, and aint going to hunt any more for them."[51]

To the dismay of all, streams were not filled with nuggets for the picking. "Gold cannot be dug from the soil, without hard work, & exposure, & various privations—as to society, there is none, but the *Gaming* Table, which is found in every other House," wrote Charles Lockwood. "This is no country to enjoy life."[52] A man may have found a solid gold nugget weighing almost fifteen pounds at Coloma late in 1849, but "if you love your family half as much as I do, if you like good victuals and nights rest, if you do not wish to make a fool of yourself stay at home," advised John L. Martin. After enduring the cold rains of two California winters, he complained everything was "like a lotery, all is a lotery, even life here is a lotery." He repeated his advice: "stay at home."[53]

Hundreds of backwoods mining camps sprang up overnight as strategic markets at Placerville, Marysville, and Nevada City boomed as trading centers. "Stockton is about as large as Milwaukee was 6 years ago," wrote Daniel Budd in 1852. "Much business doing & building fast." Scores of taverns lined "the dead-level sixty-mile road from Sacramento to Stockton."[54] Sacramento quickly became "a Callico City a whole City made of Canvas and Calico Suffitient to cover a population of from 6 to 10,000," Thomas Bedford told a relative, but it was "as much as a man can do to get there with his naked body."[55] The vast number of fortune seekers swiftly transformed California's backcountry. "Here, in this strange valley, where two months before there was not a living soul, and where the snow was twenty feet deep, we found a cluster of cabins, and cloth stores, with groceries and hotels, and the usual concomitants of a mining town—scores of monte banks," wrote Alonzo Delano at Nevada City. No matter how far miners might go into the mountains, gamblers followed to tempt them to part with their hard-earned gains in games of chance, "and they too often find willing victims to their nefarious practices.

---

[50]Spooner to "My Dear Wife," 2 March 1850, BYU Library.

[51]Blair to "Dear Brothers and Sisters," 22 January 1850, Mattes Library.

[52]Lockwood to "Respected and highly esteemed friends," 7 December 1849, Missouri Historical Society.

[53]Martin to "Dear & much beloved wife," 22 December 1849; to Rebecca, 24 March 1851, Typescript, Mattes Library.

[54]Budd, Journal, 4 September 1852, Mattes Library.

[55]Lewis, Overland to California, October 1849, Beinecke Library; Bedford to A. M. Bedford, 9 December 1849, Western Historical Manuscripts.

"Panning" on the Mokelumne

The primitive technology placer miners used to pan for gold on the Mokelumne River soon gave way to industrialized mining featuring diversion dams for "river operations," hydraulic mining using high-pressure hoses, and highly engineered hard-rock mines. From "How We Get Gold in California," *Harper's New Monthly Magazine* (April 1860): 600.

Here, too, we found families of women and children, who, despising the fatigue and dangers of the trip, left the safer and more luxurious comforts of the older towns, to grapple with the golden god."[56]

The influx of one hundred thousand young American males into the newly conquered province in 1849 created remarkable social conditions. The absence of women and their moderating influence put a rough edge on life in the "diggins." Forty-niners often commented on the honesty and order that prevailed in the early days, when workmen and merchants left tools, goods, and even their pokes of gold unprotected. When these balmy days vanished, lawlessness and rough justice triumphed. Rich diggings attracted scoundrels and blacklegs to the mining camps of the Sierra Nevada; as Gordon Cone said, "hell has sent her body guard to California."[57] Even during the purported Golden Age of 1848 and 1849, the strict morality common back in the States collapsed. "There are but few here but gamble more or less, and on the Sabbath day is the time they indulge these vices the most," wrote Henry Cox. "Men are not happy here and they seek excitement to drive away the dull monotony."[58] Joseph Wood summed up the state of affairs precisely: "Every Body is crazy."[59]

The new El Dorado's charms would soon wear thin, predicted Aaron Abbott in 1852. Abbott had "not seen a Preacher on the Plains nor since I arrived in California," but firearms were so common that he was unable to sell a rifle and revolver at Salt Lake, and in California "they are of no value in the market." He had "heard of several murders and nine cases of lynching," in which trials were "conducted with proper order." The prisoners usually "confessed their guilt and then were hung, by first running two wagons together so as to rear the tongues against each other between which the Prisoners were Swung." Abbott had seen "more Fiddles than Bibles more Cards than Hymn Books more Dirks and Pistols than Book[s] for the cultivation of morals."[60] Life in the mines took its toll on the character of many new Californians. "I give you a true picture of the America position of society in California, when I say that gamblers, swindlers and *prostitutes* form its aristocracy," wrote Adonijah Strong Welch.[61]

Despite the harsh conditions in the golden land, opportunity was plentiful for those who arrived healthy enough to work. Men who got their teams over the trail in good condition prospered as freighters. Carpenters and mechanics commanded high wages. Forty-niners found even "the Bucarios, or men who lasso the wild cattle on the Ranches, get from $200 to $300 per month, & board." Prices for basic

[56]Delano, *Life on the Plains,* 340–41.
[57]Cone, Journal, 16 April 1850, BYU Library, 95.
[58]Cox, "Letter from California," 26 September 1849, 1/3.
[59]Wood, Diary, 19 October 1849, Huntington Library.
[60]Abbott to "Dear Friends," 18 September 1852, Mattes Library.
[61]Welch, "Three Gold Rush Letters," 30 June 1850, 73.

necessities were outrageous, but with so much gold and so little to spend it on, it was hard to tell the rich from the poor. "The common dress here is a wide brimmed hat, Panama or wool, a red or brown woolen shirt with collar of same, pants with a sash or belt around the waist, boots,—and at night a coat," wrote Dr. Samuel Mathews. He feared his dress coats were out of fashion but hoped he could sell them.[62] The doctor probably kept them, since simplicity was the standard in dress and cleanliness. "I have four or five hundred dollars in my pocket every day while I am at work," Joseph Wilfrey told his wife. He had quite a pile, but acknowledged, "if you or anyone else was to see me in the states in my present garb barefooted &c you would not think I ever saw five hundred dollars."[63]

Many if not most of the gold seekers had no intention of settling permanently so far from home "and returned East after a very short trial of the hardships of mining."[64] Those who could often left immediately. "There is Hundreds of Emigrants taking Shipping for home as soon as they get here not finding the Country as they had Pictured it," John A. Richey told a friend.[65] "Some lucky fellows (who are few)," wrote George Brouster, "pick up their pile and *voomise*."[66] As gold became scarcer and local economies vacillated between boom and bust, it became harder to make money. The "Golden Sands of the Sacrimento" were "pretty well washed" when George Lawson arrived in 1850. "Some that crossed the plains this summer have got there piles & gone home, others & a good many to have gone without it."[67]

Thousands lost the perilous gamble of crossing the plains, and more felt lucky if they escaped from the mines with their lives. Nine out of ten of the men in the goldfields declared their intention to leave within two years, and "the chances are greatly on the side of their returning poorly compensated for the time spent, and the privations and hardships undergone." Most Forty-niners had "not now as much money, over the sum expended to get here, as will pay their expenses home," wrote David Willock.[68] "If a man is fortunate in this country he will make money fast, but if not, it is one of the hardest countrys in the world to make a living in," wrote George Davidson. "You hear only of those who have made their pile and gone home but nothing is said of the thousands that have not a dollar to help themselves with."[69] The exorbitant cost of plain living, not to mention the temptations of the fleshpots and gambling hells, impoverished anyone who was not lucky—and those who relied on luck squandered their futures. "Monte wins

---

[62]Mathews to "Dear Huldah," 24 September 1849, in *Mathews Family*, 308, 310.

[63]Wilfrey to "Dear wife and children," 13 October 1850, Missouri Historical Society.

[64]Abbey, *California,* editor's preface, n.p.

[65]Richey to "Friend Emmons," 3 October 1850, Missouri Historical Society.

[66]Brouster to "Dear Parents," 2 September 1850, Western Historical Manuscripts.

[67]Lawson to "Dear Parents," 15 October 1850, Huntington Library.

[68]Willock to Sosey, 24 June 1850, *Missouri Whig,* September 1850.

[69]Davidson to "Brother," 12 January 1853, Beinecke Library.

half the gold that is dug in California," wrote John M. Blair. "Going home by Ship is the talk of every one who has crossed the Plains."[70]

Aretas Blackman wrote of the trek, "Crossing the desert men suffering & animals dying with thirst [is] the best remedy for the thirst for Gold, thirst for fresh water, & traveling in the heat of the day over the blazing hot sand without a shrub or tree to rest under for a moment." He was glad he had arrived, but he voiced a refrain that became a standard lament: "All the gold in California would not tempt me to make the trip again, or so I think."[71] William Standley had only to reach Fort Laramie to regret what he had forsaken. "If I were at home again, and knowing what I know now," he wrote, "I would not again start on this trip for all the gold in the world."[72] The sentiment finds its most eloquent expression in the letters of the men who left their wives and children behind. "Oh Mary, if I were once more with you," wrote William A. Carter, "all the gold that is buried in these mountains would never induce me to leave you."[73] Only one thing would ever separate them from their loved ones again, many wandering husbands and fathers vowed: "If I live to git home I am Sertan I never shall leave you a gaine until death," James M. Walden promised his wife.[74] "If I ever get with you again nothing But de[a]th shall seperate us A gain," James E. Gale wrote from Nevada City. "I aught to Be horse whoped to deth for Ever Leaving you to Come hear."[75]

After initial discouragement, others took a longer view: despite the hardships they endured, many showed resilience and optimism. "The week did not close very encouragingly and some of our men are beginning to rail down upon California, and with no brightening hopes of a successful enterprise, begin now to despair of their bright anticipations," reported T. J. Van Dorn. Yet, he added, "Perseverance will bring all right at the end." He later concluded, "Those who emigrated to this country to make it a permanent place of residence cannot help but do well, even without going to the mines." Those who came to make money and "expected to light suddenly upon a bank of gold and return in a short time with a fat harvest" were usually disappointed. "Some few do this," Van Dorn wrote, "but many will fall short."[76]

If free land attracted Americans to Oregon, their hopes proved as illusory as the free gold of California. Superintendent of Indian Affairs Joel Palmer finally extinguished the Indian title in 1855 when he persuaded the survivors of the Kalapuya, Clackamas, Nahankhuotana, Lakmiut, Chepenafa, Molala, Nestucca, Chasta, Santiam, Chastacosta, Tumwater, Umpqua, Wapato, and Yamel peoples

---

[70]Blair to "Dear Brothers and Sisters," 22 January 1850, Mattes Library.
[71]Blackman to "Brother John," 19 August 1849, Bancroft Library.
[72]Standley, 22 June 1852, Western Historical Manuscripts.
[73]Carter to "My Beloved Wife," 11 August 1850, Western Historical Manuscripts.
[74]Walden to "Dear Polly," 6 January 1851, Western Historical Manuscripts.
[75]Gale to "Beloved Wife," 15 December 1850, Beinecke Library.
[76]Van Dorn, Diary, 16–23 September, 19 November 1849, Beinecke Library.

of western Oregon to sign treaties and agree to move to a destitute and crowded reservation in the Coastal Range. After the Donation Land Act of 1850, settlers quickly claimed what was left of Oregon's best farmland, but it was still worth substantially less than similar acreage in Missouri. Lafayette Spencer advised his brother in 1852 to avoid the long, tedious journey and stay in Iowa. "I have traveled all through the Willamette Valley. It is about 20 miles wide and is cut up with hills and mountains. All the land that is worth anything is cleaned up," he wrote. "The Umpequah Valley is not as good as the Willamette Valley, nor half as big. All of the best of the claims are taken up. I shall advise you to stay where you are." That said, by his own account Spencer lived "fat and saucy" in his new home in the West.[77]

"The land in this vicinity is mostly taken," Charles Butler wrote from Oregon City in 1853. His brother had bought a nearby 320-acre claim for only $250, but Charles was rethinking his dream of becoming a landowner. "This going into the forest and commence [sic] a farm goes a little against the grain," Butler observed. "I hear I can get $5.00 per day at the City working at my trade." He got a job building steamboats in Linn City.[78] James Miller's experience indicates Butler made the right choice. Long after proving his claim, Miller concluded his land donation was a detriment. "I could have gone to work at boating on the Willamette or Columbia River. In four years' time that I lost on the land claim, I could have earned enough to purchase three such farms."[79]

By the time the act expired in 1855, the government had given away 2,614,082.24 acres—4,084.5 square miles, an area almost the size of Jamaica—as donation land claims, yet this constituted not quite 4 percent of Oregon's terra firma. At its standard price of $1.25 an acre, the government sacrificed $3,267,602.80. Public lands still constitute more than half of the state of Oregon, so for less than the cost of a modern aircraft carrier, "the United States secured the Pacific slope," noted James M. Tompkins. The system's critics charged that a grant half the size would have attracted as many settlers, and since one man could only farm forty acres, granting a square mile of land denied homes to a dozen families. "Lands were taken without any regard to the points of compass, thus ignoring our system of land surveys, so simple and yet so beautiful," topographical engineer John Mullan complained in 1862. Gold discoveries and the markets they created did more to settle Oregon than the spirit generous spirit of the donation act, he observed.[80]

Patenting a donation claim was not as simple as it sounded, but hanging onto it proved even harder. "There are no 640-acre farms now," Isaac V. Mossman wrote in 1900. "All are divided up." Within Oregon's borders, men and women filed 7,437

---

[77]Spencer to William Spencer, 27 December 1852, in "Oregon Trail Diary," 305.

[78]Butler to "Dear Father," 11 October 1853, Beinecke Library.

[79]Miller, "Early Oregon Scenes," 161.

[80]Tompkins, "The Law of the Land," 109; Mullan, "Walla Walla to San Francisco," 213.

claims, but by 1856 only 808 of them had been surveyed and patented. Due to the incomplete survey, no public land was sold in Oregon until 1862. At century's end about two-thirds of the claims had passed from the hands of the original filers and their descendants. "While the rigors of pioneer farming ended many of those dreams," Michael Tate wrote, "the majority succumbed to fluctuating agricultural prices, unpredictable weather, and the increasing costs of mechanized farming."[81]

The West could be a hard place, but despite their troubles, California was California and Oregon was the best poor man's country in the world. The contrasting reactions to California could "be accounted for on the score of the different temperament of the writers, and the different hopes and expectations of those who come here, as well as with the success with which their various efforts are crowned," David Willock noted.[82] After their illusions vanished, dream seekers often succumbed to the region's charms. "California is every thing that the most vivid accounts you have seen describe it to be," C. F. Kirtley wrote home.[83] As its rough-and-ready society matured, so, too, did the state's attractions. Tens of thousands of trail veterans put down roots—and many of those who came overland after gold and free land disappeared were men who had already made the trek and returned west with their families. "The emigration here now is of a more permanent character. Men are bringing their families and their wives and what better can they do? Tis the best country in the tera firma," Pusey Graves rhapsodized. "Men may say what they please, *California will remain the loveliest and best country,* all things considered, this side of Jerusalem."[84]

Contemplating his own trip across the plains, Giles Isham expressed the resilience that sustained many overlanders. "There is much beautiful scenery; much to endure; much watching by day and night; much enjoyment in the many incidents that transpire; some sober moments on the reflection of home and its endearments," he wrote. "But the God of Americans is gold, a *balm* for every *wound.* So cheer up and go ahead, and enjoy the trip and get all you can."[85]

GOLD DIGGING IS ALL A LOTTERY: CONCLUSIONS

After crossing the plains, Forty-niner James M. Hutchings turned his hand to mining before abandoning hard labor to try something harder still: a literary career. *Hutchings' California Magazine* appeared monthly from 1856 to 1861. This invaluable record reflected Hutchings's relentless curiosity, which led him to take some of

[81]Mossman, "A Pioneer of 1853," 5; Johansen and Gates, *Empire of the Columbia,* 232–34; Tate, in Belshaw, "Crossing the Plains," 10.

[82]Willock, "California Letter," 15 November 1849, *Missouri Whig,* 28 February 1850.

[83]Kirtley to "My Dear Wife," October 27, 1849, "California Letters," January 1850.

[84]Graves to "Dearest Jane," 11 December 1850, Graves Collection, Earlham College Library.

[85]Isham, *Guide to California and the Mines,* 61.

the first tourists to Yosemite and preserve much of his adopted state's colorful history. During summer 1857, "anxious to obtain an excellent portrait of Mr. Marshall," he visited Coloma to photograph and interview the famed discoverer of California's gold.

Histories of western gold rushes usually begin when someone notices "flecks and nuggets of something with unsurpassed power to set people in motion—gold." In California, that someone was James Marshall. Hutchings found the taciturn carpenter as morose and as broke as ever, but Marshall told him a story. During the summer of '49, a man came to his fabled sawmill to buy a load of lumber. When he learned Edward Hargraves had come from Australia, Marshall asked, "Why don't you go and dig gold among your own mountains? for, what I have heard of that country, I have no doubt whatever that you would find plenty of it there." Hargraves did, and the British government rewarded him with fifteen thousand pounds to signal its appreciation for the million pounds sterling his discovery of Australia's goldfields had contributed to the Empire. In contrast, Marshall had been "wronged of every dollar and every foot of land which he possessed." But for the daily charity of strangers, the man who had launched "a new age—THE GOLDEN AGE" would not have a place to lay his head. Marshall refused to let Hutchings take his picture: he had a duty to himself to retain his likeness, as it was "*all I have that I can call my own,* and I feel like any other poor wretch—I want *something* for self," he explained. "I owe the country nothing." The enterprising energy of Yankeedom orators and editors celebrating California's golden days boasted about "was not national, but individual." The historic balance sheet, Marshall complained, stood thus: "Yankeedom, $600,000,000. Myself Individually, $000,000,000."[86]

"Gold digging is all a lottery," complained Elijah Spooner.[87] None of the great battles of the Civil War "broke so many heart strings and caused such widespread pain as did the Californian gold migration," but it also spared thousands from a lifetime of poverty, wrote Forty-niner John S. Hittell as the overland era ended.[88] In the century following Marshall's discovery, California produced two billion dollars' worth of gold. Such wealth transformed the state, but its land and people paid a horrendous price. The rush for riches led to the total extinction of many tribes and the near-annihilation of others and enabled land commissioners, attorneys, and Congress to deprive the old *Californios* of their land grants. Dredging, hydraulic, and hard-rock mining left "gaping holes and barren debris piles" throughout the Mother Lode. The resulting rivers of mud drove away the salmon and flooded valuable farmlands. Still, "gold was the touchstone that set California in

---

[86]West, *Contested Plains,* 13; Hutchings, "The Discovery of Gold in California," 201–202.

[87]Spooner to "My Dear Wife," 21 April 1850, BYU Library.

[88]Hittell, *The Resources of California,* xvii.

MINERS AT SPANISH FLAT

This daguerreotype, attributed to Joseph B. Starkweather, shows miners working a long tom at Spanish Flat in El Dorado County. Half of them appear to be among the six to seven hundred slaves and freemen the 1850 census counted in the Mother Lode country. Many African Americans who came overland shared the dream of "an old negress," who told Joseph Warren Wood that "if she served her master well on the road to California," she could gain her freedom and "return & claim my children that they may be free too." Courtesy California History Room, California State Library, Sacramento.

motion on the course that made her what she is today," John Caughey observed. Gold "did things for the West at large and the Pacific basin that otherwise would not have been done for a generation or perhaps at all."[89]

The tales of adventure, endurance, triumph, disaster, heartbreak, heroism, and depravity told in these pages offer a sweeping view of what it was like to travel "the plains across" to Oregon and California during the gold rush. The recurrent theme of young lives suddenly snuffed out—see the sad fates of Lewis Trimble, Dexter Tiffany, Samuel Ayres, Thomas Hudspeth, and Eliza and little Maria Terry—may or may not be good storytelling. But as professors have observed for a century, stories are not history. Their deaths illustrate the toll gold-rush trails took on some who followed them to the Pacific, but their stories are far from representative. To see the overland experience through the lens of personal tragedy is no more legitimate than to portray trails history as a triumphant episode in a great nation's march to its divine destiny, a view prosperous old pioneers promoted in dozens of smug memoirs. The gold rush had its winners as well as its losers, especially for Native peoples, but for all its disastrous consequences, the epoch and the trails it created had an enduring and often positive effect on the American West. Many of those who made the journey did not find the better life they sought, but their children and grandchildren appreciated the bounty and opportunities their sacrifices and suffering had bequeathed them.

The roads to Oregon and California first attracted hundreds, then thousands and tens of thousands, and finally hundreds of thousands of men and women seeking the American Dream—a better life for oneself and one's children. California offered hope to oppressed peoples whose futures seemed hopeless. William H. Hall returned from the goldfields rich enough to celebrate a wedding whose "splendour" was "perhaps without parallel in the history of the colored society of New York." Hall's speech on "Hopes and Prospects of Colored People in California" encouraged black emigration, as did a Philadelphia newspaper's report of the arrival of two black miners with $30,000 accumulated during their four months in El Dorado.[90]

Most of the young men who caught California fever had not the slightest intention of settling in the West. Men came to California hoping to get rich and return to a life of leisure in their old homes, not "to enjoy life, but to make money, so that they may enjoy life in some other country," John Hittell observed.[91] The trail stripped away their golden visions and changed them in so many ways that they often found they could never go home again. Their quandary transformed them and, in the process, the world around them. Their evil habits and individual

[89]Caughey, *Gold Is the Cornerstone*, 292; Caughey, *California Gold Rush*, 291–94.

[90]Lapp, *Blacks in Gold Rush California*, 22.

[91]Hittell, *The Resources of California*, 442.

squandering of wealth on fast living characterized the era and ultimately played out on a larger stage, as this rabid quest for wealth became industrialized. With the development of hydraulic and hard-rock mining, public assets became the target of ruthless exploitation in the service of enormous wealth concentrated among very few. The cycles of boom and bust that characterized mining madness became the most reliable feature of the West's economy and would be repeated in the exploitation of its timber, fisheries, and oil and gas resources.

Long after discovering gold at the foot of the Comstock Lode in 1850, when he should have been enjoying California's "palmiest days," Abner Blackburn complained, "California is not a land of gold and we are nearly all poor." Fortunes in gold dust had slipped through his fingers, but after a lifetime of backbreaking labor he survived into the twentieth century on $12 a month from a Mexican-American War pension.[92] "Why are so many of the Old-timers so poor?" asked one 1890 chronicle; Why, "when the mines were so rich, the gold so easy to get, and all kinds of business so good," were they not all wealthy? His answer was that they had spent all their money, and the gold rush "had the effect to destroy all habits or ideas of economy."[93] This was true enough, but the sorry financial fate of so many Forty-niners had more to do with how dramatically unrestrained capitalism concentrated wealth than with their personal profligacy. "It is often said that all the old Pioneers are poor men," wrote Sarah Royce in a telling observation. "Doubtless this is too sweeping."[94]

Long celebrated as a triumph of American culture and character, the rush to exploit the region's glittering mineral wealth transformed the West between 1849 and 1865. Federal judge Lorenzo Sawyer, who had crossed the plains in 1850, halted some of the most destructive mining techniques in his "gold vs. grain decision" of 1884. By then hydraulic miners had already poured 1.6 billion cubic yards of sediment into the state's waterways. In an age that has pushed the limits of what once seemed limitless resources, the human and natural costs of the Age of Gold are increasingly apparent. Gold mining moved about 5.6 billion cubic yards of California. "Hard-rock miners produced 30 million cubic yards of tailings. Dredges, which used mercury to process sand and gravel scooped from river channels and flood plains, left about 4 billion cubic yards of debris heaped alongside streams," reported journalist John Krist. "Spread a foot deep, that much debris would cover 5,424 square miles, nearly the area of Connecticut."[95]

California fever introduced something radical and new to the American

---

[92]Blackburn to Clawson, 13 April 1897, in *Frontiersman*, 220.
[93]Haskins, *The Argonauts of California*, 260, 262.
[94]Royce, *Across the Plains*, 95.
[95]Krist, "California is Haunted by Gold Rush Legacy of Toxic Mercury."

dream—the chance to get rich quickly. The fur trade and land speculation won and lost great fortunes before 1849, but the road to even modest wealth had always been a long and perilous journey only the steady and steadfast completed. The gold rush and its attendant fantasies changed all that. Now a man could go to El Dorado and in one summer pluck enough gold from its streams to keep his family in comfort for the rest of their lives. The fever proved contagious, and soon the lust for easy riches became deeply entwined with the American Dream. Like many of the dreams of the Golden West, it was mostly an illusion, but it is an illusion that lives on in the region's casinos, lotteries, racetracks, bingo halls, card rooms, and brokerage firms.

The negative impact of western mining is easy to decry, but it is pointless to long for some bucolic alternative. The agrarian Utopia of Thomas Jefferson exists only in the West of the imagination. Such visions were doomed in the arid West from the start, for harvesting its seemingly endless supply of grass, timber, and minerals provided the only practical model to drive the economic development of the region. For generations mining, grazing, and lumbering unlocked vast resources that created a better life for tens of millions of Americans.

Nothing is inevitable. The American West we know today is the creation of countless hard choices, chance events, and random results. "Remember that the outcomes were not foreordained—or, at least, they did not seem so to those who lived through them," wrote Sally Zanjani in her brilliant history of the birth of Nevada. "With the benefit of hindsight, we may conclude that strong fundamental forces produced inevitable results, but to the men of the 1850s, a broad range of possibilities—some of them quite mad to our eyes—seemed not merely visionary but likely."[96] Western romantics and idealists might passionately wish that kinder and gentler passions had created the dynamic region we call home, but our past is what it is. "It's the only history we have, and I suppose we ought to admit it and learn from it," Wallace Stegner said in the 1970s. He hoped future generations would be able to understand this past as "it ought to be dealt with: as the profound tragic drama of a high-energy civilization investing and changing and nearly destroying a virgin continent that they passionately loved." Reinterpreting and rewriting this story has its limits. "Our formerly ruthless attitudes toward Indians have largely been replaced by sentimental ones," Stegner observed. "Nevertheless, we can't deny that history, and except for a little environmental sticking plaster and a few concessions to wronged tribes we can't reverse it."[97]

The triumphs and disasters that made Westerners who and what they are were not inevitable, but they are inalterable. However much we might long for an

---

[96]Zanjani, *Devils Will Reign*, 2.
[97]Stegner, with Robinson and Robinson, "An Interview," 36.

imaginary kingdom founded on the agrarian dreams of John Sutter and Brigham Young in place of the rapacious and restless empire we inherited from Sam Brannan and Leland Stanford, we are a place and a people dedicated to the proposition that as citizens of the American West it is our birthright to get rich quick.

For the salmon that once teemed in California's golden rivers and the people who had feasted on them for millennia, the gold rush of 1849 to 1852 was an unmitigated disaster. The ratio of those whose dreams of wealth came true to those who paid for such fantasies with their lives during the frenzy did nothing to diminish the modern El Dorado's quintessential status as the Land of Dreams. The notion that anyone ever learns anything from history is dubious, but that does not prevent the past from lighting the way to a more just, tolerant, and sustainable future. We may regret the virtual devastation of the West's First Peoples and the pillaging of so much of the region's natural wealth, but we can accept our common history, try to understand how this legacy shaped today's American West, and seek to untangled our tangled heritage and its consequences.

The Indian Barrier

Three years after the Great Council of 1851, Father De Smet's optimism about the future of America's Indians had vanished. White settlers—hungry for the lands the government had divided among the Blackfeet, Gros Ventres, Assiniboines, Absarokas, Lakotas, Cheyennes, and Arapahos—cast greedy eyes on the fertile plains. Western politicians responded: "The Indian barrier must be removed," proclaimed Stephen Douglas as 1853 came to a close. "The tide of emigration and civilization must be permitted to roll onward until it rushes through the passes of the mountains, and spreads over the plains, and mingles with the waters of the Pacific." Franklin Pierce signed the senator's Kansas-Nebraska Act on 30 May 1854 and opened the Omaha, Lakota, Cheyenne, and Arapaho homelands to white settlement: whether the legislation opened the new territories to slavery remained unsettled.

"The whites continue to spread like a torrent over California, over Washington, Utah, and Oregon; over the States of Wisconsin, Minnesota, Iowa, Texas, and New Mexico; and lastly, over Kanzas and Nebraska," De Smet wrote. "The future prospect of the Indian tribes is very dark and melancholy," he said. "Their ruin appears certain. These savages disappear insensibly as the emigrations of the whites succeed each other and advance." Within fifty years, few traces of the Native races would survive: "the great tide of European emigration but makes the effect more certain." These migrations multiplied as a million Germans and half a million Britons moved to the United States during the 1850s, "and succeed like the waves of ocean," De

Smet observed. "They must find room; that room is the West." With each successive emigration, the tribes found "their grounds restricted, their hunts and fishing-places less abundant." Meaningless treaty promises of protection and privileges fell before the relentless advance of the forked-tongues, who marched in winding tracks and crooked paths to attain their objectives; resistance merely hastened the tribes' destruction. The drama's last scene would play out, the priest predicted, at "the east and west bases of the Rocky Mountains. In a few years the curtain will fall over the Indian tribes and veil them forever. They will live only in history."[98]

Many, perhaps most, emigrants agreed the peoples of the Great Plains were a doomed race. "It is upon these grounds that the wild Indian has reveled in his might, lording it over all animate beings within his reach. Here has he lived and hunted and fished, generation after generation, little dreaming that a race of 'pale faces' coming from the 'rising sun' was one day to despoil him of his home and his hunting grounds, and that his race would fade and become a shadow of the past or living only in history recorded by his enemies," John Hawkins Clark wrote in 1852. "Already has the white man taken upon himself the charge of this beautiful country," Clark noted, and the nation's warlike establishment warned the wild Indian that he "must submit to be ruled by a people of another race; and so it is. 'Manifest destiny' is spreading the white race broadcast throughout the fair fields of the great west, shedding the light of science, of civilization, and of religion, covering the dark savage superstition of the native race in the grave of the past."[99]

These were grim prophecies, but this vanishing race still defies such smug predictions.[100] By 1852—only a dozen years after Joel Walker brought the first American family overland to Oregon—a restless nation had transformed a ragged trail into a transcontinental highway. Wagon tracks had divided Indian Country, enabled the settlement of Oregon and the conquest of the Southwest, flooded California with miners and adventurers, and gave birth to cities reaching from Council Bluffs to Great Salt Lake to Portland. Wagon roads to free land, free gold, and religious freedom displaced and marginalized Native peoples as the Oregon, Mormon, and California trails transformed the nation and intensified the violent contest over who would control the American West. The new roads made the question of whether the new lands would be slave or free impossible to avoid, and answering that question during the 1850s divided the United States and challenged the republic's survival. A Golden Age was over and the best time ever made was gone, but the most important years of America's overland epoch and its most compelling stories had yet to unfold.

---

[98]De Smet, 30 December 1854, *Western Missions and Missionaries,* 213–14.
[99]Clark, "Overland to the Gold Fields," 26 May 1852, 242.
[100]The U.S. Census estimated 5.2 million Native Americans living in the United States in 2010.

Acknowledgments

It is impossible to properly express my debt to the dedicated professionals who manage the archival and published record of America's past. For a partial accounting, see the first volume of this series, which but those thanks require updating. I am especially indebted to Kay Threlkeld and Professor Robert L. Rieck for access to hundreds of transcriptions of trail narratives. Among many others who have generously shared their sources, time, and astonishing expertise are Melvin L. Bashore, Albert Edward Belanger, Don Buck, John R. Call, Stafford Hazelett, Wendell Huffman, Thomas Hunt, Kristin Johnson, Sandra Lowery, Ardis E. Parshall, Richard Silva, and Jim Tompkins. I have used and much appreciate publicly available transcriptions by Shirley R. Butler, Carolyn H. Chapman, Stephenie Flora, Janet Hauck, Molly McDade Hood, Cathy J. Labath, Robin Petersen, John C. Stone, Donnell R. Wisniewski, and Kathleen Wilham. As always, David L. Bigler, Robert A. Clark, Michael W. Homer, William P. Mackinnon, Philip F. Notarianni, and Dan Johnson provided the author with invaluable support. I owe a continuing debt to Yale University's Beinecke Rare Book and Manuscript Library, the Utah Humanities Council, the Charles Redd Center for Western Studies at Brigham Young University, and the Tanner Humanities Center and the Wallace Stegner Center at the University of Utah for their generous grants and fellowships. The staffs at Utah State History, notably Doug Misner and Alan Barnett, and at Special Collections at the University of Utah's Marriott Library, especially Walter Jones, Elizabeth Rogers, and Gregory C. Thompson have shared their photographic and manuscript treasures.

The unsparing critiques and broad perspectives of excellent scholars, particularly Kenneth N. Owens, Deborah Lawrence, and Jon Lawrence, and the late Martin Ridge, made *Golden Visions* an immeasurably better work. I must again acknowledge the National Park Service and the Bureau of Land Management—especially Jere Krakow, Lee Kreutzer, Chuck Milliken, Kim Finch, Terry Del Bene, and Craig Bromley—whose sponsorship of the original studies and continuing support made this work possible. Finally, Dawn Ollila, Alice Stanton, and especially Laura Bayer have done so much to make the Overland West volumes so much better.

Bibliography

This bibliography contains citations for every work cited in this study, with separate listings for primary sources, including executive documents, and secondary sources such as books, articles, and dissertations. Complete citations for newspaper articles are provided in the text. Full citations for more than 1,900 primary sources, with links to hundreds of online resources, will be available on the National Park Service Long Distance Trails Office website in a comprehensive "Oregon-California Trail Bibliography." See http://www.nps.gov/cali/ and http://www.nps.gov/oreg/.

Abbreviations

Beinecke Library	Western Americana Collection, Beinecke Rare Book and Manuscript Library, Yale University
Bieber Collection	Ralph P. Bieber Research Collection (in process), the Henry E. Huntington Library, San Marino, California
BYU Library	Special Collections, Harold B. Lee Library, Brigham Young University
Huntington Library	The Henry E. Huntington Library, San Marino, California
LDS Archives	Church History Department, The Church of Jesus Christ of Latter-day Saints, Salt Lake City, Utah
Missouri Historical Society	Missouri Historical Society Library and Archives, Saint Louis
Mattes Library	Merrill J. Mattes Research Library, National Frontier Trails Center (NFTC), Independence, Missouri
Oregon Historical Society	Oregon Historical Society Research Library
Society of California Pioneers	Alice Phelan Sullivan Library, the Society of California Pioneers, San Francisco
Western Historical Manuscripts	Western Historical Manuscript Collection, Ellis Library, University of Missouri–Columbia

PRIMARY SOURCES

Abbey, James. *California: A Trip across the Plains, in the Spring of 1850.* New Albany, Ind.: Kent and Norman, and J. R. Nunemacher, 1850.

Abbott, Aaron, to "Dear Friends," 18 September 1852. OCTA Manuscripts, Mattes Library.

Abbott, Carlisle S. *Recollections of a California Pioneer [1850 and 1852].* New York: Neale, 1917.

Abell, James Scott. Journal of Trip to the California Gold Fields, 1849–1850. Abell Family Papers, Minnesota Historical Society.

Adams, Cecilia McMillen. "Crossing the Plains in 1852." In Holmes, ed., *Covered Wagon Women,* 5:253–312.

Ajax, William. Journal 1862. MSS 1488, Special Collections, BYU Library.

Akin, James. "Diary" (1852). *Transactions of the 36th Annual Reunion of the Oregon Pioneer Association* (1908): 259–74.

Allen, William R., to "My Dear Brother," 4 May 1851. Mss 655, Oregon Society Library.

Anderson, William Marshall. *The Rocky Mountain Journals.* Edited by Dale L. Morgan and Eleanor Towles Harris. San Marino, Calif.: The Huntington Library, 1967.

Anonymous. "Californian Gold." *United States Magazine and Democratic Review* 24, no. 127 (January 1849): 3–13.

Anonymous. Diary from Michigan in California in 1849. OCTA Manuscripts, Mattes Library.

Anonymous. "From California," 24 August 1849, *Missouri Whig* (Palmyra), 8 November 1849. Kathleen Wilham transcription.

Anonymous. Overland Diary, 1849. In John T. Mason Diaries, Box 2, fd 11. WA MSS S-2173, Beinecke Library.

Anonymous. *St. Clair County History.* Philadelphia: Brink, McDonough, and Company, 1881.

Anonymous. Tour to California Overland, 1849. MSS SC 164 1849, BYU Library.

Anonymous. Travel Account of Journey from Indiana to Washington, ca. 1850. C3415, Western Historical Manuscripts.

Anonymous (J. E. H.). "Letter from California," 12 August 1849. *Republican Compiler* (Gettysburg, Penn.), 12 November 1849, 4/1–2. Courtesy of Kristin Johnson.

Archibald [Holmes], Julia Anna. "To Pikes Peak and New Mexico, 1858." In Holmes, ed., *Covered Wagon Women,* 7:190–215.

Arms, Cephas. *The Long Road to California in 1849.* Edited by John Cumming. Mount Pleasant, Mich: The Private Press of John Cumming, 1985.

Armstrong, J. Elza, and John Edwin Banks. *The Buckeye Rovers in the Gold Rush: An Edition of Two Diaries.* Edited by H. Lee Scamehorn, Edwin P. Banks, and Jamie Lytle-Webb. Athens: Ohio University Press, 1965.

Atkinson, Lydia B., to "Dearest Mother" (Anna Knox), 15 October 1852. Typescript, NFTC Manuscripts, Mattes Library.

Austin, Henry. Diary, 1849. MSS C-F 157, Bancroft Library.

Ayres, Dr. Samuel Matthias. Letters, 1850. Typescript, C995, V. 29, #760, Western Historical Manuscripts. Published as *Love Letters to Missouri—A Kept Promise: Trail Letters.* Edited by Gary Babler. College Station, Texas: Virtualbookworm.com Publishing, 2006.

Badman, Philip. Diary of a Journey from Pennsylvania to California, 14 April to 2 October 1849. MSS 20, Beinecke Library. Richard L. Rieck transcription.

Bang, Theodosia E. "Woman's Emancipation: A Letter From A Strong-Minded American Woman." *Punch* 21 (1851): 3.

Barnard, Frederick W. Letters, 1849–1854. MSS S-680 B254, Beinecke Library.

Batchelder, Amos. Journal of a Tour across the Continent of North America in 1849. Batchelder-Nelson Family Papers. MSS C-B 614, Bancroft Library.

Bates, John. Diary, Washington D.C., to Sacramento, California, 1849. Digital typescript, Mattes Library.

Bayley, Betsey, to Lucy P. Griffith, 20 September 1849. "Across the Plains in 1845." In Holmes, ed., *Covered Wagon Women,* 1:35–38.

Beckwith, Edward G. *Explorations and Surveys for a Railroad Route from the Mississippi River to the Pacific Ocean.* 2 vols. Washington, D.C.: A. O. P. Nicholson, Printer, 1854.

Beckwourth, James Pierson. *The Life and Adventures of James P. Beckwourth.* Edited by T. D. Bonner. New York: Harper and Brothers, 1856.

Bedford, Thomas, to A. M. Bedford, 9 December 1849, Bedford Family Papers, Western Historical Manuscripts.

Bedwell, Elizabeth K. Journal of Road to Oregon, 1852. Typescript. Original in Pendleton, Library, Oregon. Copy in OCTA Manuscripts, Mattes Library.

Belknap, Horace. "An Iowan in California, 1850." Edited by Woodrow Westholm. *Annals of Iowa* 36, no. 6 (Fall 1962): 462–65.

Belshaw, Maria Parsons. "Crossing the Plains to Oregon in 1853." Edited by Michael L. Tate. *Overland Journal* 14, no. 2 (Summer 1996): 10–42.

Bennett, William P. *The Sky-Sifter,* 275–93. Oakland, Calif.: Pacific Press., 1892.

Benson, John H. From St. Joseph to Sacramento by a Forty-niner. Typescript, Nebraska State Historical Society.

Berrien, Joseph Waring. "Overland from St. Louis to the California Gold Fields in 1849." Edited by Ted and Caryl Hinckley. *Indiana Magazine of History* (December 1960): 273–352.

Biddle, B. R. "Journey to California." Journal printed as letters to the *Illinois Daily Journal* (Springfield, Ill.), 1849. OCTA Manuscripts, Mattes Library.

Bigelow, Daniel R. Diary, 1851. MS 70, Washington State Library.

Blackburn, Abner. *Frontiersman: Abner Blackburn's Narrative.* Edited by Will Bagley. Salt Lake City: University of Utah Press, 1992.

Blackman, Aretas J. Journal and Letters of the Overland Journey to California, March 18, 1849–January 7, 1851. Blackman, Bush and Simonson Family Papers, MSS 2002/202 cz, manuscript and typescript, Bancroft Library.

Blair, John M. Letters, 1849–1850. NFTC Manuscripts, Mattes Library.

Bonniwell, George. The Gold Rush Diary, 1850. J. R. Tompkins transcription.

Booth, Edmund. *Edmund Booth (1810–1905), Forty-niner: The Life Story of a Deaf Pioneer, Including Portions of His Autobiographical Notes and Gold Rush Diary, and Selections from Family Letters and Reminiscences.* Stockton, Calif.: San Joaquin Pioneer and Historical Society, 1953.

Boyle, Charles E. Diary, 1849. *Columbus Dispatch* (Ohio), 2–28 October 1849. Republished 2 October–11 November 1949. Edited by Gerald Tebben.

Bradley, Nancy Jane, and Henry Bradley. Daily Journal, 1852. WA MSS 45, Beinecke Library. Richard L. Rieck transcription.

Brady, Charles C. "Hannibal to the Gold Fields in 1849." *Pacific Historian* 4, no. 4 (1960–61): 142–52; 5, no. 1 (1961): 5–14.

Brannan, Samuel. *Scoundrel's Tale: The Samuel Brannan Papers.* Edited by Will Bagley. Spokane, Wash.: Arthur H. Clark, 1999.

Breck, Samuel, to "Dear Father," 23 November 1849. "A Letter from California." *Chicago Commercial Advertiser,* 13 February 1850, 1.

Breyfogle, J. D., Sr., Diary, 1849. MS 165, Baker Library, Dartmouth College, Hanover, N.H. Kay
    Threlkeld transcription.
Brooks, Quincy Adams. "Letter," 7 November 1851. *Quarterly of the Oregon Historical Society* 15,
    no. 3 (September 1914): 210–15.
Brouster, George Washington. Letters, 1850. C1832, Western Historical Manuscripts.
Brown, Adam Mercer. "Over Barren Plains and Rock Bound Mountains" [1850]. Edited by David M.
    Kiefer. *Montana* 22, no. 4 (October 1972): 16–28.
Brown, John Evans. "Memoirs of an American Gold Seeker." Edited by Katie E. Blood. *Journal of
    American History* 2, no. 1 (January–March 1908): 129–54.
Brown, John Lowery. "Journal of the Cherokee Nation en Route to California in 1850." Edited by
    Muriel H. Wright. *Chronicles of Oklahoma* 12, no. 2 (June 1934): 177–213.
Brown, William R. *An Authentic Wagon Train Journal of 1853 from Indiana to California.* N.p.: Horse-
    shoe Printing, 1985.
Bruff, J. G. *Gold Rush: The Journals, Drawings, and Other Papers of J. Goldsborough Bruff, Captain, Wash-
    ington City and California Mining Association, April 2, 1849–July 20, 1851.* 2 vols. Edited by Georgia
    Willis Read and Ruth Gaines. New York: Columbia University Press, 1944.
Brush, Mary, to "Dear Parents," 27 January 1850. "Letter from California." *Weekly North-Western
    Gazette* (Galena, Ill.), 7 May 1850, 1.
Bryarly, Wakeman. In Potter, *Trail to California,* 113–211.
Buckingham, Harriet Talcott. "Crossing the Plains in 1851." In Holmes, ed., *Covered Wagon Women,*
    3:15–52.
Budd, Daniel H. Journal, Potosi, Wisconsin to California, 1852. MS Am 1878, Houghton Library,
    Harvard University. Digital transcription, Mattes Library.
Burbank, Augustus Ripley. Diary 1849. MSS P-A 304, Bancroft Library.
Burgert, Daniel, and Manlius Stone Rudy. Diary, 1849. Typescript, Mattes Library.
Burke, George William. Papers, 1850. C3796, Western Historical Manuscripts.
Burnett, Peter H. *Recollections and Opinions of an Old Pioneer.* New York: D. Appleton and Co., 1880.
Burrell, Mary. "Council Bluffs to California, 1854." In Holmes, ed., *Covered Wagon Women,* 6:255–61.
Burton, Richard F. *The City of the Saints and across the Rocky Mountains to California.* Edited by Fawn
    Brodie. New York: Alfred A. Knopf, 1963.
Bush, Charles W. Letters, 1849–1850. MSS 76/71 c, Typescripts, Bancroft Library.
Bushnell, John Corydon. The Narrative, 1853. Typescript, Lane County Pioneer-Historical Soci-
    ety, Eugene, Oregon, 1959.
Butler, C. R. Letters from Charles Rollin Butler and H. C. Butler, 1853. WA MSS S-2287 L569,
    Beinecke Library.
Byers, William N. "The Oregon Odyssey" [1852]. Edited by Merrill J. Mattes. Part 1, *Overland Journal*
    1, no. 1 (July 1983): 14–23. Part 2, *Overland Journal* 1, no. 2 (Fall 1983): 12–21. Part 3, *Overland
    Journal* 2, no. 1 (Winter 1984): 14–23. Part 4, *Overland Journal* 2, no. 2 (Spring 1984): 23–28.
Cain, Joseph, and Arieh C. Brower. *Mormon Way-bill, to the Gold Mines.* Salt Lake City: W. Rich-
    ards, 1851.
Caldwell. "Notes of a Journey to California by Fort Hall Route, June to Octr 1849 Found in the
    Mountains: By Dr. Caldwell." In Bruff, *Gold Rush,* 1:250–69.
Call, Asa C. [A.C.C.] "From Utah. Great Salt Lake City, Sept. 20, 1850." *The National Era* (Wash-
    ington, D.C.), 23 January 1851, 13. John R. Call transcription.
———. *The Diaries of Asa Cyrus Call, 1850.* Edited by John R. and Vanessa Call. Derby, Kansas:
    n.p., 1998.

Camp, Herman, to "Dear Mary, Edna, and Others," 8 July 1849. In Cumming, ed., *The Gold Rush,* 48–55.

Campbell, Robert. "Interesting News from the Plains," 7 July 1850. *Frontier Guardian,* 24 July 1850, 1–2.

Caples, Mary J. Overland Journey to California, 1849. Letter, 5 April 1911. B C244, Biographical Letter File, California State Library.

Carpenter, Dan. Dan Carpenter's Journal, 1850. Typescript, Emigrant Journal Collection, Idaho State Historical Society. Original at Special Collections, Kansas City Public Library.

Carpenter, Helen. "A Trip across the Plains in an Ox Wagon" [1857]. In Myres, ed., *Ho for California!* 92–188.

Carr, Dabney T., to "My Dear Cousin," 31 May 1850. Missouri Historical Society.

Carrington, Albert. "Diary," 28 August 1850 to 11 November 1853. In Kate B. Carter, ed., *Heart Throbs of the West,* 8:77–132. Salt Lake City, Utah: Daughters of Utah Pioneers, 1947.

Carter, William A., to "My Beloved Wife," 11 August 1850. Typescript. C542, Western Historical Manuscripts.

Cartwright, David W. "A Tramp to California in 1852." In Cartwright and Mary F. Bailey, *Natural History of Western Wild Animals,* 165–234. Toledo, Ohio: n.p., 1875.

Chamberlain, William E. Diary, April 11–August 20, 1849. Typescript, MSS C-F 163, Bancroft Library.

Chambers, Margaret White. *Reminiscences* [1851]. In Andrew Jackson Chambers, *Recollections,* 41–59. Fairfield, Wash: Ye Galleon Press, 1975.

Chalmers, Robert. "The Journal." Edited by Charles Kelly. *Utah Historical Quarterly* 20 (January 1952): 31–57.

Cheyenne. "Description of Emigration Seen at Fort Laramie," 14 May 1850, *Missouri Republican,* 9 June 1850, in Wyman, *California Emigrant Letters,* 112.

Child, Andrew. *Overland Route to California; description of the route, via Council Bluffs, Iowa; keeping the north side of the Platte River, for the whole of the distance.* Milwaukee: Daily Sentinel Steam Power Press, 1852. Reprint, Los Angeles: N. A. Kovach, 1946.

Chisholm, James. *South Pass, 1868: James Chisholm's Journal.* Edited by Lola M. Homsher. Lincoln: University of Nebraska Press, 1975.

Churchill, Stillman. Journal of Incidents and Travels to California [1849]. Vault MSS 663, vol. 1. BYU Library.

Clark, Bennett C. "A Journey from Missouri to California in 1849." Edited by Ralph P. Bieber. *Missouri Historical Review* 23, no.1 (October 1928): 3–43.

Clark, Costmor Harris. "A Trail of Hardship to 'The Land of Gold and of Plenty [1850].'" Edited by Marilyn Samuel, Noel L. Danner, and Ruth E. Danner. *Rangelands* 8, no. 4 (August 1986): 147–54.

Clark, John Hawkins. "Overland to the Gold Fields of California in 1852." Edited by Louise Barry. *Kansas Historical Quarterly* 11, no. 3 (August 1942): 227–96.

Clarke, William John, Jr. Journey to the El Dorado: Diary of William John Clarke, Jr., March 27, 1849–July 11, 1849. Typescript, Emigrant Journal Collection, Idaho State Historical Society.

Cleveland, Charles Dexter. Autobiography and Reminiscence [1849]. Typescript, Autobiographies and Reminiscences of Early Pioneers, Society of California Pioneers.

Clyman, James. *James Clyman, Frontiersman.* Edited by Charles L. Camp. San Francisco: California Historical Society, 1928. Second ed., Portland: Champoeg Press, 1960.

Cobbey, John Furmes. Journal, 1850. MSS SC 158, BYU Library.

Coffey, Alvin A. Recollection of 1849. Book of Reminiscences, California Society of Pioneers.

Coke, Henry J. *A Ride over the Rocky Mountains to Oregon and California.* London: R. Bentley, 1852.
———. *Tracks of a Rolling Stone, by the Honourable Henry J. Coke.* 2nd ed. London: Smith, Elder, 1905.
Cole, Gilbert L. *In the Early Days along the Overland Trail in Nebraska Territory, in 1852.* Compiled by Mrs. A. Hardy. Kansas City, Mo.: Franklin Hudson Publishing Company, 1905.
Coleman, Thomas, to "Dear Father," 14 April 1852. Coleman-Hayter Family Letters, Western Historical Manuscripts.
Colvig, William M. "Indian Wars of Southern Oregon." Address, 28 July 1902. *Quarterly of the Oregon Historical Society* 4, no. 3 (December 1903): 227–40.
Cone, Gordon C. Journal of Travels from Waukesha, Wisconsin, to California, by the "south pass" in the summer of 1849. Vault MSS 661, BYU Library.
Conyers, E. W. "Diary of A Pioneer of 1852." Kay Threlkeld transcription. *Transactions of the Thirty-Third Annual Reunion of the Oregon Pioneer Association* (1906): 432–512.
Cook, Thomas E., to "Dear Mother," 11 February 1850, in Mathews, ed., *Mathews Family,* 326.
Cooke, Lucy Rutledge. "Letters on the Way to California." In Holmes, ed., *Covered Wagon Women,* 4:209–95.
Coon, Polly. "Journal of a Journey over the Rocky Mountains [1852]." In Holmes, ed., *Covered Wagon Women,* 5:173–206.
Cooper, Frances Anne (Semple Van Winkle). "The Foremothers Tell of Olden Times," *San Francisco Chronicle,* 9 September 1900.
Cornell, Bertrand. Letters, 1852. Mss 2136-1, Oregon Historical Society.
Cox, Henry, to "Mr. Editor," 26 September 1849. "Letter from California." *Indiana Weekly Advertiser* (Danville), 29 December 1849, 1/1–3.
Crane, J. W., to Francis Howe, 12 June 1849. NFTC Manuscripts, Mattes Library.
Dalton, John E. Diary, 1852. Typescript, State Historical Society of Wisconsin. Kay Threlkeld transcription.
Darwin, Charles Benjamin. Diary of a Journey Overland. Huntington Library. See also " '1,000 Miles From Home on the Wild Prairie': Charles B. Darwin's 1849 Nebraska Diary." Edited by Richard E. Jensen. Kay Threlkeld transcription. *Nebraska History* 85, no. 2 (Summer 2004): 58–115.
Davidson, George Mathiot. Diary and Letters, 1849. Davidson Papers, Beinecke Library.
Davies, A. S. Journal to California, Commencing April 5 1850 and ending Nov 5th 1850. MS 2/75, Emigrant Journal Collection, Idaho State Historical Society.
Davis, George W., to Waltus Watkins, 6 December 1850. MSS S-694, Beinecke Library.
Davis, Sarah Green. "Diary from Missouri to California, 1850." In Holmes, ed., *Covered Wagon Women,* 2:171–206.
Day, Alphonse B. Journal, 1849. Vault MSS 658, BYU Library,
Dean, Thaddeus. *A Journey to California: The Letters of Thaddeus Dean, 1852.* Edited by Katharine Dean Wheeler. Tampa, Fla.: American Studies Press, 1979.
Decker, Peter. *The Diaries of Peter Decker: Overland to California in 1849 and Life in the Mines, 1850–1851.* Edited by Helen S. Griffen. Georgetown, Calif.: Talisman Press, 1966.
Delano, Alonzo. *Alonzo Delano's California Correspondence, 1849–1952.* Edited by Irving McKee. Sacramento, Calif.: Sacramento Book Collectors Club, 1952.
———. *Life on the Plains and among the Diggings.* Auburn, N.Y.: Miller, Orton and Mulligan, 1854.
De Smet, Pierre-Jean. *Western Missions and Missionaries.* New York: T. W. Strong: 1859. Reprint, with an introduction by William L. Davis, Shannon: Irish University Press, 1972.
DeWolf, David. "Diary of the Overland Trail [1849] and Letters of Captain David DeWolf." *Transactions of the Illinois Historical Society,* 1925, 184–222.

Dillard, Samantha. Great Grandmother Samantha Jane Emmons Dillard's Story [1866]. John Christopher Stone transcription.

Dinwiddie, David. "Overland from Indiana to Oregon" [of 1853]. Edited by Margaret Booth. Sources of Northwestern History (1928): 3–14.

Doty, William, to "Dear Mother," 22 November 1849. "W. Doty's Letter from California." Chicago Commercial Advertiser, 7 February 1850, 1. Bieber Collection.

Dowell, Benjamin Franklin. Daily Journal of the Trip by Ox Team, 10 May to 9 September 1850. WA MSS 142, Beinecke Library. Richard L. Rieck transcription.

Downes, Clara E. Journal across the Plains, August 1860. MSS 84/161 c, Bancroft Library.

Drake, Jefferson, to Abigail Drake. Oregon-California Papers, Missouri Historical Society.

Dresser, William. Letters, 1850. Dresser Family Papers, MSS 69/115, Bancroft Library.

Dulany, William H. F. Correspondence, 1850–1851. Dulany Papers, B-1/F-3, Missouri Historical Society.

Durban, Thomas, to "Dear Mother," 20 July 1850. "The Route to California." Zanesville Courier (Ohio), 7 November 1850, 2/3–4.

Dutton, Jerome. "Across the Plains in 1850: Journal and Letters." Annals of Iowa 9, no. 3 (October 1910): 447–84.

Easton, Langdon. "Capt. L. C. Easton's Report: Fort Laramie to Fort Leavenworth Via Republican River in 1849." Edited by Merrill J. Mattes. Kansas Historical Quarterly 20, no. 6 (May 1953): 392–416.

Edwards, Philip Leget. The Diary of Philip Leget Edwards: The Great Cattle Drive from California to Oregon in 1837. Introduction by Douglas S. Watson. San Francisco, Calif.: Grabhorn Press, 1932.

Eliot, Robert [?]. Overland to California: An Interesting History of the Trip across the Continent in 1849. Typescript, Braun Library, Southwest Museum, Los Angeles, California.

Estes Brothers to "Mother et al," 16 June 1850. NFTC Manuscripts, Mattes Library.

Evans, James W., to "Dear Brother Ellis," 27 October 1850. Autographed letter, C1872, Western Historical Manuscripts.

Evershed, Thomas. "The Gold Rush Journal." 1849. Edited by Joseph W. Barnes. Rochester History 39, nos. 1 and 2 (January and April 1977): 1–44.

Fairchild, Lucius. California Letters. Edited by Joseph Schafer. Madison: State Historical Society of Wisconsin, 1931.

Farmer, James. Journal, 1853. LDS Archives.

Farnham, Elijah Bryan. "From Ohio to California in 1849." Edited by Merrill J. Mattes and Esley J. Kirk. Indiana Magazine of History 46, nos. 3–4 (September and December 1950): 297–318, 403–20.

Farnham, Eliza W. California, In-doors and Out. New York: Dix, Edwards, 1856.

Fenn, Stephen S. Letter/Journal, 29 January 1851. Typescript, Ms2/106, Emigrant Journal Collection, Idaho State Historical Society.

Ferguson, Charles D. Experiences of a Forty-niner. Chico, Calif.: H. A. Carson, 1924.

Ferguson, Henry O. Reminiscences of 1849. Typescript, 1918, MSS C-Z 187, Bancroft Library.

Ferrill, John D. "Early Days on the Trails in 1850." Clipping, Colorado Sun, 26 June 1892, Overland Diaries Subject File, Ov2d, American Heritage Center, University of Wyoming.

Fisher, Sarah Bird Sprenger. Reminiscence, Ohio to Oregon, 1925 [1852]. Edited by Marcia Hurt Baldwin. Copy in author's possession.

Fort Laramie, Wyoming, Letters Received, 1850–1865, Record Group 393, Box 1, National Archives.

Franklin, I., to Morritz Langsdorf. Letters, 1852–1853. MSS 184, Oregon Historical Society.

Frink, Margaret A. "Adventures of a Party of Gold Seekers." In Holmes, ed., *Covered Wagon Women,*
   2:55–167.

Frizzell, Lodisa. *Across the Plains to California in 1852.* Edited by Victor Hugo Paltsits. New York:
   New York Public Library, 1915.

Fuller, Randall. "The Diary." Edited by Charles W. Martin and Thomas H. Hunt. Kay Threlkeld
   transcription. *Overland Journal* 6, no. 4 (1988): 2–34.

Galbraith, Thomas. Journal of Mess Number Twenty-seven of the PITTSBURG AND CALIFORNIA
   Enterprise Company [1849]. Typescript, OCTA Manuscripts, Mattes Library.

Gale, James E. Letters, 30 January to 15 December 1850. WA MSS S-2025 G131, Beinecke Library.

Gardner, Robert. History of Robert Gardner, Jr. [1847]. MSS SC 793, Typescript, George S. Tanner Collection, BYU Library.

Garlick, Dr. Carmi P. "A Trip Overland to California, 1850." In Garlick, ed., *Garlick Family
   History,* WA MSS S-2343 G184, Beinecke Library.

Gee, Perry. Journal of Travels, 1852. MSS 213, Beinecke Library.

Geiger, Vincent E. In Potter, *Trail to California,* 75–113.

Gifford, Samuel Kendall. Journal Book [1850]. Reminiscences, Typescript, LDS Archives.

Godfrey, James. "The Overland Diary [1849]." Edited by Peter van der Pas. Kay Threlkeld transcription. Part 1, *Nevada Country Historical Society Bulletin* 44, nos. 2–3 (April–July 1990): 10–23.
   Part 2, *Nevada Country Historical Society Bulletin* 46, nos. 3–4 (July–October 1992): 18–27.

Gold Rush Letters, *St. Louis Weekly Reveille,* 1849–50. Typescripts, Oregon-California Papers,
   1804–1876, Missouri Historical Society.

Goldsmith, Oliver. *Overland in Forty-Nine.* Detroit: n.p., 1896.

Goodell, Jotham. *A Winter with the Mormons: The 1852 Letters.* Edited by David L. Bigler. Salt Lake
   City: Tanner Trust Fund and the Marriott Library, 2001.

Gooding, J. A., to "My dear wife [Eunice]," 12 April 1849, Missouri River. Typescript, Oregon-
   California Papers, 1804–1876, Missouri Historical Society.

Goulder, William A. *Reminiscences: Incidents in the Life of a Pioneer in Oregon and Idaho* [1845]. Moscow: University of Idaho Press, 1990.

Graham, Alexander F., to "Dear Barbour [Barlow?]," 19 May 1850. WA MSS S-707 G759, Beinecke
   Library.

Grant, Richard. See Simpson, George.

Grant, Ulysses Simpson. *The Papers of Ulysses S. Grant: 1837–1861.* 31 vols. Edited by John Y. Simon.
   Carbondale, Ill.: Southern Illinois University Press, 2003.

Graves, Pusey. Diary and Letters, 1850. Typescript, Earlham College Library, Richmond, Indiana.

Gray, Charles Glass. *Off at Sunrise: The Overland Journal* [1849]. Edited by Thomas D. Clark. San
   Marino, Calif.: The Huntington Library, 1976.

Green, Edmund. "Recollections of 1849." In Edward Topham, ed., *Castles in California, 1849–1952.*
   Jackson, Calif.: Amador County Historical Society, 1952.

Grist, Franklin R. Letters, 1849. Knox Papers, Southern Historical Collection, Wilson Library,
   University of North Carolina.

Gully, Samuel, to Brigham Young, 21 May and 3 July 1849. LDS Archives.

Gunnison, John W. "Diary and Letters, 1849–1850." In Madsen, ed., *Exploring the Great Salt Lake.*
   ———. *The Mormons, or, Latter-day Saints, in the Valley of the Great Salt Lake.* 2nd ed. Philadelphia:
   Lippincott, Grambo and Co., 1860.

Hackney, Joseph. Journal, 1849. Carolyn Houghton Chapman transcription. In Elizabeth Page, ed., *Wagons West: A Story of the Oregon Trail.*. New York: Farrar and Rinehart, Inc., 1930.

Hadley, Amelia E. Hammond [Shinn]. "Journal of Travails to Oregon." In Holmes, ed., *Covered Wagon Women,* 3:53–96.

Hafford, Warren Graves. Diary Kept on His Trip to California, 1850. Rutherford B. Hayes Presidential Center.

Hale, Israel F. "Diary of a Trip to California in 1849." Kay Threlkeld transcription. *Quarterly of the Society of California Pioneers* 2, no. 2 (June 1925): 61–130.

Hall, O. J. Diary of a Forty-niner. MSS A 636, Utah State Historical Society.

Hamelin, Joseph P. Journals, 1849 and 1856. WA MSS 239, Beinecke Library.

Hamilton, Supplina, to Dr. J. M. Powell, 9 January 1900. Recollection of 1851. Copy in author's possession.

Hanna, Esther Belle. Diary, 1852. MSS P-A 313, Bancroft Library. Published as *Canvas Caravans*. Edited by Eleanor Allen. Kay Threlkeld transcription. Portland: Binfords and Mort, 1946.

Hanna, William. Diary, 1850. Typescript. MSS 693, Oregon Society Library.

Hansen, Peter Olsen. Diary, April to August 1849. LDS Archives.

Harding, B. F. "Protection Afforded by Volunteers of Oregon and Washington to Overland Immigrants in 1854." House Misc. Doc. 47 (35:2), Serial 1016.

Hardy, Francis A. Journal, 1850. WA MSS 242, Beinecke Library. Richard L. Rieck transcription.

Harris, Sarah Hollister. *An Unwritten Chapter of Salt Lake, 1851.* New York: n.p., 1901.

Harrow, Edward C. *The Gold Rush Overland Journal, 1849.* Austin, Tex.: Michael Vinson, 1993.

Hart, Thomas. "California Letter," 20 and 27 February, *Missouri Whig* (Palmyra), 1850, Kathleen Wilham transcription.

Hart, William Henry. Diaries, 1852. MSS 1411, BYU Library.

Hassenplug, Charles H. Diary of His Trip to California, 1850. Mattes Library.

Hastings, Lansford W. *The Emigrants' Guide, to Oregon and California.* Cincinnati: George Conclin, 1845.

Hatcher, Francis. "Crossing the Plains to California" [1852]. In Ruby Knifong, ed., "Moving on West," *The Knifong Family and Its Related Families*, 24. Marceline, Mo.: MBC Genealogy Publishing, 1994.

Haun, Catherine. "A Woman's Trip Across the Plains in 1849." In Schlissel, ed., *Women's Diaries of the Westward Journey,* 165–85.

Haynes, James Milton. Journal, 11 to 23 September 1849. WA MSS S-1738, Beinecke Library, Richard L. Rieck transcription.

Haze, Charles W. to "Dear friends, Father—Brothers and Sisters," 6 January 1850. Haze Papers, 851462 Ac Aa 2, Bentley Historical Library, University of Michigan.

Hearn, Fleming G. A Journal for 1850. MSS 6014, Oregon Historical Society.

Hecox, James. The Way I Went to California [1849]. Shirley Richberger Butler transcription. Copy in author's possession.

Heiskell, Hugh Brown. *A Forty-niner from Tennessee.* Edited by Edward M. Steel. Knoxville: University of Tennessee Press, 1998.

Herbert, Lemuel. Personal Diary from Delaware, Ohio, April 2, 1850 to Placerville, California and Return, 6 November 1851. G. Richard Blair Typescript. Delaware County Historical Society and Genealogical Society, Delaware, Ohio.

Hester, Sallie. "The Diary of a Pioneer Girl." In Holmes, ed., *Covered Wagon Women,* 1:231–46.

Hewitt, Randall Henry. *Across the Plains and over the Divide, 1862*. New York: Broadway, 1906.

Hickman, Richard Owen. " 'Dick's Works': An Overland Journey to California in 1852." Edited by M. Catherine White. In Hakola, *The Frontier*, 161–80.

Hill, John Berry. *A Gold Hunter: Memoirs [1850]*. Edited by Kristin Delaplane. Vacaville, Calif.: Masterpiece Memoirs, 1997.

Hillyer, Edwin. "From Waupun to Sacramento in 1849." Edited by John O. Holzhueter. *Wisconsin Magazine of History* 49, no. 3 (Spring1966): 210–44.

Hinde, Edmund Cavileer. *Overland to California in 1850*. Edited by Jerome Peltier. Fairfield, Wash.: Ye Galleon Press, 1983.

Hindman, David R. *The Way To My Golden Wedding*. Robin Petersen transcription. St. Joseph, Mo.: n.p., 1908.

Hines, Philip John. "An Ohioan's Letter from the California Gold Fields in 1850." Edited by Robert Ralph Davis. *Ohio History* 76, no. 3 (Summer 1967): 159–63.

Hittell, John S. "Reminiscences of the Plains and Mines in '49 and '50." *Overland Monthly* 9, no. 13 (February 1889): 193–205.

Hittle, Jonas. Diary 1849. Illinois State Historical Library. Richard L. Rieck transcription.

Hixson, Jasper Morris, to Robert H. Miller, 20 May 1849. Miller Papers, Missouri Historical Society.

———. "A Gold Hunter, 1849." *Los Angeles Daily Herald*, 13 January to 30 April 1890. Kay Threlkeld transcription. Excerpted in Coy, *The Great Trek*, 149–54, 177, 199–211.

Hoffman, Benjamin. Diary. "West Virginia Forty-niners." Edited by C. H. Ambler. *West Virginia History* 3, no. 1 (October 1941): 59–75.

Holcomb, William Francis. A Sketch of the Life, 1850/1888. MSS C-D 5205, Bancroft Library.

Holeman, Jacob, to Luke Lea, Letters Received 1824–1881, Utah Superintendency, RG 75, National Archives.

Hoover, Vincent A. Diary, 1849. Huntington Library.

Horn, Hosea B. *Horn's Overland Guide*. New York: J. H. Colton, 1852.

Howell, Elijah Preston. *The 1849 California Trail Diaries*. Edited by Susan Badger Doyle and Donald E. Buck. Independence: Oregon-California Trail Association, 1995.

Hoyt, D., to "Mr. Sosey," 20 January 1850, *Missouri Whig* (Palmyra). Kathleen Wilham transcription.

Hudgins, John. California in 1849. Typescript, C2189, Western Historical Manuscripts.

Hudspeth, Thomas Jefferson, to Cynthia Hudspeth, 23 October 1849. In Wilcox, *Jackson County Pioneers*, 239–40.

Hughes, Georgia. Recollections [1850], 1910. Typescript, Mss 2999, Oregon Historical Society.

Hunter, John A. "The Letters of a Missourian in the Gold Rush." Edited by David W. Francis. *Bulletin of the Missouri Historical Society* (October 1972): 41–45.

Hutchings, James Mason. *Seeking the Elephant, 1849: James Mason Hutchings' journal of His Overland Trek to California, Including His Voyage to America, 1848, and Letters from the Mother Lode*. Edited by Shirley Sargent. Glendale, Calif.: Arthur H. Clark, 1980.

———. "The Discovery of Gold in California." *Hutchings' California Magazine*, November 1857, 193–203.

Hyde, William. Private Journal. MS 1549, LDS Archives.

Ingalls, Eleazer Stillman. *Journal of a Trip to California, 1850–51*. Waukegan, Ill.: Tobey and Co., 1852.

Ingrim, Godfrey C. Reminiscences of the Clark-Brown Expedition to California in 1852. Manuscript, Kansas State Historical Society.

Isham, Giles S. *Guide to California and the Mines*. New York: A. T. Mouel, 1850.

Jackson, Edward. Journal of His Route from Fort Independence to California in 1849. MSS SC 2493, BYU Library.

James, Robert. "Correspondence of the Tribune. From the Clay Emigrants," 18 May 1850. *Liberty Tribune*, 21 June 1850, 1/3–4.

Jarrot, Vital, to Charles Tillman, 23 August 1849. Robert Forsyth Papers, Missouri Historical Society.

Jefferson, T. H. *Map of the Emigrant Road from Independence, Mo., to St. Francisco California and Accompaniment.* New York: T. H. Jefferson, 1849.

Johnston, William G. *Experiences of a Forty-niner.* Pittsburgh: n.p., 1892.

Josselyn, Amos Piatt. *The Overland Journal, April 2, 1849, to September 11, 1849.* Edited by J. William Barrett, II. Baltimore, Md.: Gateway Press, 1978.

Kauffman, Christian. "An 1852 Letter." 18 November 1852. *Overland Journal* 3, no. 2 (Spring 1985): 22–23.

Keen, Richard Augustus. Diary of a Trip to California and Return [1852]. Typescript, Iowa Historical Society.

Keith, Fleury F. Journal of Crossing the Plains in 1850. MSS SC 108 1850, BYU Library.

Kellogg, Jane D. "Memories of Jane D. Kellogg." *Transactions of the Forty-First Annual Reunion of the Oregon Pioneer Association* (1913): 86–94.

Kelly, William. *An Excursion to California.* London: Chapman and Hall, 1851.

Kelsey, Nancy. "Nancy (Roberts) Kelsey's Own Story of Her Life." Edited by Roy M. Sylar. Part 1, *Pomo Bulletin* (February 1983): 1–8. Part 2, *Pomo Bulletin* (May 1983): 9–16.

Kerns, John Tully. "Journal of Crossing the Plains to Oregon in 1852." *Transactions of the Forty-Second Annual Reunion of the Oregon Pioneer Association* (1914): 142–93.

Kilbourn, Lewis. Journal, 1850. Typescript, MSS 1508, Oregon Society Library.

Kilgore, William H. *The Kilgore Journal of an Overland Journey to California in the Year 1850.* Edited by Joyce Rockwood Muench. New York: Hastings House, 1949.

Kincade, John Thompson. From John H. Kincade, "A Sketch of the Kincade Family," 1901. NFTC Manuscripts, Mattes Library.

Kingery, Solomon. Overland Letters, 1852. WA MSS 286, Beinecke Library.

Kirtley, C. F., to "My Dear Wife," October 27, 1849, "California Letters," *Missouri Whig* (Palmyra), January 1850.

Knowlton, Chandler H. Diary, 27 April to 19 August 1852. MS SC 271, Illinois State Historical Library. Richard L. Rieck transcription.

Knox, Reuben. *A Medic Fortyniner: Life and Letters, 1849–'51* [1850]. Edited by Charles Turner. Verona, Va.: McClure Press, 1974.

Knox, William Franklin. Letters, 1849–1850. Copies of holographs, typescripts, and obituary in NFTC Manuscripts, Mattes Library.

Ladd, Horace. Letter, 8 July 1849, in Cumming, ed., *The Gold Rush,* 64–69.

Lane, Samuel A. *Gold Rush: The Overland Diary.* Akron, Ohio: Summit County Historical Society, 1984.

Langworthy, Franklin. *Scenery of the Plains, Mountains and Mines: A Diary* [1850]. Introduction by Paul C. Philips. Princeton, N.J.: Princeton University Press, 1932.

Lassen, Peter. "From the Emigrants," 16 July 1848. *The Brunswicker* (Brunswick, Missouri), 9 September 1848, 1/2. Wendell Huffman transcription.

Lawson, George. Letters, 1850. HM 50512-50517, Huntington Library.

Lee, John D. *A Mormon Chronicle: The Diaries of John D. Lee 1848–1876* 2 vols. Edited by Robert Glass Cleland and Juanita Brooks. San Marino, Calif.: The Huntington Library, 1955.

Leeper, David. *The Argonauts of 'Forty-nine: Some Recollections.* South Bend, Oreg.: J. B. Stoll and Company, 1894.

Le Poidevin, Jean, to "Dear Brother," 1852. In Marion G. Turk, ed., *The Quiet Adventurers in North America,* 34–37. Detroit: Harlo Press, 1983.

Lewelling, Seth. Excerpts from the Journal, 1850. Typescript M F865.L38, California State Library.

Lewis, Abel Franklin. An Account of the Expedition of A. F. Lewis, J. H. Royes, E. B. Lewis, P. Gregg, [and] Henry Dievendorff, Citizens of Turtleville Rock County and State of Wisconsin, 1849. MSS 90/188 c, Bancroft Library.

Lewis, Elisha B. Overland to California in 'Forty Nine. Typescript, WA MSS S-2344 L585, Beinecke Library.

Lewis, Fielding, to "Dear Cosin," 8 May 1852. NFTC Manuscripts, Mattes Library.

Linville, Augustus Joshua. Diary, 1852–1853. Mss 1508, Oregon Historical Society.

Lippincott, Benjamin S. Letters, 1847–1851. MSS 95/15 c, Bancroft Library.

Litton, Solomon, to "My Dear Wife," 30 November 1850. Typescript, C2181, Western Historical Manuscripts.

Lockwood, Chas. E., to "Respected and highly esteemed friends," 7 December 1849, 17A.3.3, Western Travel Collection, Missouri Historical Society.

Lord, Israel Shipman Pelton. *"At the Extremity of Civilization": A Meticulously Descriptive Diary, 1849.* Edited by Necia Pelton Liles. Foreword by J. S. Holliday. Jefferson, N.C.: McFarland and Company, 1995.

Lorton, William B. Diaries, September 1848–January 1850. C-F 190, Bancroft Library.

Loveland, Cyrus C. *California Trail Herd: The 1850 Missouri-to-California Journal.* Edited by Richard H. Dillon. Los Gatos, Calif.: Talisman Press, 1961.

Ludington, Hagan Z., to "My Dear Father," 4 May 1849. Typescript, Manuscript Collection, Box 13, California State Library.

Lyon, James D. "Ten Miles East of Fort Laramie," 4 July 1849. *Detroit Advertiser,* 10 September 1849, in Bruff, *Gold Rush,* 1:479n135.

M. G. D. 23 February 1850. "Letters from California." *Arkansas State Gazette,* 19 April 1850.

MacDonald, James. *The Trek of James MacDonald, 1850.* Edited by Edgar W. Stanton III. Sacramento, Calif.: Artprint Press, 1989.

Manlove, Jonathan. An Overland Trip to the California Gold Fields [1849]. Typescript, Manuscript SMCII Box 17, Folder 13, California State Library.

Manly, William Lewis. *Death Valley in '49.* San Jose, Calif.: Pacific Tree and Vine, 1894. Reprint by LeRoy and Jean Johnson, Berkeley, Calif.: Heyday Books, 2001.

Marcy, William. Report of the Secretary of War (31:2). Senate Exec. Doc. 1, Part II, Washington, D.C.: Government Printing Office, 1850.

Markle, John A. Diary, 1849. MSS C-F 126, Bancroft Library.

———. "A Letter from California." Edited by Robert Markle Blackson. *Pennsylvania Folklife* 29, no. 1 (1979): 2–12.

Martin, Dr. Solon Douglas ["Pill Box"]. Reminiscences of an Overland Trip to California in 1849 by Pill Box, 1893. NFTC Manuscripts, Mattes Library.

Martin, John L. Goldfield Letters, 1849, 1851. Typescript, NFTC Manuscripts, Mattes Library.

Mason, Dillis V., to "Dear Father & Mother," 27 July 1852. NFTC Manuscripts, Mattes Library.

Mason, J. D. "Letter from California," August 1850. *Fort Wayne Times,* 12 December 1850, 1/1–3. Courtesy of Kristin Johnson.

Mathews, Samuel. Letters and "By Wagon Train to California, 1849: A Narrative." In Dean Mathews, ed., *The Mathews Family in America,* 21–28, 273–327. Rio Verde, Ariz.: Alondra Publishing, 1996.

Maxwell, William Audley. *Crossing the Plains, Days of '57.* San Francisco: Sunset Publishing, 1915.

McAuley, Eliza Ann. "Iowa to the 'Land of Gold.'" In Holmes, ed., *Covered Wagon Women,* 4:33–81.

McCall, Ansel J. *The Great California Trail in 1849.* Bath, N.Y.: Steuben Courier Printing, 1882.

McCarty, John T. Letters to the *Indiana American* (Brookville). Bieber Collection.

McDiarmid, Finley. *Letters to My Wife.* Fairfield, Wash.: Ye Galleon Press, 1997.

McIlhany, Edward W. *Recollections of a '49er.* Kansas City, Mo.: Hailman Printing Company, 1908.

McKinstry, Byron N. *The California Gold Rush Overland Diary, 1850–1852.* Edited by Bruce L. McKinstry. Glendale, Calif.: Arthur H. Clark, 1975.

Meeker, Ezra. *Ox-team Days on the Oregon Trail.* Edited by Howard R. Driggs. Yonkers-on-Hudson, N.Y.: World Book Company, 1922.

Menefee, Arthur M. "Travels across the Plains, 1857." *Nevada Historical Quarterly* 9 (1966): 1–29.

Middleton, Joseph. The Diary and Letters: Embracing his Trip Across the Plains via the Lassen or "Death Route" Cutoff in 1849. MSS S-39, Beinecke Library. Richard L. Rieck transcription.

Miller, James D. "Early Oregon Scenes: A Pioneer Narrative," *Oregon Historical Quarterly* 31, nos. 1–3 (March–September 1930): 55–68, 160–80, 275–84. Kay Threlkeld transcription.

Millington, D. A. Diary, 1850. Typescript, NFTC Manuscripts, Mattes Library.

Minges, Abram. Journal, 8 May to 15 September 1849. 85320 AA Vault, Bentley Historical Library, University of Michigan. Richard L. Rieck transcription.

Moody, Joseph Ledlie, to "My Dear Father," 7 August 1849. "An 1849 Letter from California." *California Historical Society Quarterly* 13, no. 1 (March 1934): 84–85.

Morehead, Charles R. "Personal Recollections." In William E. Connelley, ed., *Doniphan's Expedition and the Conquest of New Mexico and California,* 600–22. Topeka, Kans.: n.p. 1907.

Morgan, Amasa. Diary, 2 April to 28 July 1849. MSS 2001/111 cz, Bancroft Library. Janice Morgan and Susan Badger Doyle transcription.

Morris, Robert M. Journal of an Overland Trip to California and other Army assignments, 1849–1853. WA MSS S-1738, Beinecke Library. Richard L. Rieck Transcription, 2003.

Morriss, Philemon D. The Diary. End of the Oregon Trail Interpretive Center. Copy in author's possession.

Moss, D. H. "Overland with a Pack Train Emigrant." 14 October 1849. In Wyman, ed., *California Emigrant Letters,* 63–67.

Mossman, Isaac Van Dorsey. "A Pioneer of 1853." *Oregon Native Son Historical Magazine* 2, no. 11 (November 1900): 299–304.

Mullan, John. "From Walla Walla to San Francisco." *Quarterly of the Oregon Historical Society* 4, no. 3 (September 1903): 202–26.

Murphy, Andrew Lopp. Diary 1849. Typescript, C2723, Western Historical Manuscripts.

Murphy, Edward. Letter, 2 September 1849. "Letters from California," *Missouri Whig* (Palmyra), 29 November 1849.

Murray, William Riley. 1849 Diary. Typescript, NFTC Manuscripts, Mattes Library.

Murrell, George McKinley. To "Dear Father [Samuel Murrell]," 17 September 1849. OCTA Manuscripts, Mattes Library.

Muscott, J. M., to Ebenezer Robbins, 10 June and 14 October 1849. Letters from the *Rome Sentinel* (New York). Typescript, California State Library.

Negley, Felix C. "Gold Fever: Diary of a Forty-Niner." Edited by Nicholas P. Ciotola. *Wild West* 17, no. 6 (April 2005): 25–31.

Newcomb, Silas. Overland Journey, 1850. WA MSS 359, Beinecke Library. Richard L. Rieck transcription.

Nichols, David Thomas. Diary, 1851. Sacramento to Dixon, Illinois. Acc 90-034, NFTC Manuscripts, Mattes Library.

Nixon, Alexander B. Diary of an Overland Journey. CF 865 N5 A3, 2 vols., California State Library.

Nobles, William H., to Secretary of the Interior Jacob Thompson, 16 April 1857. Interior Department Records, Letters received relative to the Fort Kearney, South Pass, and Honey Lake Road, RG 48, Entry 624, Box 5, National Archives.

Norton, Lewis Adelbert. *Life and Adventures*. Oakland, Calif.: Pacific Press, 1887.

Nusbaumer, Louis. Erlebnisse einer Reise nach den Goldregionen Californiens, [1849]. Diary and translation, 20 May 1849 to 19 June 1850. MSS C-F 8, Bancroft Library.

Owen, East S. Journal of an Overland Journey, 1852. MSS S-927, Beinecke Library. Richard L. Rieck transcription.

Palmer, Harriet Scott. *Crossing over the Great Plains by Ox-Wagons* [1852]. Pamphlet, Oregon Historical Society.

Parke, Charles Ross, M.D. *Dreams to Dust: A Diary of the California Gold Rush, 1849–1850*. Edited by James E. Davis. Lincoln: University of Nebraska Press, 1989.

Parkinson, John Barber. "Memories of Early Wisconsin and the Gold Mines [1852]." *Wisconsin Magazine of History* 5, no. 2 (December 1921): 124–33. Offprint, 1–25.

Parkman, Francis Jr. *Letters*. 2 vols. Edited by Wilbur R. Jacobs. Norman: University of Oklahoma Press, 1960.

Patterson, Edwin H. N. Diary and Letters [1850]. OCTA Manuscripts, Mattes Library.

Payne, James A. Saint Louis to San Francisco, 1850. Typescript, CF 593 P25, California State Library. Excerpts, *Pacific Historical Review* 9, no. 4 (December 1940): 445–59.

Peck, Washington. *On the Western Trails: The Overland Diaries*. Edited by Susan M. Erb. Norman, Okla.: Arthur H. Clark, 2009.

Pierce, E. D. *The Pierce Chronicle: Personal Reminiscences* [1849]. Edited by J. Gary Williams and Ronald W. Stark. Moscow: Idaho Research Foundation, 1975.

Perkins, Elisha Douglas. *Gold Rush Diary, 1849*. Edited by Thomas D. Clark. Lexington: University of Kentucky Press, 1967.

Phillips, Cyrus E. Diary, 1852. Vault MSS 273, BYU Library.

Phillips, M. Diary to California, 2 April to 18 November 1849. MSS 86/83c, Bancroft Library.

Philo, to "Dear Parents & Sister." California Correspondence, 1850–1855. WA MSS S-713 P548, Beinecke Library.

Pickett, Belinda Cooley. Covered Wagon Days from the Original Journal, 1853. Typescript, OCTA Manuscripts, Mattes Library.

Pike, Joseph. Diary of a Forty-niner, 1850. Typescript, CF 865 P55 1847, California State Library.

Platt, P. L., and Nelson Slater. *The Travelers' Guide across the Plains, upon the Overland Route to California Showing Distances from Point to Point, 1852*. Edited by Dale L. Morgan. San Francisco: John Howell Books, 1963.

Polk, James K. Papers. Manuscript Division, Library of Congress.

———. *The Diary, 1845 to 1849*. 4 vols. Edited by Milo Milton Quaife. Chicago: A. C. McClurg, 1910.

Potter, Theodore E. *Autobiography of Theodore Edgar Potter* [1852]. Concord, N.H.: The Rumford Press, 1913, 25–98.

Porter, Lavinia Honeyman. "By Ox Team to California [1860]." In Ridge, ed., *Westward Journeys,* 189–402.

Pratt, James. "1849 Letters." In Cumming, ed., *The Gold Rush,* 6–18, 29–39, 41–46, 57–64, 69–76, 98–117.

Pritchard, James A. *The Overland Diary, 1849.* Edited by Dale L. Morgan. Denver: Old West, 1959.

Prichet, John. "A Letter from California," 17 January 1850. *Richmond Palladium,* 3 April 1850. OCTA Manuscripts, Mattes Library.

Purdy, John H. Correspondence, 1849–1851. MSS 862, BYU Library.

Ramsay, Alexander. "Gold Rush Diary of 1849." Edited by Merrill J. Mattes. *Pacific Historical Review* 18, no. 4 (November 1949): 437–68.

Randall, J. D. Diary of an Overland Journey to California, 10 April to 28 August 1852. Typescript, Mattes Library. Kay Threlkeld transcription.

Read, George Willis. *A Pioneer of 1850.* Edited by Georgia Willis Read. Boston: Little, Brown, 1927.

Reading, Pierson B. "Journal." Edited by Philip B. Bekeart. *Quarterly of the Society of California Pioneers* 7, no. 3 (September 1930): 134–98.

Reed, Charles. Letters, 1849. Box 3, Folder 47, Kendall Papers, Newberry Library.

Reed, James Frazier. Pioneer Manuscript Collection, Box 356, Folder 63, California State Library.

Reid, Bernard J. *Overland to California with the Pioneer Line: The Gold Rush Diary.* Edited by Mary McDougall Gordon. Stanford, Calif.: Stanford University Press, 1985.

Remy, Jules, and Julius Brenchley. *A Journey to Great-Salt-Lake City.* 2 vols. London: W. Jeffs, 1861.

Reynolds, Alonzo, to "My Dear Parents," 6–17 July 1849. "From the Mountains." *Fort Des Moines Star,* 2 November 1849, 2/2. Bieber Collection.

Richardson, Albert D. "Letters on the Pike's Peak Gold Region, 1860." Edited by Louise Barry. *Kansas Historical Quarterly* 12, no. 1 (February 1943): 14–57.

Richardson, Caroline L. 1852 Journal and Commonplace Book. MSS C-F 102, Bancroft Library. Richard L. Rieck transcription.

Richey, Jno. A., to "Friend Emmons," Sacramento City, 3 October 1850. Ben L. Emmons Collection, Missouri Historical Society.

Ridge, John R. *Poems.* San Francisco: Henry Payot, 1868.

Robe, Robert. "Diary While Crossing the Plains" [1851]. *Washington Historical Quarterly* 19, no. 1 (January 1928): 42–63.

Rodmon, S. F., to "My Dear Friends," 17 August 1849. "From California," *Indiana American* (Brookville), 26 October 1849. Bieber Collection.

Rothwell, William Renfro. Notes of a Journey to California, 1850. WA MSS 409, Beinecke Library.

Royce, Sarah Eleanor. *Across the Plains: Sarah Royce's Western Narrative.* Edited by Jennifer Dawes Adkinson. Tucson: University of Arizona Press, 2009.

Savage, Americus. "Americus Savage's Journal [1851]." *Genealogical History of Freeman, Maine 1796–1938.* Edited by George A. Thompson and Janet Thompson, 3:359–69. Westminster, Md.: Heritage Books, 1996.

Sawyer, Francis Lamar. "Kentucky to California by Carriage and a Feather Bed [1852]." In Holmes, ed., *Covered Wagon Women,* 4:83–115.

Scharmann, Hermann B. *Overland Journey to California.* Translated and edited by Margaret Hoff Zimmermann and Erich W. Zimmermann. N.p.: n.p., 1918.

Schmölder, Bruno. Typescript, HM2271, Huntington Library. English translation of extracts from *Neuer praktischer Wegweiser für Auswanderer nach Nord-Amerika* taken from later German edition, *Der Führer für wanderer nach Californian.* Leipzig and Gera, Germany: I. M. C. Armbruster, 1849.

Scott, Abigail Jane [Duniway]. "Journal of a Trip to Oregon" [1852]. In Holmes, ed., *Covered Wagon Women,* 5:21–138.

Senter, Riley. *Crossing the Continent to the California Gold Fields* [1849]. Lemon Grove, Calif.: W. R. Senter, 1938.

Sharp, James Meikle. *Brief Account of the Experiences* [1852]. N.p.: n.p., 1931, 18–37.

Shaw, David Augustus. *Eldorado; or, California As Seen by a Pioneer, 1850–1900.* Los Angeles: B. R. Baumgardt & Co., 1900.

Shaw, Rueben C. *Across the Plains in Forty-nine.* Chicago: Lakeside Press, 1948.

Shepard, Hinsdale Truman. Overland Diary, 1852. Manuscript SMCII, Box 26, Folder 11, California State Library.

Shoemaker. Overland Diary, 1850. MSS SC 160 1850, BYU Library.

Shutterly, Lewis. *The Diary of Lewis Shutterly, 1849–1850.* Edited by Robert C. Black. Saratoga, Wyo.: Saratoga Historical and Cultural Association, 1981.

Simpson, George. Incoming Correspondence. R3C 1T5, Microfilm 3M94, Hudson's Bay Company Archives, Provincial Archives, Winnipeg, Manitoba, Canada.

Sloane, Oliver. Letters, 1850 and 1851. NFTC Manuscripts, Mattes Library.

Smith, Azariah. *The Gold Discovery Journal of Azariah Smith.* Edited by David L. Bigler. Salt Lake City: University of Utah Press, 1990.

Smith, Delazon. "From the Oregon Times [1852]. Letter of Hon. Delazon Smith." *The Democratic Union* (Keosauqua, Iowa), 26 February 1853.

Smith, Mary Stone. Diary 1854. [Anonymous] Travel Account of Journey from Indiana to Washington. C3415, Western Historical Manuscript Collection.

Smith, Persifor. "California—Letter from Gov. Smith." *Bangor Daily Whig and Courier* (Maine), 26 June 1849. Ardis Parshall transcription.

———. "General Smith's Correspondence." In Zachary Taylor, Message from the President. Senate Exec. Doc. 52 (31:1), Serial 561, 1850.

Smith, Samuel R., to "Dear Father and Mother," 2 September 1849. "From California: Letter from a California Emigrant." *Tioga Eagle* (Wellsboro, Pennsylvania), 11 November 1849, 4/1–3. Richard L. Rieck transcription.

Snow, Mary Augusta Hawkins. Journal, May–June 1851. Folder 1, LDS Archives, 18–79.

Spencer, Lafayette. "Lafayette Spencer's Oregon Trail Diary 1852." *Annals of Iowa* 8, no. 4 (January 1908): 304–10.

Spooner, Elijah Allen. Letters and Diary, 1849–1850. Vault MSS 662. 16 items [128 pp.], BYU Library.

St. Clair, H. C. Journal of a Tour to California, 1849. WA MSS S-1449, Beinecke Library.

Stabæk, Tosten Kittelsen. "An Account of a Journey to California in 1852." Translated by Einar J. Haugen. *Norwegian-American Studies* 4 (1929): 99–124.

Standley, William. Letters, 1852, in Papers, 1852–1853. Typescript, C2717, Western Historical Manuscripts.

Stansbury, Howard. *Exploration and Survey of the Valley of the Great Salt Lake.* Philadelphia: Lippincott, Grambo and Co., 1852.

Starr, Isaac R. Diary, 1850. Mss 2473, Oregon Historical Society. (Incorrectly listed as "J. R. Starr.") Kay Threlkeld transcription.

Stephens, Lorenzo Dow. *Life Sketches of a Jayhawker of '49.* San Jose, Calif.: Nolta Brothers, 1916.

Stine, Henry Atkinson. 1850 Journal and Letters. Missouri Historical Society.

Stockton, John K. The Trail of the Covered Wagon [1852]. Edited by Nancy Wanita Stockton Bernhardt and John P. Kirkpatrick. Copy in author's possession.

Stoddard, William Cochran [and Ezra Brown?]. Overland Diary, Kanesville, Iowa to Yreka, California, 1852. Society of California Pioneers. Richard Rieck transcription.

Stone, Sophronia Helen. Diary, 1852. Tutt Library, Colorado College, Colorado Springs, Colorado. Don Buck transcription.

Stout, Hosea. *On the Mormon Frontier: The Diary of Hosea Stout.* 2 vols. Edited by Juanita Brooks. Salt Lake City: University of Utah Press, 1964.

Stover, Samuel M. *Diary enroute to California 1849.* Elizabethtown, Tenn.: H. M. Folsom, 1939.

Sufferins, Samuel. Letter, 4 August 1849. *Richmond Palladium,* 31 October 1849; and "Wayne County's 'Forty-Niners,'" *Richmond Palladium,* 1 January 1931, 11–12.

Sullivan, Joshua. California Letters, 1849–50. Typescript, MSS 2609, Oregon Historical Society.

Summers, Joseph R., to "Esteemed Companion," 30 October 1850. Typescript, C2746, Western Historical Manuscripts.

Sumner, Cyrus. Copy of Journal to California in 1849, or Letters from Uncle Cyrus. MSS 91/25 c, Bancroft Library. Richard L. Rieck transcription.

Swain, William. In Holliday, *The World Rushed In.*

Tappan, Henry. "The Gold Rush Diary" [1849]. Edited by Everett Walters and George B. Strother. *Annals of Wyoming* 25, no. 2 (July 1953): 113–39.

Tate, James A. Diary, 1849. Typescript, C2720, Western Historical Manuscripts.

————. "One Who Went West: Letters of James Tate." *Missouri Historical Review* 57, no. 4 (July 1963): 369–78.

Taylor, Calvin. "Overland to the Gold Fields of California in 1850." *Nebraska History* 50, no. 2 (Summer 1969): 125–49. Part 2, "Overland to California." Edited by Burton J. Williams. *Utah Historical Quarterly* 38, no. 4 (Fall 1970): 312–49.

Taylor, Ossian F. Journal, April–September 1851. Marriott Library, University of Utah.

Taylor, Zachary. "California and New Mexico." House Exec. Doc. 17 (31-1), 1850, Serial 673.

Temple, William Bedford. Letters, 11 May and 2 June 1850. MSS #1508, Oregon Historical Society.

Terrell, Joseph C. "Overland Trip to California in '52." In *Reminiscences of Early Days in Fort Worth,* 76–91. Fort Worth: Texas Printing Company, 1906.

Terry, Chloe Ann. Miss C. A. Terry's Diary Kept While Crossing the Plains in 1852. Denny Papers, MsSc 100, Box 4, Folder 23, Washington State Historical Society. See also Typescript, Accession 3234, Allen Library, University of Washington. Kay Threlkeld transcription.

Thissell, G. W. *Crossing the Plains in '49* [1850]. Oakland, Calif.: n.p., 1901.

Thomas, William L. Diary, 20 May to 11 August 1849. Typescript, CB 383:1, Bancroft Library.

Thompson, William. *Reminiscences of a Pioneer* [1852]. San Francisco: n.p., 1912.

Thomson, Origen. *Crossing the Plains in 1852.* Fairfield, Wash.: Ye Galleon Press, 1983.

Thorniley, John C. Overland Diary, 4 April to 24 August 1852. California State Library.

Tiffany, Palmer C. Overland Journey from Iowa to California, 1849. WA MSS 474, Beinecke Library.

Tiffany, Pardon Dexter. Journals and Letters, 1849. Originals and Typescript, Dexter P. Tiffany Collection, 1779–1967, AMC94-001159, Missouri Historical Society. Kay Threlkeld transcription.

Tinker, Charles. "Journal: A Trip to California in 1849." Edited by Eugene H. Roseboom. *Ohio State Archaeological and Historical Quarterly* 61 (1952): 64–85.

Tolles, James S. Journal of My Travels to California. 1849. BYU Library.

Tolman, James Clark. "Pioneer Days: Judge Tolman, in 1852, Again Crosses the Plains, This Time to Oregon." Samuel A. Clarke interview, *Sunday Oregonian,* 21 March 1886, 3/6–7, 8/6–7.

Tremble, Lewis. Letters, 1849. *Illinois Republican,* 1 January 1850. Acc. 91-006, Typescript, NFTC Manuscripts, Mattes Library.

Turnbull, Thomas. "Travels from the United States over the Plains to California [1852]." Edited by Frederick L. Paxson. *Proceedings of the State Historical Society of Wisconsin, 1913* (1914): 151–225.

Turner, Charles, to "Dear Bro. & Sister," 23 August 1849. Painesville Telegraph, November 1849? In Mathews, ed., *Mathews Family,* 307–308.

Tutt, Jno. Stro., to John Dougherty, 1 July 1850. Dougherty Papers, Missouri Historical Society.

Udell, John. *Incidents of Travel to California* [1850, 1852, and 1854]. Jefferson, Ohio: Printed for the Author at the Sentinel Office, 1856.

Van Dorn, Thomas J. Diary, 1849. WA MSS S-1319, Beinecke Library.

Van Houten, Benjamin Edsell, to "My Dear Wife," 8 September 1850. Pam Arrigo typescript, NFTC Manuscripts, Mattes Library, 1–2.

Variel, William J. "A Romance of the Plains [1852]." The Grizzly Bear (July, August, September 1907). NFTC Manuscripts, Mattes Library.

Wagner, William. Journal of an Ox Team Driver, 1852. Typescript, OCTA Manuscripts, Mattes Library. Richard L. Rieck typescript.

Walden, James M. Letters 1850–1851. SUNP 4930, Western Historical Manuscripts.

Walker, William Z. Diary, 1849. MSS SC 969 1849, Special Collections, BYU Library.

Ware, Joseph E. *Emigrants' Guide to California.* Edited by John Walton Caughey. Princeton, N.J.: Princeton University Press, 1932.

Warren, William. Family Correspondence, 1850. SMCII, Box 11, Folder 8, California State Library.

Waters, Nimrod. California Gold Seekers: Diary, 1850. Gene Taylor Walters typescript. NFTC Manuscripts, Mattes Library.

Waters, William H. H. Private Journal, 5 May to 20 June 1855, 1 January 1856 to 1857. Manuscript in the possession of Stafford Hazelett.

Watson, William J. *Journal of an Overland Journey to Oregon Made in the Year 1849.* Fairfield, Wash.: Ye Galleon Press, 1985.

Webster, Kimball. *The Gold Seekers of '49.* Manchester, N.H.: Standard, 1917.

Welch, Adonijah Strong. "Three Gold Rush Letters." Edited by William H. Hermann. *Iowa Journal of History and Politics* 57, no. 1 (January 1959): 61–73.

Wellenkamp, Henry. Travel Diary, 1850. Typescript, Microfilm C995, V. 7, #187, Western Historical Manuscripts.

West, James C. to Thomas James, 17 June 1849. "From the California Emigrants," *Belleville Weekly Advocate* (Illinois), 7 August 1849. Donnell Redlingshafer Wisniewski transcription.

Whipple, Nelson Wheeler. "Journal of a Pioneer." *Instructor* (March 1947): 121–24.

Whitman, Abial. Overland Journey, 1850. WA Mss 522, Beinecke Library. Richard L. Rieck transcription.

Whitworth, George Frederick. Diary, 1853. Whitworth College Archives, Spokane, Wash. Janet Hauck transcription.

Wilfrey, Joseph, to "Dear wife and children," 13 October 1850. Typescript, Oregon-California Papers, Missouri Historical Society.

Wilkins, James F. *An Artist on the Overland Trail: The 1849 Diary and Sketches.* Edited by John Francis McDermott. San Marino, Calif.: The Huntington Library, 1968.

Willock, David. Gold Rush Letters, Missouri Whig (Palmyra), 1849–50. Donated by Boxwell Hawkins. Kathleen Wilham transcription.

Wilson, John, to Thomas Ewing, Secretary of the Interior, 22 December 1849. Letters Received, Commissioner of Indian Affairs, RG 75, National Archives.

Wilson, L. S. *Luzena Stanley Wilson, '49er: Memories Recalled Years Later.* Introduction by Francis Farquhar. Mills College, Calif.: Eucalyptus Press, 1937.

Wilson, Samuel S. Letters, 1849–1852. Western Historical Manuscripts.

Wiman, Henry E., to "Dear Parents," 25 October 1849. Robert H. Miller Papers, Missouri Historical Society.

Wistar, Isaac Jones. *Autobiography, 1827–1905.* Philadelphia: Wistar Institute, 1937.

Withers, Geo. W., to "Mr. Miller," 12 August 1849. Robert H. Miller Papers, Missouri Historical Society.

Wittenmyer, Lewis Cass. Autobiography and Reminiscence [1849]. Society of California Pioneers.

Wonderly, Pauline. *Reminiscences of a Pioneer* [1852]. Edited by John Barton Hassler. Placerville, Calif.: El Dorado County Historical Society, 1965.

Wood, D. B., to "Dear Judge," 13 September 1849. "From California." *Indiana American* (Brookville), 7 December 1849. Bieber Collection.

Wood, John. *Journal of John Wood: As Kept by Him While Traveling from Cincinnati to the Gold Diggings in California, in the Spring and Summer of 1850.* Columbus, Ohio: Nevins and Myers, 1871.

Wood, Joseph Warren. Diary, 1849. HM 318, Huntington Library. Richard L. Rieck and Kay Threlkeld transcriptions.

Wood, William W. Journal of an Overland Trip, 1850. WA MSS S-1440 W85, Beinecke Library.

Woodland, Mary. Letters, 21 June 1852, October 1852, and 29 March 1853. Transcription of originals in possession of Molly McDade Hood.

Woodruff, Wilford. *Wilford Woodruff's Journal.* 10 vols. Edited by Scott G. Kenney. Midvale, Utah: Signature Books, 1983.

Woodworth, James. *Diary: Across the Plains to California in 1853.* Eugene, Oreg.: Lane County Historical Society, 1972.

Woolley, Lell Hawley. *California, 1849–1913.* Oakland, Calif.: De Witt and Snelling, 1913.

Wright, Orin O., to "Dear Sister," 22 April 1850. Typescript. Corwith Wagner Collection, Missouri Historical Society Library and Archives.

Young, Brigham. Brigham Young Collection, MS 1234, LDS Archives.

Young, Brigham, to Superintentent of Indian Affairs, Letters Received 1824–1881, Utah Superintendency, RG 75, National Archives.

Young, Jacob. Letters, 28 March, 26 April, 7 November 1852. Young Brothers Letters, 1852–1856, California State Library.

SECONDARY SOURCES:

BOOKS, ARTICLES, MANUSCRIPT COLLECTIONS, AND DISSERTATIONS

Aldous, Jay A., and Paul S. Nicholes. "What Is Mountain Fever?" *Overland Journal* 15, no. 1 (Spring 1997): 18–23.

Arnold, Keith, and Jo Arnold. "The Lonesome Rout: The Yreka Cutoff." Edited by Richard Silva. *News from the Plains* (January 1996): 4.

Arnold, Keith, and Richard Silva. "Bloody Point—1852." *The Siskiyou Pioneer* 7, no. 1 (1998): 123–55.

Arrington, Leonard J. *Great Basin Kingdom: An Economic History of the Latter-day Saints 1830–1900.* Salt Lake City: University of Utah Press, 1993.

———. *History of Idaho.* 2 vols. Moscow: University of Idaho Press, 1994.

Bancroft, Hubert Howe. *History of California.* 7 vols. San Francisco: The History Company, 1886–1890.

———. *History of Oregon*. 2 vols. San Francisco: The History Company, 1886, 1888.

Barry, Louise. *The Beginning of the West, 1540–1854*. Topeka: Kansas State Historical Society, 1972.

Bekeart, Philip B. "Pierson B. Reading: A Biography." *Quarterly of the Society of California Pioneers* 7, no. 3 (September 1930): 134–47.

Belanger, Albert Edward. *On the Oregon Trail in 1851: Canaries, Buffalo-Chips, and Elephants in the Words of Those Who Made the Trek*. Salt Lake City: American Book Publishing, 2010.

Bieber, Ralph Paul, ed. *Southern Trails to California in 1849*. Glendale, Calif.: Arthur H. Clark, 1937.

Bigler, David L. "The Elephant Meets the Lion: Gold Rush Conflicts in the Great Basin." Paper presented at the Utah Historic Trails Consortium Symposium, 14 April 1999.

Bigler, David L., and Will Bagley, eds. *Army of Israel: Mormon Battalion Narratives*. Spokane, Wash.: Arthur H. Clark, 2000.

Blair, Roger P. "'The Doctor Gets Some Practice': Cholera and Medicine on the Overland Trails." *Journal of the West* 36, no. 1 (January 1997): 54–66.

Bleyhl, Norris A. Indian-White Relationships in Northern California 1849–1920 in the Congressional Set of United States Public Documents. Special Collections, Meriam Library, Chico State University, Chico, California.

Boag, Peter G. "Idaho's Fort Hall as a Western Crossroads." *Overland Journal* 16, no. 1 (Spring 1998): 20–26.

Boorn, Alida. "Goggles in the Rocky Mountain West." *Rocky Mountain Fur Trade Journal* 4 (2010): 126–43.

Brock, Richard K., and Donald E. Buck. *A Guide to the Applegate Trail from Lassen Meadow to Goose Lake*. Reno, Nev.: Trails West, 2004.

Brock, Richard K., and Robert S. Black, eds. *A Guide to the Nobles Trail*. Reno, Nev.: Trails West, 2008.

Brown, Randy. "Child's Cutoff." *Overland Journal* 5, no. 2 (Summer 1987): 17–22.

Browne, J. Ross. *Resources of the Pacific Slope*. New York: D. Appleton, 1869.

Browning, Peter, ed. *To the Golden Shore: America Goes to California*. Lafayette, Calif.: Great West Books, 1995.

Buck, Donald E. Where Did Emigrants Surmount the Sierra Nevada on the Truckee Trail? Summary of Don Wiggins, "Investigation of Emigrant Trails Over Passes South of Donner Pass: Interim"; and "Coldstream Pass Vs. Roller Pass: A Final Report." Unpublished ms.

———. William Nobles Itinerary in Opening the Nobles Trail From St. Paul, Minnesota Territory, to Shasta City, California, 1850–1852. Copy in author's possession.

———. A Commentary on the Bloody Point Massacre. Copy in author's possession.

Caughey, John Walton. *Gold Is the Cornerstone, with Vignettes by W. R. Cameron*. Berkeley: University of California Press, 1948.

———. *The California Gold Rush*. Berkeley: University of California Press, 1948.

Chandler, Robert J. "An Uncertain Influence: The Role of the Federal Government in California, 1846–1880." *California History* 8, nos. 3–4 (Winter 2003): 224–71.

Clark, William B. *Gold Districts of California*. Sacramento: California Division of Mines and Geology, 1998.

Cook, Sherburne F. *The Population of the California Indians, 1769–1970*. Berkeley: University of California Press, 1976.

Coy, Owen C. *The Great Trek*. San Francisco: Powell, 1931.

Culmer, Frederic A. "'General' John Wilson, Signer of the Deseret Petition." *California Historical Quarterly* 26, no. 4 (December 1947): 321–48.

Cumming, John, ed. *The Gold Rush: Letters from the Wolverine Rangers to the Marshall, Michigan* States-man, *1849–1851.* Mount Pleasant, Mich.: Cumming Press, 1974.

Curtis, Kent. "Producing a Gold Rush: National Ambitions and the Northern Rocky Mountains, 1853–1863." *Western Historical Quarterly* 50, no. 3 (Autumn 2009): 275–97.

Cutter, Donald C. "The Discovery of Gold in California." In Olaf P. Jenkins, ed., *The Mother Lode Country: Geologic Guidebook Along Highway 49—Sierran Gold Belt,* 13–17. San Francisco: California Department of Natural Resources, Division of Mines, 1948. Reprint, 1955.

Davies, J. Kenneth, and Lorin K. Hansen, *Mormon Gold: Mormons in the California Gold Rush Con-tributing to the Development of California and the Monetary Solvency of Early Utah.* North Salt Lake City, Utah: Granite Mountain Publishing Company, 2011.

Davis, Richard M. "The Walker River–Sonora Crossing: An All-But-Impossible Route." *Overland Journal* 6, no. 3 (1988): 10–28.

Decker, Dean. "Variants of the Slate Creek Cutoff." *Overland Journal* 2, no. 3 (Summer 1984): 30–35.

Delgado, James P. *To California By Sea: A Maritime History of the California Gold Rush.* Columbia: University of South Carolina Press, 1990.

Eaton, Herbert. *The Overland Trail to California in 1852.* New York: Capricorn Books, 1974.

Eichhorst, Jerry. "Pieces to the Puzzle: Rediscovering Idaho's North Alternate Oregon Trail." *Overland Journal* 28, no. 2 (Summer 2011): 48–67.

Eifler, Mark A. *Gold Rush Capitalists: Greed and Growth in Sacramento.* Albuquerque: University of New Mexico Press, 2002.

Elison, Gar. *Hudspeth Cutoff Field Guide.* Pocatello, Idaho: OCTA National Convention, 1997.

Etter, Patricia A. "HO! for California on the Mexican Gold Trail." *Overland Journal* 11, no. 3 (Fall 1993): 2–15.

———. "To California on the Southern Route—1849." *Overland Journal* 13, no. 3 (Fall 1995): 2–12.

———. *To California on the Southern Route, 1849: A History and Annotated Bibliography.* Foreword by Elliott West. Spokane, Wash.: Arthur H. Clark, 1998.

Evans, Elwood, et al. *History of the Pacific Northwest: Oregon and Washington,* 2 vols. Portland, Oreg.: North Pacific History Company, 1889.

Fairfield, Asa Merrill. *Pioneer History of Lassen County California Containing Everything That Can Be Learned About It From the Beginning of the World to the Year of Our Lord 1870.* San Francisco: H. S. Crocker, 1916.

Faragher, John Mack. *Women and Men on the Overland Trail.* New Haven, Conn.: Yale University Press, 1979.

Fey, Marshall, Joe King, and Jack Lepisto. *Emigrant Shadows: A History and Guide to the California Trail.* Virginia City, Nev.: Western Trails Research Association, 2002.

Fischer, Gayle V. *Pantaloons and Power: Nineteenth-Century Dress Reform in the United States.* Kent, Ohio: Kent State University Press, 2001.

Fleming, L. A., and A. R. Standing. "The Road to 'Fortune': The Salt Lake Cutoff." *Utah Historical Quarterly* 33, no. 3 (Summer 1965): 248–71.

Fletcher, Patricia, Jack Earl Fletcher, and Lee Whitely. *Cherokee Trail Diaries. Volume I—1849: A New Route to the California Gold Fields. Volume II—1850: Another New Route.* Caldwell, Idaho: Caxton Printers, 1999.

Folkman, David I., Jr. *The Nicaragua Route.* Salt Lake City: University of Utah Press, 1972.

Ford, Anna G. *Through the Years with the Hudspeths.* N.p.: n.p., 1971.

Foreman, Grant. "Antoine Leroux, New Mexico Guide." *New Mexico Historical Review* 16, no. 1 (January 1941): 367–78.

Fowler, Catherine S. *Tule Technology: Northern Paiute Uses of Marsh Resources in Western Nevada.* Washington, D.C.: Smithsonian Institution, 1990.

Frantz, Joe. *Gail Borden, Dairyman to a Nation.* Norman: University of Oklahoma Press, 1951.

Franzwa, Gregory M. *Maps of the Oregon Trail.* St. Louis: Patrice Press, 1990.

Gaston, Joseph. *The Centennial History of Oregon, 1811–1912.* Chicago: S. J. Clarke, 1912.

Glass, Jefferson. "Crossing the North Platte River." *Annals of Wyoming* 74, no. 3 (Summer 2002): 25–40.

Goodwin, G. G. "The First Living Elephant in America." *Journal of Mammalogy* 6, no. 4 (November 1925): 256–63.

Greever, William S. *The Bonanza West: The Story of Western Mining Rushes.* Norman: University of Oklahoma Press, 1963.

Hafen, LeRoy R., ed. *The Mountain Men and the Fur Trade of the Far West.* 10 vols. Glendale: Arthur H. Clark, 1965–1972.

Hakola, John W. *The Frontier, A Magazine of the Northwest.* Bozeman: Montana State University Press, 1962.

Hammond, Andrew. "Peter Lassen and His Trail." *Overland Journal* 4, no. 1 (Winter 1986): 33–41.

Hammond, Andrew, and Joanne Hammond. "Mapping the Beckwourth Trail." *Overland Journal* 12, no. 3 (Fall 1994): 10–28.

Hammond, George. *Who Saw the Elephant? An Inquiry by a Scholar Well Acquainted with the Beast.* Keepsake of the Wagner Memorial Dinner of the California Historical Society, September 25, 1964. San Francisco: California Historical Society, 1964.

Hannon, Jessie Gould, ed. *The Boston-Newton Company Venture: From Massachusetts to California in 1849.* Lincoln: University of Nebraska Press, 1969.

Haskins, C. W. *The Argonauts of California.* New York: Fords, Howard and Hulbert, 1890.

Hittell, John S. *The Resources of California.* San Francisco: A. Roman, 1863.

Holliday, J. S. *The World Rushed In: The California Gold Rush Experience.* Norman: University of Oklahoma Press, 2002.

Holmes, Kenneth L., ed. *Covered Wagon Women: Diaries and Letters from the Western Trails, 1840–1890.* 11 vols. Glendale, Calif., and Spokane, Wash.: Arthur H. Clark, 1983–93.

Hoshide, Robert. "Salt Desert Trails Revisited." *Crossroads* 5, no. 2 (Spring 1994): 5–9.

Hudson, Linda. *The Mistress of Manifest Destiny: Jane McManus Storm Cazneau.* Austin: Texas State Historical Association, 2001.

Hughey, Richard. "Johnson's Cutoff Led to First Link in State Highway System." *Mountain Democrat* (Placerville, Calif.), 29 April 1999.

———. "Peter Lassen and the Fandango Pass." *Mountain Democrat* (Placerville, Calif.), 19 March 1999.

Hunt, Thomas H. "Anatomy of a Massacre: Bloody Point." *Overland Journal* 7, no. 3 (Fall 1989): 2–25.

———. "Silent City of Rocks." *Overland Journal* 7, no. 4 (Winter 1989): 13–23.

———. "William Nobles and the Origins of His Trail." In Brock and Black, eds. *A Guide to the Nobles Trail,* 4–7.

Hurtado, Albert L. "Clouded Legacy: The Gold Rush and California Indians." In Owens, ed., *Riches for All,* 90–117.

———. *Indian Survival on the California Frontier.* New Haven, Conn.: Yale University Press, 1988.

Hussey, Tacitus. "The Flood of 1851." *Annals of Iowa* 5, no. 6 (July 1902): 401–24.

Jenson, Andrew. *Latter-day Saint Biographical Encyclopedia,* 4 vols. Salt Lake City: Andrew Jenson History Company, 1901.

Johansen, Dorothy O., and Charles M. Gates. *Empire of the Columbia: A History of the Pacific Northwest.* New York: Harper and Brothers, 1967.

Johnson, LeRoy, and Jean Johnson. *Escape from Death Valley: As Told by William Lewis Manly and Other '49ers.* Reno: University of Nevada Press, 1987.

Johnson, Susan Lee. *Roaring Camp: The Social World of the California Gold Rush.* New York: W. W. Norton, 2000.

Kellogg, Alice Cahail. "The Life of Dr. John Coe Kellogg." *Whidbey Island Farm Bureau News,* 1939.

Kelly, Charles. "Gold Seekers on the Hastings Cutoff." *Utah Historical Quarterly* 20 (January 1952): 3–30.

Kemble, John Haskell. *The Panama Route, 1848–1869.* Columbia: University of South Carolina Press, 1990.

Korns, Roderic and Dale L. Morgan, eds. *West from Fort Bridger.* Revised edition by Will Bagley and Harold Schindler. Logan: Utah State University Press, 1994.

Kriebl, Karen J. "From Bloomers to Flappers: The American Women's Dress Reform Movement, 1840–1920." Ph.D. diss., Ohio State University, 1998.

Krist, John. "California is Haunted by Gold Rush Legacy of Toxic Mercury." Environmental News Network, 16 August 2002.

Lamb, Blaine P. "Emigrant Aid on California Gold Rush Trails: Private Needs and Public Enterprises." *Overland Journal* 19, no. 4 (Winter 2001/2002): 122–35.

Lapp, Rudolph M. *Blacks in Gold Rush California.* New Haven, Conn.: Yale University Press, 1977.

Larsen, Dennis. "The Devil's Gangway, Searching for the Sublette Cutoff on Dempsey Ridge." *Overland Journal* 28, no. 1 (Spring 2010): 5–23.

Levy, Jo Ann. "We Were Forty-niners, Too! Women in the California Gold Rush." *Overland Journal* 6, no. 3 (1988): 29–34.

———. *They Saw the Elephant: Women in the California Gold Rush.* Hamden, Conn.: Archon Books, 1990.

Lewis, Oscar. *Sea Routes to the Gold Fields.* New York: Alfred A. Knopf, 1949.

Lyman, Edward Leo. *The Overland Journey from Utah to California: Wagon Travel from the City of Saints to the City of Angels.* Reno: University of Nevada Press, 2004.

Madley, Benjamin. "California's Yuki Indians: Defining Genocide in Native American History." *Western Historical Quarterly* 39, no. 3 (Autumn 2008): 303–32.

Madsen, Brigham D. *Gold Rush Sojourners in Great Salt Lake City, 1849 and 1850.* Salt Lake City: University of Utah Press, 1983.

Madsen, Brigham D., ed. *Exploring the Great Salt Lake: The Stansbury Expedition of 1849–50.* Salt Lake City: University of Utah Press, 1989.

Martin, Charles W., Jr. "Geology of Silent City of Rocks." *Overland Journal* 7, no. 4 (Winter 1989): 24–27.

Martin, Charles W., and Charles W. Martin, Jr. "The Fourth of July: A Holiday on the Trail." *Overland Journal* 10, no. 2 (Summer 1992): 2–20.

Mattes, Merrill J. *The Great Platte River Road: The Covered Wagon Mainline.* Lincoln: Bison Books, 1978.

———. "Joseph Robidoux's Family." *Overland Journal* 6, no. 3 (1988): 2–9.

———. *Platte River Road Narratives: A Descriptive Bibliography of Travel over the Great Central Overland Route to Oregon, California, Utah, Colorado, Montana, and Other Western States and Territories, 1812–1866.* Urbana: University of Illinois Press, 1988.

———. "Potholes in the Great Platte River Road: Misconceptions in Need of Repair." *Wyoming Annals* 65, nos. 2/3 (Summer/Fall 1993): 6–14.

McCoy, Joseph G. *Historic Sketches of the Cattle Trade*. Edited by Ralph P. Bieber. Glendale, Calif.: Arthur H. Clark, 1939.

Meacham, Alfred B. *Wigwam and War-path; or, The Royal Chief in Chains*. Boston: J. P. Dale, 1875.

Meldahl, Keith H. *Hard Road West: History and Geology along the Gold Rush Trail*. Chicago: University of Chicago Press, 2007.

Milikien, Herbert C. " 'Dead of the Bloody Flux': Cholera Stalks the Emigrant Trail." *Overland Journal* 14, no. 3 (Autumn 1996): 6–11.

Minnick, Sylvia Sun. "Never Far from Home: Being Chinese in the California Gold Rush." In Owens, ed., *Riches for All*, 142–60.

Morgan, Dale L. "Ferries on the Sublette Cutoff." *Annals of Wyoming* 32, no. 2 (October 1960): 167–201.

———. "Letters by Forty-niners." *Western Humanities Review* 3, no. 1 (April 1949): 98–116.

———. "Miles Goodyear." *Utah Historical Quarterly* 21, nos. 3 and 4 (July and October 1953): 195–218, 307–29.

———. "The State of Deseret." *Utah Historical Quarterly* 8, nos. 2, 3, and 4 (April–October 1940): 64–239.

———. *Overland in 1846: Diaries and Letters of the California-Oregon Trail*, 2 vols. Lincoln: University of Nebraska Press, 1993.

———. *Shoshonean Peoples and the Overland Trail*. Edited by Richard L. Saunders. Logan: Utah State University Press, 2007.

Murray, Keith A. *The Modocs and Their War*. Norman: University of Oklahoma Press, 1959.

Myres, Sandra L., ed. *Ho for California! Women's Overland Diaries from the Huntington Library*. San Marino: Huntington Library, 1980.

Nash, Gerald D. "A Veritable Revolution: The Global Economic Significance of the California Gold Rush." In Rawls and Orsi, *A Golden State*, 276–92.

Norton, Jack. *When Our Worlds Cried: Genocide in Northwestern California*. San Francisco: Indian Historian Press, 1979.

Owens, Kenneth N. "The Mormon-Carson Emigrant Trail in Western History." *Montana* 42 (Winter 1992): 14–27.

———. *Gold Rush Saints: California Mormons and the Great Rush for Riches*. Spokane, Wash.: Arthur H. Clark, 2004.

———. *Riches for All: The California Gold Rush and the World*. Lincoln: University of Nebraska Press, 2002.

Paden, Irene D., ed. "The Ira J. Willis Guide to the Gold Fields." *California Historical Quarterly* 32, no. 3 (September 1953): 193–207.

Paul, Rodman W. *California Gold: The Beginning of Mining in the Far West*. Cambridge, Mass.: Harvard University Press, 1947.

Paul, Rodman W., and Elliott West. *Mining Frontiers of the Far West*. Albuquerque: University of New Mexico Press, 2001.

Potter, David, ed. *Trail to California: The Overland Journal of Vincent Geiger and Wakeman Bryarly*. New Haven, Conn.: Yale University Press, 1962.

Powers, Ramon, and James N. Leiker. "Cholera among the Plains Indians." *Western Historical Quarterly* 29, no. 3 (Autumn 1998): 317–40.

Powers, Stephen. "California Indian Characteristics." *Overland Monthly* 14, no. 4 (April 1875): 297–309.

Pritzker, Barry M. *A Native American Encyclopedia: History*. New York: Oxford University Press, 2000.

Prucha, Francis Paul, ed. *Documents of United States Indian Policy*. Lincoln: University of Nebraska Press, 2000.

Rawls, James J. *California Indians: The Changing Image*. Norman: University of Oklahoma Press, 1986.

Rawls, James J., and Richard J. Orsi, eds. *A Golden State: Mining and Economic Development in Gold Rush California*. Berkeley: University of California Press, 1998.

Read, Georgia Willis. "Women and Children on the Oregon-California Trail in the Gold-Rush Years." *Missouri Historical Review* 39, no. 1 (October 1944): 1–23.

Riddle, Jeff C. *The Indian History of the Modoc War, and the Causes That Led to It*. San Francisco: Marnell and Company, 1914.

Ridge, Martin. "The Legacy of the Gold Rush." *Montana* 49, no. 3 (Autumn 1999): 58–63.

Rieck, Richard L. "A Geography of Death on the Oregon-California Trail, 1840–1860." *Overland Journal* 9, no. 1 (1991): 13–21.

———. "The Geography of Death and Graves on the Oregon/California/Mormon Trails." Paper presented at the Oregon-California Trail Association convention, Salt Lake City, 17 August 2005.

Roberts, Brigham H. *Comprehensive History of The Church of Jesus Christ of Latter-day Saints*. 6 vols. Salt Lake City: Deseret News Press, 1930.

Rogers, Fred Blackburn. "Bear Flag Lieutenant." *California Historical Society Quarterly* 30, no. 2 (June 1951): 157–75.

Rohrbough, Malcolm. *Days of Gold: The California Gold Rush and the American Nation*. Berkeley: University of California Press, 1997.

———. " 'We Will Make Our Fortunes, No Doubt of It': The Worldwide Rush to California." In Owens, ed., *Riches for All*, 55–70.

Schenck, J. S., and W. S. Rann. *History of Warren County*. Syracuse: D. Mason, 1887.

Schlissel, Lillian, ed. *Women's Diaries of the Westward Journey*. New York: Schocken Books, 1982.

Settle, Raymond W., ed. *March of the Mounted Riflemen*. Lincoln: University of Nebraska Press, 1989.

Smith, Duane A. "Mother Lode for the West: California Mining Men and Methods." In Rawls and Orsi, eds., *A Golden State*, 149–73.

———. *The Trail of Gold and Silver: Mining in Colorado, 1859–2009*. Boulder: University Press of Colorado, 2009.

Spedden, Rush. "The Fearful Long Drive." *Overland Journal* 12, no. 2 (Summer 1994): 2–16.

Sprague, Roderick, and Michael J. Rodeffer, "The Bloody Point Archaeological Investigation," *Overland Journal* 7, no. 3 (Fall 1989): 26–28.

Spence, Mary Lee, and Donald Jackson, eds. *The Expeditions of John Charles Frémont*. 4 vols., plus map portfolio. Urbana: University of Illinois Press, 1970–1984.

Steele, Volney, M.D. *Bleed, Blister, and Purge: A History of Medicine on the American Frontier*. Missoula, Mont.: Mountain Press Publishing Company, 2005.

Stegner, Wallace, with Forrest and Margaret Robinson. "An Interview with Wallace Stegner." *The American West* 15, no. 1 (January/Feburary 1978): 34–37, 61–63.

Stewart, George R. *The California Trail: An Epic with Many Heroes*. New York: McGraw-Hill, 1962.

Stillson, Richard T. *Spreading the Word: A History of Information in the California Gold Rush*. Lincoln: University of Nebraska Press, 2006.

Supernowicz, Dana E. "Surmounting the Sierra: The Opening of the Johnson Cutoff Route, 1850–1855." *Overland Journal* 13, no. 4 (Winter 1995–1996): 11–20.

Tea, Roy D. "The Limitless Plain: The Great Salt Lake Desert." Part 1, *Overland Journal* 23, no. 2 (Summer 2005): 20–38. Part 2, *Overland Journal* 23, no. 2 (Summer 2005): 61–89.

————. "The Salt Lake Desert Treadmill: The Hastings Cutoff." *Overland Journal* 18, no. 1 (Spring 2000): 3–14.

Templeton, Sardis W. *The Lame Captain: The Life and Adventures of Pegleg Smith*. Los Angeles: Westernlore Press, 1965.

Thrapp, Dan L. *Encyclopedia of Frontier Biography*. 4 vols. Glendale, Calif., and Spokane, Wash.: Arthur H. Clark, 1988, 1994.

Tompkins, James M. "The Law of the Land: What the Emigrants Knew That Historians Need to Know about Claiming Land at the End of the Oregon Trail." *Overland Journal* 19, no. 3 (Fall 2001): 82–112.

Trafzer, Clifford, and Joel Hyer, eds. *Exterminate Them: Written Accounts of the Murder, Rape, and Slavery of Native Americans during the California Gold Rush*. Lansing: Michigan State University Press, 1999.

Tullidge, Edward. "Utah and California: Original Proposition to Unite Them As One State." *Western Galaxy* 1, no. 1 (March 1888): 88–90.

Unruh, John D., Jr. *The Plains Across: The Overland Emigrants and the Trans-Mississippi West, 1840–1860*. Urbana: University of Illinois Press, 1979.

Walker, Margaret. "A Woman's Work Is Never Done." *Overland Journal* 16, no. 2 (Summer 1998): 4–13.

Watkins, Albert. "Notes of the Early History of the Nebraska Country." *Publications of the Nebraska State Historical Society* 20 (1922): 1–379.

Watson, Douglas S. "Herald of the Gold Rush—Sam Brannan." *California Historical Society Quarterly* 10, no. 3 (September 1931): 298–301.

Werner, Morris W. "Wheelbarrow Emigrant of 1850." Retrieved 19 January 2012 from Kansas Heritage website, http://www.kansasheritage.org/werner/wheemigr.html.

West, Elliot. *The Contested Plains: Indians, Goldseekers and the Rush to Colorado*. Lawrence: University of Kansas Press, 1998.

————. "Golden Dreams: Colorado, California, and the Reimagining of America." *Montana* 49, no. 3 (Autumn 1999): 3–11.

White, David A., ed. *News of the Plains and the Rockies, 1803–1865*. 8 vols. Spokane, Wash.: Arthur H. Clark, 1996–2001.

White, Richard. *It's Your Misfortune and None of My Own: A New History of the American West*. Norman: University of Oklahoma Press, 1991.

————. "The Gold Rush: Consequences and Contingencies." *California History* 77, no. 1 (Spring 1998): 42–55.

Wheat, Carl I [and Dale L. Morgan]. *Mapping the Transmississippi West*. 5 vols. San Francisco: Grabhorn Press and The Institute of Historical Cartography, 1957–1963.

Whiteley, Lee. *The Cherokee Trail: Bent's Fort to Fort Bridger*. Denver, Colo.: Posse of Westerners, 1999.

Whitmore, Eugene. "John J. Myers and the Early Trails." *Lockhart Post-Register* (Texas), November 1972. Copy in author's possession.

Wilcox, Pearl. *Jackson County Pioneers*. Independence, Mo.: Jackson County Historical Society, 1990.

Wilson, Elinor. *Jim Beckwourth: Black Mountain Man*. Norman: University of Oklahoma Press, 1972.

Wyman, Walker D., ed. *California Emigrant Letters*. New York: Bookman, 1952.

Zanjani, Sally S. *Devils Will Reign: How Nevada Began*. Reno: University of Nevada Press, 2007.

Index

References to illustrations are in italic type.

INDEX